SEX *&*
SOCIAL
JUSTICE

SEX &

SOCIAL

JUSTICE

Martha C. Nussbaum

New York   Oxford

Oxford University Press

1999

Oxford University Press

Oxford   New York
Athens   Auckland   Bangkok   Bogotá   Buenos Aires   Calcutta
Cape Town   Chennai   Dar es Salaam   Delhi   Florence   Hong Kong   Istanbul
Karachi   Kuala Lumpur   Madrid   Melbourne   Mexico City   Mumbai
Nairobi   Paris   São Paulo   Singapore   Taipei   Tokyo   Toronto   Warsaw

and associated companies in
Berlin   Ibadan

Published by Oxford University Press, Inc.
198 Madison Avenue, New York, New York 10016

Oxford is a registered trademark of Oxford University Press.

Library of Congress Cataloging-in-Publication Data
Nussbaum, Martha Craven, 1947–
Sex and social justice / Martha Craven Nussbaum.
p.   cm.
Includes bibliographical references and index.
ISBN 0-19-511032-3
1. Feminism.   2. Social justice.   3. Sex role.   I. Title.
HQ1150.N87   1998
305.42—dc21   97-50576

1 3 5 7 9 8 6 4 2

Printed in the United States of America
on acid-free paper

for
Kenneth Dover

ACKNOWLEDGMENTS

The essays in this volume were written between 1990 and 1997. I owe thanks for research support to sabbatical funding from Brown University and to summer research funding from the University of Chicago Law School. Many people have given me valuable comments on one or more of the papers, including Ronald Allen, Elizabeth Anderson, Julia Annas, Christopher Bobonich, Alan Boegehold, Diemut Bubeck, Myles Burnyeat, Victor Caston, Claudia Card, Martha Chen, Nancy Chodorow, Joshua Cohen, Scott Crider, Kenneth Dover, Jean Drèze, David Estlund, Gertrud Fremling, Robert Goodin, David Halperin, Stephen Halliwell, Virginia Held, John Hodges, Peter Hylton, Terence Irwin, Kenneth Karst, David Konstan, Andrew Koppelman, John Lawless, Catharine MacKinnon, Charles Nussbaum, Rachel Nussbaum, Sara Nussbaum, Nkiru Nzegwu, Joyce Carol Oates, Susan Moller Okin, Onora O'Neill, David Pears, Anthony Price, Hilary Putnam, Ruth Anna Putnam, John Rawls, Andrew Rehfeld, Henry Richardson, John Roemer, Sara Ruddick, Alan Soble, Richard Sorabji, Roger Scruton, Amartya Sen, Nancy Sherman, Margarita Valdés, Roop Rekha Verma, Paul Weithman, Leon Wieseltier, and Susan Wolf. I am grateful, above all, to my colleagues at the University of Chicago, some of whom have read all of these chapters at one time or another and many of whom have read far more than collegiality would require. I therefore extend extremely warm thanks to Al Alschuler, Douglas Baird, Mary Becker, Daniel Brudney, Emily Buss, David Cohen, Richard Craswell, Stephen Holmes, Elena Kagan, Dan M. Kahan, Robert Kaster, William Landes, Lawrence Lessig,

John Lott, Michael McConnell, Stephen J. Schulhofer, David Strauss, Cass Sunstein, and Candace Vogler. This is a long unwieldy manuscript, and those who have commented on the whole of it deserve especially warm thanks, so I extend those thanks to Kenneth Dover, Gertrud Fremling, Richard Posner, and Mark Ramseyer. Ross Davies provided invaluable research assistance and comments that made my thoughts sharper at many points. I am also grateful to him for preparing the indexes, and to Michelle Mason for assistance with proofreading.

I have read each of these essays in a number of places and have profited greatly from the ensuing discussions. My thanks, especially, to audiences at Oxford University; Cambridge University; Trinity College, Dublin; the Finnish Institute in Rome; the Johann-Wolfgang University, Frankfurt, Germany; the Wittgenstein Symposium, Kirchberg, Austria; the American Philosophical Association's Eastern and Central Divisions; the University of Notre Dame; the University of Minnesota; Princeton University; the University of Colorado at Boulder; Georgetown University; Bryn Mawr College; Harvard University; the University of Oklahoma; Scripps College; Stanford University; the University of California at Riverside; Brown University; Oberlin College; St. Lawrence University; St. Louis University; and the University of Chicago. Finally, I have been challenged and provoked by several groups of students, in courses on feminist philosophy and issues of social justice.

Between 1986 and 1993, I was a Research Advisor at the World Institute for Development Economics Research in Helsinki, Finland, an agency connected with the United Nations University. I spent a month every summer in Finland, working with a multinational and multidisciplinary group of researchers on a project investigating the concept of "quality of life" as used to measure development in nations. The aim of the project was to bring philosophical debates on this issue to bear on the criticism of oversimple economic models of the family and of life quality that have had widespread influence on public policy. This engagement with urgent practical issues of hunger, sex equality, and cultural and religious pluralism, and with researchers from India, Bangladesh, Nigeria, Mexico, Sri Lanka, Iran, and numerous other nations, has fundamentally changed my work as a philosopher. It has led me to tackle issues I did not write on before (including both sex equality and religion's relation to liberalism) and it has informed the abstract work that I was already doing on human functioning and the quality of life with a new sense of empirical reality and of the historical and political complexity of these issues of justice. It also led me to think that much of the work on justice and on sex equality that is produced in the American philosophical academy is too little informed by international concerns and by confrontation with complex practical situations. This, in turn, renewed my dedication to devote a good part of my career to these questions. For making these formative experiences possible I am immensely grateful to all those who welcomed me to the World Institute for Development Economics Research (WIDER): to Lal Jayawardena, its director, to Siddiq Osmani and Val Moghadam, permanent researchers, who taught me a great deal about their areas of specialization, to Martha Chen, who connected me to fieldwork in India and Bangladesh and through whose eyes and words I came to know women such as Metha Bai and Rohima, and above all to Amartya Sen, both for introducing me to WIDER and for his enormously inspiring work on our collaborative project.

During my work on ancient Greek sexuality, I began a correspondence on these topics with Sir Kenneth Dover, a scholar whom I had greatly admired for some time but had only met once. Because Dover took a keen interest in the legal issues involved in the Colorado case and their connection with both moral and historical arguments, the correspondence led to a collaboration, and we wrote jointly an appendix to the paper that appears here as chapter 12. At this same time, Dover published an extraordinary autobiography in which he describes the connection between his historical scholarship on sexuality and the opposition to prudery and narrow moralism that have characterized his life as a scholar and in the public world of academic administration. My discussion of Dover's life appears here as chapter 13. Because of my enormous respect for the dedication to truth and justice embodied in both his work and his life, and because I have so much enjoyed exchanging thoughts with him about the Greeks and about modern politics, I dedicate this volume to Sir Kenneth Dover.

Chapter 1 incorporates material from "Human Capabilities, Female Human Beings," which appeared in *Women, Culture, and Development*, ed. Martha Nussbaum and Jonathan Glover (Oxford: Clarendon Press, 1993); it is, however, basically a new essay. Chapter 2 is scheduled to appear in *Women's Voices, Women's Lives: The Amnesty Lectures 1995* (currently under contract to Westview) and appears in pamphlet form as the Lindley Lecture for 1997, University of Kansas Press. An earlier version of chapter 3 appeared in *Religion and Contemporary Liberalism*, ed. Paul Weithman (Notre Dame, IN: University of Notre Dame Press, 1997), 93–137. Portions of chapter 4 appeared in *The Boston Review* 21(5) (October/November 1996). Chapter 5 has not been previously published. A version of chapter 6 appeared in *Philosophy and Public Affairs* 22 (1993), 83–125. A version of chapter 7 appeared in *The Liberation Debate: Rights at Issue*, ed. Michael Leahy and Dan Cohn-Sherbok (London and New York: Routledge, 1996); it was paired with a response by Roger Scruton, to which I then replied; I have incorporated into the article material from that exchange. Chapter 8 appeared in *Philosophy and Public Affairs* 24 (1995), 249–91. Chapter 9 appeared in *The New Republic*, 217 (August 11/18, 1997), 36–42. Chapter 10 appeared in *Sex, Preference, and Family: Essays on Law and Nature*, ed. David Estlund and Martha Nussbaum (New York: Oxford University Press, 1996), 17–43. Chapter 11 appears in the *Journal of Legal Studies* XXVII (2) (Part 2): (University of Chicago Press, 1998), 693–724. Chapter 12 appeared in a longer version in the *Virginia Law Review* 80 (1994), 1515–1651; in its original form it was followed by a coauthored appendix written with Kenneth Dover; with Dover's permission I have incorporated parts of that document into the present form of the article. Chapter 13 appeared under the title "A Stoic's Confessions" in *Arion*, 3rd series no. 4 (1997), 149–60. Chapter 14 appeared in *The New Republic* 206 (April 20, 1992). Chapter 15 appeared in *New Literary History* 26 (1995), 731–53. All articles have been rewritten for this volume.

Chicago, Illinois   M. C. N.
March 1998

CONTENTS

SEX &
SOCIAL
JUSTICE

Woman, why are you crying?
Your tears should become your thoughts.

—Traditional song, rewritten by
the Mahila Samakhya Project,
Andhra Pradesh, India

If there had been no change, then how could I have learned
and understood all this? . . . Mother asked: "What do you see
in the books?" I said, "Ma, what valuable things there are in
the books you will not understand because you cannot read
and write." If somebody behaves badly with me, I go home
and sit with the books. When I sit with the books my mind
becomes better.

—Rohima of West Shanbandha,
Bangladesh

And there is something about creating beauty in the circumstances of shoddiness and privation that is truly exciting.

—Satyajit Ray,
"The Odds against Us"

INTRODUCTION

Feminism, Internationalism, Liberalism

Inequality, Resistance, Reversal

In 1975, near Dhaka, Bangladesh, Saleha Begum's husband became physically disabled and they lost their land. Despite local community norms against women working outside the home, Saleha decided to go to work. At first, ashamed to be seen, she worked in the fields at night, by moonlight. As she got used to working, both her fear and local criticism of her actions abated. She organized a team of female laborers to demand employment at government-sponsored food-for-work sites, where laborers moved large amounts of earth each day. Local officials refused their request, saying, "Women in Bangladesh should not work outside their homes." Saleha continued her fight. With the help of a group from the United Nations World Food Program, in consultation with the national Ministry of Relief and Rehabilitation, the women won the right to be hired. A nongovernmental organization, the Bangladesh Rural Advancement Committee (BRAC), helped organize the local women into specialized groups. In 1977, Saleha's group husked paddy and cultivated potatoes and sugar cane. Under Saleha's leadership, the women also attended BRAC's educational programs. They learned to negotiate loans, to rear poultry, to cultivate silkworms; women chosen from the group received paramedical and paralegal training. A few years later Saleha Begum was nominated for local political office. Although she lost, the narrowness of the margin was taken as a victory for women in that region.[1]

In 1975, Sareetha, a sixteen-year-old high school girl in Madras, was given in marriage by her parents to Venkata Subbaiah. They lived together for several months. Then her husband left her, after disputes with Sareetha and her family about her wish to become a film actress. They never saw each other after that. Five years later, Sareetha had become one of the most famous and admired stars of the South Indian cinema. Her husband, deciding he wanted her back, brought suit against her for "restitution of conjugal rights." A lower court judge ordered her to be returned to the conjugal home. The Andhra Pradesh High Court, however, held that the remedy of "restitution of conjugal rights" provided in the Hindu Marriage Act of 1955[2] was "a savage and barbarous remedy, violating the right to privacy and human dignity guaranteed by Art. 21 of the Constitution." The measure, the opinion continued, "deprives a woman of control over her choice as to when and by whom the various parts of her body should be allowed to be sensed" and "makes the unwilling victim's body a soulless and a joyless vehicle for bringing into existence another human being."

Judge Choudary added that although the statute is formally neutral, making a decree of restitution available to both husband and wife, the reality is that only the wife's life would be irretrievably altered by a resulting pregnancy. "As a result this remedy works in practice only as an oppression to be operated by the husband for the benefit of the husband against the wife. . . . [B]are equality of treatment regardless of the inequality of realities is neither justice nor homage to the constitutional principle."[3]

Sareetha did not win her case, however. The Supreme Court of India reversed, holding that the Hindu Marriage Act contained sufficient safeguards to prevent these abuses, since a woman who had left the marital home could not be forcibly returned if she could pay a fine. (The Court did not ask how likely it was that a woman fleeing from an abusive marriage would be able to pay the fine.) The Court praised the decree of restitution as one that "serves a social purpose as an aid to the prevention of breakup of marriage." Sareetha, being well off, paid the fine and went on making movies. The law remained unchanged.

Joe Steffan was a member of the graduating class at the United States Naval Academy in Annapolis, Maryland. An outstanding student, selected battalion commander, an honor reserved for the top ten Midshipmen, Steffan was described as a "model for his classmates and subordinates." Shortly before graduation, he told a supposed friend about his homosexual orientation, and the "friend" told Academy authorities. (At no time did Steffan state that he had committed homosexual acts, nor was any evidence of such acts ever introduced.) After a hearing, Steffan was denied the right to graduate; it was judged that he had "insufficient aptitude to become a commissioned officer in the naval service." Steffan brought suit against the Department of Defense, arguing that the navy's exclusion of homosexuals violates the Equal Protection Clause of the Fifth Amendment. At the conclusion of a trial in the U.S. District Court for the District of Columbia, the court found against Steffan; an opinion written by Judge Oliver Gasch (who had referred to Steffan during the trial using the disparaging term "homo") concluded that the naval regulations have a rational basis, one important aspect of which is the need to protect the armed services from the contagion of AIDS, "given that at least 59% of all those who have contracted HIV have done so due to homosexual or bisexual activity." When Steffan appealed, a three-member panel of the U.S. Court of Appeals found in his favor. In an opinion written by Judge Abner Mikva, the court declared the regulations without a rational basis, because they target people based on their status rather than their conduct. A majority of the judges voted to rehear the case en banc; when they did so, they found against Steffan, concluding that homosexual orientation entails an intention to commit homosexual acts. Writing in dissent, Judge Patricia Wald declared that the decision to penalize a person for acknowledging a sexual orientation "has . . . no precedent or place in our national traditions, which spring from a profound respect for the freedom to think and to be what one chooses and to announce it to the world."[4]

Human beings have a dignity that deserves respect from laws and social institutions. This idea has many origins in many traditions; by now it is at the core of modern liberal democratic thought and practice all over the world. The idea of human dignity is usually taken to involve an idea of *equal* worth: rich and poor, rural and urban, female and male, all are equally deserving of respect, just in virtue of being human, and this respect should not be abridged on account of a characteristic that is distributed by the whims of fortune. Often, too, this idea of equal worth is connected to an idea of liberty: to respect the equal worth of persons is, among other things, to promote their ability to fashion a life in accordance with their own view of what is deepest and most important.

But human dignity is frequently violated on grounds of sex or sexuality. Many women all over the world find themselves treated unequally with respect to employment, bodily safety and integrity, basic nutrition and health care, education, and political voice. In many cases these hardships are caused by their being women, and in many cases laws and institutions construct or perpetuate these inequalities. Sex is involved in inequality in other ways as well. Many women and many men are treated unequally on the basis of their sexual inclinations, the types of acts and partners they choose or even mentally desire. Sometimes these inequalities are pervasive, extending to "an almost limitless number of transactions and endeavors that constitute ordinary civic life in a free society."[5]

Such women and men are resisting inequality and claiming the right to be treated with respect. Sometimes they succeed, and sometimes they do not. But what does it mean to respect the dignity of a human being? What sort of support do human capacities demand from the world, and how should we think about this support when we encounter differences of gender or sexuality? What types of legal and political treatment are required to treat people as dignified and equal in the modern world, and how might a deeper understanding of sex and gender help us answer that question? How, finally, should we think about each other across the divisions that a legacy of injustice has created? How, we might ask—given the ample grounds history gives people for suspicion, anger, and even, perhaps, hatred—might we overcome hatred by love?

A Conception of Feminism

The essays in this volume try to answer these questions, articulating a distinctive conception of feminism. The feminism defended here has five salient features: It is *internationalist, humanist, liberal, concerned with the social shaping of preference and desire,* and, finally, *concerned with sympathetic understanding.* These five elements are not usually found together, and some of them are widely thought to be at odds with others. I shall argue, however, that a coherent and powerful picture emerges from their combination. Among the advantages of the combination is an opportunity to link feminist inquiry closely to the important progress that has been made during the past few decades in articulating the elements of a theory of both national and global justice.

Internationalism

Feminism begins from the real lives of women, and the lives of women are highly varied. It is myopic to focus only on conditions and problems that are shared by a local or national group while neglecting the very different gender-related problems that may be faced by women in very different political and economic circumstances. Feminists in the United States have long acknowledged that arguments based on the experiences of white middle-class women are incomplete without the insights and experiences of women from other racial and ethnic groups. Too often, however, this admirable curiosity has not extended to the world outside the United States. The isolationist habits of our nation lead us to focus inward rather than on urgent needs at a distance. Thus, by now there is a rich feminist literature on questions such as rape and sexual harassment, which are common concerns of women all over the world. Much less is known and said about women's hunger, about sex-selective infanticide and abortion, about the denial of the right to work, about sex discrimination in religious courts of family law.

This volume takes its start from such urgent questions and from the experiences of women who are grappling with them in many places. It has been important to me to work in close partnership with women and men who do empirical fieldwork and to hear, through these partnerships, the voices of women fighting against hunger and illiteracy and inherently unequal legal systems. This volume contains far more empirical material than is common in a work of political philosophy because one of its central aims is to let reality speak for itself. I present both statistical material about the situation of women and also case studies of particular women and groups and their legal and political struggles.

The internationalism of this volume's method is linked to views about global justice that I do not develop fully here. I believe that individuals have moral obligations to promote justice for people outside their national boundaries and that their governments do also. In this volume I focus on the obligations of each nation to secure a basic level of functioning for its citizens, and also on universal obligations to protect and promote human dignity through the international human rights movement and through support for international agencies. I do not articulate principles of international distributive justice for material resources, although I think this immensely important and necessary to a complete account of justice for the world's women. That is a large question that goes beyond the scope of the present inquiry. But at least a beginning of the larger inquiry is made by thinking about the facts of human inequality in basic life chances, and by attempting to remedy some of these through domestic and private strategies. When we become able to conceive of the humanity of distant human beings, of their dignity and their needs, we at least begin to ask the hard questions about the contingency that affects people's lives more than any other, the contingency of birth location. Although I shall be focusing on differences in life chances between the sexes, we should never forget that the difference in life expectancy at birth between Iceland (78.2) and Sierra Leone (39.0) is enormously greater than that between females and males in any nation,[6] and so it goes for all the indicators of quality of life. One might therefore feel that the biggest question of distributive justice is lurking around the edges of these essays and is not addressed within them. True, and yet I hope that the method of my inquiry makes it at least audible.

Because many of these essays take their start from experiences of women in developing countries, and because economics is the intellectual discipline that has so far had the largest public impact on the lives of such women, development economics is an important part of this volume. My coworkers and I have been highly critical of conventional approaches in development economics. Convinced that development is a normative notion and that normative argument can be rational rather than merely subjective, we have also been concerned to develop that normative structure and to criticize irrationalist approaches that dismiss it—both those deriving from neoclassical economics, with its subjectivism about value, and those that derive from postmodernism. (Several of the essays develop this critique, and chapter 5 shows how subjectivism about preferences has increasingly been assailed from within economics itself.) But it is very important for feminist philosophers to care about and to study economics because no normative project, however valuable, can be pursued and implemented without adequate formal models. For philosophers to turn in disdain from economic modeling on the grounds that the foundations of existing models are philosophically crude is one way of guaranteeing that their work will have no impact on the real world.

Humanism

The view developed here seeks justice for human beings as such, believing all human beings to be fundamentally equal in worth. It also holds that human beings have common resources and common problems wherever they live, and that their special dilemmas can best be seen as growing out of special circumstances, rather than out of a nature or identity that is altogether unlike that of other humans. This is not to say that historical, social, political, and natural circumstances do not shape extremely different lives for people in different parts of the world. But it is to say that there is likely to be a good deal of overlap of problems within those lives, and also a good deal of commonness about what people must have if they are to be capable of living well.

The problems people face wherever they live include scarce resources, competition for resources, and the shortness of life. These have been called "the circumstances of justice,"[7] circumstances that make it incumbent upon us to develop an account of what is due to people and to their dignity. We might hold that people share common problems but that the solutions that are proper vary from region to region and group to group. To some extent, we should hold this, in the sense that any good solution to a problem must be responsive to the concrete circumstances for which it is designed. But it is a long step from that sensible interest in specificity to a normative cultural relativism, according to which the ultimate standard of what is right for an individual or group must derive from that group's internal traditions. The approach defended here refuses to take that step, arguing that an account of the central human capacities and functions, and of the basic human needs and rights, can be given in a fully universal manner, at least at a high level of generality, and that this universal account is what should guide feminist thought and planning. The essays are strongly critical of forms of both descriptive and normative relativism deriving from postmodernism. They try to show that a universal account of human justice need not be insensitive to the variety of traditions or a mere projection of narrow Western values onto groups with different concerns.

One crucial step in defending a universalist project is to point to the variety within groups, cultures, and traditions. The relativist move of deferring to "local knowledge" is not very plausible even initially: For why shouldn't we think from the start that traditions can be evil as well as good, a view most people hold about their own traditions? But it begins to lose whatever appeal it had once we begin to reflect that traditions are not monoliths. Any living culture contains plurality and argument; it contains relatively powerful voices, relatively silent voices, and voices that cannot speak at all in the public space. Often some of these voices would speak differently, too, if they had more information or were less frightened—so part of a culture, too, is what its members *would* say if they were freer or more fully informed. When women are at issue, we should be especially skeptical of deferring to the most powerful voices in local tradition. In most parts of the world, that voice is especially likely to be a male voice, and that voice may not be all that attentive to the needs and interests of women. One may also find that a voice that is in some sense foreign proves to be essential to the self-expression of a marginalized or oppressed group: for people often appropriate good ideas from outside and vindicate their dignity by pointing to examples of respect elsewhere.

A vivid example of this last point occurred at a conference in Beijing in June 1995, which brought Western feminist philosophers together with Chinese scholars in women's studies.[8] Most of the Chinese scholars were harshly critical of the Confucian tradition as a tradition that subordinates women. One paper was different. Presented by a young scholar from Hong Kong, it argued that one could mine the Confucian tradition for values of community and solidarity that could be used in building a Chinese feminism. The Chinese women reacted with unanimous negativity, saying that this was a "Western paper." She could not have said that, they said, had she not been from Hong Kong. For these women, the Confucian tradition was a living source of humiliation and disempowerment. It was not their voice, and it spoke politically against them even in 1995, defending the "women go home" policy that is responsible for many layoffs of female workers. Where did they locate their tradition? In their own critical thought and work, in the efforts of women to win respect within history—but also in John Stuart Mill, whose *The Subjection of Women*, translated into Chinese early in the twentieth century, is a primary source of the Chinese feminist tradition.[9]

What is East and what is West? What is the tradition of a person who is fighting for freedom and empowerment? Why should one's group be assumed to be the ethnic or religious group of one's birth? Might it not, if one so chooses, be, or become, the international group of women—or of people who respect the equality and dignity of women?

In an important sense, the views expressed in this volume are not really about women at all but about human beings and about women seen as fully human. The focus on women is justified, it seems to me, by the urgency of the problems facing women in today's world and by the sorry record of our dealings with (and evasions of) these problems. But no theory of justice could plausibly call itself such if it did select out one group for favorable treatment on the basis of a contingency of birth. This, then, is a theory of human justice, and of feminism as a humanism.[10] It ought to prompt reflection about hunger more generally, about the relief of poverty and misery more generally. As I said, it leaves a tremendous question, that of the global redistribution of wealth, waiting in the wings.

Universalist views, applied to women, are frequently suspected of being the projections of a male view onto women, or of the views of well-educated Western white women onto women of diverse backgrounds and cultures. I try to answer this concern through my method, which lets the voices of many women speak and which seeks collaboration with women and men from many different regions in the process of forming a view. The universals defended here are the fruit of many years of collaborative international work. I also try to answer it in the details of my proposal, with its emphasis on a positive role for knowledge of local circumstances. Nonetheless, another most important way to answer this worry is to insist on the universal importance of protecting spheres of choice and freedom, within which people with diverse views of what matters in life can pursue flourishing according to their own lights. We can hardly be charged with imposing a foreign set of values upon individuals or groups if what we are doing is providing support for basic capacities and opportunities that are involved in the selection of any flourishing life and then leaving people to choose for themselves how they will pursue flourishing. Any universalism that has a chance to be persuasive in the modern world must, it seems to me, be a form of political liberalism.

Liberalism

The liberal tradition in political philosophy has frequently been thought to be inadequate for the goals of feminism. One central purpose of the volume is to answer that charge, defending a form of liberalism (deriving, in different ways, from Kant, Mill, and Aristotle) that can answer the feminist charges that are legitimate and show why other charges are not legitimate. The version of liberalism here begins from the idea of the equal worth of human beings as such, in virtue of their basic human capacities for choice and reasoning. All, in virtue of those human capacities, are worthy of equal concern and respect: Thus, the view is at its core antifeudal, opposed to the political ascendancy of hierarchies of rank, caste, and birth. The crucial addition liberal feminism makes to the tradition is to add sex to that list of morally irrelevant characteristics. It should have been there all along, for no liberal thinker ever presented a cogent argument to justify the subordination of women to men while opposing feudalism and monarchy. Subordination by sex was simply seen as natural, and the entire topic was basically ignored in theories of political justice. This was a profound inconsistency in the liberal tradition, as J. S. Mill powerfully showed already in 1869, but we have had to wait until the present decade for serious and sustained work on the justice of family arrangements that is beginning to make the promise of liberalism real for the world's women.

The basic argument I make, then, is that the liberal tradition of equal concern and respect should, and in all consistency must, be extended to women and to the relations between women and men in the family. In the process, we should not be quick to dismiss the often-criticized individualism of the liberal tradition. I argue that liberal individualism does not entail egoism or a preference for the type of person who has no deep need of others. Many liberal thinkers have made compassion, care, and love an essential part of their normative program. What does distinguish liberalism from other political traditions is its insistence on the separateness of one life from another, and the equal importance of each life, seen on its own terms rather than as part of a larger organic or corporate whole. Each human being should be regarded as an end rather than as a means to the ends of others. The liberal insists that the goal of politics should be the amelioration of lives taken one by one and seen as separate ends, rather than the amelioration of the organic whole or the totality. I argue that this is a very good position for women to embrace, seeing that women have all too often been regarded not as ends but as means to the ends of others, not as sources of agency and worth in their own right but as reproducers and caregivers.

The form of liberalism endorsed here is fully compatible with ascribing great importance to care and love. But it suggests a way in which the commitment to care should be qualified. Emotions of love and care, like other emotions, have in part a social origin, but this means that they are only as reliable as the social norms that give rise to them. The common propensity of women to subordinate themselves to others and to sacrifice their well-being for that of a larger unit may in many cases be morally admirable, but this should by no means be taken for granted. Such dispositions have been formed, often, in unjust conditions and may simply reflect the low worth society itself has placed on women's well-being. My view urges that all such emotions be valued with the constraints of a life organized by critical reasoning. The same, I argue, is true of sexual desire and emotion: Insofar as these are shaped by unjust social conditions, they should not be relied on as unproblematic guides to a flourishing life. The norm, here as elsewhere, should be the idea of being treated as an end rather than a means, a person rather than an object.

Liberalism concerns itself with freedom and with spheres of choice. As I conceive it, this does not mean maximizing the sheer numbers of choices people get to make for themselves. The idea of liberty should be understood in close conjunction with the idea of equal worth and respect: The choices that liberal politics should protect are those that are deemed of central importance to the development and expression of personhood. In this sense, liberalism has to take a stand about what is good for people, and I argue that it needs a somewhat more extensive conception of the basic human functions and capacities than many liberal thinkers have used if it is to provide sufficient remedies for entrenched injustice and hierarchy. But the goal should always be to put people into a position of agency and choice, not to push them into functioning in ways deemed desirable. I argue that this is no mere parochial Western ideology but the expression of a sense of agency that has deep roots all over the world; it expresses the joy most people have in using their own bodies and minds. Rohima, quoted in the epigraphs to this volume, discovered that literacy was a powerful source of selfhood and joyful expression, because for the first time she was using her capacities on her own hook rather than merely executing the will of others. It is this experiential idea of choice on which I rely in defending choice as goal, and no argument has yet shown that there is any human being who does not desire choice so construed.

Concern with the Social Shaping of Preference and Desire

Among the most significant charges feminists have made against the liberal tradition is its neglect of the social formation and deformation of preference, emotion, and desire. It is indeed true that some offshoots of the tradition, in particular neoclassical economics (until recent years), have indeed treated people's subjective preferences and desires as simply given, a bedrock external to law and public policy. Economists have typically understood the goal of public policy to be the satisfaction of preference, regarded as antecedently given and more or less impervious to policy.

Such a view is exceedingly myopic and ultimately indefensible. Empirically, it has been amply demonstrated that people's desires and preferences respond to their beliefs about social norms and about their own opportunities. Thus people usually adjust their desires to reflect the level of their available possibilities: They can get used to having luxuries and mind the absence of these very much, and they can also fail to form desires for things their circumstances have placed out of reach. People from groups that have not traditionally had access to education, or employment outside the home, may be slow to desire these things because they may not know what they are like or what they could possibly mean in lives like theirs. Even at the level of simple bodily health and nutrition, people who have been malnourished all their lives may not know what it would be like to feel strong. Especially if they have been told that women are weaker than men, they may not be able to form a desire for the health and strength of which they are capable. The absence of such a desire should not convince policymakers that health and strength are not important goals to be promoted for these people.[11]

Conceptually, the traditional economic picture is also naive. For centuries philosophers and others have debated about the nature of experiences such as emotion, desire, and pleasure. A considerable consensus has emerged that emotions, at any rate, are at least in part made up out of evaluative judgments; these judgments are likely to have been learned in society and shaped by that society's norms of appropriateness. It was on this basis, for example, that the Greek and Roman Stoics criticized the prevalence of anger in their society, holding that a change in social norms could make people less obsessed with slights to their honor and therefore less prone to rage. As for desire and pleasure, arguments of great power, beginning with Plato if not earlier, urge us to see these experiences, too, as infused by judgments of value and appropriateness, and thus responsive in at least some measure to changes in social norms. (Acceptance of such a view need not involve denying that emotions are grounded in biological tendencies; societies deal in many different ways with the tendencies in their members' biology, shaping expression and choice of objects, and at times either repressing or encouraging the entire emotion category.[12])

If these arguments are sound, they mean a good deal for justice between the sexes. For they suggest that appeals to an unchanging human nature, in the context of defending a traditional pattern of family love and fear, may posit an immutable bedrock where reality presents us with many possibilities for change. If many actual women are fearful and dependent, it may in part be because they have been formed to be that way. If many men are possessive and tyrannical, it may be less because of unchanging male aggression than because society gives permission to males to form and to express such attitudes. The philosophical tradition suggests that even something as apparently deepseated as the character of a person's erotic desire may contain a socially learned component. It may therefore be not too utopian to imagine a culture in which men's sexual desire for women will not commonly be associated with projects of possession and control, and in which female sexual agency will not inspire fear and suspicion.

Some feminists have thought the recognition of a social dimension in desire alien to the liberal tradition of political philosophy; it is not. Following the Roman Stoics, Adam Smith developed a powerful critique of socially learned greed and excessive anger, proposing norms of rational self-scrutiny that should move each person nearer to an appropriate balance in passion.[13] The contemporary Kantian tradition represented in John Rawls's *A Theory of Justice* focuses intently on the social origins of envy and fear, insisting that mutable social conditions are in large part responsible for the genesis of these destructive passions.[14] John Stuart Mill anticipated the arguments of leading modern feminists such as Catharine MacKinnon and Andrea Dworkin when he argued that the nature of both male and female sexuality has been shaped by long habits of domination and subordination. To call women's sexual personalities "natural" is about as plausible, he says, as to put a tree one half in a vapor bath and the other half in the snow—and then, seeing that one half is withered and the other half luxuriant, to declare that it is the "nature" of the tree to grow that way.[15]

Mill understood, too, that a moral critique of deformed desire and preference is not antithetical to liberal democracy; it is actually essential to its success. Children learn how to be good citizens in families; what they see in the demeanor of those closest to them shapes their citizenship powerfully for good or for ill. At present, he argues, the family is "a school of despotism," where male children learn that just in virtue of being born male they are the superiors of one half of the human race. This cannot be a good preparation for political equality in the rest of life. "The family, justly constituted," he concludes, "would be the real school of the virtues of freedom." But the just constitution of the family requires a reform of moral education on a large scale, and this reform must be facilitated by at least some changes in laws and institutions, especially those concerning marital rape, domestic violence, and women's legal rights over children.

It therefore seems crucial for an inquiry into gender justice to investigate the social origins of desire, preference, and emotion, both through refined conceptual analysis and through empirical study, drawing on the excellent work that has recently been done in these areas in cognitive psychology and in anthropology. Liberalism cannot make sense of its own subject matter unless it looks deeper into these questions than some liberal thinkers have.

Concern with Sympathetic Understanding

Women are often valued as creatures of care and sympathy. Often they are devalued for the same characteristics. Sometimes, too, women's propensity to care for others veers over into an undignified self-abnegation in which a woman subordinates her humanity utterly to the needs of another or others. It is tempting to praise women for their ability to care and to sympathize and to suggest that men have a great deal to learn from their example. It is also tempting to criticize women for their frequent passivity and lack of autonomy and to suggest that they have at least something to learn from the example of men. Some feminists deeply concerned with women's dignity and agency, for example, Catharine MacKinnon and Claudia Card, have questioned the validity of women's instincts of care, suggesting that those "instincts" are actually constructs of women's subordination, which frequently serve male interests and work against women. Other feminists, such as Carol Gilligan and Virginia Held, have suggested that women's ability to love and care for others is at the core of morality, and should be emulated by all.[16] To Gilligan's claim that women speak in a "different voice," the voice of care, MacKinnon responds with skepticism: "If you will take your foot off our necks, then you will hear in what voice women speak."[17]

Anyone who believes, as I do, that emotions are in part made up out of socially learned beliefs is likely to share MacKinnon's suspiciousness of emotions formed under conditions of injustice. It seems wrong to observe the way women are under injustice and to conclude directly from this that they should and must be that way. Nonetheless, duly scrutinized and assessed, emotions of care and sympathy lie at the heart of the ethical life. No society can afford not to cultivate them, and certainly a society that is struggling to overcome a legacy of great injustice needs all the love and sympathy it can muster. Many feminists have believed that the record of injustice erodes, practically speaking, all possibility of sympathy, trust, and love between women and men. Or at least—as few real women actually believe something so extreme—many feminists feel that it is politically valuable to call for the repudiation of trust and the refusal of sympathy and mercy. I dispute this claim.

I try here, however uneasily, to combine a radical feminist critique of sex relations with an interest in the possibilities of trust and understanding. Each reader must judge in the light of his or her own sense of life the odd combination that results—of Kant with D. H. Lawrence, of MacKinnon with Virginia Woolf. To some the moral interest in sympathy and forgiveness will seem like a kind of collaboration with oppression. And indeed, who knows at what point patience becomes masochism or sympathy self-torment. These questions are rightly pressed by MacKinnon and Dworkin. It would be naive to claim to have definitive answers. But one important ingredient of a response is the reminder that cultures are not monoliths; people are not stamped out like coins by the power machine of social convention. They are constrained by social norms, but norms are plural and people are devious. Even in societies that nourish problematic roles for men and women, real men and women can also find spaces in which to subvert those conventions, resourcefully creating possibilities of love and joy. (And some societies offer their members more space than others: Mill's England is not 1999 America, and we should be clear about these differences.)

In the spring of 1989, the distinguished classical scholar John J. Winkler delivered the Charles Alexander Robinson lecture at Brown University, a lecture endowed by Robinson's widow Celia Stillwell, who always attended the lecture. Winkler, an expert on ancient homosexuality, chose to honor the donor (and to surprise the audience) by lecturing on the possibilities of heterosexuality. Focusing on the love of Penelope and Odysseus in Homer's *Odyssey*, he argued that even in that most hierarchical of societies a man and a woman could create a relationship of equality and mutuality. Winkler drew attention to the long simile at the poem's end, when the two embrace for the first time after their long separation, a simile that begins in his mind, expressing his joy at having escaped so many perils, and ends up in her mind, expressing her joy at having found him at last. Here, he said, the poet is saying that a man and a woman can be equal. As he lectured with his usual grace and élan, a gay man already ill with the AIDS of which he died a year later, he wore an AZT pill box strapped to his waist, equipped with a beeper reminding him to take his medication halfway through the talk. He too was improvising a life of joy and sympathy in the face of great odds. As Satyajit Ray said, (describing the possibilities of Bengali filmmaking): "[T]here is something about creating beauty in the circumstances of shoddiness and privation that is truly exciting."

Gay Rights and Women's Rights

This volume is centrally about the situation of women; it also focuses on the political and legal situation of lesbians and gay men. How are these two themes connected? Some feminists have connected them by arguing that feminism can best be advanced by lesbian separatism, that women can only remove themselves from male domination turning their erotic attention to one another. This volume does not so argue, and one of its emphases is on creating possibilities of justice and equality within heterosexual relationships. What connection, then, is drawn between justice for women and justice for lesbians and gay men?

The traditional Western heterosexual family—consisting of male breadwinner, female homemaker, and several children—is rapidly becoming less common in the United States. (Of course in many parts of the world it never existed, and one dividend of thinking about feminism internationally is that one comes to see the many different ways in which children have been cared for with good results.) Some view its decline with alarm, and some with approval. Two social movements that have been implicated in the decline are feminism and the lesbian/gay rights movement. Feminism has led women to ask whose interests the traditional hierarchical structure served and to demand changes that give women a greater measure of economic and personal independence. Once they have become more independent in the larger society, women have been reluctant to accept bad bargains, and they have therefore avoided early marriage and childbearing and have been quicker to seek or accept divorce.[18] Defenders of the hierarchical nuclear family rightly see women's autonomy, and the feminism that supports it, as a threat to that structure.

The gay rights movement is another such threat. If economic and political equality remove women to some extent from male domination, lesbianism does so in a more radical way. The idea of a woman who does not need or desire men is therefore a threatening idea for many traditional men. As for gay men, they are often seen as men who refuse the civilizing influence of the female, and who pursue pleasure at the expense of social responsibility as parents. They are also widely seen as men who want to do to other men what men traditionally do to women—and this, too, inspires fear in many men, usually a deeper fear, for whatever reason, than the fear of lesbian women. The widespread stereotyping of both feminists and gays and lesbians as underminers of the traditional social order gives us one strong reason to study the two sets of issues together, asking what definitions of maleness and femaleness underlie both the fear of feminism and the opposition to equal civil rights for lesbians and gay men.

Thus, legal theorists have recently argued that resistance to full equality for gays is a form of sex discrimination in the sense that it is a device for maintaining fixed divisions between the male and the female, which, in turn, are traditionally linked with a hierarchical placement of male over female. If we ask what is really at stake in the ban on gay marriage, such theorists maintain, it is the desire to shore up an institution that perpetuates traditional sex roles and to resist change in those roles.[19]

If we study sexuality in a historical and cross-cultural manner, both sets of issues are simultaneously illuminated. For we gain thereby a much greater understanding of the variety of ways in which laws and institutions have categorized people and acts in the sexual sphere, the great variety of demarcations that have appeared to make sense in people's lives. We also see that what we find "natural" and "unnatural" in this domain may be very different from what another culture finds natural, and thus we acquire a healthy skepticism about our own use of such labels, which often are ways of wrapping the deeply habitual in a mantle of sanctity. We discover, finally, that women and men find love and pursue justice in many different ways. We learn, it seems to me, that it is usually best to look at the whole of an individual case before making moral judgments, that the labels we commonly apply to people usually show us very little about the quality of an individual relationship of desire and love.

One final reason for feminists to study the history of homosexuality is given by the fact that lesbian and gay relationships, throughout history, have frequently, though certainly not always, been less hierarchical than male-female relationships, more characterized by genuine reciprocity in both passion and daily life. I read Plato's *Phaedrus* while in high school in the 1960s, surrounded by relationships that defined the woman as homemaker, the male as breadwinner/lawyer/professor/pursuer of truth. By day we did our schoolwork apart from men, and in the evening we were warned not to talk too much or the boys would not like us. Reading the *Phaedrus* I discovered the paradigm of a relationship that combines intense mutual erotic passion with a shared pursuit of truth and justice. This seemed to me enormously exciting, and I wondered whether it might not be possible to find such a relationship in the real world. It did not seem easy. Shortly after that, I met openly gay men for the first time, as an actress, and saw that they were treated with opprobrium by the surrounding society. This seemed to me highly irrational and outrageous given the view that I had formed of the possibilities of those relationships, so much more promising, I thought, than the heterosexuality defined by the high school prom and the debutante party. Perhaps, I thought, the world as a whole could learn a thing or two from Plato's *Phaedrus*.

Discrimination against gay men and lesbians still seems to me irrational and outrageous, and I still think we have a lot to learn from the *Phaedrus*, though I think we should criticize Plato's generally hostile account of the bodily desires. We can also learn by examing the lives of same-sex couples in our own world, who in general divide domestic duties more equally than opposite-sex couples,[20] and who have shown a remarkable loyalty and tenacity in the face of great social odds.

Sex and the Sexual

Saleha Begum denied employment in the fields, Sareetha seeking the freedom to work as an actress: These cases raise issues of discrimination on the basis of sex. But what do they have to do with the sexual domain of life? Some essays in the volume focus on the specifically sexual domain, and on respect for human dignity there; others focus on many apparently nonsexual ways in which women are abused and exploited and in which they resist exploitation. How do I connect the sexual domain with the other areas of women's inequality?

This is a huge, mysterious question, and there is probably no single answer to it. Many complicated empirical questions are involved, and we do not yet have good answers to them, so our best conjectures are likely to be speculative. On the one hand, it seems plausible that women's inequality in other areas of social life contributes to the sexual mistreatment of women. As Mill argued in 1869, marital rape would be far less likely to occur if it were illegal, and if women were in general the legal equals of men. More broadly, the perception that women are not the legal and social equals of men feeds into many ways of viewing women as sexual objects that deny them full humanity and agency. Thus, in Sareetha's case, Judge Choudary referred to "our Hindu culture," in which women are not in general the social equals of men, to explain why the officially neutral remedy of "restitution" was in fact a source of sexual oppression and brutalization for women at the hands of men. But the causal relationship has two directions: traditions of viewing women as sexually whorish and childish and desires for sexual control over them helped to shape the *Laws of Manu* that denied women legal equality, creating the social regime within which Sareetha's case unfolds.[21] Similarly in our own culture, Thomas Jefferson wrote that the reason to deny women political equality was a sexual reason, "to prevent depravation of morals and ambiguity of issue."[22] Certainly the desire to control women's reproductive functioning and to maintain control over their sexuality has been a major impetus behind various restrictions on women's public role, ranging from seclusion and veiling to more subtle pressures and disincentives.

On the other hand, it is not to be assumed that all reasons for women's inequality are sexual reasons. Some, long ago in history, were reasons of physical strength. Others probably derive from the exhaustions and strains of childbearing. Still others may derive, especially in the modern world, where slavery does not exist and domestic servants are becoming rarer, from the desire of men to have a permanent support system for the needs and functions of daily life, including child care, housework, and clerical work. Laws and institutions shape these questions for better or for worse, by giving or not giving parental leave, by supporting or not supporting systems of child care.

As Mill already stressed, motives connected with sexuality interact in complex ways with motives connected with women's more general subordination. If women do not have careers and their useful role is confined to that of domestic labor, they will be more likely, Mill argued, to rely on their sexuality for power, developing arts of flattering and pleasing those on whose sufferance they entirely depend. On the other hand, he also argued, their learned habits of sexual submissiveness reinforce their inferior status in the household and the community.

Like Mill, I believe that there are both sexual and nonsexual reasons for women's subordinate status, and that these reasons interact and reinforce one another in many different ways. Because I also agree with Mill that sexual desire itself is shaped by structures of power and subordination, I don't think that the distinction between the "sexual" and the "nonsexual" is, or should be, a sharp one. Nor do I think that the question which of these forces is primary is very useful. It seems most productive to examine women's subordination in the many areas in which it occurs, looking to see in each case what its likely causes and content are. Thus, some of the essays will focus on sex, others on apparently nonsexual matters, still others on a combination of both. I do not assume that motives connected with sex are primary, nor do I claim that they are ever out of the picture altogether.

Victims and Agents

These days we commonly hear an oversimple contrast between two types of feminism. One, the story goes, urges women to see themselves as victims, powerless to change their situation, and to blame men for putting them in this bad position. The other urges women to see themselves as agents, to take responsibility for what happens to them, and to seek power. The former is thought to be connected with hating men and sex, the latter with loving men and being optimistic about partnerships with men.[23] Thus, because Catharine MacKinnon and Andrea Dworkin insist on the harms women have suffered and dramatize the extent of their legal, material, and sexual inequality, they are widely portrayed as haters of all men and hostile to female responsibility and agency. The presence of such oversimple categories also leads to misperceptions in the opposite direction: Any woman who likes men and who emphasizes the resourcefulness of women under difficult conditions is assumed by believers in these categories to be a person who denies that women have suffered gross harms at the hands of men. Because this volume both emphasizes the resourcefulness of women in conditions of hardship and also argues for radical change in the relation of women to men worldwide, it seems important to comment on this common set of perceptions.

Why are such categories oversimple? Consider Saleha Begum. This woman showed enormous resourcefulness. Untrained and uneducated, opposed in her efforts to work both by government policy and by local custom, she eventually got work, education, and even political voice. But the moral of this story is not that social and political conditions do not matter, that our own nation's emphasis on equal employment rights and on compulsory primary and secondary education for both females and males is a bad thing. One could certainly say that our customs treat women like victims, because they treat women as people who cannot go out and fight for literacy and employment against the most adverse of conditions. And, of course, women can do this; sometimes they succeed. But it would be very odd to conclude that the only way to respect people's dignity as agents is to create an uphill unequal struggle for them at every turn in the road. It would be odd to conclude that treating people with equal respect for their dignity is a way of turning them into victims rather than agents. Laws protect all citizens from theft, assault, and fraud, and yet it is rarely suggested that such laws turn men into victims.

Women do overcome the greatest of obstacles, showing an amazing courage and resourcefulness. So much was true of Saleha Begum. But this is no reason not to change the conditions that placed these obstacles in their way, especially when the conditions are unequally experienced by women just because they are women. Men did not have to fight against cultural opprobrium and political opposition to get jobs; men did not have to struggle to get an education. (An earlier generation of men did, if they came from a lower caste: And their struggles against caste required state assistance then, just as women's struggles do now.) Just think what a courageous woman like Saleha might have done had the state provided her with equal primary and secondary education, had society offered her equal opportunities for work, had her nutrition and health care been equal to that of a middle-class person in the United States. It seems a fair bet that she would not have collapsed into an armchair saying, "I am a victim and society owes me a living." She would have gotten on with some useful occupation, probably one that would have employed her considerable talents to better advantage (for herself and for the Bangladeshi economy) than carrying earth in the fields or husking paddy. Just think, too, of the many women who die early fighting Saleha's fight, because they are not quite as physically strong as she was, or as lucky. Many highly gifted and intelligent women and men are not physically strong enough to survive a prolonged regimen of carrying forty cubic feet of earth per day. Are we showing disdain for their agency by saying that society should make other options to them on an equal basis so that they can use the talents they have to promote their own survival and flourishing?

Consider, now, the basic political liberties. People have frequently overcome religious intolerance and barriers to the freedom of expression. Artists show resourcefulness and agency when they fight to publish and disseminate their work in regimes that impose censorship. Religious believers show courage when they hold secret services in regimes that make their mode of worship illegal. But how many of us would conclude from this that legal guarantees of freedom of expression are unnecessary, or even bad because they turn people into victims? Nietzsche did think something like this: He wrote that the liberties of expression, press, and assembly undermine "the will to assume responsibility for oneself," making people "small, cowardly, and hedonistic."[24] Calling Mill a "flathead," he prounounced that "[t]he highest type of free men should be sought where the highest resistance is constantly overcome: five steps from tyranny, close to the threshold of the danger of servitude."[25] But this is an adolescent view of what liberty means. Legal guarantees do not erode agency: They create a framework within which people can develop and exercise agency. No doubt all Americans are dependent on the freedom of worship in the sense that we do not have well-developed capacities to conceal our religious affiliations and carry on in secret; we are also dependent on the freedom of the press. The question is, Is this a bad thing, or is the denial of expressive liberty rather like an ugly disease, something that no human being should have to face if we can prevent it?

In short, no human being should be expected to overcome all potential life obstacles, and people who have to fight for the most basic things are precluded by that struggle from exercising their agency in other more fulfilling and socially fruitful ways. Someone who is struggling for minimal subsistence, or who is beaten every day, probably cannot at the same time be a lawyer or a parliamentary representative. Someone who has to fight to go to a meeting where she will see other women probably will not at the same time be running a primary school or leading a food relief movement. Social support for basic life functions, including prominently the basic liberties, is what we owe to people's humanity and dignity. It also makes good social sense, freeing people to be agents in socially productive ways. Every society, then, needs to decide what struggles people should not have to fight for themselves without social support. The rhetoric of victimology simply distracts us from asking the real question, which is what people are entitled to claim from their society. I argue that people should not have to fight exhausting personal struggles to get support for a small list of basic human capacities. Thus, society owes people, including women, a basic level of support for nutrition, health, shelter, education, and physical safety, and it also owes them effective guarantees of the major liberties of expression, conscience, and political participation.

In my view, the radical feminism of MacKinnon makes just such a demand for equal respect, asking that laws and institutions truly acknowledge women's equal worth in ways they have not previously done. In so arguing, MacKinnon, far from turning women into victims, is making the Kantian demand that women be treated as ends in themselves, centers of agency and freedom rather than merely as adjuncts to the plans of men. That it takes legal change to fulfill this demand does not mean that women are not seen as resourceful and active—any more than the fact that I give my daughter three meals a day means that I do not conceive of her as an active being. Thus, to create laws against sexual harassment is not to say that women cannot surmount such obstacles. We frequently have done so. We also surmount robbery and assault, which are illegal in every society. It is to say that no woman should have to surmount that particular obstacle, that the dignity of a person demands that she not be treated this way, that this is simply not one of the life struggles that our democracy thinks it valuable for people to be fighting on their own one by one without legal aid. Laws against robbery express a sense of the vulnerability of victims; they say that robbery does real harm. So too do laws against sexual harassment; they say that sexual harassment is not pleasing, that it does real harm. In that sense, such laws portray people as victims: They are shown not to be invulnerable to harm. But such harms are bad because people are seen as having a worth and dignity that means that they should not suffer that—so at the same time such laws express a sense of people as agents.

To insist on the real harms that women suffer is, then, not to undermine their dignity. It is to say what recognition of that dignity entails. If we are to think well about feminism, we need to learn to think better than we usually do about the complex interrelationship between agency and need, between harm and humanity.

Political and Personal

Most of these essays are concerned with developing an account of women's equality for use in the public political domain. Because, with many contemporary political theorists, I hold that the family is part of the basic structure of political society, in the sense that it is among the legally shaped institutions that most pervasively shaped individuals' capacities for flourishing, I take legal reform of the family to be a part of political justice. I believe that liberal political theory can remain true to a central commitment of liberalism, the protection of spheres of choice, while still ensuring a just starting point for male and female children by appropriate legal reforms.

There are, however, areas in which, as a liberal, I have definite views and make arguments that I think cogent, while believing that it would be inappropriate to make my views part of a shared public political conception. On certain basic matters we must reach a social consensus if political justice is ever to get off the ground. In that sense, a liberal can reasonably ask nonliberals to go along with a shared structure of laws and institutions if she can convince the nonliberal that these give appropriate opportunities for the nonliberal as well as the liberal to pursue human flourishing according to their own lights. For example, the liberal principle of religious toleration ought to be acceptable to members of nonliberal religions because it gives them the best shot at pursuing their own way of life free from interference. On the other hand, there are views a liberal might hold about religion—say, that religions should have respect for human reason, refusing to subordinate moral reasoning to religious authority—that should not be turned into public laws binding on all religions. As a liberal Jew, I will pursue those ideas within my religion and make such headway as I can. But it is altogether different to recommend that religions be legally repressed if they do not contain this principle, and a political liberal will not make this suggestion.

Sex poses delicate challenges for a political liberal who also holds liberal views (views about the importance of choice and freedom) concerning the conduct of life more generally. To what extent should she insist that such views be made part of the public political culture, even if they clash with the beliefs of other traditions present in the society, and to what extent should she draw a line between the political and the rest of life, making recommendations in the latter that she would not be prepared to commend as law in the former?

I argue that the equality of the sexes should be a prominent part of the public political culture, and that religions that dispute sex equality should not have the option of making law to that effect, as of course they do in very many nations of the world, including quite a few that have constitutional guarantees of sex equality. I also believe that in some areas of the religion's daily life, it ought to be held to public laws protecting sex equality (e.g., in the hiring of workers and in matters of sexual harassment). On the other hand, it seems to me that it would be unacceptably intrusive for the law to require the Roman Catholic Church to make women priests, a matter going to the heart of worship, although there are certainly impressive religious and moral arguments in favor of opening the priesthood to women. In general, individuals and groups may choose to view and treat one another in all sorts of hierarchical ways without legal interference, although there may be good moral arguments against such conduct.

In the sphere of sexual activity, we have similar questions to handle. To what extent should a moral argument, however well considered, be permitted to ground a legal restriction on sexual conduct? To what extent should we refuse to allow legal interference with people's sexual choices, however immoral? Once again, I follow Mill on this point. Two issues are salient: consent and harm. It seems wrong to interfere legally with the consensual sexual activities of adults unless there is a clear showing of harm (as distinct from offense) to nonconsenting third parties. Thus, I argue that laws criminalizing sodomy and fornication are indefensible, whereas there are strong reasons for laws criminalizing marital rape, child sexual abuse, and sexual harassment. It is important to bear in mind that Mill linked his concept of liberty closely to an idea of the dignity of the person: Regulations seemed to him incompatible with equal respect for persons if they constrained individuals in their personal choices in ways that imply that they are incompetent to decide what is right for themselves.[26] Where there is no consent, by contrast, we probably do not even need to show harm to intervene legally: The theft of a useless item from a prosperous person is still theft.

On many issues, then, I have strong moral views that I would not be prepared to commend as law in the public realm. "Objectification" discusses moral norms for sexual conduct but opposes legal restrictions on people whose conduct is blameworthy by those standards, except in the cases of harm already mentioned. Just as a nonliberal religious person ought to be able to accept a liberal principle of religious toleration as the one that best supports her ability to live a life in accordance with her own conscience, so too, it seems to me, a nonliberal in the sexual sphere should support the removal of sodomy laws and other related laws as unacceptably intrusive, even if she should believe sodomy immoral. A Millean no-harm principle in the sexual domain seems the one that best supports our desire to conduct our lives in accordance with our own moral views and our sense of our equal dignity as citizens, in a society that contains much disagreement about these issues.

In both religion and sex, the nonliberal may worry that the liberal political principle will lead to contamination of the young. A young Roman Catholic in a tolerant pluralistic society will grow up seeing Jews and Muslims and Protestants respected; she will associate with them in school and on the playground. Won't this undermine her allegiance to Catholicism? Similarly, the person who thinks homosexual acts immoral may worry that a regime of toleration and nondiscrimination poses a threat to her children: Won't they lose hold of the moral teaching when they see such people respected and not penalized for what they do? To both questions we should answer, yes, that is a risk people run in a liberal democracy. But it gives them some important benefits as well, prominent among which is not getting imprisoned and humiliated themselves should their opponents get the upper hand. More important, such a regime of noninterference expresses respect for the dignity of human beings, which ought to be something both liberals and nonliberals can agree about in a political way. If people are told what not to do with their lives in the intimate area of sexual conduct, this seems especially invasive of their humanity, and it would seem that from a variety of different viewpoints we could all agree not to invade people in those ways.

Pornography poses especially difficult problems for the political liberal. For it appears to cause harms to third parties, not only through its reinforcement of injurious stereotypes but in more direct ways: Through its effect on men who abuse women and, in many cases, through harmful exploitation of actresses and models in the making of it.[27] I discuss these issues in chapter 9, clarifying the proposals made by MacKinnon and Dworkin and examining various reasonable and unreasonable objections to them. I argue that MacKinnon and Dworkin have identified the correct moral target, as current obscenity law does not, but that their proposed remedy (a civil ordinance under which women can sue the makers and distributors of pornography for damages caused by its use) is probably not a good idea because it is likely to be badly implemented in practice and because it may exert a stifling effect on some valuable speech, including the feminist critique of pornography.

Prostitution is another of the most difficult issues faced by the Millean liberal. Once again, it is an institution that undeniably causes harms to women, and the question of consent is a complicated one because most women who enter prostitution, even when they are not literally forced (as is often the case internationally), have such a reduced menu of options that they can be said to have chosen only in a reduced sense. It is not clear, however, that criminalization is a good way to remedy these harms. In chapter 11, I argue that prostitution should not be considered apart from a wide range of cases in which people sell their bodily services. It is especially important to link the analysis to a consideration of the economic options of poor women; one should also attempt to separate criticisms that are based on puritanism and a distaste for female sexuality from criticisms based on a concern for women's dignity and autonomy. I argue that the continued criminalization of prostitution almost certainly makes both economic problems and dignity problems worse, and that the best approach to the issue is through providing poor women with a wider range of educational and employment opportunities.

Historical Antecedents: Aristotle, Stoics, Kant, Mill

My arguments are shaped by the many years I have spent writing about the history of Western philosophy, especially ancient Greek and Roman philosophy. Most obvious, perhaps, is the influence of Aristotle, who is the source for the conception of human functioning and capability that forms the core of the political argument, as it did of my work in the United Nations quality-of-life project. Aristotle is the source, as well, for the account of equitable judgment and mercy in chapter 6 (though his view needs help from Seneca), and for a general approach to the sympathetic perception of complex particulars that informs my writing as a whole. Finally, I owe to Aristotle the picture of justification within which I work: the idea that our aim is not to anchor our conclusions to extrahistorical first principles but, rather, to seek the best comprehensive fit among principles and concrete judgments, "preserving the greatest number and the most basic."

Aristotle offers a lot to liberal political theory, which needs a richer account of human needs for functioning than it usually has. But Aristotle is no liberal in matters of freedom and dignity; this volume is therefore centrally shaped, as well, by the tradition of Kantian liberalism represented, today, in the writings of John Rawls, who is central to more than one chapter. Rawls's thought has been variously interpreted and misinterpreted, and I do not focus on exegesis here. But I do owe to Kant and Rawls the notions of dignity and liberty, and the equal worth of liberty, that inform my discussions of women's equality and women's human rights in chapters 1, 2, and 3 and the discussion of women as ends rather than means in chapters 8 and 9.

These ideas of dignity and equal worth themselves have historical antecedents. Kant was profoundly influenced by the thought of the ancient Greek and especially Roman Stoics, whose ideas about obligation to humanity have been the central topic of my research in the history of philosophy for the past ten years or so.[28] In chapter 6 I investigate some related aspects of Stoic thought; and chapter 8 illustrates the considerable influence of Stoic notions of dignity on Kant's thought about sex relations.

In the course of defending a Kantian liberalism, I make a number of arguments against elements of the utilitarian tradition. But Mill has been a very important figure for me because he is the only major thinker in the modern Western philosophical tradition who devoted a major part of his energies to the injustice suffered by women, in collaboration with his wife, Harriet Taylor. *The Subjection of Women* is a wonderful work that says most of the most important things about sex equality. It is not a utilitarian work, and it is fully compatible with the Kantian/Aristotelian liberalism I develop. (In fact, I believe that it is generally best to think of Mill as an Aristotelian eudaimonist rather than as a Benthamite Utilitarian.) I also owe to Mill the libertarian view of sexual expression that I pursue throughout my discussions of gay rights and morals legislation.

It is easy to see how these philosophers could be sources for material about justice. But sex, one might ask? And it is certainly true that philosophy in most of the Western tradition has had little of interest to say about the sexual domain of life. The Roman Stoics presented a moving picture of marriage as a partnership, but about its sexual aspect they had little to offer but warnings against self-indulgence. Kant contributes some good insights about objectification, but otherwise most of what he says is highly bizarre. Few readers, for example, will share his judgment that masturbation is "the most abominable conduct of which man can be guilty,"[29] and most readers will think this an extraordinary judgment in someone who spent a great part of his career thinking about (and condemning) aggressive war, genocide, colonial conquest, and slavery. Mill is right on target about the formation of sexual desire, but about sex itself he is, following the custom of Victorian Britain, altogether silent. Aristotle probably discussed these matters in work now lost to us. His stray surviving remarks, combined with his wonderful writings on friendship, suggest that (if we can overlook his foolish views about women's capacities) he may have discussed them very well.[30] Joyce certainly thought so when he named Aristotle as the source for his own assault on doctrines of original sin and bodily impurity; to some extent I follow his lead.

Philosophers who lack good philosophical models frequently turn to examples based on familiar experiences. But this is especially unlikely to be a good way to proceed with this topic because, apart from the obvious issues of privacy and reticence, people do not always understand themselves very well in this domain of life, and any single person's experience, even if well understood, is bound to be highly selective. I have therefore turned to social science for empirical data, and to works of literature for an understanding of the phenomena deeper than that offered by the philosophers. One obvious gap is the lack of any systematic cross-cultural study of sexual experience and the value seen in it. Even at the level of literary description I do not pursue that project, nor do I think it would be at all feasible to do so without deep immersion in a particular culture. So, for the most part I confine myself to ancient Greece/Rome and to modern Britain/America, in the latter case choosing James Joyce, D. H. Lawrence, and Virginia Woolf as very different but mutually illuminating thinkers who provide good starting points for a discussion of some aspects, at least, of sexual experience.

PART I

Justice

1

WOMEN AND CULTURAL UNIVERSALS

We shall only solve our problems if we see them as human
problems arising out of a special situation; and we shall not
solve them if we see them as African problems, generated by
our being somehow unlike others.
—Kwame Anthony Appiah,
Africa in the Philosophy of Cultures

Being a woman is not yet a way of being a human being.
—Catharine MacKinnon

I. A Matter of Survival

"I may die, but still I cannot go out. If there's something in the house, we eat.
Otherwise, we go to sleep." So Metha Bai, a young widow in Rajasthan, India,
with two young children, described her plight as a member of a caste whose
women are traditionally prohibited from working outside the home—even when,
as here, survival itself is at issue. If she stays at home, she and her children may
shortly die. If she attempts to go out, her in-laws will beat her and abuse her
children. For now, Metha Bai's father travels from 100 miles away to plow her
small plot of land. But he is aging, and Metha Bai fears that she and her children
will shortly die with him.[1]

In this case, as in many others throughout the world, cultural traditions pose
obstacles to women's health and flourishing. Depressingly, many traditions
portray women as less important than men, less deserving of basic life support
or of fundamental rights that are strongly correlated with quality of life, such
as the right to work and the right to political participation. Sometimes, as in the
case of Metha Bai, the women themselves resist these traditions. Sometimes,
on the other hand, the traditions have become so deeply internalized that they
seem to record what is "right" and "natural," and women themselves endorse
their own second-class status.

Such cases are hardly confined to non-Western or developing countries. As recently as 1873, the U.S. Supreme Court upheld a law that forbade women to practice law in the state of Illinois, on the grounds that "[t]he constitution of the family organization, which is founded in the divine ordinance, as well as in the nature of things, indicates the domestic sphere as that which properly belongs to the domain and functions of womanhood."[2] And in 1993, a woman who was threatened and grossly harassed by her male coworkers, after becoming the first woman to work in the heavy metal shop in the General Motors plant in Indiana, was described by a federal district judge as having provoked the men's conduct by her "unladylike" behavior—behavior that consisted in using a four-letter word a few times in a five-year period.[3] Clearly our own society still appeals to tradition in its own way to justify women's unequal treatment.

What should people concerned with justice say about this? And should they say anything at all? On the one hand, it seems impossible to deny that traditions, both Western and non-Western, perpetrate injustice against women in many fundamental ways, touching on some of the most central elements of a human being's quality of life—health, education, political liberty and participation, employment, self-respect, and life itself. On the other hand, hasty judgments that a tradition in some distant part of the world is morally retrograde are familiar legacies of colonialism and imperialism and are correctly regarded with suspicion by sensitive thinkers in the contemporary world. To say that a practice endorsed by tradition is bad is to risk erring by imposing one's own way on others, who surely have their own ideas of what is right and good. To say that a practice is all right whenever local tradition endorses it as right and good is to risk erring by withholding critical judgment where real evil and oppression are surely present. To avoid the whole issue because the matter of proper judgment is so fiendishly difficult is tempting but perhaps the worst option of all. It suggests the sort of moral collapse depicted by Dante when he describes the crowd of souls who mill around in the vestibule of hell, dragging their banner now one way, now another, never willing to set it down and take a definite stand on any moral or political question. Such people, he implies, are the most despicable of all. They cannot even get into hell because they have not been willing to stand for anything in life, one way or another. To express the spirit of this chapter very succinctly, it is better to risk being consigned by critics to the "hell" reserved for alleged Westernizers and imperialists—however unjustified such criticism would in fact be—than to stand around in the vestibule waiting for a time when everyone will like what we are going to say. And what we are going to say is: that there are universal obligations to protect human functioning and its dignity, and that the dignity of women is equal to that of men. If that involves assault on many local traditions, both Western and non-Western, so much the better, because any tradition that denies these things is unjust. Or, as a young Bangladeshi wife said when local religious leaders threatened to break the legs of women who went to the literacy classes conducted by a local NGO (nongovernmental organization), "We do not listen to the *mullahs* any more. They did not give us even a quarter kilo of rice."[4]

The situation of women in the contemporary world calls urgently for moral standtaking. Women, a majority of the world's population, receive only a small proportion of its opportunities and benefits. According to the *Human Development Report*, in no country in the world is women's quality of life equal to that of men, according to a complex measure that includes life expectancy, educational attainment, and GDP (gross domestic product) per capita.[5] Some countries have much larger gender disparities than others. (Among prosperous industrial countries, for example, Spain and Japan perform relatively poorly in this area; Sweden, Denmark, and New Zealand perform relatively well.[6]) If we now examine the Gender Empowerment Measure, which uses variables chosen explicitly to measure the relative empowerment of men and women in political and economic activity,[7] we find even more striking signs of gender disparity. Once again, the Scandinavian nations do well; Japan and Spain do relatively poorly.[8]

If we turn our attention to the developing countries we find uneven achievements but, in the aggregate, a distressing situation. On average, employment participation rates of women are only 50% those of men (in South Asia 29%; in the Arab states only 16%).[9] Even when women are employed, their situation is undercut by pervasive wage discrimination and by long hours of unpaid household labor. (If women's unpaid housework were counted as productive output in national income accounts, global output would increase by 20–30%.) Outside the home, women are generally employed in a restricted range of jobs offering low pay and low respect. The percentage of earned income that goes to women is rarely higher than 35%. In many nations it is far lower: in Iran, 16%; Belize, 17%; Algeria, 16%; Iraq, 17%; Pakistan, 19%. (China at 38% is higher than Japan at 33%; highest in the world are Sweden at 45%, Denmark at 42%, and the extremely impoverished Rwanda at 41%, Burundi at 42%, and Mozambique at 42%.) The situation of women in the workplace is frequently undermined by sex discrimination and sexual harassment.

Women are much less likely than men to be literate. In South Asia, female literacy rates average around 50% those of males. In some countries the rate is still lower: in Nepal, 35%; Sierra Leone, 37%; Sudan, 27%; Afghanistan, 32%.[10] Two-thirds of the world's illiterate people are women. In higher education, women lag even further behind men in both developing and industrial nations.[11]

Although some countries allowed women the vote early in this century, some still have not done so. And there are many informal obstacles to women's effective participation in political life. Almost everywhere, they are underrepresented in government: In 1980, they made up only around 10% of the world's parliamentary representatives and less than 4% of its cabinet officials.[12]

As Metha Bai's story indicates, employment outside the home has a close relationship to health and nutrition. So too, frequently, does political voice. And if we now turn to the very basic issue of health and survival, we find compelling evidence of discrimination against females in many nations of the world. It appears that when equal nutrition and health care are present women live, on average, slightly longer than men—even allowing for a modest level of maternal mortality. Thus, in Europe the female/male ratio in 1986 was 105/100, in North

America 104.7/100.[13] But it may be objected that for several reasons it is inappropriate to compare these developed countries with countries in the developing world. Let us, therefore, with Jean Drèze and Amartya Sen, take as our baseline the ratio in sub-Saharan Africa, where there is great poverty but little evidence of gender discrimination in basic nutrition and health.[14] The female/male ration in 1986 was 102.2/100. If we examine the sex ratio in various other countries and ask the question, "How many more women than are now in country C would be there if its sex ratio were the same as that of sub-Saharan Africa?," we get a number that Sen has graphically called the number of "missing women." The number of missing women in Southeast Asia is 2.4 million; in Latin America, 4.4; in North Africa, 2.4; in Iran, 1.4; in China, 44.0; in Bangladesh, 3.7; in India, 36.7; in Pakistan, 5.2; in West Asia, 4.3. If we now consider the ratio of the number of missing women to the number of actual women in a country, we get, for Pakistan, 12.9%; for India, 9.5%; for Bangladesh, 8.7%; for China, 8.6%; for Iran, 8.5%; for West Asia, 7.8%; for North Africa, 3.9%; for Latin America, 2.2%; for Southeast Asia, 1.2%. In India, not only is the mortality differential especially sharp among children (girls dying in far greater numbers than boys), the higher mortality rate of women compared to men applies to all age groups until the late thirties.[15]

Poverty alone does not cause women to die in greater numbers than men. This is abundantly clear from comparative regional studies in India, where some of the poorest regions, for example, Kerala, have the most equal sex ratios, and some far richer regions perform very poorly.[16] When there is scarcity, custom and political arrangement frequently decree who gets to eat the little there is and who gets taken to the doctor. And custom and political arrangement are always crucial in deciding who gets to perform wage labor outside the home, an important determinant of general status in the family and the community. As Sen has argued, a woman's perceived contribution to the well-being of the family unit is often determined by her ability to work outside, and this determines, in turn, her bargaining position within the family unit.[17] Custom and politics decree who gets access to the education that would open job opportunities and make political rights meaningful. Custom and politics decree who can go where in what clothing in what company. Custom and politics decree who gets to make what sorts of protests against ill treatment both inside and outside the family and whose voice of protest is likely to be heard.

Customs and political arrangements, in short, are important causes of women's misery and death. It seems incumbent on people interested in justice, and aware of the information about women's status that studies such as the *Human Development Reports* present, to ask about the relationship between culture and justice and between both of these and legal-political arrangements. It then seems incumbent on them to try to work out an account of the critical assessment of traditions and political arrangements that is neither do-gooder colonialism or an uncritical validation of the status quo.

One might suppose that any approach to the question of quality of life assessment in development economics would offer an account of the relationship between tradition and women's equality that would help us answer these questions. But in fact such an account is sorely lacking in the major theoretical approaches that, until recently, dominated the development scene. (Here I do not even include what has been the most common practical approach, which has been simply to ask about GNP (gross national product) per capita. This crude approach does not even look at the distribution of wealth and income; far less does it ask about other constituents of life quality, for example, life expectancy, infant mortality, education, health, and the presence or absence of political liberties, that are not always well correlated with GNP per capita.[18] The failure to ask these questions is a particularly grave problem when it is women's quality of life we want to consider. For women have especially often been unable to enjoy or control the fruits of a nation's general prosperity.)

The leading economic approach to the family is the model proposed by Nobel Prize–winning economist Gary Becker. Becker assumes that the family's goal is the maximization of utility, construed as the satisfaction of preference or desire, and that the head of the household is a beneficent altruist who will adequately take thought for the interests of all family members.[19] In real life, however, the economy of the family is characterized by pervasive "cooperative conflicts," that is, situations in which the interests of members of a cooperative body split apart, and some individuals fare well at the expense of others.[20] Becker deserves great credit for putting these issues on the agenda of the profession in the first place. But his picture of male motivation does not fit the evidence, and in a way substantial enough to affect the model's predictive value—especially if one looks not only at women's stated satisfactions and preferences, which may be deformed by intimidation, lack of information, and habit,[21] but at their actual functioning.[22] Furthermore, the model prevents those who use it from even getting the information about individual family members on which a more adequate account might be based.[23]

Suppose we were to retain a utilitarian approach and yet to look at the satisfactions of all family members—assuming, as is standardly done in economics, that preferences and tastes are exogenous and independent of laws, traditions, and institutions rather than endogenously shaped by them. Such an approach—frequently used by governments polling citizens about well-being—has the advantage of assessing all individuals one by one. But the evidence of preference endogeneity is great, and especially great when we are dealing with people whose status has been persistently defined as second class in laws and institutions of various sorts. There are many reasons to think that women's perception even of their health status is shaped by traditional views, such as the view that female life is worth less than male life, that women are weaker than men, that women do not have equal rights, and so forth. In general, people frequently adjust their expectations to the low level of well-being they think they can actually attain.[24] This approach, then, cannot offer a useful account of the role of tradition in well-being, because it is bound by its very commitments to an uncritical validation of the status quo.

More promising than either Becker's model or the standard utilitarian approach is one suggested by John Rawls's liberalism, with its account of the just distribution of a small list of basic goods and resources.[25] This approach does enable us to criticize persistent inequalities, and it strongly criticizes the view that preferences are simply given rather than shaped by society's basic structure. But in one way the Rawlsian approach stops short. Rawls's list of "primary goods," although it includes some capacity-like items, such as liberty and opportunity, also includes thing-like items, particularly income and wealth, and it measures who is least well off simply in terms of the amount of these thing-like resources an individual can command. But people have varying needs for resources: a pregnant woman, for example, needs more calories than a nonpregnant woman, a child more protein than an adult. They also have different abilities to convert resources into functioning. A person in a wheelchair will need more resources to become mobile than a person with unimpaired limbs; a woman in a society that has defined employment outside the home as off limits to women needs more resources to become a productive worker than one who does not face such struggles. In short, the Rawlsian approach does not probe deeply enough to show us how resources do or do not go to work in making people able to function. Again, at least some of our questions about the relationship between tradition and quality of life cannot be productively addressed.

Workers on such issues have therefore increasingly converged on an approach that is now widely known as "the capabilities approach." This approach to quality-of-life measurement and the goals of public policy[26] holds that we should focus on the question: What are the people of the group or country in question actually able to do and to be? Unlike a focus on opulence (say, GNP per capita), this approach asks about the distribution of resources and opportunities. In principle, it asks how each and every individual is doing with respect to all the functions deemed important. Unlike Becker's approach, the capability approach considers people one by one, not as parts of an organic unit; it is very interested in seeing how a supposed organic unit such as the family has constructed unequal capabilities for various types of functioning. Unlike a standard utilitarian approach, the capability approach maintains that preferences are not always reliable indicators of life quality, as they may be deformed in various ways by oppression and deprivation. Unlike the type of liberal approach that focuses only on the distribution of resources, the capability approach maintains that resources have no value in themselves, apart from their role in promoting human functioning. It therefore directs the planner to inquire into the varying needs individuals have for resources and their varying abilities to convert resources into functioning. In this way, it strongly invites a scrutiny of tradition as one of the primary sources of such unequal abilities.[27]

But the capabilities approach raises the question of cultural universalism, or, as it is often pejoratively called, "essentialism." Once we begin asking how people are actually functioning, we cannot avoid focusing on some components of lives and not others, some abilities to act and not others, seeing some capabilities and functions as more central, more at the core of human life, than others. We cannot avoid having an account, even if a partial and highly general account, of what functions of the human being are most worth the care and attention of public planning the world over. Such an account is bound to be controversial.

II. Anti-Universalist Conversations

The primary opponents of such an account of capability and functioning will be "antiessentialists" of various types, thinkers who urge us to begin not with sameness but with difference—both between women and men and across groups of women—and to seek norms defined relatively to a local context and locally held beliefs. This opposition takes many forms, and I shall be responding to several distinct objections. But I can begin to motivate the enterprise by telling several true stories of conversations that have taken place at the World Institute for Development Economics Research (WIDER), in which the anti-universalist position seemed to have alarming implications for women's lives.[28]

At a conference on "Value and Technology," an American economist who has long been a leftwing critic of neoclassical economics delivers a paper urging the preservation of traditional ways of life in a rural area of Orissa, India, now under threat of contamination from Western development projects. As evidence of the excellence of this rural way of life, he points to the fact that whereas we Westerners experience a sharp split between the values that prevail in the workplace and the values that prevail in the home, here, by contrast, exists what the economist calls "the embedded way of life," the same values obtaining in both places. His example: Just as in the home a menstruating woman is thought to pollute the kitchen and therefore may not enter it, so too in the workplace a menstruating woman is taken to pollute the loom and may not enter the room where looms are kept. Some feminists object that this example is repellant rather than admirable; for surely such practices both degrade the women in question and inhibit their freedom. The first economist's collaborator, an elegant French anthropologist (who would, I suspect, object violently to a purity check at the seminar room door), replies: Don't we realize that there is, in these matters, no privileged place to stand? This, after all, has been shown by both Derrida and Foucault. Doesn't he know that he is neglecting the otherness of Indian ideas by bringing his Western essentialist values into the picture?[29]

The same French anthropologist now delivers her paper. She expresses regret that the introduction of smallpox vaccination to India by the British eradicated the cult of Sittala Devi, the goddess to whom one used to pray to avert smallpox. Here, she says, is another example of Western neglect of difference. Someone (it might have been me) objects that it is surely better to be healthy rather than ill, to live rather than to die. The answer comes back; Western essentialist medicine conceives of things in terms of binary oppositions: life is opposed to death, health to disease.[30] But if we cast away this binary way of thinking, we will begin to comprehend the otherness of Indian traditions.

At this point Eric Hobsbawm, who has been listening to the proceedings in increasingly uneasy silence, rises to deliver a blistering indictment of the traditionalism and relativism that prevail in this group. He lists historical examples of ways in which appeals to tradition have been politically engineered to support oppression and violence.[31] His final example is that of National Socialism in Germany. In the confusion that ensues, most of the relativist social scientists—above all those from far away, who do not know who Hobsbawm is—demand that Hobsbawm be asked to leave the room. The radical American economist, disconcerted by this apparent tension between his relativism and his affiliation with the left, convinces them, with difficulty, to let Hobsbawm remain.

We shift now to another conference two years later, a philosophical conference on the quality of life.[32] Members of the quality-of-life project are speaking of choice as a basic good, and of the importance of expanding women's sphere of choices. We are challenged by the radical economist of my first story, who insists that contemporary anthropology has shown that non-Western people are not especially attached to freedom of choice. His example: A book on Japan has shown that Japanese males, when they get home from work, do not wish to choose what to eat for dinner, what to wear, and so on. They wish all these choices to be taken out of their hands by their wives. A heated exchange follows about what this example really shows. I leave it to your imaginations to reconstruct it. In the end, the confidence of the radical economist is unshaken: We are victims of bad universalist thinking, who fail to respect "difference."[33]

The phenomenon is an odd one. For we see here highly intelligent people, people deeply committed to the good of women and men in developing countries, people who think of themselves as progressive and feminist and antiracist, people who correctly argue that the concept of development is an evaluative concept requiring normative argument[34]—effectively eschewing normative argument and taking up positions that converge, as Hobsbawm correctly saw, with the positions of reaction, oppression, and sexism. Under the banner of their fashionable opposition to universalism march ancient religious taboos, the luxury of the pampered husband, educational deprivation, unequal health care, and premature death.

Nor do these anti-universalists appear to have a very sophisticated conception of their own core notions, such as "culture," "custom," and "tradition." It verges on the absurd to treat India as a single culture, and a single visit to a single Orissan village as sufficient to reveal its traditions. India, like all extant societies, is a complex mixture of elements[35]: Hindu, Muslim, Parsi, Christian, Jewish, atheist; urban, suburban, rural; rich, poor, and middle class; high caste, low caste, and aspiring middle caste; female and male; rationalist and mystical. It is renowned for mystical religion but also for achievements in mathematics and for the invention of chess. It contains intense, often violent sectarianism, but it also contains Rabindranath Tagore's cosmopolitan humanism and Mahatma Gandhi's reinterpretation of Hinduism as a religion of universal nonviolence. Its traditions contain views of female whorishness and childishness that derive from the Laws of Manu[36]; but it also contains the sexual agency of Draupadi in the *Mahabharata*, who solved the problem of choice among Pandava husbands by taking all five, and the enlightened sensualism and female agency of the *Kama Sutra*, a sacred text that foreign readers wrongly interpret as pornographic. It contains women like Metha Bai, who are confined to the home; it also contains women like Amita Sen (mother of Amartya Sen), who fifty years ago was among the first middle-class Bengali women to dance in public, in Rabindranath Tagore's musical extravaganzas in Santiniketan. It contains artists who disdain the foreign, preferring, with the Marglins, the "embedded" way of life, and it also contains Satyajit Ray, that great Bengali artist and lover of local traditions, who could also write, "I never ceased to regret that while I had stood in the scorching summer sun in the wilds of Santiniketan sketching *simul* and *palash* in full bloom, *Citizen Kane* had come and gone, playing for just three days in the newest and biggest cinema in Calcutta."[37]

What, then, is "the culture" of a woman like Metha Bai? Is it bound to be that determined by the most prevalent customs in Rajasthan, the region of her marital home? Or, might she be permitted to consider with what traditions or groups she wishes to align herself, perhaps forming a community of solidarity with other widows and women, in pursuit of a better quality of life? What is "the culture" of Chinese working women who have recently been victims of the government's "women go home" policy, which appeals to Confucian traditions about woman's "nature"?[38] Must it be the one advocated by Confucius, or may they be permitted to form new alliances—with one another, and with other defenders of women's human rights? What is "the culture" of General Motors employee Mary Carr? Must it be the one that says women should be demure and polite, even in the face of gross insults, and that an "unladylike" woman deserves the harassment she gets? Or might she be allowed to consider what norms are appropriate to the situation of a woman working in a heavy metal shop, and to act accordingly? Real cultures contain plurality and conflict, tradition, and subversion. They borrow good things from wherever they find them, none too worried about purity. We would never tolerate a claim that women in our own society must embrace traditions that arose thousands of years ago—indeed, we are proud that we have no such traditions. Isn't it condescending, then, to treat Indian and Chinese women as bound by the past in ways that we are not?

Indeed, as Hobsbawm suggested, the vision of "culture" propounded by the Marglins, by stressing uniformity and homogeneity, may lie closer to artificial constructions by reactionary political forces than to any organic historical entity. Even to the extent to which it is historical, one might ask, exactly how does that contribute to make it worth preserving? Cultures are not museum pieces, to be preserved intact at all costs. There would appear, indeed, to be something condescending in preserving for contemplation a way of life that causes real pain to real people.

Let me now, nonetheless, describe the most cogent objections that might be raised by a relativist against a normative universalist project.

III. The Attack on Universalism

Many attacks on universalism suppose that any universalist project must rely on truths eternally fixed in the nature of things, outside human action and human history. Because some people believe in such truths and some do not, the objector holds that a normative view so grounded is bound to be biased in favor of some religious/metaphysical conceptions and against others.[39]

But universalism does not require such metaphysical support.[40] For universal ideas of the human do arise within history and from human experience, and they can ground themselves in experience. Indeed, those who take all human norms to be the result of human interpretation can hardly deny that universal conceptions of the human are prominent and pervasive among such interpretations, hardly to be relegated to the dustbin of metaphysical history along with recondite theoretical entities such as phlogiston. As Aristotle so simply puts it, "One may observe in one's travels to distant countries the feelings of recognition and affiliation that link every human being to every other human being."[41] Kwame Anthony Appiah makes the same point, telling the story of his bicultural childhood. A child who visits one set of grandparents in Ghana and another in rural England, who has a Lebanese uncle and who later, as an adult, has nieces and nephews from more than seven different nations, finds, he argues, not unbridgeable alien "otherness," but a great deal of human commonality, and comes to see the world as a "network of points of affinity."[42] But such a metaphysically agnostic, experiential and historical universalism is still vulnerable to some, if not all, of the objections standardly brought against universalism.

Neglect of Historical and Cultural Differences

The opponent charges that any attempt to pick out some elements of human life as more fundamental than others, even without appeal to a transhistorical reality, is bound to be insufficiently respectful of actual historical and cultural differences. People, it is claimed, understand human life and humanness in widely different ways, and any attempt to produce a list of the most fundamental properties and functions of human beings is bound to enshrine certain understandings of the human and to demote others. Usually, the objector continues, this takes the form of enshrining the understanding of a dominant group at the expense of minority understandings. This type of objection, frequently made by feminists, can claim support from many historical examples in which the human has indeed been defined by focusing on actual characteristics of males.

It is far from clear what this objection shows. In particular it is far from clear that it supports the idea that we ought to base our ethical norms, instead, on the current preferences and the self-conceptions of people who are living what the objector herself claims to be lives of deprivation and oppression. But it does show at least that the project of choosing one picture of the human over another is fraught with difficulty, political as well as philosophical.

Neglect of Autonomy

A different objection is presented by liberal opponents of universalism. The objection is that by determining in advance what elements of human life have most importance, the universalist project fails to respect the right of people to choose a plan of life according to their own lights, determining what is central and what is not.[43] This way of proceeding is "imperialistic." Such evaluative choices must be left to each citizen. For this reason, politics must refuse itself a determinate theory of the human being and the human good.

Prejudicial Application

If we operate with a determinate conception of the human being that is meant to have some normative moral and political force, we must also, in applying it, ask which beings we take to fall under the concept. And here the objector notes that, all too easily—even if the conception itself is equitably and comprehensively designed—the powerless can be excluded. Aristotle himself, it is pointed out, held that women and slaves were not full-fledged human beings, and because his politics were based on his view of human functioning, the failure of these beings (in his view) to exhibit the desired mode of functioning contributed to their political exclusion and oppression.

It is, once again, hard to know what this objection is supposed to show. In particular, it is hard to know how, if at all, it is supposed to show that we would be better off without such determinate universal concepts. For it could be plausibly argued that it would have been even easier to exclude women and slaves on a whim if one did not have such a concept to combat.[44] On the other hand, it does show that we need to think not only about getting the concept right but also about getting the right beings admitted under the concept.

Each of these objections has some merit. Many universal conceptions of the human being have been insular in an arrogant way and neglectful of differences among cultures and ways of life. Some have been neglectful of choice and autonomy. And many have been prejudicially applied. But none of this shows that all such conceptions must fail in one or more of these ways. At this point, however, we need to examine a real proposal, both to display its merits and to argue that it can in fact answer these charges.

IV. A Conception of the Human Being: The Central Human Capabilities

The list of basic capabilities is generated by asking a question that from the start is evaluative: What activities[45] characteristically performed by human beings are so central that they seem definitive of a life that is truly human? In other words, what are the functions without which (meaning, without the availability of which) we would regard a life as not, or not fully, human?[46] We can get at this question better if we approach it via two somewhat more concrete questions that we often really ask ourselves. First is a question about personal continuity. We ask ourselves which changes or transitions are compatible with the continued existence of that being as a member of the human kind and which are not. Some functions can fail to be present without threatening our sense that we still have a human being on our hands; the absence of others seems to signal the end of a human life. This question is asked regularly, when we attempt to make medical definitions of death in a situation in which some of the functions of life persist, or to decide, for others or (thinking ahead) for ourselves, whether a certain level of illness or impairment means the end of the life of the being in question.[47]

The other question is a question about kind inclusion. We recognize other humans as human across many differences of time and place, of custom and appearance. We often tell ourselves stories, on the other hand, about anthropomorphic creatures who do not get classified as human, on account of some feature of their form of life and functioning. On what do we base these inclusions and exclusions? In short, what do we believe must be there, if we are going to acknowledge that a given life is human?[48] The answer to these questions points us to a subset of common or characteristic human functions, informing us that these are likely to have a special importance for everything else we choose and do.

Note that the procedure through which this account of the human is derived is neither ahistorical nor a priori. It is the attempt to summarize empirical findings of a broad and ongoing cross-cultural inquiry. As such, it is both open-ended and humble; it can always be contested and remade. Nor does it claim to read facts of "human nature" from biological observation; it takes biology into account as a relatively constant element in human experience.[49] It is because the account is evaluative from the start that it is called a conception of the good.

It should also be stressed that, like John Rawls's account of primary goods in *A Theory of Justice*,[50] this list of good functions, which is in some ways more comprehensive than his own list, is proposed as the object of a specifically political consensus.[51] The political is not understood exactly as Rawls understands it because the nation state is not assumed to be the basic unit, and the account is meant to have broad applicablity to cross-cultural deliberations. This means, given the current state of world politics, that many of the obligations to promote the adequate distribution of these goods must rest with individuals rather than with any political institution, and in that way its role becomes difficult to distinguish from the role of other norms and goals of the individual. Nonetheless, the point of the list is the same as that of Rawlsian primary goods: to put forward something that people from many different traditions, with many different fuller conceptions of the good, can agree on, as the necessary basis for pursuing their good life. That is why the list is deliberately rather general.[52] Each of its components can be more concretely specified in accordance with one's origins, religious beliefs, or tastes. In that sense, the consensus that it hopes to evoke has many of the features of the "overlapping consensus" described by Rawls.[53]

Having isolated some functions that seem central in defining the very presence of a human life, we do not rest content with mere bare humanness. We want to specify a life in which fully human functioning, or a kind of basic human flourishing, will be available. For we do not want politics to take mere survival as its goal; we want to describe a life in which the dignity of the human being is not violated by hunger or fear or the absence of opportunity. (The idea is very much Marx's idea, when he used an Aristotelian notion of functioning to describe the difference between a merely animal use of one's faculties and a "truly human use."[54]) The following list of central human functional capabilities is an attempt to specify this basic notion of the good: All citizens should have these capabilities, whatever else they have and pursue.[55] I introduce this as a list of capabilities rather than of actual functionings, because I shall argue that capability, not actual functioning, should be the goal of public policy.

Central Human Functional Capabilities

1. *Life.* Being able to live to the end of a human life of normal length[56]; not dying prematurely or before one's life is so reduced as to be not worth living

2. *Bodily health and integrity.* Being able to have good health, including reproductive health; being adequately nourished[57]; being able to have adequate shelter[58]

3. *Bodily integrity.* Being able to move freely from place to place; being able to be secure against violent assault, including sexual assault, marital rape, and domestic violence; having opportunities for sexual satisfaction and for choice in matters of reproduction

4. *Senses, imagination, thought.* Being able to use the senses; being able to imagine, to think, and to reason—and to do these things in a "truly human" way, a way informed and cultivated by an adequate education, including, but by no means limited to, literacy and basic mathematical and scientific training; being able to use imagination and thought in connection with experiencing and producing expressive works and events of one's own choice (religious, literary, musical, etc.); being able to use one's mind in ways protected by guarantees of freedom of expression with respect to both political and artistic speech and freedom of religious exercise; being able to have pleasurable experiences and to avoid nonbeneficial pain

5. *Emotions.* Being able to have attachments to things and persons outside ourselves; being able to love those who love and care for us; being able to grieve at their absence; in general, being able to love, to grieve, to experience longing, gratitude, and justified anger; not having one's emotional developing blighted by fear or anxiety. (Supporting this capability means supporting forms of human association that can be shown to be crucial in their development.[59])

6. *Practical reason.* Being able to form a conception of the good and to engage in critical reflection about the planning of one's own life. (This entails protection for the liberty of conscience.)

7. *Affiliation.* (a) Being able to live for and in relation to others, to recognize and show concern for other human beings, to engage in various forms of social interaction; being able to imagine the situation of another and to have compassion for that situation; having the capability for both justice and friendship. (Protecting this capability means, once again, protecting institutions that constitute such forms of affiliation, and also protecting the freedoms of assembly and political speech.) (b) Having the social bases of self-respect and nonhumiliation; being able to be treated as a dignified being whose worth is equal to that of others. (This entails provisions of nondiscrimination.)

8. *Other species.* Being able to live with concern for and in relation to animals, plants, and the world of nature[60]

9. *Play*. Being able to laugh, to play, to enjoy recreational activities
10. *Control over one's environment*. (a) *Political*: being able to participate effectively in political choices that govern one's life; having the rights of political participation, free speech, and freedom of association (b) *Material*: being able to hold property (both land and movable goods); having the right to seek employment on an equal basis with others; having the freedom from unwarranted search and seizure.[61] In work, being able to work as a human being, exercising practical reason and entering into meaningful relationships of mutual recognition with other workers.

The "capabilities approach," as I conceive it,[62] claims that a life that lacks any one of these capabilities, no matter what else it has, will fall short of being a good human life. Thus it would be reasonable to take these things as a focus for concern, in assessing the quality of life in a country and asking about the role of public policy in meeting human needs. The list is certainly general—and this is deliberate, to leave room for plural specification and also for further negotiation. But like (and as a reasonable basis for) a set of constitutional guarantees, it offers real guidance to policymakers, and far more accurate guidance than that offered by the focus on utility, or even on resources.[63]

The list is, emphatically, a list of separate components. We cannot satisfy the need for one of them by giving a larger amount of another one. All are of central importance and all are distinct in quality. This limits the trade-offs that it will be reasonable to make and thus limits the applicability of quantitative cost-benefit analysis. At the same time, the items on the list are related to one another in many complex ways. Employment rights, for example, support health, and also freedom from domestic violence, by giving women a better bargaining position in the family. The liberties of speech and association turn up at several distinct points on the list, showing their fundamental role with respect to several distinct areas of human functioning.

V. Capability as Goal

The basic claim I wish to make—concurring with Amartya Sen—is that the central goal of public planning should be the *capabilities* of citizens to perform various important functions. The question that should be asked when assessing quality of life in a country—and of course this is a central part of assessing the quality of its political arrangements—is, How well have the people of the country been enabled to perform the central human functions? And, have they been put in a position of mere human subsistence with respect to the functions, or have they been enabled to live well? Politics, we argue (here concurring with Rawls), should focus on getting as many people as possible into a state of capability to function, with respect to the interlocking set of capabilities enumerated by that list.[64] Naturally, the determination of whether certain individuals and groups are across the threshold is only as precise a matter as the determination of the threshold. I have left things deliberately somewhat open-ended at this point, in keeping with the procedures of the *Human Development Report*, believing that the best way to work toward a more precise determination, at present, is to focus on comparative information and to allow citizens to judge for themselves whether their policymakers have done as well as they should have. Again, we will have to answer various questions about the costs we are willing to pay to get all citizens above the threshold, as opposed to leaving a small number below and allowing the rest a considerably above-threshold life quality. It seems likely, at any rate, that moving all citizens above a basic threshold of capability should be taken as a central social goal. When citizens are across the threshold, societies are to a great extent free to choose the other goals they wish to pursue. Some inequalities, however, will themselves count as capability failures. For example, inequalities based on hierarchies of gender or race will themselves be inadmissible on the grounds that they undermine self-respect and emotional development.

The basic intuition from which the capability approach starts, in the political arena, is that human capabilities exert a moral claim that they should be developed. Human beings are creatures such that, provided with the right educational and material support, they can become fully capable of the major human functions. That is, they are creatures with certain lower-level capabilities (which I call "basic capabilities"[65]) to perform the functions in question. When these capabilities are deprived of the nourishment that would transform them into the high-level capabilities that figure on my list, they are fruitless, cut off, in some way but a shadow of themselves. They are like actors who never get to go on the stage, or a person who sleeps all through life, or a musical score that is never performed. Their very being makes forward reference to functioning. Thus, if functioning never arrives on the scene they are hardly even what they are. This may sound like a metaphysical idea, and in a sense it is (in that it is an idea discussed in Aristotle's *Metaphysics*). But that does not mean it is not a basic and pervasive empirical idea, an idea that underwrites many of our daily practices and judgments in many times and places. Just as we hold that a child who dies before getting to maturity has died especially tragically—for her activities of growth and preparation for adult activity now have lost their point—so too with capability and functioning more generally: We believe that certain basic and central human endowments have a claim to be assisted in developing, and exert that claim on others, and especially, as Aristotle saw, on government. Without some such notion of the basic worth of human capacities, we have a hard time arguing for women's equality and for basic human rights. Think, for example, of the remark of Catharine MacKinnon that I quoted as my epigraph. If women were really just trees or turtles or filing cabinets, the fact that their current status in many parts of the world is not a fully human one would not be, as it is, a problem of justice. In thinking of political planning we begin, then, from a notion of the basic capabilities and their worth, thinking of them as claims to a chance for functioning, which give rise to correlated political duties.

I have spoken both of functioning and of capability. How are they related? Getting clear about this is crucial in defining the relation of the capabilities approach to liberalism. For if we were to take functioning itself as the goal of public policy, the liberal would rightly judge that we were precluding many choices that citizens may make in accordance with their own conceptions of the good. A deeply religious person may prefer not to be well nourished but to engage in strenuous fasting. Whether for religious or for other reasons, a person may prefer a celibate life to one containing sexual expression. A person may prefer to work with an intense dedication that precludes recreation and play. Am I saying that these are not fully human or flourishing lives? Does the approach instruct governments to nudge or push people into functioning of the requisite sort, no matter what they prefer?

Here we must answer: No, capability, not functioning, is the political goal. This is so because of the very great importance the approach attaches to practical reason, as a good that both suffuses all the other functions, making them human rather than animal,[66] and figures, itself, as a central function on the list. It is perfectly true that functionings, not simply capabilities, are what render a life fully human: If there were no functioning of any kind in a life, we could hardly applaud it, no matter what opportunities it contained. Nonetheless, for political purposes it is appropriate for us to shoot for capabilities, and those alone. Citizens must be left free to determine their course after that. The person with plenty of food may always choose to fast, but there is a great difference between fasting and starving, and it is this difference we wish to capture. Again, the person who has normal opportunities for sexual satisfaction can always choose a life of celibacy, and we say nothing against this. What we do speak against, for example, is the practice of female genital mutilation, which deprives individuals of the opportunity to choose sexual functioning (and indeed, the opportunity to choose celibacy as well).[67] A person who has opportunities for play can always choose a workaholic life; again, there is a great difference between that chosen life and a life constrained by insufficient maximum-hour protections and/or the "double day" that makes women in many parts of the world unable to play.

The issue will be clearer if we recall that there are three different types of capabilities that figure in the analysis.[68] First, there are *basic capabilities*: the innate equipment of individuals that is the necessary basis for developing the more advanced capability. Most infants have from birth the basic capability for practical reason and imagination, though they cannot exercise such functions without a lot more development and education. Second, there are *internal capabilities*: states of the person herself that are, as far as the person herself is concerned, sufficient conditions for the exercise of the requisite functions. A woman who has not suffered genital mutilation has the internal capability for sexual pleasure; most adult human beings everywhere have the internal capability to use speech and thought in accordance with their own conscience. Finally, there are *combined capabilities*, which we define as internal capabilities *combined with* suitable external conditions for the exercise of the function. A woman who is not mutilated but is secluded and forbidden to leave the house has internal but not combined capabilities for sexual expression (and work and political participation). Citizens of repressive nondemocratic regimes have the internal but not the combined capability to exercise thought and speech in accordance with their conscience. The aim of public policy is the production of *combined capabilities*. This means promoting the states of the person by providing the necessary education and care; it also means preparing the environment so that it is favorable for the exercise of practical reason and the other major functions.[69]

This clarifies the position. The approach does not say that public policy should rest content with *internal capabilities* but remain indifferent to the struggles of individuals who have to try to exercise these in a hostile environment. In that sense, it is highly attentive to the goal of functioning, and instructs governments to keep it always in view. On the other hand, we are not pushing individuals into the function: Once the stage is fully set, the choice is up to them.

The approach is therefore very close to Rawls's approach using the notion of primary goods. We can see the list of capabilities as like a long list of opportunities for life functioning, such that it is always rational to want them whatever else one wants. If one ends up having a plan of life that does not make use of all of them, one has hardly been harmed by having the chance to choose a life that does. (Indeed, in the cases of fasting and celibacy it is the very availability of the alternative course that gives the choice its moral value.) The primary difference between this capabilities list and Rawls's list of primary goods is its length and definiteness, and in particular its determination to place on the list the social basis of several goods that Rawls has called "natural goods," such as "health and vigor, intelligence and imagination."[70] Since Rawls has been willing to put the social basis of self-respect on his list, it is not at all clear why he has not made the same move with imagination and health.[71] Rawls's evident concern is that no society can guarantee health to its individuals—in that sense, saying that our goal is full combined capability may appear unreasonably idealistic. Some of the capabilities (e.g., some of the political liberties) can be fully guaranteed by society, but many others involve an element of chance and cannot be so guaranteed. We respond to this by saying that the list is an enumeration of political *goals* that should be useful as a benchmark for aspiration and comparison. Even though individuals with adequate health support often fall ill, it still makes sense to compare societies by asking about actual health capabilities, because we assume that the comparison will reflect the different inputs of human planning and can be adjusted to take account of more and less favorable natural situations.

Earlier versions of the list appeared to diverge from the approach of Rawlsian liberalism by not giving as central a place as Rawls does to the traditional political rights and liberties—although the need to incorporate them was stressed from the start.[72] This version of the list corrects that defect of emphasis. These political liberties have a central importance in making well-being human. A society that aims at well-being while overriding these has delivered to its members a merely animal level of satisfaction.[73] As Amartya Sen has recently written, "Political rights are important not only for the fulfillment of needs, they are crucial also for the formulation of needs. And this idea relates, in the end, to the respect that we owe each other as fellow human beings."[74] This idea has recently been echoed by Rawls: Primary goods specify what citizens' needs are from the point of view of political justice.[75]

The capability view justifies its elaborate list by pointing out that choice is not pure spontaneity, flourishing independently of material and social conditions. If one cares about people's powers to choose a conception of the good, then one must care about the rest of the form of life that supports those powers, including its material conditions. Thus the approach claims that its more compre-

hensive concern with flourishing is perfectly consistent with the impetus behind the Rawlsian project, which has always insisted that we are not to rest content with merely formal equal liberty and opportunity but must pursue their
fully equal worth by ensuring that unfavorable economic and social circumstances do not prevent people from availing themselves of liberties and opportunities that are formally open to them.

The guiding thought behind this Aristotelian enterprise is, at its heart, a profoundly liberal idea,[76] and one that lies at the heart of Rawls's project as well:
the idea of the citizen as a free and dignified human being, a maker of choices.
Politics has an urgent role to play here, getting citizens the tools they need, both
to choose at all and to have a realistic option of exercising the most valuable
functions. The choice of whether and how to use the tools, however, is left up to
them, in the conviction that this is an essential aspect of respect for their freedom. They are seen not as passive recipients of social planning but as dignified
beings who shape their own lives.[77]

Let us now return to the Marglins and to Metha Bai. What would this universalist approach have to say about these concrete cases? Notice how close the
Marglin approach is, in its renunciation of critical normative argument, to the
prevailing economic approaches of which it presents itself as a radical critique.
A preference-based approach that gives priority to the preferences of dominant
males in a traditional culture is likely to be especially subversive of the quality
of life of women, who have been on the whole badly treated by prevailing traditional norms. And one can see this clearly in the Marglins' own examples. For
menstruation taboos, even if endorsed by habit and custom, impose severe restrictions on women's power to form a plan of life and to execute the plan they
have chosen.[78] They are members of the same family of traditional attitudes that
make it difficult for women like Metha Bai to sustain the basic functions of life.
Vulnerability to smallpox, even if someone other than an anthropologist should
actually defend it as a good thing, is even more evidently a threat to human
functioning. And the Japanese husband who allegedly renounces freedom of
choice actually shows considerable attachment to it, in the ways that matter, by
asking the woman to look after the boring details of life. What should concern
us is whether the woman has a similar degree of freedom to plan her life and to
execute her plan.

As for Metha Bai, the absence of freedom to choose employment outside the
home is linked to other capability failures, in the areas of health, nutrition,
mobility, education, and political voice. Unlike the type of liberal view that focuses on resources alone, my view enables us to focus directly on the obstacles
to self-realization imposed by traditional norms and values and thus to justify
special political action to remedy the unequal situation. No male of Metha Bai's
caste would have to overcome threats of physical violence in order to go out of
the house to work for life-sustaining food.

The capabilities approach insists that a woman's affiliation with a certain group
or culture should not be taken as normative for her unless, on due consideration,
with all the capabilities at her disposal, she makes that norm her own. We should
take care to extend to each individual full capabilities to pursue the items on the

list—and then see whether they want to avail themselves of those opportunities. Usually they do, even when tradition says they should not. Martha Chen's work with widows like Metha Bai reveals that they are already deeply critical of the cultural norms that determine their life quality. One week at a widows' conference in Bangalore was sufficient to cause these formerly secluded widows to put on forbidden colors and to apply for loans; one elderly woman, "widowed" at the age of seven, danced for the first time in her life, whirling wildly in the center of the floor.[79] In other cases, especially when a woman must negotiate a relationship with a surviving husband, it takes longer for her real affiliations and preferences to emerge. Chen's related study of a rural literacy project in Bangladesh[80] shows that it took a good deal of time for women previously illiterate to figure out, in consultation with development workers, that literacy might offer something to their own concrete lives. Nonetheless, what we do not see in any of these cases is the fantasy that the Marglins describe, a cultural monolith univocally repudiating the outsider and clinging to an "embedded way of life." Why should women cling to a tradition, indeed, when it is usually not their voice that speaks or their interests that are served?

VI. Answering the Objections: Human Functioning and Pluralism

We still need to show that this approach has answers to the legitimate questions that confronted it. Concerning *neglect of historical and cultural difference,* we can begin by insisting that this normative conception of human capability is designed to make room for a reasonable pluralism in specification. The capabilities approach urges us to see common needs, problems, and capacities, but it also reminds us that each person and group faces these problems in a highly concrete context. The list claims to have identified in a very general way some components that are fundamental to any human life. But it makes room for differences of context in several ways. First, it is open ended and nonexhaustive. It does not say that these are the only important things, or that there is anything unimportant (far less, bad) about things not on the list. It just says that this is a group of especially important functions on which we can agree to focus for political purposes.

Further, the list allows in its very design for the possibility of multiple specifications of each of the components. Good public reasoning about the list will retain a rich sensitivity to the concrete context, to the characters of the agents and their social situation. Sometimes what is a good way of promoting education in one part of the world will be completely ineffectual in another. Forms of affiliation that flourish in one community may prove impossible to sustain in another. Arriving at the best specification will most reasonably be done by a public dialogue with those who are most deeply immersed in those conditions. We should use the list to criticize injustice, but we should not say anything at all without rich and full information.

We see this, for example, in Martha Chen's account of the Bangladeshi literacy project.[81] An initial approach that simply offered the women adult literacy materials met with no response. It was only after a period of "participatory dialogue," during which the local women told their stories and the development workers gave them rich narrative information about the lives of women elsewhere, that a picture of literacy for these women in these circumstances began to emerge and to make sense. Given the opportunity, they made for themselves a concrete local specification of this vague end. And it was clearly no external imposition: The women's narratives express a joy in self-command and agency that seems to come from something very deep in themselves. Rohima, of the West Shanbandha women's group, comments:

> Even my mother said yesterday: "You did not use to visit others' homes, did not speak to others. How have you learnt to speak so many things?" I said: "Ma, how I have learnt I cannot say. Whenever I am alone I sit with the books." Mother asked: "What do you see in the books?" I said: "Ma, what valuable things there are in the books you will not understand because you cannot read and write." If somebody behaves badly with me, I go home and sit with the books. When I sit with the books my mind becomes better.[82]

The books had to have some relation to the women's concrete situation, but it was equally important that the development workers did not back off when they saw that the women's local traditions contained no history of female literacy.

We can say the same of the related value of autonomy. It would have been very wrong to assume, with the Marglins, that these women did not want separateness and choice, that they really wanted to submerge their own aims in those of husband and family. This, again, emerges retrospectively, in their moving accounts of their newfound feeling of selfhood and mental awareness. "My mind was rusty," says one young wife, "and now it shines." On the other hand, it also would have done no good to go into that village and deliver a lecture on Kant—or on human capabilities! The universal value of practical reason and choice would have meant little in the abstract. To make sense, it had to become concretely situated in the stories they told about themselves and their lives.

If we turn to the difficult story of Metha Bai, something similar emerges. Metha Bai's is the story of age-old traditions regarding widowhood in India.[83] Any approach to her situation would have to be based on an understanding of these traditions and their special connection with issues of caste in an upwardly mobile Hindu family. Talk of "the right to work" would have been no use without a concrete local understanding. On the other hand, if the workers in the widows project had simply backed off, saying that the local values did not include a value of right to work for widows, they would have missed the depth at which Metha Bai herself longed for choice and autonomy, both as means to survival for herself and her children and as means to selfhood. These are typical examples of the fruitful ways in which an abstract value can be instantiated in a concrete situation, through rich local knowledge.

One further observation is in order. This objector is frequently worried about the way in which universalist projects may erode the values that hold communities together. We have already seen that traditional community values are not always so good for women. We can now add that universalist values build new types of community. All the women studied by Chen stressed the solidarity promoted by the literacy project, the comfort and pleasure they had in consulting with a group of women (some local, some from the development project) rather than each being isolated in the home. Mallika, a young widow in Dapunia, vigorously expresses this idea:

> The group helped us and taught us many things. I have learned how to live unitedly. Before if any rich person abused or criticized, we could not reply. But now if anybody says anything bad, we, the 17 members of the group, go together and ask that person why he or she passed this comment. This is another kind of help we have gotten. Before we did not know how to get together and help each other. . . . Each one was busy with their own worries and sorrows, always thinking about food for their children and themselves. Now we, the 17 members of the group, have become very close to one another.[84]

This story is no isolated phenomenon. In women's groups I have visited in both India and China, the first benefit that is typically mentioned is that of affiliation and friendship with other women in pursuit of common goals. This shows us something highly pertinent to the Marglins' nostalgic tale of embeddedness. We do not have to choose between "the embedded life" of community and a deracinated type of individualism. Universal values build their own communities, communities of resourcefulness, friendship, and agency, embedded in the local scene but linked in complex ways to groups of women in other parts of the world. For these women the new community was a lot better than the one they had inhabited before.

The liberal charges the capability approach with *neglect of autonomy*, arguing that any such determinate conception removes from the citizens the chance to make their own choices about the good life. We have already said a good deal about this issue, but let us summarize, stressing three points. First, the list is a list of capabilities, not a list of actual functions, precisely because the conception is designed to leave room for choice. Government is not directed to push citizens into acting in certain valued ways; instead, it is directed to make sure that all human beings have the necessary resources and conditions for acting in those ways. By making opportunities available, government enhances, and does not remove, choice.[85] It will not always be easy to say at what point someone is really capable of making a choice, especially when there are traditional obstacles to functioning. Sometimes our best strategy may well be to look at actual functioning and infer negative capability (tentatively) from its absence.[86] But the conceptual distinction remains critical. Even in the rare case in which the approach will favor compulsory measures—particularly in primary and secondary education—it does so because of the huge role education plays in opening other choices in life.

Second, this respect for choice is built deeply into the list itself, in the role it gives to practical reasoning, to the political liberties, and also to employment, seen as a source of opportunity and empowerment. One of the most central capabilities promoted by the conception will be the capability of choosing itself.[87]

The examples we have considered show the truth of these claims. In the literacy project, a concern for autonomy was fundamental in the method of participatory dialogue itself, which constructed a situation free from intimidation and hierarchy in which the women's own concerns could gradually emerge and develop on the basis of the information they received. Their ex post facto satisfaction with their new situation, in which life choices were greatly enhanced, indicates, I believe, that the focus on a general capability goal was not a violation of their autonomy. (Rohima comments: "It is good now. . . . As my knowledge and understanding are good now, I will be able to do many things gradually."[88]) Indeed, we can see in the project as a whole the construction of full autonomy out of a more inchoate sense of the self. Metha Bai already had a robust sense of her own interests and how they diverged from the expectations of those around her. But the widows project, which extended her thoughts by providing information and advice, was crucial to the further development of her own conception of life.

Finally, the capability view insists that choice is not pure spontaneity, flourishing independently of material and social conditions. If one cares about autonomy, then one must care about the rest of the form of life that supports it and the material conditions that enable one to live that form of life. Thus, the approach claims that its own comprehensive concern with flourishing is a better way of promoting choice than is the liberal's narrower concern with spontaneity alone, which sometimes tolerates situations in which individuals are cut off from the fully human use of their faculties.

We now face the objection about *prejudicial application*. Catharine MacKinnon once claimed that "being a woman is not yet a way of being a human being."[89] As this remark suggests, most traditional ways of categorizing and valuing women have not accorded them full membership in the human species, as that species is generally defined. If this is so, one might well ask, of what use is it to identify a set of central human capabilities? For the basic (lower-level) capacity to develop these can always be denied to women, even by those who grant their centrality—for example, by denying women "rational nature," or by asserting that they are connected to dangerous or unclean animality. Does this problem show that the human function idea is either hopelessly in league with patriarchy or, at best, impotent as a tool for justice?

I believe that it does not. For if we examine the history of these denials we see, I believe, the great power of the conception of the human as a source of moral claims. Acknowledging the other person as a member of the very same kind would have generated a sense of affiliation and a set of moral and educational duties. That is why, to those bent on shoring up their own power, the stratagem of splitting the other off from one's own species seems so urgent and so seductive. But to deny humanness to beings with whom one lives in conversation and interaction is a fragile sort of self-deceptive stratagem, vulnerable to sustained and consistent reflection, and also to experiences that cut through self-deceptive rationalization. Any moral conception can be withheld, out of ambition or hatred or shame. But the conception of the human being, spelled out, as here, in a roughly determinate way, seems much harder to withhold than others that have been made the basis for ethics, such as "rational being" or "person."

VII. Women and Men: Two Norms or One?

But should there be a single norm of human functioning for men and women? One might grant that human capabilities cross cultures while still maintaining that in each culture a division of labor should be arranged along gender lines.

One such position, which I shall call Position A, assigns to both males and females the same general normative list of functions but suggests that males and females should exercise these functions in different spheres of life: men in the public sphere, for example, and women in the home. The second, which I shall call Position B, insists that the list of functions, even at a high level of generality, should be different: for men, citizenship and rational autonomy; for women, family love and care.

Position A is compatible with a serious interest in equality and in gender justice. For what it says, after all, is that males and females have the same basic needs for capability development and should get what they need. It is determined to ensure that both get to the higher (developed) level of capability with respect to all the central functions. It simply holds that this can (and perhaps should) be done in separate spheres. Is this any more problematic than to say that human functioning in India can, and even should, take a different concrete form from functioning in England? Or that some people can realize musical capacities by singing; others by playing the violin?

The trouble comes when we notice that Position A usually ends up endorsing a division of duties that is associated with traditional forms of hierarchy. Even Mill, who made so many fine arguments against women's subordination, did not sufficiently ask how the very perpetuation of separate spheres of responsibility might reinforce subordination. It is hard to find plausible reasons for perpetuating functional distinctions that coincide with traditional hierarchy. Even in the fourth century B.C.E., Plato was able to see that women's role in childbearing does not require, or even suggest, that women be confined to the home.[90] Advances in the control of reproduction are making this less and less plausible. The disability imposed by childbearing on a member of the labor force is to a large extent socially constructed, above all by the absence of support for child care, from the public sphere, from employers, and from male partners.

Sometimes clinging to traditional divisions is a prudent way of promoting social change. Neither Chen nor her colleagues proposed to jettison all gender divisions within the Bangladeshi villages. Instead, they found "female jobs" for the women that were somewhat more dignified and important than the old jobs, jobs that looked continuous with traditional female work but were outside the home and brought in wages. The "revolution" in women's quality of life never would have taken place but for the caution of the women, who at each stage gave the men of the village reason to believe that the transformations were not overwhelmingly threatening and were good for the well-being of the entire group. But such pragmatic decisions in the face of recalcitrant realities do not tell us how things ought to be. And it is likely that women's subordination will not be adequately addressed as long as women are confined to a sphere traditionally devalued, linked with a low "perceived well-being contribution."[91] The *Human Development Report's* Gender Empowerment Measure rightly focuses, therefore, on the ability of women to win entry into the traditional male spheres of politics and administration.

I turn, then, to Position B, which has been influentially defended by many philosophers, including Rousseau and some of his followers in today's world.[92] Insofar as B relies on the claim that there are two different sets of basic innate capacities, we should insist, with John Stuart Mill, that this claim has not been borne out by any responsible scientific evidence. Experiments that allegedly show strong gender divisions in basic (untrained) abilities have been shown to contain major scientific flaws; these flaws removed, the case for such differences is altogether inconclusive.[93] Experiments that cross-label babies as to sex have established that children are differentially handled, played with, and talked to straight from birth, in accordance with the handler's beliefs about the child's biological sex. It is therefore impossible at present to separate "nature" from "culture."[94] There may be innate differences between the sexes, but so far we are not in a position to know them—any more than we were when Mill first made that argument in 1869.[95]

Second, we should note that even what is claimed in this body of scientific material without substantiation usually does not amount to a difference in what I have been calling the central basic capabilities. What is alleged is usually a differential statistical distribution of some specific capacity for a high level of excellence, not for crossing a basic threshold, and excellence in some very narrowly defined function (say, geometrical ability), rather than in one of our large-scale capabilities such as the capability to perform practical reasoning. Thus, even if the claim were true it would not be a claim about capabilities in our capacious sense; nor, because it is a statistical claim, would it have any implications for the ways in which individuals should be treated. The political consequences of such alleged sex differences in our scheme of things, even had they been established, would be nil.

But we can also criticize Position B in a different way, arguing that the differentiated conceptions of male and female functioning characteristically put forward by B are internally inadequate and fail to give us viable norms of human flourishing.[96]

What do we usually find, in the versions of B that our philosophical tradition bequeaths to us? (Rousseau's view is an instructive example.) We have, on the one hand, males who are "autonomous," capable of practical reasoning, independent and self-sufficient, allegedly good at political deliberation. These males are brought up not to develop strong emotions of love and feelings of deep need that are associated with the awareness of one's own lack of self-sufficiency. For this reason they are not well equipped to care for the needs of their family members or, perhaps, even to notice those needs. On the other hand, we have females such as Rousseau's Sophie,[97] brought up to lack autonomy and self-respect, ill equipped to rely on her own practical reasoning, dependent on males, focused on pleasing others, and good at caring for others. Is either of these viable as a complete life for a human being?

It would seem not. The internal tensions in Rousseau's account are a good place to begin.[98] Rousseau places tremendous emphasis on compassion as a basic social motivation. He understands compassion to require fellow feeling and a keen responsiveness to the sufferings of others. And yet, in preparing Emile for autonomous citizenship, he ultimately gives emotional development short shrift, allocating caring and responsiveness to the female sphere alone. It appears likely that Emile will be not only an incomplete person but also a defective citizen, even by the standards of citizenship recognized by Rousseau himself.

With Sophie, things again go badly. Taught to care for others but not taught that her life is her own to plan, she lives under the sway of external influences and lacks self-government. As Rousseau himself shows in his fascinating narrative of the end of her life,[99] Sophie comes to a bad end through her lack of judgment. Moreover, in the process she proves to be a bad partner and deficient in love. For love, as we come to see, requires judgment and constancy. Thus each of them fails to live a complete human life, and each fails, too, to exemplify fully and well the very functions for which they were being trained, because those functions require support from other functions for which they were not trained. The text leads its thoughtful reader to the conclusion that the capabilities that have traditionally marked the separate male and female spheres are not separable from one another without a grave functional loss. Society cannot strive for completeness by simply adding one sphere to the other. It must strive to develop in each and every person the full range of the human capabilities.

This more inclusive notion of human functioning admits tragic conflict. For it insists on the separate value and the irreplaceable importance of a rich plurality of functions. And the world does not always guarantee that individuals will not be faced with painful choices among these functions, in which, in order to pursue one of them well they must neglect others (and thus, in many cases, subvert the one as well). But this shows once again, I believe, the tremendous importance of keeping some such list of the central functions before us as we assess the quality of life in the countries of the world and strive to raise it. For many such tragedies—like many cases of simple capability failure—result from unjust and unreflective social arrangements. One can try to construct a society in which the tragic choices that faced Emile and Sophie would not be necessary, in which both males and females could learn both to love and to reason.

In April 1994, Metha Bai went to Bangalore for the widows' conference. She met widows from all over India, and they spent a week discussing their common problems. During that week, Metha Bai began to smile a lot. She bought beads in the forbidden color of blue, and she seemed pleased with the way she looked. With advice from a local NGO involved in the conference, she applied for and obtained a loan that enabled her to pay off the mortgage on the small property she still owns. Although her economic situation is not secure and she still does not hold a job outside the home, she has managed to stave off hunger. Like many women all over the world, she is fighting for her life, with resilience and fortitude.

Women belong to cultures. But they do not choose to be born into any particular culture, and they do not really choose to endorse its norms as good for themselves, unless they do so in possession of further options and opportunities—including the opportunity to form communities of affiliation and empowerment with other women. The contingencies of where one is born, whose power one is afraid of, and what habits shape one's daily thought are chance events that should not be permitted to play the role they now play in pervasively shaping women's life chances. Beneath all these chance events are human powers, powers of choice and intelligent self-formation. Women in much of the world lack support for the most central human functions, and this denial of support is frequently caused by their being women. But women, unlike rocks and plants and even horses, have the potential to become capable of these human functions, given sufficient nutrition, education, and other support. That is why their unequal failure in capability is a problem of justice. It is up to all human beings to solve this problem. I claim that a conception of human functioning gives us valuable assistance as we undertake this task.

2

THE FEMINIST CRITIQUE
OF LIBERALISM

Women around the world are using the language of liberalism. Consider some representative examples from recent publications:

1. Roop Rekha Verma, philosopher and grass-roots activist from Lucknow, India, speaks about the many ways in which Indian religious traditions have devalued women. She concludes that the largest problem with these traditions is that they deprive women of "full personhood." "What is personhood?" Verma asks. "To me three things seem essential for [full personhood]: autonomy, self-respect, and a sense of fulfillment and achievement."[1]

2. Nahid Toubia, the first woman surgeon in the Sudan and woman's health activist, writes of the urgent need to mobilize international opposition to the practice of female genital mutilation (FGM), especially when it is performed on young girls without their consent. "International human rights bodies and organizations," she concludes, "must declare FGM to be violence against women and children and a violation of their rights. . . . If women are to be considered as equal and responsible members of society, no aspect of their physical, psychological, or sexual integrity can be compromised."[2]

3. Describing a meeting at the Indian Institute of Management in Bangalore that brought together widows from all over India for a discussion of their living conditions, *The Hindu Magazine* reports as follows:

Throughout the week they came to realise many things about themselves and their lives—especially how much they had internalised society's perceptions of them as daughters, wives, mothers and widows (their identity invariably defined in terms of their relationship to men). . . . They were encouraged to see themselves as persons who had a right to exist even if their husbands were dead, and as citizens who had a right to resources—such as land, housing, employment, credit and ration cards—which would enable them to live and bring up their children (if any) with dignity and self-respect.[3]

Personhood, autonomy, rights, dignity, self-respect: These are the terms of the liberal Enlightenment. Women are using them, and teaching other women to use them when they did not use them before. They treat these terms as though they matter, as though they are the best terms in which to conduct a radical critique of society, as though using them is crucial to women's quality of life.

This situation looks in some respects deeply paradoxical, because liberalism has been thought by many feminists to be a political approach that is totally inadequate to the needs and aims of women, and in some ways profoundly subversive of those aims. Over the past twenty years, feminist political thinkers have put forward many reasons to reject liberalism and to define feminism to some extent in opposition to liberalism. In 1983, in *Feminist Politics and Human Nature*, one of the most influential works of feminist political theory, Alison Jaggar concluded that "the liberal conception of human nature and of political philosophy cannot constitute the philosophical foundation for an adequate theory of women's liberation."[4] Many influential feminist thinkers have agreed with Jaggar, treating liberalism as at best negligent of women's concerns and at worst an active enemy of women's progress.

But liberalism has not died in feminist politics; if anything, with the dramatic growth of the movement to recognize various women's rights as central human rights under international law, its radical feminist potential is just beginning to be realized. So it is time to reassess the charges most commonly made in the feminist critique.

Why should this reassessment matter? It is obvious that the activists from whom I have quoted have gone about their business undaunted by the feminist critique, and they will not be daunted now, if feminists once again tell them that autonomy and personhood are bad notions for feminists to use. In that sense a philosophical investigation could be seen as beside the point. But the international political situation is volatile, and the liberal discourse of personhood and rights has come under attack from many directions, some of them practical and influential.[5] Looking at the case for the defense is therefore not simply a scholarly exercise but also a contribution to practical politics.

In general, I shall argue, liberalism of a kind can be defended against the charges that have been made. The deepest and most central ideas of the liberal tradition are ideas of radical force and great theoretical and practical value. These ideas can be formulated in ways that incorporate what is most valuable in the feminist critique—although liberalism needs to learn from feminism if it is to formulate its own central insights in a fully adequate manner. Taking on board the insights of feminism will not leave liberalism unchanged, and liberalism needs to change to respond adequately to those insights: But it will be changed in ways that make it more deeply consistent with its own most foundational ideas. Another way of putting this is to say that there have been many strands within liberalism; thinking about the feminist critique proves important in choosing among these because feminism shows defects in some forms of liberalism that continue to be influential. Some feminist proposals do resist incorporation even into a reformulated liberalism, but I shall argue that these are proposals that should be resisted by anyone who seeks justice for the world's women.

There is danger in speaking so generally about "liberalism," a danger that has often plagued feminist debates. "Liberalism" is not a single position but a family of positions; Kantian liberalism is profoundly different from classical Utilitarian liberalism, and both of these from the Utilitarianism currently dominant in neoclassical economics. Many critiques of liberalism are really critiques of economic Utilitarianism, and would not hold against the views of Kant or Mill. Some feminist attacks oversimplify the tradition, and in responding to them I run a grave risk of oversimplification myself. When I speak of "liberalism," then, I shall have in mind, above all, the tradition of Kantian liberalism represented today in the political thought of John Rawls, and also the classical Utilitarian liberal tradition, especially as exemplified in the work of John Stuart Mill. I shall also refer frequently to some major precursors, namely, Rousseau,[6] Hume, and Adam Smith. It seems reasonable to assess the feminist critique by holding it up against the best examples of liberal political thought; any critique of liberalism that cannot be taken seriously as a criticism of Kant or Mill probably is not worth discussing.

The thinkers I have chosen are not in agreement on many important matters, but a core of common commitments can be scrutinized with the interests of feminism in mind. At the heart of this tradition is a twofold intuition about human beings: namely, that all, just by being human, are of equal dignity and worth, no matter where they are situated in society, and that the primary source of this worth is a power of moral choice within them, a power that consists in the ability to plan a life in accordance with one's own evaluations of ends.[7] To these two intuitions—which link liberalism at its core to the thought of the Greek and Roman Stoics[8]—the liberal tradition adds one more, which the Stoics did not emphasize: that the moral equality of persons gives them a fair claim to certain types of treatment at the hands of society and politics. What this treatment is will be a subject of debate within the tradition, but the shared starting point is that this treatment must do two closely related things. It must respect and promote the liberty of choice, and it must repect and promote the equal worth of persons as choosers.[9]

To what is liberalism, so conceived, opposed? Here again we must begin crudely, with some rough intuitions that we will try to render more precise as we go on. Liberalism is opposed, first of all, to any approach to politics that turns morally irrelevant differences into systematic sources of social hierarchy.[10] It is opposed, then, to the naturalizing of hierarchies—to feudalism and hereditary monarchy, to the caste system characteristic of traditional Indian society, to related caste hierarchies created in many times and places by differences of race and class and power and religion.[11] It is opposed, second, to forms of political organization that are corporatist or organically organized—that seek a good for the group as a whole without focusing above all on the well-being and agency of individual group members.[12] Finally, it is opposed to a politics that is ideologically based, in the sense that it turns one particular conception of value—whether utopian or religious or traditional—into a mandatory standard imposed by authority on all citizens. Religious intolerance, the establishment of a single church, or the establishment of a single utopian political vision of the good—all these strike the liberal as embodying unequal respect for persons, who ought to be free to follow their conscience in the most important matters. Liberalism is thus opposed to Marxism, to theocratic social orders, and to many forms of authoritarian or tradition-based conservatism.[13]

Liberalism so conceived is centrally about the protection of spheres of choice—not, I claim, in a purely negative way, maximizing the sheer number of choices people get to make for themselves but rather in a way closely tied to the norm of equal respect for personhood. The choices that get protection will be those deemed to be of crucial importance to the protection and expression of personhood. Thus, it would be perfectly consistent for a liberal, beginning from these intuitions, to support certain forms of interference with choice if it could be successfully argued that such interference promotes equal respect rather than undermining it, or, even, that the interference makes no difference to personhood one way or another. All liberal views accept some interference with choice, whether to promote more choice, or to constrain force and fraud, or to produce greater overall prosperity or greater fairness. Starting from the same basic intuitions, then, liberals can end up in very different positions about many matters, such as the justice of various types of economic redistribution or the appropriateness of various types of paternalistic legislation. They will differ about these policies because they differ about what is crucial to respect the equal worth of persons and to give the power of choice the support that is its due. On this account, both John Rawls and Robert Nozick are liberals because both share a central commitment to liberty and equal respect, although they disagree profoundly about the permissibility of economic redistribution—Rawls holding that it is required to show equal respect for persons; Nozick holding that it is incompatible with such equal respect.[14] Many such disagreements arise within liberalism. They involve, often, not only disagreement about means to shared ends but also different concrete specifications of some highly general ends.[15] On the other hand, it would be hard to conceive of a form of liberalism in which religious toleration was not a central tenet, or one that did not protect certain basic freedoms associated with personal choice, such as freedoms of expression, press, and assembly.[16]

Feminists have made three salient charges against this liberal tradition as a philosophy that might be used to promote women's goals. They have charged, first, that it is too "individualistic": that its focus on the dignity and worth of the individual slights and unfairly subordinates the value to be attached to community and to collective social entities such as families, groups, and classes. They have charged, second, that its ideal of equality is too abstract and formal, that it errs through lack of immersion in the concrete realities of power in different social situations. Finally, they have charged that liberalism errs through its focus on reason, unfairly slighting the role we should give to emotion and care in the moral and political life. All these alleged failings in liberalism are linked to specific failings in the tradition's handling of women's issues. It has frequently been claimed that liberalism cannot atone for these defects without changing utterly, and that feminists interested in progress beyond the status quo would be better off choosing a different political philosophy—whether a form of socialism or Marxism or a form of communitarian or care-based political theory. Let us examine these charges.

Individual and Community

The most common feminist charge against liberalism is that it is too "individualistic." By taking the individual to be the basic unit for political thought, it treats the individual as prior to society, as capable, in theory if not in fact, of existing outside all social ties. "Logically if not empirically," writes Jaggar of the liberal view, "human individuals could exist outside a social context; their essential characteristics, their needs and interests, their capacities and desires, are given independently of their social context and are not created or even fundamentally altered by that context"(29).[17] Jaggar later restates this liberal "metaphysical assumption" in an even stronger form: "[E]ach human individual has desires, interests, etc. that in principle can be fulfilled quite separately from the desires and interests of other people" (30). Jaggar later describes this as the liberal assumption of "political solipsism, the assumption that human individuals are essentially self-sufficient entities" (40). She holds that this starting point makes liberals characterize "community and cooperation . . . as phenomena whose existence and even possibility is puzzling," if not downright "impossible" (41).

Described this way, liberal individualism lies perilously close to two positions most feminists agree in rejecting: *egoism* and *normative self-sufficiency*. If liberals really did hold, as Jaggar suggests, that the most basic desires of human beings not only are not shaped by society but also are desires that can be satisfied independently of the satisfactions of desires and interests of others, they would indeed be close to endorsing *psychological egoism*, the view that people are all motivated to pursue their own self-interest above all else. And this, of course, is a view that makes cooperation and community at least somewhat puzzling. On the basis of Jaggar's belief that such self-centered desires and interests are given special weight in liberal politics, she apparently takes the liberal view to lie close to *normative ethical egoism* as well,[18] that is, to a view that it is always best to promote the satisfaction of one's own self-interest—though such a conclusion is rather puzzling given that the political theories she discusses, both Utilitarian and Rawlsian, aim, by Jaggar's own account, at satisfying *everyone's* interests, not just the interests of a single agent. This would seem to make them far from egoistic.[19]

The charge of egoism is unconvincing. Some liberal thinkers do assume a form of psychological egoism, and it is right of both feminists and others to call that assumption into question. Jaggar cites Amartya Sen's article "Rational Fools,"[20] which criticizes economic Utilitarianism for underrating the importance of sympathy and commitment as motives; she is right to find this a powerful objection to some dominant modes of economic modeling. But she herself admits that this view of human motivation is far from universal in the liberal tradition: that John Rawls has a nonegoistic account of human psychology, and that Mill and Kant think of the human being as moved by both egoistic and nonegoistic motives.[21] She does not give us any reason to believe that the egoism she criticizes in economic Utilitarianism is entailed or even encouraged by anything deep in liberalism itself.

Indeed, even Jaggar's weaker psychological claim about the solitary character of basic desires in liberalism appears to be inaccurate. Liberal theorists vary, and no doubt some, in particular Hobbes[22] and Bentham in their different ways, come close to imagining the human individual as having no natural love of others. Kant, because he holds that all sensuous inclinations are accidents of individual endowment, is agnostic on the matter and thinks that we should not rely on such motives too much if we want to promote benevolence. But other liberal thinkers, such as Mill, Hume, Smith, and Rawls, have an evidently social and other-inclusive psychology, building affiliation with and need for others into the very foundations of their accounts of human motivation and denying that individuals can satisfy their basic desires independently of relationship and community. In a very important way Kant himself agrees: For although he holds that with respect to liking and pleasure and other forms of sensuous inclination we are not reliably inclined toward one another, he holds at the same time that the identity of a human being is given in the most fundamental terms by its membership in a certain sort of community, namely, the kingdom of ends, the community of free rational beings who regard one another with respect and awe and who are committed to promote one another's happiness and well-being because of the respect they feel for one another. Rawls, similarly, imagines the agents in the "original position" as held together by a concern for building a community in which they will live together on terms of mutual cooperation.

As for normative ethical egoism, one could not even begin to argue plausibly that either the Utilitarian or the Kantian tradition is guilty. The essential emphasis of liberal individualism is on respect for *others* as individuals; how can this even initially be thought to involve egoism? Both theories are extremely exigent in the demands they make of moral agents in respect of altruism and duties to others. Utilitarianism holds that an action is right only if it maximizes total or average utility—of all the world's people, in its strictest version; some utilitarians would extend the requirement to animals as well. Clearly this is a theory that demands enormous sacrifices of agents and is very far from letting them go about their self-interested business. Kantian duties to others are not quite as severe, because "imperfect duties" of benevolence have much elasticity, and the Kantian agent is allowed to give preference on many occasions to the near and dear. Nonetheless, it would be utterly implausible to call Kant's an egoistic moral theory; duties to promote the happiness of others are at its very core.[23]

More initially plausible is the suggestion that liberalism, by conceiving the human being in a way that imagines her cut off from all others and yet thriving, encourages normative projects of self-sufficiency—urges people, that is, to minimize their needs for one another and to depend on themselves alone. This, I think, is what Jaggar is really worried about when she speaks of "political solipsism." This is certainly one of the charges feminists commonly think true of liberalism, and one of the ways in which feminists have connected liberalism with common male attitudes and concerns. Feminists hold that by encouraging self-sufficiency as a goal, liberalism subverts the values of family and community, ends that feminists rightly prize. What should we say about this charge?

First, we should note that the normative goal of self-sufficiency is not one that feminists should dismiss without argument. The figures in the Western philosophical tradition who have defended some form of detachment and self-sufficiency as goals—in particular, the Stoics and Spinoza—have done so using powerful arguments, in particular arguments that connect the aim of self-sufficiency with the elimination of anger and revenge and the creation of a just and merciful society. Even if feminists want to reject those arguments, they need to grapple with them rather than viewing them as so many signs of heedless maleness.[24] They also need to grapple with the fact that some feminists, especially in the developing world, endorse self-sufficiency as an appropriate goal. To give just one example, the Self-Employed Women's Association in India (SEWA), one of the most successful feminist employment and credit projects worldwide, makes self-sufficiency one of its ten normative points for women, following Gandhi's use of this concept in the struggle against Britain.[25] These feminists do not take self-sufficiency to entail neglect of others, but they do hold that women care for others best when they are economically situated so that they can survive on their own.

Second, we should observe that the ethical aim of self-sufficiency and detachment is not strongly linked to individualism, that is, to the view that the primary focus of ethical and political thought should be the individual, understood as a separate unit. Indeed, in its most influential world form, in the Buddhist and to some extent also Hindu traditions, the normative doctrine of self-sufficiency and detachment presupposes the recognition that individuals as such do not really exist; it is precisely this recognition that grounds indifference to events, such as deaths of loved ones, that might be thought to matter deeply. Individualism, with its focus on what happens here and now in one's very own life, would seem to have an uphill battle in order to cultivate detachment from such external events.[26]

Next, even if the psychology of liberalism were as described, that is, even if liberals did hold that our most basic desires can be satisfied independently of relationships to others, the normative conclusions about self-sufficiency would not follow. For moral theories frequently demand of people things that go against the grain, and we could demand great concern for others from people to whom such concern does not seem to come naturally. Such appears to have been the enterprise of Jeremy Bentham, who combined an extremely self-centered psychology with an exigent normative altruism. Kant, too, was ready to demand of agents that they disregard their most powerful desires; he famously holds that even a man in whose heart nature has placed little sympathy for others can still be expected to be absolutely committed to their good. Kant certainly believes that all altruistic commitment and loving concern in marriage goes against the grain, given the extremely solipsistic tendencies he imputes to sexual desire, but he expected individuals to live up to those commitments, rather than to seek self-sufficiency.[27] Liberals, then, can and do highly value benevolence, family concern, and social/political involvement, even if they should hold that individuals must control strong selfish inclinations. And, as I have argued, liberalism typically endows individuals with powerful other-regarding motives also.

Liberal individualism, then, does not entail either egoism or normative self-sufficiency. What does it really mean, then, to make the individual the basic unit for political thought? It means, first of all, that liberalism responds sharply to the basic fact that each person has a course from birth to death that is not precisely the same as that of any other person; that each person is one and not more than one, that each feels pain in his or her own body, that the food given to A does not arrive in the stomach of B. The separateness of persons is a basic fact of human life; in stressing it, liberalism stresses something experientially true and fundamentally important. In stressing this fact, the liberal takes her stand squarely in the camp of this worldly experience and rejects forms of revisionary metaphysics (e.g., forms of Buddhism or Platonism) that would deny the reality of our separateness and our substantial embodied character.[28] It rejects the Buddhist picture of persons as mere whorls in the ceaseless flux of world energy and the feudal picture of persons as fundamentally characterized by a set of hierarchical relations. It says that the fundamental entity for politics is a living body that goes from here to there, from birth to death, never fused with any other—that we are hungry and joyful and loving and needy one by one, however closely we may embrace one another.[29] In normative terms, this commitment to the recognition of individual separateness means, for the liberal, that the demands of a collectivity or a relation should not as such be made the basic goal of politics: collectivities, such as the state and even the family, are composed of individuals, who never do fuse, who always continue to have their separate brains and voices and stomachs, however much they love one another. Each of these is separate, and each of these is an end. Liberalism holds that the flourishing of human beings taken one by one is both analytically and normatively prior to the flourishing of the state or the nation or the religious group: analytically, because such unities do not really efface the separate reality of individual lives; normatively because the recognition of that separateness is held to be a fundamental fact for ethics, which should recognize each separate entity as an end not as a means to the ends of others. The central question of politics should not be, How is the organic whole doing?, but rather, How are X and Y and Z and Q doing? The central goal for politics will be some sort of amelioration in the lives of X and Y and Z and Q, where a larger amount of happiness for X, where X might be the ruler, does not compensate for a larger amount of misery for Q, where Q might be a poor rural woman.[30]

Putting things this way does not require us to deny that X might love Y intensely and view his life as worthless without Y; it does not require that Z and Q do not plan their lives together and aim at shared ends; it does not require us to hold that all four do not need one another profoundly or vividly hold the pleasure and pain of one another in their imaginations. It just asks us to concern ourselves with the distribution of resources and opportunities in a certain way, namely, with concern to see how well *each and every one of them* is doing, seeing each and every one as an end, worthy of concern.

Put this way, liberal individualism seems to be a good view for feminists to embrace. For it is clear that women have too rarely been treated as ends in themselves, and too frequently treated as means to the ends of others. Women's individual well-being has far too rarely been taken into account in political and economic planning and measurement. Women have very often been treated as parts of a larger unit, especially the family, and valued primarily for their contribution as reproducers and caregivers rather than as sources of agency and worth in their own right. In connection with this nonindividualistic way of valuing women, questions about families have been asked without asking how well each of its individual members are doing. But conflicts for resources and opportunities are ubiquitous in families around the world, and women are often the victims of these conflicts. When food is scarce in families, it is frequently women, and especially girls, who get less, who become malnourished and die. When there is an illness and only some children can be taken to the doctor, it is frequently girls who are neglected. When only some children can go to school, it is frequently the girls who are kept at home.[31]

Again, when there is violence in the family, women and girls are overwhelmingly likely to be its victims. Sexual abuse during childhood and adolescence, forced prostitution (again, often in childhood), domestic violence and marital rape, and genital mutilation all are extremely common parts of women's lives. Many of the world's women do not have the right to consent to a marriage, and few have any recourse from ill treatment within it. Divorce, even if legally available, is commonly not a practical option given women's economic dependency and lack of educational and employment opportunities.[32]

To people who live in the midst of such facts, it is important to say, I am a separate person and an individual. I count for something as such, and my pain is not wiped out by someone else's satisfaction. When we reflect that a large number of the world's women inhabit traditions that value women primarily for the care they give to others rather than as ends, we have all the more reason to insist that liberal individualism is good for women.

There is no doubt that liberalism deserves feminist criticism on this point. For, as many feminists have long pointed out, where women and the family are concerned, liberal political thought has not been nearly individualist enough. Liberal thinkers tended to segment the private from the public sphere, considering the public sphere to be the sphere of individual rights and contractual arrangements, the family to be a private sphere of love and comfort into which the state should not meddle. This tendency grew, no doubt, out of a legitimate concern for the protection of choice—but too few questions were asked about whose choices were thereby protected. This meant that liberals often failed to notice the extent to which law and institutions shape the family and determine the privileges and rights of its members. Having failed to notice this, they all too frequently failed to ask whether there were legal deficiencies in this sphere that urgently needed addressing. In 1869, John Stuart Mill already urged British law to address the problem of marital rape, which, he said, made the lot of women lower than that of slaves:

> Hardly any slave . . . is a slave at all hours and all minutes. . . . But it cannot be so with the wife. Above all, a female slave has (in Christian countries) an admitted right, and is considered under a moral obligation, to refuse to her master the last familiarity. Not so the wife: however brutal a tyrant she may unfortunately be chained to—though she may know that he hates her, though it may be his daily pleasure to torture her, and though she may feel it impossible not to loathe him—he can claim from her and enforce the lowest degradation of a human being, that of being made the instrument of an animal function contrary to her inclinations.[33]

Though Mill seems excessively sanguine here about the female slave,[34] he is right on target about the wife, and he sees what a deep violation of basic liberal tenets is involved in the failure to legislate against marital rape. Again, in the same passage, he argues that the laws that deny the wife equal legal rights over children are also a profound violation of personhood and autonomy.[35] In a similar way, he diagnoses other distortions of the family structure caused by male power and the laws that express it, arguing for women's full equality in all that relates to citizenship and therefore for many changes in disabling family laws.

Mill supports his argument in part by appeal to consistency, saying that liberalism cannot plausibly deny women the rights it vindicates for men. But he also argues that *male* citizenship in a liberal regime is ill served by a mode of family organization based on subordination. For such a family order is a vestige of monarchical power and raises up despots who are ill prepared to respect the rights of their fellow citizens.

> Think what it is to a boy, to grow up to manhood in the belief that without any merit or any exertion of his own, though he may be the most frivolous and empty or the most ignorant and stolid of mankind, by the mere fact of being born a male he is by right the superior of all and every one of an entire half of the human race: including probably some whose real superiority to himself he has daily or hourly occasion to feel. . . . Is it imagined that all this does not pervert the whole manner of existence of the man, both as an individual and as a social being? It is an exact parallel to the feeling of a hereditary king that he is excellent above others by being born a king, or a noble by being born a noble. The relation between husband and wife is very like that between lord and vassal, except that the wife is held to more unlimited obedience than the vassal was. However the vassal's character may have been affected, for better or worse, by his subordination, who can help seeing that the lord's was affected greatly for the worse? . . . The self-worship of the mon-

arch, or of the feudal superior, is matched by the self-worship of the male. Human beings do not grow up from childhood in the possession of unearned distinctions, without pluming themselves upon them.

In short, Mill argues, the stability of a liberal regime demands legal reform of the family. All liberals should and must seek the "advantage of having the most universal and pervading of all human relations regulated by justice instead of injustice."[36]

Mill's arguments in *Subjection* showed that a concern for the individual well-being of family members and a determination to use law to further that concern were in no way alien to liberalism. Indeed, they grew naturally, as he shows, out of liberalism's concern for the fair treatment of each and every individual and its disdain for feudalism and monarchical power, the caste-like ascendancy of morally irrelevant distinctions. But most of the liberal tradition did not follow Mill's lead. Thus, John Rawls, while envisaging a society in which each individual's well-being would be a matter of social concern, still imagined the contracting individuals as heads of households, who would be expected to take thought altruistically for the interests of family members.[37] Here Rawls adopted a strategy similar to that of economist Gary Becker when he assumed that the head of the household is a beneficent altruist who will adequately take thought for the interests of all family members.[38] Liberal reluctance to interfere with the family has run very deep; dispiritingly, many liberal thinkers have failed to notice that the family is not always characterized by a harmony of interests.[39] No model of the family can be adequate to reality if it fails to take into account competition for scarce resources, divergent interests, and differences of power.[40]

Liberalism has much to learn from feminism in this area. It should begin by learning the facts of women's hunger, domestic violence, marital rape, and unequal access to education. It should go on to correct these facts by laws and by moral education. It should also consider the implications of women's individuality for many traditional areas of law and policy, prominently including divorce and taxation.[41] But notice that, as Mill already argued, what we see here is not a failure intrinsic to liberalism itself. It is, in fact, a failure of liberal thinkers to follow their own thought through to its socially radical conclusion. What is wrong with the views of the family endorsed by Becker, Rawls, and others is not that they are too individualist but that they are not individualist enough. They assume too much organic unity and harmony. They give people too much credit for altruism and are not worried enough about the damages of competition. For this reason they fail to ask rigorously their own question, namely, How is each and every individual doing? They fail to ask this, perhaps, because they are focused on the autonomy and freedom of males, and they want to give these males plenty of scope for planning their lives in the private sphere. But that is not the liberal tradition, when this freedom is bought at the expense of violence and death to other individuals. To treat males this way is, as Mill said, tantamount to treating them as kings, who have a hereditary title to subordinate others. To treat any group or person this way runs counter to the deepest instincts of the liberal tradition.

For these reasons, theorists eager to remedy the wrongs done to women in the family have been able to propose internal criticisms of liberalism, rather than its wholesale rejection. Susan Moller Okin's *Justice, Gender, and the Family* criticizes liberal theory severely for its failure to consider injustice in the family. But she argues, plausibly, that John Rawls's theory of justice can be reformulated—along lines suggested by Rawls himself when he insisted that the family was one of the institutions that is part of the "basic structure of society," to be ordered in accordance with principles of justice.[42] In this feminist reformulation, parties in the original position would be individuals, rather than representatives of household units[43]; and parties in the original position, in addition to being ignorant of their wealth, class, and conception of the good, would also be ignorant of their sex. Okin argues that this would lead them to design institutions in which the influence of gender (i.e., of the social hierarchies correlated with biological sex) was minimized, and opportunities and resources would be equitably distributed within the family.[44] Rawls has now accepted many parts of this proposal.[45]

In economics, too, approaches to the family have responded to feminist criticism by becoming more rather than less individualistic. Becker himself has now acknowledged that his model assumed too much altruism and that other motives should be ascribed to family members.[46] Although he has not explicitly urged the disaggregation of the family unit into its individual bargaining agents, such a "bargaining model of the family" is by now increasingly dominant in mainstream economics.[47]

In a very similar manner, international women's activists, taking international human rights agencies to task for their neglect of issues such as marital rape, domestic violence, marital consent, and women's hunger, have not moved to jettison the language of human rights. Instead, they have insisted that the major rights already on the agenda be vindicated for women, and also that rights of women to be free from gender-specific abuses be added to the list of human rights. Once again, the defect found in international agencies such as the United Nations is not that they have stressed individualism too much but that, deferring to tradition and male power, they have not done so consistently and deeply enough. Charlotte Bunch, who coordinated the Global Campaign for Women's Human Rights at the United Nations 1993 World Conference on Human Rights, eloquently describes the feminist liberal program: "The concept of human rights, like all vibrant visions, is not static or the property of any one group; rather, its meaning expands as people reconceive of their needs and hopes in relation to it. In this spirit, feminists redefine human rights abuses to include the degradation and violation of women."[48]

This liberal program is already producing transformations in many countries. Some rights language in constitutions and statutes around the world is vague and aspirational, of little practical help. But there is real change. With increasing success in many countries, women are claiming rights of bodily integrity within their marriages[49]; with the help of international agencies and legal reform, they are also achieving a stronger economic bargaining position as family members.[50] In a wide variety of areas, including education, reproduction, and nutrition, they have been winning the right to be recognized as separate beings whose well-being is distinct from that of a husband's. Just so, the widows who gathered in Bangalore were learning to think of themselves not as discarded adjuncts of a family unit, half dead things, but as centers of thought and choice and action, citizens who could make claims against the state for respect and resources. All this is liberal individualism, and liberal individualism, consistently followed through, entails a radical feminist program.

A deep strategic question arises at this point. When liberal people and states prove obtuse, refusing women's legitimate demands to be treated as ends, at what point should women—in pursuit of that liberal end—prefer revolutionary strategies that depart from liberal politics? Many feminists have discovered that Mill is correct: "The generality of the male sex cannot yet tolerate the idea of living with an equal." In consequence, legitimate arguments are met, again and again, not with rational engagement but with a resistance that keeps "throwing up fresh intrenchments of argument to repair any breach made in the old" but is in actuality quite impervious to reason.[51] This sort of thing makes revolutionary collective action deeply attractive to many women. And indeed, in many parts of the world, women have to at least some extent advanced their well-being through alliance with Marxist movements. It is beyond my scope here to give an account of when it is acceptable to use illiberal means for liberal ends, or to give advice to women who are faced with real choices between obtuse liberalism and profeminist collectivism. Even in the United States and Europe, the repeated experience of male irrationality may legitimately cause many feminists to find liberal politics insufficiently radical. In the long run, however, it is unlikely that liberal ends will be effectively served by collectivist means. Any noble ideal, furthermore, can be used as a screen by those who wish to do harm. The right response is to expose the abusers, not to discard the ideal.

Abstraction and Concrete Reality

Closely related to the feminist critique of liberal individualism is the criticism that liberalism's vision of persons is too abstract. By thinking of individuals in ways that sever them from their history and their social context, liberal thinkers have deprived themselves of crucial insights. I believe that there are two different criticisms here. The first has great power but can be addressed within liberalism; the second is a genuine attack upon liberalism but does not have great power.

The first attack is pressed by Catharine MacKinnon, Alison Jaggar, and a number of other feminist thinkers.[52] Their claim is that liberalism's disregard of differences between persons that are a product of history and social setting makes it adopt an unacceptably formal conception of equality, one that cannot in the end treat individuals as equals given the reality of social hierarchy and unequal power. Notice that if this were so, it would be an extremely serious *internal* criticism of liberalism, whose central goal is to show equal respect for persons despite actual differences of power. What do these feminist critics have in mind?

It seems plausible that the liberal principle of formally equal treatment, equality under the law, may, if it is applied in an excessively abstract or remote manner, end up failing to show equal respect for persons. For example, one might use basically liberal language to justify schooling children of different races in separate schools: As long as the schools are equal, the children have been treated as equal; and if any disadvantage attaches to the separation, it is an equal disadvantage to them both. This, in fact, was the reasoning of Herbert Wechsler in a famous article critical of the reasoning in *Brown v. Board of Education*, the landmark school-desegregation case.[53] Insisting on abstraction for reasons of liberal equality and neutrality, Wechsler held that the introduction into evidence of the history of racial stigmatization and inequality was illegitimate and could only result in a biased judgment "tailored to the immediate result." Similar reasoning has been used in cases involving gender. In the Indiana sexual harassment case discussed in chapter 1, the lower court judge insisted on abstracting from the asymmetry of power between Mary Carr and her male coworkers, holding that the continual use of obscenities toward Carr by the male workers was exactly the same as the occasional use of a four-letter word by Carr. Judge Posner, overruling the lower court judge on the findings of fact, held that the asymmetry of power—including its social meaning in historical terms—was a crucial part of the facts of the case.[54] Their use of language was harassing and intimidating in a way that hers could not be. If liberal neutrality forbade one to recognize such facts, this would indeed be a difficulty for liberalism.

In general, liberalism has sometimes been taken to require that the law be "sex blind," behaving as if the social reality before us were a neutral starting point and refusing to recognize ways in which the status quo embodies historical asymmetries of power. Feminists have worried, for example, that this sort of neutrality will prevent them from demanding pregnancy and maternity leaves as parts of women's equality of opportunity.[55] Again, if liberal feminism would prevent the government of Bangladesh from investing its money disproportionately in literacy programs aimed at women, this would lose liberalism the regard of most feminists in international politics.[56]

It seems mistaken, however, to think that liberalism has ever been committed to this type of unrealistic and ahistorical abstraction.[57] MacKinnon is correct that some liberal legal thinkers and some important Supreme Court decisions have been guilty of this error; her critique of liberal equality theory is a valuable critique of positions that have been influential in the law. But liberal philosophers have, on the whole, seen more deeply—and, I would say, more consistently—when they have rejected the purely formal notion of equality. Liberals standardly grant that the equality of opportunity that individuals have a right to demand from their governments has material prerequisites, and that these prerequisites may vary depending on one's situation in society. My own preferred way of expressing this (see chapter 1) is to say that liberalism aims at equality *of capabilities*: The aim is not just to distribute some resources around but also to see that they truly go to work in promoting the capacity of people to choose a life in accordance with their own thinking.[58] Even Rawls, with his somewhat greater abstemiousness about the role played by a view of the good in society's basic structure, nonetheless provides political thought with ample resources to think well about difference and hierarchy. He emphasizes a distinction between merely formal equal liberty and what he calls the "equal worth of liberty" and also between formal equality of opportunity and truly fair equality of opportunity; the latter members of each pair have material prerequisites that are likely to involve redistribution.[59]

One very good example of a liberal appeal to the worth of equality, used to oppose purely formal equality, is in the 1983 Indian case discussed in the Introduction, which declared unconstitutional the portion of the Hindu Marriage Act that mandated the restitution of conjugal rights. Judge Choudary noted that the remedy of restitution is available to both men and women—but, given the asymmetries of power in Indian society, the remedy is likely to be used only by males against females, and the resulting burdens (including nonconsensual pregnancy) borne only by females. He concludes:

> Thus the use of remedy of restitution of conjugal rights in reality becomes partial and one-sided and available only to the husband. The pledge of equal protection of laws is thus inherently incapable of being fulfilled by this matrimonial remedy in our Hindu society. As a result this remedy works in practice only as an oppression, to be operated by the husband for the husband against the wife. By treating the wife and the husband who are inherently unequal as equals, Section 9 of the Act offends the rule of equal protection of laws.[60]

One could not have a better expression of MacKinnon's critique—in the context of a liberal legal conception, in which the right of all citizens to autonomy and privacy is the central issue in question.[61]

Liberals will continue to differ about the topic of differential treatment, especially in the area of affirmative action. Libertarian liberals allow wide latitude for advantages that individuals derive from morally irrelevant attributes of birth and social location but are strict on the rules that should govern benefits, insisting on a type of neutrality in which morally irrelevant characteristics play no role in the design of distributive policies and programs. Rawlsian liberals, noting that individuals arrive in society with many advantages that they have already derived from morally irrelevant characteristics, think it not just reasonable but morally required to readjust things in order that individuals should not be kings and princes; they therefore permit themselves a more extensive scrutiny of the history of group hierarchy and subordination, rejecting abstractness at this point as incompatible with a fully equal treatment. Feminist liberals have typically followed this strand of liberal thinking,[62] and their criticisms of other ideas of neutrality have been very important in generating legal change.

The criticism, then, is a serious criticism of some parts of the liberal political and legal tradition and of the obtusely remote language this tradition has sometimes chosen to characterize human affairs, but it can be and frequently has been accommodated within liberalism. To address it well, however, liberalism needs to pay close attention to history and to the narratives of people who are in situations of inequality. This it will do best if, in the spirit of Rousseau's *Émile*, it allows a generous role for the imagination in the formulation and the writing of liberal theory.

Another criticism of liberal abstractness cuts deeper.[63] Many communitarian thinkers, among them some feminists, have held that liberalism's determination to think of persons in abstraction from allegedly morally irrelevant features, such as birth, class, ethnicity, gender, religion, and race, entails a pernicious form of "essentialism" that disregards the extent to which people are deeply identified with their religious heritage, their ethnicity, and so forth, and the extent to which these social and historical differences shape people. In one sense, we could say again that this is just a mistake: liberalism is very interested in knowing these historical facts of difference in order to ensure fair equality of opportunity.[64] But there is a deep point that is correct: Liberalism does think that the core of rational and moral personhood is something all human beings share, shaped though it may be in different ways by their differing social circumstances. And it does give this core a special salience in political thought, defining the public realm in terms of it, purposefully refusing the same salience in the public political conception to differences of gender and rank and class and religion.[65] This, of course, does not mean that people may not choose to identify themselves with their religion or ethnicity or gender and to make that identification absolutely central in their lives.[66] But for the liberal, choice is the essential issue; politics can take these features into account only in ways that respect it. This does not mean treating these features of people's lives as unimportant; indeed, in the case of religion it is because they are regarded as so important that any imposition on a person's conscience on these matters is seen as inappropriate in the public political conception.[67]

At this point deep conflicts arise between liberalism and various religious and traditional views of life, insofar as the latter hold that freedom of choice is not a central ethical goal. Even if those views are accommodated respectfully within a liberal polity, their adherents may feel that respectful accommodation within a regime of toleration and free choice is not accommodation enough. Many delicate legal and political issues arise at this point, some of which I pursue in the following chapter.

The more urgent question for our purposes is, What values prized by feminists are likely to be slighted in this liberal emphasis on choice? If women are understood to be, first and foremost, members of families, or members of religious traditions, or even members of ethnic groups—rather than, first and foremost, as human centers of choice and freedom—is this likely to be in any way better for women than is the "abstract individualism" of liberalism? Better in whose terms, we have to ask, and of course we encounter at this point many religious women who sincerely hold that the account of their identity given in the Laws of Manu,[68] or the *Analects*, or the *Koran*, is superior to the account given in Kant and Mill. We cannot follow out all those lines of argument here, except to note that a political type of liberalism such as the type defended in chapter 1 strives to leave space for these other identities.[69]

But we can ask how wise antiliberal feminists are to jettison the liberal account of the human essence in favor of an account that gives more centrality to "accidental" features of religion or class or even gender. These features are especially likely not to have been chosen by the women themselves and to embody views of life that devalue and subordinate them. Even feminists who are themselves communitarians should be skeptical about accepting uncritically this feature of communitarian thought. Communitarianism need not be altogether uncritical of the status quo, as many traditions have an internal critical strand. But feminists who are generally critical of tradition should still be skeptical of communitarian antiessentialism. The idea that all human beings have a core of moral personhood that exerts claims on government no matter what the world has done to it is an idea that the women of the world badly need to vindicate their equality and to argue for change. It is the disparity between humanity and its social deformation that gives rise to claims of justice. And the communitarian vision of persons, in which we are at heart and essentially what our traditions have made us, is a vision that leaves reduced scope for feminist critique.[70]

We can make one further reply to feminists who stress the importance of recognizing differences of race and class. The liberal approach is a principled approach that addresses itself to issues of human dignity in a fully general way. As a liberal feminist, one is also, by the entailment of one's very feminist position, also an antiracist, a defender of religious toleration, and a supporter of fair equality of opportunity across classes. One's feminism is not mere identity politics, putting the interests of women as such above the interests of other marginalized groups. It is part of a systematic and justifiable program that addresses hierarchy across the board in the name of human dignity. To that extent, the liberal feminist is in a better position than are many others to show her fellow women that she has not neglected claims that are peculiar to their own class-, religion-, or race-based identities.

Feminism needs to operate with a general notion of the human core, without forgetting that this core has been differently situated and also shaped in different times and places. We should not overlook the questions raised by these differences, and we cannot formulate a just social policy if we do. But insofar as feminism denies the value of the whole idea of a human core, it gives up something vital to the most powerful feminist arguments.

Reason and Emotion

Liberalism traditionally holds that human beings are above all reasoning beings, and that the dignity of reason is the primary source of human equality. As Jaggar puts it, "Liberal political theory is grounded on the conception of human beings as essentially rational agents."[71] Here liberal thinkers are not alone: They owe much to their forebears in the Western philosophical tradition, in particular the Greek and Roman Stoics, whose conception of the dignity of reason as a source of equal human worth profoundly influenced Kant, Adam Smith, and others. Continuing the Stoic heritage, liberalism typically holds that the relevant type of reason is practical reason, the capacity for understanding moral distinctions, evaluating options, selecting means to ends, and planning a life. Thinkers differ in the relative weight they assign to these different components, but not in their choice of practical over theoretical reasoning power as the essential mark of humanity.

Modern feminist thinkers usually grant that this liberal move has had at least some value for women in seeking to secure their equality. They point out that earlier feminists, from Cartesian philosopher Mary Astell to Mary Wollstone-craft, were able to appeal to women's rational capacity as a ground for claims to full political and moral equality. (They could indeed go much further back in history to support this claim: for Astell's arguments are closely related to the arguments of the Greek and Roman Stoics.[72]) And they could reflect that the decision to base moral and political claims on an innate capacity of persons, rather than on social endowments or relations, is one that opens the door to radical claims of empowerment for the disempowered.

On the other hand, feminists have worried that liberalism is far too rational-ist: that by placing all emphasis on reason as a mark of humanity, it has empha-sized a trait that males traditionally prize and denigrated traits, such as emotion and imagination, that females traditionally prize. This emphasis has permitted men to denigrate women for their emotional natures and to marginalize them on account of their alleged lack of reason. This would not have been possible, the argument goes, had political philosophy been grounded in a conception that gave, at least, equal weight to reason and to emotion.

Most feminists who make such claims do not argue for innate differences between the sexes, although some do.[73] Their argument is, more frequently, that women, as a result of their experiences of mothering and of family love, have rightly valued some important elements in human life that men often under-value.[74] Liberal philosophy is accused of making that male error in a way that contributes to the denigration of women.

This is a complicated issue. Grappling with it fully would require us to argue for an account of what emotions are. The objection, as I have stated it, drawing a strong contrast between reason and emotion, suggests that emotions are not forms of thought or reasoning. But is this true? Both the history of philosophy and contemporary psychology debate the issue. On the whole, the dominant view, both in the Western philosophical tradition and in recent cognitive psy-chology, is that emotions such as fear, anger, compassion, and grief involve evaluative appraisals, in which people (or animals) survey objects in the world with an eye to how important goals and projects are doing. If one holds some such view of what emotions involve, the entire distinction between reason and emotion begins to be called into question, and one can no longer assume that a thinker who focuses on reason is by that move excluding emotion.[75] So we must proceed cautiously, looking both at the view of the emotion-reason contrast a thinker holds and also at the normative judgments the thinker makes about how good or valuable emotions are. This is tricky, because in the liberal tradition these positions cut across one another: Thinkers who hold a strong form of the emo-tion-reason contrast disagree about the value they attach to emotions, as do thinkers who consider emotions to involve thought and evaluation. By trying to keep these distinctions straight we can make some progress in understanding the force of the feminist objections.

First, then, we do discover in the liberal tradition some philosophers who conceive of emotions as impulses distinct from reason, unintelligent forces that push the person around. On this basis, they endorse a contrast between reason and emotion. Kant and Hume (to some extent) are very different examples of this tendency. A strong feminist objection to such elements in the liberal tradition is that this is an indefensible picture of what emotions are.[76] To put a complex issue very briefly, it is implausible because it neglects the extent to which perceptions of an object and beliefs about the object are an intrinsic part of the experience of a complex emotion such as grief or fear. Grief, for example, is not simply a tug at the heartstrings: It involves the recognition that an object of great importance has been lost. Emotions involve ways of seeing.[77] This objection has been made by many philosophers and psychologists independently of feminist concerns, but the fact that the oversimple pictures were not criticized sooner may be explained in part by a cultural suspiciousness of emotions as female.[78]

But even Kant and Hume, whatever the deficiencies in their analysis of emotions, are far from dismissing emotions from their normative picture of the moral life. Kant is guarded about the contribution of emotions to moral motivation, but even he sees a necessary role for pity in motivating benevolence. Hume sees the emotions as the source of all the ends that morality pursues. Modern feminist Annette Baier has recently defended Hume's conception of the passions as the one feminists ought to use.[79] Although I am far from agreeing with Baier, because I think Hume's conception indefensible,[80] I think she is right to acknowledge the central place Hume gives to passion in his account of human nature. So even if major liberal thinkers have failed to appreciate sufficiently the amount of intelligence involved in emotion, it has not altogether stopped them from valuing the contribution of emotion to our moral choices.

Let me now turn to the cognitive conceptions of emotion. Quite a few philosophers who focus on reason, and who make reason a hallmark of the human, have a strongly cognitive conception of emotion and see emotions as activities of the rational faculty. Among these are some ancestors of liberalism, such as the Stoics and Spinoza. The Stoics and Spinoza dislike the emotions intensely; they do so, however, not on the grounds that emotions are not reason based but because they believe that the emotions involve confused reasoning, which ascribes to persons and things outside our control more importance than they actually possess. They hold this because of their normative views about individual self-sufficiency; as I have argued, these views are not widely shared in the liberal tradition.[81]

The position that many feminists would favor as doing most justice to women's experience of the value of emotional attachment would be a position that first analyzes emotions as containing cognition and then evaluates them positively, as having at least some value in the ethical life. This position is powerfully represented in the liberal tradition—to some extent under the influence of Aristotle. Both Jean-Jacques Rousseau and Adam Smith seem to have held that emotions involve thought and imagination; they also hold that the capacity for sympathy is a central mark of both private and public rationality, and indeed of humanity as such. Rousseau holds that a person who has no capacity for feeling pain at the distress of others is not fully human, that this capacity for imaginative response is the essential thing that draws us together in community and makes political thought possible in the first place. Smith's entire account of the "judicious spectator"—his model of good public judgment—is preoccupied with ascertaining the correct balance in the passions of anger and sympathy and love that such a public actor will feel; he explicitly criticizes his Stoic forebears for their normative doctrine of self-sufficiency and passionlessness. These thinkers hold conventional and nonprogressive views of women, but their positions on emotion offer what feminists have demanded. To this pair we may add Mill, whose *Autobiography* provides a moving testament to the barrenness of a rationality starved of emotional attachment and imaginative stimulation.

What, then, is the issue? What does this liberal tradition assert about emotions, that feminist thinkers might still wish to deny? The liberal tradition holds that emotions should not be trusted as guides to life without being subjected to some sort of critical scrutiny. Emotions are only as reliable as the evaluations they contain, and because such evaluations of objects are frequently absorbed from society, they will be only as reliable as those social norms. To naturalize them would be to naturalize the status quo. In general, emotions, like other forms of thought and imagination, should be valued as elements in a life governed by critical reasoning.

Some feminists, however, hold that this entire idea of subjecting emotion to rational appraisal is mistaken, an imposition of a male norm of cool rationality on the natural vigor of the passions. Unlike other feminist objections to liberal views of reason and emotion—which, as I have argued, inaccurately characterize the strongest liberal positions—this one directly assails a central tenet of liberalism. In her influential book *Caring*,[82] Nel Noddings holds that women's experience of mothering reveals a rich terrain of emotional experience into which judgment and appraisal do not and should not enter. For example, the primitive bond of joy and love between mother and child would be sullied by reflection, and this primitive unscrutinized love should be the model for our social attachments. From the perspective of a moral view such as Noddings's, liberalism, by urging people to ask whether their emotions are appropriate, robs moral life of a spontaneous movement toward others that is at the very core of morality.[83] Unless we give ourselves away to others without asking questions, we have not behaved in a fully moral way. It is the very unreasoning and unjudicious character of maternal love and care that make it a fitting paradigm for social life.

Noddings appeals, here, to images of selfless giving that lie deep in the Jewish and Christian traditions, though her view would certainly be controversial in both.[84] She holds that her maternal paradigm of care is incompatible with norms of reflective caring that are preferred by liberalism. And she is correct. The liberal tradition is profoundly opposed to the idea that people should spontaneously give themselves away without reflection, judgment, or reciprocity. We have finally identified a position about the emotional life that is truly opposed to liberalism; it puts itself forward as a feminist position because it appeals to maternal experience as a paradigm for all human concern.

Liberalism says to let them give themselves away to others—provided that they so choose in all freedom. Noddings says that this is one thought too many: love based on reflection lacks some of the spontaneity and moral value of true maternal love.

What should feminists say about this? First of all, we should ask some questions about Noddings's claim that maternal love and joy can and should be innocent of appraisal and judgment. She gives an example that makes at least one mother doubt.

> There is the joy that unaccountably floods over me as I walk into the house and see my daughter asleep on the sofa. She is exhausted from basketball playing, and her hair lies curled on a damp forehead. The joy I feel is immediate. . . . There is a feeling of connectedness in my joy, but no awareness of a particular belief and, certainly, no conscious assessment.[85]

Noddings concludes that such moments in which consciousness is emptied of focus and the personality flows toward another in a condition of fusion lie at the core of morality.

Let us consider this allegedly thoughtless and objectless joy. Noddings thinks nothing; she simply basks in the fused experience of maternal caring.[86] But can it really be the case that she has no thoughts at all? Doesn't Noddings have to have, in fact, the belief that her daughter is alive and asleep on the couch, rather than dead? Change that belief and her emotion would change from joy to devastating grief. She may not have to stop to ponder such a fact, but when her daughter was a baby she probably did.[87] Again, doesn't her joy presuppose the recognition that it is her daughter there on the couch rather than, say, a burglar? Doesn't its intensity also presuppose a recognition of the importance of her daughter in her life? To some extent, then, the view seems just wrong of the case as characterized.

But to the extent to which Noddings does give in to a joy without thought, how wise is she to do so? It does not occur to her, for example, to ask whether her daughter is sleeping from a drug or alcohol overdose, or following risky sex with a boyfriend, or sexual abuse from a relative. Assuming things are as she thinks, her joy is fine, and her maternal reactions appropriate. But aren't there circumstances in which the erasure of thought (which, as we see, is not complete even in the example) could be pushed too far? If her daughter really is unconscious from an overdose, or from sexual abuse, Noddings's joy would be inappropriate and her maternal responses harmful. Such heedless caring is dangerous in a world where many of the forces affecting children are malign. Noddings may live in a world in which she may safely bracket those concerns, but most mothers do not.

As Nietzsche wrote in a related connection: Blessed are the sleepy ones—for they shall soon nod off.[88]

A child is not an arm or a leg or a wish but a separate person. This person lives in a world full of both delight and danger. Therefore, the mother had better think, and she had better teach her child how to think. And she had better think critically, asking whether the norms and traditions embodied in the emotions of fear and shame and honor in her society—and in her own emotions as well—are reasonable or unreasonable norms. What shall she teach her child to fear, and what not to fear? How shall she urge her child to see the stranger who offers her an ice cream, or the teacher who caresses her, or the friend who says that people with black skin are bad? Unless society is perfect, as it probably is not, critical thought needs to inform emotional development and response. This liberal idea seems a better recipe for maternal care than Noddings's emphasis on thoughtless giving.

Even were symbiotic fused caring a good thing in the mother-child relationship, a very different sort of care seems required in the political life. Here indiscriminate self-giving-away seems a very bad idea, especially for women, who have frequently been brought up to think that they should sacrifice their well-being to others without demanding anything for themselves. This has frequently served male interests and harmed women. A little reflection, far from representing "one thought too many,"[89] might provide the saving distance between social norms and one's own selfhood. Noddings and her allies risk turning some of the pathologies of women's lives into virtues. Even in the family, there is no reason why women should simply give themselves away without demanding a just distribution of resources.

Recall, now, the widows at the conference in Bangalore. Having spent most of their lives thinking of themselves as mere adjuncts of a family, with no rights and no separate identity, they started to learn not to give themselves away without thinking. And this looked like a good thing. The women themselves were delighted with their newfound self-expression and freedom, and the expansion in their set of choices itself seems a definite good. But still, we might ask: Aren't these women being brainwashed by these liberal ideas? The widows in Bangalore gathered under the auspices of regional development workers,[90] who had some goals in mind, liberal goals. The *Hindu* article reports that the women were "urged" to think of themselves in a certain way; Noddings would presumably object that this way of thinking involves giving up a valuable kind of organic unity within the family that women had previously prized. Indian feminist Veena Das develops a similar position, arguing that the notion of personal welfare is alien to Indian women.[91] If a typical Indian rural woman were to be asked about her personal "welfare," Das claims, she would find the question unintelligible, except as a question about how the family is doing. The thinking of these women, Das holds, exemplifies a valuable type of devotion, which would be destroyed by liberal scrutiny.

Here we must distinguish several different aspects of these women's familial devotion. Liberal individualism, I have argued, does not ask a woman to become an egoist, putting her own gratification first and others' second. As far as liberalism is concerned, she may be (and in most versions ought to be) a committed altruist, even to the point of making considerable sacrifices of her own personal welfare for the sake of others. Nor, so far as liberalism is concerned, need she be dedicated to self-sufficiency, to minimizing her needs from others—although, as I have noted, some Indian feminist programs, following a Gandhian anti-

colonialist model, do endorse this as a feminist goal. As a liberal, she may continue to place friendship and love squarely at the heart of her plan. What liberalism asks, however, is that the woman *distinguish* her own well-being from
the well-being of others, noticing what tensions might exist between the two,
even if they are bound up in one another. Liberalism asks, further, that a woman
reflect and choose for herself the extent to which she will indeed sacrifice her
own well-being for others—that she do so not out of habit or convention but as
the result of an individual decision, freely made. It is of course a large matter to
spell out the conditions under which such choices would count as freely made,
but we can at least agree that many conditions under which women make sacrifices (such as conditions of malnutrition, intimidation, lack of education, and
lack of political power) are not such conditions. It is common for people to internalize the roles society gives them and to act unreflectively in accordance with
these roles. People also adjust their desires and preferences to what is possible,
so that they may even in a limited sense be content with their lot. But in circumstances of traditional hierarchy and limited information, we surely should
not assume that the sacrifices of well-being a woman makes are freely chosen,
whatever account of free choice and autonomy we ultimately prefer. And this
does matter. As Smith and Mill advise: Let her love others and give herself
away—provided she does so freely and judiciously, with the proper critical scrutiny of social norms. I believe that this proposal, far from killing love through
excessive male rationality, indicates the conditions under which love is a healthy
part of a flourishing life.[92]

In fact, the most powerful feminist criticism of liberal views of reason and
emotion points in the opposite direction to Noddings's. Made most influentially
by Catharine MacKinnon and Andrea Dworkin, and by now commonly accepted
in at least some form, the argument is that emotion, desire, and preference are
not given or "natural" but shaped by social norms and appraisals—and that many
emotions of both men and women are shaped by norms that subordinate women
to men.[93] MacKinnon has argued that not only male aggression and female
timidity but also the character of both male and female sexual desire are shaped
by the social norm that women ought to be the subordinates of men. Men eroticize domination and learn to achieve sexual satisfaction in connection with its
assertion. Women eroticize submission and learn to find satisfaction in giving
themselves away. This, MacKinnon has argued, harms both individuals and
society.

MacKinnon's insistence on criticizing socially deformed preferences goes
against one strand in contemporary liberalism, namely, the part of economic
utilitarianism that sees preferences as given, a bedrock to which law and politics respond rather than material that is itself shaped by law and politics. Economics is increasingly calling these views into question.[94] They have always
been at odds with the Kantian liberal tradition, which insists that individuals'
desires are frequently distorted by self-interest. They are even more clearly
at odds with Smith and Rousseau, both of whom were highly critical of diseased emotions and desires and blamed bad social arrangements for those dis-

eases. Rousseau vividly shows how differences of rank corrupt human sympathy, preventing nobles from seeing their own pain in the pain they inflict on a peasant.[95] Smith shows how society, attaching importance to money and status, corrupts anger and sympathy, producing bad citizens.[96] Both follow the ancient Stoic tradition, according to which human beings are born good and envy and malice result from social deformation.[97]

Nor are such insights foreign to the utilitarian tradition. Mill recognized that gender hierarchy deformed the desires of both men and women. Women, he held, internalize their inferior status in ways that shape their desires and choice, and many of these ways are very damaging to them and to society. He held that "what is now called the nature of women is an eminently artificial thing—the result of forced repression in some directions, unnatural stimulation in others." It is, he says, as if one had grown a tree half in a vapor bath and half in the snow, and then, noting that one part of it is withered and another part luxuriant, had held that it was the nature of the tree to be that way.[98] Mill draws special attention to the way in which society eroticizes female "meekness, submissiveness and resignation of all individual will" as "an essential part of sexual attractiveness," whereas strength of will is eroticized in the case of men (16). Given the upbringing of women, it would be "a miracle if the object of being attractive to men had not become the polar star of feminine education and formation of character" (16), and equally miraculous if this object had not been understood to entail subordination. Here again, Mill makes a judicious comparison to feudalism: To both nobles and vassals, domination and subordination seemed natural, and the desires of both were shaped by this sense of the natural. Equality always seems unnatural to the dominator; this is why any departure from women's subjection to men appears unnatural. "But how entirely, even in this case, the feeling is dependent on custom, appears by ample experience" (12–13).

What is new and remarkable in the work of MacKinnon and Dworkin is the insight that even sexual desire—which has often been thought to be natural and presocial, even by thinkers who would not hold this of envy and fear and anger[99]—is socially shaped, and that this shaping is often far from benign. Their central idea is already in Mill, but they have developed it much further, given that they can discuss sexual matters with a candor unavailable to Mill. One may differ with many of their analyses and conclusions, but it seems hard to avoid granting that they have identified a phenomenon of immense human importance, one that lies at the heart of a great deal of human misery. Insofar as liberalism has left the private sphere unexamined, this critique of desire is a critique of liberalism. It challenges liberalism to do for desire what it has often done with greed and anger and envy—that is, to conduct a rigorous examination of its social formation and to think of the moral education of children with these aims in mind. As Mill shows us, such scrutiny of desire is right in line with liberalism's deepest aspirations.

Doesn't this ruin sex? As in the case of maternal caring, so here: Doesn't the liberal ask women to have "one thought too many"? Doesn't sex at its best involve a heedless giving away of oneself to the other, an erasing of conscious reflection? Yes and no. Liberal feminism—and here I believe it is right to treat MacKinnon as a kind of Kantian liberal, inspired by a deep vision of personhood and autonomy[100]—does not ask women not to abandon themselves to and in pleasure, any more than it asks them not to invest themselves deeply in caring for children and loved ones. Once again, however, it says: Fine, so long as you think first. Abandon yourself, as long as you do so within a context of equality and noninstrumental respect.[101] In some areas of life, perhaps, noninstrumental respect can be taken for granted. In this one, because of its history of distortion, it cannot be, and so you must think. If, as Mill plausibly suggests, "the generality of the male sex cannot yet tolerate the idea of living with an equal" (53), this thinking may cause pain. The liberal holds that this pain should be risked rather than endure the hidden pain that arises from subordination.

In short, wherever you most mistrust habit, there you have the most need for reason. Women have lots of grounds to mistrust most habits people have had through the centuries, just as poor people have had reason to mistrust the moral emotions of kings. This means that women have an especially great need for reason. Males can at least take consolation from the thought that the habits they live by have been formed by them, whether for good or for ill. Women should recognize that where the voice of tradition speaks, that voice is most often male, and it has even invented a little squeaky voice for women to speak in, a voice that may be far from being their own true voice, whatever precise content we attach to that idea.

In an age skeptical of reason, as Mill rightly argues, we have a hard time unmasking such deeply habitual fictions. Thus the romantic reaction against reason that he saw in his own time seemed to him profoundly subversive of any critique of established custom. "For the apotheosis of Reason," he concludes, "we have substituted that of Instinct; and we call everything instinct which we find in ourselves and for which we cannot trace any rational foundation." Contemporary feminism should beware of making the same error.

Two things fill the mind with ever-increasing awe, wrote Kant: "the starry sky above me, and the moral law within me."[102] In that famous statement we see the radical vision of liberalism. Think what real people usually hold in awe: money, power, success, nice clothes, fancy cars, the dignity of kings, the wealth of corporations, the authority of despots of all sorts—and, perhaps most important of all, the authority of custom and tradition. Think what real women frequently hold in awe, or at least in fear: the physical power of men, the authority of men in the workplace, the sexual allure of male power, the alleged maleness of the deity, the control males have over work and shelter and food. The liberal holds none of these things in awe. She feels reverence for the world, its mystery and its wonder. And she reveres the capacity of persons to choose and fashion a life. That capacity has no gender, so the liberal does not revere established distinctions of gender any more than the dazzling equipment of kings. Some liberal thinkers have in fact revered established distinctions of gender. But, insofar as they did, they did not follow the vision of liberalism far enough. It is the vision of a beautiful, rich, and difficult world, in which a community of persons regard one another as free and equal but also as finite and needy—and therefore strive to arrange their relations on terms of justice and liberty. In a world governed by hierarchies of power and fashion, this is still, as it was from the first, a radical vision, a vision that can and should lead to social revolution. It is always radical to make the demand to see and to be seen as human rather than as someone's lord or someone's subject. I believe it is best for women to embrace this vision and make this demand.

3

RELIGION AND WOMEN'S HUMAN RIGHTS

The *mullahs* say: "When they will die we shall not bury them."
Villagers say, "Wherever they want, they go. They do not
cover their heads. They talk with men. They will be sinners."
I said: "If Allah does not see us when we stay hungry then
Allah has sinned."
—A Bangladeshi wife, participant in a literacy and skills
program sponsored by the Bangladesh Rural Advancement
Committee (cited in M. A. Chen, *A Quiet Revolution*)

The Liberal Dilemma

Political liberals characteristically defend two theses that appear to be closely
related. First, liberals hold that religious liberty, or more generally the liberty
of conscience, is among the most important of the human freedoms and must
be given a very strong degree of priority in the basic structure of a political regime. This is frequently understood to entail that the freedom of religious exercise can permissibly be infringed upon only when there is an imminent threat
to public order.[1] Second, liberals hold that human beings have various other
rights, including rights to freedom of movement, freedom of assembly, freedom
of speech, equal political participation, equal treatment under the law, both civil
and criminal, and, finally, various rights to the integrity and inviolability of the
person.

In a sense, there seems to be a strong complementarity between the first thesis and the second. For we know well that the rights on the list given in the second thesis have all too often been denied to individuals on grounds of religious
membership; one clear sign of a regime's failure to honor the first thesis is its
discriminatory behavior toward religious groups with respect to a wider spectrum of human rights. Thus, the German Nazi regime, unlike that of medieval
Spain, was not preoccupied with the specific task of impeding the Jews' freedom

to worship. They pursued their campaign through the denial of other human rights, such as the equal right to contract a marriage; the right to mobility, assembly, and choice of occupation; and, of course, ultimately, the right to life. True religious liberty required that these other basic freedoms not be impaired on a discriminatory basis.

On the other hand, the two theses can also generate a tension, which poses difficult questions for contemporary law and political thought. For the world's major religions, in their actual human form, have not always been outstanding respecters of basic human rights or of the equal dignity and inviolability of persons. Some, indeed, have gone as far as to create systems of law that deny the equal rights of persons and justify violations of their dignity and their person. Apart from law, influential religious discourse in many parts of the world threatens the bodily integrity and equal dignity of persons—and sometimes, even, their equal liberty of worship. Consider the following six examples.

(1) In a village in rural Bangladesh in the early 1980s, impoverished women leave their homes to meet in a group organized by the Bangladesh Rural Advancement Committee. They are learning to read, to keep accounts, and to pursue various forms of work outside the home—all important ingredients in improving nutrition and health for themselves and their children. The local *mullahs* (Islamic religious leaders) make speeches saying that women who work outside the house and talk with men other than their husbands are whores. They threaten them with religious and communal ostracism (refusal to officiate at any of the woman's social or religious functions), and even with physical violence. ("If you go into the field, your legs will be broken."[2]) Although most of the women continue with the literacy project, they fear for their status in the community, their well-being (which, so far, is entirely dependent on their relation to men), and their physical safety.[3]

(2) In Pakistan, again in the early 1980s, a young blind girl named Safia Bibi complained of rape. Because she was a minor, her father filed a complaint. Under the recently promulgated Hudood Ordinance, rape convictions require four male witnesses, and complainants who fail to produce the necessary testimony may then be prosecuted for fornication (*zina*). The Sessions Court found Safia in violation of the *zina* ordinance, sentencing her to three years hard labor in prison, despite her blindness. After a storm of national and international protest, the Federal Shariat Court set the case aside on technical grounds but refused to prosecute the accused rapist.[4]

(3) In Madhya Pradesh, India, in 1975, a Muslim woman named Shah Bano was thrown out of her home by her husband, a well-to-do lawyer, after forty-three years of marriage and five children.[5] As required by Islamic personal law, he returned Rs. 3000 (about $300), which had been her marriage settlement from her family in 1932. Rather than accept this settlement, inadequate for survival, she sued for maintenance under Section 125 of the Criminal Procedure Code, which requires a person of adequate means to protect relations from destitution and vagrancy.[6] (India has a uniform criminal code, although it does not have a uniform civil code; civil matters are handled by many distinct religious systems of law.) As a result, she was awarded Rs. 180 ($18) per month, hardly "a princely

sum," but an improvement. Her husband, however, appealed this judgment to the Supreme Court of India, holding that as a Muslim he was bound only by Islamic law. In 1985, the Supreme Court held that the provisions of the Criminal Procedure Code regarding maintenance of destitute relations were applicable to members of all religions and that a person should not lose simply by being a Muslim. In his opinion Chief Justice Chandrachud alluded to a provision of the Constitution that had instructed the state to "endeavour to secure" a uniform civil code; he deplored its failure to have done so. The Muslim Personal Law Board and other religious leaders vehemently criticized the ruling, using public rhetoric to persuade followers that their religion was in grave danger unless the government should decide to exempt Muslim women from the provisions of Section 125.[7] Responding to this campaign, the government of Rajiv Gandhi passed the Muslim Women (Protection of Rights on Divorce) Bill of 1986, which deprived divorced Muslim women of their right of maintenance under the criminal code[8]—at the same time recommending that by the year 2000 the nation adopt a uniform civil code.[9] Hindu political activists subsequently complained that the new law discriminated against Hindus by giving Muslims "special privileges."[10]

(4) In 1955, the Indian Parliament passed the Hindu Marriage Act, which for the first time gave women the right to divorce and remarriage, which men had long enjoyed. (Indeed, previously men could marry an unlimited number of times without getting divorced, although the reforms of 1955 and 1956 ruled out polygamy for Hindu men.) Conservative Hindu members of Parliament claimed that the bill had been passed to "wound the religious feeling of the Hindus" and was "against the fundamental principles of Hinduism."[11]

(5) In contemporary Iran, the penalty for women who do not adhere to the dress code is between thirty-four and seventy-four lashes with a whip. The actual penalties are more varied. Some women get off with a cash fine. "But, just as commonly, women who do not adhere to the dress code are punished with acts of extreme cruelty: their feet may be put in a gunny sack full of mice and cockroaches, their faces splashed with acid or cut with razor blades."[12] So terrifying are the penalties that in 1991, a thirteen-year-old girl who was found in violation committed suicide by throwing herself out a fifth-floor window. On August 15, 1991, the Prosecutor-General, Abolfazl Musavi-Tabrizi, addressing the controversy occasioned by this death, declared that "anyone who rejects the principle of the *Hijab* [dress code] is an apostate and the punishment for apostasy under Islamic Law is death."[13]

(6) In 1993, two groups of women attempted to hold prayer services at the Western Wall (the "Wailing Wall") in Jerusalem. Although they did not challenge the traditional separation of male and female prayer spaces—and thus were not in violation of any explicit provision of religious law—they did wear prayer shawls and read from the Torah scroll, which is not conventionally appropriate within Orthodox Judaism. The official in charge, representing the Ministry of Religious Affairs, forbade them to continue, holding that it would undermine custom and violate the religious feelings of orthodox worshippers. They were even labeled "provocateurs" for their organized singing. The Supreme

Court of Israel dismissed the women's petition for freedom of religious exercise, recommending that the government establish a commission to look into the issue.[14]

In all these cases we see an apparent dilemma for the modern liberal regime. For if the people who claim to speak for the religious traditions in these examples are to be accepted as their representatives and their claims as legitimate claims of religious liberty (and we shall see that this is not an uncomplicated matter), then there really is a tension between respect for religious liberty and respect for the basic human rights of many citizens. This tension finds its sharpest form wherever the religious traditions have arrogated to themselves, and have been permitted, the right to make law, but it arises, as well, in more informal ways, when the highly influential discourse of religious leaders poses problems for the equal worth of basic liberties—usually already guaranteed in the constitutions (or the legal traditions) of the nations in question, as well as in their commitment to the Universal Declaration of Human Rights and, in most cases, the Convention on the Elimination of All Forms of Discrimination Against Women (CEDAW), a multilateral treaty ratified by 131 countries.[15] If the government defers to the wishes of the religious group, a vulnerable group of individuals will lose basic rights; if the government commits itself to respecting equal human rights of all individuals, it will stand accused of indifference to the liberty of conscience. Often government actors, like Rajiv Gandhi, make a mere pretense of serious engagement with the problem—satisfying the religious group, seeing that it is far more politically powerful than women, but saying, at the same time, that something must surely be done about this by someone in the future.

Nor is this dilemma troubling only for the liberal state: It also vexes the religions themselves. An especially poignant statement of its force can be found in the Pope's October 1995 address to the United Nations General Assembly. On the one hand, this address contained a very strong injunction to respect the world's major religions and a ringing defense of "the fundamental right to freedom of religion and freedom of conscience, as the cornerstones of the structure of human rights and the foundation of every truly free society."[16] These sentiments are exactly those of John Rawls, who writes that "the question of equal liberty of conscience is settled. It is one of the fixed points of our considered judgments of justice."[17] At the same time, however, the Pope vigorously endorsed the United Nations Universal Declaration of Human Rights as "one of the highest expressions of the human conscience of our time," and he spoke of a worldwide movement toward universal respect for the dignity and inviolability of the human person. His more recent "Letter to Women," issued just before the Beijing Women's Conference, makes it clear that he considers many of the rights at issue in my examples to be central human rights: He mentions freedom from sexual violence (including, it would appear, marital rape), equality in family rights, equality in political duties and responsibilities, equality under the law, and equality in the workplace.[18] Although his list does not contain all the rights that all advocates of women's rights have sought, it includes enough of them to generate the dilemma, simply by its juxtaposition with the urgent injunction to respect the answers given by each religious tradition.

The dilemma studied here does arise in the United States as well; as I follow the international issues I shall allude to aspects of those debates. But, given that the United States has a Bill of Rights that is effective, not merely aspirational (as are relevant constitutional provisions in many other nations[19]), and given that by now the major religions in the United States have long accepted some fundamental shared ideas about the equal dignity and liberty of persons, such a focus cannot address the most problematic aspects of the relationship between political liberalism and religion. We simply do not hear any influential religious voice in the United States proposing, at this time, that women's legal testimony be judged unequal to that of men, that women be severely punished for dressing in a particular way, that their legs be broken for working outside the house, or that they be denied a right to divorce equal to that granted a man. None of these cases is totally discontinuous with our own past and even present; the practical difficulty of complaining of rape, for example, and the punishment meted out to women who do so complain, are real and recent, in some cases current (see chapter 5). Further back in our history all the mentioned inequalities in family law could be attested, often buttressed by appeals to religion.[20] Certainly Christianity and Judaism are far from blameless in the global history of women's unequal treatment, as my Israeli case attests, although in Europe and North America they have adopted a more liberal form recently, as a result of both internal criticism and legal constraint. My international examples manifest, I believe, what parts of most religious traditions (as well as many nonreligious traditions) will try to do when they are not so shaped by liberal traditions. I believe, therefore, that a focus on current international issues is valuable to give us a vivid sense of the reality of our topic. Without this focus, we might fail to acknowledge that religions (like many nonreligious political actors) can propose atrocities; we might therefore fail to ask what liberals who care about religion should say when they do.

It is useful to focus on this topic for another reason as well: because these violations do not always receive the intense public concern and condemnation that other systematic atrocities against groups often receive—and there is reason to think that liberal respect for religious difference is involved in this neglect.[21] The worldwide mobilization against South African Apartheid was not accompanied by any similar mobilization to divest stock holdings in nations that treat women as unequal under the law. Indeed, these inequalities are often cheerfully put up with, as part of legitimate differences—as when our troops were asked to fall in with Saudi customs regarding women's dress while serving in the Gulf. One reason for the reluctance of Western liberals to face such harms and to take appropriate political action is surely the political hopelessness of it all—for how could we hope to convince our nation to take economic action against so many oil-rich nations? There may be several other reasons.[22] Among them, however, is surely the role of religion in the debate: Liberals who do not hesitate to criticize a secular government that perpetrates atrocity are anxious and reticent when it comes to vindicating claims of justice against major religious leaders and groups. They are hesitant, I suggest, because they hold that the liberty of conscience is among the fixed points in our considered judgments of justice, and they are at a loss to see how they could in good conscience ask religious people to acquiesce in a judgment about sex equality that is foreign to that religious tradition. This suggests that sorting out the liberal dilemma may contribute to greater political clarity in an area where we urgently need it.

I shall focus on cases in which religions threaten basic human rights. This is because it is these cases that generate the dilemma with which I am concerned, not because I believe that this is the primary relation religions have had to human rights. It is obvious that religious discourse has been among the major sources of support for human rights around the world, and I have focused on the Pope's statement partly to keep this fact before our minds.

We must also keep reminding ourselves that cultures are complex. It is generally very difficult to determine to what extent the religions in a nation reflect influences from other aspects of the culture and to what extent they influence the culture. In nations such as Iran, we can contrast the situation prior to the control of religious fundamentalists with the current situation; usually such assessments are more elusive, and we must exercise caution in drawing conclusions. The problem is compounded, in a nation such as India, by sharp regional variations that reflect many different cultural and political factors; differences across religions are less sharp than such regional differences, though religion appears to have some independent explanatory weight.[23]

Our assessments are made still more complex by the fact that when religions act politically their religious discourse is often powerfully colored by issues of political power. Thus, the Hinduism represented today in India by the Bharatiya Janata Party (BJP, the leading Hindu nationalist party) is not very much like the inclusive, loosely defined, polytheistic Hinduism of earlier tradition; political and cultural forces are likely to have shaped the BJP's selection of religious principles and emphases.[24] Very different political aims shaped Mahatma Gandhi's characterization of the essence of Hinduism, when he said, "If I were asked to define the Hindu creed, I should simply say: Search after truth through nonviolent means."[25] Where women are concerned, the same has been true over the years. The Hindu tradition, as we noted in chapter 1, offers many different and contradictory pictures of women's sexual agency. An investigation of cultural context would be likely, here too, to reveal political influences at work shaping and reshaping the religious tradition; more important for our purposes, the contemporary choice to stress one aspect of the tradition rather than another itself often expresses political aims.[26]

Similarly, the Islamic fundamentalism characteristic of the Iranian regime has little in common with the tolerant and pluralistic form of Islam espoused by Iranian writer Alberuni, who traveled to India in the eleventh century, or with that implemented politically by the tolerant Moghul emperor Akbar in the sixteenth century.[27] Islam contains fundamentalists who are intolerant of other religions, but it also contains some of the earliest expressions of toleration and the transcendence of sectarian boundaries—in, for example, the great medieval religious poet Kabir, who wrote, "Kabir is the child of Allah and of Ram: He is my Guru, he is my Pir."[28] In India today, Muslims include liberals and conservatives, feminists and traditionalists. Similarly, the contemporary Iranian regime interprets Islam in ways that do not reflect the entirety of that tradition, in connection with its political goals. Many devout Muslims today support more liberal views and policies. In nations such as Indonesia and Tunisia, liberalization has had large political effects. Most of us are aware that Judaism and Christianity contain such complexities; we should not refuse this recognition to religions we know less well.[29]

Thus the criticisms we may make of "religious practices" and "religious discourse" will be criticisms of human beings, often vying for political power; they do not presuppose that any of these religions has an unchanging and unchangeable core of misogyny, or even that the misogynistic elements are religiously central rather than political in origin. Nonetheless, because we are interested in the rights of individuals, we must approach the religions where they, or their representatives, threaten these rights.

In what follows, I do not ignore, though I shall not directly address, the difficulties involved in defining the notion of a "human right" or specifying the conditions under which a person can be said to have a right to a certain type of treatment. Clearly, given that I shall be urging legal change to do justice to women's human rights, I do not accept a positivist analysis, according to which a person has a right if and only if the law in her country has recognized such a right. I understand a human right to be a claim of an especially urgent and powerful sort, one that can be justified by an ethical argument that can command a broad cross-cultural consensus, and one that does not cease to be morally salient when circumstances render its recognition inefficient. A human right, unlike many other rights people may have, derives not from a person's particular situation of privilege or power or skill but, instead, just from the fact of being human. In my understanding, articulated in chapter 1, there is a very close relationship between a list of basic human rights and a list of basic human capabilities to function that is also very close to the Rawlsian list of "primary goods," that is, things that all persons may be presumed to need in order to carry out their plans of life, whatever the plan is. Human rights are, in effect, justified claims to such basic capabilities or opportunities.[30]

Women's Human Rights: The Problem Areas

CEDAW defines "discrimination against women" as follows:

> Any distinction, exclusion or restriction made on the basis of sex which has the effect or purpose of impairing or nullifying the recognition, enjoyment or exercise by women, irrespective of their marital status, on a basis of equality of men and women, of human rights and fundamental freedoms in the political, economic, social, cultural, civil or any other field.

By ratifying CEDAW—as most of the nations under discussion have—states pledge (1) to embody "the principle of the equality of men and women" in their national Constitutions or other appropriate legislation; (2) to legislate against discrimination against women, providing appropriate sanctions; (3) to "establish legal protection of the rights of women on an equal basis with men" and to ensure this protection through "competent national tribunals and other public institutions"; (4) to ensure that public authorities do not discriminate against women; (5) to take "all appropriate measures" to eliminate existing discrimination "by any person, organization or enterprise"; (6) to change or abolish any existing discriminatory "laws, regulations, customs and practices"; and (7) to repeal all provisions of the penal law that are discriminatory.[31] Article 5 of CEDAW elaborates these duties by explaining that state parties agree to confront and modify "customary and all other practices" that are based on the idea of the inferiority or superiority of one sex to the other, or on ideas of stereotyped roles for men and women. Let us keep these norms in mind as we briefly survey eleven problem areas for women's human rights (closely connected to chapter 1's account of the basic capabilities) in which religious discourse, and often action, has been a major influence.

1. Life and Health

Women's lives are unequally at risk in many parts of today's world. Statistics continue to show that women suffer unequally from hunger and malnutrition and from unequal access to basic health care.[32] Although it is difficult to pin down the origins of practices of unequal feeding and care, cultural systems that portray female life as unequal in worth to male life must bear some of the responsibility for this egregious situation. Religious discourse has played a substantial role here: Although it is difficult to distinguish between a religion and the cultural traditions that surround it, the Hindu, Islamic, and Confucian traditions have all, with some plausibility, been accused of denigrating the value of female life in ways that have undermined women's claim to basic goods of subsistence.[33]

Of equal or greater importance, religious discourse has played a major and undisguised role in confining women to the home in many parts of the world, and in denying them opportunities to earn wages outside. Islamic ideas of a woman's proper role returned thousands of women to the home in Iran and, more recently, in Afghanistan; they keep women in the home in Bangladesh, India, and many other nations. Hindu caste traditions, similarly, are often invoked to resist a woman's attempt to seek outside employment. It is especially common that middle-rank "upwardly mobile" caste families will invoke norms of the Brahmin ideal of woman to forbid their women employment, thus defining the family as "Brahminizing."[34] Confucian values, as we saw in chapter 1, are also publicly invoked to return women to the home from the public sector. But the fact is that wage labor outside the home is highly correlated with a woman's ability to command food and other goods within it. Sometimes the connection is direct: In Rajasthan, Metha Bai, a young Hindu widow, was starving because her Brahminizing in-laws refused to let her earn money to feed herself and her children, threatening to beat her if she went out.[35] Sometimes it is more indirect, through a perception of a woman's importance to the future of the family. Because housework is usually not perceived as making a great contribution to the family's well-being, whereas cash wages are, women who work outside do better at commanding food in times of shortage, and the general perception of a daughter's worth is similarly affected by her future employment opportunities.[36] Religious discourse is thus heavily implicated in many female deaths.

At times, religion directly urges female death. The Indian practice of *sati*, or the immolation of a widow following her husband's death, is certainly religious in origin. The practice has dwindled but has not disappeared completely. On September 4, 1987, in Deorala, Rajasthan, an eighteen-year-old university student named Roop Kanwar was burned alive on her husband's funeral pyre.[37] (Her husband, when he died, was an unemployed university undergraduate.) Some say that she died willingly; others that she was coerced by family pressure.[38] Pilgrims flocked to Deorala, revering Roop as a goddess and believing that offerings at her shrine would cure cancer. A huge public controversy erupted. Three months later the Indian Parliament passed a tough new law extending the domain of criminal culpability with respect to *sati*, even though an old law already made the practice illegal. The new law prohibits the "glorification" of *sati*, defining "glorification" to include the justification or support of the practice of *sati*, the eulogizing of a person who has committed *sati*, holding any ceremony or procession in connection with *sati*, or collecting funds to construct a temple or place of worship in connection with *sati*.[39] Rajiv Gandhi, decisive in this case, pronounced the practice "utterly reprehensible and barbaric." Traditionalist Hindus, however, attacked the government. "A leading Hindi journal pointed an accusing finger at secular, western-educated intellectuals, arguing that only godless people who did not believe in reincarnation would denigrate Roop's brave act."[40]

It is an understatement to say that most Indian widows do not commit *sati*. More common are crimes involving dowry: killings of women to get hold of their dowry or beating and threats to murder to extract further payments from the woman's family. Laws directed specifically against these abuses, in India and Bangladesh, testify to the problem they pose. Indeed, India made the entire practice of dowry illegal, starting in 1961, to cope with the abuses, which, nonetheless, persist.[41] One 1986 Bangladeshi case illustrates the common sordid pattern. Ferdousi Begum brought a modest dowry into her marriage with Jahangir Alam, including a 14" black and white TV set, some personal items of jewelry for the marriage, a wrist watch, a table fan, a sofa set, and "various items of wooden furniture." Her husband's family knew, however, that her father and brothers had a good income and could perhaps pay more. They therefore began a campaign of psychological and physical intimidation, with a view to augment this dowry. As the judge remarks, "Accused Md. Jahangir Alam was found after marriage to be a ruthless, cruel and greedy person. . . . All the accused persons in collusion with each other started torturing complainant Ferdousi Begum both mentally and physically immediately after the marriage with a view to squeeze money (as dowry) from the guardians of complainant Ferdousi Begum. . . ." One morning in 1985, her husband asked his wife Ferdousi Begum to "bring 20" Coloured T.V. set, Radio, Wrist Watch, and cash money amounting to Taka 25,000 from her brothers (as dowry for the marriage)." When she said her broth-

ers could not meet this demand, he became furious and the whole group of relatives began to beat her "with rod, lathi, etc." Her husband then attempted to
murder her by throttling her; he kicked her, pressed her down on the floor, and
dragged her out of the house by her hair. At this point the accused relatives
snatched the gold jewelry off Ferdousi Begum's body and beat her further,
until she lost consciousness. After she was taken to her father's house, medical
examination revealed that she had received severe injuries to the legs, "trau-
matic collapse" of the spinal column, and a permanent hearing loss in one ear.
The husband and relatives were tried under the 1983 Cruelty to Women Act,
which forbids murder, attempted murder, or grave bodily harm in connection
with dowry payments. A local ward chairman dismissed the complaint observing arbitrarily that the complainant Ferdousi Begum had "lodged the complaint
falsely to suppress the fact of her own guilt; but the Ward Chairman has not
stated what was her guilt." Judge F. H. M. Habibur Rahman of the Chittagong
Bench reinstated her complaint.[42]

This sad case shows how difficult it is for women to protect themselves from
violence, even when a special law targets these offenses. Notice that a woman's
life counts less, in the thought of Jahangir Alam and his relatives, than the difference between a 14" black-and-white TV set and a 20" color TV set. Religion is not
directly involved in such dowry deaths, but it is an important part of a cultural
system that supports these traditions, making women highly vulnerable.

But even these much publicized dowry crimes are few and largely middle class.
Dramatic cases involving upper-class or middle-class women tend to attract more
press coverage and more public protest than the "endemic but quiet deprivations"[43] that are the lot of a large proportion of widows, especially in rural areas.
A large majority have very insecure and limited property rights; because they
remain in their husband's place of residence, they can expect little care or support either from their birth family or their in-laws, who frequently mistreat
them; they may have no freedom to work, even if this causes malnutrition or
starvation.[44] As Metha Bai said to Martha Chen, "I may die, but still I cannot go
out. If there is something in the house we eat; otherwise we go to sleep."[45] Many
factors are implicated in this situation, including a traditional gendered division
of labor and customs of patrilocal residence and patrilineal inheritance. Religious
discourse about widowhood (according to which the widow is virtually dead at
the husband's death) is, then, not the only cause of these ills; it is, however,
among the causes.

2. The Right to Bodily Integrity

Women suffer many abuses that violate their bodily integrity. These include rape,
marital rape, other sexual abuse, domestic violence, and genital mutilation.

Rape is an underreported and underpunished crime the world over; it is more
likely to be unreported when religions have constructed norms that make rape
a sign of impurity. Stranger rape sometimes has a religious rationale, as in the
large number of rapes and abductions that accompanied the Hindu-Muslim
Partition Riots in India/Pakistan in 1947. Rape was seen as a type of forced con-

version and was condemned as such in the position statement of the All India Congress Committee that met to consider the problem.[46] The total number of women raped on both sides may have been as high as 100,000.[47] More commonly, religion, although not directly urging stranger rape, promulgates norms of female purity and submissiveness that are used to justify the rape of women who defy such conventions. Religious discourse is heavily implicated in creating the picture of women as either chaste or "fallen" that makes prosecution very difficult. The Iranian Prosecutor-General believes that any woman who violates the dress code deserves death; he is not likely, then, to deter the common practice of police rape of women under detention for such violations. There is widespread evidence of police abuse of women in Pakistan[48]; in India the law of rape has been rewritten for police custody cases, to shift the burden of proof onto the defendant (to deter examinations of women without female witnesses), and special women's courts have been established to hear charges of rape.[49] More generally, the requirements on rape evidence under Islamic laws that prevail in many nations (four male witnesses) make an accusation extremely difficult (as the Safia Bibi case shows) and highly contingent upon the good will of family members.[50] In Pakistan, with its Catch-22 according to which an unsuccessful accusation of rape constitutes a confession to fornication, an offense punishable by whipping, few women will complain of rape, and few men will be deterred from raping.

Domestic violence is one of the gravest problems faced by women the world over. Religions sometimes call directly for corporal punishment of a disobedient spouse: Islamic law explicitly countenances this remedy, allowing the wife to petition for divorce only if the beating is especially prolonged or severe.[51] Even more often, religious discourse promulgates norms of male authority—and also pictures of female wantonness and childishness[52]—that support these practices. (This is as true of Western as of non-Western religions.) Nations that allow the religions to take charge of family law often move very slowly to counter this problem. In India, women have long sought a civil law against domestic violence; a major obstacle is the fact that, in the absence of a uniform civil code, such laws would have to be separately made for Hindus, Muslims, and Parsis.[53] In both Hindu and Islamic communities, unequal access to divorce and the remedy of "restitution of conjugal rights" frequently confines women to a scene of domestic violence and sexual imposition.

The very concept of marital rape is foreign to many religious traditions, which give a husband limitless sexual access to the wife. The concept is a recent one in European and North American culture and religion and still is not recognized in many jurisdictions (see chapter 5). Indeed, the concept of "restitution of conjugal rights" that is frequently invoked in Indian and Bangladeshi family courts is of British origin and was retained in the Hindu Marriage Act and the Special Marriage Act of 1954. Nonetheless, at this point, religious law and discourse, including the Hindu and Islamic, are heavily implicated in maintaining marital rape as an option for men.

There has been opposition. The "Introduction" discussed *T. Sareetha v. T. Venkata Subbaiah* (1983),[54] in which Judge Choudary of the Andhra Pradesh

High Court, in an eloquent opinion, held that the remedy of "restitution of conjugal rights violates the right to privacy and human dignity guaranteed by and contained in Article 21 of our Constitution," depriving a woman of both sexual choice and control over her reproductive functioning.[55] Although religious issues were not directly pertinent to his constitutional argument, which rested on issues of both privacy and equal protection, Judge Choudary did address the religion question, arguing that the "restitution" remedy was not entailed by "our ancient Hindu system of matrimonial law." In that tradition, the wife has a duty to "surrender to her husband," but it is "an imperfect obligation incapable of being enforced against her will."[56] He traces the forcible remedy to medieval English ecclesiastical law, noting that the British abolished it only in 1970.

Thus, if we agree with Judge Choudary, there is no absolutely binding religious claim at issue here, although the law supports religion, enforcing what religion considers to be a duty. But the very fact of separate religious courts, and of their perceived importance in constituting a religious identity, leads to a demand for enforcement, even against the woman's admitted constitutional rights. And there is no doubt that the worth of the constitutional rights in question in Sareetha's case is severely limited by the insistence of religious courts on maintaining their separate domains of authority. Indeed, because of those claims, Sareetha ultimately lost: The Supreme Court reversed, praising the remedy of restitution as one that "serves a social purpose as an aid to the prevention of break-up of marriage."[57] The Court (perhaps influenced by Sareetha's evident autonomy) did not take cognizance of the likely financial position of most women in her position, many of whom would be forced to return to marriages from which they had fled, often for reasons of violence; nor did the Supreme Court effectively respond to the constitutional questions. In other related decisions, the Court has opined that a Hindu woman's duty is to live with her husband in the matrimonial home.

Similar cases can be found on the Islamic side. In Bangladesh, a woman who had suffered from domestic violence left the conjugal home and filed for divorce; her husband brought suit for restitution of conjugal rights.[58] A lower court held that the woman had "no right to divorce at her own sweet will and without any reasonable excuse." In this case, however, the High Court vindicated her rights, commenting on the inconsistency between the restitution remedy and the equality provisions in Bangladesh's constitution:

> The very concept of the husband's unilateral plea for forcible restitution of conjugal rights had become outmoded and . . . does not fit with the State and Public Principle and Policy of equality of all men and women being citizens equal before the law and entitled to be treated only in accordance with the law as guaranteed in Articles 27 and 31 of the Constitution. . . . A reference to Article 28(2) of the Constitution of Bangladesh guaranteeing equal rights of women and men in all spheres of the State and public life would clearly indicate that any unilateral plea of the husband for forcible restitution of conjugal rights as against a wife unwilling to live with her husband is violative of the accepted State and Public Principle and Policy.

In these two contested cases we see our liberal dilemma. Both India and Bangladesh have sought to combine a secular liberal constitution, including guarantees of sex equality, with religious courts of family law. In both cases it remains ambiguous to what extent the equality provisions of the constitution apply to the protected family sphere. In such a situation, women's constitutional rights are bound to be fragile and contestable; sometimes things work out one way, sometimes the other.

Female genital mutilation is frequently defended with discourse that appeals to its basis in Islam. It would appear that these appeals are at the very least tendentious, given that there is no authentic religious argument supporting the compulsory practice (see chapter 4). Nonetheless, religious discourse of a kind has been powerful in defending the practice and branding the attack on it as Westernizing.

The right to bodily integrity is also compromised by degrading punishments. A number of international human rights instruments speak of a right against "cruel, inhuman, or degrading treatment or punishment."[59] A number of punishments mandated in the Koran and Shari'a have been regarded as problematic under this description, including the mandated one hundred lashes for *zina* or fornication. These punishments are in essence religious, justified at their core by their religious textual rationale.[60] Even Muslims who privately view them as cruel and inhuman cannot risk the consequences of openly questioning the will of God; indeed, to dispute the binding authority of the Koran is to be liable for the death penalty for apostasy.[61] On the other hand, liberal Islamic thinkers agree that a great deal can be done, even within religious orthodoxy, to restrict the implementation of these punishments in practice, by stressing elements of the texts that insist they should not be inflicted if there is any doubt; a broad concept of doubt may be developed that blocks implementation in a variety of cases.[62]

There can be no doubt that the control of women's bodies has been a central preoccupation of many, if not most, religions of the world. These controls have usually been asymmetrical and, from the point of view of justice, discriminatory. In a wide range of cases, they violate some of the most basic rights of a human being, without which, as Judge Choudary says, human bodily life becomes degraded to a merely animal level of existence.

3. Employment Rights

Women should have the right to seek employment outside the home without intimidation or discrimination. CEDAW states that the rights to seek employment, to nondiscrimination in hiring, to free choice of occupation, and to equal pay for work of equal value are all fundamental rights that women enjoy equally with men.[63] Religious discourse, as I have already indicated, is prominently used to oppose women's efforts to seek and retain employment outside the home. In the Rajasthan inhabited by Metha Bai, in the Bangladeshi village described by Martha Chen, in Islamic Iran, in the contemporary Chinese workplace—in all these places, religious norms about women's proper place are working to deny women equality and in many cases totally to deny them access to employment. At the time of Iran's Islamic revolution, the regime fired more than 40,000 women working as elementary and high school teachers, as well as many others; women's employment fell in five years by 50% and reached a low point of 6.2%.[64] The 1995 United Nations *Human Development Report* gives 19% as the figure for women's economic activity, but this figure includes unpaid agricultural labor and is therefore difficult to compare with the earlier figures. The Ayatollah Mutahari, one of the architects of Islamist policy, wrote that "the specific task of women in this society is to marry and bear children. They will be discouraged from entering legislative, judicial, or whatever careers may require decision making, as women lack the intellectual ability and discerning judgement required for these careers."[65] More recently, the Taliban in Afghanistan has banned women from working outside their homes, exempting only a small number of female doctors and nurses from the decree.[66]

These views of women are similar to those that were defended by appeal to Christian norms in earlier American cases—for example, the famous *Bradwell* case in 1873 in which a woman was denied the right to practice law, in an opinion that mentioned "the divine ordinance" as a source for the view that women were naturally unsuited for the professions.[67] Employment rights are a central source of genuine equality for women in a modern liberal regime. They are also frequently essential for well-being and often for survival.

4. Mobility and Assembly Rights

It is obvious that women who are confined to the home and threatened with harm or opprobrium by religious leaders should they walk outside are being deprived of an essential right. It is difficult to conceive of the meaning and extent of this deprivation. Cornelia Sorabji, the first woman to take a degree in law at Oxford and the first woman admitted to the bar in India, dedicated her career to representing women who were not permitted to see a man other than their husband. (As a Parsi, Sorabji was in an unusually advantaged position, because Parsis of that era held more liberal views about women's mobility.) She reports that when she brought a rose to one young wife and mentioned having plucked it from a bush outside, the wife reacted with puzzlement. Having been married as a small child, she had never been in contact with growing things of any kind; she believed that roses lie on the ground and are picked up like stones.[68] The Bangladeshi women described by Martha Chen are not exactly in that position—one reason for this being that they are too poor not to have to go outside for some purposes. But their lives were utterly circumscribed by religious threats of ostracism and physical violence if they walked around in the streets and talked to males. The dress codes that obtain in Iran and, in an even more extreme form, in Taliban-ruled Afghanistan impose great restrictions on women's mobility, as do other related provisions of these regimes, such as the requirement that Iranian women sit in the back of the bus and the recent restriction on female bicycling in Teheran, now confined to a fence-enclosed trail.[69] In 1990, the Saudi government justified a ban against women driving as flowing from Islamic morality and principles.[70]

In all countries governed in whole or part by Islamic law, women are under some form of male guardianship, and this, again, imposes various limits on mobility. To take many trips, especially trips abroad, women must secure written permission from a male. In Saudi Arabia, for example, women may not leave the country without permission of a father or husband—and female visitors are not allowed in unless accompanied by a male family member.[71] In the Sudan, the Personal Law for Muslims Act directs the husband to grant permission "within reason" for a woman to visit parents and relatives for short periods, but she may never travel on her own. If she is under fifty, she must be accompanied by a male relative to whom she could not legally be married; if she is over fifty, another sort of "trustworthy companion" may, with the guardian's permission, be selected. Exit visas require written permission of the guardian.[72]

As to assembly rights, it is of course true that in regimes that are not liberal and democratic nobody has very secure freedom of assembly, especially when political protest is involved, but assembly rights are also denied to women, further, on a discriminatory basis. When Saudi women demonstrated against the ban on driving, the government responded by prohibiting all future demonstrations by women.[73] In Egypt, the prominent Arab Women's Solidarity Association was suppressed in 1992, with reference to religious norms: The organization had "threatened the peace and political and social order of the state by spreading ideas and beliefs offensive to the rule of Islamic *shari'a* and the religion of Islam."[74] Particular reference was made to the group's criticisms of established laws regulating marriage and divorce. In China, it is similarly impossible for any independent women's organization to exist, but it is unclear to me whether religious discourse has been used to justify the repression.

Even in the constitutional democratic regimes, such discrimination in assembly rights is well-known. The women described by Chen drew the opposition of the *mullahs* primarily on the ground that they were going to meet in an organized group to mobilize for common action. Even had the women complained of a constitutional violation, it is unlikely that this complaint would have been effectual given the way religious power dominates the local scene.

5. Rights of Political Participation and Speech

Again, these rights are severely curtailed for all citizens in many of the nations under discussion. Are they unusually curtailed for women in ways that show the influence of religious norms? The Egyptian case involves suppression of speech as well as assembly. All countries that impede women from going outside the home create barriers to political speech and participation, as do those that create barriers to women's literacy. Nations that effectively enforce constitutional guarantees of free press and free political speech, for example, India, do not often suppress women's speech or speech about women's issues in a discriminatory way. On the other hand, the fear of offending religious authorities does at times pose acute threats to speech—consider various democratic governments' willingness to ban *The Satanic Verses*, and the relative absence of official protest against the *fatwahs* directed against authors Salman Rushdie and Taslima Nasrin, both critics of Islamic traditions regarding women. The most pervasive impediments to women's speech in the democratic nations are, however, the indirect and unseen obstacles imposed by poverty, malnutrition, impediments to mobility outside the home, illiteracy, and an exhausting round of duties. In the nondemocratic nations, speech is not free for anyone, but it is especially unfree for women who might be inclined to criticize the prevailing view of women's role—recall the Saudi ban on demonstrations by women.

As to political participation: In Iran, women were for a time banned totally from employment in government and are heavily discouraged from entering politics. Only 3% of parliamentary seats are held by women (as contrasted with 12% in Jamaica, 16% in Nicaragua, 18% in Trinidad and Tobago, 24% in South Africa, 20% in Guyana, 33% in Denmark, 39% in Finland and Norway, 34% in Sweden, 29% in the Netherlands, and 20% in Germany[75]), and there are no female ministers. Although women notoriously play leading roles in government in India, Pakistan, and Bangladesh, their situation is far from representative of the average women in their nations: In Pakistan 2% of parliamentary seats are held by women, in India 7%, in Bangladesh 10%. It is very difficult to gauge actual participation in elections, but we can infer that poverty, illiteracy, and lack of mobility are grave impediments to women's equal participation. Religious doctrines to the effect that women are unsuited for political functions are invoked in many nations and play at least some part in bringing about this situation.

6. The Right of Free Religious Exercise

Once again, there is no recognition of such a right in many of the nations under discussion, a fortiori none for women. In India, however, such a right is given prominent constitutional recognition,[76] giving rise to many dilemmas, as we have said. The entire Indian system of civil law may be held to violate the free exercise of religion.[77] Individuals must be classified at birth into one of the religious systems, and it is very difficult to extricate oneself from the system to which one is assigned, particularly because ancestral property can never be extricated. Conversion to a religion of one's choice is therefore greatly impeded by the legal structure. Religions that are not among the traditional religions of India, and therefore lack a legal system, are under strong disabilities. The choice to be nonreligious is even more impeded, because, although secular marriage and divorce exist, there is no secular law that can govern hereditary property; thus, individuals are forced to deal with religion, whether they wish to or not. All these provisions would be unconstitutional under our own free exercise and nonestablishment jurisprudence.

Israel faces similar problems. As is well-known, the rights of conservative and reform Jews are severely curtailed under law and may become even more so. Moreover, there are no secular marriage and divorce at all, a more serious assault on free exercise for secular people than we encounter in India. The very idea of a Jewish state violates nonestablishment, and infringements of free exercise are not far away. In my opening example, the women's free exercise of a right to worship was indeed infringed, with appeal to majority religious norms; it seems very likely that the behavior of the guard would have been declared unconstitutional under U.S. law. The fact that Israel at that time had no written constitution made the situation of basic rights, including religious rights, unclear. This indicates that whatever the tensions and confusions between the claims of free exercise and the claims of nonestablishment in our own jurisprudence, we have chosen a wise course in giving both of these values strong protection, because they support one another. It is very difficult to maintain free exercise for minorities when one has established a single religion and given it considerable political and legal power.

7. Rights of Property and Civil Capacity

Article 15 of the Women's Convention insists on women's equality with men before the law, on their full legal capacity, and on their equal opportunities to exercise that capacity. Women are to have equal rights to make contracts, equal treatment before courts and tribunals, equal property rights, and rights to administer property. This is simply not the case for very many of the world's women, frequently on account of religious discourse and religious law. Under traditional Islamic law, women are explicitly unequal. A woman must have a male guardian to perform many contracts, including a marriage contract for herself. A woman's testimony in court is regarded as half as weighty as the testimony of a man; in the case of rape and adultery, women are forbidden to give evidence. Witnesses to contracts and other documents may be either two men or one man and two women. States vary in the degree to which this religious discourse and the laws based on it have full effect: Some, like Iran, Pakistan, and the Sudan, are quite thoroughly Islamicized—though even among these there are differences of degree; in others, such as Egypt, there is an unpredictable mixture of elements; in India and Bangladesh, there is a putative distinction between private law, which is governed by religious norms, and other affairs, which are in the charge of the secular state. In none are women's human rights to legal equality fully respected.

Once again, the Indian situation provides instructive examples of the conflict between constitutional guarantees of sex equality and religious legal systems.[78] Because we have focused until now on Hindu and Muslim law, let us turn, for a change, to the situation of India's Christian women. Christians in India (2.4% of the population in 1981) are governed by a bewildering variety of distinct regional codes. Catholic Christians in Goa, for example, are still governed by the Portuguese Civil Code. Until recently, Christians from Kerala were governed by the Cochin Christian Succession Act of 1921 and the Travancore Christian Act of 1916. In 1983, a Syrian Christian woman named Mary Roy challenged the Travancore Act in the Supreme Court on the grounds that it violated the sex equality guarantee by denying equal inheritance rights to daughters and sons. The Supreme Court did not declare the Act unconstitutional, but overturned it on a technicality, ruling that Christians in Kerala should henceforth be governed by the Indian Succession Act of 1925, which grants daughters and sons equal rights.[79] The Christian community in Kerala has continued to protest this judgment as an inappropriate interference with their religious prerogatives, adding that it would "open up a floodgate of litigation and destroy the traditional harmony and goodwill that exists in Christian families."[80] The Synod of Christian Churches has supported these protests, arranging for legal counsel to help draft wills to disinherit female heirs.[81] Such clashes between constitutional rights and religious law are common throughout the Indian legal system.

8. Nationality

The Women's Convention insists (in Article 9) that women and men be fully equal in matters of their own and their children's nationality. All nations that, relying on Islamic law, require a woman to obtain a guardian's permission before moving abroad are in violation of this fundamental right. In addition, quite a few nations have laws forbidding women from passing their own nationality on to their children. Although a landmark case testing such a law derives from Botswana and involves no religious element,[82] religious discourse is heavily implicated, elsewhere, in the maintenance of this form of discrimination against women.

9. Family Law

This is an especially large and complex area of women's inequality; religious norms and laws play a direct role in it. Religious systems of family law, Islamic, Hindu, Jewish, and other, may severely limit women's degree of choice in and consent to marriage, their rights to control the lives of their children during a marriage and of child custody if the marriage ends, their access to divorce and the type of evidence required to get a divorce, and their right of maintenance after a divorce. Polygamy, insofar as it continues to exist, is a structurally unequal practice: Plural marriages are unavailable to women.[83]

A few examples of these practices must suffice to indicate the whole. In the Sudan (whose Personal Law for Muslims Act is closely based on the *shari'a*) a woman's guardian had absolute authority to decide on a marital partner—until a rash of suicides by young girls forced a change. Now the woman's consent is required. In the Sudan, again, a man may divorce a wife simply by saying, "You are divorced." A woman must go to court and establish a basis, such as impotence, cruelty, or inability to provide. Most religiously grounded systems of personal law are asymmetric in a similar way. In India, secular marriage is available as an option, but secular divorce is not: A couple must appeal for divorce to the religion of their birth. As to the important issue of maintenance, so dramatically exposed in the *Shah Bano* case, the uniform civil code in India that might adjust the plight of such women is very far in the distance, even as the year 2000 rapidly approaches.

In nations governed by Islamic law, deviation from religious orthodoxy may force a divorce. In Cairo in August 1996, the Court of Cassation, Egypt's top appeals court, rejected the appeal of Nasr Abu Zeid, a professor of Arabic, against a ruling ordering his separation from his wife, Ibtihal Younis, also a professor. Islamic fundamentalists claimed that Mr. Zeid's writings make him an unbeliever; Zeid denies this, claiming that fundamentalist clerics have quoted texts out of context and made factual errors. (The couple has now moved to the Netherlands, where they have accepted teaching jobs.) The Secretary General of the Egyptian Organization for Human Rights calls the ruling "a slap in the face of civil society in Egypt."[84]

In most systems of Islamic law, a woman is guardian of a male child only until he is seven years old. In a recent Bangladeshi case, however, the high court ruled that a mother might retain custody of her eight-year-old son, who was afflicted with a rare disease. (The mother, a doctor, was able to give him expert care and she had also financed his medical treatment.) The judge remarked, "The principle of Islamic law has to be regarded, but deviation therefrom would seem permissible as the paramount consideration should be the child's welfare."[85] But the judge was also in a relatively easy position: He pointed out that this was an issue on which there was no rule in either the Koran or the Sunnah; the rule resulted from a Hanafi interpretation, not agreed to by other traditions of Islamic legal interpretation. Thus he was able to say that the rule "would not seem to have any claim to immutability." Nor did he make any general conclusion about mothers' rights: He rested his analysis on the unusual facts of the case. As for India's Hindu law, the father is regarded as natural guardian of the child, except for children under the age of five, or when the father is away. Only an illegitimate child can remain in its mother's custody.[86]

The right to adopt a child, a right important to many women, is another matter that is decisively affected by the domination of religion in codes of personal law. The Hindu Adoptions and Maintenance Act, passed in 1956, was for many years the only statutory law of adoptions in India. This law applies only to Hindus. Thus for many years only Hindus could adopt a child, and only a Hindu child could be adopted. Attempts in both 1972 and 1980 to enact a uniform adoption act met with determined resistance from Muslim leaders, who hold adoption to be forbidden by the Koran. (This is not a universal opinion: Tunisia in 1958 enacted a law of adoption whose provisions were very similar to the 1972 Indian Adoption Bill.) The 1980 bill was passed—thus granting Jews, Christians, Parsis, and others adoption rights—but only after Muslims were explicitly exempted.[87] Tariq Mahmood, of the Faculty of Law at the University of Delhi, summarized the matter well in a public letter to the Indian Council for Child Welfare:

> Even if it is accepted that Islamic law prohibits adoption, how can the Muslims prevent enactment of a secular law of adoption which will be applicable only to those who wish to adopt a child? If Islamic law does not permit adop-

tion, the Muslims need not make use of the Indian adoption law. That law will certainly not impose on any person a duty to adopt. . . . If Islam does not recognize a social or economic concept, the state cannot compel every Muslim to keep away from it. If that were possible, our banking laws should not be available to any Muslim, since Islam does prohibit interest on money. . . . The demand that a special saving clause exempting the entire Muslim community from its application be inserted in the Bill cannot be accepted. There are some Muslims who do not share the belief that their personal law prohibits adoption; and there are many who do not consider personal law as a part of their religion at all. To them the benefit of the adoption law cannot be denied.[88]

This sensible conclusion seems right for the whole area of family law: Loyal members of a religious group should remain at liberty to follow its teachings in such matters, but this does not justify imposing such teachings on people who do not so choose, especially when imposition is unequal and when it violates a fundamental right of choice.

10. Education Rights

Nothing is more important to women's life chances than education. With literacy, a woman may consider her options and to some extent shape her future. She may question tradition and discover how women in other parts of the world are managing to live. She may discover that women are actually able to achieve well in many of life's functions; that the female body is not as weak as has sometimes been said. With literacy, she may do her own accounts, read a bill, read an important notice that comes to her in the mail,[89] and enter trades that require literacy.

Women's educational opportunities and achievements are dramatically limited in many nations in the world. Adult female literacy rates, in the developing countries, range from 96.7% (Guyana) and 94.2% (Cuba) all the way down to 5.8% (Niger) and 8.0% (Burkina Faso). Among the nations under discussion here, we find Pakistan at 22.3%, India at 35.2%, Bangladesh at 24.4%, Afghanistan at 12%, and the Sudan at 30%; China does considerably better at 69%[90]; Saudi Arabia, at 40%, is extremely low among the countries sharing its general level of economic development, as is Iran at 55%. In all these cases, women are doing considerably worse than men. In Pakistan, the female literacy rate is 56% that of males; in India, 55%; in Bangladesh, 51%; Afghanistan, 29%; the Sudan, 56%; China, 79%; Saudi Arabia, 66%; and Iran, 74%.[91]

The reason for disproportionaly low female attainments are not always religious, but in many cases one can see clearly that religious discourse has played a major part. The *mullahs* in the village described by Chen set out to oppose women's literacy—by insults to the women's moral character and, if necessary, by threats to their physical safety. As Cornelia Sorabji's memoir attests, denial of literacy has strong conventional links to *purdah* and to general notions of women's purity that are at least in part religious. In Afghanistan, the Islamic fundamentalism of the Taliban has led to a ban on women going to school. In

India, women's education is opposed or neglected for all sorts of reasons, some economic, some customary, but the major religions certainly play their role in creating an image of a woman's role. Although regional differences in policy and culture are important in explaining these differences, religion also seems to play at least some independent causal role.[92] In Iran, related ideas of women's proper role have led to severely curtailed educational opportunities at the level of higher education. Women are excluded from 79 of 157 courses of study in the university, including 55 of 84 courses in math and technology; they are forbidden to study, among other things, archaeology, cinematography, and graphic design.[93] In the United States, the successful attempt of the Wisconsin Amish community to keep their teenage children out of the last years of required schooling has a differential impact on boys and girls: Boys learn skills (such as carpentry) that are marketable outside the community; girls, confined to the home, will have a harder time leaving should they want to leave.[94]

And one must ask, as well, what is being taught when girls are taught. In the ultraorthodox communities of Jerusalem, all children attending state-supported schools are permitted to follow a curriculum that contains absolutely no information about world history or about the life of the world outside (just as at home television and radio are entirely forbidden). They do learn modern math and science, but women are carefully shielded from any image of a woman's proper role that is not that of the ultraorthodox community. They will not be in a position to choose their own way of life as the result of their very own reflection.

11. Reproductive Rights

This is such a familar contested area that it seems unnecessary to discuss it at length. International human rights activists agree, with few exceptions, that women's access to contraception is an extremely important ingredient of their own well-being, both because of reproductive control and because of AIDS. They agree, further, that promoting women's control of their own reproduction (along with women's education more generally) is the most effective way to control world population without unacceptable infringements of liberty.[95]

Both Islamic and Roman Catholic discourse have been involved in opposition to such policies, as the Cairo conference made clear, although the primary emphasis of the Catholic position was access to abortion. I know of no corresponding discourse from the Jewish or Hindu traditions, though clearly the ultraorthodox Jewish community, in Israel and to some extent elsewhere, does have a strong pronatalist bias and for its own members opposes contraception. It seems plausible that unimpeded access to contraception is a basic human right of women.[96] It is especially urgent to protect this right for women who have no economic or social alternative to marriage and no recourse against enforced intercourse within it.

As for abortion, the issue cuts both ways where women's human rights are concerned. On the one hand, many defenders of such rights do hold that abortion rights, at least in the first trimester, are basic to women's equality; I myself would defend such a right for the United States on such grounds.[97] On the other hand, abortion has very often been used sex-selectively, to destroy female fetuses; in that sense it can also be a dangerous instrument of women's inequality. Right now it is possible to prevent the abuse without restricting abortion rights, by forbidding access to amniocentesis and by forbidding late abortions, as some governments have done, but this balancing act will not endure long into the future, as information becomes more readily available and at an earlier date. Some Indian feminists therefore favor removing the abortion right—indeed, some would like to jail women who seek abortions.[98] The issues are so difficult and have generated such intense, subtle, and lengthy debate that it would be foolish of me to attempt, here, to determine what an advocate of women's human rights should say.

Addressing the Dilemma

My starting point is a simple one: It is that human beings should not be violated, and that the protection of the basic human rights should have a very strong degree of priority, even when this interferes with some elements of traditional religious discourse and practice. To those who object that violating others is part of the free exercise of their religion, we should reply as we do when a murderer claims that God told him to do it (and he may sincerely believe this to be true): Never mind, we say, there are some things we do not allow people to do to other people. Or, as the Bangladeshi wife said in my epigraph, if Allah really said that, then he is dead wrong. (What we really mean by saying such things is that a just God cannot possibly have said such things.[99])

Beyond this, we can say more about the list of basic rights that has just been enumerated. These rights, like (and closely related to) John Rawls's list of primary goods, would appear to be necessary for all people if they are to carry out their plans of life, whatever they are. They therefore have a strong claim to be recognized politically as basic in a pluralistic society, whatever the commitments of its constitutive religious groups. Because of their fundamental role, a liberal society should commit itself to protecting these rights for all individuals, regardless of whether it contains groups that do not like individuals (their own members or members of other groups) to have these rights. The list is somewhat more extensive than Rawls's list and closely related to the list of basic human capabilities defended in chapter 1.

In the view I have defended in chapters 1 and 2, the fundamental bearer of rights is the individual human being. This seems right: A violation of a person is no better when it comes from some group to which the person belongs than when it comes from the state. The hunger of A is made not less but more morally offensive when we learn that A is a loving girl child in a family in which there is, overall, enough food to go round. The rape of B is made not less and quite likely more offensive when we discover that the rapist is B's husband and therefore a member of an allegedly altruistic organic unit together with B. Nor is the bodily integrity of B a merged part of a larger whole; B's body is B's body, the only one she will ever have.

The rights, furthermore, should not be regarded as isolated atoms, which can be given or withheld independently of one another. Because they interact and support one another in so many ways, we should think in terms of a total system of liberties and opportunities and refuse to compromise on any one item not only because of its intrinsic worth but also because of the way it affects the other items on the list. Education is closely correlated with meaningful opportunities for employment, and both of these with nutrition and health. The right to protect one's bodily integrity is closely connected to, and derives support from, equality in family law and rights to mobility and assembly. The right to contraception is closely associated with increased abilities to pursue education and employment, with political participation and with health, and so forth. We want, then, to secure to individuals not only one or two liberties but a total system of liberties, and not merely the liberties in name only (as some words in a constitution) but their fully equal worth, meaning the capability to avail oneself of them.

I shall now make some normative suggestions; in a concluding section I shall ask what practical action is available.

Religion and the Structure of the Legal System

Basically, no systems of religious law should be permitted to interfere with the basic human rights of citizens. It is especially obvious that intolerant sectarian regimes, such as those of Iran, the Sudan, and Pakistan, and in some respects Israel, are unacceptable. Such systems do not raise our liberal dilemma because their violations of other human rights are accompanied by equally serious violations of the liberty of conscience—either for members of minority religions (witness, as one egregious example, the Iranian persecution of the Baha'i) or for nonorthodox members of the dominant religion.

At times, a tolerant liberal regime has an established state religion but protects the rights and liberties of all citizens—as is the case, in general, in today's Britain and Scandinavia. Such arrangements, I would argue, are not necessarily unacceptable, but always raise serious moral questions. In the British case, the unsavory history of discrimination against dissenters, Jews, and Roman Catholics colors the social meaning of the innocuous and bland pronouncements of the Anglican Church; its established status, even if it does nothing wrong, may still be expected to affect the self-respect of members of these minorities, and nonreligious people as well, despite liberal policies. This suggests that establishment by itself raises problems for a liberal political understanding,[100] although the Scandinavian cases perhaps show an acceptable form of establishment, dedicated to the protection of minority religions. (Norway's current opposition to Islamic schools suggests, however, that even benign establishment is a dangerous policy.) On the other hand, the problems are certainly different in kind from those that obtain where recognition of equal protection of the law for all citizens is not a fundamental political commitment. In Israel, there is, of course, an intense struggle over just this issue of equal citizenship, and the religious nature of the state makes its resolution extremely difficult.

For our questions about women's rights, however, the most complex and interesting situations are those in countries such as Bangladesh and India, where a basically liberal constitutional order (nominally secular, in the Indian case) has allowed the religions to take charge of part of the legal system, creating systems of religious law. Here we see the liberal dilemma in its sharpest form. Such regimes are problematic in a number of ways. First, they are simply unwieldy, creating tremendous administrative costs and inconsistencies. Second, they treat nonreligious citizens very unfairly, forcing them to deal with religion in important areas of their lives whether or not they want to. Third, they treat citizens unequally on the basis of the chance of their birth into a given religious community. Shah Bano did worse because she was a Muslim than had she been a Hindu, and she had no option of going to a different court if she did not like the way Islamic law handled things. Fourth, they encourage the maintenance of practices that are in direct violation of equality provisions recognized in many constitutions and implicit in the legal system of some nations that lack a written constitution. It is less than ideal for India to guarantee women all sorts of rights in the Constitution and then turn the all-important sphere of family law over to codes that explicitly deny women the equal protection of the laws. All such elements in religious law codes should be reformed to bring them into accord with the Constitution's list of Fundamental Rights of citizens. Finally, such systems are highly divisive politically, as we see from the endless negotiations in which the Indian government has had to engage.

The example of India[101] illustrates the way in which a keen sensitivity to our liberal dilemma has led, years later, to an unfortunate situation. The Indian Constitution abolishes "untouchability," arguably a core feature of Hinduism, boldly and decisively, in Article 17 of the Constitution itself, at the same time creating constitutional protections for affirmative action toward previously oppressed caste groups.[102] These decisive steps have led, forty years later, to a situation in which no religious leader urges the restoration of caste hierarchy; it is simply off limits as an area of legitimate free religious exercise.

Where sex equality and the separate courts of religious law were concerned, however, the framers decided to leave crucial issues for later resolution. In the original constitutional debates, Muslim leaders repeatedly held that retention of the personal laws is "a part of the fundamental right to religious freedom."[103] Therefore, the directive that the state shall "endeavour to secure" a uniform civil code was placed in Article 44 of the Constitution, among the unenforceable Directives of State Policy. The words "endeavour to secure" were chosen deliberately to contrast with the words "shall enact," and essentially the idea of Article 44 was that the state should gradually prepare the population to accept a uniform code at some future date. On the other hand, it is perfectly plain that the enumerated Fundamental Rights include a right for all persons to the equal protection of the laws and also a right to nondiscrimination on the grounds of religion, caste, sex, or place of birth, and Article 13(1) rendered void all "laws in force" that were inconsistent with the enumerated Fundamental Rights; at the same time, Article 13(2) forbade the state to introduce any new law abridging a Fundamental Right.

Thus a contradiction was created because the existing (and also the subsequently introduced, i.e., reformed) personal laws of both Hindus and Muslims do violate the constitutional guarantee of sex equality, and in some respects the guarantee of religious equality as well. It would thus appear that the framers deliberately left in place a route whereby such personal laws could be deemed unconstitutional—although in a 1952 decision in *State of Bombay v. Narasu Appa Mali*, two especially eminent judges held that the term "laws in force" did not include the personal laws, which he held to be distinct from other "laws in force" in that they are not just the result of legislative enactments but are grounded in religious texts. This seems perfectly beside the point, in a liberal constitutional regime with no established state religion. Clearly the state should strongly urge the internal reform of personal laws until they are in conformity with the list of Fundamental Rights.

Does this nullify the whole project of having distinct systems of personal law? Modern defenders of secularism insist that the ideal of secularism requires only symmetrical treatment of the religions, and that this can in principle be fulfilled in quite a few different ways.[104] We must remember, however, that the fundamental bearer of rights is the individual citizen, and that any system of personal law that groups individuals in accordance with their religious origins runs a great risk of disadvantaging those individuals who do not particularly rejoice in that classification, whether because they are nonreligious or because they do not agree with the dominant group in their own religion, or because they would prefer to make their fundamental affiliation one with a professional or gender-based group. In India, religious classifications do not require any statement of membership, belief, or enthusiasm: One is classified by origin, and everyone is put into one box or another. One does not, similarly, have the option to participate in feminist law courts, even though that affiliation might in fact be the most fundamental in one's life. Secular marriage, divorce, and property laws exist, but people whose property is tied up in one of the religious systems can rarely avail themselves of these alternatives. To reform those portions of the separate religious codes that treat citizens unequally on grounds of their religious background and membership would seem to be the bare minimum that would be compatible with justice.

More important for our purposes, a guarantee of nondiscrimination on the basis of sex, such as the one enacted in the list of Fundamental Rights in India's constitution, requires the reform of many of the provisions of most of the separate codes, in regard to marriage, divorce, and maintenance. In all the heated debate about Indian laws of marriage and divorce, the fundamental interest of women in equality before the law was rather neglected—Muslims claiming violation of religious freedom if they were held to the uniform provisions of maintenance under the criminal code; Hindus claiming that the exemption of Muslims from these provisions violated their equality rights as Hindus. In effect, they were haggling over how not to be required to pay a destitute woman $18 per month. The woman's fundamental rights under the constitution were not taken to represent fundamental interests of either religious group. But such debates can and should be cut short by pointing to the fundamental role of the

constitutional guarantee of sex equality. If codes agree in doing away with hierarchies of gender, caste, race, and so on, then the case for allowing differences that
reflect different traditions will be far stronger.

The founders clearly believed that such uniformity could not be implemented
overnight in nations that contain groups with traditional hostilities. At every
step in the unfolding debate about personal law, opposition to a uniform civil
code was vigorous from some quarters of both Muslim and Hindu communities. On the other hand, at every stage, defenders of constitutional uniformity
also included prominent members of these religious traditions. Muslim lawyer
Chowdhry Hyder Hussain strongly defended a uniform civil code already in
1949, arguing that separate codes were a vestige of British rule and "wholly a
medieval idea [that] has no place in the modern world."[105] Twenty years later
another distinguished Muslim jurist, M. C. Chagla, held that an acceptable
legal system was one that "applies to every individual whatever his religion or
his community. . . . The Constitution was enacted for the whole country, it is
binding on the whole country, and every section and community must accept
its provisions and its directives."[106] Such influential voices, which have been
heard continuously throughout the post-Independence period, show that strong
rights-oriented constitutionalism is not generally opposed by Muslims any more
than it is by Hindus. It is not clear, even in strategic terms, that the right choice
was made. Decisive action on untouchability has created a solid social consensus in the next generation; indecisiveness on civil law has made the question of
the uniform code a political football for fractious and self-interested actors. At
this point, it is virtually impossible for liberals and feminists to support a uniform civil code, given that the cause of the uniform code is now championed by
the BJP as part of their projected assault on the equality of Muslim citizens.

The claim that the uniform protection of the rights of individuals infringes
legitimate prerogatives of free religious exercise is itself a contentious and highly
political claim. Religious liberty is a right of persons, like other rights. How, then,
can the religious liberty of a person possibly be infringed by the determination
to protect all individual rights of the religion's members on an equal basis? The
liberty to treat your co-religionists unequally is simply not a legitimate prerogative of religious freedom. The order to pay alimony to Shah Bano did not restrict her husband's freedom of worship; indeed, one may more easily argue that
her freedom of worship was compromised by not getting alimony and thus
being in a state of "destitution and vagrancy." The fact that Mary Roy's female
descendants will now inherit equally with males does not compromise Christian worship; actions of the Christian church protesting this constitutional judgment seem related more to power than to freedom of conscience. Similarly, denial of the right to force Sareetha to return to his home does not seem to have
impeded the ability of Venkata Subbaiah to worship in accordance with his conscience. It simply diminishes the power of the Hindu courts, which is a very
different matter. The right to divorce does not force anyone to get divorced; the
right to contraception does not force contraceptive use; the right to adopt, as
Muslim jurist Mahmood eloquently insists, does not force anyone to adopt a
child against his or her religious principles. The fact that prominent spokesmen

for the major religions agree with this liberal principle should be insisted on, as one makes this argument. The liberal should emphasize this individualistic concept of basic rights and religious liberty, insisting on uniform codes of law that give individuals broad latitude to choose forms of life in accordance with the dictates of their religion. We should not accept the idea that denying any fundamental right of any individual is a legitimate prerogative of a religious group. As Zoya Hasan, convener of the Committee for Protection of Rights of Muslim Women, commented on the Shah Bano case, "In the guise of freedom of religion, Muslim women are being denied constitutional and human rights. . . . It is not [a] question of the personal law of the community, but that of the abandoned getting social justice."[107] Danial Latifi went even further, calling the 1986 law "obnoxious to Islamic principles" and "an insult to the traditions of Islamic civilization."[108] In a recent statement shortly after the death of the aged Shah Bano, he writes that Muslim legal scholars who support it "have forgotten the dictum of the Prophet Mohammed who spoke as follows: 'heed the cry of the oppressed; for these shake the very Throne of God.'"[109]

Indeed, we should not even grant that such cases raise our liberal dilemma: The legal claims of the religious courts conflict with individual liberty of conscience as much as they do with other basic rights. The very same system that denies Shah Bano equal rights as a citizen also denies her, effectively, the option to define herself as a Christian, or an atheist, should she so choose; furthermore, it discriminates against her on the basis of her religious membership. If the system of personal laws were modified to allow the latitude for mobility in accordance with conscience that religious liberty itself would seem to require, we might well get the desirable result that the religions would compete with one another to attract female members by instituting sex equality, a situation now heavily promoted by feminist legal scholars.[110]

In general, then, when any democratic government or government actor takes an action or makes a law that violates the equal rights of its citizens in response to pressure from a religious party or group, this action should be regarded as incompatible with the basic rights of citizens in a liberal democratic regime, and steps should be taken to change this practice. This is what happened in the case of Shah Bano—before Rajiv Gandhi's intervention. It is the way Judge Choudary argued in Andhra Pradesh, defending Sareetha's privacy and equality rights—until the Supreme Court intervened, defending the Hindu Marriage Act. It is what happened in the High Court in Bangladesh, in a similar case. It is what happened in Bangladesh, again, in the child custody case, in which the judged dared to opine that deviation from Islamic legal tradition "would seem permissible" for the sake of a child's well-being. It is what happened in India's Supreme Court in the case of Mary Roy, when the unequal inheritance rights mandated by the Travancore Christian Act were declared henceforth inapplicable. It is what happened in the Unity Dow case in Botswana, not religious but a precedent for many cases involving religion because the Women's Convention was interpreted as binding on state actors.

In a related way, the Israeli public school setup should be held unlawful and presumably would be unconstitutional if Israel had a constitution enumerating basic rights in keeping with the Women's Convention. There are many issues here, including the egregious separate and unequal treatment of Arab children. But let me focus for now on the case of Jerusalem's ultraorthodox community, permitted to receive state funding for schools that produce gross ignorance of the modern world. This is inappropriate for all sorts of reasons, but in keeping with my theme let me simply focus on the fact that such systems prevent women from having access to information about their role in the world and norms of sex equality in modern democratic constitutions. They are thus a kind of *purdah*, and this ought to be deemed a violation of education rights. Were a religious school to operate in this manner in the United States, it probably would not win accreditation by any regional or local agency, much less receive public funding.

Special issues arise when a nation-state contains within its borders a distinct national minority that has in effect been conquered and subdued and now claims the right to a separate legal system. Will Kymlicka has given an extensive analysis of the situation of tribal populations in Canada, urging that in such cases broader latitude be granted to such groups to form distinct political communities. If such groups rule illiberally, violating individual rights, he holds that it is legitimate for constitutional arrangements to immunize them from judicial review at the federal level. Liberals should hold that such a minority acts unjustly, should speak out against such injustices, and should promote the development of international human rights policies that would ultimately give international courts the power to handle complaints of rights violations from such communities. But intervention from the federal level in the internal affairs of a minority would be justified, he argues, only in cases of "gross and systematic violation of human rights, such as slavery or genocide or mass torture and expulsions, just as these are grounds for intervening in foreign countries."[111] Remarks elsewhere in the chapter indicate that Kymlicka does not regard the denial of legal and political rights to women as the type of "gross and systematic" violation that would justify intervention.[112]

This position seems to me totally inadequate. It is of course desirable that ultimately international courts should become strong defenders of individual rights. But what is to happen in the meantime with women who are not only suffering what ought to be called gross and systematic rights violations but, precisely on account of those deprivations (of political voice, mobility, assembly, education, often equal nutrition, and health care), also are unable to move their own community in the direction of change? Should this subgroup within the nation even be thought of as "their" community, just because they are in it and unable to leave? We think that the family is a type of community. Nonetheless, if a husband beats a wife or tries to prevent her from voting or going out of the house, we do not hesitate to intervene—or if we do hesitate, we should not. I see no reason why a tribal or religious group should have any more latitude than a family in abridging the fundamental rights of adult citizens.

It is of course another matter to decide how to implement that judgment politically. Kymlicka seems right that such cases are less tractable than the Indian case, in which the two largest religious groups have been intertwined for years and each has considerable political power at the federal level. In India, it seems plausible for defenders of a unified civil code to say, with Muslim jurist M. C. Chagla, that Muslims who wish to influence the law are already empowered to do so: "After all fifty million Muslims[113] have a voice in the election of that Parliament through adult suffrage."[114] The election of 1996 showed the world exactly how decisive that power can be: Muslim parties form a major part of the coalition that eventually managed to form a government, after the BJP was unable to do so.[115] (Today, that political power is in jeopardy; Islamic courts should therefore probably be protected, though also urged to reform.) In Kymlicka's case, by contrast, the tribal peoples are few, uninfluential, and bitterly opposed to cooperation with the former oppressor. But it is hard to understand how the sad history of a group can provide a philosophical justification for the gross denial of individual rights and liberties to members of the group. What is a "group" anyway? As Joyce's Leopold Bloom said of that equally overrated concept "nation," it is neither more nor less than "the same people living in the same place"[116] (or, as the case may be, not in the same place). A "group" is, then, not a fused organism but a plurality of individuals, held together in some ways but usually differing in many others. The voices that are heard when "the group" speaks are not magically the voice of a fused organic entity; they are the voices of the most powerful individuals; these are especially likely not to be women. So why should we give a particular group of men license to put women down, just because they have managed to rise to power in some group that would like to put women down, if we have concluded that women should have guarantees of equal protection in our nation generally?[117] To do so is condescending to that group—we don't hold them up to the same moral standard to which we hold ourselves—and it is grossly unfair to the women, who are simply being told that because they are tribal women, or whatever, they do not enjoy the same guarantees of liberty that other women do. (And what of the "group" of women? Are they not as much a group as the tribe? And do they not have their own sad tale to tell?)

No religious group, then, should maintain a separate system of law that either violates the basic rights of any citizen, as specified above, or involves the religions in inequality vis-à-vis one another. If all this is firmly guaranteed, the case for permitting religions some latitude in areas such as marriage and divorce contract may at least be argued. For example, it ought to be possible, as it is virtually everywhere, to enter into a religious marriage contract—provided that the state guarantees equality of treatment to all citizens regardless of religion in areas such as consent, divorce, and maintenance, provided that secular marriage also exists and is regulated in an evenhanded way by the state, and provided that individuals of religious origin may choose whether or not to avail themselves of religious marriages when they marry. In such cases, the devotional and spiritual meaning of religious marriage and divorce may still be great; what is important is that these rules do not impose an obligation on citizens in violation of their equal rights and liberties. (Thus, a religious Roman Catholic may decide to regard the availability of secular divorce as spiritually unimportant and may focus on annulment as the only way in which a marriage may be validly terminated; what is important is that the state does not impose these Roman Catholic views on all people of Catholic origin but maintains a secular system of divorce open to all citizens.)

Religions Actors under the Legal System

Religious actors should be governed by the same legal system as everyone else. This is not always the case. In Thailand, Buddhist monks can be indicted and tried only by courts composed of themselves; they may not be indicted by the general legal system. They tend, however, to hang together. In a recent case, a monk charged with sexual harassment and refusing to support an illegitimate child (he had allegedly told various women that their spiritual status was in grave jeopardy if they did not sleep with him) could not be publicly prosecuted, and the other monks refused to prosecute him. Only after a prolonged scandal did the Ministry of Education order the monk to take a DNA paternity test[118] or risk being defrocked, and even then its authority to do anything was in doubt.[119] Needless to say, this should not be permitted to happen.

Should religious organizations and their members be treated as unequal under the law for certain purposes connected with gender? United States constitutional law has standardly granted special latitude to religion, by contrast with other forms of commitment and affiliation. Religious reasons for exemption from military service,[120] or for refusing to work on a particular day,[121] are granted a latitude that is not granted to other forms of conscientious commitment, such as the familial or the artistic or even the ethical. This remains controversial for the way it appears to privilege religion over nonreligion and thus, it might seem, to violate the Establishment Clause. The future of this issue remains uncertain, and this is not the place to make a normative argument on such a complex and vexed matter. Suffice it to say that such privileges given to religion, though highly contestable, can be strongly supported by pointing to the special importance of the liberty of conscience as a fundamental right and the consequent need to give religious freedom special protection from the incursions that, throughout history, have threatened it.

Religious bodies have also claimed exemption from certain laws of general applicability, including nondiscrimination laws. A Catholic church may refuse to accept a Jew as a member just because she is a Jew; such action, usually unconstitutional, seems perfectly legitimate here. The crucial question is how many jobs within a religious organization should be covered by such an exemption. Currently, Title VII permits discrimination on the basis of religion when it is a "bona fide occupational qualification reasonably necessary to the normal operation" of the enterprise, and it makes a specific exemption for religious educational institutions, permitting them to discriminate on the basis of religion in the hiring of "employees." This seems excessively broad. While it seems reasonable (though controversial) that Notre Dame should seek a "preponderant number" of Catholics on its faculty, it hardly seems reasonable that janitors and construction workers should be so selected. Some clearer demarcation of the exemption is in order.

More difficult still—and more important for our purposes—are demands by religious groups to be exempted from the reach of other nondiscrimination statutes, for example, those dealing with gender and sexual orientation. The state does not require the Roman Catholic Church to admit women to the priesthood on equal terms, although in almost all other occupations a denial on the basis of sex would be illegal. But this affects other appointments, as when the president of a Roman Catholic university is required by statute to be a member of a particular order of priests. One can argue that the priesthood lies within the core of worship and should be protected on that account; the presidency of a university seems hard to defend on this basis, especially when it has been granted that female faculty and administrators are a valued part of the institution.

As for sexual orientation, some local nondiscrimination laws on sexual orientation, for example, that of the city of Denver, have exempted religious institutions. These are borderline cases, difficult to distinguish from those of private clubs and educational institutions, whose liberty to discriminate on grounds of religion and gender has steadily eroded. Again, the legal questions are complex; we can only gesture in the direction of a recommendation. But a promising approach would be to insist that any form of discrimination on the basis of gender, race, or sexual orientation should face heightened scrutiny under the Equal Protection Clause—or the analogue of this in the legal system in question: Only a compelling state interest can justify such restrictions. On the other hand, it should be possible to hold in some cases that the protection of religious liberty may supply such a compelling interest, as long as the law in question is narrowly tailored to protect that particular interest.[122] My own view is that such narrow tailoring should involve specifying which functions lie within the core of worship and which are other activities that happen to be undertaken by a religious body.

A further area of controversy is the role of state benefits and subsidies: Should the state be permitted to grant tax-exempt status to an institution that does engage in discriminatory activity? In *Norwood v. Harrison*,[123] the Court held that a state-supported textbook program was unconstitutional as applied to schools with racially discriminatory policies. In *Bob Jones University v. United States*,[124] the Court upheld the Internal Revenue Service's denial of tax-exempt status to a religiously grounded institution[125] that had a racially discriminatory admissions policy.[126] The Court argues that "[t]he Government's fundamental, overriding interest in eradicating racial discrimination in education substantially outweighs whatever burden denial of tax benefits places on petitioners' exercise of their religious beliefs. Petitioners' asserted interests cannot be accommodated with that compelling governmental interest, and no less restrictive means are available to achieve the governmental interest" (2020–2021). A religious institution that refused to admit women, or treated them in a discriminatory way, might possibly receive similar treatment, and state subsidies to such institutions might be struck down, although this is unclear. The question is, however, what other practices of religious institutions qualify as discriminatory for these purposes? Hardly any religion fails to allow women in as members; the question is, how does it treat them when they are there? Should the Roman Catholic Church lose its tax-exempt status because women are not admitted to the priesthood? Should the University of Notre Dame lose federal funds because only a male can serve as its president? Such questions may well be answered in favor of broad latitude for the religious group, but they must be honestly confronted and debated. If we take them off the table, we suggest that such forms of discrimination, unlike racial discrimination or religious discrimination, are permissible and innocuous expressions of cultural variety—and that, I think, is an assumption from which women have suffered far too long. If we debate these questions openly, we will come to a better shared understanding of the limits of religious liberty even in voluntary organizations, within a liberal regime committed to the protection of fundamental rights.

There are many other controversial issues of religious free exercise that bear on sex discrimination: those, especially, involving parental rights to control children's schooling in accordance with religious beliefs and practices. This complex issue needs full and separate treatment; suffice it to say that one important issue, not always sufficiently stressed in such cases, will be the quality of education granted to girls, and its relation to their equal rights to education that will fit them for employment and citizenship.

Are there, and should there be, any legal restrictions on the speech of religious actors? Any form of religious discourse that constitutes a threat of violence against an individual or group should be, and probably already is, illegal under the state's system of criminal law. It is obvious that proposing a *fatwah* should be an illegal act, and that all who had a part in it are international criminals and villains, but because they are also the makers of law in their country, we cannot use their case to speak about how a constitutional democracy should operate its legal system.[127]

Let us therefore turn to cases that arise within democracy. The *mullahs* who threatened to break women's legs should have been arrested. The fact that they are *mullahs* should give them no special rights; insofar as they are advocating leg breaking, they are no different from Mafia crime bosses making similar threats. What is their crime? Presumably assault: Take, for example, the Model Penal Code's definition, according to which one sufficient condition for assault is that the person "attempts by physical menace to put another in fear of imminent serious bodily injury" (211.1.c). Given that the actions of the *mullahs* restrained women from going outside to seek education, we might also focus on the crime of "felonious restraint," which occurs if a person "(a) restrains another unlawfully in circumstances exposing him to risk of serious bodily injury or (b) holds another in a condition of involuntary servitude" (212.2). Other statutory solutions could involve notions of stalking, harassment, and so forth that have more recently been developed. Probably their threat of social ostracism should receive similar treatment, because in that situation it was like a death threat.

In a gray area is discourse that incites other people to commit violent acts against women. This is a large and heterogeneous class. The case of *sati* is instructive. Direct incitement to commit *sati* (itself illegal as a form of suicide) was illegal under Indian law for some time; and similar acts can be criminalized in the United States. But the new law passed after Roop Kanwar's death criminalized a far broader area of speech: "glorifying," "eulogizing," and holding ceremonies and processions in connection with *sati*. Some of this speech, at least, lies within the core of political speech protected by our First Amendment; the Indian Constitution explicitly permits the State to "impose reasonable restrictions on the exercise of the right" of free speech "in the interests of the sovereignty and integrity of India, the security of the state, friendly relations with foreign States, public order, decency or morality, or in relation to . . . incitement to an offense." The prohibition is thus more likely defensible within this constitutional regime. Although we may find the Indian restriction overly broad, it must be interpreted within the history of tremendous religious violence and violence against women; the judgment was that only such a restriction could prevent a widespread outbreak of a practice that would put many women in jeopardy.

Similarly in a gray area are speeches saying that women who do thus and so (say, dress in a certain way, or talk immodestly) deserve to die; speeches saying that such women are whores and fair game for rape; speeches simply saying that such women are whores; speeches saying that widows are virtually dead and their wishes do not count; speeches saying that women are childlike and immoral and in need of stern home discipline; and a host of others. Such incitements are a major cause of battery, rape, and even death of women: At what point should the religious speaker be held to have committed a criminal offense? It seems obvious, here again, that the strongest case for criminality exists when the incitement is directly targeted at a particular individual and is an incitement to immediate action. For example, a brother whose sister has gone off to work in the big city and comes home in short skirts is told that a woman like her deserves to die without further ado,[128] or a man is told by a religious leader that he should assert his domestic authority more and a little thrashing when he gets home today won't hurt, or village men are urged by *mullahs* to feel free to beat up these particular women as they go to school. Just in this way, the Cruelty to Women laws in both India and Bangladesh criminalized mental as well as physical abuse of women in connection with extraction of dowry. Even when no threat is involved, expressions of hate targeted narrowly against a particular individual may legitimately be criminalized.[129]

When threatening speech or hate speech is more general, we should be cautious. Much speech against women's equality is political speech, and general expressions of a political sentiment, however odious, should receive a high degree of protection. And yet, a country may legitimately, in keeping with its particular history, judge that some forms of speech expressing hatred and stirring up hostility are too dangerous not to be made illegal. Most European nations, including Britain with its Race Relations act, set narrower limits to hate speech than does the United States. In Germany, anti-Semitic speech is illegal, even if it is clearly political or religious speech and would obviously, as such, be protected under the U.S. Constitution. Such a course seems right, given Germany's particular history. A nation in which millions of women are "missing" might legitimately judge that some forms of speech denigrating the value of female life are to be forbidden, even if the speech is religious and, indeed, the expression of a deeply rooted religious tradition. In practical terms, such laws are likely to cause more problems than they solve—for the religious groups in question, unlike the Nazis, are not defeated and mostly dead and therefore will make no end of trouble with clever use of ideas of free speech. Nonetheless, it seems important to point out that there is a moral case to be made for such laws. India has possibly gone too far in restricting speech in some areas, with the ample laws against blasphemy that permitted suppression of Rushdie's novel. But it is obvious that such line drawing must be done with a concrete understanding of the threats to public order faced by each nation, and therefore it is unwise to comment further here.[130] This large and controversial topic deserves separate treatment.

Moral Constraints on Religious Discourse in the Public Realm

Even when religious discourse is not legally regulable, it may still be judged immoral in some cases. Here, finally, we approach the topic of most of the current U.S. debate. In a constitutional or otherwise democratic regime that has adopted a guarantee of sex equality or ratified the Women's Convention, it should be straightforwardly immoral and inappropriate, though legally protected, to speak in ways that contradict or undermine these fundamental rights. Thus, any discourse that denies women's equal humanity (or, indeed, the equal humanity of all citizens); any discourse that portrays women as by nature whorish or childish or unfitted for citizenship; any defense of practices that violate women's human rights as guaranteed in the constitution, such as marital rape or female genital mutilation—all should be deemed highly inappropriate. (And I do mean to include here any religious speech attacking contraception in international fora, because, as I have said, I take contraception to be a basic human right of women.) We could legitimately view a history of such speech as a reason against confirming a judge for office; a religious leader who uses such speech in the public realm should be strongly criticized as a subverter of the constitution.

As for other forms of religious discourse, my view is essentially that of John Courtney Murray (and close to the view defended in the new paper edition of John Rawls's *Political Liberalism*[131]): that such discourse is appropriate, even in debates about basic constitutional issues, provided it can be made publicly assessible and intelligible to citizens who do not share the speaker's religious starting point, and provided it takes care to indicate its harmony with the fundamental principles of the constitution (or the principles implicit in the democratic political culture, if there is no written constitution). Thus, the Pope's address to the United Nations[132] seems to me fully appropriate, because he is always at pains to make his moral argument available to others who may come to the issue from a different metaphysical starting point, and because he is careful to show its consistency with fundamental principles of, in this case, international law and morality.

Special care should be taken, however, to avoid offense to minorities: Thus, a judge in India who cites the *Ramayana*, however compatibly with the principles I have set forth, may send a political signal that many will construe, in the present climate of opinion, as denigrating Muslims and expressing the sentiment that India is basically a Hindu society[133]; a judge who cites the *Laws of Manu*, even as a storehouse of wisdom of the ages, could be suspected by some feminists of holding its views regarding women, even if the portion he has cited has nothing to do with women's issues; a Hindu judge who criticizes a portion of Islamic scripture unwisely suggests that he is exercising authority over a minority group in an intimate area of religious self-definition.[134]

Are these acceptable constraints? Certainly they will not be acceptable to many participants in many religions because they involve the curtailment of traditional prerogatives. We should insist, however, that there is a basic core of international morality that constrains all religious actors in the public realm, that to be held to this morality in the ways I have described is no more violative of religious free exercise than is the requirement to obey the criminal law.

If any of these proposals should be greeted with charges of "Westernizing," liberals should insist, once again, that the loudest voices in a religious tradition do not define the totality of its possibilities; that political actors use religious appeals as a vehicle for their own power, not always as legitimate attempts to capture the essence of the tradition in question; that all religions are plural and contain argument and dissent; and finally, that all religions contain the voices of women, which have not always been heard in the statements that are usually taken to define what the religion is and requires. It is, moreover, just false, and chauvinistic, to hold that the idea of the fair treatment of the diverse groups comprising a population is Western in origin. It has been on the Indian agenda since the edicts of Ashoka in the fourth century B.C., and ideas of toleration were elaborately developed in the legal system under the Moghul emperors, well before the European Enlightenment. An Indian judge who extends these ideas to women is not borrowing an external concept but extending one that has deep roots in Indian history.

What Can Be Done

One form of action in which liberals concerned with religion can very definitely engage is to encourage pluralistic and comparative religious discourse on these topics, discourse that brings to light and publicizes the plurality of views on all these matters within the religious traditions and also brings members of the different traditions together for consultation and comparative discussion.[135] In the process, many appeals to religion that do violate women's rights will be exposed as at the least narrow and partial accounts of a tradition, and often as simple misrepresentations—as has been happening with the relation of Islam to female genital mutilation. This is one area in which the old adage that it is best to drive out bad speech with more speech seems to be just right. Religious discourse, if a villain in many of my examples, is also, in multiple and powerful ways, a major source of hope for women's future. We should therefore not accept any solution to the liberal dilemma that unduly marginalizes religious speech or asks people to cut themselves off from humanitarian motivations that may motivate them in a specifically religious form. I believe that my own proposal does not do this.

It is, moreover, a legitimate function of a liberal state to encourage the liberal elements in the religious traditions. Here I agree with John Courtney Murray and with Rawls: By giving prominence to the type of religious speech that accords with constitutional fundamentals and to its speakers, a state legitimately strengthens the political consensus around these fundamentals and dramatizes to citizens the fact that religious argument in the major traditions can support them. Thus, in India, it would be highly advisable for major state actors to spend time insisting (as intellectuals such as Tariq Mahmood and Amartya Sen have long insisted) that both Islamic and Hindu traditions are diverse and plural and contain prominent liberal elements. Such public emphasis weakens the claim of antiliberal parties and individuals to speak for the entirety of a religious tradition.

Beyond this, it seems crucial for all who are concerned with these facts to promote and support local forms of group action that are the most promising avenues of change. This means supporting NGOs like the Bangladesh Rural Advancement Committee (organizer of the literacy project), which are free from government pressure and able to pursue a highly effective grass roots agenda. At the same time, recognizing that governments are more fully accountable to people than are NGOs, especially international ones, women and their supporters should also try to bring pressure to bear on governments and on multinational corporations to alter the problematic aspects of women's situation, as was done so successfully in the case of South Africa. Women from other nations may join a domestic struggle if they do so with proper deference and sensitivity. Women who are fighting these injustices on the spot need reinforcement. Frequently, too, the fact that an international body or a foreign government has made compliance with certain human rights practices a condition of some form of economic or diplomatic cooperation gives women a way to support such changes without fear.

Meanwhile, in acute cases, individuals who suffer human rights violations on account of being female should be granted political asylum, as in the case of Fauziya Kassindja, who fled to the United States to avoid genital mutilation (see chapter 4). Clearly, however, we should not rely on this remedy, which is arbitrary in its benefits (it helps only those people who can get on a plane and go somewhere), and which can hardly address problems that affect millions of people.

The best way to promote the role for religious discourse defended in this chapter is to produce active, unintimidated, educated democratic citizens. Such citizens will be likely to demand that religious discourse play a role compatible with constitutional guarantees of human equality. And this means that their role toward their own religious tradition will also be active and reflective, not merely submissive to the powerful interpreters of the moment. In many parts of the world, women have not been encouraged to become such citizens. But this situation is changing. At the conclusion of the literacy project, some women said that they no longer took advice from the local religious leaders. One woman said that she still went to get advice. Asked whether she found the advice helpful, she replied, "I will think myself whether he gives me good suggestions or bad ones. If he gives me a good suggestion, I will try to understand how far it is good for me. Or whether it is a bad suggestion." This clearly did not mean that the speaker was losing her religious convictions: She was the one in the group still interested in religious advice. It meant that she had ceased to assume that male religious leaders are infallible, and she had adopted a reflective attitude to her own religious practice. This is exactly the response that a society truly committed to religious liberty should encourage.

4

JUDGING OTHER CULTURES

The Case of Genital Mutilation

In June 1997, the Board of Immigration Appeals of the United States Immigration and Naturalization Service (INS) granted political asylum to a nineteen-year-old woman from Togo who had fled her home to escape the practice of genital mutilation.[1] Fauziya Kassindja is the daughter of Muhammed Kassindja, a successful owner of a small trucking business in Kpalimé. Her father opposed the ritual practice: He remembered his sister's screams during the rite and her suffering from a tetanus infection she developed afterwards. Hajia, his wife, recalled the death of her older sister from an infection associated with the rite; this tragedy led Hajia's family to exempt her from cutting, and she, too, opposed the practice for her children. During his lifetime, Muhammed, being wealthy, was able to defy the tribal customs of the Tchamba-Kunsuntu, to which he belonged. Both illiterate themselves, the Kassindjas sent Fauziya to a boarding school in Ghana, so that she could learn English and help her father in his business. Meanwhile, her four older sisters married men of their own choice, genitals intact.

Fauziya's family was thus an anomaly in the region. Rakia Idrissou, the local genital exciser, told a reporter that girls usually have the procedure between the ages of four and seven. If weak, they are held down by four women; if stronger, they require five women, one to sit on their chests and one for each arm and leg. They must be kept still, she said, because if they jerk suddenly the razor blade used for the surgery can cut too deep.

When Fauziya was fifteen, however, her father died. Her mother was summarily turned out of the house by hostile relatives, and an aunt took control of the household, ending Fauziya's education. "We don't want girls to go to school too much," this aunt told a reporter from *The New York Times*. The family patriarch then arranged for Fauziya to become the fourth wife of an electrician; her prospective husband insisted that she have the genital operation first. To avoid the marriage and the mutilation that would have preceded it, Fauziya decided to leave home; her mother gave her $3,000 of the $3,500 inheritance that was her only sustenance. On her wedding day, Fauziya left her aunt's house, flagged down a taxi, and, with nothing but the clothes on her back, asked the driver to take her across the border into Ghana, some twenty miles away. Once in Ghana, she got on a flight to Germany; with help from people who befriended her there, she got a flight to the United States.

On landing in Newark she confessed that her documents were false and asked for political asylum. After weeks of detention in an unsanitary and oppressive immigration prison, she got legal assistance—again with the help of her mother, who contacted a nephew who was working as a janitor in the Washington area. Scraping together $500, the nephew hired a law student at American University, Ms. Miller Bashir, to handle Fauziya's case. At first, Bashir was unsuccessful, and a Philadelphia immigration judge denied Fauziya's request for asylum. Through the determined efforts of activists, journalists, and law faculty at American University, she successfully appealed the denial. The appellate ruling stated that the practice of genital mutilation constitutes persecution and concluded: "It remains particularly true that women have little legal recourse and may face threats to their freedom, threats or acts of physical violence, or social ostracization for refusing to undergo this harmful traditional practice, or attempting to protect their female children."

In recent years, the practice of female genital mutilation has been increasingly in the news, generating a complex debate about cultural norms and the worth of sexual functioning. This chapter attempts to describe and to sort out some aspects of this controversy. First, however, a word about nomenclature. Although discussions sometimes use the terms "female circumcision" and "clitoridectomy," "female genital mutilation" (FGM) is the standard generic term for all these procedures in the medical literature. "Clitoridectomy" standardly designates a subcategory, described shortly. The term "female circumcision" has been rejected by international medical practitioners because it suggests the fallacious analogy to male circumcision, which is generally believed to have either no effect or a positive effect on physical health and sexual functioning.[2] Anatomically, the degree of cutting in the female operations described here is far more extensive. (The male equivalent of the clitoridectomy would be the amputation of most of the penis. The male equivalent of infibulation would be "removal of the entire penis, its roots of soft tissue, and part of the scrotal skin."[3]) This discussion is confined to cases that involve substantial removal of tissue and/or functional impairment; I make no comment on purely symbolic procedures that involve no removal of tissue, and these are not included under the rubric "female genital mutilation" by international agencies that study the prevalence of the procedure.[4]

Three types of genital cutting are commonly practiced: (1) In *clitoridectomy*, a part or the whole of the clitoris is amputated and the bleeding is stopped by pressure or a stitch. (2) In *excision*, both the clitoris and the inner lips are amputated. Bleeding is usually stopped by stitching, but the vagina is not covered. (3) In *infibulation*, the clitoris is removed, some or all of the labia minora are cut off, and incisions are made in the labia majora to create raw surface. These surfaces are either stitched together or held in contact until they heal as a hood of skin that covers the urethra and most of the vagina.[5] Approximately 85% of women who undergo FGM have type 1 or type 2; infibulation, which accounts for only 15% of the total, nonetheless accounts for 80 to 90% of all operations in certain countries, for example, the Sudan, Somalia, and Djibouti.

The practice of female genital mutilation remains extremely common in Africa, although it is illegal, and widely resisted, in most of the countries where it occurs.[6] The World Health Organization estimates that overall, in today's world between 85 and 115 million women have had such operations. In terms of percentages, for example, 93% of women in Mali have undergone genital cutting, 98% in Somalia, 89% of women in the Sudan, 43% in the Central African Republic, 43% in the Ivory Coast, and 12% in Togo.[7] Smaller numbers of operations are now reported from countries such as Australia, Belgium, France, the United Kingdom, and the United States.

Female genital mutilation is linked to extensive and in some cases lifelong health problems. These include infection, hemorrhage, and abscess at the time of the operation; later difficulties in urination and menstruation; stones in the urethra and bladder due to repeated infections; excessive growth of scar tissue at the site, which may become disfiguring; pain during intercourse; infertility (with devastating implications for a woman's other life chances); obstructed labor and damaging rips and tears during childbirth.[8] Complications from infibulation are more severe than those from clitoridectomy and incision; nonetheless, the false perception that clitoridectomy is "safe" frequently leads to the ignoring of complications.

Both in the implicated nations and outside, feminists have organized to demand the abolition of this practice, citing its health risks, its impact on sexual functioning, and the violations of dignity and choice associated with its compulsory and nonconsensual nature. These opponents have been joined by many authorities in their respective nations, both religious and secular. In Egypt, for example, both the Health Minister, Ismail Sallem, and the new head of Al Azhar, the nation's leading Islamic institution, support a ban on the practice. The World Health Organization has advised health professionals not to participate in the practice since 1982 and repeated its strong opposition in 1994; the practice has also been condemned by the U.N. Commission on Human Rights, UNICEF, the World Medication Organization, Minority Rights Group International, and Amnesty International.[9]

At the same time, however, other writers have begun to protest that the criticism of genital mutilation is inappropriate and "ethnocentric," a demonizing of another culture when we have many reasons to find fault with our own.[10] They have also charged that the focus on this problem involves a Western glamorization of sexual pleasure that is inappropriate, especially when we judge other cultures with different moral norms. To encounter such positions we do not need to turn to scholarly debates. We find them in our undergraduate students, who are inclined to be ethical relativists on such matters, at least initially, hesitant to make any negative judgment of a culture other than their own. Because it seems important for anyone interested in political change in this area to understand these views in their popular and nonacademic form, I shall illustrate them from student writings I have encountered both in my own teaching and in my research for a book on liberal education, adding some points from the academic debate.[11]

Many students, like some participants in the academic debate, are general cultural relativists, holding that it is always inappropriate to criticize the practices of another culture, and that cultures can appropriately be judged only by their own internal norms. That general position would indeed imply that it is wrong for Westerners to criticize female genital mutilation, but not for any reasons interestingly specific to genital mutilation itself. For that reason, and because I have already considered that family of views in chapter 1, discussing the views of relativists in anthropology and development policy, I shall focus here on four criticisms that, while influenced by relativism, stop short of the general relativist thesis:

(1) It is morally wrong to criticize the practices of another culture unless one is prepared to be similarly critical of comparable practices when they occur in one's own culture. (Thus, a typical student reaction is to criticize the "ethnocentrism" of a stance that holds that one's own culture is the benchmark for "the principles and practices that are appropriate for all people.")[12]

(2) It is morally wrong to criticize the practices of another culture unless one's own culture has eradicated all evils of a comparable kind.[13] (Thus, a typical undergraduate paper comments that criticism of genital mutilation is unacceptable "when one considers the domestic problems we are faced with in our own cultures.")

(3) Female genital mutilation is morally on a par with practices of dieting and body shaping in American culture. (I observed quite a few courses in which this comparison played a central role, and the comparison has often been suggested by my own students. In a similar vein, philosopher Yael Tamir writes that "Western conceptions of female beauty encourage women to undergo a wide range of painful, medically unnecessary, and potentially damaging processes."[14])

(4) Female genital mutilation involves the loss of a capacity that may not be especially central to the lives in question, and one to which Westerners attach disproportionate significance. Thus "references to clitoridectomy commonly reveal a patronizing attitude toward women, suggesting that they are primarily sexual beings."[15]

These are significant charges, which should be confronted. Feminist argument should not be condescending to women in developing countries who have their own views of what is good. Such condescension is all the more damaging when it comes from women who are reluctant to criticize the flaws in their own culture, for then it is reminiscent of the worst smugness of "white man's burden" colonialism. Our students are surely right to think that withholding one's own judgment until one has listened carefully to the experiences of members of the culture in question is a crucial part of intelligent deliberation. On the other hand, the prevalence of a practice, and the fact that even today many women endorse and perpetuate it, should not be taken as the final word, given that there also many women in African cultures who struggle against it, and given that those who do perpetuate it may do so in background conditions of intimidation and economic and political inequality. How, then, should we respond to these very common charges?

The first thesis is true, and it is useful to be reminded of it. Americans have all too often criticized other cultures without examining their own cultural short-comings. It is less clear, however, that lack of self-criticism is a grave problem for Americans on such issues. We find no shortage of criticism of the ideal fe-male body image, or of practices of dieting intended to produce it. Indeed, Ameri-can feminists would appear to have devoted considerably more attention to these American problems than to genital mutilation, to judge from the success of books such as Naomi Wolf's *The Beauty Myth* and Susan Bordo's *Unbearable Weight*. Indeed, a review of the recent feminist literature suggests the problem may lie in exactly the opposite direction, in an excessive focusing on our own failings. We indulge in moral narcissim when we flagellate ourselves for our own errors while neglecting to attend to the needs of those who ask our help from a distance.

The second thesis is surely false. It is wrong to insist on cleaning up one's own house before responding to urgent calls from outside. Should we have said "Hands off Apartheid," on the grounds that racism persists in the United States? Or, during the Second World War, "Hands off the rescue of the Jews," on the grounds that in the 1930s and 1940s every nation that contained Jews was im-plicated in anti-Semitic practices? It is and should be difficult to decide how to allocate one's moral effort between local and distant abuses. To work against both is urgently important, and individuals will legitimately make different decisions about their priorities. But the fact that a needy human being happens to live in Togo rather than Idaho does not make her less my fellow, less deserving of my moral commitment. And to fail to recognize the plight of a fellow human being because we are busy moving our own culture to greater moral heights seems the very height of moral obtuseness and parochialism.

We could add that FGM is not as such the practice of a single culture or group of cultures. As recently as in the 1940s, related operations were performed by U.S. and British doctors to treat female "problems" such as masturbation and lesbianism.[16] Nor is there any cultural or religious group in which the practice is universal. As Nahid Toubia puts it, "FGM is an issue that concerns women and men who believe in equality, dignity and fairness to all human beings, re-gardless of gender, race, religion or ethnic identity. . . . It represents a human tragedy and must not be used to set Africans against non-Africans, one religious group against another, or even women against men."[17]

If the third thesis were true, it might support a decision to give priority to the local in our political action (though not necessarily speech and writing): If two abuses are morally the same and we have better local information about one and are better placed politically to do something about it, that one seems to be a sensible choice to focus on in our actions here and now. But is the third thesis true? Surely not. Let us enumerate the differences.

1. Female genital mutilation is carried out by force, whereas dieting in response to culturally constructed images of beauty is a matter of choice, however seductive the persuasion. Few mothers restrict their children's dietary intake to unhealthy levels in order to make them slim; indeed most mothers of anorexic girls are horrified and deeply grieved by their daughters' condition. By contrast, during FGM small girls, frequently as young as four or five, are held down by force, often, as in Togo, by a group of adult women, and have no chance to select an alternative. The choices involved in dieting are often not fully autonomous: They may be the product of misinformation and strong social forces that put pressure on women to make choice, sometimes dangerous ones, that they would not make otherwise. We should criticize these pressures and the absence of full autonomy created by them. And yet the distinction between social pressure and physical force should also remain salient, both morally and legally. (Similarly, the line between seduction and rape is difficult to draw; frequently it turns on the elusive distinction between a threat and an offer, and on equally difficult questions about what threatened harms remove consent.) Nonetheless, we should make the distinction as best we can, and recognize that there remain relevant differences between genital mutilation and dieting, as usually practiced in America.

2. Female genital mutilation is irreversible, whereas dieting is, famously, far from irreversible.

3. Female genital mutilation is usually performed in conditions that in and of themselves are dangerous and unsanitary, conditions to which no child should be exposed; dieting is not.

4. Female genital mutilation is linked to extensive and in some cases lifelong health problems, even death. (In Kassindja's region, deaths are rationalized by the folk wisdom that profuse bleeding is a sign that a girl is not a virgin.) Dieting is linked to problems of this gravity only in the extreme cases of anorexia and bulimia, which, even, then, are reversible.

5. Female genital mutilation is usually performed on children far too young to consent even were consent solicited; dieting involves, above all, adolescents and young adults.[18] Even when children are older, consent is not solicited. Typical is the statement of an Ivory Coast father of a twelve-year-old girl about to be cut. "She has no choice," he stated. "I decide. Her viewpoint is not important." His wife, who personally opposes the practice, concurs: "It is up to my husband," she states. "The man makes the decisions about the children."[19]

6. In the United States, as many women as men complete primary education, and more women than men complete secondary education; adult literacy is 99% for both females and males. In Togo, adult female literacy is 32.9% (52% that of men); in the Sudan, 30.6% (56% that of men); in the Ivory Coast, 26.1% (56%); in Burkina Faso, 8% (29%). Illiteracy is an impediment to independence; other impediments are supplied by economic dependency and lack of employment opportunities. These facts suggest limits to the notions of consent and choice, even as applied to the mothers or

relatives who perform the operation, who may not be aware of the extent of resistance to the practice in their own and relevantly similar societies. To these limits we may add those imposed by political powerlessness, malnutrition, and intimidation. The wife of the patriarch in Fauziya Kassindja's clan told a reporter that she is opposed to the practice and would have run away like Fauziya had she been able—but nonetheless, she will allow the operation for her infant daughter. "I have to do what my husband says," she concludes. "It is not for women to give an order. I feel what happened to my body. I remember my suffering. But I cannot prevent it for my daughter."

7. Female genital mutilation means the irreversible loss of the capability for a type of sexual functioning that many women value highly, usually at an age when they are far too young to know what value it has or does not have in their own life. In the rare case in which a woman can make the comparison, she usually reports profound regret. Mariam Razak, a neighbor of the Kassindjas, was fifteen when she was cut, with five adult women holding her down. She had had sex with the man who is now her husband prior to that time and found it satisfying. Now, they both say, things are difficult. Mariam compares the loss to having a terminal illness that lasts a lifetime. "Now," her husband says, "something was lost in that place. . . . I try to make her feel pleasure, but it doesn't work very well."[20]

8. Female genital mutilation is unambiguously linked to customs of male domination. Even its official rationales, in terms of purity and propriety, point to aspects of sex hierarchy. Typical is the statement of Egyptian farmer Said Ibrahim, upset about the government ban: "Am I supposed to stand around while my daughter chases men?" To which Mohammed Ali, age seventeen, added, "Banning it would make women wild like those in America." Sex relations constructed by the practice are relations in which intercourse becomes a vehicle for one-sided male pleasure rather than for mutuality of pleasure.[21]

By contrast, the ideal female body image purveyed in the American media has multiple and complex resonances, including those of male domination, but also including those of physical fitness, independence, and boyish nonmaternity.

These differences help explain why there is no serious campaign to make ads for diet programs, or the pictures of emaciated women in *Vogue*, illegal, whereas FGM is illegal in most of the countries in which it occurs.[22] (In the Sudan, the practice is punishable by up to two years' imprisonment.) Such laws are not well enforced, but their existence is evidence of a widespread movement against the practice in the countries implicated. Women in local regions where the practice is traditional give evidence of acquiescing, insofar as they do, out of intimidation and lack of options; women in adjacent regions where the practice is not traditional typically deplore it, citing health risks, loss of pleasure, and unnecessary suffering.[23]

These differences also explain why Fauziya Kassindja was able to win political asylum. We shall not see similar arguments for political asylum for American women who have been pressured by the culture to be thin—however much it remains appropriate to criticize the norms of female beauty displayed in *Vogue* (as some advertisers have begun to do), the practices of some mothers, and the many covert pressures that combine to produce eating disorders in our society. Similarly, whereas the prospect of footbinding of the traditional Chinese type (in which the bones of the feet were repeatedly broken and the flesh of the foot became rotten[24]) would, in my view, give grounds for political asylum; the presence of advertisements for high-heeled shoes surely would not, however many problems may be associated with the fashion. Even the publication of articles urging women to undergo FGM should be seen as altogether different from forcing a woman to undergo the procedure.

How, then, is FGM traditionally justified, when it is? In social terms, it is highly likely that FGM emerged as the functional equivalent to the seclusion of women. African women, unlike their counterparts in India, Pakistan, and elsewhere, are major agricultural producers. There is no barrier to women's work outside the home, and indeed the entire organization of agriculture in Africa traditionally rests on the centrality of female labor.[25] In India, women's purity is traditionally guaranteed by seclusion; in Africa, this guarantee was absent, and another form of control emerged. But this functional history clearly does not justify the practice. What arguments are currently available?

It is now generally agreed that there is no religious requirement to perform FGM. The prophet Mohammed's most cited statement about the practice (from a reply to a question during a speech) makes the process nonessential, and the force of his statement seems to have been to discourage extensive cutting in favor of a more symbolic type of operation.[26] The one reference to the operaation in the *hadith* classifies it as a *makrama*, or nonessential practice. FGM is not practiced at all in many Islamic countries, including Pakistan, Algeria, Tunisia, Saudia Arabia, Iran, and Iraq. Defenses appealing to morality (FGM keeps women from extramarital sex) have resonance because they connect with the practice's likely original rationale, but they presuppose an unacceptable picture of women as whorish and childish. However sincerely such arguments are addressed, they should not be accepted by people with an interest in women's dignity. Defenses in terms of physical beauty are trickier, because we know how much cultures differ in what they regard as beautiful, but even perceptions of beauty (also at issue in Chinese footbinding) should yield before evidence of impairment of health and sexual functioning. Arguments claiming that without the practice women will not be acceptable to men may state something true in local circumstances (as was also the case with footbinding) and may therefore provide a rationale for individual families to defer to custom as the best of a bad business (although this is less true now than formerly, given the widespread resistance to the practice in most areas where it occurs). Such arguments, however, clearly cannot justify the practice in moral or legal terms; similarly, arguments advising slaves to behave themselves if they do not want to be beaten may give good advice but cannot justify the institution of slavery.

The strongest argument in favor of the practice is an argument that appeals to cultural continuity. Jomo Kenyatta and others have stressed the constitutive role played by such initiation rites in the formation of a community and the disintegrative effect of interference.[27] For this reason, Kenyatta opposed criminalization of the surgery and recommended a more gradual process of education and persuasion. Although one must have some sympathy with these concerns, it is still important to remember that a community is not a mysterious organic unity but a plurality of people standing in different relations of power to one another. It is not obvious that the type of cohesion that is effected by subordination and functional impairment is something we ought to perpetuate. Moreover, sixty years after Kenyatta's ambivalent defense, we see widespread evidence of resistance from within each culture, and there is reason to think that the practice is kept alive above all by the excisers themselves, paramedical workers who enjoy both high income and high prestige in the community from their occupation. These women frequently have the status of priestesses and have great influence over social perceptions.[28] Countries that move against the practice should certainly make provision for the economic security of these women, but this does not mean taking them as unbiased interpreters of cultural tradition. To the extent that an initiation ritual is still held to be a valuable source of cultural solidarity, such rituals can surely be practiced (as they already are in some places) using a merely symbolic operation that does not remove any tissue.

Let me now turn to the fourth thesis. A secondary theme in recent feminist debates about FGM is skepticism about the human value of sexual functioning. Philosopher Yael Tamir, for example, argues that hedonistic American feminists have ascribed too much value to pleasure. She suggests that it is men, above all, whose interests are being served by this, because female sexual enjoyment in our society is "seen as a measure of the sexual power and achievements of men," and because men find women who do not enjoy sex more intimidating than those who do.

I am prepared to agree with Tamir to this extent: The attention given FGM seems to me somewhat disproportionate, among the many gross abuses the world practices against women: unequal nutrition and health care, lack of the right to assemble and to walk in public, lack of equality under the law, lack of equal access to education, sex-selective infanticide and feticide, domestic violence, marital rape, rape in police custody, and many more. Unlike Tamir, I believe that the primary reason for this focus is not a fascination with sex but the relative tractability of FGM as a practical problem, given the fact that it is already widely resisted and indeed illegal, and given that it is not supported by any religion. How much harder to grapple with women's legal inequality before Islamic courts, their pervasive hunger, their illiteracy, their subjection to battery and violence. But surely Tamir is right that we should not focus on this one abuse while relaxing our determination to make structural changes that will bring women closer to full equality worldwide. And she may also be right to suggest that the fascination with FGM contains at least an element of the sensational or even the prurient.

Tamir, however, does not simply criticize the disproportionate focus on FGM: She offers a more general denigration of the importance of sexual pleasure as an element in human flourishing. This part of her argument is flawed by the failure to make a crucial distinction: that between a function and the capacity to choose that function. Criticizing her opponents for their alleged belief that the capacity for sexual pleasure is a central human good, she writes:

Nuns take an oath of celibacy, but we do not usually condemn the church for preventing its clergy from enjoying an active sex life. Moreover, most of us do not think that Mother Teresa is leading a worse life than Chichulina, though the latter claims to have experienced an extensive number of orgasms. It is true that nuns are offered spiritual life in exchange for earthly goods, but in the societies where clitoridectomy is performed, the fulfilling life of motherhood and child bearing are offered in exchange. Some may rightly claim that one can function as a wife and a mother while still experiencing sexual pleasures. Others believe that full devotion to God does not require an oath of celibacy. Yet these views are, after all, a matter of convention.[29]

There are a number of oddities in this argument. (It is hard, for example, to know what to make of the assertion that the possibility of combining sexual pleasure with motherhood is a mere "matter of convention.") More centrally, however, Tamir mischaracterizes the debate. No feminist opponent of FGM is saying or implying that celibacy is bad, that nuns all have a starved life, that orgasms are the be-all and end-all of existence. I know of no opponent who would not agree with Tamir's statement that women "are not merely sexual agents, that their ability to lead rich and rewarding lives does not depend solely on the nature of their sex life." But there is a great difference between fasting and starving; just so, there is also a great difference between a vow of celibacy and FGM. Celibacy involves the choice not to exercise a capability to which nuns, insofar as they are orthodox Roman Catholics, ascribe considerable human value.[30] Its active exercise is thought good for all but a few of those humans, and even for them it is the choice not to use a capacity one has (as in the case of fasting) that is deemed morally valuable. (A Catholic should hold that a survivor of FGM cannot achieve the Christian good of celibacy.) FGM, by contrast, involves forgoing altogether the very possibility of sexual functioning—and, as I said, well before one is of an age to make such a choice.[31] We all know that people who are blind or unable to walk can lead rich and meaningful lives; nonetheless, we would all deplore practices that deliberately disabled people in those respects, nor would we think that critics of those practices are giving walking or seeing undue importance in human life.

Can even the mothers of these girls make an informed choice as to the value of female sexual pleasure? They have been immersed in traditional beliefs about women's impurity; lacking literacy and education, as a large proportion do, they have difficulty seeking out alternative paradigms. As the immigration report points out, their situation is made more difficult by fear and powerlessness. Equally important, their own experience of sexual life cannot have contained orgasmic pleasure if they themselves encountered FGM as girls; even if they did not, they are highly likely to have experienced marriage and sexual life as a series of insults to their dignity, given the ubiquity of domestic violence and marital rape. Should they believe that FGM is a bad thing for their daughters— as a remarkable proportion of the women interviewed in the recent stories clearly do—they have no power to make their choices effective and many incentives to conceal the views they hold. Such facts do not show that women who have had a more fortunate experience of marriage and sexuality are making a mistake when they hold that the capacity for sexual pleasure should be preserved for those who may choose to exercise it. There is certainly something wrong with any social situation in which women are viewed only or primarily as sex objects; but criticizing such perceptions has nothing to do with defending FGM.

Nor does Tamir give us any reason to suppose that the importance of women's sexual pleasure is a mythic construct of the male ego. Many women have reported enjoying sex a good deal, and there is no reason to think them all victims of false consciousness. It is probably true that some men find women who do not enjoy sex more intimidating than those who do, but it would be more than a little perverse to deny oneself pleasure simply in order to intimidate men. Moreover, in the situation we are contemplating in the case of FGM, the operative male fear is surely that of women's sexual agency, which is a sign that the woman is not simply a possession and might even experience pleasure with someone other than her owner. It would be highly implausible to suggest that African women can gain power and intimidate men by undergoing FGM. The attack on FGM is part and parcel of a more general attempt by women to gain control of their sexual capacities; it is thus a relative of attacks on rape, marital rape, sexual harassment, and domestic violence. It is precisely this challenge to traditional male control that many men find threatening.

In the concluding section of her discussion of FGM, Yael Tamir imagines a country called Libidia, where women with unnaturally enlarged clitorises find they cannot do anything else but have sex and therefore seek to remove the clitoris in order to have better lives. In this way she suggests that sexual pleasure undermines other valuable human functions—so one might plausibly deem its removal a helpful thing, rather like a trip to the dentist to get rid of a diseased tooth. She here expresses a Platonic idea about the relation between continence and intellectual creativity that may be true for some individuals at some times but is surely not a universal datum of human experience. Plato did indeed hold in the *Phaedo* that mental life would be much better if the bodily appetites could be put to one side insofar as possible—though even he did not maintain this position with absolute consistency, nor did he suggest genital mutilation as a remedy.[32] Aristotle, on the other hand, held that someone who was insensible to the full range of the bodily pleasures would be "far from being a human being." We do not need to decide which thinker is right—or indeed for which people each of them is right—to decide sensibly that FGM is not like an appendectomy—that it involves the removal of a capability for whose value history and experience have had a great deal to say. Individuals may then choose whether and how to exercise it, just as we also choose whether and how to use our athletic and musical capacities.

Internal criticism is slowly changing the situation in the nations in which FGM has traditionally been practiced. The eighteen-year-old son of the patriarch of the Kassindja family told reporters that he wanted to marry a woman who had not been cut, because teachers in his high school had influenced his thinking. The patriarch himself now favors making the practice optional, to discourage more runaways who give the family a bad name. The very fact that the age of cutting in Togo has been moving steadily down (from twelve to four), in order (the exciser says) to discourage runaways, gives evidence of mounting resistance to the practice. But many of the women and men in the relevant nations who are struggling against this practice are impoverished or unequal under the law or illiterate or powerless or in fear—and often all of these. There is no doubt that they wish outside aid. There is also no doubt that they encounter local opposition—as is always the case when one moves to change a deeply entrenched custom connected with the structures of power. (As I have suggested, some of the people involved have strong personal economic and status interests in the status quo.) Suzanne Aho, director of Togo's Office for the Protection and Promotion of the Family, explains that she tries to counsel men about women's rights of choice, but she encounters the dead weight of custom. Of the Kassindja patriarch she says: "'You cannot force her,' I told him. He understood, but he said it is a tradition."

These upholders of tradition are eager, often, to brand their internal opponents as Westernizers, colonialists, and any other bad thing that may carry public sentiment. Even so, Fauziya's father was accused of "trying to act like a white man." But this way of deflecting internal criticism should not intimidate outsiders who have reasoned the matter out, at the same time listening to the narratives of women who have been involved in the reality of FGM. The charge of "colonialism" presumably means that the norms of an oppressor group are being unthinkingly assimilated, usually to curry favor with that group. That is not at all what is happening in the case of FGM. In the United Nations, in Human Rights Watch, in many organizations throughout the world, and in countless local villages the issue has been debated. Even the not very progressive Immigration and Naturalization Service (INS) has been swayed by the data it collected. The vigor of internal resistance should give confidence to those outside who work to oppose the practice. Frequently external pressure can assist a relatively powerless internal group that is struggling to achieve change.

In short, international and national officials who have been culpably slow to recognize gender-specific abuses as human rights violations are beginning to get the idea that women's rights are human rights, and that freedom from FGM is among them. Without abandoning a broader concern for the whole list of abuses women suffer at the hands of unjust customs and individuals, we should continue to keep FGM on the list of unacceptable practices that violate women's human rights, and we should be ashamed of ourselves if we do not use whatever privilege and power has come our way to make it disappear forever.

5

AMERICAN WOMEN

Preferences, Feminism, Democracy

*You know you want to, Marianne—why'd you come with me
if you don't?*
I'm not gonna hurt you for Christ's sake. Come on!
Nobody plays games with me.

And this was a strangeness she'd recall: how when she entered
her room which was exactly as she'd left it the day before, yet
irrevocably changed, she'd known what a long time she'd been
away, and such a distance. As if she'd left, and could not now
return.

—Joyce Carol Oates, *We Were the Mulvaneys*

I. Illiberal Feminism?

American feminists are illiberal and antidemocratic, committed to a radical
program of social change whose roots lie in discredited totalitarian ideologies.
Humorless and angry, they have abandoned the Enlightenment values of liberty and equality that were dear to an earlier generation of feminists, the ones
who won women the vote. Bent on controlling the minds of the younger generation, they systematically distort the truth in public reporting on women's
issues, particularly sexual violence. They reject marriage and the family, romantic
love, and, in short, the values of the vast majority of American women, holding
that society is dominated by a vicious "sex-gender system" that damages women
both physically and psychologically. They are fanatically dedicated to the overthrow of this system. As a result, feminists are widely, and rightly, perceived as
dangerous extremists, and feminism has almost entirely lost its popularity. This
is unfortunate, because it is possible to be a feminist, in favor of legal equality,
without holding such radical and unpalatable views.

These charges against feminism are becoming a pervasive feature of our popu-
lar political culture. A particularly vivid example is the recent book *Who Stole
Feminism? How Women Have Betrayed Women*, by philosopher Christina Hoff
Sommers.[1] I shall focus on Sommers in what follows because she states the

charges clearly and with specific theoretical issues in view. .
to confront the substance of the charges, which are widesprea
detailed critique of Sommers's work.

The charge of unpopularity is, initially, difficult to reconcile
of danger. If feminism has lost its constituency, it is hard to see h
a threat to democracy. The most plausible way to reconcile the two
understand the claim to be that a narrow academic elite has lost touch
lar values, and that this feminist elite is nonetheless dangerous be.   .s
dominant in the academy and therefore in the training of many leade.s of the
next generation.

These charges need to be confronted by anyone concerned with the future of
feminism. They raise at least the following questions:

1. What do American women have to complain of?
2. Has the thought of radical feminist thinkers made a positive contribution
   to social justice and to the well-being of American women?
3. Does the common feminist claim that many women's preferences and
   desires are distorted by a legacy of injustice pose a threat to democracy?

It is particularly important to confront these charges if one holds, as I do, that
feminism should become less insular and more international, more attentive to
the urgent problems of unequal hunger, unequal health care, and lack of political equality that are the daily lot of women in many parts of the world. A feminist with these commitments should indeed ask what American women have to
complain of. That there are certain bad things that they do not have to complain
of should be obvious from the analysis of the previous chapters. American women
do not suffer from the pervasively unequal nutrition and health care that are
the cause of so many female deaths worldwide. American female children are
not often victims of sex-selective infanticide or of grossly disproportionate passive neglect. American women are entitled to vote, to hold office, to enter the
occupation of their choice, to travel without a male, to assemble and organize
politically. They are, at least formally, equal under the law: The unequal rules
of evidence and systems of family and property law that are so pervasive in the
world would not be constitutional here. Moreover, American women enjoy a
high living standard by comparison to most of the world's women. Although
many lack adequate economic, educational, and employment options—and although this situation leads many American women to enter ways of life, such
as prostitution, that damage their dignity (see chapter 11)—they almost never
live in regions that completely lack schools, or reliable electricity, or a clean water
supply, all common lacks in developing countries.

It is quite wrong, however, to think (as Sommers seems to) that American
women have no urgent complaints to press. Focusing on the area of sexual intimidation and violence to which she herself devotes central emphasis, I shall
suggest that recent improvements in our (still problematic) situation in these
areas are owed largely to the efforts of the very feminists Sommers criticizes as
dangerous to democracy. These feminists have won public recognition for important truths about rape, domestic violence, and sexual threats, making women

mewhat more free to avail themselves of life's opportunities without fear. Moreover, by forging the concept and the law of sexual harassment, they have made equal opportunity for employment and promotion more nearly a reality. Thus, although American women still have much to complain of in this area, they are closer to the equality they seek. Further pursuit of these insights, not their abandonment, is what is required if further progress is to be made.

A crucial step in this thoroughly democratic social movement has been the recognition that the preferences of both men and women are in some respects distorted by a legacy of injustice and hierarchy. Such a recognition, I shall argue, is not intrinsically undemocratic: indeed, when appropriately constrained, it is at the heart of the most profound liberal-democratic thought in both the Utilitarian and the Kantian traditions. Understanding this is important not just because it helps us read the past correctly but, above all, because it helps us choose directions for the future.

II. Two Types of Feminism

Central to Sommers's argument are two concepts: the "equity feminist" and the "gender feminist." Sommers counts herself as an "equity feminist." Equity feminists hold that women should have full legal equality with men, but that once that battle is won (in particular, by giving women the vote, the one case of legal reform on which she speaks clearly) nothing further should be demanded. Sommers quotes Elizabeth Cady Stanton, who said in 1854, "We ask no better laws than those you have made for yourselves. We need no other protection than that which your present laws secure to you." This equity agenda, she says, is by now "a great American success story" (22).

It would seem that Sommers, then, supports formal equality for women without special privileges. But this by itself tells us little about how she would view legal developments aimed at securing full political and social equality for women that go beyond the "present laws" mentioned here: laws against sexual harassment and marital rape, for example, antidiscrimination laws for gender, or the effective prosecution of domestic violence as a criminal offense. We do not know her view about the developments in interpretation of the Equal Protection Clause of the Fourteenth Amendment that, beginning in 1971,[2] led to the treatment of gender as a "quasi-suspect" classification and thus gave women broad protection against gender-based inequalities. Such legal developments certainly involve going beyond the "success story" to which Sommers repeatedly refers. (Indeed, in one key case, the Supreme Court explicitly claimed that, despite recent improvements in women's situation, "women still face pervasive, although at times more subtle, discrimination in our educational institutions, in the job market and, perhaps most conspicuously in the political arena."[3]) They also involve the recognition of an asymmetry of power between women and men in our society, something to which Sommers appears to be persistently opposed.[4] On the other hand, it would not be implausible to think of them as essential parts of any "equity agenda." Until the reader knows what Sommers thinks about such laws, which have proven extremely valuable resources for countless American women, it is difficult to tell how close she really is to the "grass-roots constituency" that she claims to be representing. It is not only women in the academic elite who wish to be able to call the police when battered in the home; who wish to be able to bring a charge of rape without testifying to their prior sexual history; who wish to avoid sexual harassment in the workplace; who wish to have fully equal treatment in matters relating to the administration of estates and the receipt of medical benefits.[5] If Sommers holds that a woman such as Mary J. Carr, who successfully brought charges of sexual harassment against General Motors (GM) after a five-year campaign of threats and obscenities, is not an "equity feminist" but a supporter of a suspect radical agenda, it would appear to be Sommers who has lost touch with what American women want. And yet, the concept of asymmetry of power, which Sommers apparently rejects, was a crucial part of Judge Richard Posner's reasoning when he decided in favor of Carr and against GM.[6]

If the category of "equity feminist" is unclear, the category of "gender feminist" is even more elusive. A gender feminist is sometimes identified by the way she behaves—with anger and resentment against men, with little respect for the truth or scholarship. But because it is supposed to be the *conclusion* of the book that these are properties of gender feminists, one would hope that gender feminist is at some point defined in a logically independent manner. If we search the text for such an independent specification, we appear to find that a gender feminist, for Sommers, is any thinker about women's issues who believes that (1) women's suffrage did not remove a systematic asymmetry of power between women and men in our society, and/or (2) the existing preferences of women and men in our society concerning gender issues may be corrupted by social forces and are not always reliable bases for the formation of social policy. We shall see that this definition is not ultimately helpful in sorting feminists into two categories because it fits almost all contemporary social thinkers in political thought and economics. Nonetheless, it gives us a way of rephrasing the questions we have posed:

1. Do American women have complaints that have not been adequately addressed by the agenda of "equity feminism"? In other words, do they have good reasons to become "gender feminists"?
2. Does the thought of radical feminist thinkers make a valuable contribution to addressing those complaints?
3. Do the views of these "gender feminist thinkers" about preferences and desires pose a threat to democracy?

I shall now argue that the answer to the first two questions is an emphatic "yes," and that the answer to the third question is "no."

III. Gender Gaps in the United States

We could address the first question in many ways. I have said that in some respects American women are clearly doing well by comparison to women in many other regions of the world. And yet American women, like women the world over, are not equal to men in many of the areas that international agencies measure when they measure quality of life. According to the 1995 and 1996 *Human Development Reports*,[7] U.S. women do quite well in basic health, nutrition, and life expectancy. There are 106 women in the United States to every 100 men, a sex ratio that is generally agreed to represent equal nutrition and health care (because women have a slight longevity edge, probably as a result of cardiovascular fitness); as I have argued in chapter 1, many regions of the world have a very different sex ratio, giving evidence of discrimination against females in matters of basic health and nutrition. In these very important matters, then, U.S. women do as well (compared to men) as the women of any nation in the world. They also do absolutely well, with a life expectancy exceeded by only fifteen nations in the world (though we should note that this is not great, given that the United States ranks second overall in life quality).[8] The maternal mortality rate of U.S. women is 8 per 100,000 live births, worse than the rate in Canada, Norway, Spain, Sweden, Australia, Belgium, Switzerland, Germany, Denmark, Ireland, Italy, Israel, Greece, Hong Kong, and Kuwait, tied with Austria and the United Kingdom, and ahead of all other nations. In educational attainment, U.S. women do well. Female secondary school participation is 97 percent that of males, and female "tertiary" educational participation is 119 percent that of males. In the secondary area, all other nations in the top twenty-four overall have a female participation that exceeds that of males, but when we get to the tertiary area, the United States does comparatively better, ranking in the middle of the top group with respect to this ratio. If we consider total enrollment as a ratio of the female population (combining all three levels of education), the United States surpasses all nations in the world, with the exception of Canada and Finland.

In the economy, we begin to see evidence of unequal attainment. Women have an employment participation rate of 50%, or 65% that of males; this is right in the middle for the group of highly developed nations. Among these nations, U.S. women do relatively well in getting professional and technical positions, holding 52.7% of these positions: only Canada, Norway, Finland (at 62.3%), Sweden (64.4%), and Denmark have higher ratios among the most highly developed nations; Switzerland is the lowest in this group, at 23.8%. (Other nations where women do well in this area relative to men include Israel, Barbados, the Bahamas, Uruguay, Trinidad and Tobago, Thailand, Brazil, Bulgaria, Botswana, and the Philippines [62.7%].) If we turn to administrative and managerial positions, U.S. women still do comparatively well, holding 42.0% of the positions, as compared with 8.5% for Japan. Only Canada and Australia are higher in the top group; among less developed countries, only Hungary.

The proportion of earned income that goes to females is 40.1%—as compared to 33.0% for Japan, 37% for Canada, 41.5% for Norway, 41.6% for Denmark, 41.2% for Finland, 44.9% for Sweden, 38.3% for France, 33.2% for the Netherlands, 34.2% for the United Kingdom, 28.4% for Spain, 29.9% for Switzerland, and 24.8% for Ireland. Thus, in the most developed group of nations, only the four Scandinavian nations do better in wage equality. (Other less developed nations that have a higher female earned income percentage include Slovakia, Russia, Bulgaria, Estonia, Lithuania, Vietnam [47.3%], Kenya, Ghana, Tanzania [47.5%], Benin, Uganda, Malawi, Guinea, Burundi, and Mozambique.) These optimistic data should not conceal, however, the fact that poverty in the United States is a gender-linked condition. Some 25% of all U.S. children are being raised in single female–headed households, which include three fifths of all chronically poor households with children.

Among the areas studied by the *Human Development Report*'s new Gender Empowerment Measure, the one in which U.S. women perform worst is that of political representation. They hold only 10.4% of seats in Congress, as contrasted with 28.4% in parliament in the Netherlands, 39.4% in Norway, 33.5% in Finland, 40.4% in Sweden, 33.0% in Denmark, and 25.5% in Germany. Other nations that exceed the U.S. figure include Canada, Spain, Australia, Belgium, Austria, New Zealand, Switzerland, Ireland, Italy, Barbados, Bahamas, Luxembourg, Costa Rica, Trinidad and Tobago, Hungary, Mexico, Malaysia, Poland, Bulgaria, Belize, South Africa, Guyana, El Salvador, Namibia, Zimbabwe, Cameroon, Lesotho, Bangladesh, Burundi, and Mozambique.[9] Parliamentary representation is not an infallible sign of political influence, especially in a parliamentary system, but we can also point to the fact that nations such as Israel, Bangladesh, India, Pakistan, Turkey, and Sri Lanka have had female heads of state (the recent election in Bangladesh gave the voters a choice between two women), whereas the United States is a long way from having a female presidential candidate. It is striking that with very high economic and educational attainments, U.S. women have still not achieved a proportional measure of political influence.

In short, U.S. women are doing relatively well in many areas. This is not to say, however, that many U.S. women do not face grave economic problems. Indeed, the economic situation of many U.S. women is in some respects comparable to that of the women in developing nations who have been the primary subjects of chapters 1 and 2.[10] In the United States, as elsewhere, the fact that women still are expected to perform most unpaid housework and child care constrains women's access to employment and their productivity within it. It also contributes to a perception of women's lesser "usefulness" and productivity that injures women's access to many opportunities and resources. As Susan Okin writes, summarizing a number of empirical studies, "The *perception* that women's work is of less worth, largely because either unpaid or poorly paid (despite the fact that in most places they do more of it, and it is crucial to the survival of household members) contributes to women's being devalued and having less power within the family and outside of the household" (284). This perception, in turn, further reinforces women's economic dependence on men. Unlike women in some developing nations, U.S. women are never actually *forbidden* to work outside the home. Nor, in the home, do they usually have to carry water from a distance, to cook without electricity, to fight contagion without adequate sanitary facilities. These are real and significant differences. Nonetheless, their real equal access to employment opportunities may be severely constrained relative to those of men.

Similarly, the economic situation of U.S. women following a divorce is not as bad as that of Shah Bano, because a U.S. woman in her position would be likely to be literate and suited for at least some employment. But their situation is certainly threatening, and many U.S. women are, like Shah Bano, forced to support themselves after having been the mainstays of the male-headed household, with either no return or a blatantly insufficient return for their years of unpaid work.

One area in which it seems highly plausible to say that many people's preferences and judgments are distorted by habits of hierarchy and subordination is, then, household labor and its worth. In the United States, as in many parts of the world, people neglect the worth of this work and fail to respect and to compensate those who perform it. In the United States, as elsewhere, the likely cause of this neglect is habit and the sense of the overwhelming naturalness of things being this way. It would appear that this sense of the natural undermines democracy by denying women the equal worth of their liberties and opportunities. To draw attention to these distortions would, then, be a considerable service to democracy.

IV. Sexual Violence and Preference-Deformation

Let us now, however, turn to an area of female misery in which the United States may lead the world: sexual violence. The United States has 90,400 reported adult rapes in a representative year, as compared with 20,500 in Canada and much lower rates in other nations. Rape is an underreported crime; it is probably less underreported in the United States than in countries in which feminist complaints have not altered police behavior.[11] It is difficult even to know how underreported rape is, although we are on safe ground in concluding that it is a very serious problem in the lives of American women.[12]

Sexual violence is a central focus of Sommers's analysis. She argues as follows: American women do indeed suffer violence, but not disproportionately. The United States is a violent nation, with the highest rates of violent crime for all violent crimes. In general, vulnerability to sexual violence is a problem of "poor urban communities." The incidence of rape elsewhere has been grossly exaggerated, often in ways that suggest the desire to make a political point. In particular, the occurrence of acquaintance rape has been very much distorted, giving rise to a culture of victimhood.

It is admittedly difficult to elicit accurate figures on sexual force by survey or interview techniques, and Sommers is right to question some aspects of previous surveys.[13] But what does the best recent empirical study of sexual violence tell us? The survey of American sexual behavior by Edward Laumann and his collaborators is, among surveys in this area, the most comprehensive and carefully crafted, according to standards emphasized by Sommers herself.[14] It is a significant advance over previous studies of sexuality both because of its carefully random sample selection and because of its questionnaire, which was designed to address the most common problems with interview data gathering, and does so to an impressive degree.

While concluding that data on both adultery and homosexuality have been considerably exaggerated in recent reports, Laumann and his coauthors do find a strikingly high incidence of forced sexual activity, especially between close acquaintances. Most striking, they find an alarming disparity between the proportion of women who report that they have been forced to do something sexual that they did not want to do and the proportion of men who state that they have committed such an act.[15] Whereas Sommers concludes that the problem of date and acquaintance rape has been vastly exaggerated, Laumann and his coauthors find that codes such as the much-ridiculed Antioch rules, which require explicit consent at every stage in the process of sexual interaction, "may have arisen from a valid problem":

> Although, clearly, sexual interactions between men and women are fraught with ambiguity and potential conflicts, there is something more going on than a few misunderstandings. There seems to be not just a gender gap but a gender chasm in perceptions of when sex was forced. We find that large numbers of women say they have been forced by men to do something sexually that they did not want to do. But very few men report ever forcing a woman. The differences that men and women bring to the sexual situation and the differences in their experiences of sex sometimes suggest that there are two separate sexual worlds, his and hers.[16]

Specifically, 22% of women were forced sexually at some time after age thirteen (and only .6% were forced by another woman). Only 2% of men were forced. All but 4% of these women knew the man who was forcing them and nearly half said they were in love with him. Furthermore, the survey found a substantial positive correlation between the experience of force and general unhappiness in life.[17]

Men, by contrast, overwhelmingly denied using force: Only 3% said they forced a woman and .2% said they forced a man. Some may be lying, but the authors plausibly hold that the huge disparities cannot be explained away in this manner. They suggest that a more likely explanation is that "most men who forced sex did not recognize how coercive the women thought their behavior was" (229). They imagine the husband who comes home drunk from a night out with the boys, wanting sex now and thinking it his due; the young man on a date with a sexy woman who makes and accepts some advances but says no to intercourse: "He thinks the sex they have was consensual. She thinks it was forced."

If these plausible scenarios are as common as Laumann's data suggest, the feminists Sommers attacks are right to consider that we have a problem of major proportions, and one that will require massive educational efforts to address. (Indeed, his conclusion lies very close to the analysis of our sexual norms proposed by radical feminist Andrea Dworkin in a recent book,[18] when she claims that America's great problem is that violence by males is taken to be normal, "boys will be boys," something women just have to put up with.) There may be problems in the survey: We would expect underreporting of morally problematic and potentially criminal acts (although we would also expect at least some underreporting of having been the victim of such an act, given the stigma our society attaches to being a rape victim). Nor do their findings at all confirm Sommers's contention that rape is a problem of "poor urban communities": The perceptual disparity crosses all strata of society.[19] Sommers did not have these data. But they show that one should not be hasty in claiming that a problem has been manufactured by ideological feminists bent on telling "noble lies," as Sommers appears to claim; they show that feminists who kept insisting on the problem were in fact on the right track.[20]

Let us turn, however, to the central issue, that of distorted desire and preference. To understand how the situation described by Laumann may have arisen, we need to step back in history. And we must begin by mentioning some legal facts, which may be familiar but which bear repeating. Blackstone defined rape as "carnal knowledge of a woman forcibly and against her will."[21] The standard elements of rape in criminal law, following this definition, are (1) intercourse, (2) force, and (3) nonconsent.[22] Standardly these have been treated as independent elements: Thus, the presence of force is not by itself evidence of nonconsent. Traditionally, rape also includes a mental element, although there has been controversy about how this element of criminal intent should be defined. Before 1976, it was generally understood that only a reasonable belief that the woman had consented was a defense to a charge of rape. In 1976, in *Regina v. Morgan*,[23] the House of Lords set, instead, the weaker standard of "honest belief." (The case concerned a woman whose husband falsely told his friends that she liked to play rape games; they gang-raped her and claimed that they believed this was what she wanted. Their belief was held to be unreasonable but honest.) Controversy over this case led to a change in British law, making recklessness as to the woman's intent sufficient for the requisite mental element. Most U.S. states have not required proof of recklessness but have permitted conviction on the basis of negligence, permitting a mistake defense only when the defendant's error is both nonnegligent and reasonable. This, however, still leaves many problems in place because what is often at issue is precisely what a reasonable belief *is* in this situation—to whom is it reasonable and why?[24]

Before the feminist challenge to criminal law that began in the 1970s, a woman complaining of rape was required to show that the man involved had used physical force, and force additional to the force requisite to consummate the sexual act itself. The mere threat of force was often considered insufficient, although the threat of death or grave bodily injury usually was. Usually, too, the woman had to show that she had resisted, even in the face of force or the threat of force, because only this was taken to give evidence of nonconsent. Some states made resistance a formal statutory requirement, but more often it was read into statutes as a requirement implicit in the notions of force and/or nonconsent. The old requirement was that the victim resist "to the utmost"; more recently, this was replaced by terms such as "reasonable resistance" or "earnest resistance." Typical of its period was a New York statute of 1965 saying that rape is committed only when the man uses "physical force that overcomes earnest resistance" or makes a threat of "immediate death or serious physical injury." A woman who did not resist physically, or who succumbed to lesser threats, was treated as consenting, and the man's conduct was not criminal at all. The standard produced bizarre results. In one case, the victim said she submitted to intercourse because the man threatened her with a knife or box cutter. She got the weapon away from him, then submitted to intercourse a second time when he choked her and told her he could kill her. A 1973 New York appellate court set aside the man's conviction, saying, "[R]ape is not committed unless the woman opposes the man to the utmost limit of her power. The resistance must be genuine and active. It is difficult to conclude that the complainant here waged a valiant struggle to uphold her honor."[25]

These stringent requirements have long been criticized by law enforcement professionals, who believe it unwise for women to fight back in situations of attack.[26] Nonetheless, even in 1981, in a case in which the defendant took away a woman's car keys in a dangerous area of town, "lightly choked" her, and made menacing gestures, a lower court concluded that the woman had not resisted sufficiently to establish nonconsent. Although the conviction was reinstated on appeal, a three-vote minority, in the 4–3 decision, said of the victim, "She must follow the natural instinct of every proud female to resist, by more than mere words, the violation of her person by a stranger or an unwelcome friend."[27] A 1982 Hawaii case still required for conviction a showing of "genuine physical effort on the part of the complainant to discourage and to prevent her assailant from accomplishing his intended purpose."[28] In 1983, an appellate court in Illinois reversed a rape conviction in a case in which a large and powerful man (6'3", 185 pounds) carried a small woman (5'2", 100 to 105 pounds) bodily into the woods, lifting her off her bicycle, and asked her to lie on the ground while he had intercourse with her. The woman's failure to struggle was taken as evidence of consent, despite the discrepancy of size, the male's threatening behavior and statements (such as "I don't want to hurt you"), and the deserted nature of the wooded area in which the sex act took place, in which screaming would have been futile and might have provoked further violence. The court stated that the woman's "failure to resist when it was within her power to do so conveys the impression of consent."[29]

Notice the strange asymmetry between this treatment of sexual crime and our standard attitudes about property crime. If I remove your wallet without your express permission, I am committing a crime. I cannot defend myself by pointing to the fact that you failed to put up a fight. But if a man had nonconsensual intercourse with a woman, invading her intimate bodily space, our system thought it a crime only if she offered physical resistance, frequently in the face of danger. Nor does a conviction of theft require a showing that the thief used more force than was necessary to accomplish the theft itself (although such force may be an aggravating factor). But it was only in 1992, in an unusual ruling, that a New Jersey court held (explicitly rejecting prior tradition) that the element of "force" in rape was established simply by "an act of non-consensual penetration involving no more force than necessary to accomplish that result."[30]

Moreover, a woman who brought a rape charge would typically be subjected to humiliating questioning about her sexual history. It was oddly assumed that the fact that a woman was not chaste was evidence of consent to the particular sexual act in question. Why would such an assumption be made? When we encounter a friend dining at a fine restaurant, for example, we usually do not infer that he would love to have a plate of rancid broccoli rammed down his throat.

And yet it is just this sort of "reasoning" that pervaded most rape trials. It would appear that the inference reflects an underlying picture of women as divided into two groups: either chaste or whores with whom anything is permitted. These pictures of women have deep roots in our entire culture, coloring the ways in which we see, or missee, particular events. As eminent a cultural authority as Samuel Johnson once said to Boswell, "The one great principle that a woman should learn is to keep her legs together. When once a woman has given up that principle, she has given up every other." This idea is surely at work in the perception that a woman who does not struggle, at some risk to herself, has consented and has no right to complain. Such phrases as "a valiant struggle to uphold her honor" and "the natural instinct of every proud female to resist" show us that the world of the judiciary in the 1970s and 1980s is not so very far from Dr. Johnson's world.

These judgments about women also colored the interpretation of the mental element of rape. Men who hold these stereotypical views of women—widely disseminated in our society through pornographic depictions of women and many other cultural sources—may actually come to believe that a woman who says no is consenting to intercourse. The question the law typically had to face, as we have seen, is whether such beliefs were reasonable. The standard of the "reasonable" is notoriously elusive and frequently serves as a screen onto which judges project their own (generally male) ideas of appropriate social norms. Most readers will recall the rape trial of Mike Tyson, at which he claimed (unsuccessfully) that the willingness of D. W. to accompany him to his room was sufficient to make his belief in her consent reasonable, despite the evidence of her vigorous objections and her attempts to escape.[31] Such beliefs about consent were not found reasonable in 1993; earlier they probably would have been. In a 1982 case, in which a group of Boston doctors took a nurse bodily to a car, drove her up to Rockport, and had sex with her over her repeated protests, Justice Brown of the Appeals Court of Massachusetts commented that it was high time to reject the defense of reasonable mistake as to consent in cases such as this:

> It is time to put to rest the societal myth that when a man is about to engage in sexual intercourse with a "nice" woman, "a little force is always necessary."
> . . . I am prepared to say that when a woman says "no" to someone[,] any implication other than a manifestation of non-consent that might arise in that person's psyche is legally irrelevant, and thus no defense. . . . In 1985, I find no social utility in establishing a rule defining non-consensual intercourse on the basis of the subjective (and quite likely wishful) view of the more aggressive player in the sexual encounter.[32]

As Justice Brown recognizes, men often indulge in wishful thinking about women's wishes and (whether hypocritically or sincerely) convince themselves that aggressive behavior is what the situation calls for. If we interpret the "reasonable" in line with prevailing male social norms, we encourage this sort of wishful thinking. Justice Brown announces a truly radical conclusion: When a woman says "no," it is never reasonable to believe that she means "yes."

The judgments criticized by Justice Brown were distorted judgments. So too was the closely related judgment that a woman sexually active with others will "do it" with anyone. Such judgments relied, quite simply, on a set of false beliefs about women's behavior and desires: a "societal myth," as Justice Brown asserts. To say that women who are not sexually abstinent are still usually highly selective about their partners is to state the obvious. And there is probably no woman in the world who "is asking for" any form of sexual behavior, however brutal. Even women whose work involves admitting a wide range of sexual partners are not unselective: Prostitutes frequently express the desire for greater control over their working conditions, precisely to be in a position to refuse violent customers. Women whose nonchastity implies consent to anything and everything exist in pornography, but they do not exist in reality—except in the limiting case of a person whose selfhood is so broken down by repeated ill treatment that she can no longer assert choice and selfhood at all. The corresponding picture of males as creatures who cannot control themselves once aroused is also false. Women who, on saying no, have heard men complain (as they often do) that they have to have intercourse because they "cannot stop" also know, if they are not intimidated by such claims, that the claims are not true: The man can either stop or, if he does not want to stop, can deal with the problem without intercourse with the woman in question. Most men do control themselves, and all can; arousal is no justification for the use of force, although many men grew up believing that it was, or at least talking as if they believed that it was.

These false beliefs had a large effect on law and public policy. They informed men's sexual desires and sexual behavior—as when the knowledge that a woman is not chaste gave rise to an assumption that she would "do it" with anyone,[33] as when arousal by a woman's clothing, gestures, or kissing was taken to license the use of sexual force. They also shaped the desires and preferences of women, in many harmful ways. Women who had been raped, however violent and nonconsensual the incident, felt shamed and sullied and frequently did not even consider turning to the law for help. Often guilt about their own sexual desires, or about having consented to kissing or petting, made women feel that they had "asked for it," even when the rape involved violence and substantial physical damage. In addition, women who had consented to intercourse but who had not consented to acts of violence within intercourse also felt it impossible to complain because the reigning view was that a woman who said yes to intercourse had no right to complain about any abuse that ensued. Such a woman would surely have been treated with mockery and abuse by the police had she complained of assault.

For examples of these distortions and the damage they caused, most women who grew up in that era have only to consult their own histories and those of their friends. As Laumann's data suggest, a large proportion of women living in the United States today have encountered sexual force, often from an acquaintance. Those who lack such experiences can find vivid accounts of these attitudes in history, in fiction, and in the law.

As one remembers or reads about this strange era, what is most difficult to understand is the failure of women to be angry and to complain, their feeling (shared, frequently, by parents, friends, and the surrounding society) that their own sexuality is a provocation for male violence. Especially frequently, women who had consented to some sexual activity, such as petting or kissing, blamed themselves for forced intercourse if that ensued, and women who had consented to intercourse blamed themselves for violent sexual acts to which they had not consented. Those who did not live through that era, or who were fortunate enough not to encounter sexual violence, may think that only neurotic or ill-informed women reacted in this way. But those of us who have lived through one or more violent episodes are aware of how ubiquitous these reactions were, even in people who had every advantage of family love and education. These frequently tragic reactions were caused by a kind of distortion in belief and desire that the feminist movement of the 1970s exposed, arguing repeatedly that female sexual desire and attractiveness are not a way of "asking for it," that the only thing that counts as "asking for it" is a woman's expressed consent to the acts in question—just as the only way of "asking for" someone to take your wallet is to take it out and give it to that person, without intimidation or threat, either explicit or implicit. It seems clear that this critique has exposed damaging falsehoods—although much more work needs to be done to achieve a legal system that adequately protects women's autonomy.

Under the pressure of this feminist critique, rape law has changed considerably, increasingly reflecting the insight that a woman's "no" means that she does not consent, and does not mean that she is "playing games" and "asking for it," and that her prior sexual history is irrelevant to the question of consent on a particular occasion. Change has been slow, and there are many problems to solve. The new emphasis on "no means no" does not yet enable the law to grapple well with cases in which the victim is silent out of fear (as in *Warren*, the case of the small Illinois biker), and a tendency remains to suppose that silence expresses consent. Note that we would never think that a patient's silence in response to a question about whether he wanted a medical procedure was evidence of consent to that procedure; a doctor would be culpable if he or she simply went ahead and did the procedure, claiming that the patient had expressed consent by silence.[34] Our failure to think similarly about women probably betrays the legacy of the "societal myth" that good women will fight to the utmost. The law has not yet figured out how to articulate the idea of consent in a consistent manner that protects a woman's autonomy in cases such as *Warren*.[35]

It is not my intention here to offer a review of these highly complicated legal changes, which are still in progress and which exhibit much variation from state to state. Suffice it to say that this is an area in which the feminist critique has transformed and continues to transform law in a way that has won the widespread approval of women in the United States as a recognition of truths about their lives. The data Laumann discovers come as no surprise to professionals in the criminal justice system, who have been grappling with such "societal myths" for years. They suggest, as Laumann himself interprets them, that these recognitions have not yet influenced men's understanding of their actions as much as they have influenced women's understanding of what has happened to them. But this hardly shows that feminists who have pressed for these changes are out of step with women's lives in the United States, lives that are still pervasively threatened by sex-linked violence from both acquaintances and strangers.

One of the oldest distortions in this area is the idea that rape within marriage is not possible, and one of the most important contributions of the radical feminist critique of existing norms has been its attack on this idea. The marital exemption from rape and sexual assault was until very recently a standard feature of legal systems. At common law, it was not possible to try a man for raping his wife. In the nineteenth century, when the United States began to create criminal codes based on English common law, they incorporated this exemption. Even in the 1950s, the Model Penal Code recommended retaining it, and even expanding it to include couples who cohabit without marrying. In the 1970s, however, feminists launched a persuasive and powerful attack on the existing norm, pointing out that once one discards the legal fiction that man and wife are "one person," there is much less reason for refusing to recognize rape within marriage. Even the evidential problems, which remain, are now widely seen as no more serious than they are in rape generally.[36] Moreover, rape within marriage, studies demonstrated, is not a rare phenomenon, but "frequent enough to constitute a significant social problem."[37] Its long-term psychological effects, moreover, appear to be more serious than those of stranger rape.[38] Once again, it is the recognition of a women's right of autonomous choice that is crucial here: For apart from damage to autonomy, and assuming there is no additional physical violence, the nature of the harm inflicted by one more episode of intercourse with a man with whom the woman has had intercourse many times may seem obscure. Marital rape can produce an unwanted pregnancy, a very severe difficulty for the woman's autonomy; apart from this, it also represents a surrender of control over a woman's sexual choices, something modern women view as a serious harm. By now, most states have either repealed or qualified the marital exemption. Some have repealed it only for spouses who are under court-ordered separations or are living apart. Others require a greater showing of force for marital than for other rape or treat it as a lesser offense. Twenty-three states and the District of Columbia have eliminated the exemption completely.[39] Sommers, who holds that "[a]s a crime against the person, rape is uniquely horrible in its long-term effects" (209), is totally silent about these legal changes and the feminist pressures that produced them.

As Mill already observed in 1869, marital rape never was welcome to women: Indeed, it represented a surrender of dignity so complete that it made her lot similar to (Mill says worse than) that of a slave. But the idea that men had a right to such conduct exercised a powerful hold over the imaginations of men, helping them to rationalize conduct that might trouble them, and over the imaginations of women, making many, at least, suppose that they were fulfilling a duty and had no right to demand change.[40] In Diana Russell's study, *Rape in Marriage*, couples interviewed frequently stated that they thought men were exercising marital rights and duties. Said one forty-eight-year-old woman, "I was protesting and pleading and he was angry because he said I was his wife and had no right to refuse him." A husband stated, "At the time I felt men had the 'right' to do this with their wives." The changes in law that have been inspired by the feminist critique of marital rape have removed many of these distortions. As Officer Dave Hanczuk of the training section on domestic violence at the Los Angeles Police Academy said of wife-beaters in 1993, "When two big guys come to their houses, handcuff 'em, and take them down to the station for the night, they start to wonder whether or not it's really o.k. to hit their wives."[41] It is plausible to think that the removal of the marital exemption will lead to at least some similar attitudinal changes in the case of rape in marriage, although many problems are likely to remain.

Finally, a major contribution of the feminist movement of the 1970s is in the area of sexual harassment in the workplace. All workplaces face these problems, but let me simply focus on the academy, which is representative enough. The world in which I was a graduate student, in the early 1970s, was a world in which more or less every graduate student woman I knew at some time suffered some unwanted sexual attentions from men in positions of power and authority over her. Sometimes these attentions were accompanied by explicit threats of bad grades or failure to support for a job. Sometimes they were not so accompanied, and the man made an effort to be fair to the woman who said no. Even in these cases, however, the existence of the sexual pressures compromised the dignity of working relations, made women feel unprofessional, and created awkward inequalities in the classroom, as women wondered whether the ones who said yes were getting either undue favoritism or, less commonly, undue harsh treatment on that account. Women were not without resources: They could change supervisors, fields, or institutions if the pressures became too uncomfortable. But they should not have had to do this. To point to the resourcefulness of women who surmount these obstacles hardly shows that the obstacles were not a disgrace, nor does saying that they are a disgrace turn women into victims. Women should have been able to stay right where they were, doing their work. There were, however, no formal grievance procedures for sexual harassment in any university. There was no official concept of it, no name for it. And even men of good will were reluctant to hear complaints about it. There was a general atmosphere of shame and embarrassment. When the rare woman did bring a complaint to her department chair, not only the chair but most other women felt that she was doing something rather tasteless and unnecessarily punitive. That is how far women were from fully respecting themselves as professionals and their own workplace as a professional workplace.

All this began to change in the late 1970s, with the publication of *Sexual Harassment of Working Women*,[42] and the accompanying publicity drawn to the issue, as MacKinnon (as their lawyer) and the late John J. Winkler, a Professor of Classics (as their faculty adviser) helped a group of Yale undergraduates bring a complaint against Yale University that it had failed to protect them from sexual harassment. What they described was a series of incidents that ranged from rape to threats of low grades. What they demanded was that Yale set up a grievance procedure to hear such charges. The case was settled, and Yale now has such a grievance procedure, as does almost every university and college. (Harvard was the first, adopting in 1984 a policy banning all sexual relations between teachers and students whom they either taught or supervised. Many policies are less explicit and take the form of loosely formulated recommendations.[43]) By now, any law library contains shelves of publications relating to sexual harassment, and a wide range of court cases has progressively described the boundaries of permissible and impermissible conduct.

What MacKinnon's book and related feminist legal arguments stressed was the way in which an asymmetry of power corrupts sexual consent and creates threatening conditions for women in a workplace. Women had known this for a long time. It did not feel romantic and great to be approached with a quid pro quo or an implicit threat of the withdrawal of professional support. Women knew that this was wrong—but they thought they had to put up with it. Men, in many cases, did not even see the problem. Typical of an earlier era, though for its own time somewhat extreme, is a 1993 statement made by a professionally well-regarded English professor at the University of Massachusetts (Amherst), William Kerrigan, in a forum in *Harper's Magazine*[44]:

> [T]here is a kind of student I've come across in my career who was working through something that only a professor could help her with. I'm talking about a female student who, for one reason or another, has unnaturally prolonged her virginity. . . . There have been times when this virginity has been presented to me as something that I . . . half an authority figure, can handle—a thing whose preciousness I realize. . . . These relationships exist between adults and can be quite beautiful and genuinely transforming. It's very powerful sexually and psychologically, and because of that power, one can touch a student in a positive way.

Kerrigan's complacent pride in his paternal helpfulness is far from unusual, although few male professors today would speak so freely of the way in which they act out their sexual fantasies. But he simply fails to understand what the problem at issue is. Even if he extracts no quid pro quo (he denies that he has ever conditioned grades on sex), his very authority creates a type of pressure that a student in a course of his cannot easily deal with. Even if he is not going to penalize her, she is likely to fear that he will, or at least that he will withdraw his support. Suppose she does not want sex (and note that he speaks of the need to use his authority to remove the "unnaturally prolonged" virginity): Will she feel free to say no? Suppose she wants to break it off when he does not: Will she be able to do so without fear? And what about his other female (and male) students: How do they feel about the fact that one of their number has been singled out for an intimate relationship with the well-known professor?

Many cases of academic sexual harassment are worse than this: For it is still common to find sex traded for grades or other favors. Others look more innocuous: Young assistant professors, for example, dating graduate students in their own department. These cases raise legitimate issues of personal freedom because adults are often brought together in a working environment by their common interests. But most standard policies would allow such dating, provided that the professor carefully avoided teaching the graduate student, supervising his or her work, and participating in any departmental decisions concerning him or her.

These conditions set reasonable boundaries, expressing ideas about when an asymmetry of power corrupts a working environment.

By now the law, too, has begun to take cognizance of the issue of imbalance of power and its connection with workplace harassment. A judge applying the Title VII law[45] must be able to ask whether a form of sexual conduct created a hostile or intimidating working environment.[46] And in order to do this, as has recently been held in finding for Mary Carr against General Motors (discussed earlier) he or she may even be required to take cognizance of the asymmetry of power between women and men as a part of the facts of the case.[47] The problem of harassment remains, and there is still no general agreement in our society about exactly what the boundaries should be between acceptable and unacceptable conduct. But male awareness of the problem has increased, and women, who were usually aware of it all along, no longer think that it is just part of life, that they have no right to complain. These developments, which are widely welcomed by women working everywhere in America, are due to the feminist movement of the 1970s, which went well beyond the "equity feminism" described by Sommers to recognize ways in which intimidation and threat taint sexual situations of many kinds.

Prior to the feminist movement of the 1970s, our society had areas of irrationality in its thought about the sexes that had not been exposed to reflection and criticism. "Societal myth[s]," about what women really want and about what conduct is really threatening and assaultive, have now begun to be challenged, and the preferences and desires that were based on these false myths have to some extent altered, but the process is an ongoing one in which we encounter considerable backsliding and uncertainty. The idea that myths are justified to the extent that they become embedded in preferences and desires is a big obstacle to sorting out what we really want to say. Preferences are not innate or unchangeable, a bedrock of "nature" exogenous to law and public policy; they are themselves in countless ways shaped by laws and policies. Those that are based on false beliefs should be criticized, just as we criticize any false belief.

V. Preference-Deformation, Feminism, and Liberty

Sommers, however, is a philosopher, and the essence of her argument against "gender feminism" is philosophical. We have seen some reasons for thinking that the problem of distorted preferences in the sexual sphere is a serious one, and that the feminist movement of the 1970s has made a valuable contribution to its diagnosis. But we cannot respond well to the argument without addressing its philosophical core; we have not yet given an account of what preferences are, of what factors may be taken to distort them, or of how these distorting factors are related to democratic debate.

The notion of a "preference" is a somewhat obscure one; economists who use the notion usually do not define it and rarely, if ever, comment on its relationship to a number of other notions commonly used, and defined, by philosophers—such as desire, emotion, choice, and evaluative belief. But two broad schools of thought may be identified in the literature. According to one view, preferences are not psychological factors lying behind choices but are contained in the actual choices a person makes. (Typically, Samuelson and others who hold this view say that preferences are "revealed" in choice, but because they do not want to admit that preferences are identifiable independently of choice, the language of revelation is misleading.) The other view, shared by economists as otherwise diverse as Gary Becker and Amartya Sen, is that it is most illuminating to think of preferences as psychological items that lie behind choices and influence them, but in many different ways. There are very good reasons to prefer this account, because preferences construed in Samuelson's way do not obey a number of important axioms, such as transitivity.[48] Without going into this, I simply state that I follow the Becker-Sen view, and think of "preference" as a genus of evaluative attitudes some species of which will be desires, emotions, and appetites.

At the heart of Sommers's argument is a surprising claim, though one commonly made against feminists. This is the thesis that any criticism of existing preferences and desires as irrational, or deformed by malice or resentment or hierarchy, is in itself undemocratic and, indeed, dangerous to democracy. This argument needs close scrutiny, for it is the central route by which Sommers arrives at the conclusion that gender feminism is not just silly or mistaken but a profound threat to cherished American ways of life. Because her view is by no means idiosyncratic but is found, in one or another form, in a good deal of the recent criticism of feminism, it is worth trying to state it clearly and to criticize it in detail.

The argument proceeds in two stages. In the first phase, Sommers cursorily reports the views of a mixed group of feminist writers who describe ways in which women are led by social forces to internalize and endorse images of themselves that impose hardship and deform self-expression. She mentions in particular the views of Naomi Wolf and Susan Faludi that women frequently suffer losses of self-esteem when they internalize popular norms of a woman's worth as dependent on her achievement of an ideal type of bodily beauty. To these she adds MacKinnon's view that women easily learn to find being dominated sexy, again with frequent bad consequences for their own self-esteem and self-expression. This idea that social norms can deform preferences, creating internal forces that militate against one's own happiness, Sommers then traces to Michel Foucault (229)—although Foucault, as she acknowledges, is not mentioned by any of these writers as the source of these views. (Only Wolf even mentions him in her bibliography. MacKinnon has written attacking postmodernism, which she calls "a hazardous departure for feminism," and defending a universalist view of human rights.[49]) Foucault's views about the social deformation of preferences are then held to depend on the idea that we all live in something like an "authoritarian" (229) police state. After pointing out that respected liberal social theorist Michael Walzer once characterized Foucault's view as "infantile leftism" (in connection with his general neglect of individual liberty, however, not his account of deformed preference), Sommers concludes: "It would be a mistake to think that the idea of a tenacious internalized power that is keeping women subjugated is on the fringe of the New Feminism and not at its center" (231). Her conclusion: The New Feminism ignores the difference between democracy and a police state and rejects liberty in a way that is both implausible and dangerous.

In the second phase of her argument, in a chapter entitled "The Gender Wardens," Sommers returns to the question of women's preferences, focusing on the common feminist claim that many women who endorse their own inequality do so in a way that does not express their own true or authentic preferences. "Respect for people's preferences is generally thought to be fundamental for democracy" (258), she observes; any feminist who holds that on occasion women may be wrong about their true interests is "prepared to dismiss popular preferences in an illiberal way." She now quotes a passage from feminist philosopher Marilyn Friedman that expresses the allegedly illiberal view:

> Liberal feminists can easily join with other feminists in recognizing that political democracy by itself is insufficient to ensure that preferences are formed without coercion, constraint, undue restriction of options, and so forth. Social, cultural, and economic conditions are as important as political conditions, if not more so, in ensuring that preferences are, in some important sense, authentic.

Friedman is "quite wrong," says Sommers: "anyone, liberal or conservative, who believes in democracy will sense danger in" her ideas. "Who," she asks, "will 'ensure' that preferences are 'authentic'? What additions to political democracy does Friedman have in mind? A constitutional amendment to provide reeducation camps for men and women of false consciousness?" (259).

Such ideas about preferences, she continues, might have had some truth in the days when John Stuart Mill uttered them—for in those days women were not only taught that their own subjugation was "fitting and natural" (259), they were also prevented from changing things by voting. But now that women have the vote, "their preferences are being taken into account." So we must reject the idea that any criticism of their preferences is appropriate or even admissible. "Since women today can no longer be regarded as the victims of an undemocratic indoctrination, we must regard their preferences as 'authentic.' Any other attitude to American women is unacceptably patronizing and profoundly illiberal" (260).

This second phase of the argument is interesting, first of all, for the way in which it casts doubt on the first: For Sommers now admits that the ideas she criticizes are to be found in Mill, perhaps the greatest of the liberal political philosophers, and are not the private property of a radical thinker such as Foucault. Thus she can no longer damn the view merely by association. And, of course, Mill did not believe that women's preferences were deformed merely by the fact that they did not have the vote, or that the suffrage would correct the situation. The denial of suffrage explained why their preferences were not duly *recorded*. But Mill's account of why these preferences were in any case *distorted* is a different matter altogether. Here he speaks of a multitude of factors: the absence of equal education; the absence of accurate information about women's potentialities and abilities; the hierarchical behavior of men, who treat women with condescension and cast aspersions on their achievements; the pervasive social teaching that women are fit only or primarily for domestic and nonintellectual functions; women's own justified fear of questioning authority, which leads them to shy away from new functions and pursuits; their equally justified fear of moving from a position of comfortable inequality to a position that would be both unprotected and still unequal. Men's preferences, too, were corrupt, he argued: For to be taught that without any personal distinction, just in virtue of being male, one is superior to the most talented woman is the source of a view of oneself and one's conduct that is diseased, and that leads men to endorse diseased and self-protective social choices.

In short, Mill thought that a liberal democracy—even one with women's suffrage—could contain preferences deformed by a legacy of social hierarchy and inequality. His analysis identifies the same sources of distortion that appeared in the history of thinking about sexual violence and intimidation I sketched earlier. There, too, we were confronted with distortions of desire, evaluative belief, and emotion produced by (1) lack of information or false information about fact—as, for example, when men mistakenly assumed that women who are not chaste are likely to consent to any sexual act, and this influenced their erotic imagination and their conduct; (2) lack of reflection or deliberation about norms—as, for example, when the absence of public debate about the idea that a husband has a right to force his wife, the idea that a boss has the right to demand sex from an employee, shaped men's desires and choices; (3) lack of options—as when the fact that a woman had no realistic option to prosecute a rapist, or to complain of sexual harassment, led her to make the best of a bad business rather than complain.

Because of the priority Mill attached to liberty, he did not argue that people with diseased preferences should suffer political disabilities. But he did believe that, insofar as possible, social policy should not be based on those diseased preferences. How was this to be accomplished without illiberal restrictions on liberty? By intensive attention to the education of the young, and by the force of public persuasion and public argument. Our history supports Mill, suggesting that persuasion can bring about many changes, and that the absence of a public critique of these distortions does grave disservice to democracy. It would surely be implausible to claim that democracy was better off when women were afraid to complain of rape, or when they could be ridiculed for complaining of sexual harassment.

Mill's idea is at the heart of respectable Utilitarian thought of the present day, both in philosophy and in economics. Utilitarians, unlike some other types of democratic political thinker, do hold that at the end of the day social policy should be based on the preferences and desires of individuals. But most Utilitarian thinkers recognize that preferences may be distorted by a variety of factors in such a way that they will fail to be the individual's own "true" or "authentic" preferences. And most hold that democratic deliberation must try very hard to separate the "authentic" from the "inauthentic" preferences, basing social choice on the former rather than the latter when this can be done.

A representative, and especially clear, formulation of the problem is that given by Nobel Prize–winning economist John Harsanyi, in an article entitled "Morality and the Theory of Rational Behaviour" published in the highly regarded collection on utilitarianism edited by philosopher Bernard Williams and economist/philosopher Amartya Sen.[50] Harsanyi insists, so far in agreement with Sommers, that "in deciding what is good and what is bad for a given individual, the ultimate criterion can only be his own wants and his own preferences" (55). But, he immediately continues:

> Any sensible ethical theory must make a distinction between rational wants and irrational wants, or between rational preferences and irrational preferences. It would be absurd to assert that we have the same moral obligation to help other people in satisfying their utterly unreasonable wants as we have to help them in satisfying their very reasonable desires. (55)

It might seem that a preference-based theory will have difficulty making this distinction. Not so, continues Harsanyi:

> In actual fact, there is no difficulty in maintaining this distinction even without an appeal to any other standard than an individual's own personal preferences. All we have to do is to distinguish between a person's manifest preferences and his true preferences. His manifest preferences are his actual preferences as manifested by his observed behaviour, including preferences possibly based on erroneous factual beliefs, or on careless logical analysis, or on strong emotions that at the moment greatly hinder rational choice. In contrast, a person's true preferences are the preferences he *would* have if he had all the relevant factual information, always reasoned with the greatest possible care, and were in a state of mind most conducive to rational choice. (55)

Social policy, Harsanyi continues, should be based, insofar as possible, on the true preferences of individuals. And not on all of these, for some true preferences are "antisocial," deformed by "sadism, envy, resentment, and malice" (56). These, he concludes, "must be altogether excluded from our social-utility function" (56). Such an analysis has obvious pertinence to feminism. It is precisely the contention of Catharine MacKinnon, the feminist thinker most strongly criticized by Sommers, that men's preferences are frequently deformed by "sadism, envy, resentment, and malice," women's preferences by adaptation to (even eroticization of) a state of affairs in which men's desire for control governs the course of life. One can of course argue about whether the case for seeing various preferences of women and men as distorted in this way has been made out, and one can certainly argue that there is danger in leaping prematurely to such a conclusion. But my point is that insofar as they can be shown to be so deformed, it is a standard conclusion of Utilitarian liberalism that such preferences should be suspect, when social policy is formed. Once again, utilitarian thinkers do not suggest that we should deny such people the vote; they do suggest that a reflective democracy should criticize such people, instill suspicion of such preferences in the young, and view the signs of preference deformation in the proponents as a strong reason for skepticism about the merits of a proposed law or a policy. At times, democracy may judge that the harms done to nonconsenting third parties are too great to allow such preferences to determine social choice: Thus, our society decided that the preferences of southern white parents for segregated schools should not be permitted to determine the type of public schools children would attend.

Let us now consider another type of preference-deformation, by now familiar in the economic literature, which also has implications for feminist analysis. This is the phenomenon of "adaptation," in which an individual's preferences are shaped to accord with the (frequently narrow) set of opportunities she actually has. (Jon Elster[51] has called this the "sour grapes" phenomenon, although this is perhaps a misleadingly narrow term, because "sour grapes" implies that one has previously been aware of and consciously desired the grapes and subsequently adapts to their unavailability, whereas in many cases adaptation takes place in situations in which there is no good information about other opportunities and possibilities.) Economist Amartya Sen has argued that women in many parts of the world exhibit preferences that are deformed in this way, even when very basic matters such as physical health, nutrition, and security are concerned.[52] If one does not know what it is like to feel well nourished, it is especially easy to be content with the undernourished state in which one lives; if one has never learned to read and is told that education is not for women, it is very easy to internalize one's own second-class status and learn not to strive for, or even desire, what tradition has put out of reach. The existence of such "adaptive preferences," Sen argues, gives us strong reasons to be highly mistrustful of existing preferences in choosing social policies. We have good reasons, for example, to support public investment in female literacy, even in the absence of young girls' demand for such programs.

Such a suggestion is fully compatible with democracy; indeed it coexists, in Sen's thought, with a strong defense of liberal political freedoms and of democratic procedures.[53] Indeed, the point about female literacy has been supported by libertarian economist Gary Becker, writing in *Business Week*.[54] Democratic choice need not be understood as the aggregation of uncriticized preferences, and most theorists of democracy, even those in the utilitarian tradition, by now do not so construe it. A growing number of theorists construe choice, instead, as a more reflective exercise, in which we attempt to ascertain which among our preferences are conducive to the general welfare.[55] Indeed, it is also a familiar point in democratic political theory that liberal/democratic institutions themselves shape, and ought to shape, the preferences citizens have. Under conditions of stably guaranteed equal liberty and material adequacy, for example, citizens may be less likely to form "strong and inordinate desires" to have more wealth than others. In general, liberal/democratic institutions influence people's basic aspirations and shape their character and aims.[56]

Does this mean that Sommers is right to suggest that when women have the vote, this very fact removes the problem of adaptive preference and desire? Few democratic theorists would come to that conclusion. Certainly the right to vote is one important determinant of a citizen's character and aspirations, but Mill seems correct to think that it does not by itself undo the other sources of distortion in desire. It is jejune to suppose that the existence of women's suffrage in India has removed the problem of adaptive preference and desire; Sen's data show clearly that women misperceive their own health and nutritional status, the likely worth of literacy for their own future, and so forth. And although the position of women in our own society is different in many important respects from the position of women in India—American women, for example, are on average well ahead of Indian women with respect to basic health and nutrition, with respect to literacy and education, and with respect to employment rights—nonetheless it would be extremely naive, and more than a little chauvinistic, to assume that the problem of adaptive preference could not possibly exist in our own democracy, with regard to many important elements of a human being's quality of life. Quite a few feminist thinkers have given interesting arguments to show that this problem is present, for example, in women's attitudes to demanding physical tasks, to careers in science and mathematics, and to their own autonomy and equality more generally.

Indeed, a view related to Sen's has been endorsed as true of our own society by an economist whom Sommers would perhaps have difficulty linking with the radical left, namely, Becker, who made an account of adaptive choice-deformation central to his Nobel Prize address, with explicit reference to women's lives and choices.[57] Becker argued that social prejudices of various sorts, especially "the *beliefs* of employers, teachers, and other influential groups that minority members are less productive," can be self-fulfilling, causing the members of the disadvantaged group to "underinvest in education, training, and work skills"—and this underinvestment does subsequently make them less productive. In short, disadvantaged groups—among which Becker includes "blacks, women, religious groups, immigrants, and other"—internalize their second-class status in ways that cause them to make choices that perpetuate that second-class status.[58] Any theory of social rationality, Becker holds, implicitly agreeing with Sen, should be alert to and critical of these facts. Although in this paper Becker, unlike Sen, does not draw any inferences for public policy, it would not be hard to conclude from his analysis that it can be risky for a democracy to build policy on all existing preferences in a society, especially when it contains traditional hierarchies of race or gender.

Nor is the recognition of diseased preferences a new discovery. It is a pervasive feature of the most prominent accounts of emotion and desire in the Western philosophical tradition. Cultural forces, including ideas of self and other imparted through moral teaching, are widely held to produce emotions and desires that are inauthentic in the sense of being inimical to self-development, self-expression, and rational autonomy. As I have said, these views are prominently found in Mill, a liberal democrat. They are also found, in one or another form, in thinkers as diverse as Plato, Aristotle, Thomas Aquinas, Epicurus, the Greek and Roman Stoics, Spinoza, Kant, and many others. Kant is especially important in this history for the way in which he criticizes sexual desire itself for leading people to treat one another as objects, in an argument that is the direct ancestor of the arguments of MacKinnon, whom Sommers derides.[59] Some of these thinkers, above all Plato, did indeed hold that this problem made democracy unworkable. (In an earlier phase of her argument Sommers actually labeled her feminist opponents "Platonists."[60]) But of course one need not reach this conclusion, and one will not reach it if one is convinced, as are, in different ways, Aristotle,

Kant, and Mill, of the overwhelming importance of individual choice and self-determination. Instead, one will tend to focus on the role of public persuasion and moral education, hoping that inappropriate preferences, whether competitive or acquisitive or sexist or racist, can be eradicated through a voluntary program of reform within a democratic society. When serious harms to nonconsenting parties are present, law may be invoked, as it has been in the area of racial discrimination, marital rape, and sexual harassment. But the central focus of the democratic critic of preferences will be on persuasion rather than coercion. In that same earlier article, Sommers called herself an "Aristotelian," defining that as one who believes that the commonsense ordinary beliefs of a society should not be criticized. But of course this was far from being Aristotle's view. He held, in fact, that a program of moral education should play a central role in changing diseased preferences for money, status, and aggressive success, and that social policy should not be built on such diseased preferences. So, although there are many differences of substance among the thinkers I have mentioned—Aristotle and Gary Becker will not agree, for example, about whether the preference for the accumulation of wealth should be understood as diseased or healthy, and certainly most modern democrats will be at odds with Aristotle over the limits of government intervention with personal choice[61]—there is general agreement that this is an urgently important question for public policy to answer, and that it can be put at the center of political deliberation without giving up on democracy.

In short, the feminist views attacked by recent critics are not the monopoly of a sect of radical extremists. They are commonplace in mainstream liberal, and even some libertarian, thought. These theoretical ideas have a very close relationship to the critique of existing preferences that led to the critique of rape law and to the demand for laws and policies dealing with sexual harassment in the workplace. These changes certainly seem to have enhanced democracy rather than to have undermined it—for surely it is not better for democracy that women should suffer from violence and intimidation without the opportunity to complain. Complaint is not a solution to the problems, and women continue to face many grave problems of sexual harassment and sexual violence. But complaint is surely far better than silent intimidation, and the right to complain does not turn women into pathetic victims—any more than the right to complain when someone steals a wallet turns men into pathetic victims.

We may now return to the questions with which we began. American women have much to complain of. They are far too often victims of rape, of sexual coercion of many kinds, of sexual harassment and discrimination in the workplace. Moreover, the underlying attitudes that made these problems so difficult persist, producing pain of many kinds. On the other hand, the feminist movement that began in the 1970s has made considerable progress in articulating the underlying problems and in proposing legal solutions. This has happened in large part through a criticism of the myths that underlay many men's (and women's) beliefs about sexual violence and its causes.[62] Such criticism, far from treating people like victims or children, treats them like adults who are capable of reflection, and capable of deciding that they were wrong on an important matter even when their own emotions and desires are at stake.

6

EQUITY AND MERCY

... we stomp on the rape magazines or we invade where they
prostitute us, where we are herded and sold, we ruin their
theatres where they have sex on us, we face them, we scream
in their fucking faces, we are the women they have made
scream when they choose. ...We're all the same, cunt is cunt
is cunt, we're facsimiles of the ones they done it to, or we are
the ones they done it to, and I can't tell him from him from
him ... so at night, ghosts, we convene; to spread justice,
which stands in for law, which has always been merciless,
which is, by its nature, cruel.

—Andrea Dworkin, *Mercy*

This second doctrine [of mercy]—counterdoctrine would be
a better word—has completely exploded whatever coherence
the notion of "guided discretion" once had. ... The requirement [of mitigation] destroys whatever rationality and pre-
dictability the ... requirement [of aggravation] was designed
to achieve.

—Justice Scalia,
in *Walton v. Arizona*

"O child ... do not cure evil with evil. Many people have
preferred the more equitable to the more just."

—Herodotus, *History*

I. Mercy and Retribution

I begin with the plot of a novel whose title is *Mercy*.[1] By the author's deliberate
design, it is not really a novel, and there is no mercy in it. These facts are connected. To pursue the connection is my plan. The author of this novel, or antinovel, is the feminist writer and antipornography activist Andrea Dworkin. Its
narrator is also named Andrea—a name that, as she tells us, means "courage"
or "manhood." At the age of nine, Andrea is molested by an anonymous man
in a movie theater. At fourteen, she is cut with a knife by a sadistic teenage lover.
At eighteen she sleeps with many men for money; she finds a tender black lover
but is brutally raped by his roommate. Jailed for antiwar activity, she is sexually abused by prison doctors. She goes to Crete and has a passionate loving
relationship with a Greek bartender—but when he discovers that she has been
making love casually with many men he rapes her and gives her up. Returning
to New York, she lives a marginal life of sex, drink, and drugs. Threatened by a

gang one night, she tries to make peace with its leader. He holds her hostage at knifepoint in her own bed. Apparently rescued by a man who turns up at her door, she finds herself raped by her rescuer.

At twenty-two she marries a tender young revolutionary. As soon as they are husband and wife, he finds himself unable to make love without tying her up and hitting her. She leaves him for street life. Some years later, after many other abuses, she takes karate lessons and becomes adept at kicking drunken homeless men to death. We encounter at this point the passage that I quoted as an epigraph to this chapter; it expresses Andrea's angry refusal of mercy, her determination to exact retribution without concern for the identity of the particulars. ("I can't tell him from him from him.") Although one might wonder whether the point is that terrible experiences have corrupted Andrea's perceptions, it appears that her refusal of mercy is endorsed by the novel as a whole.

This novel does not read like a traditional novel because its form expresses the retributive idea that its message preaches. That is, it refuses to perceive any of the male offenders—or any other male—as a particular individual, and it refuses to invite the reader into the story of their lives. Like Andrea, it can't tell him from him from him. The reader hears only the solitary voice of the narrator; others exist for her only as sources of her pain. Like the women in the male pornography that Dworkin decries, her males have no history, no psychology, no concrete reasons for action. They are just knives that cut, arms that beat, penises that maim by the very act of penetration. Dworkin's refusal of the traditional novelist's attention to the stories of particular lives seems closely connected with her heroine's refusal to be merciful to any of those lives, with her doctrine that justice is cruel and hard.[2] But the nature of the connection between mercy and a vision of the particular is not yet evident; my hope is to make it evident—and, in the process, to make a case for the moral and legal importance of the novelist's art.

In order to do this, however, I must begin with a historical inquiry into the origins, in the Western tradition, of the close connection between equitable judgment—judgment that attends to the particulars—and mercy, defined by Seneca as "the inclination of the mind toward leniency in exacting punishment." I begin with a puzzle in ancient Greek thought about law and justice. Solving this puzzle requires understanding some features of the archaic idea of justice that turn out to be highly pertinent to Andrea Dworkin's project. This sort of justice is soon criticized, with appeal both to equity and to mercy. After following the arguments of Aristotle and Seneca on this question, I shall return to contemporary issues, using these ideas to make a case for the moral and legal importance of narrative art in several areas of contemporary legal and political relevance, defending the equity/mercy tradition as an alternative both to retributive views of punishment and to some modern deterrence-based views.

II. Mercy and Particularity: A Puzzle

There is a puzzle in the evidence for ancient Greek thought about legal and moral reasoning. Two concepts that do not appear to be at all the same are treated as so closely linked as to be aspects of the same concept, and introduced together by one and the same moral term. The moral term is *epieikeia*.[3] The concepts are the two that I have already identified as my theme: the ability to judge in such a way as to respond with sensitivity to all the particulars of a person and situation and the "inclination of the mind" to leniency in punishing—equity, and mercy.[4] From the beginning, the idea of flexible particularized situational judgment is linked with leniency. *Epieikeia*, which originally designates the former, is therefore said to be accompanied by the latter: It is something mild and gentle; something contrasted to the rigid or harsh. The Herodotean father, in my epigraph, contrasts the notion of strict retributive justice with *epieikeia*, at a time when that word was already clearly associated with situational appropriateness.[5] The orator Gorgias, praising the civic character of soldiers fallen in battle, says of them that "on many occasions they preferred the gentle equitable (*to praon epieikes*) to the harshly stubborn just (*tou authadous dikaiou*), and appropriateness of reasoning to the precision of the law, thinking that this is the most divine and most common law, namely to say and not say, to do and to leave undone, the thing required by the situation at the time required by the situation."[6] He too, then, links the ability to do and say the right thing in the situation with a certain mildness or softness; opposed to both is the stubborn and inflexible harshness of law. By this time, the original and real etymology of the word *epieikeia*—from *eikos*, the "plausible" or "appropriate"[7]—is being supplemented by a popular derivation of the term from *eikô*; "yield," "give way." Thus, even in writing the history of the term, Greek thinkers discover a connection between appropriate judgment and leniency.[8]

The puzzle lies, as I have said, in the unexplained connection between appropriate situational judgment and mercy. One might well suppose that a judgment that gets all the situational particulars correct will sometimes set the level of fault high up and sometimes low down, as the situation demands. If the judgment is a penalty-setting judgment, it will sometimes set a heavy penalty and sometimes a light one, again as the situation demands. If the equitable judgment and/or penalty is being contrasted with a general principle designed beforehand to fit a large number of situations—as is usually the case—we might expect that the equitable will sometimes be more lenient than the generality of the law but sometimes harsher. For, as that not-very-merciful philosopher Plato puts it in his *Laws*, sometimes the offender turns out to be unusually good for an offender of that sort, but sometimes, too, unusually bad.[9] Plato has a modern ally in Justice Scalia, who feels that it is absurd that aggravation and mitigation should be treated asymmetrically in the law. The very same requirements should hold for both—and, presumably, once we begin looking at the specific circumstances, we will be about as likely to find grounds for the one as for the other.[10]

But this is not what many Greek and Roman thinkers seem to think. They think that the decision to concern oneself with the particulars is connected with taking up a gentle and lenient cast of mind toward human wrongdoing. They endorse the asymmetry that Justice Scalia finds absurd and incoherent. We must now ask on what grounds, and with what rationality and coherence of their own, they do so.

III. Retribution and Particular Perception

We can make some progress by looking at what *epieikeia* opposes or corrects. We see in our passages a contrast between *epieikeia* as flexible situational judgment and the exceptionless and inflexible mandates of law or rule. We also find these laws or rules described as "harsh," "harshly stubborn," a "cure of evil with evil." This goes to the heart of our puzzle, clearly: For what we need to know is how that sort of justice comes to be seen as *harsh* in its lack of fit to the particulars rather than simply imprecise.

Let us think, then, of the archaic conception of justice. And let us take the first surviving philosophical text to use the notion of justice: For in its metaphorical application of *dikê* to cosmic process, it illustrates very vividly what *dikê*, in human legal and moral matters, was taken to involve. Writing about the cyclical changes of the basic elements into one another—as the hot, the cold, the wet, and the dry succeed one another in the varying combinations that make up the seasons of the year—the sixth-century B.C. philosopher Anaximander writes, "They pay penalty and retribution (*dikên kai tisin*) to one another in accordance with the assessment of time."[11]

What does Anaximander describe? He describes a process in which "encroachments" by one element are made up in exact proportion, over time, by compensatory "encroachments" of the corresponding opposite element. We are, it seems to imagine as the neutral state, a state of balance in which each element has, so to speak, its own—its due sphere, its due representation in the sphere of things. Next the balance is thrown off in that one or more of the elements goes too far, trespasses on the preserve of the other—as, for example, winter is an invasion by the cold and the wet into the due preserve of the warm and the dry. (Thus the root notion of injustice, already in the sixth century, is the notion of *pleonexia*, grasping more than one's due share, the very notion that Plato exploits in the *Republic*, trying to capture its opposite with the notion of "having and doing one's own."[12]) Winter is an imbalance, and for justice or *dikê* to be restored, retribution (*tisis*) must take place, or, in other words, the elements that encroached must "pay justice and retribution" to the ones they squeezed out. What this seems to mean is that a corresponding encroachment in the other direction must take place in order that "the doer should suffer."[13] Summer is the due retribution for the imbalance of winter; mere springtime would not right the balance because cold and wet would not be duly squeezed out in their turn.

In short, this cosmology works with an intuitive idea that derives from the legal and moral sphere. It is the idea that for encroachment and pain inflicted, a compensating pain and encroachment must be performed. The primitive sense of the just—remarkably constant from several ancient cultures to modern intuitions such as those illustrated in our passage from Andrea Dworkin—starts from the notion that a human life (or, here, the life of the cosmos) is a vulnerable thing, a thing that can be invaded, wounded, violated by another's act in many ways. For this penetration, the only remedy that seems appropriate is a counterinvasion, equally deliberate, equally grave. And to right the balance truly, the retribution must be exactly, strictly proportional to the original encroachment. It differs from the original act only in the sequence of time and in the fact that it is response rather than original act—a fact frequently obscured if there is a long sequence of acts and counteracts.

This retributive idea is committed to a certain sort of neglect of the particulars. For Anaximander, it hardly matters whether the snow and rain that get evaporated are in any sense "the same" snow and rain that did the original aggressing. The very question is odd, and Anaximander seems altogether uninterested in the issues of individuation and identity that would enable us to go further with it. Nor are things terribly different in the human legal-moral applications of retributive *dikê*. For very often the original offender is no longer on the scene, or is inaccessible to the victim: And yet the balance still remains to be righted. What then happens is that a substitute target must be found, some member of the offender's family. The crimes of Atreus are avenged against Agamemnon; Agamemnon's offense burdens Orestes. The law that "the doer must suffer" becomes, in this conception of justice as balanced retribution, the law that for every bad doing some surrogate for the doer must suffer: And, like Andrea Dworkin's narrator, the ancient concept of *dikê* can't "tell him from him from him." A male has raped Andrea: Then another male will get a karate kick. The substitution is usually justified through an intuitive notion that the real offender is "the line of X" or "the house of X," or, in Dworkin, "the gender of X." But this alleged justification entails neglect of the particularity of the so-called offender; it neglects, too, questions of motive and intention that one might think crucial in just sentencing.

A closely related sort of neglect can arise even if the original offender is around to receive the punishment. For suppose that the offender committed an act that is in some sense heinous but did so with extenuating circumstances. (Oedipus committed both parricide and incest, but with an excusable ignorance of crucial factual information.) *Dikê* says: There have been parricide and incest here, and things can never be the same. The balance must be righted. The eyes that saw their mother's naked body must be blinded.[14] Now in this case the doer and the sufferer are the same individual. But notice that Oedipus' particularity is still in a significant sense neglected. For he is being treated the same way, by *dikê*, as a true or voluntary parricide would be treated: And crucial facts about *him*, about his good character, innocent motives, fine intentions, are neglected. But to neglect all this is to neglect *him*: substitution again, though of a more subtle sort.

If we start thinking this way, the asymmetry we asked about naturally begins to arise. For looked at in this way, *dikê* is always harsh and unyielding. Sometimes the harshness is merited; sometimes excessive. But it is rarely too soft—for it begins from the assumption that the doer *should* suffer, that any wrong should be "made up" by a penalty that befits a deliberate wrong. The particulars of the case, more closely inspected, lead in the directly of extenuation or mitigation far more frequently than in the opposite direction. If *dikê* has got the right person, well and good; nothing more need be added. If, however, *dikê* has got hold of the wrong person, a more flexible and particularized judgment will let that person off. So too in the Oedipus-type case: For *dike* assumes that Oedipus *is* a parricide; there is nothing more we can find out about him that will aggravate his offense. We can and do, on the other hand, find out that in a most relevant sense he is *not* a parricide because the act he intended and chose was not that act. Once again, the more flexible judgment of *epieikeia* steps in to say, Be gentle with this man, for we cannot assume without looking further that he really did the awful thing for which strict justice holds him responsible. Getting the right life and getting the life right are not two separate issues but two aspects of a single process of appropriate scrutiny.

In effect, the asymmetry arises from the fact that the circumstances of human life throw up many and various obstacles to meeting the tough standards of justice; if we set a high standard of good action, the very course of life will often make it difficult for mere human beings to measure up. To put it another way, the asymmetry arises from a certain view about the common or likely causes of wrongdoing: The asymmetrist claims that a certain number of wrongful acts are fully deliberate wrongs and that a certain number are produced by obstacles such as failure of knowledge, mistaken identification, bad education, or the presence of a competing moral claim. There may be some cases of parricide and incest that are produced by an especially or unusually blameworthy degree of hatred or wickedness, going beyond the responsible deliberateness assumed by the law, but the claim is that this is likely to be a smaller class than the Oedipus-type class, given the character of human life and the nature of human motivation.

The world of strict *dikê* is a harsh and symmetrical world in which order and design are preserved with exceptionless clarity. After summer comes fall, after fall comes winter, after day comes the night, and the fact that Agamemnon was not the killer of Thyestes' children is as irrelevant to *dikê* as the fact that the night did not deliberately aggress against the day; the fact that Oedipus acted in ignorance is as irrelevant to *dikê* as the fact that the winter came in ignorance of its crimes against the summer. It is a world in which gods are at home, and in which mortals often fare badly. As a fragment of Sophocles puts it, "The god before whom you come . . . knows neither equity nor grace (*oute toupieikes oute tên charin*), but only cares for strict and simple justice (*tên haplôs dikên*)."[15] The world of *epieikeia* or equity, by contrast, is a world of imperfect human efforts and complex obstacles to doing well; a world in which humans sometimes deliberately do wrong but sometimes also get tripped up by ignorance, passion, poverty, bad education, circumstantial constraints of various sort; a world in which bad things are sometimes simply bad, sometimes extremely bad—but sometimes, and more often, when one goes into them, somewhat less bad, given the obstacles the person faced on the way to acting properly. *Epieikeia* is a gentle art of particular perception, a temper of mind that refuses to demand retribution without understanding the whole story; it responds to Oedipus' demand to be seen for the person he is.

IV. Equity and Justice: Aristotle

So far we are still dealing with a contrast between the equitable and the just. Justice itself is still understood as strict retribution, and therefore the equitable, insofar as it recognizes features of the particular case that the strict law does not cover, stands in opposition to the just. But justice or *dikê* is by the fifth century a venerated moral norm, associated in general with the idea of giving to each his or her due. We would expect, then, as the conflict between equity and strict retributive justice assumed prominence, an attempt to forge a new conception of justice, one that incorporates the insights of equity. This project was pursued to some extent by Plato, in his late works the *Statesman* and the *Laws*.[16] Even more significant for our purposes, it was pursued, albeit unsystematically, by the Attic orators, in their actual arguments about particular cases in front of citizen juries.[17] But it was Aristotle who made the major contribution.

Aristotle's discussion of the equitable in the *Nicomachean Ethics* occurs within his account of justice. It begins with an apparent dilemma. The *epieikes*, he says, is neither strictly the same as the just nor altogether different in kind (*Nicomachean Ethics* 1137a33–4). On the one hand, it looks as if it would be strange to separate *epieikeia* from justice. For we praise both people and their judgments for the quality of *epieikeia*, recognizing it as a normatively good thing. But in that case, it will be odd if it turns out to be altogether opposed to the just. Then we would either have to say that justice is not a normatively good quality, or withdraw our normative claims for *epieikeia* (1137a34–b8).[18] Aristotle's solution to the dilemma is that equity is a kind of justice, but a kind that is superior to and frequently opposed to another sort, namely, strict legal justice (1137b8–34). It may be regarded as a "correcting" and "completing" of legal justice.[19]

The reason for this opposition, he continues, is that the law must speak in general terms and therefore must err in two ways: both leaving gaps that must be filled up by particular judgments, and sometimes even getting things wrong. Aristotle says that this is not the fault of the lawgiver but in the very nature of human ethical life: The "matter of the practical" can be grasped only crudely by rules given in advance and adequately only by a flexible judgment suited to the complexities of the case. He uses a famous image. The good architect does not measure a complicated structure (e.g., a fluted column) with a straight edge. Or, if he did, he would get a woefully inadequate measurement. Instead, he uses a flexible strip of metal that "bends to the shape of the stone and is not fixed" (1137b30–32). Even so, particular judgments, superior in flexibility to the general dictates of law, bend round to suit the case.[20]

Aristotle ends the discussion with some remarks that seem ill-suited to their context. But by now we should be prepared to understand how they fit in:

> It is also clear from this [sc. account of the equitable] what sort of person the equitable person is. For a person who chooses and does such things, and who is not zealous for strict judgment in the direction of the worse, but is inclined to mitigation, even though he can invoke the law on his side—such a person is equitable, and this trait of character is equity, being a kind of justice and not a distinct trait of character. (1137b34–1138a3)

Here Aristotle alludes to and endorses the tradition that links perception of the particular with mitigation. By now we can see on what grounds he does so. But he makes a new contribution: for he insists that this is the way a truly *just* person is. In keeping with his insistence throughout his ethical and political writings that justice, as a virtue of character, is a peculiarly human virtue, one that gods neither possess nor comprehend,[21] and indeed would think "ridiculous" (*EN* 1178b11), he now gives the just a definition suited to an imperfect human life.

In the *Rhetoric* discussion of *epieikeia*, having given a very similar account of the equitable as that which corrects or supplements—and thereby fulfills— the written law, he adds a somewhat more detailed account of equitable assessment, telling us that the equitable person is characterized by a forgiving attitude to "human things." He uses the word *suggnômê*, "judging with," which typically suggests the idea of forgiveness, in a way that connects it etymologically with the idea of sharing the other person's point of view.[22] He links this ability with particular perception, and both of these with the ability to classify actions in accordance with the agent's motives and intentions (1374b2–10[23]). Elsewhere, Aristotle links *suggnômê* closely with sympathy or compassion (*eleos*), an attitude he defines as requiring the thought that one's own possibilities are in significant ways shared with those of the person one contemplates, and that this person was overwhelmed by obstacles not of his own making.[24]

The logic of these connections seems to be as follows. To perceive the particular really accurately, one must not simply be concerned with retribution.[25] One must, in addition, "judge *with*" the agent who has done the alleged wrong. One must, that is, see things from that person's point of view—for only then will one begin to comprehend what obstacles that person faced as he or she tried to act. In that sense, it takes *suggnômê* to deliver a "correct discrimination" of the equitable. And when one looks at the person's case with *suggnômê*, certain distinctions that do not play a part in the archaic conception of *dikê* assume a remarkable salience. Equity, like the sympathetic spectatorship of the tragic audience, accepts Oedipus' plea that the ignorant and nonvoluntary nature of his act be duly acknowledged; it acknowledges, too, the terrible dilemmas faced by characters such as Agamemnon, Antigone, and Creon, the terrible badness of all their options. Recognizing the burden of these "human things," the equitable judge is inclined not to be "zealous for strict judgment in the direction of the worse" but to prefer merciful mitigation.

I have already illustrated Aristotle's argument by speaking about tragedy and tragic spectatorship. And because I shall go on to develop my own account of the equitable with reference to literature, it seems well worth pointing out that Aristotle's account of *suggnômê* and *epieikeia* in these passages has close links with his theory of tragedy. For in his theory, the spectator forms bonds of both sympathy and identification with the tragic hero.[26] This means that "judging with" is built into the drama itself, into the way in which the form solicits attention. If I see Oedipus as one whom I might be, I will be concerned to understand how and why his predicament came about; I will focus on all those features of motive and agency, those aspects of the unfortunate operations of chance, that I would judge important were I in a similar plight myself. I would ask *how* and *why* all this came about—and ask not from a vantage point of lofty superiority but seeing his tragedy as something "such as might happen" in human life, in my own life.[27] Tragedy is thus a school of equity, and therefore of mercy. If I prove unable to occupy the equitable attitude, I will not even enjoy tragedy: For its proper pleasure requires emotions of pity and fear that only *suggnômê* makes possible.

Aristotle's attitude to law and equity was not simply a theoretical fiction. There is evidence that it both shaped legal practice and, even more clearly, built on an already developed and developing tradition of Athenian legal thought.[28] We have, of course, almost no records of the actual *outcomes* of jury trials, and no record at all of the deliberation of jurors. The process did not encourage lengthy or communal deliberation, as each juror cast a separate vote after hearing the various arguments, apparently without much mutual consultation.[29] We do, however, have many examples of persuasive speeches delivered to such juries. And because the orator's reputation rested on his ability to persuade a jury of average citizens, chosen by lot, we can rely on these speeches for evidence of widespread popular beliefs about legal and ethical concepts. These speeches show the orators relying on a concept of law and even of justice that is very much like the one that Aristotle renders explicit and systematic. Thus litigants frequently call for a justice tailored to the circumstances of their own case, and they frequently use the expression *ta dikaia* ("those things that are just") in that sense.[30] And they often proceed as if the written law is understood to be a set of guidelines with gaps, to be filled in, or corrected, by equity argumentation.[31] In this process, frequent appeal is made to the juror's sense of fairness, as if, once the particular circumstances of the case are understood, they can be expected to see that justice *consists in* an equitable determination.

This is a deep insight, and one that I support. For it seems wrong to make a simple *contrast* between justice and equity,[32] suggesting that we have to choose between the one and the other. Nor, in a deep sense, do we have to choose between equity and the rule of law as understandings of what justice demands. The point of the rule of law is to bring us as close as possible to what equity would discern in a variety of cases, given the dangers of carelessness, bias, and arbitrariness endemic to any totally discretionary procedure. But no such rules can be precise or sensitive enough, and when they have manifestly erred, it is justice itself, not a departure from justice, to use equity's flexible standard.

V. Equity and Mercy: Seneca

We are still not all the way to a doctrine of mercy. For what Aristotle recommends is a precise attention to the circumstance of offense and offender, both in ascertaining whether or not there is any guilt and in assessing the penalty if there is. He is prepared to let people off the hook if it can be shown that their wrongdoing is unintentional, or to judge them more lightly if it is the result of something less than full deliberate badness. But the point of this is to separate out the fully and truly guilty from those who superficially resemble them. In effect, we are given a more precise classification of offenses, a classification that takes intention and motive into account. But once a particular offense is correctly classified, the offender is punished exactly in proportion to the actual offense.

By contrast to the archaic conception of justice, this is indeed merciful, but it does not suffice, I think, for all that we mean by mercy—which seems to involve a gentleness going *beyond* due proportion, even to the deliberate offender. With his emphasis on sympathetic understanding, Aristotle is on his way to this idea. And he insists that the virtuous disposition in the area of retributive anger is best named "gentleness" (using the same word that Gorgias had used in connection with *epieikeia*). He stresses that "the gentle person is not given to retribution [*timôrêtikos*], but is rather inclined to sympathetic understanding [*suggnômonikos*]" (*EN* 1126a2–3). But retribution will still play an important role where the circumstances demand it. For "people who do not get retributively angry[33] at those at whom they should look like fools. . . . For they seem to have no perception and no feeling of pain . . . and to allow oneself and one's loved ones to be kicked around, and overlook it, is slavish" (1126a4–8). The demand to avoid the slavish is certain to play a role in the public world of the law, as well as in the private world of the family. This demand makes Aristotelian *suggnômê* stop short of mercy. For the full development of that idea, we must wait for Roman Stoicism, and for Seneca.[34]

Stoic moral theory accepts and builds on the Aristotelian insight that rules and precepts are useful only as guidelines in both private and public thought. Any fully adequate moral or legal judgment must be built on a full grasp of all the particular circumstances of the situation, including the motives and intentions of the agent. Like Aristotle, Stoics are fond of using an analogy between medicine and ethics to illustrate this point: General ethical or legal rules are about as useful as are medical rules and precepts—which is to say, useful as outlines, but no substitute for a resourceful confrontation with all the circumstances of the case. Both the Greek and the later Roman Stoics stress the fact that an act is a fully correct and moral act, what they call a *katorthôma*, only if it is done with the appropriate motives and the appropriate knowledge; a *kathêkon* or (in Latin) *officium* is an act of (merely) the right general type, without consideration of the agent's thoughts and motivations. Rules can tell you what the *kathêkonta* are, but to get all the way to a full *katorthôma* you need to become a certain sort of person. The same goes in reverse for bad actions. This means that the Aristotelian idea of justice as equity is already built into the moral schema from the beginning; it will automatically influence the classification of offenses in public reasoning and in the law.[35]

The Greek Stoics stop there, and in their moral rigor they explicitly reject any application of *epieikeia* that goes beyond the careful classification of offenses. The soul of the good Stoic judge is a hard soul that protects itself from all impulses that might sway it from the strict path of virtue and duty. "All wise men," they announce, "are harshly rigorous [*austêroi*] ."[36] They "never permit their soul to give way or to be caught by any pleasure or pain."[37] And this hardness cordons them off from any yielding response to the defects of another person. The wise man, they announce, does not forgive those who err, and he never waives the punishment required in the law. An unyielding judge, the Stoic will do exactly what strict justice requires. In this connection, *epieikeia* is explicitly rejected: He will never waive the punishment that is mandated for that particular type of offense.[38]

Many Greek Stoic texts show us this attitude of detachment and hardness to offenders, an attitude far removed from the Aristotelian norm of *suggnômê*. One can see this emerge with particular clarity in the treatment of tragedy, which Stoics are permitted to watch, provided that they watch it from a vantage point of secure critical detachment—like Odysseus, they say, lashed to the mast so that he can hear, but not be swayed by, the sirens' song.[39] From this secure vantage point they view the disasters and vulnerabilities of ordinary mortals with amusement, and even scorn, defining tragedy as what happens "when chance events befall fools."[40] To Oedipus, the wise man says, "'Slave, where are your crowns, where your diadem?'" To Medea, the wise man says, "'Stop wanting your husband, and there is not one of the things you want that will fail to happen.'"[41] There is no inevitability in tragedy: For if one has the proper moral views there is no contingency in the world that can bring one low.[42]

Here Seneca steps in, perceiving a serious tension in the Greek Stoic position. On the one hand, Stoicism is deeply committed to the Aristotelian position that good moral assessment, like good medical assessment, is searchingly particular, devoted to a deep and internal understanding of each concrete case. On the other hand, the Stoic norm of critical detachment withholds psychological understanding, treating deep and complex predicaments as easily avoidable mistakes, simply refusing to see the obstacles to good action from the erring agent's own viewpoint.

Seneca opts for the medical side of this dilemma, offering a complex account of the origins of human wrongdoing that leads to a new view of the proper response to wrongdoing. Seneca begins his argument in *On Anger* as an Aristotelian would, asking the judge to look at all the circumstances of the offense (I.19.5–8). At this point he still seem to be a symmetrist, urging that sometimes a closer look makes the person look better, and sometimes worse. But he then continues his reflections, in the second book, in a manner that makes our asymmetry open up. People who do bad things—even when they act from bad motives—are not, he insists, simply making a foolish and easily corrigible error. They are yielding to pressures that lie very deep in the fabric of human life. Many of these pressures are social. Before a child is capable of the critical exercise of reason, he or she has internalized a socially taught scheme of values that is in many ways diseased, giving rise to diseased passions: the excessive love of money and honor, angers connected with slights to one's honor; excessive attachment to sex, and especially to romanticized conceptions of the sexual act and the sexual partner; anger and violence connected with sexual jealousy; the list goes on and on.[43]

These cultural forces are in error, and in that sense someone who is in their grip is indeed a "fool," as Epictetus holds. But there is not much point in giving a little sermon to Medea as to a docile child; for such errors, taught from an early age, take over the soul, and can be eradicated, if at all, only by a lifetime of zealous and obsessive self-examination. And, furthermore, Seneca suggests that anger and the desire to inflict pain—the worst, in his opinion, of the errors of the soul—are not in any simple way just the result of a corrigible error, even at the social level. He firmly commits himself to the view that they do not result from innate instinct. On the other hand, they "omit no time of life, exempt no race of human beings" (*De Ira* III.22).

In a crucial passage, Seneca says that the wise person is not surprised at the omnipresence of aggression and injustice, "since he has examined thoroughly the circumstances of human life" (*condicio humanae vitae*, II.10). Circumstances, then, and not innate propensities, are at the origins of vice. And when the wise person looks at these circumstances clearly, he finds that they make it extremely difficult not to err. The world into which human beings are born is a rough place, one that confronts them with threats to their safety on every side. If they remain attached to their safety and to the resources that are necessary to protect it—as is natural and rational—that very attachment to the world will almost certainly, in time, lead to competitive or retaliatory aggression. For when goods are in short supply and people are attached to them, they compete for them. Thus aggression and violence grow not so much inside our nature as from an interaction between nature and conditions that is prior to and more deeply rooted than any specific form of society.

Seneca now uses this view as the basis for his argument against retributive anger and in favor of mercy. Given the omnipresence of aggression and wrongdoing, he now argues, if we look at the lives of others with the attitudes typical of the retributive tradition of justice—even in its modified particularistic form— if, that is, we are determined to fix a penalty precisely proportionate to the nature of the particular wrongdoing, then we will never cease to be retributive and to inflict punishment, for everything we see will upset us. But this retributive attitude, even when in some sense justified, is not without its consequences for the human spirit. For a person who notes and reacts to every injustice, and who becomes preoccupied with assigning just punishments, becomes, in the end, oddly similar to the raging ungentle people against whom he reacts. Retributive anger hardens the spirit, turning it against the humanity it sees. And in turning against humanity, in evincing the rage and hardness of the angry, one then becomes perilously close to the callous wrongdoers who arouse rage in the first place. Thus in Seneca's examples we find acts of horrifying vindictivenes and cruelty committed by people whose anger is in the first place justified, according to a precise assessment of the nature of the crime. Sulla's acts of retribution were initially directed against legitimate enemies; they ended in the murder of innocent children (II.34). Caligula was justified in his anger over the imprisonment of his mother, and yet this led him to cruelty and destruction. Cambyses had just cause of battle against the Ethiopians, but in his obsession with revenge he led his men on a fatal campaign that ended in cannibalism (III.20). Andrea Dworkin's heroine would be right at home here, for she reacts in some sense appropriately to real wrongs but becomes in the process an engine of revenge, indifferent to the face of humanity.[44]

Seneca's famous counterproposal, announced at the very end of *On Anger*, is that we should "cultivate humanity" (*colamus humanitatem*, III.43). He elsewhere describes this as the proposal to "give a pardon to the human species" (II.10). It is this attitude that he now calls by the name of mercy—translating Greek *epieikeia* with the Latin word *clementia*. Rejecting the austerity and rigor of the Greek Stoic, he makes a sympathetic participatory attitude central to the norm of good judging. Senecan *clementia* does not fail to pass judgment on wrongdoing; this is continually stressed. Seneca does not hold that the circumstances of human life remove moral and legal responsibility for bad acts. We may still convict defendants who fulfill some basic conditions of rationality in action. But, looking at the circumstances of human life, one comes to understand how such things have happened.[45] And this "medical" understanding leads to mercy.

Clementia, mercy, is even defined in a manner that makes its difference from Greek Stoic harshness evident: For it is an "inclination of the soul to mildness in exacting penalties," and also "that which turns its course away this side of that which could be justly determined" (*Clem.* II.3). The Greek Stoic soul, by contrast, never bends aside, never inclines away from hardness. The somewhat more gentle Aristotelian soul does bend, but inconstantly, conscious always that it is slavish to allow oneself and one's loved ones to be kicked around. Given that Seneca defines mercy as the opposite of cruelty, and given that cruelty is held to be a frequent outgrowth of retributive anger, we can say, putting all this together, that mercy, *clementia*, is opposed at one and the same time both to strictness in exacting penalties and also to retributive anger, as if that strictness does indeed lie very close to anger in the heart. As Seneca says, "It is a fault to punish a fault in full" (*culpa est totam persequi culpam*, *Clem.* II.7, fragment).[46]

One might, of course, adopt this attitude as a practical strategy to keep the self pure from anger, without endorsing it as *just* or *correct* toward the offender. Seneca sometimes appears to oscillate between these two positions, because he can commend the practical strategy even to those who do not accept his position about correctness. But in the end his position clearly is that it is right and correct to assign punishments in accordance with mercy, both because of what it means for oneself and because of what it says about and to the offender.

The merciful attitude, as Seneca develops it, entails regarding each particular case as a complex narrative of human effort in a world full of obstacles. The merciful judge will not fail to judge the guilt of the offender, but she will also see the many obstacles this offender faced on the way to being just—as a member of a culture, a gender, a city or country, and, above all, as a member of the human species, facing the obstacles characteristic of human life in a world of scarcity and accident. The starting point is a general view of human life and its difficulties, but the search for mitigating factors must at every point be searchingly particular. The narrative/medical attitude asks the judge to imagine what it was like to have been that particular offender, facing those particular obstacles with the resources of that history. Seneca's bet is that once one performs this imaginative exercise one will cease to have the strict retributive attitude to the punishment of the offender. One will be inclined, in fact, to gentleness and the waiving of the strict punishment mandated in the law. And the punishments that one does assign will be chosen, on the whole, not for their retributive function but for their power to improve the life of the defendant.[47]

This merciful attitude requires, and rests on, a new attitude to the self. The retributive attitude has a we/them mentality, in which judges set themselves against offenders, looking at their actions as if from a lofty height and preparing to find satisfaction in their pain. The good Senecan judge, by contrast, has both identification and sympathetic understanding. Accordingly, a central element in Seneca's prescription for the judge is that he should remind himself at every turn that he himself is capable of the failings he reproves in others. "If we want to be fair judges of all things, let us persuade ourselves of this first: that none of us is without fault. For it is from this point above all that retributive anger arises: 'I did nothing wrong,' and 'I did nothing.' No, rather, you don't admit to anything" (II.28).

This part of Seneca's argument reaches its conclusion in a remarkable passage in which Seneca confronts himself with the attitude of merciful judgment that he also recommends, describing his own daily practice of self-examination in forensic language that links it to his public recommendations:

> A person will cease from retributive anger and be more moderate if he knows that every day he has to come before himself as judge. What therefore is more wonderful than this habit of unfolding the entire day? How fine is the sleep that follows this acknowledgment of oneself, how serene, how deep and free, when the mind has been either praised or admonished, and as its own hidden investigator and assessor has gained knowledge of its own character? I avail myself of this power, and plead my cause daily before myself. When the light has been removed from sight, and my wife, long since aware of this habit of mine, has fallen silent, I examine my entire day and measure my deeds and words. I hide nothing from myself, I pass over nothing. For why should I fear anything from my own errors, when I can say, "See that you don't do that again, this time I pardon you." (III.36)

Seeing the complexity and fallibility of his own acts, seeing those acts as the product of a complex web of highly particular connections among original impulses, the circumstances of life, and the complicated psychological reactions life elicits from the mind, he learns to view others, too, as people whose errors emerge from a complex narrative history. Seneca's claim is that he will then moderate his retributive zeal toward the punishment of their injustices and intensify his commitment to mutual aid.

This part of Seneca's work seems very private. But there is no doubt that the primary aim of this work, and of the later De Clementia as well, is the amelioration of public life and public judgment. The De Ira was written at the start of the reign of the emperor Claudius. It responds to a well-known speech by Claudius on the subject of anger and irascibility and obviously contains advice for the new regime.[48] Moreover, its explicit addressee and interlocutor is Novatus, Seneca's own brother, an aspiring orator and public man. Thus its entire argumentative structure is built around the idea of showing a public judge that the retributive attitude is unsuitable for good judging. As for the De Clementia, its explicit addressee is none other than the new emperor Nero Caesar himself, and its explicit task is to persuade this young man to use his immense power in merciful, rather than retributive, ways. The private material provides the basis for a new sort of public and judicial life.

VI. Mercy and the Literary Imagination

But instead of pursuing this history further, I want now to suggest some implications of these ideas for contemporary political and legal issues. First I shall develop a general thesis; then I shall apply it to some particular questions. The general thesis concerns the connection between the merciful attitude and the literary imagination. The Greco-Roman tradition already made a close connection between equity and narrative. The person who "reads" a complex case in the manner of the reader of a narrative or the spectator at a drama is put in contact—by the structure of the forms themselves, as they solicit the reader's or spectator's attention—with two features of the equitable: its attentiveness to particularity and its capacity for sympathetic understanding. But this means that the spectator or reader, if he or she reads well, is already prepared for equity and, in turn, for mercy.

I could illustrate these points about the relationship between form and content in many ways. Instead I want to choose just two examples, which show with particular clarity the connection between mercy and the art of the novelist. For the novel has been in recent times an especially vigorous popular literary form. And it goes beyond tragic drama in its formal commitment to following complex life histories, looking at the minute details of motive and intention and their social formation—all that Seneca would have the good judge examine. This means that the novel, even more than tragic drama, is an artificial construction of mercy.

My first example is from Charles Dickens's *David Copperfield*.[49] James Steerforth, we know, is a bad person, one who deserves blame for some very serious bad actions. He humiliates the kind teacher, Mr. Mell; he uses his charm to get power over those younger and weaker than himself; he uses his wealth to escape discipline and criticism. And, above all, he destroys the life of Em'ly, who falls in love with him—betraying, in the process, both David's trusting friendship and the simple kindness of the Peggotty family. These bad actions are seen and judged by Agnes Wickfield in the straightforward way characteristic of the strict moral code that is her guide in life. A reader of religious books rather than of novels and stories, Agnes has no interest in the psychology of Steerforth's acts, or in seeing them from his point of view. She simply judges him, and judges him harshly, calling him David's "bad angel," and urging David (even before the serious crime) to have no further association with him. (It is a subtle point in the novel that moralism here allies itself with and provides a screen for the operations of jealousy: For Agnes resents the romantic hold that Steerforth has over David and uses her moral condemnation to get revenge.) David's view is more complex.

The novel—a novel represented as written by David some years after the event, during a tranquil marriage to Agnes—does present its reader with Agnes's moral judgment of Steerforth and the reasons for that judgment. The reader is led, at times—even as David shows himself being led—into the strict moral point of view, and is inclined at such times to judge Steerforth harshly. But these times are moments within the novel; they are not the overall attitude with which the novel leaves us. David tells and shows the reader that the novelist's imagination is of a certain sort—very different, in fact, from the moral imagination of Agnes. And this imagination leads to a different way of judging.

The central characteristic of the narrative imagination, as David depicts it, is that it preserves as a legacy from childhood an ability to attend closely to the particulars and to respond to them in a close and accurate manner. Like our ancient tradition, David immediately goes on to link this "power of observation" with gentleness: Adults who retain it retain also "a certain freshness, and gentleness, and capacity of being pleased, which are also an inheritance they have preserved from their childhood (61)."[50] The nature of the connection is apparent in the manner in which the character David sees Steerforth, and in which the mature novelist David depicts him for the reader's imagination.[51] For, as I say, we do become aware of Steerforth's crimes. But we see them as episodes in the life of an extremely complicated character, who has enormous ability, awesome powers of attraction, great kindness and beneficence to his friends—and an extremely unfortunate family history. We do judge Steerforth's arrogance, duplicity, and self-destructiveness. But we know also, as readers of the novel, that he grew up with no father to guide him, and with the misguided and uncritical affection of a willful and doting mother who indulged his every whim. We know, too, that his position and wealth compounded this ill fortune, exempting him for too long from the necessity to discipline his character and to cooperate with others. We are led to see his crimes as deliberate in the immediate sense required by strict legal and even moral judgment, but we also know that behind these crimes is a tangled history that might have been otherwise, a history that was not fully chosen by Steerforth himself. We imagine that with a different childhood Steerforth might have made an altogether different use of his abilities—might have had, in short, a different character. Like Seneca's reader, we are led to see character itself as something formed in society and in the family, something for which strict morality rightly holds individuals responsible, but something over which, in the end, individuals do not have full control.[52]

The result of all this is mercy. Just before Steerforth leaves to run off with Em'ly—in, then, the last conversation he has with David—we have the following exchange:

"Daisy, if anything should ever separate us, you must think of me at my best, old boy. Come! Let us make that bargain. Think of me at my best, if circumstances should ever part us!"

"You have no best to me, Steerforth," said I, "and no worst. You are always equally loved, and cherished in my heart." (497)

David keeps the bargain, loving Steerforth with the unconditional attention and concern of his narratorial heart. When, years later, the tempest washes Steerforth's body ashore and he recognizes it, David exclaims:

"No need, O Steerforth, to have said, when we last spoke together, in that hour which I so little deemed to be our parting-hour—no need to have said, "Think of me at my best!" I had done that ever; and could I change now, looking on this sight!" (866)

Just as the character David suspends punitive judgment on Steerforth's acts, so the imagination of the narrator—and of the reader—is led to turn aside, substituting for punishment an understanding of Steerforth's life story. David makes it very clear that the activity of novel writing causes him to relive this moment of mercy,[53] and that its "freshness and gentleness" can be expected to be, as well, its reader's experience. In this sense the novel is about itself, and the characteristic moral stance of its own production and reception. That stance is the stance of equity, and of mercy.

My second example is contemporary. In 1992, the novelist Joyce Carol Oates visited my seminar at Brown to speak about the moral and political dimensions of her fiction. As we discussed her recent novel *Because It Is Bitter and Because It Is My Heart*, a student, silent until then, burst in with a heated denunciation of Oates's character Leslie, a well-meaning but ineffectual liberal photographer. Isn't his life a complete failure really? Isn't he contemptible for his inability to *do* anything significant out of his antiracist intentions? Isn't he to be blamed for not more successfully combatting racism, in his family and in his society? Oates was silent for a time, her eyes peering up from behind her round glasses. Then she answered slowly, in her high, clear girlish voice. "That's not the way I see it, really." She then went on to narrate the story of Leslie's life, the efforts he had made, the formidable social and psychological obstacles in the way of his achieving more, politically, than he had—speaking of him as of a friend whose life inhabited her own imagination and whom, on that account, she could not altogether dismiss or condemn. Here, I believe, was mercy; and, lying very close to it, the root of the novelist's art. The novel's structure is a structure of *suggnômê*—of the penetration of the life of another into one's own imagination and heart. It is a form of imaginative and emotional receptivity, in which the reader, following the author's lead, comes to be inhabited by the tangled complexities and struggles of other concrete lives.[54] Novels do not withhold all moral judgment, and they contain villains as well as heroes. But for any character with whom the form invites our participatory identification, the motives for mercy are engendered in the structure of literary perception itself.

VII. Mercy and Legal Thought

Now to contemporary implications.

Until now, I have been talking about a moral ideal, which has evident implications for publicly promulgated norms of human behavior, and for public conduct in areas in which there is latitude for judicial discretion. I have suggested that in many ways this norm fulfills and completes a conception of justice which lies, itself, at the basis of the rule of law: For it was to prevent incomplete, defective, and biased discretionary reasoning that the rule of law was introduced and defended. But at this point and for this reason caution is in order; for the moral ideal should not be too simply converted into a norm for a legal system. First of all, a legal system has to look out for the likelihood that the moral ideal will not always be perfectly realized, and it should protect against abuses that moral arbitrariness and bias can engender. This suggests a large role for codified requirements in areas in which one cannot guarantee that the equity ideal will be well implemented; the equity tradition supports this. Second, a system of law must look to social consequences as well as to the just judgment on particular offenders; thus it may need to balance an interest in the deterrent role of punishments against the equity tradition's interest in punishments that suit the agent. Both the balance between codification and discretion and the balance between equity and deterrence are enormously complex matters, with which my analysis here cannot fully grapple. What I do wish to offer here are some representative suggestions of what the equity tradition has to offer us, as we think about these issues.

A Model of Judicial Reasoning

In other recent work,[55] I have been developing the idea that legal, and especially judicial, reasoning can be modeled on the reasoning of the concerned reader of a novel.[56] Following in some respects the lead of Adam Smith, in *The Theory of Moral Sentiments*,[57] I argue that the experience of the concerned reader is an artificial construction of ideal moral and judicial spectatorship, with respect both to particularity of attention and to the sort and range of emotions that will and will not be felt. Identifying with a wide range of characters from different social circumstances, and concerning oneself in each case with the entire complex history of their efforts, the reader comes to have emotions both sympathetic and participatory toward the things that they do and suffer. These emotions will be based on a highly particularized perception of the character's situation. On the other hand, because the reader is not herself a character in the story, except in the Henry Jamesian sense of being a "participator by a fond attention,"[58] she will lack emotions relating to her own concrete placement in the situation with regard to which she is asked to judge; her judgments will thus, I argue, be both sympathetically emotional and, in the most appropriate sense, neutral.

My current inquiry into mercy takes the model one step further, where judgment on the wrongdoing of others is concerned, going, with this step, beyond Smith's rather austere construction of emotional spectatorship. For it construes the participatory emotion of the literary imagination as emotion that will frequently lead to mercy, even when a judgment of culpability has been made. And this merciful attitude derives directly, we can now see, from the literary mind's keen interest in all the particulars, a fact not much stressed by Smith in his account of the literary (perhaps because he focuses on classical drama, in which the concrete circumstances of daily life are not always so clearly in view). My literary judge sees defendants as inhabitants of a complex web of circumstances, circumstances which often, in their totality, justify mitigation of blame and/or punishment.[59]

This attitude on the part of my ideal judge is unashamedly mentalistic. It does not hesitate to use, and to use centrally, the notions of intention, choice, reflection, deliberation, and character that are part of a nonreductive intentionalist psychology. Like the novel, it treats the inner world of the defendant as a deep and complex place, and it instructs the judge to investigate that depth. This approach is opposed, in spirit if not always in outcome, to an approach to the offender articulated in some well-known writings of Justice Holmes and recently further developed by Richard Posner.[60] According to this approach, the offender should be treated as a thing with no insides to be scrutinized from the internal viewpoint—but simply as a machine, whose likely behavior, as a result of a given judgment or punishment, we attempt, as judges, to predict.[61] The sole proper concern of punishment becomes deterrence; as law becomes more sophisticated, and our predictive ability improves, states of mind play a smaller and smaller role in judgment.

Holmes's defense of this idea takes an interesting form, from our point of view. For it begins from an extremely perceptive description and criticism of the retributive idea of judgment and punishment.[62] His own deterrence-based view is advanced as an alternative—he seems to think it the only plausible one—to retributivism; and much of the argument's force comes from the connection of the positive recommendation with the effective negative critique. The trouble begins when he conflates the retributive idea with the idea of looking to the wrongdoer's state of mind, implying that an interest in the "insides" invariably brings retributivism with it.[63] As we have seen, matters are far more complicated, both historically and philosophically. It is, I think, in order to extricate judging from the retributive view—felt by Holmes, rightly, to be based on metaphysical and religious notions of balance and proportion and to be an outgrowth of passions that we should not encourage in society[64]—that he feels himself bound to oppose all mentalistic and intention-based notions of punishing. In "The Common Law," Holmes argues that so far from considering "the condition of a man's heart or conscience" in making a judgment, we should focus on external standards that are altogether independent of motive and intention. And here he insists on the very sort of strict assessment, without mitigation, that the entire mercy tradition opposes:

> [The external standards] do not merely require that every man should get as near as he can to the best conduct possible for him. They require him at his own peril to come up to a certain height. They take no account of incapacities, unless the weakness is so marked as to fall into well-known exceptions, such as infancy or madness. They assume that every man is as able as every other to behave as they command. If they fall on any one class harder than on another, it is on the weakest. (253)

But from our viewpoint, this dichotomy between intentionalism and retributivism leaves out the real opponent of retributivism, both historical and philosophical—simply putting in its place a strict external assessment that looks suspiciously like the old Anaximandrean *dikê* in modern secular dress, despite its evident differences.

Posner follows Holmes's view in most essential respects, developing it in much more detail, with appeal to modern behaviorist theories of mind. Like Holmes, Posner is motivated above all by the wish to describe an alternative to retributivism, which he criticizes eloquently, with appeal to both history and literature.[65] His argument is highly complex and cannot even be accurately summarized, much less appropriately criticized, in the space available here. What is most important for our purposes is that Posner makes explicit the fact that his behaviorist view of the criminal law requires rejecting—for legal purposes—the Kantian idea that people are to be treated as ends rather than means. It requires, in fact, treating them as objects that, through their behavior, generate either good or bad social consequences. This, we can easily see, is profoundly opposed to the stance of the literary judge, who may differ from some Kantians in her focus on particular circumstances but who certainly makes the Kantian insight about human beings central to her entire project. Posner also makes it clear that the case for his account of the external standards to be applied stands or falls with the case for behaviorism (perhaps eliminative materialism as well?) as an adequate and reasonably complete theory of human behavior. Because I think it is fair to say that the best current work in the philosophy of mind and in cognitive psychology—like the best work on mind in classical antiquity—finds serious flaws in the behaviorist and reductionist views, this explicitness in Posner makes the vulnerable point in the Holmes/Posner argument especially plain. On the other hand, unlike Holmes, Posner does not seem to claim that the behaviorist view is the only available alternative to retributivist views of punishment. He shows an awareness, in fact, of the mercy tradition—strikingly enough, not in the chapter dealing with the criminal law but in his chapter dealing with "Literary and Feminist Perspectives."[66] He shows some sympathy with this tradition, arguing that what the law should really seek is an appropriate balance between strict legal justice and a flexible and merciful discretion.[67] He is, however, pessimistic about the role that latitude for mercy is likely to play in actual cases, holding that a discretionary approach on the part of judges will frequently be harsher to defendants—especially minority defendants—than will an approach based on strict rules.[68] This is a valuable insight, and I shall return to it shortly. But first I must conclude the story, where Holmes is concerned.

Holmes's "The Common Law" was written in 1881, "The Path of the Law" (where Holmes argues for a related view[69]) in 1897. It is worthy of note that toward the end of his life, in a remarkable letter, Holmes appears to endorse the mercy tradition—as a result of his reading of Roman philosophy. Writing on March 28, 1924, to his friend Harold Laski,[70] Holmes begins by speaking of the large impression made on him by Seneca's "cosmopolitan humanity"; he suggests (correctly) that this notion came to Christianity from Roman philosophy, rather than vice versa. He confirms the impression by reading Plutarch, in order to get the Greek perspective. After making an obligatory shocking remark—that "the literature of the past is a bore"—he vigorously praises Tacitus. Then, appended to the account of his Roman reading, comes the arresting insight: "Before I leave you for the day and drop the subject let me repeat if I have said it before that I think the biggest thing in antiquity is 'Father forgive them—they know not what they do.' There is the modern transcending of a moral judgment in the most dramatic of settings. . . ."

It is not terribly clear to what extent Holmes means to connect this remark about Jesus with his observations concerning the debt owed by Christianity to Roman thought. My argument has shown that he certainly could do so, with justice. Nor is it clear how, or whether, he would apply his insight to concrete issues in the law. What is clear is that by this time in his life Holmes has recognized that the transcendence of strict moralism that he has recommended throughout his career need not be captured through a reliance on external behavioral standards. It seems to him to be most appropriately captured in the "dramatic setting" in which Jesus takes up, toward his enemies, the attitude of Senecan mercy.[71] I think that he is right.[72]

In short, to depart from a retributivism that is brutal in its neglect of human complexity, we do not need to embrace a deterrence-only view that treats people as means to society's ends, aggregating their good and ill without regard to what is appropriate for each. The deterrence view is all too close to the retributive view it opposes[73] in its resolute refusal to examine the particularities of motive, intention, and story; in its treatment of people as place holders in a larger social or cosmic calculus. A merciful judge need not neglect issues of deterrence, but she is above all committed to an empathetic scrutiny of the "insides" of the individual life.

Mercy and the Criminal Law

The implications of the mercy tradition for issues in the criminal law are many and complex. The criminal law has long had a profound commitment to Aristotelianism—that is, to the proposition that we should in most cases take cognizance of the accused person's motives and intentions in determining guilt or innocence and in fixing the level of wrongdoing. This Aristotelian tradition treats people as, on the whole, the authors of their own characters. Thus a genuinely angry person will be able to claim "reasonable provocation," and thus get a reduction, for example, from first-degree murder to manslaughter, only if he or she can show that the anger that produced the crime was that of a "reasonable person." As one Pennsylvania court expressed this idea, when confronted with a defendant who made a plea of unusual irascibility, "Suppose then we admit testimony that the defendant is quick-tempered, violent and revengeful; what then? Are these an excuse for, or do they even mitigate crime? Certainly not, for they result from a want of self-discipline; a neglect of self-culture that is inexcusable."[74] This demand for appropriate "self-culture" leads, in general, to the rejection of pleas for mitigation or exculpation when the defendant acted out of motives that are not thought to be part of a good character. Thus racial hatred, however deeply and sincerely felt, will not be regarded as mitigating a crime and may even appropriately be regarded as an aggravating feature.[75]

Is the law, then, Aristotelian rather than Senecan? Once bad character is on the scene, is there no room for mercy? What does it say where we have reason to believe, with Seneca, that people form their characters in circumstances that may deform their aspirations? Consider Bigger Thomas, the hero of Richard Wright's novel *Native Son*, an impoverished and undereducated African American who eventually commits two violent criminal acts, at least one of which (the killing of his lover Bessie) is clearly a murder. Throughout the novel, Wright prevents us from having easy sympathy for Bigger by showing him as someone whose emotions are deformed and inappropriate. At the same time, Wright makes us feel discomfort with our urge to condemn Bigger by showing us in detail how his character and emotions have been shaped by both poverty and racism, how shame at the color of his skin, fear of the dominant white community, and rage at his unequal and immobilized situation all interact in the daily events of Bigger's life. We are led to think that he did not have the degree of control over his character development that we usually do, given the extremely closed and unequal situation in which he lives. If we look at his crime as Aristotle recommends, we will find him guilty and refuse to ask further questions. But Seneca, like the novelist's vision, prompts a deeper inquiry; admitting his culpability, we are urged to see with sympathy the road that led him to become a person of this sort.

In fact, the criminal law is Senecan as well as Aristotelian. In determining an offender's guilt or innocence and the grade of her offense, the law evaluates her actions, including her motives and character; at this point the law is usually unconcerned with how the defendant came to be the way she is. But during the sentencing process the law has traditionally permitted the story of the defendant's character formation to come before the judge or jury, in all its narrative complexity, in such a way as to manifest any factors that might, once presented, give rise to sympathetic assessment and to a merciful mitigation of punishment. Indeed, a long tradition has held that we owe it to the dignity and humanity of the defendant to make this individualized inquiry. This tradition was well articulated in a 1976 capital-sentencing case:

> A process that accords no significance to relevant facets of the character and record of the individual offender or the circumstances of the particular offense excludes from consideration in fixing the ultimate punishment of death the possibility of compassionate or mitigating factors stemming from the diverse frailties of humankind. It treats all persons convicted of a designated offense not as uniquely individual human beings, but as members of a faceless, undifferentiated mass to be subjected to the blind infliction of the penalty of death.[76]

Woodson does not explicitly say that the tradition is asymmetrical, as in Seneca. But we can see that it is by focusing on a pair of more recent cases involving the death penalty, which raise issues of mitigation and aggravation in connection with discretionary sentencing. One is *Walton v. Arizona*[77]; the other is *California v. Brown*.[78] At stake are the role to be played by discretion in deciding capital cases and the criteria to be used in analyzing the aggravating and mitigating features of the case. Walton was convicted by a jury of first-degree murder and sentenced to death by the judge, in accordance with an Arizona statute that requires the judge first to ascertain whether at least one aggravating circumstances is present—in this case two were found[79]—and then to consider all the alleged mitigating circumstances advanced by the defendant, imposing a death sentence if he finds "no mitigating circumstances sufficiently substantial to call for mercy." The defendant is required to establish a mitigating circumstance by the preponderance of the evidence—and it was this that was the central issue in Walton's appeal. Because previous Supreme Court decisions had rejected a requirement of unanimity for mitigation,[80] Walton contended that the preponderance of the evidence test was also unconstitutional. His claim was rejected by a plurality of the court. My concern is not so much with the result as with some interesting issues that emerge from the opinions.

First, it is plain that the Arizona system, which the decision in effect upholds, establishes a lexical ordering in which a finding of aggravation—which must be based on criteria explicitly enumerated in the law—is used to classify an offense as a potential death-penalty offense; mitigation is then considered afterwards, in a discretionary manner. In other words, the whole range of potentially mitigating circumstances will be brought forward only when it has already been established that an offense falls into a certain class of extremely serious offenses. And discretionary concern for the entirety of the defendant's history will enter the picture only in the mitigation phase. Justice Stevens comments on this feature in his dissenting opinion, arguing that once the scope of capital punishment is so reduced, the risk of arbitrariness in sentencing is sufficiently reduced as well to permit very broad discretion and individuated decision making with the remaining class. This seems to be a correct and valuable observation. Indeed, the mercy tradition stresses that merciful judgment can be given only when there is time to learn the whole history of the life in question, with great complexity, and also inclination to do so in a sympathetic manner, without biases of class or race. The tradition wholeheartedly endorses decision making by codified requirement when these requirements cannot be met. (Here Posner's warnings about arbitrariness in equity seem perfectly appropriate, and they are reflected in the move away from unguided discretion represented by the Federal Sentencing Guidelines.[81]) We should not, however, say, as Stevens seems to, that the main function of such criteria is to reduce the *number* of cases that are eligible for the death penalty. What they do is, of course, more substantial: They eliminate from the death-eligible group many cases for which death would *clearly* not be an *appropriate* penalty, leaving the judge free to turn his or her attention to those that are more problematic, requiring a more fine-tuned deliberation.[82]

A second significant feature, and a more problematic one, is the plurality's unquestioning acceptance of the preponderance of the evidence test—which, as Allen has shown here and elsewhere, has grave defects when we are dealing with a case having multiple relevant features.[83] For suppose a defendant advances three grounds for mitigation, each of which is established to a .25 probability, and therefore to be thrown out under Arizona's rule. The probability that at least one of the factors is true, assuming they are independent,[84] is, as Allen shows, .58. If each of three factors is proved to a probability of .4, the probability that at least one is true is .78. On the other hand, if the defendant proves just one of the mitigating factors with a probability of .51 and the others with probability

0, he is successful, even though the probability that the decision is correct is in fact lower here than in the previous cases. And so forth.[85] The law asks the judge to treat each feature one by one, in total isolation from any other. But human lives, as the literary judge would see, consist of complex webs of circumstances, which must be considered as a whole.

This same problem is present in Justice Scalia's scathing attack on the whole notion of mitigation. For Scalia thinks it absurd that we should have codified criteria for aggravation, apply these, *and then* look with unguided discretion to see whether a mitigating factor is present. If the criteria for aggravation are enumerated in the law, so too should be the criteria for mitigation. Only this explicitness and this symmetry can prevent total irrationality. Scalia here ignores the possibility—which Stevens recognizes—that the functions of aggravation criteria and of mitigation are not parallel: Aggravation places the offense in the class to which mitigation is relevant.[86] And, furthermore, in ridiculing the entire notion of discretionary mercy, Scalia adamantly refuses the forms of perception that we have associated with the literary attitude. That is, he treats mitigating factors as isolated units, unconnected either to one another or to the whole of a life. It is in this way that he can arrive at the conclusion that unbridled discretion will (absurdly) be permitted to treat traits that are polar opposites as, both of them, mitigating; for example, "that the defendant had a poor and deprived childhood, or that he had a rich and spoiled childhood."[87] His assumption is that both of these cannot be mitigating, and that it is a sign of the absurdity of the current state of things that they might both be so treated. But the alleged absurdity arises only because he has severed these traits from the web of circumstances in which they actually figure. In connection with other circumstances, either a trait or its opposite might, in fact, be mitigating.[88] This, in Allen's argument and in mine, is the reason why categories for mitigation should not be codified in advance, for it will be impossible for such a code to anticipate adequately the countless ways in which factors interweave and bear on one another in human reality. Telling the whole story, with all the particulars,[89] is the only way to get at that.[90]

In reality, of course, the mercy tradition has serious reservations about the whole idea of capital punishment. Although some of its major exponents, including Seneca, endorsed it, they did so on the basis of very peculiar arguments comparing it to euthanasia (see n. 47). If we reject these arguments, we are left, I think, with no support for capital punishment from within that tradition and strong reasons to reject retributivist justifications. Indeed, the tradition strongly suggests that such punishments are always cruel and excessive. The question would then have to be whether the deterrence value of such punishments by itself justifies their perpetuation, despite their moral inappropriateness, and the deterrence-based argument has never been made out in a fully compelling way.

California v. Brown raises a different issue: the issue of jury instruction, where emotion is concerned.[91] The Court reviewed a state jury instruction stipulating that the jury in a capital case (in the sentencing phase) "must not be swayed by mere sentiment, conjecture, sympathy, passion, prejudice, public opinion or public feeling." From the point of view of our account of literary judging, this instruction is a peculiar and inappropriate mixture. For the juror as "judicious spectator" and merciful reader would indeed disregard conjecture, prejudice, public opinion, and public feeling. On the other hand, sentiment, passion, and sympathy would be a prominent part of the appropriate (*and* rational) deliberative process, where those sentiments are based in the juror's "reading" of the defendant's history, as presented in the evidence. It would of course be right to leave aside any sentiment having to do with one's own involvement in the outcome—but we assume that nobody with a personal interest in the outcome would end up on the jury in any case. It would also be correct to leave aside any mere gut reaction to the defendant's appearance, demeanor, or clothing—anything that could not be made a part of the "story" one tells about the case, giving reasons. But the vast majority of the passional reactions of a juror hearing a case of this kind will be based on the story that is told: In this sense, the law gives extremely bad advice.[92] The Court, however, approved the instruction, concluding that "A reasonable juror would . . . understand the instruction . . . as a directive to ignore only the sort of sympathy that would be totally divorced from the evidence adduced during the penalty phase."[93] On the one hand, this seems to me a perfectly reasonable way of articulating the boundaries of appropriate and inappropriate sympathy. On the other hand, the likelihood is so high that the sentiments of the juror would be of the appropriate, rather than the inappropriate, sort—for what else but the story told them do they have to consider?—that approving the regulation creates a misleading impression that some large and rather dangerous class of passions is being excluded.[94] The other opinions in the case confirm the general impression of confusion about and suspicion of the passions. Thus Justice O'Connor argues that "the sentence imposed at the penalty stage should reflect a reasoned *moral* response to the defendant's background, character, and crime rather than mere sympathy or emotion." She goes on to state that "the individualized assessment of the appropriateness of the death penalty is a moral inquiry into the culpability of the defendant, and not an emotional response to the mitigating evidence."[95] This contrast between morality and sympathy is a nest of confusions, as our argument by now should have shown. Justice Brennan, too, holds that "mere sympathy" must be left to one side—though he does hold (dissenting) that the instruction prohibits the juror from considering exactly what it should consider, and although he does demonstrate with a wealth of examples that the instruction has been frequently abused by prosecutors, who convince juries that they should disregard all sympathy.[96] Justice Blackmun does somewhat better with the concepts, defending the juror's ability to respond with mercy as "a particularly valuable aspect of the capital sentencing procedure." But he, too, contrasts rationality with mercy, even in the process of defending the latter: "While the sentencer's decision to accord life to a defendant at times might be a rational or moral one, it also may arise from the defendant's appeal to the sentencer's sympathy or mercy, human qualities that are undeniably emotional in nature."[97] The confusion persists: In a more recent case, the Court now speaks even more suspiciously and pejoratively of the juror's emotions, contrasting them with the "actual evidence regarding the crime and the defendant"[98]—as if these were not the source of and basis for these emotions.

In short, the insights of the mercy tradition can take us a long way in understanding what is well and not well done in recent Supreme Court writings about sentencing. It can help us to defend the asymmetry between mitigation and aggravation that prevailed in *Walton*, as well as *Walton's* moderate defense of discretion. But it leads to severe criticism of the categories of analysis deployed in the juror-instruction cases, which employ defective conceptions of the rational.

It is important, however, to notice that, even in the midst of conceptual confusion, the Court is unhesitatingly Senecan about the penalty phase. All the opinions in *California v. Brown* agree that we owe it to the defendant to hear the whole story and to look for mitigating factors; they disagree only about whether the instruction, as written, is likely to mislead.

Legal mercy is not and should not be the same as mercy in the moral life. According to Seneca, if we look hard enough at any case of individual wrongdoing we are likely to discover factors that lead to mercy. His plausible view about the causes of human error makes it likely that we will find ignorance, or bad cultural and parental influence, or some type of suffering and deprivation, behind any bad act. But in the law we set the penalties for bad acts in a way that presupposes a norm of "self-culture" and a sense of what conditions normally enable the requisite amount of self-culture. (If we are Senecan about the normal case, this will give us reasons to resist extremely harsh penalties generally, or to favor those that are likely to reform and educate.) What we are looking for in the penalty phase, then, is the atypical case—the person who, like Bigger Thomas, has suffered an unusual degree of either cultural or personal deprivation and whose process of character formation therefore seems unusually deformed. In giving mercy to such a defendant we recognize that all citizens in our society do not have equal opportunities to become good; to see this is to see something true about our world, and to acknowledge incentives to change it.

It has recently been argued that those who admit the narrative voice of the defendant in a criminal trial must, in all consistency, admit the narrative voice of the victim, in the form of a "victim impact" statement.[99] Is this true? The claim is that if the defendant has a chance to bid for the sympathy of the judge or jury, the victim should have an equal chance—and the victim is often no longer around to tell his or her own story. It is simply arbitrary politics to admit the one story and to exclude the other.

This argument is not convincing. A criminal trial is about the defendant and the crime he or she has committed. The question before the court is what the defendant did; the function of narrative is to illuminate the character and origins of that deed. What has to be decided is not what to do about the victim but what to do about the defendant. Everything about the victim that is relevant to the crime is already included in the evidence—including not only the immediate impact of the defendant's actions on the victim but also such further consequences as whether the victim ultimately died. For this we do not need a victim impact statement. Furthermore, in the penalty phase of a trial the sentencing guidelines direct the judge's or jury's attention to certain further facts about the victim. In sentencing a defendant convicted of blackmail, for example, the judge is instructed by the Federal Sentencing Guidelines to consider whether he or she preyed on an "unusually vulnerable victim."[100] This seems relevant to assessing the defendant's crime because it sheds light on the level of malice involved in the crime. But why should we go beyond this? There is no requirement that narratives be symmetrical in the sense that Gewirtz suggests because a criminal trial is not symmetrical: It is focused from the start on the fate of the defendant.[101]

What more might we hope to gain from the victim impact statement? Such statements typically shed light on the upstanding nature of the victim, and they elicit sympathy in ways closely related to the victim's social class and character, treating the well-placed and the homeless or outcast victim differently. They also focus on the pain and suffering of children or relatives—thus skewing the process in favor of people who happen to have families and against those who are alone. In both of these ways the process treats victims unequally, in a manner that is repugnant to our democratic traditions, according to which the rich and the poor, the married and the unmarried, the well housed and the homeless, should stand as equals before the law. Nor is it fair that a defendant should fare worse because he happens to kill a rich person: Such bias is endemic in criminal trials anyway, and it should be the business of the legal system to counteract it, not to magnify it.

Susan Bandes has raised a further issue in her excellent article, "Empathy, Narrative, and Victim Impact Statements." In the penalty phase of a criminal trial, it is usually difficult for the judge or jury to have sympathetic understanding of the defendant, who has not only been convicted of a serious offense but is likely to be from a different socioeconomic milieu from that of the jurors. By contrast, "the feeling of identification with the victim of a crime often comes naturally," because most people readily fear being in similar circumstances.[102] The introduction of victim impact statements does not simply add one more voice, thus completing the jury's understanding. More often, it provides a distraction from the difficult task of understanding the defendant, diverting the jury into a perspective on the events that is much easier for them to assume and that may block their attempt to understand the defendant. As Bandes concludes, "It is the defendant who is at a disadvantage, and who needs rules and structures to enable the jury to make the empathetic connection with him" (403). I conclude, with Bandes, that we should admit all evidence about the victim that is relevant to establishing what happened and what the defendant did—and then no more. In the penalty phase, the jury or judge should turn to the difficult task of understanding the character of the criminal, because the penalty phase is about his fate. The additional information imported by victim impact statements seems to function primarily by giving vent to the passion for revenge against such offenders, and it is this passion that, as I have argued, the criminal justice system should seek to counteract.

Feminist Political Thought

It is now time to return to Andrea Dworkin, and to feminism. Dworkin's novel *Mercy* has been in the background throughout this chapter, providing us with a striking modern example of the strict retributivist position, and showing us how the retributive imagination is opposed to the literary imagination. But Dworkin's book is, after all, called a novel. And so one might well wonder how I can so easily say that the novel as form is a construction of mercy.

The problem is only apparent. For Andrea Dworkin's "novel" is formally not a novel but an antinovel. By the author's deliberate design, it does not invite its reader to occupy the positions of its characters, seeing their motivations with sympathy and with concern for the entire web of circumstances out of which their actions grew. It does not invite its reader to be emotionally receptive. In the case of its central figure it does do this to a limited degree. But this figure is such a solipsistic self-absorbed persona that to identify with her is to enter a sealed world of a peculiar sort, a world in and from which the actions of others appeal only as external movement, without discernible motive. And as for the men who people the novel, the reader is enjoined to view them as the narrator views them—as machines that produce pain. We are forbidden to have an interest in their character, origins, motives, points of view. We are forbidden all sympathy and even all curiosity. We are refused perception of the particular—for, as in the male pornography that Dworkin's activism opposes,[103] her male characters are not particulars but generic objects. In effect, we are refused novelistic readership.

Indeed, the very form of Dworkin's work causes us, as readers, to inhabit the retributive frame of mind and to refuse mercy. The inclination to mercy is present in the text only as a fool's inclination toward collaboration and slavery. When the narrator, entering her new profession as a karate-killer of homeless men, enunciates "the political principle which went as follows: It is very important for women to kill men,"[104] a voice within the text suggests the explanations that might lead to mercy. As the return of the narrator quickly makes clear, this is meant to be a parody voice, a fool's voice, the voice of a collaborator with the enemy:

> He didn't mean it; or he didn't do it, not really, or not fully, or not knowing, or not intending; he didn't understand; or he couldn't help it; or he won't again; certainly he will try not to; unless; well; he just can't help it; be patient; he needs help; sympathy; over time. Yes, her ass is grass but you can't expect miracles, it takes time, she wasn't perfect either you know; he needs time, education, help, support; yeah, she's dead meat; but you can't expect someone to change right away, overnight, besides she wasn't perfect, was she, he needs time, help, support, education; well, yeah, he was out of control; listen, she's lucky it wasn't worse, I'm not covering it up or saying what he did was right, but she's not perfect, believe me, and he had a terrible mother; yeah, I know, you had to scrape her off the ground; but you know, she wasn't perfect either, he's got a problem; he's human, he's got a problem. (329)

The only alternative to the retributive attitude, Dworkin implies, is an attitude of foolish and hideous capitulation. According to Dworkin, the style of perception characteristic of the novel is in league with evil.

There are some reasons to think this a psychologically accurate portrayal of the ways in which women who are repeatedly brutalized by men lose the ability to see particularity and to give and receive love; as the novel's amorphous sentences show, they may even lose the ability to grasp causal connections and temporal sequence.[105] Read in that way, the novel would be profoundly tragic, for it would tell us that there are things that happen to people that do in fact destroy the world.[106] But it remains unclear whether this is the spirit in which the novel is written. Its double ending, in which Andrea both immolates herself and dedicates herself to revenge on homeless men, does not clarify the stance of the authorial presence, and a plausible reading of the text as it stands is that the projects of revenge are endorsed as an appropriate, rather than a tragic, response to the evils that Andrea has suffered. Probably it is supposed to be both, and the tragedy lies in the fact that women are in a position where only the retributive response is appropriate, if one does not commit suicide. But such a despairing depiction of our situation obscures prospects of progress and reconciliation that we need to be able to contemplate if we are to take political action to right these wrongs.

Because the emotional and political stance of the novel as a whole remains so unclear, the novel seems to me not entirely successful. And yet it is in another way an important book—for it brings to the surface for scrutiny the strict retributive attitude that animates some portions of our moral and legal tradition and allows us to see this attitude as a reasonable response to terrible wrongs. Dworkin is correct in stressing the pervasiveness of male violence against women, and correct, too, in insisting that to deny and conceal these wrongs is to condemn women of the present and future to continued bodily and psychological suffering. She is correct in protesting loudly against these wrongs and in refusing to say that they are not wrongs. The only remedy, Dworkin (or at least her heroine) suggests (if one does not commit suicide), is to refuse all sympathy and all particular perception, moving over to a conception of justice so resolute in its denial of particularity that it resembles Anaximandrean *dikê* more than it resembles most modern retributive schemes. The narrator announces, "None of them's innocent and who cares? I fucking don't care." And it is Dworkin's position, repeatedly announced in the novel as in her essays, that the social norms of the American heterosexual male are in some ways those of a rapist, and that, to the extent that society endorses these norms, rape is not abnormal but "normal" heterosexual intercourse. This does not mean that there are no individual exceptions, but it does mean that the norm itself is guilty *and* that it is appropriate to act politically against that generalized target. In this sense, there really is no difference between him and him, and to refuse to see this is to collaborate with evil.

But Dworkin is wrong. Retributivism is not the only alternative to cowardly denial and capitulation.[107] Seneca's *On Anger* is hardly a work that denies evil where it exists: Indeed, it is a work almost as relentlessly obsessed with narrating tales of evil as is Dworkin's work. Like Dworkin's work, it insists on the pervasiveness of evil, the enormous difficulty of eradicating it, the necessity of bringing it to judgment. Mercy is not acquittal. In what, then, does its great difference from Dworkin's work consist? In two things, I think. First of all, it does not exempt itself. It takes the Dworkin parody line, "She wasn't perfect either," very seriously, urging that all human beings are the products of social and natural conditions that are, in certain ways, subversive of justice and love, that need slow, patient resistance. And this interest in self-scrutiny already gives it a certain gentleness, forces it out of the we/them mentality characteristic of retributivism. Second, it is really interested in the obstacles to goodness that Dworkin's narrator mocks and dismisses—the social obstacles, deeply internalized, that cannot be changed in an instant, the other more circumstantial and particular obstacles that stand between individuals and justice to those they love. It judges these social forces and commits itself to changing them, but, when judgment on the individual is concerned, it yields in mercy before the difficulty of life. And if you really open your imagination and heart to admit the life story of someone else, it becomes far more difficult to finish that person off with a karate kick. In short, the text constructs a reader who, while judging justly, remains capable of love.

Feminist thought should retain those complex capacities: It should not ignore the evidence, or fail to say that injustice is injustice, evil evil[108]—but, drawing on the resources of the novelist's art, it should remain capable of *suggnômê* and therefore of *clementia*.

Toward the end of his address to Nero Caesar, Seneca asks the young man a pointed question: "What . . . would living be if lions and bears held the power, if serpents and all the most destructive animals were given power over us?" (*Clem.* I.26.3) These serpents, lions, and bears, as Seneca well knows, inhabit our souls—in the form of our jealous angers, our competitiveness, our retributive harshness.[109] These animals are as they are because they are incapable of receiving another creature's life story into their imagination and responding to that history with gentleness. But those serpents, lions, and bears in the mind still play a part today, almost two thousand years after Seneca's treatise was written, in determining the shape of our legal institutions—as the merciful attitude to punishment still comes in for ridicule, as the notion of deliberation based on sentiment still gets repudiated and misunderstood, as a simple form of retributivism has an increasing influence on our legal and political life. With Seneca, I argue that we should oppose the ascendancy of these more obtuse animals[110]—and, while judging the wrong to be wrong, still cultivate the perceptions and capacities of mercy.

7

A DEFENSE OF LESBIAN
AND GAY RIGHTS

Now in my own cases when I catch a guy like that I just pick
him up and take him into the woods and beat him until he can't
crawl. I have had seventeen cases like that in the last couple
of years. I tell that guy if I catch him doing that again I will
take him out to the woods and I will shoot him. I tell him that
I carry a second gun on me just in case I find guys like him
and that I will plant it in his hand and say that he tried to kill
me and that no jury will convict me.
                    —Police officer in a large industrial city
            in the United States, being interviewed about his
        treatment of homosexuals (Westley, "Violence and the
                    Police," quoted in G. D. Comstock,
                Violence against Lesbians and Gay Men)

I. The "Death of Dialogue"?

In 1960, E. M. Forster wrote a Terminal Note to his novel *Maurice*, written in
1913, to explain why the novel still could not be published. The reason, he
said, was the happiness of its central characters: "If it ended unhappily, with a
lad dangling from a noose or with a suicide pact, all would be well, for there is
no pornography or seduction of minors. But the lovers get away unpunished
and consequently recommend crime."[1] American society in the 1990s, much
like Forster's Britain in 1960, appears willing to tolerate, somewhat grudgingly,
the existence of lesbians and gay men—provided that it does not have to put
up with their happiness, that is (as a minimum necessary condition), their enjoyment of full equality in all the major areas of life that are affected by law
and public policy. As long as various burdens of discrimination can be imposed
upon them, reminding them that they are not to demand the happy endings
reserved for heterosexuals in film and story, thus far their presence can be
countenanced. So burdened, they do not constitute an advertisement for their
form of life.

But the time has now come when the question of fully equal rights for lesbians and gay men can no longer be avoided. In 1996, an overwhelming majority
in both houses of Congress voted to support the Defense of Marriage Act, a law

that defines marriage as a relationship between a man and a woman. (This law is intended to facilitate other states' denial of recognition to same-sex marriages contracted in Hawaii) The very title of the law, together with the rhetoric that surrounded it, suggested that equal marriage rights for same-sex couples pose a dire threat to cherished American ways of life.

But 1996 also saw a near majority in the Senate voting to support a law forbidding discrimination in the workplace on grounds of sexual orientation. And it also saw *Romer v. Evans*, a landmark Supreme Court decision striking down Colorado's Amendment 2, a law passed by referendum that forbade local communities and state agencies to enact nondiscrimination laws protecting the rights of gays, lesbians, and bisexuals.[2] Justice Kennedy's majority opinion concluded that this law was unacceptable in the light of our constitutional commitment to giving all citizens the equal protection of the laws. "It is not within our constitutional traditions to enact laws of this sort. . . . A law declaring that in general it shall be more difficult for one group of citizens than for all others to seek aid from the government is itself a denial of equal protection of the laws in the most literal sense" (1628).

American society, in short, is both confused and deeply divided about what its traditions support, and about whether the guidance of tradition is, in any case, good guidance. In his dissenting opinion in *Romer*, Justice Scalia sarcastically states that support for lesbian and gay civil rights derives from "the views and values of the lawyer class from which the Court's Members are drawn" (1636). But in fact people at all levels of American society are debating these issues—in families, in churches, in local civic groups, in government agencies, and, yes, in universities. All major religious denominations in the United States contain intense controversy about sexual orientation; there is none in which the position Justice Scalia ascribes to "the lawyer class" does not find at least some strong support. It seems important, then, to keep setting out the arguments on both sides of the issue as clearly as possible, in such a way that citizens from a wide variety of starting points may be able to reach a consensus—if not about all concrete conclusions, at least about what the issues are and about which solutions are unacceptable in the light of our commitment to values of equal liberty and equality.

Rational argument on this issue will not resolve all controversy because it is very likely that the resistance to full equality for gays has deep psychological roots. Fear of the erosion of traditional distinctions and boundaries, fear of a type of female sexuality that is unavailable to men, fear of a type of male sexuality that is receptive rather than assertive—all these probably play a role in making the current debate as ugly and irrational as it is. In such a situation, as John Stuart Mill observed, discussing arguments about women's equality, clarity of argument frequently serves only to intensify the force of opposition:

> So long as an opinion is strongly rooted in the feelings, it gains rather than loses in stability by having a preponderating weight of argument against it. . . . [T]he worse it fares in argumentative contest, the more persuaded its adherents are that their feeling must have some deeper ground, which

the arguments do not reach; and while the feeling remains, it is always throwing up fresh intrenchments of argument to repair any breach made in the old.[3]

Much of the congressional debate on the Defense of Marriage Act conformed to Mill's description. The possibility of irrational opposition to a new movement for social equality did not, however, cause Mill to conclude that reason is irrelevant to the resolution of public controversies about sexuality. To expose the irrational for what it is, in the process engaging constructively with the plausible and rational arguments that have been made on both sides of a divisive issue, could, he concluded, still play a valuable public role. It can play the same role today. If we conclude that reason is no use when fear, disgust, and hatred are so prominently calling the tune, we cede the debate to those forces. Instead, we may hope to show that these passions are grounded in appraisals that cannot be rationally defended—and this may cause them to lose their hold on the minds of many people of goodwill. As Roman Catholic theologian John Courtney Murray famously wrote, "Civility dies with the death of dialogue." In a political climate already far too uncivil, we should attempt to preserve and expand the areas within which reasoned dialogue is possible.

Whose rights are we talking about, then, when we talk about "lesbian and gay rights?" And what are the rights in question? First, I take on the surprisingly difficult task of identifying the people. Next, I discuss a number of the most important rights that are at issue, including (1) the right to be protected against violence and, in general, the right to the equal protection of the law; (2) the right to have consensual adult sexual relations without criminal penalty; (3) the right to nondiscrimination in housing, employment, and education; (4) the right to military service; (5) the right to marriage and/or its legal benefits; and (6) the right to retain custody of children and/or to adopt.

II. Whose Rights?

This is no easy question. Legal and political disputes sometimes speak of "gays and lesbians," sometimes of "gays" only, sometimes of "gays, lesbians, and bisexuals." Moreover, there are two different ways of defining these groups, each of which contains an internal plurality of frequently conflicting definitions. One broad class focuses on *conduct*, one on *orientation*.

Conduct first. Frequently, at least in American law, gay and lesbian people are taken to be all and only those people who commit "sodomy." Sodomy is usually defined today as a sex act in which the genital organs of one partner make contact with the mouth or anus of the other. (Earlier, this was not the case. Fellatio is a relatively late addition to U.S. sodomy law and has never been considered "sodomy" in England: An 1885 statute criminalizing "gross indecency" between men was added to cover it. Female-female sex acts have never been illegal in Britain.[4]) However, this definition is both overinclusive and underinclusive: underinclusive because many gay males and lesbians have sex but do not commit these acts, especially in the age of AIDS; overinclusive because these acts are extremely common in male-female relations as well. The famous U.S. case *Bowers v. Hardwick*,[5] in which the Supreme Court upheld the constitutionality of a Georgia sodomy law, originally included a heterosexual couple as plaintiffs alongside Hardwick, because the Georgia law as written plainly covered them. (Their case was dismissed for lack of standing; they were said to be in no danger of prosecution.) At one point, too, Hardwick's lawyers moved to disqualify any member of the Georgia attorney general's office who had ever committed sodomy. Had the motion succeeded, we could have expected a large number of heterosexual disqualifications. (More than 70% of Americans, both male and female, have engaged in heterosexual oral sex during their lifetime; approximately one fourth have engaged in heterosexual anal sex.[6]

More promising, then, would be a definition in terms of the biological sex of the actors: Gays and lesbians are all and only those people who commit sex acts with partners of the same biological sex. Once again, however, there are problems: (1) What acts? and (2) How many such acts? Some accounts limit the acts to acts actually terminating in orgasm for one or both parties; some instead include all acts *intended* to induce orgasm in one or both parties (an elusive concept). But given the frequent lack of access to evidence about orgasmic reality or intent, the zeal of the American prosecutorial mind has found other more sweeping categorizations. Thus, the old U.S. Army regulation under which Sgt. Perry Watkins, described by his commanding officer as "one of our most respected and trusted soldiers," was ejected from the military referred to "bodily conduct between persons of the same sex, actively undertaken or passively permitted, with the intent to obtain or give sexual gratification." The act alleged in Watkins's discharge proceedings was described as "squeezing the knee of another male soldier." (All through his army career, as well as before it, Watkins publicly declared his sexual identity and practices, but his own evidence was considered insufficient because he was suspected of trying to avoid military service.)[7] The new U.S. military policy goes still further, defining "homosexual conduct" as "a homosexual act, a statement that the member is homosexual or bisexual, or a marriage or attempted marriage to someone of the same gender"; hand holding and kissing "in most circumstances" are explicitly mentioned as examples of "homosexual acts"—though it was determined that a person may visit a gay bar, march in a gay pride rally in civilian clothes, or list a person of the same sex as an insurance beneficiary without thereby committing a homosexual act.[8]

Frequently the law has considered the definition in terms of acts unsatisfactory—both because of the evident problem of vagueness and, more significantly, because many people who commit the prohibited acts are not the people against whom policy is really being directed. The U.S. Army, for example, is well aware that many soldiers engage in same-sex sexual acts. (Watkins points out that he never had to approach anyone for sex: Once his reputation was established, all kinds of men who would never have called themselves "gay" came to him for oral sex.[9]) So the old policy, while specifying "homosexual act" in the loose way I have described, actually made the basis for discharge "homosexual orientation" rather than homosexual acts, used acts only as evidence of orientation, and defined "orientation" in terms of the "desire" for any of the large menu of acts.

(A still larger menu of evidentiary acts is used by the U.S. Department of Defense: In a recent case membership in a gay organization was sufficient to brand one a "homosexual."[10])

Because such an account might prove overinclusive—presumably the men who repeatedly asked Watkins for sex desired what they got—Army policy allows that a soldier who has committed a homosexual act may escape discharge if he can show that the conduct was "a departure from the soldier's usual and customary behavior" that "is unlikely to recur because it is shown, for example, that the act occurred because of immaturity, intoxication, coercion, or a desire to avoid military service." Another section adds "curiousity" [sic] to the list of extenuating motives. The regulation expressly states that "[t]he intent of this policy is to permit retention *only* of *nonhomosexual* soldiers who, because of extenuating circumstances, engaged in, attempted to engage in, or solicited a homosexual act."[11] Still, there are problem cases. Think what the Army would say about one lover of Watkins, who, asked why he had sex with Watkins every day, replied, "Well, I like a good blow job, and the women downtown don't know how to suck dick worth a damn. But this man happens to suck mine better than anyone I have ever found in the world."[12] We shall never know the Army's verdict, because Watkins did not name names. But the odds are that this man, who considered himself "straight," would be retained by some reading of the rules. (Curiosity, as Aristotle informs us, is a regular self-renewing part of our human equipment.)

Finally, in the course of arguing a recent case in which the plaintiff had admitted only to homosexual orientation and had never been known to engage in sexual acts of any kind, the Department of Defense argued that the crucial defining chracteristic was a "desire" to commit the forbidden acts, and that a crucial distinction should be drawn between "attraction" and "desire." A person might be "attracted" to members of the same sex and yet not "desire" to engage in homosexual conduct; such persons were described by Counsel for the Secretary of Defense as "celibate homosexuals." As Judge Abner Mikva points out in his opinion, there is no known case in which a service member seeking to remain in the military has invoked "this purported defense," nor was the distinction between "attraction" and "desire" explained in any of the directives.[13]

We might suppose that we are dealing here with the stuff of high comedy, or even farce. Such definitions, however, determine the course of many lives, not only in the military, and they create an atmosphere within which the violence endemic to American life can very easily direct itself against these people— whoever, more precisely, they are. (Nor is this just the line-drawing problem the law typically has with most offenses: For here, the problem of definition is caused by a desire to exempt people who commit identical acts but are viewed as desirable for other reasons.)

Can we ourselves define the category in a useful way? Any good definition should recognize that sexual orientation is itself multiple and complex. The types of sexual actors recognized, and the basis for the assignment of individuals to types, has varied greatly in history. The biological sex of the partner may be just one part of what an individual desires in a partner. In many cultures, both historical and modern, biological sex is traditionally considered less salient than sexual role (e.g., the active or the passive).[14] At the same time, few real people would be willing to make love with any willing member of a given sex. Most people's "orientation" has other desiderata, often inscrutable and complex: persons of a certain ethnic type, or a certain level of intelligence, or a certain way of laughing, or a certain resemblance to a parent. In many individuals and cultures, such desiderata are at least as revealing and interesting as biological sex. American culture's focus on the sex of the partners seems no more timeless than its equally obsessive focus on their race. (In the case of both homosexuality and miscegenation, it has been similarly argued that "nature" forbids the unions in question.[15]) However, to be crudely practical, let us define gays, lesbians, and bisexuals, the class of persons with a "homosexual or bisexual orientation" (now the most common formulation in nondiscrimination law), as those who stably and characteristically desire to engage in sexual conduct with a member or members of the same sex (whether or not they also desire sexual conduct with the opposite sex) and let us adopt a difficult-to-ascertain but not impossibly broad definition of same-sex conduct, namely, that it is bodily conduct intended to lead to orgasm on the part of one or both parties. Notice, then, that we are talking about the rights both of people who frequently perform these acts and also of those who desire to but do not. "Stably and characteristically" is tricky still, but perhaps we can live with it, knowing that it excludes a person who experimented a few times in adolescence, or who has not desired such conduct for a good many years. On the other hand, it includes people who regularly have sex with partners of both sexes, the so-called bisexuals. This definition clearly includes all the people against whom the Army policies are directed. Does it also include Watkins's friend, whom the Army would probably wish to retain? I think it should—he had regular access to women but still repeatedly chose Watkins; on the other hand, notice that his desire, completely impersonal and self-referential, had little to do with Watkins's sex—so he is in that way different from a person who has an actual *preference* for a partner of a certain sex. (It seems a bit odd for the Army to prefer him to Watkins, if indeed it would, just on the grounds of the total nonselectivity of his desire.)

This definition, though it seems the best available at present, does not make a great deal of progress beyond the confused and confusing accounts now being used by the military. It embodies no real understanding of individual people, and, like most definitions in areas of intimate expression, it cuts things up in far too crude a way. It does give us a general starting point to explore the social issues. But when we notice how crude even a relatively careful definition is, and how little real understanding—historical, cultural, and personal—it encompasses, we have strong reasons to refrain from using such categorizations to interfere with people's lives, or to inflict legal and civic disadvantages on them.

Why are lesbians and gay men as they are? (This question is rarely asked about heterosexuals, because that way of being is assumed to be neutral and natural.[16]) Few questions in this area are more hotly disputed. There is considerable evidence in favor of some kind of biological explanation for sexual preference, though there are serious flaws with all the research done until now.[17]

But one thing that seems clear is that sexual orientation, if not innate, is formed very early in life, certainly before the age of ten, and after that time proves highly resistant to change, despite all the countless therapies that have been devised to change it. (It may, of course, not be exclusive, and, especially in these cases, it may alter with stage of life.) Another thing that is becoming increasingly clear from empirical research is that a child's sexual orientation is not a function of that of its parents or guardians.[18]

III. What Rights?

The Right to be Protected against Violence

Gays, lesbians, and bisexuals are targets of violence in America. 24% of gay men and 10% of lesbians, in a recent survey, reported some form of criminal assault because of their sexual orientation during the past year (as compared to general-population assault rates in a comparable urban area of 4% for women and 6% for men). [All data here and to follow are from Gary David Comstock's valuable book, *Violence against Lesbians and Gay Men*.] A Massachusetts study found that 21% of lesbian and gay students, compared to 5% of the entire student body, report having been physically attacked. An average of five recent U.S. non-college surveys on anti-gay/lesbian violence show that 33% of those surveyed had been chased or followed; 23% had had objects thrown at them; 18% had been punched, hit, kicked or beaten; 16% had been victims of vandalism or arson; 7% had been spat on; and 7% had been assaulted with a weapon.[19] To live as a gay or lesbian in America is thus to live with fear. As one might expect, such violence is not unknown in the military. Most famous, but not unique, was the 1992 death of navy radioman Allen Schindler at the hands of three of his shipmates who, unprovoked, stalked and then fatally beat him—and later blamed their crime on the presence of gays in the military.

Who are the perpetrators? They are more likely than average assault perpetrators are to be strangers to their victims. 94% of them are male (as compared with 87% for comparable crimes of violence); 46% are under twenty-two years of age (as compared with 29% for comparable crimes); 67% are white. They do not typically exhibit what are customarily thought of as criminal attitudes. "Many conform to or are models of middle-class respectability" (91–2). The arresting officer in a Toronto incident in which five youths beat a forty-year-old gay man to death remarked, "If you went to [a shopping mall] and picked up any group of young males about the same age as these boys— that is what they were like. Average" (93). The data suggest that gay beatings, including the most lethal, are often in essence "recreational": groups of adolescent men, bored and intoxicated, seek out gays not so much because they have a deep-seated hatred of them as because they recognize that this is a group society has agreed to dislike and not to protect fully (94). A California perpetrator of multiple anti-gay beatings, interviewed by Comstock, cited as reasons for his acts boredom, the desire for adventure, a belief in the wrongness of homosexuality, and, finally, attraction to the men he and his friends attacked.

He told Comstock that they "were probably attacking something within ourselves" (171–2).

Physical assaults are crimes as defined by the laws of every state in the United States. In that sense, the right to be protected against them is a right that gays and lesbians have already. But there is ample evidence that the police often fail to uphold these rights. They may indeed actively perpetrate violence against gays, in unduly violent behavior during vice arrests, and so on. Such violence is illegal if it exceeds the requirements of arrest, but it is widely practiced. Even more common is the failure of police to come promptly to the aid of gays and lesbians who are being assaulted. A Canadian study finds that in 56% of cases in which gays sought police protection, the behavior of the responding officers was "markedly unsatisfactory" (151–62).

In numerous U.S. jurisdictions, moreover, killers of gays have successfully pled "reasonable provocation," alleging that the revulsion occasioned by a (noncoercive and nonviolent) homosexual advance, or even by witnessing gay sexual acts, justified a homicidal response; there is no corresponding tradition of a "heterosexual advance" defense. In a 1990 Pennsylvania case[20] in which a drifter shot two lesbians whom he saw making love in the woods, fatally wounding one of them, the court refused to allow the defendant to introduce evidence of "reasonable provocation," saying that the law "does not recognize homosexual activity between two persons as legal provocation sufficient to reduce an unlawful killing . . . from murder to voluntary manslaughter." Invoking the traditional standard of the "reasonable man," the court concluded that "[a] reasonable person would simply have discontinued his observation and left the scene; he would not kill the lovers" (1363–5).

In many such cases, however, a provocation defense is permitted, and the most deliberate killing is determined to be only voluntary manslaughter.[21] David Thacker met Douglas Koehler in a bar and invited him to his apartment. There Koehler allegedly attempted to kiss Thacker, who became enraged and insisted that Koehler leave. Later in the evening, still angry, Thacker recruited his roommate to help him track Koehler down. When they found him, Thacker shot Koehler in the face, killing him. Prosecutors permitted Thacker to plead guilty to manslaughter, and the judge sentenced him to a mere six years. Explaining the lenient sentence, the judge stated that the unusual circumstances of the killing made it a "one-time tragedy" and that he was "confident Mr. Thacker would not kill again."[22] In a 1988 Texas case in which a man was convicted of brutally killing two homosexuals, Judge Jack Hampton issued a thirty-year sentence instead of the life sentence requested by the prosecution. He commented: "[I] put prostitutes and gays at about the same level . . . [and] I'd be hard put to give somebody life for killing a prostitute."[23] In a California case in which a homosexual-advance defense was accepted and the jury returned a manslaughter verdict, Superior Court Judge Daniel Weinstein commented that the victim "'contributed in large part to his own death' by his 'reprehensible conduct.'"[24]

There is a good case for linking rights involving protection against violence to others as yet not universally recognized. As long as no laws protect gays against discrimination in other areas of life and guarantee their equal citizenship, as long as their sex acts can be criminalized, as long they are displayed as second-class citizens, they are natural targets of violence for those in search of "recreational" violence, even when the crimes are not specifically prompted by hatred. We may expect the rights they do have to go on being underenforced and violence against them to remain a common fact. In 1987, after Daniel Wan was brutally beaten outside a gay bar by men who called him "faggot," Circuit Judge Daniel Futch jokingly asked the prosecutor, "That's a crime now, to beat up a homosexual?" The prosecutor replied, "Yes sir. And it's a crime to kill them." To that, the judge commented, "Times really have changed."[25] They have not changed enough.

My discussion of violence has not addressed the emotional harm done to lesbians and gay men by the perception that they are hated and despised. Emotional damage can be as dangerous, ultimately, as physical violence: Gay and lesbian youth are a group at high risk for suicide, two to three times more likely to commit suicide than other young people. They may comprise 30% of youth suicides annually.[26] Studies of this problem attribute the high suicide rate to conflicts with their families and to the "outcast" status of lesbian and gay youth in the school culture. If these teenagers remain closeted, they face enormous internal psychological pressure. If they are open about their sexual orientation, they "can expect harassment and abuse in junior high and high schools."[27] Teachers and other school officials all too frequently fail to protect these students from harassment, and sometimes abet it by taunting and ridiculing gay teenagers.[28]

Some influential conservative thinkers encourage this conduct: Roger Scruton, for example, recently argued that schools should teach revulsion toward homosexuality, on the ground that the perpetuation of this revulsion is "a human good."[29] This argument is astonishing. Given the overwhelming evidence that sexual orientation is formed very early in life, Scruton cannot mean that this teaching will produce more heterosexuals. Teaching children to be revolted by homosexuality is teaching them to feel disgust for themselves or for their gay and lesbian peers. Such teaching causes untold misery and pain. How does such teaching contribute to "the human good"? It would seem best to teach all children to respect themselves and one another as human beings, regardless of the traits with which they happen to be born. Then we will be far more likely to produce a society capable of cooperative engagement for the sake of the "human good."

This issue too can be addressed by law and public policy. By enacting nondiscrimination laws (such as the law recently enacted in Massachusetts, which forbids discrimination against lesbian and gay students in the school system[30]) we can at least alter the behavior that causes these harms. Perhaps eventually the perception that gay and lesbian youth are respected as equals by the legal system may begin to alter the attitudes themselves. Hatred and disgust for groups are not innate and immutable parts of the personality. They have their basis in the images and language we use, the ways we learn to see others—as helpful, as a threat, as perverted or diseased. Both by shaping norms of behavior and by shaping attitudes and images more directly, law can address the very roots of discrimination.[31]

The Right to Have Consensual Adult Sexual Relations
without Criminal Penalty

Consensual sexual relations between adult males were decriminalized in Britain in 1967. In the United States, six states criminalize only same-sex sodomy;[32] seventeen states plus the District of Columbia criminalize sodomy (usually now understood to include both anal-genital and oral-genital intercourse) for all.[33] In addition, California restricts sodomy within state prisons; Florida has a vague statute referring to "any unnatural and lascivious act with another person"— and then goes on to clarify that "a mother's breast feeding of her baby does not violate this section"; South Carolina's statute mentions only "buggery," thus apparently including both heterosexual and male-male anal sex but exempting lesbian acts. Five state sodomy laws have recently been judicially repealed, as has a Massachusetts law prohibiting "unnatural and lascivious act[s]." (But Massachusetts retains its law prohibiting "crime against nature.") These laws are rarely enforced, but such enforcement as there is is highly selective, usually against same-sex conduct, and usually for conduct in a semipublic location, such as a rest room. Penalties are not negligible: The maximum penalty for consensual sodomy in Georgia is twenty years' imprisonment.

Although sodomy laws are, as I have argued, both under- and overinclusive for same-sex conduct, it is frequently assumed that sodomy defines gay or lesbian sexual life. Thus, the laws, in addition to their use in targeting the consensual activities of actual sodomites, can also be used to discriminate against gay and lesbian individuals who have never been shown to engage in the practices in question—as when Robin Shahar lost her job in the office of Georgia Attorney General Michael J. Bowers for announcing a lesbian marriage. It was claimed that she could not be a reliable enforcer of the state's sodomy statute.[34] (All heterosexual intercourse outside marriage is criminal "fornication" in Georgia, and yet there is no evidence that Bowers ever denied employment to heterosexual violators of either that law or the sodomy law.)

The case against sodomy laws is strong. Rarity of enforcement creates a problem of arbitrary and selective police behavior. This problem was conspicuous, for example, in the famous case of Michael Hardwick, who was arrested in his own home, which the police officer had entered using a warrant that had expired three weeks previously and that probably resulted from harassment in the first place: Hardwick worked in a gay bar, and a police officer, driving by, arrested him for "drinking in public" when he saw Hardwick throw a beer bottle in a trash can near the back door of the bar.[35] Although neither all nor only homosexuals are sodomites, the laws are overwhelmingly used to target them, and the fact that some of their acts remain criminal is closely connected with the perception that they are acceptable targets of violence, and with other social exclusions as well. For example, "[t]here is . . . a natural reluctance . . . to appoint to judicial positions people who have committed hundreds or even thousands of criminal acts"[36]—unjustified as this reluctance may be, and also arbitrary, given that the judiciary is no doubt full of heterosexual perpetrators of sodomy and criminal fornication.[37]

Most important, such adult consensual sexual activity does no harm. There is thus no public benefit to offset the evident burdens these laws impose. As Judge Posner concludes, such laws "express an irrational fear and loathing of a group that has been subjected to discrimination."[38] We have no need of such laws in a country all too full of incitements to violence.

The Right to Be Free from Discrimination in Housing, Employment, and Education

Gays, lesbians, and bisexuals suffer discrimination in housing and employment. Many U.S. states and local communities have responded to this situation by adopting nondiscrimination laws. (Such laws have for some time been in effect in some European countries and in some Australian states.) Recently in the United States, efforts have also been made to prevent local communities from so legislating, through referenda amending the state's constitution to forbid the passage of such a local law. The most famous example is that of Amendment 2 in Colorado, which nullified antidiscrimination laws in three cities in the state and prevented the passage of any new ones. I believe that there is no good argument against such nondiscrimination laws, and there are many reasons to believe them important sources of protection. (The repeated suggestion that such protection against discrimination would lead to quotas for this group and would therefore injure the prospects of other minorities was especially invidious and misleading; none of the local ordinances had even suggested quota policies.)

The state's principal argument in defense of Amendment 2 was that it does nothing more than to put lesbians and gay men in the same position as all other citizens and therefore does nothing more than to deny them "special rights." This argument was rejected by the U.S. Supreme Court in *Romer v. Evans*. Amendment 2, the Court concluded, puts homosexuals in "a solitary class with respect to transactions and relations in both the private and the governmental spheres. The amendment withdraws from homosexuals, but no others, specific legal protection from the injuries caused by discrimination, and it forbids reinstatement of these laws and policies."[39] The areas of life affected by Amendment 2, the Court observed, include public accommodations, housing, sales of real estate, insurance, health and welfare services, private education, and employment.

> We find nothing special in the protections Amendment 2 withholds. These are protections taken for granted by most people either because they already have them or do not need them; these are protections against exclusion from an almost limitless number of transactions and endeavors that constitute ordinary civic life in a free society. (1627)

After rejecting the state's "special rights" argument, the Court went on to argue that the amendment is in fundamental tension with the basic idea of "equal protection of the laws," because it identifies persons by a single characteristic and then denies them protection across the board[40]:

> The resulting disqualification of a class of persons from the right to seek specific protection from the law is unprecedented in our jurisprudence. . . . It is

not within our constitutional traditions to enact laws of this sort. Central both to the idea of the rule of law and to our own Constitution's guarantee of equal protection is the principle that government and each of its parts remain open on impartial terms to all who seek its assistance. . . . A law declaring that in general it shall be more difficult for one group of citizens than for all others to seek aid from the government is itself a denial of equal protection of the laws in the most literal sense. (1628)

The Court's reasoning in *Romer* leaves many questions unanswered.[41] Its extraordinary silence about *Bowers v. Hardwick* leaves us with the anomalous situation that a state may still criminalize homosexual activity but may not place special barriers in the way of nondiscrimination ordinances targeted at sexual preference. Nor is it altogether clear precisely on what basis the Court concluded that the amendment lacks a "rational relationship to a legitimate government purpose."[42] The opinion is probably best read as suggesting that the sweeping character of the amendment's prohibitions outruns any even initially plausible purpose (e.g., protecting landlords' freedom of association); thus the amendment gives rise to "the inevitable inference that it is born of animosity toward the class that it affects" (1622). This contrast between legitimate purpose and animosity is, it seems, fundamental in justifying the conclusion reached. A "bare desire to harm a politically unpopular group," the Court writes, citing an earlier case, "cannot constitute a legitimate government interest" (1628). But this contrast, especially the notion of the "bare desire to harm" a group, needs much more development and precision before we can be sure precisely what its constitutional scope may prove to be, and what types of discrimination on the basis of sexual orientation might still be allowed to express a legitimate government purpose.

In a recent analysis of the case, Cass Sunstein convincingly argues that the heart of the matter is that a state may no longer discriminate against homosexuals as a class, in a broad and sweeping way, simply because it wishes to discourage a type of conduct of which it disapproves. Linking *Romer* with *Cleburne*, a case involving fear and dislike of the mentally retarded, Sunstein concludes that

polygamists, adulterers, and fornicators are punished through law or norms because of what they do; homosexuals are subject to a deeper kind of social antagonism, connected not only with their acts but also their identity. It is this status feature that links discrimination on the basis of sexual orientation with discrimination on the basis of race or sex. Here, as with the mentally retarded, we can find a desire to isolate and seal off members of a despised group whose characteristics are thought to be in some sense contaminating or corrosive. In its most virulent forms, this desire is rooted in a belief that members of the relevant group are not fully human. On this count, *Cleburne* and *Romer* are one.[43]

Sunstein's analysis accords well with the history of Amendment 2, which was passed through a campaign that included widespread circulation of pamphlet material portraying gays as in various ways monstrous—for example, claims that they eat feces and drink raw blood. Such claims are reminiscent of the history of medieval and modern anti-Semitism and represent an attempt to demonize a class of persons in ways that go beyond their specific acts.

Having already argued that sodomy laws are unacceptable, we can find additional reasons for the result in *Romer*, reasons that were not available to the Court, because they were writing in the wake of *Bowers* and had decided not to overrule *Bowers* for the time being. Nonetheless, it seems very important to say that even should we accept the constitutionality of laws forbidding homosexual acts, a measure like Amendment 2 can still be judged to lack a legitimate state purpose.

Are there special areas of employment in which a general policy of nondiscrimination does not make sense? Even in the sensitive area of primary and secondary education, there is no evidence to show that the presence of gay and lesbian teachers harms children or adolescents. Gays are at least no more likely, and in some studies less likely, to molest children than are heterosexual males;[44] nor is there evidence to show that knowing or respecting a gay person has the power to convert children to homosexuality (any more than being taught by heterosexuals has converted gay youths to heterosexuality). The sexual harassment of students or colleagues should be dealt with firmly wherever it occurs. Beyond that, what one's colleagues do in bed should be irrelevant to their employment.

One further educational issue remains: the right to have opportunities to learn about lesbian and gay people. This right is of special interest to lesbian and gay students, but it is also, importantly, a right of all students, all of whom are citizens and need to learn something about their fellow citizens, especially as potential voters in referenda such as the one in Colorado. The study of homosexuality—historical, psychological, sociological, legal, literary—is now a burgeoning field of research. Do students of various ages have the right to learn about this work?[45] In the United States, the First Amendment makes a flat prohibition of such teaching unlikely (not impossible, because the First Amendment is not binding on private institutions), though teachers may be subtly penalized for introducing such material into their courses. In Britain, a 1986 law forbids local governments to "intentionally promote homosexuality or publish material with the intention of promoting homosexuality" or to "promote the teaching in any maintained school of the acceptability of homosexuality as a pretended family relationship."[46]

This law would very likely be unconstitutional in the United States. It is also, I think, morally repugnant for several reasons. First, it inhibits the freedom of inquiry. Second, it inhibits the freedom of political debate. Third, it creates just the sort of atmosphere of taboo and disgust that fosters discrimination and violence against gays and lesbians. Furthermore, I believe it to be counterproductive to the proponents' own ostensible goals of fostering morality as they understand it. For a moral doctrine to announce publicly that it needs to be backed up by informational restrictions of this sort is a clear confession of weakness. And Judge Richard Posner has cogently argued that such policies actually increase the likelihood that gay sex will be casual and promiscuous, presumably something the law's partisans wish to avoid. Deprived of the chance to learn about themselves in any way other than through action, Posner argues, young gay people will in all likelihood choose action earlier than they might have otherwise. The atmosphere of concealment also makes courtship and dating difficult— so "they will tend to substitute the sex act, which can be performed in a very short time and in private, for courtship, which is public and protracted."[47]

The most serious issue that arises with regard to nondiscrimination laws is that of religious freedom. Both institutions and individuals may sincerely believe that to be required to treat lesbians and gays as equal candidates for jobs (or as equal prospective tenants) is to be deprived of the freedom to exercise their religion. This argument seems more pertinent to some occupations than to others. To hire someone as a teacher may plausibly be seen as conferring a certain role-model status on that person; to hire someone as an accountant can hardly be seen in this light. And it is unlikely that a landlord's freedom to worship in his or her chosen way is compromised by being forced to consider on an equal basis tenants he or she may deem immoral. (The U.S. Supreme Court recently refused to hear an appeal of an Alaska decision against a landlord who refused to rent on religious grounds to an unmarried heterosexual couple.)

Various responses are possible. The Denver ordinance exempted religious organizations from its nondiscrimination provisions. The American Philosophical Association refused to exempt religious institutions from its (nonbinding) nondiscrimination policy for hiring and promotion, except in the case of discrimination on the basis of religious membership—and not when such membership is defined in accordance with discrimination against persons under one of the other rubrics of the nondiscrimination statement.[48] I believe that we should combine these two approaches: Religious organizations should in some cases be allowed greater latitude to follow their own beliefs, but in publicly funded and in large professional organizations, with sexuality as with race, freedom to discriminate, for religious member institutions, should be limited by shared requirements of justice. We should also discriminate among functions, treating differently those that are plausibly argued to be central to worship in each case. Thus it would be wrong to require the Roman Catholic Church to ordain women as priests, however deeply we may deplore the fact that it does not; it would be equally wrong for the Church to object if it was held to a local nondiscrimination law when the hiring of janitorial or secretarial staff is in question. When the city nondiscrimination law in Washington, D.C., forced Georgetown University to give official recognition to its student gay and lesbian organization, this seemed, though a hard case, to be the right result. But it would be wrong to require a religious body to ordain open and practicing homosexuals, nor would any local government be likely to do so. These are difficult questions, and we should recognize that many people of good faith with deep religious convictions are likely to disagree with some of these judgments.

The Right to Military Service

It is clear enough that gays and lesbians can serve with distinction in the military, because many of them have done so.[49] Furthermore, the armies of quite a few nations have successfully integrated open homosexuals into the service: France, Germany, Israel, Switzerland, Sweden, Denmark, Norway, Finland, the Netherlands, Belgium, Australia, Spain, and recently Canada. As Posner writes, "The idea that homosexuals will not or cannot fight seems a canard, on a par with the idea that Jews or blacks will not or cannot fight" (317). Nor are they security risks if they openly announce their homosexuality. Nor are they to be excluded because some of them might commit acts of sexual harassment. If this were so, by parity of reasoning we should much more readily exclude all heterosexual males. The "Tailhook" scandal in the U.S. Navy was recently followed by an even more extensive scandal involving sexual harassment in the U.S. Army, and it is now evident that the sexual harassment of women by men in the armed services is extraordinarily ubiquitous and unrestrained. Sexual harassment should be dealt with firmly wherever it occurs; this has nothing to do with the issue of lesbian and gay rights.

The real issue that keeps coming up is that heterosexual males do not want to be forced to associate intimately with gay males, especially to be seen naked by them. The psychology of this intense fear of the gaze of the homosexual is interesting. (It has even been attempted as a legal defense in gay-bashing cases, under the description "homosexual panic.") This fear may have something to do with the idea expressed by Comstock's gay-basher, when he perceptively noted that his aggression assailed something within himself. It may also be connected with the thought that this man will look at me in the way I look at a woman (i.e., not in a respectful or personal way, but a way that says, "I want to fuck you") and that this gaze will somehow humiliate me. Judge Oliver Gasch, for example, argued that the "quite rational assumption" in the Navy is that "with no one present who has a homosexual orientation, men and women alike can undress, sleep, bathe, and use the bathroom without fear or embarrassment that they are being viewed as sexual objects."[50]

What should be noted, however, is that this fear goes away when it needs to, and quite quickly too. Any frequenter of health clubs can easily note that in that setting both males and females undress all the time in front of other patrons, many of whom they can be sure are gay. Frequently it is clear through conversation who the gays and lesbians are. Nonetheless, we do not observe an epidemic of muscular failure. Straight men do not leap off the treadmill or drop their barbells in panic. They know they cannot root out and eject these people, so they forget about the issue, and just do what they came there to do. We should also note that openly gay officers have been included in the police forces of New York City, Chicago, San Francisco, Los Angeles, and probably others by now, without incident. During wartime, moreover, when the need for solidarity and high morale is greatest, toleration of gays and lesbian soldiers has gone up, not down.[51] It seems likely that gays could be integrated relatively painlessly into the U.S. Armed Forces if firm leadership were given from the top. The unfortunate fact, however, is that, here as with the harassment of women, high-ranking officers do not give the requisite leadership. As Judge Posner writes, "[I]t is terrible to tell people they are unfit to serve their country, unless they really are unfit, which is not the case here."[52] Evidence is strong that the recent "don't ask, don't tell" policy has actually increased the number of discharges for homosexuality, and the policy still permits the discharge of soldiers without evidence of actual homosexual acts, on the basis of the ascription of a "propensity" to commit such acts.[53]

To such arguments, Roger Scruton has recently replied that there is no such thing as a right to military service. There is only a duty to serve if called on. He concludes that I have "conjure[d] this right from the metaphysical ether."[54] This is obtuse. Of course, there is no blanket right to serve in the military; there is no blanket right to be a typist either. But if someone who is a qualified typist is fired on account of race or gender, that is a violation of his or her rights. It has been argued that similar legal issues are at stake in the military cases, and this is what concerns me. The rights in question are not ethereal but all too palpable: the right not to be tossed out of one's military job on account of one's sexual orientation if one has served adequately, or even, like Sgt. Perry Watkins, with distinction, the right to get a diploma from one of the military academies if one has satisfied all the graduation requirements, the right to keep one's ROTC scholarship,[55] and so forth. Courts have long been hearing cases dealing with these very earthly rights.

We have already considered the case of Sgt. Perry Watkins, a highly rated soldier who was told, after many years of doing his job with distinction, that he had no right to do so. Let us now consider one more recent case, that of Midshipman Joseph Steffan. Steffan was a member of the graduating class at the U.S. Naval Academy in Annapolis, Maryland. He was an outstanding student who had won numerous honors and had been selected Battalion Commander, an honor reserved for the top ten midshipmen. He was described as a "model for his classmates and subordinates," who would "undoubtedly make an outstanding naval officer."[56] A few months before graduation, he told a supposed friend about his homosexual orientation. The "friend" then told authorities. (At no time did Steffan state that he had committed homosexual acts, nor was any evidence of such acts ever introduced.) After a hearing, Steffan was denied the right to graduate; it was judged that he had "insufficient aptitude to become a commissioned officer in the naval service."[57] Steffan brought suit against the Department of Defense, alleging that the Navy's exclusion of homosexuals violated the Equal Protection Clause of the Fifth Amendment. At the conclusion of a trial in the U.S. District Court for the District of Columbia, the court found against Steffan. The opinion, written by Judge Oliver Gasch, argued (1) that homosexuals were not a class deserving heightened scrutiny, and (2) that the military regulations have a rational basis. Judge Gasch concluded that one important aspect of this rational basis was the need to protect the Armed Services from the contagion of AIDS, "given that at least 59% of all those who have contracted HIV have done so due to homosexual or bisexual activity. . . ."[58] (He did not explain why this line of argument would not justify the ejection of Jews, or African Americans, or males, or females—all groups that can be shown to be at increased risk for some deadly disease or diseases.) Gasch's participation in the case remains controversial because, during the discovery process, he referred to the plaintiff using the disparaging word "homo."[59] He refused to recuse himself from the case.

When Steffan appealed, his case was heard by a three-member panel of the U.S. Court of Appeals for the District of Columbia Circuit. The panel, in an opinion written by Judge Abner Mikva, declared the regulations under which Steffan was dismissed unconstitutional, unable to survive even rational basis review. Mikva emphasized that the directives focused on orientation, not conduct, and that no evidence of conduct had been presented. "America's hallmark," he concluded, "has been to judge people by what they do, and not by who they are. Just as Mr. Steffan won his Battalion Commander ranking by his conduct, so must he be judged by his conduct."[60]

The panel's decision did not prevail, however. A majority of the judges voted to rehear the case en banc, and when they did so they concluded that "the class of self-described homosexuals was sufficiently close to the class of those who engaged or intended to engage in homosexual conduct for Navy Academy regulations to survive rational basis review."[61] Through an argument that reads orientation as implying desire, and reads desire as equivalent to an intention to commit acts,[62] the majority rejected the panel's attempt to drive a wedge between orientation and conduct. A dissenting opinion written by Judge Patricia Wald vigorously restated the panel's position:

> For the government to penalize a person for acknowledging his sexual orientation runs deeply against our constitutional grain. It has, we believe, no precedent or place in our national traditions, which spring from a profound respect for the freedom to think and to be what one chooses and to announce it to the world.[63]

Wald's reason, like Mikva's, brings the Steffan case into close connection with the recent Supreme Court opinion in *Romer*, which also stressed the distinction between conduct and orientation. The point, once again, is that even if we should accept for the purposes of argument the constitutionality of laws and regulations forbidding homosexual acts, we should not target an entire group of persons on the unsupported hypothesis that they will be bound to commit such acts. For the time being, however, such reasoning seems to have lost the day in the military; Joe Steffan will not receive his diploma.

The Right to Marriage and/or the Legal and Social Benefits of Marriage

Gays and lesbians in Denmark, Sweden, Norway, and the Netherlands can form a registered partnership that gives all the tax, inheritance, and other civic benefits of marriage; similar legislation is soon to be passed in Finland. Many businesses, universities, and other organizations within other nations, including the United States, have extended their marriage benefits to registered same-sex domestic partners. Same-sex marriage is currently a topic of intense debate in Judaism and in every major branch of Christianity.

Why are marriage rights important to lesbians and gay men? Legally, marriage is a source of many benefits, including favorable tax, inheritance, and insurance status; immigration and custody rights; the right to collect unemployment benefits if one partner quits a job to move to be where his or her partner has found employment; the spousal privilege exception when giving testimony; the right to bring a wrongful death action upon the negligent death of a spouse; the right to the privileges of next-of-kin in hospital visitations, decisions about burial, and so forth.[64] Many gays and lesbians have discovered in the most painful way that they lack these rights, although they may have lived together loyally for years. By contrast, states do not deny marriage licenses to "[c]onvicted felons, divorced parents who refuse to pay child support, delinquent taxpayers, fascists, and communists." Nor, moreover, do states deny marriage licenses to many people who are generally considered sexually deviant:

> Pedophiles, transvestites, transsexuals, sadists, masochists, sodomites, and hermaphrodites can get marriage licenses in every state—so long as they can persuade the state that they are heterosexual pedophiles, transvestites, transsexuals, sadists, masochists, sodomites, and hermaphrodites. . . . Gay people constitute virtually the only group in America whose members are not permitted to marry the partner they love."[65]

Some of the civil benefits of marriage are already available to same-sex couples, because many businesses, local governments, and voluntary organizations have extended medical, tuition, and other benefits to same-sex domestic partners. (The University of Chicago was the first major U.S. university to do so, with a committee chaired by libertarian thinker Richard Epstein taking the initiative.[66]) The success of these measures as devices to promote recruitment and retention of talented employees gives us a sign that the world does not collapse when equal privileges are extended in this way. Nations that do extend all the civil benefits of marriage to same-sex couples have done so without widespread social upheaval; there is no pressure on the relevant governments to repeal such laws. It is both simple justice and wise social policy to follow their lead— and, I would argue, to do so through the institution of marriage rather than by creating an extra institution of registered partnership, whose only function would seem to be to create barriers for gays to full social equality.[67]

Emotionally and morally, being able to enter a legally recognized form of marriage means the opportunity to declare publicly an intent to live in commitment and partnership. Although many lesbian and gay people consider themselves married and have frequently solemnized their commitment in ceremonies not recognized by the state, they still seek to do so in a recognized manner because they attach importance to the public recognition of their union and to the expressive act of declaring a commitment in the presence of others.

As the Norwegian Ministry of Children and Family Affairs writes, supporting Norway's 1993 law, "It can be detrimental for a person to have to suppress fundamental feelings concerning attachment and love for another person. Distancing oneself from these feelings or attempts to suppress them may destroy one's self respect."[68] Noting that 92% of gays and lesbians polled in a comprehensive Swedish survey were either part of a registered couple or stated that they would like to be, the Ministry concluded that the primary obstacle to stable marital unions in the gay community is "negative attitudes from the social environment."

These seem to be very plausible views. And yet gay marriage is widely opposed. On what grounds? On what account of marriage is it an institution that should remain closed to lesbians and gay men? The basis of marriage in the United States and Europe is generally taken to be a stated desire to live together in intimacy, love, and partnership and to support one another, materially and emotionally, in the conduct of daily life.[69] Of course, many people enter marriage unprepared, and many marriages fail, but the law cannot and should not undertake a stringent inquiry into the character and behavior of the parties before admitting them to the benefits of that status.

Many people do believe that a central purpose of marriage is to have and to educate children. But (apart from the fact that many lesbian and gay people do have and raise children, whether their own from previous unions or conceived by artificial insemination within the relationship) nobody has seriously suggested denying marriage rights to postmenopausal women, to sterile individuals of any age, or to people who simply know (and state) that they do not want children and will not have them. It therefore seems flatly inconsistent and unjust to deny these rights to other individuals who wish to form exactly this type of committed yet childless union.

No doubt the extension of marriage rights to gays and lesbians will change the way we think about "the family." On the other hand, "the family" has never been a single thing in American, far less in world, history.[70] Although Roger Scruton sentimentally refers to its nuclear heterosexual form as an institution that has "shown us the way to happiness,"[71] the fact is that the nuclear family unit headed by two parents of the opposite sex has been associated with grave moral problems, including child abuse, marital rape, domestic violence, and other types of gender inequality. There is no reason to sentimentalize it as a morally perfect institution. Studies have shown that households established by same-sex couples, both male and female, have a more equal division of domestic labor than do heterosexual ones.[72] Thus, they may even have valuable contributions to make to our understanding of what commitment and marital fairness are, as we seek to respond to the challenge of combining intimate love with a respect for personal equality.

The denial of marriage rights to same-sex couples has socially undesirable consequences. It reinforces stereotypes of lesbians and gay men as rootless, antisocial, and subversive, thus contributing further to their marginalization and isolation. It also treats them as second-class citizens, denying them a privilege that many nonideal people routinely get; once again, this pattern contributes to a climate that isolates gays and makes them ready targets of discrimination and harassment in other areas of life. By contrast, encouraging gay marriages will help to remove stereotypes of gays as promiscuous and culturally subversive.[73] Moreover, if gays cannot legally get married, their efforts to live in stable committed partnerships are discouraged, and a life of rootless or even promiscuous noncommitment is correspondingly encouraged. Thus a form of discrimination that has its roots in a stereotype may cause the stereotype to become, in some measure, true. But this state of affairs is irrational: Society has strong reasons to encourage the formation of stable domestic units by both heterosexual and homosexual couples.[74]

One further legal issue should now be considered: It is the connection between the ban on same-sex marriage and sex discrimination. In *Loving v. Virginia*,[75] the famous case in which state miscegenation laws were declared unconstitutional, the state attempted to argue that the ban on interracial marriage was not racist in character because both races were equally forbidden. This argument failed: The Supreme Court concluded that racial caste and hierarchy were at the very heart of the prohibition. Similarly, the argument that a ban on same-sex marriage imposes an equal disadvantage on all parties—males are forbidden to marry males, females females—seems not clearly convincing. But what should we say the relevant sort of hierarchy is? If we say what seems most obvious, that the ban puts at a disadvantage all and only those persons seeking same-sex marriages, we encounter difficulty making a constitutional argument because homosexuality has never been recognized to be a "suspect classification" for the purposes of equal-protection review; therefore the ban needs only to withstand rational basis review. Several legal scholars have therefore recently taken a different tack. Andrew Koppelman, Sylvia Law, and Cass Sunstein have all argued that the ban on same-sex marriage is a form of sex discrimination. To put the point purely formally, the ground on which X, a female, is forbidden to marry Y, another female, is her sex. To approach the issue at a deeper level, such classifications, it is argued, are ultimately an extension of a system of sex discrimination, because the ban on same-sex marriage is at its root a way of maintaining sharp binary boundaries between the sexes and enshrining the institution of the patriarchal heterosexual couple as the central recognized unit.[76] Thus, the ban is a sex-based classification serving sexist goals.

There is much sociological support for these connections.[77] And it seems right to push this legal theory as far as it can be pushed; in the Hawaii case it proved decisive. We should not, however, allow the peculiarities of current equal-protection law to make us lose sight of the fact that it is wrong to deny marriage rights on the basis of sexual orientation, *whether or not* the asserted link with sex hierarchy remains true. If at some point men and women should be fully equal in our society, it would still be wrong to ban same-sex marriages because the choice of a marital partner is a fundamental person-defining choice with which the state should not interfere.[78]

Marriage has three aspects: the civil, the emotional, and the sacramental. I have argued that there is no good reason to deny same-sex couples the benefit of the civil and emotional benefits of marriage. It is now time to turn to the sacramental. Scruton assumes that extending marriage rights to gays will cause marriage to be "suddenly deprived of its sacramental character." But this is far from being the case. Many lesbians and gay men are religious. Every major religion has recently confronted the issue of same-sex marriage, and there is none in which there is not a segment that strongly supports such marriage rights.

Scruton hazards the guess that no Catholic natural law thinker has supported same-sex marriage.[79] But even here he is in error: In an elegant argument, University of Notre Dame philosopher Paul Weithman has convincingly argued that the notion of sexual complementarity relied on in influential statements of the natural-law position on marriage cannot be consistently articulated in a way that fails to include same-sex couples.[80] Because the recent controversy over same-sex marriage has generated such a great outpouring of writing from within the religious traditions, we can now see exactly how divided major traditions are on this matter, and how strong the support actually is for the extension to same-sex couples of the sacramental benefits of marriage.[81] Same-sex commitment ceremonies are regularly performed with the support of religious leaders. A salient but not atypical case is that of my University of Chicago Law School colleague Mary Becker, who in 1996 solemnized her commitment to her same-sex partner in Bond Chapel of the University of Chicago, in a ceremony at which a Roman Catholic priest officiated. The only thing lacking was the term "marriage," and it is not always lacking in other denominations in which individual leaders have broad discretion. (Reconstructionist Judaism has recognized such marriages for some time; recently Reform Judaism appears to be taking the same step.)

In short, the relationship between same-sex couples and the established churches is in flux, and no doubt many such couples have severed their ties with the religions of their upbringing because these religions refuse to recognize their unions. But nobody could deny that the desire to win religious marriage is extremely strong among such couples, or that many do obtain the sacramental benefits of religious marriage.

The Right to Retain Custody of Children and/or to Adopt

Gays and lesbians have and raise children. In a 1970 California survey, 20% of male homosexuals and more than a third of female homosexuals have been married, and many of those have had children. Lesbian couples can have children through artificial insemination or sex with a male; a gay man can obtain a child through some sort of surrogacy arrangement. Should these things be (or remain) legal? Experience shows that children raised in homosexual households showed no differences from other groups, either in sexual orientation or in general mental health or social adjustment. Indeed, evidence shows that children raised by an unmarried heterosexual woman had more psychological problems than others.[82] We need more research on these issues, clearly; samples have been small and have covered a relatively short time span. But so far there is no evidence to justify a court in removing a child from its parent's custody simply on the grounds that he or she is living in a homosexual union. And this has frequently happened. To mention just one notable case, Bottoms v. Bottoms, [83] in 1995 the Virginia Supreme Court upheld the denial of custody of her child to Sharon Bottoms, who was living in a committed same-sex relationship, and awarded custody to the child's grandmother. The court held that a lesbian mother, even one living in a committed relationship, was presumptively unfit to have custody of her child.

What argument might possibly justify such a position? The court in *Bottoms* cited the fact that "[c]onduct inherent in lesbianism is punishable as a Class 6 felony in the Commonwealth . . . thus, that conduct is [an] important consideration in determining custody" (108). But I have argued that there is an extremely strong case against the retention of these invidious laws. (Moreover, the court's position seems somewhat hypocritical, because the criminal acts in question were explicitly said to be oral sex acts, but we know that such acts take place in a large proportion of heterosexual relationships, and the Virginia sodomy law applies to heterosexual acts as well.) As to the court's contention that lesbianism as such renders a mother an unfit parent,[84] there is no evidence that same-sex parents are worse parents than heterosexual parents.

If one were to argue that such a child will inevitably be the target of social prejudice, no matter how well its parent is doing,[85] it seems plausible that the Constitution will intervene to block that argument. In a 1984 case, *Palmore v. Sidoti*,[86] in which a child was removed from its (white) mother's custody because she had remarried to a black man—grounds for change of custody being that such a child will suffer from public racial prejudice—the U.S. Supreme Court returned custody to the child's mother, holding that the law may not give public legitimacy to private prejudices. This case was cited as a precedent in a 1985 Alaska decision granting custody to a lesbian mother. The court held that a court could not rely on "any real or imagined social stigma" attaching to a parent's homosexual status when deciding the best interests of a child in a custody case.[87] In Florida, in 1991, a state court found the state's law banning adoptions by homosexuals in violation of the Florida Constitution's privacy provisions, as well as federal and state due process and equal protection clauses. Thus these constitutional avenues, too, deserve to be explored further.[88] In general, it seems especially important that children should not be removed from the custody of parents who love and care for them successfully, without compelling reason.

Recently the Intermediate Court of Appeals of Hawaii reviewed this whole matter because the state had made parental fitness the linchpin of its case for denial of same-sex marriage. The court concluded, reviewing the social science evidence presented on both sides, that "gay and lesbian parents and same-sex couples can be as fit and loving parents as non-gay men and women and different-sex couples" and that "[t]he sexual orientation of parents is not in and of itself an indicator of the overall adjustment and development of children." What was most striking about the evidence presented in the case was that even the expert witnesses for the state agreed that gay and lesbian parents "are as fit and loving parents as non-gay persons and couples."[89]

As for adoption and foster parenting, courts should probably take a case-by-case approach, rejecting a flat ban. Frequently, especially where foster parenting is concerned, such a placement might be a child's best chance for a productive home life.[90] Even when that is so, gay and lesbian parents have to fight an uphill battle to win adoption rights. Consider the 1990 Ohio case *In re Adoption of Charles B*,[91] in which the Ohio Supreme Court reversed a court of appeals decision denying the adoption of a child by a gay man. Charles B., an eight-year-old boy suffering from both physical disease (leukemia) and mental retardation (produced by fetal alcohol syndrome), had been in at least four different foster homes, and several adoptive placements had failed. Mr. B., a psychological counselor with degrees in child psychology and family life education, lives with Mr. K., a research scientist. Mr. B. met Charles as a counselor but soon developed a close and supportive relationship with him: "The evidence presented showed that Mr. B. has been the one consistent and caring person in the life of Charles B" (884). His efforts to adopt Charles were supported by a guardian appointed by the court, who noted that the boy himself would prefer this placement. Nonetheless, the Department of Human Services opposed Mr. B.'s effort, and appealed after a trial court had supported Mr. B. Noting that Ohio makes the "best interest of the child" the "polestar" governing decisions about adoption, the court insisted that each such decision must be based on "the facts of each individual case." Noting that Mr. B. had the support of his mother and sister, who had testified as witnesses in his support, and noting that psychological witnesses who had examined the child concurred in supporting Mr. B., the Supreme Court concluded that the "best interests" standard clearly supported placement with Mr. B.

This case shows how hard it is for a gay parent to adopt: Even when all the evidence was decisively on one side (the Supreme Court noted that the agency's sole argument was the submission of an ideal description of the sort of "child-centered" heterosexual family a child should allegedly have), even when no heterosexual family was willing to adopt the particular child, nonetheless, Mr. B. had to struggle for years to win adoption rights. This was so even given his possession of specialized expertise relevant to the child's mental problems, and even given the energetic support of his mother and sister, which convinced the court that the boy would have "sufficient female role models" (887). And even then, a dissenting opinion observed that a child with an immune system that had probably been suppressed by treatment for leukemia should not be living in "a homosexual household" (891). The interests of children are indeed best served by a flexible case-by-case approach—but not by one that imposes such enormous burdens on concerned gay and lesbian adults and couples. And once again, the reason for refusing a homosexual couple must not be the existence of public prejudice against homosexuality; as yet, no feature intrinsic to homosexuality as such has been demonstrated to have a detrimental effect on children.

IV. Roger Scruton's Counterargument

It is frequently held, against gay rights of various sorts, that gay sex relationships are unusually likely to be promiscuous and/or superficial. This has rarely been claimed about lesbian relationships. But the image of the gay male bathhouse is often paraded before voters as a scare image. Conservative philosopher Roger Scruton recently argued that "[t]here is in homosexual union between men a vector which tends to promiscuity," and that any society that treats gays as equal must therefore "school itself to regard promiscuity—with all that it means by way of social breakdown, impermanence and the loss of care—as morally neutral."[92] What should we say about this?

To begin with, we have no reliable data. The only data about sexual behavior in the United States that are even remotely reliable are those in the recent Laumann/Chicago survey.[93] Because of funding difficulties resulting from conservative congressional opposition to the study, Laumann could not study a large enough sample of homosexuals to draw conclusions about their number of sex partners. His results show, however, that many if not most common beliefs in this general area are false, and that most types of people have far fewer sex partners than popular belief supposes. (The alleged promiscuity of black males, for example, turns out to be a complete myth: Black males and white males have, on average, exactly the same number of lifetime sexual partners.[94] Indeed, the only variable that proved to have a strong positive correlation with a higher number of lifetime sexual partners is a higher level of education.[95])

One might well hold that a person's promiscuity is not the business of the law, unless he harms others, and should not have any relevance to deliberations about basic legal rights. But large numbers of people do think that the alleged connection between male homosexuality and promiscuity is pertinent to deliberations about such rights as the rights to marriage and adoption, and perhaps certain employment rights as well. We should therefore address these concerns.

First, we should insist that straight men are allowed to get married and to obtain the legal, emotional, and religious benefits of marriage; gay men are not, and their stable committed unions have to fight against public denial and opprobrium. Furthermore, no evidence about the behavior of a group that is currently the target of social opprobrium and violence is a reliable predictor of the way in which those same people would behave in better social circumstances.

Next, we have to note that we are talking about males raised in a culture that has generally taught men to value self-sufficiency and the uncommitted state, women to value intimacy and commitment. It is not surprising that sometimes putting two males together doubles the "maleness" of the relationship. But should that be blamed on the same-sex character of the relationship, or on its maleness? Scruton suggests the latter, and therefore casts doubt on the idea that his argument is really about same-sex conduct at all. And is the remedy to be found (if one is wanted) in yet more measures against same-sex individuals, or does it lie in the discouragement of promiscuous conduct, and, as well, in the reformation of the moral education of males?

Like any statistical argument, Scruton's argument cannot serve as a justification for denying any right to an entire group. If the mobility and assembly rights of all males were curtailed on the ground that males commit a high proportion of our society's violent crimes, we would view that as an outrage. If heterosexual males were forbidden to marry women on the ground that such a high proportion of domestic violence is committed by males, we would again view that as absurd. We should therefore repudiate any attempt to deny rights to gays on grounds of the (alleged) promiscuity of some or even many gays. If the law wishes to discourage promiscuity, there are steps that can be taken without removing anyone's civil rights (although even such steps should be controversial): tax incentives for married couples, public rhetoric of a hortatory sort,

above all the legalization of gay and lesbian marriage.[96] There is no need to target a group already targeted. It is inaccurate, and it is unjust.

In his earlier book *Sexual Desire,* Scruton advanced a somewhat more subtle
version of his argument, focusing on superficiality rather than promiscuity.[97]
The argument is as follows: When one makes love with someone of the opposite gender, one is dealing with a different, mysterious world; by contrast, the
world of one's own gender is familiar and well-known. (Scruton seems to me to
give people undue credit for self-knowledge.) The willingness to put one's being
at risk toward a world so profoundly other is morally valuable and imparts depth
to the relationship; same-sex relationships lack this risky openness; this lack of
openness is connected with their (alleged) greater superficiality. This may help
us to see that male gay sex (Scruton explicitly exempts lesbian relationships) is,
if not perverted or depraved, still morally inferior.

A number of problems arise. First, Scruton uses the unclear notion of "gender" rather than the somewhat clearer notion of biological sex. This is important because knowing one's own gender is supposed to be a matter of not just
knowing what it is like to have a certain sort of genital organ but of knowing a
whole way of being in the world. But even within a single culture, most individuals will find themselves in both conformity and nonconformity with any
list of gender attributes one might construct. And even if one's attributes on the
whole conform to the stereotype, one need not find the other gender's world
unfamiliar if one works with many people of that gender and has intimate friendships with some of them. I suspect, in fact, that Scruton's idea that the world of
the female is mysterious to men (an idea I have heard from quite a number of
men) is not easily separable from its cultural context, in which single-sex education and the sparse representation of women in the professions have made it
hard for men to have female friends.

Next, the argument is more sweeping than Scruton appears to realize, in two
ways. First, if we follow it we shall be led to find superior moral value in any
relationship in which a barrier of experiential difference is crossed. This ought
to mean that relationships between the Chinese and the British, or the sighted
and the blind, or the aged and the youthful, have greater moral value than relationships between two Britons or two sighted people or two young people. I doubt
that Scruton would actually hold this. I think Scruton is actually thinking not
of qualitative differences of this sort but of the mystery of intimacy with any
world that is separate from one's own. But that is a challenge that exists in any
intimate human relationship.

Second, if we really direct disapproval against those who are (for whatever
reason) unwilling to be vulnerable and at risk in their sexual relationships, preferring contacts of a superficial sort, we will have to exclude from the targeted
group many homosexuals, both female and male, and include many heterosexuals, well exemplified by Watkins's satisfied friend, whose desires were as superficial and narcissistic as anyone's could be. Indeed, common attitudes of men
toward women throughout much of history have been just this self-centered,
and even more possessive.

Would it make any sense to say that people inclined to superficiality in sex could not serve in the armed forces? The U.S. Navy's shameful Tailhook scandal (in which crude harassment of women was revealed as endemic to naval life), and the recent discovery of pervasive patterns of sexual exploitation in the U.S. Army, show the broad sweep of promiscuous attitudes about sex, even at the highest levels of the services. Indeed, it appears that such attitudes are actively encouraged, in order to promote male group solidarity. It seems pathetic to lay all this at the door of the one group that is not allowed to serve and can least be blamed for the current situation. Where marriage rights are concerned, it might make *moral* sense to dissuade a person prone to superficial sexual contacts from marrying, given the likelihood that the partner might be disappointed. But surely this makes no *political* sense as a basis for the denial of the marriage license. The inquiries that would then be required would be unmanageable and incredibly prone to abuse, vindictive ex-spouses offering testimony about their ex's superficial attitudes and his or her unwillingness to be "at risk" toward the "other," all to impede a marriage to the hated rival. Or, if a putative statistical correlation between (male) homosexuality and superficiality should be used as criterial, why not deny marriage licenses to all males on the grounds that they are far more likely than females to abuse their children? This is surely worse than superficiality. Where adoption is concerned, certainly let us look hard at the life of the individual couple—but let us look at the *individual* couple and not assume beforehand, what is perfectly false, that all and only same-sex couples are unsuitable. (Scruton already concedes the suitability of female couples, thus casting doubt on whether his argument is really about homosexuality.)

Thus, it appears that Scruton's argument gets at something deep about sex when we take him to be talking about separateness or "otherness" rather than mere qualitative difference. But the argument seems to have no bearing on the legal and moral issues before us.

Forster famously dedicated *Maurice* "to a Happier Year." He concluded his "Terminal Note" of 1960, however, with a gloomy prognosis. Some gay men, he says, had hoped that greater public openness about the topic of homosexuality would bring a "generous recognition" of the emotional depth of their sexual orientation, and consequent social acceptance. He himself, although less optimistic, had at least hoped that "knowledge would bring understanding." What he discovered instead, he writes, was that the new openness brought only "the change from ignorance and terror to familiarity and contempt," and that having to deliberate in public about the topic made politicians more simplistic and wooden rather than more understanding. He therefore predicted that the recommendations of the Wolfenden report (which urged the decriminalization of consensual homosexual relations) would be "indefinitely rejected," and that selective police prosecutions would continue, usually targeting poor working-class men: "Clive on the bench will continue to sentence Alec in the dock" (255).

But Forster's pessimistic prediction was wrong about Britain, which did put the recommendations of the Wolfenden Report into law only seven years later, although gay men and lesbians still encounter many forms of discrimination. His gloomy view is more appropriate to the United States, where sodomy laws are still constitutional, and where public debate has not, so far, produced an abundance of either generosity or understanding. We can respond, however, by pointing out that the United States has not yet really tried to have a civil public dialogue on this issue, laying out the arguments calmly and seeking both generosity and understanding. Let us see what happens when we do.

PART II

Sex

8

OBJECTIFICATION

> It is true, and very much to the point, that women are objects, commodities, some deemed more expensive than others—but it is only by asserting one's humanness every time, in all situations, that one becomes someone as opposed to something. That, after all, is the core of our struggle.
>
> —Andrea Dworkin,
> *Woman Hating*

Sexual objectification is a familiar concept. Once a relatively technical term in feminist theory, associated in particular with the work of Catharine MacKinnon and Andrea Dworkin, the word "objectification" has by now passed into many people's daily lives. It is common to hear it used to criticize advertisements, films, and other representations and also to express skepticism about the attitudes and intentions of one person to another, or of oneself to someone else. Generally it is used as a pejorative term, connoting a way of speaking, thinking, and acting that the speaker finds morally or socially objectionable, usually, though not always, in the sexual realm. Thus, Catharine MacKinnon writes of pornography, "Admiration of natural physical beauty becomes objectification. Harmlessness becomes harm."[1] The portrayal of women "dehumanized as sexual objects, things, or commodities" is, in fact, the first category of pornographic material made actionable under MacKinnon and Dworkin's proposed Minneapolis ordinance.[2] The same sort of pejorative use is common in ordinary social discussions of people and events.

Feminist thought, moreover, has typically represented men's sexual objectification of women as not a trivial but a central problem in women's lives, and the opposition to it as at the very heart of feminist politics. For Catharine MacKinnon, "women's intimate experience of sexual objectification . . . is definitive of and synonymous with women's lives as gender female." It is said to yield an exis-

213

tence in which women "can grasp self only as thing."[3] Moreover, this baneful experience is, in MacKinnon's view, unavoidable. In a most striking metaphor, she states that "[a]ll women live in sexual objectification the way fish live in water"—meaning by this, presumably, not only that objectification surrounds women but also that they have become such that they derive their very nourishment and sustenance from it. But women are not fish, and for MacKinnon objectification is bad because it cuts women off from full self-expression and self-determination—from, in effect, their humanity.

But the term "objectification" can also be used, somewhat confusingly, in a more positive spirit. Indeed, one can find both of these apparently conflicting uses in the writings of some feminist authors, for example, legal theorist Cass Sunstein, who has been generally supportive of MacKinnon's critique of sexuality. Throughout his earlier writings on pornography, Sunstein speaks of the treatment of women as objects for the use and control of men as the central thing that is bad in pornographic representation.[4] On the other hand, in a recent, mostly negative, review of a recent book by Nadine Strossen defending pornography,[5] Sunstein writes the following:

> People's imaginations are unruly. . . . It may be possible to argue, as some people do, that objectification and a form of use are substantial parts of sexual life, or wonderful parts of sexual life, or ineradicable parts of sexual life. Within a context of equality, respect and consent, objectification—not at all an easy concept to define—may not be so troublesome.[6]

To be sure, Sunstein expresses himself very cautiously, speaking only of an argument that might be made and not indicating his own support for such an argument. Nonetheless, to MacKinnon and Dworkin, who have typically represented opposition to objectification as at the heart of feminism, this paragraph might well seem puzzling. They might well wish to ask: What does Sunstein wish to defend? Why should "objectification and a form of use" ever be seen as "wonderful" or even as "ineradicable" parts of sexual life? Wouldn't it always be bad to use a "someone" as a "something"? And why should we suppose that it is at all possible to combine objectification with "equality, respect, and consent"? Isn't this precisely the combination we have shown to be impossible?

My hunch, which I shall pursue, is that such confusions can arise because we have not clarified the concept of objectification to ourselves, and that once we do so we will find out that it is not only a slippery but also a multiple concept. Indeed, I shall argue that there are at least seven distinct ways of behaving introduced by the term, none of which implies any of the others, though there are many complex connections among them. Under some specifications, objectification, I shall argue, is always morally problematic. Under other specifications, objectification has features that may be either good or bad, depending on the overall context. (Sunstein was certainly right to emphasize the importance of context, and I shall dwell on that issue.) Some features of objectification, furthermore, I shall argue, may in fact in some circumstances, as Sunstein suggests, be either necessary or even wonderful features of sexual life. Seeing this requires, among other things, seeing how the allegedly impossible combination between (a form of) objectification and "equality, respect, and consent" might after all be possible.

I begin with a series of examples, to which I shall return in what follows. All are examples of what might plausibly be called the objectification of one person by another, the seeing and/or treating of someone as an object. In all cases the objectified person is a sexual partner or would-be sexual partner, though the sexual context is not equally prominent in all the cases. Deliberately, I have chosen examples from a wide variety of styles, and I have not restricted my sample to the male objectification of women because we need to be able to ask how our judgments of the cases are influenced by larger issues of social context and social power.

> His blood beat up in waves of desire. He wanted to come to her, to meet her. She was there, if he could reach her. The reality of her who was just beyond him absorbed him. Blind and destroyed, he pressed forward, nearer, nearer, to receive the consummation of himself, be received within the darkness which should swallow him and yield him up to himself. If he could come really within the blazing kernel of darkness, if really he could be destroyed, burnt away till he lit with her in one consummation, that were supreme, supreme. (D. H. Lawrence, *The Rainbow*)

> Yes because he must have come 3 or 4 times with that tremendous big red brute of a thing he has I thought the vein or whatever the dickens they call it was going to burst though his nose is not so big after I took off all my things with the blinds down after my hours dressing and perfuming and combing it like iron or some kind of a thick crowbar standing all the time he must have eaten oysters I think a few dozen he was in great singing voice no I never in all my life felt anyone had one the size of that to make you feel full up he must have eaten a whole sheep after whats the idea making us like that with a big hole in the middle of us like a Stallion driving it up into you because thats all they want out of you with that determined vicious look in his eye I had to halfshut my eyes still he hasn't such a tremendous amount of spunk in him. (James Joyce, *Ulysses*)

> She even has a sheet over her body, draped and folded into her contours. She doesn't move. She might be dead, Macrae thinks. . . . Suddenly a desire to violate tears through his body like an electric shock, six thousand volts of violence, sacrilege, the lust to desecrate, destroy. His thumbs unite between the crack of her ass, nails inwards, knuckle hard on knuckle, and plunge up to the palms into her. A submarine scream rises from the deep green of her dreaming, and she snaps towards waking, half-waking, half-dreaming with no sense of self . . . and a hard pain stabbing at her entrails . . . Isabelle opens her eyes, still not knowing where or what or why, her face jammed up against the cracking plaster . . . as Macrae digs deeper dragging another scream from her viscera, and her jerking head cracks hard on the wall . . . and her palms touch Macrae's hands, still clamped tight around her ass, kneading, working on it, with a violence born of desperation and desire, desire to have her so completely . . . that it seems as if he would tear the flesh from her to absorb it, crush it, melt it into his own hands. . . . And Isabelle . . . hears a voice calling out "don't stop; don't stop," a voice called from somewhere deep within

her from ages past, ancestral voices from a time the world was young, "don't stop, don't stop." It's nearer now, this atavistic voice, and she realises with surprise that it is coming from her mouth, it is her lips that are moving, it is her voice. (Laurence St. Clair, *Isabelle and Véronique: Four Months, Four Cities*)

Why We Love Tennis. (A caption for three pictures of actress Nicollette Sheridan playing at the Chris Evert Pro-Celebrity Tennis Classic, her skirt hiked up to reveal her black underpants, *Playboy*, April 1995)

At first I used to feel embarrassed about getting a hard-on in the shower. But at the Corry much deliberate excitative soaping of cocks went on, and a number of members had their routine erections there each day. My own, though less regular, were, I think, hoped and looked out for. . . . This naked mingling, which formed a ritualistic heart to the life of the club, produced its own improper incitements to ideal liaisons, and polyandrous happenings which could not survive into the world of jackets and ties, cycle-clips and duffel-coats. And how difficult social distinctions are in the shower. How could I now smile at my enormous African neighbour, who was responding in elephantine manner to my own erection, and yet scowl at the disastrous nearly-boy smirking under the next jet along? (Alan Hollinghurst, *The Swimming-Pool Library*)

She had passed her arm into his, and the other objects in the room, the other pictures, the sofas, the chairs, the tables, the cabinets, the "important" pieces, supreme in their way, stood out, round them, consciously, for recognition and applause. Their eyes moved together from piece to piece, taking in the whole nobleness—quite as if for him to measure the wisdom of old ideas. The two noble persons seated, in conversation, at tea, fell thus into the splendid effect and the general harmony: Mrs. Verver and the Prince fairly "placed" themselves, however unwittingly, as high expressions of the kind of human furniture required, aesthetically, by such a scene. The fusion of their presence with the decorative elements, their contribution to the triumph of selection, was complete and admirable; though to a lingering view, a view more penetrating than the occasion really demanded, they also might have figured as concrete attestations of a rare power of purchase. There was much indeed in the tone in which Adam Verver spoke again, and who shall say where his thought stopped? "*Le compte y est.* You've got some good things." (Henry James, *The Golden Bowl*[7])

Most of the works and authors are familiar. Hollinghurst's novel of gay London before AIDS has been widely hailed as one of the most important pieces of erotic writing in the 1980s. To those who are unfamiliar with the *oeuvre* of Laurence St. Clair, it is probably sufficient to point out that St. Clair is a pseudonym of James Hankinson, scholar in ancient Greek philosophy and Professor of Philosophy at the University of Texas at Austin, who wrote this novel for a standard hard-core pornographic series, and was later publicized as its author.

So: we have five examples of conduct that seems to deserve, in some sense, the name of "objectification." In each case, a human being is being regarded and/ or treated as an object, in the context of a sexual relationship. Tom Brangwen sees his wife as a mysterious inhuman natural force, a "blazing kernel of darkness." Molly reduces Blazes Boylan to his genital dimensions, regarding him as somewhat less human than the stallion to which she jokingly compares him. Hankinson's hero Macrae treats the sleeping Isabelle as a prehuman preconscious being ripe for invasion and destruction, whose only quasi-human utterance is one that confirms her suitability for the infliction of pain. The *Playboy* caption reduces the young actress, a skilled tennis player, to a body ripe for male use: It says, in effect, she thinks she is displaying herself as a skilled athletic performer but all the while she is actually displaying herself to *our* gaze as a sexual object. Hollinghurst's hero represents himself as able to see his fellow Londoners as equal interchangeable bodies or even body parts, under the sexual gaze of the shower room, a gaze allegedly independent of warping considerations of class or rank. Maggie and Adam contemplate their respective spouses as priceless antiques whom they have collected and arranged.

In all such analyses of literary works, we need to distinguish the objectification of one character by another character from the objectification of persons by a text taken as a whole. Both are of interest to me as examples of morally assessible human conduct, and, given the connections of my analysis to the debate over pornography, I shall be concerned with the morality of the conduct that consists in representing,[8] as well as with the morality of represented conduct. Both sorts of conduct can be morally assessed, but they should be kept separate. Frequently it is difficult to do this, but the attempt must be made, given that important moral issues clearly turn on the difference, and in dealing with literary examples we must grapple with it. Fortunately, ethical criticism of literature has by now developed a rich set of distinctions to assist us. Especially helpful is Wayne Booth's threefold distinction between (1) the *narrator* of a text (and/or its other characters); (2) the *implied author*, that is, the sense of life embodied in the text taken as a whole; and (3) the *real-life author*, who has many properties lacked by the implied author, and may lack some that the implied author has.[9] Booth argues, and I agree, that the ethical criticism of the action represented in a text is one thing, and criticism of the text as a whole another; to get to the second we need to focus on the *implied author*, asking ourselves what sort of interaction the text as a whole promotes in us as readers, what sorts of desires and projects it awakens and constructs. In this way, ethical criticism of texts can be both sensitive to literary form and continuous with the ethical appraisal of persons.[10]

Here what we should probably say is that Brangwen's way of viewing his wife is exemplary of attitudes that Lawrence advocates in his text taken as a whole, and in other related texts; that Molly Bloom's attitude to Boylan is far from being the only attitude to sexual relations that Joyce depicts, even in his portrayal of Molly's imagining; that Hankinson's entire text objectifies women in the manner of the passage cited, which is but the first of a sequence of increasingly violent episodes that, strung together, constitute the whole of the "novel"[11]; that *Playboy*'s typical approach to women's bodies and achievements is well captured in my example; that Henry James's novel, by contrast, awakens serious moral criticism of its protagonists by portraying them as objectifiers. Hollinghurst is the most puzzling example, and it remains to me quite unclear what attitude the text as a whole invites us to assume to its protagonist and his fantasies.

To give a suggestion of my reaction to the texts: I think that although none of them is without moral complexity, and none will be to everyone's taste, there are two examples of conduct in them, perhaps three, that stand out as especially sinister. (The James characters are the ones of whom I would be most ready to use the term "evil.") At least one of the texts shows how objectification of a kind might be quite harmless and even pleasant, and at least one, perhaps more than one, shows what might lead someone to suggest that it could be a wonderful part of sexual life. Taken as a group, the examples invite us to distinguish different dimensions of objectification and to notice their independence from one another. When we do so, I shall argue, we discover that all types of objectificaiton are not equally objectionable, that the evaluation of any of them requires a careful evaluation of context and circumstance, and that, once we have made the requisite distinctions, we will see how at least some of them might be compatible with consent and equality, and even be "wonderful" parts of sexual life.

Seven Ways to Treat a Person as a Thing

Now we need to begin the analysis. I suggest that in all cases of objectification what is at issue is a question of treating one thing as another: One is treating *as an object* what is really not an object, what is, in fact, a human being. The notion of humanity is involved in quite a Kantian way in the Dworkin quotation that is my epigraph, and I think that it is implicit in most critiques of objectification in the MacKinnon/Dworkin tradition. Beyond this, however, we need to ask what is involved in the idea of treating *as an object*. I suggest that at least the following seven notions are involved in that idea:

1. *Instrumentality*. The objectifier treats the object as a tool of his or her purposes
2. *Denial of autonomy*. The objectifier treats the object as lacking in autonomy and self-determination
3. *Inertness*. The objectifier treats the object as lacking in agency, and perhaps also in activity
4. *Fungibility*. The objectifier treats the object as interchangeable (a) with other objects of the same type and/or (b) with objects of other types
5. *Violability*. The objectifier treats the object as lacking in boundary integrity, as something that it is permissible to break up, smash, break into
6. *Ownership*. The objectifier treats the object as something that is owned by another, can be bought or sold, etc.
7. *Denial of subjectivity*. The objectifier treats the object as something whose experience and feelings (if any) need not be taken into account[12]

Each of these is a feature of our treatment of things, though of course we do not treat all things as objects in all these ways. Treating things as objects is not objectification, because, as I have suggested, objectification entails making into a thing, treating *as* a thing, something that is really not a thing. Nonetheless, thinking for a bit about our familiar ways of treating things will help us to see that these seven features are commonly present and distinct from one another. Most inanimate objects are standardly regarded as tools of our purposes, though some are regarded as worthy of respect for their beauty, age, or naturalness. Most inanimate objects are treated as lacking autonomy, though at times we do regard some objects in nature, or even some machines, as having a life of their own. Many objects are inert and/or passive, though not by any means all. Many are fungible with other objects of a similar sort (one ballpoint pen with another), and also, at times, with objects of a different sort (a pen with a word processor), though many, of course, are not. Some objects are viewed as "violable"[13] or lacking in boundary integrity, though certainly not all: We allow a child to break and destroy relatively few things in the house. Many objects are owned, and are treated as such, though many again are not. (It is interesting that the unowned among the inanimate objects—parts of nature for the most part—are also likely to be the ones to which we especially often attribute a kind of autonomy and an intrinsic worth.) Finally, most objects are treated as entities whose experiences and feelings need not be taken into account, though at times we are urged to think differently about parts of the natural environment, whether with illicit anthropomorphizing or not I shall not determine here. In any case, we can see on the list a cluster of familiar attitudes to things, all of which seem to play a role in the feminist account of the objectification of persons. What objectification is, is to treat a human being in one or more of these ways.

Should we say that each is a sufficient condition for the objectification of persons? Or do we need some cluster of the features, in order to have a sufficient condition? I prefer not to answer this question, because I believe that use is too unclear. On the whole, it seems to me that "objectification" is a relatively loose cluster term, for whose application we sometimes treat any one of these features as sufficient, though more often a plurality of features is present when the term is applied. Clearly there are other ways we standardly treat things— touching them, seeing them—that do not suggest objectification when we apply the same mode of treatment to persons, so we have some reason to think that these seven items are at least signposts of what many have found morally problematic. And there are some items on the list—especially denial of autonomy and denial of subjectivity—that attract our attention from the start because they seem to be modes of treatment we would not bother discussing much in the case of mere things, where questions of autonomy and subjectivity do not arise; they seem most suited to the thing-like treatment of persons. This suggests that they may be of special interest to us in what follows, suggesting that we are going to be at least as interested in the treatment that is denied to persons as in the treatment that is accorded them.[14]

How are the features connected? It will be helpful to turn, first, to two examples from the thing world: a ballpoint pen and a Monet painting. The way in which a ballpoint pen is an object involves, it would seem, all the items on this list, with the possible exception of violability. That is, it might be thought inappropriate or at least wasteful to break up ballpoint pens, but I do not think that worry would rise to great moral heights. Certainly it seems that to treat the pen as a tool, as nonautonomous, as inert, as fungible (with other pens and at times with other instruments or machines), as owned, and as lacking in subjectivity— all this is exactly the standard and appropriate way to treat it. The painting, on the other hand, is certainly nonautonomous, owned, inert (though not passive), and lacking in subjectivity; it is definitely not fungible, either with other paintings or, except in the limited sense of being bought and sold, which does not imply thoroughgoing fungibility, with anything else either; its boundaries are precious, and there is a real question whether it is simply a tool for the purposes of those who use and enjoy it. What this tells us already is that objects come in many kinds. Some objects are precious objects, and these will usually lack fungibility and possess some boundary integrity (inviolability).[15] Others are not so precious and are both fungible and all right to break up.

The items on the list come apart in other ways as well. We see from the case of the painting that lack of autonomy does not necessarily imply instrumentality, though treating as instrumental may well imply treating as nonautonomous; the fact that most objects are inert should not conceal from us, for our later purposes, the fact that inertness is not a necessary condition of either lack of autonomy or instrumentality. Precisely what is useful about my word processor, what makes it such a good tool for my purposes, is that it is not inert. Nor does instrumentality entail lack of consideration for feelings and subjectivity—for one's purpose in using a tool may turn out to require concern for its experiences (as our pornographic examples will clearly show). As for violability, it is not entailed, it would seem, by any of the other six items. Even fungible items are not generally regarded as all right to break or smash, though the ones that are all right to smash are usually of the fungible sort, perhaps because it seems clear that they can be replaced by others of the kind.

Again, the fact that most objects are owned should not conceal from us the fact that ownership is not entailed by any of the other items on the list. Does it entail any of the others? Not fungibility, as is shown by the case of the painting. Not violability, not inertness, and probably not instrumentality, as our attitudes to household pets and even plants show us clearly. (We do not think they are just tools of our own purposes.) But probably ownership does entail lack of self-determination and autonomy; indeed it seems conceptually linked to that absence, though an item may certainly lack autonomy without being owned.

Finally, a thing may be treated as something whose experiences and feelings need not be taken into account without being treated as a mere tool, without being treated as fungible, without being seen as violable—all these are shown in the Monet painting case; also, without being seen as owned (the Grand Canyon, the Mojave Desert), and, it seems clear, without being seen as inert (my word processor). If one treats an object as something whose feelings and experiences need not be taken into account, is that consistent with treating as autonomous? I think very likely not. Again, it seems that there is a conceptual connection here.

In fact, what we are discovering is that autonomy is in a certain sense the most exigent of the notions on our list. It seems difficult if not impossible to imagine a case in which an inanimate object is treated as autonomous, though we can certainly imagine exceptions to all the others. And treating an item as autonomous seems to entail treating it as noninstrumental, as not simply inert, as not owned, and as not something whose feelings need not be taken into account. The only kind of objectification that seems clearly consistent with treating as autonomous, in fact, seems to be treating as fungible, and this in the limited sense of treating as fungible with other autonomous agents. This turns out to be highly pertinent to Hollinghurst, and to a well-developed ideology of gay male promiscuity, best exemplified, perhaps, in Richard Mohr's *Gay Ideas*[16] where fungibility objectification is linked with democratic equality. To this I shall return. Treating as violable, as lacking boundary integrity, may well also be consistent with treating as autonomous, and it is a prominent claim of defenders of consensual sadomasochism (e.g., lesbian and gay writers Gayle Rubin and Richard Mohr) that this is so. Interestingly enough, the same claim has been defended by conservative political philosopher Roger Scruton, in an eloquent and surprising argument.[17] (In fact, Scruton's entire analysis has a great deal to offer the person who tries to think about this subject, and it is certainly the most interesting philosophical attempt to date to work through the moral issues involved in our treatment of persons as sex partners.)

On the other hand, there is one way in which *instrumentality* seems to be the most morally exigent notion. We can think of many cases in which it is permissible to treat a person or thing as nonautonomous (the Monet painting, one's pets, one's small children) and yet inappropriate to treat the object merely or primarily as a tool of our own purposes. That, I have said, would be a bad attitude to the painting, even though the painting hardly displays autonomy. What is interesting is to see how few of the other forms of object treatment are clearly ruled out by the decision not to treat a thing as instrumental. What more, in fact, is entailed by the decision to treat a thing as, to use the Kantian phrase, an end in itself? Not treating as autonomous, I have said, though this does not rule out the possibility that treating as autonomous would be a necessary feature of the noninstrumental treatment *of adult human beings*. Not treating as noninert, in the case of the painting; though again, it is at least arguable that noninstrumentality for adult humans entails recognition of agency and activity. Not treating as nonfungible, or at least not clearly so. I may view each one of many pieces of fine silver flatware as precious for its own sake and yet view them as exchangeable one for another. Not treating as having subjectivity, or not generally (the painting again); though once again, it might turn out that to treat an adult human being as an end in him- or herself does entail recognition of subjectivity. And, finally, it seems quite unclear whether treating as an end in itself requires seeing as inviolable. That all seems to depend on the nature of the object. (Some experimental artworks, for example, invite breakage.) On the whole, though, there may be a conceptual connection between treating as an end in itself and treating as inviolable in the sense that to break up or smash an object is usually to use it in accordance with one's own purposes in ways that negate the natural development and may even threaten the existence of the object.

I now pass over the fascinating issues of objectification raised by our treatment of plants and other animals and move on to some cases involving the treatment of human beings by human beings. Let us for the moment avoid the sexual realm. And let us consider first of all the relationship between parent and child. The treatment of young children by their parents almost always involves a denial of autonomy; it involves some aspects of ownership, though not all. On the other hand, in almost all times and places it has been thought bad for parents to treat their children as lacking in bodily integrity—battery and sexual abuse, though common, are more or less universally deplored. Nor would it be at all common to find children treated as inert and lacking in activity. On the other hand, the extent to which children may be used as tools of their parents' purposes, as beings whose feelings need not be taken into account, and even as fungible,[18] has varied greatly across place and time. Modern American views of childrearing would view all three of these forms of objectification as serious moral wrongs; in other times and places, they have not been so regarded.

Let us now consider Marx's account of the object-like treatment of workers under capitalism (abstracting from the question of its truth).[19] Absence of true autonomy is absolutely crucial to the analysis, as is also instrumentality and absence of concern for experiences and feelings (although Marx seems to grant that workers are still treated with some lingering awareness of their humanity and are not regarded altogether as tools or even animals).[20] Workers are also treated as quite thoroughly fungible, both with other able-bodied workers and at times with machines. They are not, however, treated as inert: Their value to the capitalist producer consists precisely in their activity. Nor, whatever other flaws Marx finds with the system, does he think they are treated as physically violable. The physical safety of workers is at least nominally protected, though of course it is not all that well protected, and the gradual erosion of health through substandard living conditions may itself be regarded as a kind of slow bodily violation. Spiritual violation, on the other hand, lies at the heart of what Marx thinks is happening to workers when they are deprived of control over the central means of their self-definition as humans. Finally, workers are not exactly owned, and are certainly morally different from slaves, but in a very profound sense the relationship is one of ownership—in the sense, namely, that what is most the worker's own, namely, the product of his labor, is what is most taken away from him. MacKinnon has written that sexuality is to feminism what work is to Marxism: In each case something that is most oneself and one's own is what is seen by the theory to have been taken away.[21] We should remember this analogy when we enter the sexual domain.

Now let us think of slavery. Slavery is defined as a form of ownership. This form of ownership entails a denial of autonomy, and it also entails the use of the slave as a mere tool of the purposes of the owner. (Aristotle defines the slave as "an animate tool.") This is true as far as the institution is concerned, and (as even Aristotle granted) is not negated by the fact that on occasion noninstrumental friendships may exist between slave and owner. (As Aristotle says, in that case the friendship is not with the slave *qua* slave but with the slave *qua* human, meaning that the relationship constructed by the institution itself cannot be friendship, though occasionally one may glimpse the human being despite the constraints of the institution.[22]) Why so, given that I have noted that in the case of paintings, house plants, and pets, treating as owned need not entail treating as instrumental? I believe that it is something about the type of ownership involved in slavery, and its relation to the humanity of the slave, that makes this connection. Once one treats a human being as a thing one may buy or sell, one is ipso facto treating that human being as a tool of one's own purposes. Perhaps this is because, as I have suggested, the noninstrumental treatment of adult human beings entails recognition of autonomy, as is not the case for paintings and plants, and ownership is by definition incompatible with autonomy.

On the other hand, slaves are certainly not treated as inert; far from it. Nor are they necessarily treated as fungible in the sense that they may be specialized in their tasks. On the other hand, the very tool-like treatment inherent in the institution entails a certain sort of fungibility in the sense that a person is reduced to a set of body parts performing a certain task and under that understanding can be replaced by another similar body, or by a machine. Slaves are not necessarily regarded as violable; there may even be laws against the rape and/or bodily abuse of slaves. On the other hand, it is easy to see how the thing-like treatment of persons inherent in the institution led, as it so often did, to the feeling that one had a right to use the body of that slave in whatever way one wished. Once one treats as a tool and denies autonomy, it is difficult to say why rape or battery would be wrong except in the sense of rendering the tool a less efficient tool of one's purposes. Slaves, finally, are not always denied subjectivity; one may imagine them as beings mentally well suited to their lot; one may also think with a limited empathy about their pleasure or pain. On the other hand, once again, the very decision to treat a person as not an end in himself or herself but as a mere tool leads rather naturally to a failure of imagination. Once one makes that basic move it is very easy indeed to stop asking the questions morality usually dictates, such as, What is this person likely to feel if I do X? What does this person want, and how will my doing X affect her with respect to those wants? And so on.

This example prepares us for the MacKinnon/Dworkin analysis of sexuality, because it shows us how a certain sort of instrumental use of persons, negating the autonomy that is proper to them as persons, also leaves the human being so denuded of humanity, in the eyes of the objectifier, that he or she seems ripe for other abuses as well—for the refusal of imagination involved in the denial of subjectivity,[23] for the denial of individuality involved in fungibility, and even for bodily and spiritual violation and abuse, if that should appear to be what best suits the will and purposes of the objectifier. The lesson seems to be that there is something especially problematic about instrumentalizing human beings, something that involves denying what is fundamental to them as human beings, namely, the status of being ends in themselves. From this one denial, other forms of objectification that are not logically entailed by the first seem to follow.

Notice, however, that instrumentalization does not seem to be problematic in all contexts. If I am lying around with my lover on the bed and use his stomach as a pillow, there seems to be nothing at all baneful about this, provided I do so with his consent (or, if he is asleep, with a reasonable belief that he would not mind), and without causing him unwanted pain, provided, as well, that I do so in the context of a relationship in which he is generally treated as more than a pillow.[24] This suggests that what is problematic is not instrumentalization per se but treating someone *primarily* or *merely* as an instrument. The overall context of the relationship thus becomes fundamental, and I shall return to it.

Kant, Dworkin, and MacKinnon

We are now beginning to get a sense of the terrain of this concept and to see how slippery, and how multiple, it is. We are also beginning to approach, I think, the core idea of MacKinnon's and Dworkin's analysis. As Barbara Herman has argued in a remarkable article,[25] this core notion is Kantian. Central to Kant's analysis of sexuality and marriage is the idea that sexual desire is a very powerful force that conduces to the thing-like treatment of persons, by which he means, above all, the treatment of persons not as ends in themselves but as means or tools for the satisfaction of one's own desires.[26] That kind of instrumentalizing of persons is very closely linked, in his view, to both a denial of autonomy—one wishes to dictate how the other person will behave, so as to secure one's own satisfaction—and also to a denial of subjectivity—one stops asking how the other person is thinking or feeling, bent on securing one's own satisfaction. It would appear that these three notions are the ones in which Kant is interested. Inertness, fungibility, ownership, and even violability do not seem to interest him, although one can easily see how the instrumentalization he describes might lead, here as in the case of the slave, to the view that the other body can be violated or abused, as long as that secures the agent's own pleasure. Certainly Dworkin, when she follows him, does make this connection, tracing the prevalence of sex abuse and sadistic violence to the initial act of denying autonomy and end-like status.[27]

Why does Kant think that sex does this? His argument is by no means clear, but we can try to elaborate it. The idea seems to be that sexual desire and pleasure cause very acute forms of sensation in a person's own body; that these sensations drive out, for a time, all other thoughts, including the thoughts of respect for humanity that are characteristic of the moral attitude to persons. Apparently he also thinks that they drive out every end-like consideration of the pleasure or experience of the sex partner and cause attention to be riveted on one's own bodily states. In that condition of mind, one cannot manage to see the other person as anything but a tool of one's own interests, a set of bodily parts that are useful tools for one's pleasure, and the powerful urge to secure one's own sexual satisfaction will ensure that instrumentalization (and therefore denial of autonomy and of subjectivity) continues until the sexual act has reached its conclusion. At the same time, the keen interest both parties have in sexual satisfaction will lead them to permit themselves to be treated in this thing-like way by one another, indeed, to volunteer eagerly to be dehumanized in order that they can dehumanize the other in turn.[28] Kant clearly believes this to be a feature of sexuality generally, not just of male sexuality, and he does not connect his analysis to any issues of social hierarchy or the asymmetrical social formation of erotic desire. He seems to think that in a typical sex act both parties eagerly desire both to be objectifiers and to be objects.

MacKinnon and Dworkin in a way follow Kant but in a very important way depart from him. Like Kant, they start from the notion that all human beings are owed respect, and that this respect is incompatible with treating them as instruments, and also with denials of autonomy and subjectivity.[29] Unlike Kant, however, they do not believe that these denials are intrinsic to sexual desire itself. They do not have a great deal to say about how sexual desire can elude these problems, but the more overtly erotic parts of Dworkin's fiction suggest that it is possible to aim, in sex, at a mutually satisfying fused experience of pleasure in which both parties temporarily surrender autonomy in a good way (a way that enhances receptivity and sensitivity to the other) without instrumentalizing one another or becoming indifferent to one another's needs. Because she is clearly much influenced by Lawrence, I shall return to these issues when I discuss him later. Moreover, in her discussions of James Baldwin in *Intercourse* (47–61), Dworkin makes it clear that she thinks that the lovemaking of gay men can right now, in our society, exemplify these good characteristics, because their relationships need not be deformed by social hierarchy. The problem derives not from any obtuseness in sexual desire itself but from the way in which we have been socialized erotically, in a society that is suffused with hierarchy and domination. Men learn to experience desire in connection with paradigm scenarios of domination and instrumentalization. (The fact that pornography is, for both MacKinnon and Dworkin, a primary source of these paradigm scenarios is what explains the importance of pornography in their thought.) Women learn to experience desire in connection with these same paradigm scenarios, which means that they learn to eroticize being dominated and being turned into objects. Thus objectification for MacKinnon and Dworkin is asymmetrical: On the one side the objectifier, on the other side, the volunteer for object status. And this means that it is only the female for whom sex entails a forfeiture of humanity, being turned into something rather than someone. MacKinnon and Dworkin sometimes suggest that this objectification involves elements of inertness,[30] fungibility, and ownership,[31] but it seems to me clear that the central core of the concept, as they use it, is in fact that of instrumentality, connected in a Kantian way to denials of autonomy and subjectivity, and in a related way to the possibility of violation and abuse.[32]

Kant's solution to the problem of sexual objectification and use is marriage.[33] He argues that objectification can be rendered harmless only if sexual relations are restricted to a relationship that is structured institutionally in ways that promote and, at least legally if not morally, guarantee mutual respect and regard. If the two parties are bound to support one another in various ways, this ensures a certain kind of respect for personhood that will persist undestroyed by the ardors of lovemaking, though it is apparently Kant's view that this respect and "practical love" can never color or infuse the lovemaking itself.[34] Characteristically, Kant is not very much worried about the asymmetrical or hierarchical nature of marriage, or about its aspects of ownership and denial of autonomy. These aspects he sees as fitting and proper, and he never suggests that sexual objectification derives support from these institutional arrangements.

For Dworkin and MacKinnon, by contrast, hierarchy is at the root of the problem. The lack of respect that much lovemaking displays is not, as I have argued, a feature of sexuality in itself; it is created by asymmetrical structures of power. Marriage, with its historical connotations of ownership and nonautonomy, is one of the structures that makes sexuality go bad. We see this, for example, in Dworkin's *Mercy*, in which the mutually satisfying passionate sexual relationship between Andrea and the young revolutionary turns sour as soon as they are man and wife. Encouraged by the institution, he begins to need to assert his dominance sexually, and the relationship degenerates into a terrible saga of sadism and abuse. In this morality tale Dworkin illustrates her belief that institutions maim us despite our best intentions, causing the eroticization of forms of sexual conduct that dehumanize and brutalize. The remedy for this state of affairs, it is suggested, is no single institution but rather the gradual undoing of all the institutional structures that lead men to eroticize power. Thus the critiques of sexual harassment, of domestic violence, and of pornography hang together as parts of a single program of Kantian moral/political reform.

Failure to sort out the different aspects of the concept of objectification leads at times to obscurity in MacKinnon's and Dworkin's critique. Consider, for example, the following passage from Dworkin's analysis of *The Story of O*:

> O is totally possessed. That means that she is an object, with no control over her own mobility, capable of no assertion of personality. Her body is *a* body, in the same way that a pencil is a pencil, a bucket is a bucket, or, as Gertrude Stein pointedly said, a rose is a rose. It also means that O's energy, or power, as a woman, as Woman, is absorbed. . . . The rings through O's cunt with Sir Stephen's name and heraldry, and the brand on her ass, are permanent wedding rings rightly placed. They mark her as an owned object and in no way symbolize the passage into maturity and freedom. The same might be said of the conventional wedding ring.[35]

Here we have inertness, fungibility, and ownership, all treated as if they are more or less inevitable consequences of an initial denial of autonomy (mixed up, clearly, with instrumentalization). It may be true that the novel makes these connections, and that the particular way in which Sir Stephen possesses O is in fact incompatible with active agency, with qualitative individuality, or with nonownership. But it is important to insist that these are logically independent ideas. One may deny autonomy to a beloved child without these other consequences. So what we want to know is, How are they connected here? What should make us believe that a typical male way of relating to women as nonautonomous brings these other consequences in its train? (For it is clear, as the wedding ring remark indicates, that for Dworkin *The Story of O* is a paradigm of a type of relationship prevalent in our culture.) If we are contemplating institutional and/ or moral change, we need to understand these connections clearly so that we will have a sense of where we might start.

What brings these different aspects of the concept together is, I believe, a certain characteristic mode of instrumentalization and use that is alleged to lie behind the male denial of autonomy to women. For Sir Stephen, O exists only as something to be used to gratify his own pleasure (and, as Dworkin perceptively points out, as a surrogate for the male René, whom he loves but will not approach physically). Apart from that she is O, zero. So she is not like a beloved child, who may be denied autonomy but retain individuality and agency. She is just a set of bodily parts, in particular a cunt and an anus[36] to be entered and used, with nothing of salience over and above them, not even the individuality and agency of those parts. It is in this way, I believe, that Dworkin (and at times MacKinnon) makes the further step from the core concepts of instrumentalization and denial of autonomy to the other aspects of the concept of objectification. They believe that these connections are ubiquitous. This, they suggest, is the sum total of what women are under male domination. But once we have noticed that the connections are not as conceptually tight as they suggest, we are led to ask how pervasive in fact they are. And we are led to ask whether and to what extent women and men can combine these features in different ways in their lives, uncoupling passivity from instrumentality, for example, or fungibility from the denial of autonomy.

A Wonderful Part of Sexual Life?

Before returning to the passages, we must observe one fundamental point: In the matter of objectification, context is everything. MacKinnon and Dworkin grant this when they insist, correctly, that we assess male-female relations in the light of the larger social context and history of female subordination and insist on differentiating the meaning of objectification in these contexts from its meaning in either male-male or female-female relations. But they rarely go further, looking at the histories and the psychologies of individuals. (In fact, in judging literary works they standardly refuse appeal to the work-as-a-whole test; even where narrative is concerned, context is held to be irrelevant.[37]) In a sense the fine details of context are of little interest to them, involved as they are in a political movement; on the other hand, they are of considerable interest to us, for I shall argue that in many if not all cases, the difference between an objectionable and a benign use of objectification will be made by the overall context of the human relationship in question.

This can be seen easily if we consider a simple example. W, a woman, is going out of town for an important interview. M, an acquaintance, says to her, "You don't really need to go. You can just send them some pictures." If M is not a close friend of W, this is almost certain to be an offensively objectifying remark. It reduces W to her bodily (and facial) parts, suggesting, in the process, that her professional accomplishments and other personal attributes do not count. The remark certainly seems to slight W's autonomy; it treats her as an inert object, appropriately represented by a photograph; it may suggest some limited sort of fungibility. It may also, depending on the context, suggest instrumentalization: W is being treated as an object for the enjoyment of the male gaze. Suppose, now, M is W's lover, and he says this to her in bed. This changes things, but we really don't know how, because we don't know enough. We don't know what the interview is for (a modeling job? a professorship?). And we don't know enough about the people. If M standardly belittles her accomplishments, the remark is a good deal worse than the same remark made by a stranger, and more deeply suggestive of instrumentalization. If, on the other hand, there is a deeply understood mutual respect between them and he is simply finding a way of telling her how attractive she is, and perhaps of telling her that he doesn't want her to leave town, then things become rather different. It may still be a risky thing to say, far more risky than the very same thing said by W to M, given the social history that colors all such relationships. Still, there is the sense that the remark is not reductive—that instead of taking away from W, the compliment to her appearance may have added something. (Much depends on tone of voice, gesture, sense of humor.) Consider, finally, the same remark made to W by a close friend. W knows that this friend respects her accomplishments and has great confidence in his attitude toward her in all respects pertinent to friendship, but she wishes he would notice her body once in a while. In this case, the objectifying remark may come as a pleasant surprise to W, a joke embodying a welcome compliment. Though we still need to know more about what the interview is all about, and how it is related to W's capacities (and though we still should reflect about the fact that it is extremely unlikely, given the way our society currently is, that such a remark will ever be made by W to M), it may well seem to her as if the remark has added something without taking anything away. It is possible, of course, that W reacts this way because she has eroticized her own submission. Such claims, like all claims of false consciousness, are difficult to adjudicate. But it seems to me implausible that all such cases are of this sort. To these human complexities Dworkin and MacKinnon frequently seem to me insufficiently sensitive.

Let us now turn to the examples of objectification presented at the start of this chapter. Lawrence focuses, here as often, on the willing resignation of autonomy and, in a sense, of subjectivity. The power of sexuality is most authentically experienced, in his view, when the parties do put aside their conscious choice making, and even their inner life of self-consciousness and articulate thought, and permit themselves to be, in a sense, object-like, natural forces meeting one another with what he likes to call "blood knowledge." Thus, Brangwen feels his blood surging up in a way that eclipses deliberation, that makes him "blind and destroyed." His wife at this moment does appear to him as a mysterious thing-like presence—in the striking metaphor, a "blazing kernel of darkness" (indicating that the illumination that comes from sexuality requires, first, the blinding of the intellect). This thing-like presence summons him—not, however, to instrumental use of it but to a kind of surrender of his own personhood, a kind of yielding abnegation of self-containment and self-sufficiency. This sort of objectification has its roots, then, in a mutual denial of autonomy and subjective self-awareness. It has links with inertness, understood as passivity and receptivity, as both surrender agency before the power of the blood. It has links, as well, with fungibility: For in a certain sense, Lydia's daily qualitative individuality does vanish before his desire, as she becomes an embodiment of something primal; and he puts aside his daily ways of self-definition, his own idiosyncrasies, before the dark presence that summons him. And there is also a link with violability: For in the sway of desire, he no longer feels himself clearly individuated from her, he feels his boundaries become porous, he feels the longing to be "destroyed" as an individual, "burnt away."[38] Lawrence, like (and influenced by) Schopenhauer, sees a connection between the ascendancy of passion and the loss of definite boundaries, the loss of what Schopenhauer calls the *principium individuationis*.

All this is objectification. And whether or not one finds Lawrence's prose, or even his ideas, to one's taste, it seems undeniable that it captures some profound features of at least some sexual experiences. (As I have said, it is this very idea of sexuality that animates the fiction of Andrea Dworkin, and it is this wonderful possibility that she hates sexism for destroying.) If one were to attribute a sense to Sunstein's remark that objectification might be argued to be a wonderful part of sexual life, one might begin to do so along these lines. Indeed, one might go so far as to claim, with Schopenhauer, that it is a necessary feature of sexual life—though Lawrence seems to me to make a more plausible claim when he indicates that such resignation of control is not ubiquitous and can in fact be relatively rare, especially in a culture very much given to self-conscious aloofness and the repression of feeling.

It is worth noting that Lawrentian objectification is frequently connected with a certain type of reduction of persons to their bodily parts and the attribution of a certain sort of independent agency to the bodily parts. Consider this scene from *Lady Chatterley*:

> "Let me see you!"
>
> He dropped the shirt and stood still, looking towards her. The sun through the low window sent a beam that lit up his thighs and slim belly, and the erect phallus rising darkish and hot-looking from the little cloud of vivid gold-red hair. She was startled and afraid.
>
> "How strange!" she said slowly. "How strange he stands there! So big! and so dark and cocksure! Is he like that?"
>
> The man looked down the front of his slender white body, and laughed. Between the slim breasts the hair was dark, almost black. But at the root of the belly, where the phallus rose thick and arching, it was gold-red, vivid in a little cloud.
>
> "So proud!" she murmured, uneasy. "And so lordly! Now I know why men are so overbearing. But he's lovely, really, like another being! A bit terrifying! But lovely really! And he comes to me—" She caught her lower lip between her teeth, in fear and excitement.
>
> The man looked down in silence at his tense phallus, that did not change. . . . "Cunt, that's what tha'rt after. Tell lady Jane tha' wants cunt. John Thomas, an' th' cunt o' lady Jane!—"
>
> "Oh, don't tease him," said Connie, crawling on her knees on the bed towards him and putting her arms round his white slender loins, and drawing him to her so that her hanging swinging breasts touched the top of the stirring erect phallus, and caught the drop of moisture. She held the man fast.

Here there is a sense in which both parties put aside their individuality and become identified with their bodily organs. They see one another in terms of those organs. And yet Kant's suggestion that in all such focusing on parts there is denial of humanity seems quite wrong. Even the suggestion that they are *reducing* one another to their bodily parts seems quite wrong, just as I think it seemed wrong in my simple photograph example. The intense focusing of attention on the bodily parts seems an addition, rather than a subtraction, and the scene of passion, which is fraught for Constance with a sense of terror, and the fear of being overborne by male power, is rendered benign and loving, is rendered in fact liberating, by this very objectification, in the manner in which Mellors undertakes it, combining humor with passion.

Why is Lawrentian objectification benign, if it is? We must point, above all, to the complete absence of instrumentalization, and to the closely connected fact that the objectification is symmetrical and mutual—and in both cases undertaken in a context of mutual respect and rough social equality.[39] The surrender of autonomy and even of agency and subjectivity are joyous, a kind of victorious achievement in the prison house of English respectability. Such a surrender constitutes an escape from the prison of self-consciousness that, in Lawrence's quite plausible view, seals us off from one another and prevents true communication and true receptivity. In the willingness to permit another person to be this close, in a position in which the dangers of being dominated and overborne are, as Constance knows, omnipresent, one sees, furthermore, enormous trust, trust that might be thought to be impossible in a relationship that did not include at least some sort of mutual respect and concern—although in Lawrence's depictions of a variety of more or less tortured male-female relationships we discover that this is complex. When there is loss of autonomy in sex, the context is, or at least can be, one in which, on the whole, autonomy is respected and promoted; the success of the sexual relationship can have, as in Constance's case, wide implications for flourishing and freedom more generally. We do not need to find every single idea of Lawrence's about sexuality appealing to see in the scene something that is of genuine value. Again, when there is a loss in subjectivity in the moment of lovemaking, this can be and frequently is accompanied by an intense concern for the subjectivity of the partner at other moments, because the lover is intensely focused on the moods and wishes of that one person, whose states mean so much for his or her own. Brangwen's obsession with his wife's fluctuating moods shows this very clearly.

Finally, we see that the kind of apparent fungibility involved in identifying persons with parts of their bodies need not be dehumanizing at all but can coexist with an intense regard for the person's individuality, which can even be expressed in a personalizing and individualizing of the bodily organs themselves, as in the exchange between Mellors and Constance. Giving a proper name to the genital organs of each is a way of signifying the special and individual way in which they desire one another, the nonfungible character of Mellors's sexual intentionality.[40] It is Mellors's way of telling Constance what she did not know before (and what MacKinnon and Dworkin seem at times not to know), that to be identified with her genital organs is not necessarily to be seen as dehumanized meat ripe for victimization and abuse but can be a way of being seen more fully as the human individual she is. It is a reminder that the genital organs of people are not really fungible but have their own individual character, and are in effect parts of the person, if one will really look at them closely without shame.[41]

We are now in a position to notice something quite interesting about Kant. He thinks that focusing on the genital organs entails the disregard of personhood—because he apparently believes that personhood and humanity, and, along with them, individuality, do not reside in the genital organs; the genital organs are just fungible nonhuman things, like so many tools. Lawrence says, that is a response that itself dehumanizes us, by reducing to something subhuman what properly is a major part of the humanity in us, and the individuality as well. We are a certain type of animal, and animality is part of our personhood, complexly interwoven with individuality and personality. We have to learn to call our genital organs by proper names—that would be at least the beginning of a properly complete human regard for one another.

Thinking about Lawrence can make us question the account of the deformation of sexuality given by MacKinnon and Dworkin. For Lawrence suggests that the inequality and, in a sense, dehumanization of women in Britain—which he does frequently acknowledge, not least in *Lady Chatterley*—rests on and derives strength from the denial of women's erotic potentiality, the insistence that women be seen as sexless things and not identified also with their genital organs. Like Audré Lorde among contemporary feminists,[42] Lawrence shows how a kind of sexual objectification—not, certainly, a commercial sort, and one that is profoundly opposed to the commercialization of sex[43]—can be a vehicle of autonomy and self-expression for women, how the very surrender of autonomy in a certain sort of sex act can free energies that can be used to make the self whole and full.[44] In effect, Mellor is the only character in that novel who sees Connie as an end in herself, and this noninstrumentalization, and the attendant promotion of her autonomy, is closely connected to his sexual interest.

MacKinnon and Dworkin would surely object that both Lawrence and Lorde are somewhat naive in their assumption that there is a domain of "natural" sexuality behind cultural constructions, which can be liberated in a sex act of the right sort. They would argue that this underestimates the depth to which sexual roles and desires are culturally shaped and therefore infected by the ubiquitous distortions of gender roles. It is beyond the scope of this essay to adjudicate this large controversy, but I can at least indicate the direction my reply would take. I believe that it is correct that Lawrence's romantic rhetoric of nature and blood knowledge probably is naive, underestimating the depth of socialization and, more generally, of cognitive awareness, in sexual life. Nor do I sympathize with Lawrence's idea that sexuality is better the freer it is of both culture and thought. On the other hand, I think that his larger case for the value of a certain type of resignation of control, and of both emotional and bodily receptivity, does not depend on these other theses, and that one can defend a kind of Lawrentian sexuality (as, indeed, Andrea Dworkin herself does, in the early chapters of *Mercy* and in her essays on Baldwin) without accepting them. Such a stance does involve the recognition that our culture is more heterogeneous and allows us more space for negotiation and personal construction than MacKinnon and Dworkin usually allow.[45]

We turn now to Molly Bloom. Molly regards Blazes Boylan as a collection of outsized bodily parts. She does so with humor and joy, though at the same time with certain reservations about the quality of Boylan's humanity. Her objectification of Boylan has little to do with either denial of his autonomy or instrumentalization and use—certainly not with inertness either, or ownership, or violability. It focuses on features of denial of subjectivity (she never in the entire monologue wonders about what he feels, as she so frequently does about Poldy), fungibility (he is just an especially large penis, "all right to spend time with as a joke," almost interchangeable with a stallion, or an inanimate dildo-like crowbar). This is far from being a profound Lawrentian experience. It is a little unsatisfying, in its absence of depth, to Molly herself—whose ambiguous use of the word "spunk" to mean both "semen" and "character" shows us throughout the monologue her own confusion about the importance of this physical joy by comparison to her physically unsatisfying but loving relationship with Poldy. On the other hand, it seems that Molly's delight in the physical aspects of sex (which was found especially shocking by prudish attackers of the novel) is at least a part of what Lawrence and André Lorde want women to be free to experience, and it seems wrong to denigrate it because of its incompleteness. (Indeed, one might say that the theme of the novel as a whole is the acceptance of incompleteness, and what Joyce would most profoundly be opposed to would be a moralizing Lawrentian romantic denigration of Molly's pleasure on account of the fact that it was not especially earthshaking.[46]) So here we have quite a different way in which objectification may be a joyous part of sexual life—and maybe this sort of mythic focusing on body parts is even a regular or necessary feature of it, though Molly's comic exaggeration is not.

What is especially important to notice, for our purposes, is the way in which our reaction to Molly's objectification of Boylan is conditioned by context. Molly is socially and personally quite powerless, except through her powers of seduction. She is also aware that Boylan does not have an especially high regard for her—he is, like so many other men, using her as a sex object—"because thats all they want out of you." There is a retaliatory self-protective character to her denial of subjectivity that makes it seem right and just in a way that it might not be if it were Boylan thinking about Molly.

Hankinson's hard-core "novel" is both a typical example of the genre attacked by MacKinnon and Dworkin and, in itself, quite an interesting case in its pseudo-literary aspects. For if one holds this passage up next to *The Rainbow*, as the customer of the Blue Moon Press is not very likely to do, one notices the way in which Hankinson has borrowed from Lawrence and has incorporated into his narrative of violence and abuse features of the Lawrentian "blood knowledge" and denial of autonomy that serve as legitimating devices for the violence that ensues. We said that Lawrentian sexuality involves the surrender of individuation and a certain sort of porousness of boundaries that can border on violability. Lawrence certainly depicts the willingness to be penetrated as a valuable aspect of sexual receptivity. The question then is (1) can sadomasochistic sexual acts ever have a simply Lawrentian character, rather than a more sinister character? and (2) is Hankinson's narrative a case of that benign sort? (Here I shall not be able to say much about the characters and their conduct without focusing on the way in which the "implied author" has structured the narrative as a whole, because the "novel" is exceedingly formulaic and lacking in complex characterization.)

There seems to be no a priori reason why the answer to (1) cannot be "yes." I have no very clear intuitions on this point, and here I am going to have to own to limits of experience and desire, but it would seem that some narrative depictions of sadomasochistic activity do plausibly attribute to its consensual form a kind of Lawrentian character in which the willingness to be vulnerable to the infliction of pain, in some respects a sharper stimulus than pleasure, manifests a more complete trust and receptivity than could be found in other sexual acts. Pat Califia's disturbing short story "Jenny" is one example of such a portrayal.[47] And Hankinson certainly positions his narrative this way, suggesting that there is a profound mutual desire that leads the two actors to seek an absence of individuation. The Lawrentian "atavistic voice" speaking from within Isabelle asks for the continuation of violence, and Hankinson suggests that in asking this she is making contact with some depth in her being that lies beneath mere personality. All this is Lawrence, and Schopenhauer, in Blue Moon Press clothing.

What makes the difference, clearly, are context and intention. For the answer to (2) is clearly "no." Not only the character Macrae but Hankinson's text as a whole represents women as creatures whose autonomy and subjectivity do not matter at all, insofar as they are not involved in the gratification of male desire. The women, including whatever signs of humanity they display, are just there to be used as sex objects for men in whatever way suits them. The eroticization of the woman's inertness, her lack of autonomy, her violability—and the assuaging fiction that this is what she has asked for, this is what nature has dictated for her—all these features, which make the example a textbook case of MacKinnon's views, also make it crucially unlike Lawrence, in which vulnerability and risk are mutually assumed and there is no malign or destructive intent.[48] In Lawrence, being treated as a cunt is a permission to expand the sphere of one's activity and fulfillment. In Hankinson, being treated like a cunt is being treated like something whose experiences do not matter at all. The entire novel, which is nothing but a succession of similar scenes, conceals the subjectivity of women from the reader's view and constructs women as objects for male use and control. There is a ghastly way in which subjectivity does figure, for Macrae's desire is a desire "to violate . . . to desecrate, destroy." It is a desire that would not have been satisfied by intercourse with a corpse, or even an animal. What is made sexy here is precisely the act of turning a creature whom in one dim corner of one's mind one knows to be human into a thing, a something rather than a someone. And to be able to do that to a fellow human being is sexy because it is a dizzying experience of power.

John Stuart Mill vividly described the distorted upbringing of men in England, who are taught every day that they are superior to one half of the human race, even though at the same time they see the fine achievements and character of women daily before their eyes. They learn that just in virtue of being male they are superior to the most exalted and talented woman, and they are corrupted by this awareness.[49] Consider in this light the education of Hankinson's reader, who learns (in the visceral way in which pornography leaves its impress, forming patterns of arousal and response[50]) that just in virtue of being male he is entitled to violate half of the human race, whose humanity is at the same time dimly presented to his vision. To the extent that he immerses himself in such works and regularly finds easy and uncomplicated satisfaction in connection with the images they construct, he is likely to form certain patterns of expectation regarding women—that they are for his pleasure, to be taken in this way. The work as a whole, which contains no episodes that are not of this kind, strongly encourages such projections.[51] Unlike MacKinnon and Dworkin, I do not favor any legal restrictions on such work, on balance not even the civil ordinance they propose, because I believe it would be ill administered in practice and would jeopardize expressive interests that it is important to protect.[52] I also think that the availability of this work has moral value, because we learn a lot about sexism from studying it. But I would certainly take it away from any young boy I know, I would protest against its inclusion on a reading list or syllabus—except in the way I recommend our reading it here[53]—and I would think that an ethical critique of it, which needs to be given again and again, is indeed, as Andrea Dworkin says in my epigraph, "at the heart of our struggle."

Playboy is more polite, but ultimately similar. Here again I agree with MacKinnon and Dworkin, who have repeatedly stressed the essential similarity between the soft-core and the hard-core pornography industries. The message given by picture and caption is, Whatever else this woman is and does, for us she is an object for sexual enjoyment. Once again, the male reader is told, in effect, that he is the one with subjectivity and autonomy, and on the other side are things that look very sexy and are displayed out there for his consumption, like delicious pieces of fruit, existing only or primarily to satisfy his desire.[54] The message is more benign because, as a part of the Playboy "philosophy," women are depicted as beings made for sexual pleasure, rather than for the infliction of pain, and their autonomy and subjectivity are given a nodding sort of recognition. Playboy could be said to be part of the movement for women's liberation in the sense suggested by Lawrence and Lorde. Insofar as women's full autonomy and self-expression are hindered by the repression and denial of their sexual capacities, thus far the cheery liberationist outlook of Playboy might be said to be feminist.

However, the objectification in Playboy is in fact a profound betrayal not only of the Kantian ideal of human regard but also, and perhaps especially, of the Lawrence/Lorde program. For Playboy depicts a thoroughgoing fungibility and commodification of sex partners and, in the process, severs sex from any deep connection with self-expression or emotion. Lorde argues plausibly when she suggests that this dehumanization and commercialization of sex is but the modern face of an older puritanism, and the apparent feminism of such publications a mask for a profoundly repressive attitude toward real female passion.[55] Indeed, Hankinson could argue that Playboy is worse than his novel, for his novel at least connects sexuality to the depths of people's dreams and wishes (both female and male) and thus avoids the reduction of bodies to interchangeable commodities, whereas in Playboy sex is a commodity and women become very like cars, or suits, namely, expensive possessions that mark one's status in the world of men.

Who is objectified in Playboy? In the immediate context, it is the represented woman who is being objectified and, derivatively, the actress whose photograph appears. But the characteristic Playboy generalizing approach ("why we love tennis," or "women of the Ivy League") assisted in no small measure by the magazine's focus on photographs of real women, rather than on paintings or fictions, strongly suggests that real-life women, relevantly similar to the tennis player, can easily be cast in the roles in which *Playboy* casts its chosen few. In that way it constructs for the reader a fantasy objectification of a class of real women. Used as a masturbatory aid, it encourages the idea that an easy satisfaction can be had in this uncomplicated way, without the difficulties attendant on recognizing women's subjectivity and autonomy in a more full-blooded way.[56]

We can now observe one further feature of Lawrence that marks him as different from the pornographer. In Lawrence, the men whose sexual behavior is approved are always remarkably unconcerned with worldly status and honor. The last thing they would think of would be to treat a woman as a prize possession, an object whose presence in their lives, and whose sexual interest in them, enhances their status in the world of men. (Indeed, that sort of status-centered attitude to women is connected by Lawrence with sexual impotence, in the character of Clifford Chatterley.) One cannot even imagine Mellors boasting in the locker room of the "hot number" he had the previous night, or regarding the tits and ass or the sexual behavior of Connie as items of display in the male world. What is most characteristic of Mellors (and of Tom Brangwen) is a profound indifference to the worldly signs of prestige, and this is a big part of the reason why both Connie Chatterley and the reader have confidence that his objectification of her is quite different from commodification (in my vocabulary, instrumentalization/ownership).

Playboy, by contrast, is just like a car magazine, only with people instead of cars to make things a little sexier—in the Hankinson way in which it is sexier to use a human being as a thing than to simply have a thing, because it manifests greater control, it shows that one can control what is of such a nature as to elude control. The magazine is all about the competition of men with other men, and its message is the availability of a readily renewable supply of more or less fungible women to men who have achieved a certain level of prestige and money—or, rather, that fantasy women of this sort are available, through the magazine, to those who can fantasize that they have achieved this status. It is not in that sense very different from the ancient Greek idea that the victorious warrior would be rewarded with seven tripods, ten talents of gold, twenty cauldrons, twelve horses, and seven women.[57] Objectification means a certain sort of self-regarding display.

The one further thing that needs to be said about the picture is that in the *Playboy* world it is sexier, because more connected with status, to have a woman of achievement and talent than an unmarked woman, in the way that it is sexier to have a Mercedes than a Chevrolet, in the way that Agamemnon assures Achilles that the horses he is giving him are prize-winning race horses and the women both beautiful and skilled in weaving. But a sleek woman is even more sexy than a sleek car, which cannot really be dominated because it is nothing but a thing. For what *Playboy* repeatedly says to its reader is, Whoever this woman is and whatever she has achieved, for you she is cunt, all her pretensions vanish before your sexual power. For some she is a tennis player—but you, in your mind, can dominate her and turn her into cunt. For some, Brown students are Brown students. For you, dear reader, they are *Women of the Ivy League* (an issue prepared at regular intervals, and a topic of intense controversy on the campuses where models are sought[58]). No matter who you are, these women will (in masturbatory fantasy) moan with pleasure at your sexual power. This is the great appeal of *Playboy* in fact, for it satisfies the desires of men to feel themselves special and powerful, by telling them that they too can possess the signs of exalted status that they think of as in real life reserved for such as Donald Trump. This, of course, Lawrence would see as the sterile status-seeking of Clifford Chatterley, in a modern guise.

Playboy, I conclude, is a bad influence on men[59]—hardly a surprising conclusion. I draw no legal implications from this judgment, but, as in the case of Hankinson, I think we should ponder this issue when we educate boys and young men and meet the prevalence of that style of objectification with criticism—the most powerful form of which is, as Andrea Dworkin said, the assertion of one's own humanity at all times.

Hollinghurst is a case full of fascinating ambiguity. On its surface, this scene, like many in the novel, manifests the exuberant embrace of sexual fungibility that characterized parts of the male gay subculture in the pre-AIDS era. It seems like a very different sort of eroticizing of bodily parts from the sort that goes on in Hankinson and *Playboy*, more like Molly Bloom, in fact, in its delight in the size of organs, coupled with a cheerful nonexploitative attitude, albeit an emotionally superficial one, to the people behind the parts. Richard Mohr has written eloquently of this sort of promiscuous sexuality that it embodies a certain ideal of democracy, because couplings of the anonymous bathhouse sort neglect distinctions of class and rank. In a rather Whitmanesque burst of enthusiasm, he concludes that "Gay sexuality of the sort that I have been discussing both symbolizes and generates a kind of fundamental equality—the sort of fundamental equality that stands behind and is necessary for justifications of democracy."[60] The idea is that anonymous couplings establish that in an especially fundamental matter everyone really is equal to everyone else. Mohr makes it very clear that this can happen among men because they are already acknowledged socially as more than just bodies, because the social meaning of objectification among men is altogether different from its meaning between men and women. This being the case, promiscuous and anonymous sex can exemplify a norm of equality.

Mohr does seem to have gotten at something important about democracy, something about the moral role of the fungibility of bodies that is probably important in both the utilitarian and the Kantian liberal traditions. Certainly the fact that all citizens have similar bodies subject to similar accidents has played an important role in the thought of democratic theorists as diverse as Rousseau and Walt Whitman. Some such egalitarian idea animates Hollinghurst as well at some moments. On the other hand, it is a little hard to know how the sexual scene at issue really is supposed to show the sort of equal regard for bodily need that underlies this democratic tradition. Notice how distinctions of class and rank are omnipresent, even in the prose that pushes them aside. The narrator is intensely conscious of racial differences, which he tends, here as elsewhere, to associate with stereotypes of genital organ size. Nor are the cycle clips and duffle coats that mark the lower middle classes ever out of mind, even when they are out of sight—and the disdainful description of the small genitalia of the "smirking" neighbor strongly suggests the disdain of the "jacket and tie" for these signs of inferiority. We notice, in fact, that all the genitalia described are stereotypes, and none is personalized with the regard of Mellors for the "cunt of Lady Jane."

Now the question is, How is this connected with the emphasis on fungibility? Mohr would say, presumably, that there is no connection—that this narrator, an upper-class Englishman, has just not managed to enter fully enough into the democratic spirit of the bathhouse world. But the suspicion remains that there may after all be some connection between the spirit of fungibility and a focus on these superficial aspects of race and class and penis size, which do in a sense dehumanize and turn people into potential instruments. For in the absence of any narrative history with the person, how can desire attend to anything else but the incidental, and how can one do more than use the body of the other as a tool of one's own states?[61] The photographs used by Mohr to illustrate his idea focus intently on hypermasculine characteristics of musculature and penis size, which presumably are not equally distributed among all citizens of this world, and indeed one imagines that the world so constructed is likely to be one in which morally irrelevant characteristics count for everything, rather than nothing, an extremely hierarchical world, rather than one without hierarchy. Maybe this just means that people are not after all treated as fungible, and that if they were to be more fully treated as fungible, things would be well. But the worry is that in a setting that, in order to construct a kind of fungibility, denies all access to features of personhood that are at the heart of the real democratic equality of persons, it is hard to see how things could turn out otherwise. This is not a knockdown argument showing that Mohr's Whitmanesque ideal is doomed to failure. The connection between fungibility and instrumentality is loose and causal rather than conceptual. But it is a worry that would, I think, be shared by MacKinnon and Dworkin with Lorde and Lawrence: Can one really treat someone with the respect and concern that democracy requires if one has sex with him in the anonymous spirit of Hollinghurst's description?

We arrive, finally, at the end of *The Golden Bowl*. This is, to my mind, the most sinister passage on my list if we focus on the conduct of the characters rather than the implied author, and the one that most clearly depicts a morally blameworthy instrumentalization of persons—though of course it is the business of the novel as a whole to question this behavior. Treating their respective spouses as fine antique furniture is, for Adam and Maggie, a way of denying them human status and asserting their right to the permanent use of those splendidly elegant bodies. This use involves denial of autonomy—Charlotte has to be sent off to the museum in America to be "buried," the Prince has to be turned into an elegant if flawed domestic object—and also denial of subjectivity. To appreciate them as antique furniture is to say that we do not have to ask ourselves whether they are in pain. We can just look at them and neglect the claims that they actively make. The *sposi* are rendered inert, morally and emotionally, and as in a sense, fungible—for from the outset Maggie has noted that to treat her husband as a work of art is to neglect his personal uniqueness.[62] In fact, we see every item on our list except physical violability—and emotional violation is amply attested.

What this should tell us is that the dehumanization and objectification of persons has many forms. It is not obvious that the "core" of such objectification is sexual, or that its primary vehicle is the specifically erotic education of men and women. Mill tells us that the entire education of men in his society teaches the lesson of domination and use; he does not put the blame at the door of the specifically sexual education. Here we are reminded that there can be morally sinister objectification without any particular connection to sex, or even to gender roles. Maggie and Adam learned their attitudes to persons by being rich collectors. Their attitude probably has consequences for sex, but it has its roots elsewhere, in an attitude about money and other things that James associates with America. All things, in the rich American world, are regarded as having a price, as being essentially controllable and usable, if only one is wealthy enough. Nothing is an end in itself because the only end is wealth.[63] The skeptical incursion of the narrator, with his "lingering view, a view more penetrating than the occasion demanded" points out that what we really see here is the "concrete attestatio[n]" of "a rare power of purchase."

This complicates our question, for it tells us that we should question the claim of Kant, Dworkin, and MacKinnon that the deformation of sexual desire is prior to, and causes, other forms of objectification of the sexual partner. It also seems possible that in many cases an antecedent deformation of attitudes to things and persons infiltrates and poisons desire.[64] I shall not be able to pursue this question further. I leave it on the table, in order to suggest the next chapter that would need to be written in any story of sexual objectification in our world.

To conclude, let me return to the seven forms of objectification and summarize the argument. It would appear that Kant, MacKinnon, and Dworkin are correct in one central insight: The instrumental treatment of human beings, the treatment of human beings as tools of the purposes of another, is always morally problematic; if it does not take place in a larger context of regard for humanity, it is a central form of the morally objectionable. It is also a common feature of sexual life, especially, though not only, in connection with male treatment of women. As such, it is closely bound up with other forms of objectification, in particular with denial of autonomy, denial of subjectivity, and various forms of boundary violation. In some forms, it is connected with fungibility and ownership or quasi-ownership: the notion of "commodification."

On the other hand, there seems to be no other item on the list that is always morally objectionable. Denial of autonomy and denial of subjectivity are objectionable if they persist throughout an adult relationship, but as phases in a relationship characterized by mutual regard they can be all right, or even quite wonderful in the way that Lawrence suggests. In a closely related way, it may at times be splendid to treat the other person as passive, or even inert. Emotional penetration of boundaries seems potentially a very valuable part of sexual life, and some forms of physical boundary penetration also, though it is less clear which ones these are. Treating as fungible is suspect when the person so treated is from a group that has frequently been commodified and used as a tool, or a prize; between social equals these problems disappear, though it is not clear that others do not arise.

As for the etiology of objectification, we have some reasons by now to doubt Kant's account, according to which the baneful form of use is inherent in sexual desire and activity themselves. We have some reason to endorse MacKinnon and Dworkin's account, according to which social hierarchy is at the root of the deformation of desire, but Lorde and Lawrence show us that the deformation is more complicated than this, working not only through pornography but also through puritanism and the repression of female erotic experience.[65] In that sense it may be plausible to claim, as Lawrence does, that a certain sort of objectifying attention to bodily parts is an important element in correcting the deformation and promoting genuine erotic equality. Finally, we should grant that we do not really know how central sexual desire is in all these problems of objectification and commodification, by comparison, for example, to economic norms and motives that powerfully construct desire in our culture.

The concept of objectification is complex and requires much further investigation, as does its relationship to other concepts, such as autonomy, exploitation, and commodification. This preliminary mapping, however, shows, at least, how much work there is to be done; in that way it indicates that analytic philosophy (of, admittedly, an expanded and rather atypical kind) is not without its benefits for feminist politics.

9

RAGE AND REASON

I. Prophecy and Philosophy

Prophets don't write like philosophers. Why not, since they seem to have a common goal? Since Socrates, philosophers, like prophets, have been dedicated foes of ethical complacency and of the many forms of moral disease complacency conceals. Socrates' call to the examined life was inspired by a concern for the health of souls. He once described the insides of his interlocutor as filled with tumorous growths, his arguments as purgative drugs that would carry away the diseased material.[1] This vivid sense of the ugliness of evil and the urgency of ethical change makes itself felt in the arguments of many of the greatest moral philosophers, including, in different ways, Plato, Spinoza, Kant, and John Stuart Mill. Even when philosophers write calmly, as they usually do, an intense engagement with corruption can frequently be detected beneath the serene surface. It would not be wrong, for example, to see the arguments of John Rawls, a deliberately abstract, cool philosopher, as motivated by the ugliness of human dignity violated and a longing for the world that would be constructed by "purity of heart, if one could attain it."[2]

And yet, as I have said, philosophers do not write like prophets. If they excoriate evil, or call the heart to an acknowledgment of its transgressions, this is not their immediate business. This lies in the construction and dissection of theories and arguments, often intricate and rather removed from the urgent practical matters that were their starting point. They address the reader not with a cascade of resonant denunciation but with delicacy and logic; not with "Woe unto you," but with "Many different kinds of things are said to be just and unjust" (Rawls, in an Aristotelian mode[3]).

Why do philosophers proceed in this way, when real evil is at hand? Sometimes it is because they are profoundly unworldly people who just don't know how to confront bad things. (Thus Edmund Husserl, completely bewildered by the evil of Nazism, wrote, shortly before his death in 1938, that he hoped soon to be in a "realm of truth," where such matters don't exist.) Sometimes, too, it is because they are gentle, polite people who don't feel comfortable denouncing others, even if they know there is evil at hand. Often, though, there is a better reason: because they share with Socrates a commitment to reason as an indispensable instrument in the struggle for good.

What do philosophers have to believe about people, in order to believe that a logical argument can produce a result in calling the soul to an acknowledgment of its own deficiencies? They have to believe, I think, that at least a part of evil is not innate or necessary, that at least a good part of it is based on error, whether societal or personal. (These errors may of course be very deep-rooted, shaping emotions as well as thoughts.) They also have to believe that people have many good beliefs and good intentions, so that there is at least a good chance that, confronted with an argument that reveals hidden contradictions in their view, they will select the better and reject the worse. They probably need to believe, too, that reason is a morally good way to approach adversaries, one that shows respect for their humanity. Finally, they also need to believe that the patient work of theory construction can deliver a practical benefit in the long run, systematizing the best of our beliefs and intuitions in a way that reveals new possibilities for politics or morality.

All these beliefs, of course, are questionable. No philosopher's work can prove that the conditions for the worth of philosophizing are satisfied in the world, and to that extent all the work of philosophy is built on what Kant would call a "practical postulate," a faith in a kind of goodness that is not empirically verifiable.

Prophets, by contrast, believe that the urgency and magnitude of the evils they see admit of no delay, no calm and patient dialogue. They believe that only by violently shaking the heart can they ever make progress against the complacency that is evil's great ally. Argument looks too unengaged, theory construction too remote from the urgent practical task. Jeremiah did not write a theory of justice, nor did Isaiah address the Israelites with Socratic dialectic. Even the philosopher's interest in the nuances of individual cases seems to prophets a dangerous detour when by and large things are so hideously bad. Suppose Jeremiah had said, "The heart of Israel is corrupt utterly, but on the other hand there are some very nice people there." Suppose Frederick Douglass had excoriated the evils of slavery but pointed to the moral goodness of certain individual slave owners. These delicate philosophical tactics would have undermined their prophetic purpose, which is to terrify, prompting tears and repentance.

In any movement for social justice, then, philosophers and prophets are likely to be to some extent at odds. To prophets, philosophical patience looks like collaboration with evil. (This impression is magnified when, as frequently happens, philosophical calm brings academic security, while the prophet is a despised outcast.) Philosophers, on the other hand, are likely to conclude that prophets don't get to the root of the problem because they aren't patient enough to do the necessary analytical work. They will be suspicious of the prophet's lack of attention to variety and nuance. They may sense that the prophet's way of speaking shows insufficient respect for the adversary's dignity. It just isn't true that people are utterly corrupt, and we get the best out of our dealings with them by proceeding on the assumption that they want to think well and to be good.

On the other hand, it is also possible for philosophers and prophets to be (uneasy) allies. Philosophers may judge that their own tactics aren't the only ones we need to approach human beings in a time of moral unrest, and they may grant that change sometimes requires a more confrontational style of discourse. (Mill's *The Subjection of Women* didn't have much influence with its calm rational arguments, and its failure cannot be ascribed to Mill's philosophical insufficiency.) They may also feel some doubts about their practical postulate itself, wondering whether it is merely a convenient way of justifying a personal preference for detachment from politics, or even for personal comfort.

The whole idea of a feminist philosopher can thus be seen, by these philosophers themselves, as a problematic one, and the feminist prophet can thus prove as compelling as she is disturbing. Is it really right to proceed as if one can make progress by calmly arguing with men? Should one really assume that they are basically good, so that argument can change them? Should one say, "Yes, some are corrupt, but others are very nice"—or isn't that the very cop-out Jeremiah rejected?

II. Dignity and Objectification

Andrea Dworkin knows that good men exist. Indeed, among the most moving passages in the autobiographical essay that opens her new book (alongside portraits of strong women who inspired or helped her) is the portrait of her father, a gentle man who adored her and treated her intelligence and will with respect, challenging her socratically to debate and argument.[4] Once in high school, asked to give an example of a great man in history, she named her father and was ridiculed. "But I meant it—that he had the qualities of true greatness, which I defined as strength, generosity, fairness, and a willingness to sacrifice self for principle." Dworkin also warmly praises her only brother, a Jewish scientist who married an Austrian Catholic, also a scientist. They transcended "cultural differences and historical sorrow," she writes, "through personal love, the recognition of each other as individuals, and the exercise of reason, which they both, as scientists, valued." At his funeral, the chief rabbi of Vienna officiated and her father sat with the women, in protest against the Orthodox separation of the sexes. And finally, there is John Stoltenberg, with whom Dworkin has lived for twenty years:

"I love John with my heart and soul. . . . We share a love of writing and of equality; and we share each and every day. He is a deeply kind person, and it is through the actual dailiness of living with him that I understand the spiritual poverty and the sensual stupidity of eroticizing brutality over kindness."

So: Dworkin, whose history includes child molestation by a stranger, sexual abuse by prison guards, domestic violence, and prostitution, also knows that the world is complex, containing some very good male people. She knows, too, that reason may do some good in this complex world. (Both her father and brother are portrayed, sympathetically, as reason-loving types. And her Jewish education is praised for teaching her the argumentative skills that enabled her to conduct a critique of, among other things, Jewish sectarianism and antiuniversalism.) But Dworkin aims to deliver shocks to the heart. Her political hero is not Socrates or Kant, it is Frederick Douglass, "someone whose passion for human rights was both visionary and rooted in action," whose political speech "was suffused with emotion: indignation at human pain, grief at degradation, anguish over suffering, fury at apathy and collusion."

Dworkin's prose is a powerful prophetic instrument. (Less so in her fiction, with its frequently turgid stream of consciousness.) She is inspired to indignation and grief by the evils of violence against the female body, in rape, in domestic violence, in prostitution, and by the sheer fact that women throughout so much of the world's history have been understood to be mere objects for the use of men. To make a difference (she reports her own earlier reasoning), she will need to write in a way that strikes readers as "nightmarish and impolite," denying them the option of seeing themselves as "innocent bystander[s]." And she will have to give up "sentimentality" toward men in favor of a "militarist's" strategizing. What this means, among other things, is a focus on the evils perpetrated by "the collective him" and a refusal of sympathy, and of mercy, to many individual hims, each of whom a philosopher might hold to be basically good at heart, and capable of being persuaded.

Life and Death returns to some of the topics of *Woman Hating, Pornography*, and *Intercourse*, and adds some new topics—the status of women in Israel, the Holocaust Memorial Museum in Washington. But its primary focus is physical violence against women—stalking, misogynistic homicide, rape, and, above all, domestic violence. (There is a fine piece on Nicole Brown Simpson.) Dworkin's essays have provoked much hostility, inside feminism and outside it. She is frequently called a man-hater, a foe of free speech, and many other things that are more expressive than precise. So any critical response should begin by trying to get clear about what she has actually claimed.

At the heart of Dworkin's thought are two theses, one normative and one diagnostic. The normative thesis is that women deserve to be treated with a dignity equal to that of men, and given rights fully equal to those of men. This idea is unmistakably Kantian. The words "dignity," "human rights," "equality," and "fairness" suffuse this text, making Dworkin's affiliations with a certain type of radical Enlightenment vision clear. As for Kant, so too for Dworkin, the central moral sin is treating a human being as a mere object, a tool for the ends of others.

Objectification, as Dworkin defines it, has a number of different aspects, which are not always clearly distinguished. Sometimes to objectify someone is to deny the person's autonomy; sometimes, to show indifference to the person's feelings and experiences; sometimes, to proceed as if the person's boundaries are not deserving of the same respect that one's own deserve; sometimes, to treat the person as fungible, easily replaceable by other similar objects. (Of course these different ideas are closely linked, and one can well see how one might lead to the others.) But the core concept, I think, is that of instrumental use: What is always morally problematic, for Dworkin, is to treat other human beings as mere tools rather than as ends in themselves. "The issue here," she concludes, "is the rights of human beings. And if you understand that women are human beings you must ask: what is the right and honorable and proper way for this person to be treated by that person?"

Why would a person treat another person as a mere thing? Of course, there may be many reasons in different contexts, but Kant held that this happens inevitably between men and women in the context of a sexual relationship. Sexual desire, he believed, makes people lose their grip on the moral point of view: "[A]s soon as a person becomes an Object of appetite for another, all motives of moral relationship cease to function." The intense sensations of sex drive out, for a time, all thought of respect for humanity as an end, leading partners to treat one another as mere tools of their own urgent desires for pleasure. At the same time, their keen interest in pleasure leads them to permit themselves to be used as things by one another, indeed, to volunteer eagerly to be dehumanized so that they can dehumanize in turn.

Kant apparently thought that this tendency was intrinsic to sexual desire itself. This view led him to conclude that desire should only be expressed within a relationship (marriage, as he saw it) that constructs moral regard institutionally by making the parties promise to care for one another. This proposal completely ignored the asymmetrical character of marriage and the extent to which its conception of women as property reinforces the thing-like treatment of women, giving men limitless sexual rights over women's bodies and making it very unlikely that the law will intervene to protect the women's boundaries from violence.

Without explicitly discussing Kant, Dworkin departs from the Kantian view in two important respects. First, she denies that the baneful tendencies Kant imputes to sexual desire belong to it inevitably or as such. Indeed, Dworkin thinks that it is always a mistake to read existing social behavior as reflecting desire's underlying "nature," given the depth at which social and political structures contribute to shaping what we find desirable in a partner. And apart from social deformations caused by asymmetrical structures of power, Dworkin clearly holds that sexual relationships can express regard for humanity.

Second, she focuses, as Kant does not, on the role of male-female asymmetry in constructing a pernicious form of sexual exchange in which men come to be aroused by the idea of turning a woman into a thing, and women come to find excitement in the thought of volunteering to be used as things. Here Dworkin's analysis lies close to that of Mill, who argued in *The Subjection of Women* that men, wishing to make willing rather than unwilling slaves of women, have "put everything in practice to enslave their minds," teaching women that "meekness, submissiveness, and resignation of all individual will" is "an essential part of sexual attractiveness." The idea that women's current behavior reveals their "nature" is scoffed at as much by Mill as by Dworkin when he says that this is just like putting a tree half in a vapor bath and half in the snow, and then, seeing that one part is luxuriant and the other part withered, saying that it is "the nature of the tree" to be that way.

Dworkin does not speculate about how the sexual objectification of women began, though she suggests (again with Mill) that it is greatly helped along by the legal construction of marriage as involving limitless rights of sexual access. (Mill already argued in 1869 that the absence of laws against marital rape made women's status lower that that of slaves. Today many U.S. states still have some form of spousal exemption for rape.) What she does emphasize—this is her diagnostic thesis—is that men have been pervasively socialized to think that aggression, violence, and the treatment of women as objects are just normal male attitudes, "boys being boys," and that women just have to put up with that. Given our society's tendency to glorify and eroticize male violence, men frequently learn, as well, to find sexual satisfaction only in situations of dominance. The cultural portrayal of intercourse as conquest has deformed sexual relations, making it difficult for men to accept women both as sexual partners and as equals. "In order to get a response from men, one has to be the right kind of thing." And "[w]hen you enter the sexual agreement to be a thing, you then narrow your own possibilities for freedom."

Dworkin has frequently been portrayed as holding that all sexual intercourse is rape. Some of her more sweeping statements have supported such a reading. She should have been more circumspect here, demarcating her claims more precisely. Still, examining her rhetoric with care, one may discern a far more plausible and interesting thesis: that the sexualization of dominance and submission, and the perpetuation of these structures through unequal laws (such as the failure to criminalize marital rape or to prosecute domestic violence effectively), have so pervasively infected the development of desire in our society that "you cannot separate the so-called abuses of women from the so-called normal uses of women." This sentence certainly does not say that all acts of intercourse are abuses. It does say that the dominant paradigms of the normal are themselves culpable, so we can't simply write off the acts of rapists and batterers by saying that they are "abnormal." Gendered violence is too deep in our entire culture.

Dworkin observes that no matter how often males use violence against other males, nobody concludes that men like being beaten up, or that it is in the nature of men to provoke violence by their bodily appearance. But women who do not leave abusive marriages, whether on account of economic dependence or terror or a conviction that they will die sooner or later anyway, are often portrayed as wanting abuse, and the abuse is often portrayed as a natural reflex of the jealous male nature. Again, until very recently it was standard courtroom policy to portray a rape victim as someone who "asked for it"; such judgments are rarely made about men who get mugged. "There's a different standard of dignity," Dworkin concludes. What we should say, in both cases equally, is that human rights have been violated. But we do not say that frequently enough about women.

Up to this point in her argument, Dworkin says what few feminists today would find controversial. The legal proposals that her arguments have promoted or supported now enjoy widespread support in our society. Most feminists welcome the changes that have made it possible to complain of sexual harassment in the workplace and to demonstrate that an asymmetry of power is frequently at the root of what creates a "hostile work environment." These concepts, pioneered by Dworkin and Catharine MacKinnon, are now commonplace in our legal culture and have been validated recently in workplace opinions by such nonradical judges as William Rehnquist and Richard Posner. Most feminists, again, would hardly wish to return to the situation of thirty years ago, where a raped woman would have to show that she resisted "to the utmost" or was physically harmed in a struggle, and where a woman's prior sexual history would be used against her as evidence in a rape trial, to show that she "asked for it." Most feminists also gladly concur with Dworkin's central conclusion in the present book: that the laws against domestic violence should be far more effectively enforced and that our society should intervene in many more ways to provide women with alternatives to staying in abusive relationships. Dworkin's suggestion that women who retaliate violently against their batterers should in some cases be allowed to plead self-defense also enjoys widespread support.

It is a curious feature of feminism today that one repeatedly encounters women who denounce MacKinnon and Dworkin as man-haters but who gladly enjoy, and even take credit for, the legal reforms that were made possible only through concepts they introduced. Dworkin and MacKinnon are radicals, but their radicalism has proven broadly acceptable, in large part because they call a culture based on rights and equal dignity to full consistency with itself.

III. Pornography and Women's Dignity

Pornography is a different matter. *Life and Death* describes the episode in Dworkin's career that has, more than any other, led to widespread vilification: her association with MacKinnon working for legal changes in this area. It is extremely common to hear the two assailed as apostles of censorship, but often the ideas themselves are not described with any precision.

Dworkin's persuasive argument about cultural patterns of objectification prompts an obvious question: How are these bad attitudes about women reproduced, in a culture that in some respects accords women equal dignity as persons? Dworkin answers that a key part of the causal story is violent and humiliating pornography. Pornographic images repeatedly portray women as dirty and debased, as asking to be raped, as deserving violent or abusive treatment. Pornography standardly portrays the will of women from a fictive male viewpoint, expressing the thought that they *want* to be used as things for male pleasure. Describing a photograph in which a pregnant woman gleefully sticks a hose up herself, Dworkin comments, "This is not a human being. One cannot look at such a photograph and say, This is a human being, she has rights, she has freedom, she has dignity, she is someone. One cannot. That is what pornography *does* to women."

In Dworkin's view, of course, our whole culture is suffused with such attitudes, and pornography is far from being their only source. Yet she argues, drawing both on experimental evidence and on testimony from women whose batterers made them reenact pornographic scenarios, that it is a prominent part of the causal story behind the "boys-will-be-boys" indifference to violence. (It is hard not to think this way when Larry Flynt, who portrayed the dismemberment of a woman in a meat grinder as arousing, is canonized as a saint of free speech, while the Nazis who marched in Skokie are regarded as despicable scum whose rights nevertheless just might be protected by the First Amendment. What does this difference show us about ourselves?) Regarding pornography as rather like a dangerous drug that causes harms, she and MacKinnon have attempted to create a legal remedy for women who are victims of these harms.

Neither MacKinnon nor Dworkin recommends using the criminal law to punish the makers or distributors of pornography. Nor have they called for censorship of pornographic materials. What they have proposed (with brief success in Indianapolis, before a federal appellate court ruled against them) is a civil ordinance under which women who have been harmed by pornography can sue its makers and distributors for damages and asks an administrative agency to issue an injunction against the offenders. The potential plaintiffs were envisaged as of two types: actresses who are harmed while making pornographic films, and battered women who can show a sufficient causal connection between the abuse and the man's use of pornographic materials. The category of material that would be potentially actionable is both narrower and broader than the materials potentially illegal under current obscenity law: narrower because sexual explicitness by itself is not found problematic if there is no humiliation and/or violence; broader because there is no escape clause for redeeming social value, and no permissible appeal to the sense of the work as a whole to establish such redeeming value.

People who attack this proposal simply on the grounds that they are in favor of the First Amendment are not saying anything intellectually respectable. The First Amendment has never covered all speech; bribery, threats, extortionate offers, misleading advertising, perjury, and unlicensed medical advice are all unprotected. Indeed, in 1918 (when Eugene Debs went to jail for sedition on account of speeches urging people to resist military service) it was not even held to cover the type of political speech that is currently recognized as lying at its very core. Thus the argument cannot be that pornography is speech, so it must be protected. Instead, the argument must be made that it is the type of speech that ought to be protected by the First Amendment.

Such an argument against Dworkin must be based on extensive legal analysis, something that Dworkin's opponents (with a small group of exceptions) fail to offer. They need to grapple also with the fact that we currently have a legal obscenity standard that renders illegal (on other grounds) most of the materials that concern Dworkin, and that we also have a variety of other laws—against cigarette and alcohol advertising, for example—that reflect our society's view that some speech is harmful and needs regulation. Moreover, we now permit people harmed by tobacco products and the advertising surrounding them to sue the makers of those products for damages. Under certain circumstances, sellers of alcohol are also liable for damages their products have caused. (But we currently do not allow damage suits against those who write or speak in praise of alcohol or tobacco.) Most Western democracies, furthermore, allow more regulation of hate speech than we do: Germany's restrictions on anti-Semitic speech and Britain's Race Relations Act, for example, need to be considered as we ponder what we really want to say. What we need to hear from objectors is subtle discussion of how the Dworkin/MacKinnon proposal relates to this whole range of cases, not vilification without analysis.

How might one object to the MacKinnon/Dworkin proposal? Certainly one should begin by acknowledging that it addresses the right moral target in the sense that material depicting abuse and violence against women as sexy is morally problematic in a way that the traditional category of the "obscene" does not seem to be. (Defined in terms of the vague notion of appeal to "prurient interest," that category has frequently led to a focus on depictions of reciprocal sex that are just a little too frank for some judge's taste—as with *Lady Chatterley's Lover*.) And one should grant that such representations of women as made for abuse are likely to contribute in some way to the general climate of violence against women that is among our pressing social problems. But there are some respectable objections that should now be weighed.

One reasonable objection might be that MacKinnon and Dworkin have never satisfactorily articulated a theory of the distinction between law and morals, and that we need a general account of this notoriously problematic line in order to carry the argument further. Many bad things aren't, and shouldn't be, illegal. Even under Mill's "harm" principle, a case can surely be argued for some regulation of pornography. But Dworkin never argues such a case, though she seems to agree with Mill's objection to laws against the merely offensive. More argument would have clarified her position.

Next, given the ubiquity of violence in our society, the causal links between pornography and any particular case of harm may simply be too difficult to establish. With cigarette smoking, we have a control group of nonsmokers to examine. Men in the United States have been exposed to a wide range of images of women, in the media, in advertising, and, in many cases, in pornography. Perhaps we cannot adequately distinguish the contributions of these different sources, showing that in a given case of abuse pornography, and not the man's earlier socialization, was the primary cause.

Third, it is unclear under what circumstances we should hold the producer of a work liable for harms it inflicts. Dostoyevsky's *Crime and Punishment* gave rise to copycat murders. Nietzsche's writings influenced the Nazis. In both these cases the murderers are to some extent misreading the work, whereas the batterer who imitates a violent porn book or video is not misinterpreting (except in the sense that the maker of the work plainly aimed at masturbation, not real-life enactment). But MacKinnon and Dworkin probably cannot use this distinction, given their rejection of the appeal to the sense of the work as a whole. It seems plausible, then, that making authors liable for what copycat criminals do will exert a stifling effect on some valuable speech.

Fourth, we might object that such an ordinance is very likely to be abused in practice. Judges are likely to prove bad judges of sexual stereotypes and their effect. The history of obscenity law shows us that work of high human value is likely to be targeted while much harmful trash escapes unscathed.

Indeed, insofar as they refuse appeal to the sense of the work as a whole, MacKinnon and Dworkin make it possible to indict some feminist work, for example, Dworkin's fiction, which graphically portrays the sexual abuse of women, with the overall purpose of sensitizing us to its terrible character. James Lindgren has shown that 63% of students shown an extract from Dworkin's *Mercy* ranked it as pornographic under MacKinnon and Dworkin's own definition of pornography (almost as high a proportion as *The Story of O*, one of Dworkin's central examples of pornography)—although, interestingly, they did not rank it as obscene under a modified version of the current Supreme Court obscenity test.

This points to another and more fundamental issue. There is value in Dworkin's prophetic examination of the pornographic, both in her fiction and in her critical discussions of particular pornographic works. The ability to study troubling cultural representations without fear of legal penalty is an important part of effecting social change; so even someone convinced of the moral case against the pornographic might plausibly be disturbed by the legal pressures such an ordinance might create.

But should we accept Dworkin's moral thesis? Many objectors have defended the value of a type of pornography that she does not attack (works involving consensual, nonhumiliating activity that would be far more likely to be targeted by the current obscenity test than by her test). Others have simply refused to acknowledge that there is any moral problem in the representation of women as meant for abuse and humiliation—and this, I think, is an implausible position. But there is another position, one that appeals, again, to the all-important issue of context and sense in the work as a whole. Sexual objectification of various types occurs within many relationships that are, in their larger structure, relationships of equality and respect. Within such an established context, forms of treatment that might otherwise undermine dignity (e.g., treating a person, for a time, as identical with his or her bodily parts) do not undermine dignity. One might reformulate Kant's position, plausibly, as the claim that one moral goal of an intimate relationship is to establish a context within which respect can be taken on trust and acts that would elsewhere mean domination and subordination do not, therefore, mean this. Dworkin's position on penetrative intercourse seems compatible with such an insight, for, as I have said, she speaks about social norms, allowing that in individual lives penetration and receptivity may have other meanings. But the ordinance itself makes no distinctions of context and thus might be used to target representations that even a sympathizer with Dworkin's argument might judge morally good.

For a combination of these reasons, I am inclined to oppose the MacKinnon/ Dworkin ordinance as a legal remedy for the harms of violent pornography. Nonetheless, Dworkin has identified an urgent problem that needs to be treated with moral seriousness. Feminists who deny this should ask whether women can really make progress in areas such as rape law and the prosecution of domestic abuse, when a jury of their peers has been raised on images that depict such abuses as exactly what women are about.

IV. Reason and Retribution

Prophets may be false prophets. That is how many feminists view Dworkin's attacks on sexual corruption. A calm examination of Dworkin's views can help to articulate more precisely the sense of her claims and to show what is plausible and valuable in them. At this point, however, there are some general worries about the nature of Dworkin's undertaking that must be faced.

The first worry concerns Dworkin's obsessive focus on the sexual as the locus of women's subordination and her apparent indifference to economic analysis. Dworkin holds that it is because men view women as sex objects that women do not enjoy equal dignity. She therefore sees a change in socially constructed forms of sexual desire as the key to women's equality. Yet men have traditionally viewed women in other ways as well: as bearers of, and carers for, children; as homemakers; as performers of domestic labor. It is plausible to think that these powerful interests reinforce and perpetuate the more narrowly sexual forms of subordination and may even collude in their creation.

If one sees things this way, one will think that the key to women's equality is to promote their economic advantage, focusing on employment, credit, land rights, and other issues of daily self-sufficiency. In developing countries today, feminists are split over these issues—some rejecting projects as nonfeminist if they do not focus, Dworkin style, on the critique of sex roles; others insisting that this critique can never bear fruit unless women first enjoy greater economic self-sufficiency. There is no necessary incompatibility between the two approaches, but Dworkin's failure to acknowledge the economic aspect of inequality means that she offers very uncertain guidance for practical change, especially in the developing world.

Another worry concerns Dworkin's attitude to reasoned persuasion. In her new book, one finds less hostility to argument than in her other writings, but Dworkin's contemptuous attitude to her opponents, and her failure to engage in calm exchanges of ideas, has not disappeared, and it is troubling. Maybe Dworkin is right: Maybe most people are so distracted, or obtuse, or jaded, that only highly colored rhetoric can shake them, and a calm argument will leave their prejudices untouched. But it seems more productive to believe that people are innocent of the refusal of reason until proven guilty over a long period of time, and that we should always make the first move toward them on the assumption that they would like to search along with us for an adequate account. Doesn't prophetic rhetoric of Dworkin's sort objectify people in its own way, reducing them to their sins rather than regarding them with respect as ends in themselves? At any rate, the assumption that they are rational creatures seems likely to create a more fruitful type of community with them than the assumption that they are not.

I have referred to Dworkin's "fire-and-brimstone" rhetoric. My deepest concern about her project lies precisely here. Dworkin's attitude to men exemplifies traits standardly, and falsely, imputed to the Jewish god: a focus on retributive justice, a total absence of compassion and mercy. Her novel *Mercy* is all about why it is correct to refuse mercy to men and best to regard them in the light of strict retributive justice, paying them back in kind for the wrongs that they have done to women. Like most old-time retributivists, Dworkin doesn't even think it terribly important which individual gets the punishment, because the sins are understood to belong to the whole "house" or race, and individuals are guilty in virtue of this membership.

Life and Death, too, contains the denunciation of evil without the vision of reconciliation, fury without mercy, hatred without love. Indeed, Dworkin repeatedly expresses sympathy with violent extralegal resistance against male violence: "If we have to fight back with arms, then we have to fight back with arms. One way or another we have to disarm men." Dworkin is of course right to claim that feminists have used "extraordinary patience and self-restraint" by responding with words and not with violence, as have most other oppressed groups. But this does not mean that a commitment to nonviolence is not a good feminist choice rather than a source of shame. ("I have a long history of violence against me, and I say, to my increasing shame, that everyone who has hurt me is still walking around.")

One might be in favor of legal and nonviolent means while still being a strict retributivist, opposed to sympathy and mercy. Kant, who denied a right to revolution, also held that only the retributive attitude expresses respect for the criminal's personhood. Pleas for sympathy (attributing the wrong, for example, to bad cultural forces rather than personal evil) are seen as diminishing personhood by negating responsibility. (Justice Thomas has recently followed Kant's lead in his remarks about criminal sentencing of minority defendants.) But sympathy and mercy need not diminish personhood. They may simply express the thought that all human beings are weak and fallible, in part the creation of their social milieu and not fully culpable for evils that are bred into them by the unjust conditions they inhabit.

Such an idea is a valuable one for a prophet of social change, for it can forge a link between the corrupt world the prophet decries and a new world of equality and respect. Martin Luther King understood this well. He saw that a prophet must lead people out of something bad but at the same time into something good. His use of prophetic language created a space within which love might come to exist, and a world made ugly by hierarchy might be redeemed by the beauty of equality. By contrast, Dworkin's rhetoric contains no such space for reconciliation, no positive vision. Her nonforgiveness toward men, like her refusal of reason, is itself an act of violent aggression, expressing the thought that men will be punished forever for their bad acts by being refused entry into any world that is good.

This is a message that is ultimately at odds with Dworkin's own view of the possibilities of human life, though it is perhaps entailed by her decision to talk about a "collective him" rather than to make more fine-grained distinctions.

Certainly it is a vision that cripples social progress by identifying the call for justice with a state of permanent hostility. Mercy may be given from a position of weakness because one has been taught that women are sympathetic creatures who shouldn't demand their rights. But it may also be given from a position of strength because one is confident that one has dignity, and one has some (perhaps naive) confidence in the possibilities of reason and reconciliation. Nietzsche once said that mercy toward the aggressor is "the self-overcoming of justice." Dworkin gives us the call for justice without any space for its self-overcoming.

10

CONSTRUCTING LOVE, DESIRE, AND CARE

I. Nature and Culture

Like most of us, the ancient Greeks tended to think that where sex is concerned some things are natural and other things are not, some up for grabs as expressions of personal preference and others ruled out (or in) by our universal animal nature itself. Like most civilizations, they had strong views about what "nature" was in this domain, and they were prepared to argue for these views using examples from the animal kingdom. Consider the following passage from Philo's *On Animals*, written in the first century A.D., in which Philo "proves" the naturalness of having heterosexual sex relations only for reproductive purposes, and "proves," too, the naturalness of male self-restraint, which subdues female greediness:

> Not only among animals domesticated and reared by us but also among the other species there are those which appear to have self-restraint. When the Egyptian crocodile . . . is inclined to copulate, he diverts the female to the bank and turns her over, it being natural to approach her (when she is) lying on her back. After copulating, he turns her over with his forearms. But when she senses the copulation and the impregnation, she becomes malicious in purpose and pretends to desire copulation once more, displaying a harlot-like affection and assuming the usual position for copulation. So he immediately comes to ascertain, either by scent or by other means, whether the invitation

is genuine or merely pretense. By nature he is alert to hidden things. When the intent of the action is truly established by their looking into each other's eyes, he claws her guts and consumes them, for they are tender. And unhindered by armored skin or hard and pointed spines, he tears her flesh apart. But enough about self-restraint.[1]

The very biological implausibility of this story is suggestive: for it shows us how much the picture of "nature" has been shaped by assumptions deriving from culture. Philo appeals to the animal kingdom to demonstrate that male control over female sexual greed is grounded in nature. When we look at the crocodile world, we are supposed to discover that there is one natural position for intercourse (did the crocodiles get it from the missionaries, or the missionaries from the crocodiles?[2]); that it is natural for males to initiate and control sexual activity; that reproduction is the single legitimate purpose for heterosexual intercourse; that females are rapacious and that males need to keep them in line, by bloody means if necessary. But of course the modern reader (to whom such assumptions are not as customary as they were in Philo's time) finds in the very concocted character of Philo's account of the crocodile world reasons to call the whole set of "nature" claims into question. He has clearly been none too neutral a student of animals, projecting onto that prepolitical domain customs and laws of his own Jewish-Greek milieu. Because we stand at a distance from Philo, we can easily see this dynamic operating, when we might be inclined to miss it in the work of biologists of our own era. "Nature" is the name Philo gives to the firmest of the cultural assumptions, those he does not intend to question. We are prompted to ask whether the same is true of our own practices of distinguishing between the "natural" and the "unnatural."

Consider now a passage from Xenophon's *Hieron*, in which the poet Simonides and the ruler Hieron are conversing about erotic passion. Both have been introduced by Xenophon as high-minded, morally sensitive figures. The two men discuss nature and its compulsions:

> "How do you mean, Hieron? Are you telling me that erotic passion for young men does not grow by nature in a ruler, as it does in other people? How is it then that you are in love with Dailochos?" "My erotic passion for Dailochos is for what human nature perhaps compels us to want from the beautiful, but I have a very strong desire to attain the object of my passion only with his love and consent."[3]

Hieron insists that his strong premoral desire for the beautiful young man is suitably constrained by social morality: Though he is extremely passionate about him, he will hold off until he has consent and (friendly) love. But consider Hieron's view about what lies in the realm of the "natural," behind social convention, a view that both his interlocutor and the author seem to find unremarkable. The view is that "nature" compels a normal adult man to want sex with beautiful young men. But this desire and its expression are considered "unnatural" by many societies, including a large segment of our own. This striking divergence in ideas of what lies in "nature," behind the social and customary realm, does not show us that there is no such realm or that it too is shaped by social forces. But it prompts us to raise those questions. If what Hieron and Xenophon think paradigmatically natural is what we frequently think paradigmatically unnatural in sex, maybe the whole idea of the "natural" deserves our critical scrutiny. Maybe there is more custom and law in nature than we usually think.

We use the term "nature" in multiple and slippery ways.[4] When we say that a certain way of doing things exists "by nature," we sometimes mean that this is the way things are given in our innate equipment, without the transformative influence of human choice and effort. Sometimes we simply mean that this is a deeply habitual way for things to be, that anything else seems weird. Sometimes we mean that things cannot be otherwise. Sometimes, finally, we mean that it is fitting and proper that they should be this way. ("Unnatural" here means "to be shunned.") All four meanings are logically independent: The fact that something is customary does not imply that it is given in our innate equipment, nor does an innate basis always imply customariness. (We are born with many tendencies that we alter or remove as we mature.) Neither of these implies that the way of proceeding is necessary and immutable. And, finally, none of the other three implies that the way of proceeding is right and proper. Innate tendencies can be defective or bad: We seek to correct myopia and other bodily defects; we teach children not to put their own concerns at the center of the universe. So too with customs: We criticize them if they do not seem to promote well-being or justice. The necessary character of bodily weakness and death is not usually thought to make them good things. And the fact that something is fitting and proper does not by itself show that it is innate, customary, or necessary.

And yet we often argue badly, sliding from one sense of "nature" to another: inferring from the habitual character of something that it has its roots in innate biology, inferring from the biological rootedness of something that it is fitting and proper, inferring from the fact that many people think a custom fitting and proper that it is unchangeable and must remain as it is. Philo imputes to our biological nature certain behavioral tendencies that he evidently prizes and wishes to validate; to show crocodiles behave this way is supposed to show us that people who do not act like this are shameful and bad. (To such an argument, citing roosters instead of crocodiles, the father in Aristophanes' *Clouds* replied, "If you imitate roosters in everything, why don't you eat shit and sleep on a perch?" (1430–31)) Hieron imputes to biology a desire customary among males of his class but whose full description could probably not be given in neutral trans-cultural language, so thoroughly is it shaped by the institutions and categories of Greek homosexuality. Unlike Philo, he seems to think the desire itself neither good nor bad, because he holds that the appropriateness of the action depends on precisely how the desire is expressed.[5] The two cases are similar, however, in that the elements of human life that are traced to biology seem to be in part artifacts of custom and social norms.

In this chapter I shall investigate the philosophical basis for the thesis that human love, desire, and sexuality are "socially constructed." We need to look clearly at the philosophical arguments involved and at the bearing of historical and cross-cultural data on such arguments. I shall begin with the case of love and other related emotions, because here the issues seem to me somewhat clearer than in the case of sexual desire, where biological arguments begin to complicate the issue. I shall then turn to sexual desire itself and the related issues of sexual preference and gender structure, assessing the strength of the case that these phenomena too are "socially constructed." This will involve looking at the status of the sexual body and the sexual organs, asking whether even these are in some significant sense social and historical artifacts. I shall then draw on all this material to make some concluding remarks about the social construction of the family.

My general thesis will be that in many central respects, the sexual domain of human life, and its close relative, the domain of the family, are domains of symbolic cultural interpretation, shaped by historical and institutional forces, though within constraints imposed by biology; that cultural formations affect not just the theoretical explanation of desire but the very experience of desire, and of oneself as a desiring agent; that such considerable overlap as one does encounter among cultures in these areas can best be explained by the considerable overlap in the problems with which different human societies must grapple as they try to get on in the world[6]; that the feeling most human beings have that certain ways of doing things sexually are "natural" and necessary is often best explained not by biology but by the depth of social conditioning in the life of every human being, in giving a sense of what is possible and impossible, what is an available role, and what is not. Finally, I shall argue that recognizing the depth of interpretation in sexuality does not remove rational debate or force us into a rootless relativism; instead, it opens up a space for normative argument, political criticism, and reasoned change.

These claims will sound peculiar to some and excessively familiar to others. To those who find them overly familiar, from the large "cultural studies" literature that has investigated them for some time, I can only say that I believe this literature has not set out the philosophical arguments surrounding the issue as clearly as might be done, and that I shall try in that way to take the investigation further; nor has it connected questions about the constructedness of desire and sexuality to a study of the cultural construction of emotion, a comparison I believe to be very illuminating.

When we speak of "social construction" or "cultural construction," we should be careful not to suggest that cultures are monoliths. The account presented here will be one that makes a great deal of room for plurality, contestation, and individual variety within cultures, and for overlap and borrowing among cultures. This very fact makes it likely that we will find less impenetrable foreignness in the emotions and desires of other societies than some anthropological accounts at times suggest; as I shall argue, the fact that all human beings face similar problems as they try to get around in the world makes for even less foreignness and more convergence.

II. Emotions and their Social Form

The thesis that emotions are to some extent socially constructed, in the form in which I shall defend it, rests on a cognitive view of emotion—a view, that is, that holds that perceptions and beliefs of a certain sort play a central role in emotional experience.[7] We shall see that a cognitive view, although necessary for the social-construction thesis in the form in which I shall defend it, is not sufficient for that thesis. I shall add further arguments to get to that thesis, holding that human cognition in the relevant area is socially shaped. But we can best begin by articulating and defending the cognitive view itself. This view, in turn, can best be understood by beginning with its theoretical adversary—which is also the thesis most commonly held by opponents of social construction.[8]

The adversary claims that emotions such as grief, anger, fear, and love do not involve any form of cognitive interpretation of the world: They are just unthinking energies that push a person around. Like gusts of wind or the currents of the sea, they move, and move the person, but obtusely, without a vision of an object or beliefs about it. The view is frequently linked with the idea that emotions are "natural," "innate," or "bodily," rather than learned—for this seems to be the adversary's characteristic way of explaining how these unthinking forces got there and why most people seem to have them. The adversary's view has had a certain influence in behaviorist experimental psychology and also in popular talk and thought about the emotions.[9] But it never fared well in philosophy, where most major writers, in the Western tradition, and in what is known to me of non-Western traditions,[10] have endorsed some form of cognitive analysis. And by now it has been thoroughly repudiated in anthropology, in psychoanalysis, and even in cognitive psychology—where, as one major theorist[11] ironically observes, the field has just managed to fight its way back to the position defended in Aristotle's *Rhetoric*. What are the reasons for this shift? For if we see what has led to the current consensus about a cognitive analysis for emotion—which, as I have said, is a necessary, if not a sufficient, condition for a social-constructionist project of the sort I shall describe[12]—we will be in a better position to understand the arguments in favor of that project. We need an example: I shall take one from Euripides' tragedy, *The Trojan Women*.

Hecuba kneels in front of the shield of her dead son Hector.[13] On the shield is the dead body of her little grandson Astyanax. The victorious Greek commanders, fearing that this royal child might later cause them political trouble, have arranged for him to be thrown from the walls of the Trojan city. Hecuba pours out her grief in a speech of intense passion and lyrical beauty, as she remembers how each bodily part that now lies dead used to be full of hope, and brightness, and humor, and love, as she sees how the face that once smiled at her is now just a mass of splintered bones and blood. She angrily denounces the Greeks for their cruelty and their cowardice. She observes that human life is in general ferociously unstable, and all the most important things are beyond our control, without any firm foundation. What makes Hecuba's emotions here so different from the mindless currents hypothesized by the adversary?

First of all, Hecuba's emotions have an object: Her grief is for the death of her grandson, and her anger is at his killers. They are *about* these objects, in a way that a wind is not *about* the tree against which it strikes. Internal to the emotion itself is a focusing on the object, and the emotion contains a representation of the object, seeing it in the way in which the person interprets and sees it. Hecuba's grief sees Astyanax as both enormously important and as irrevocably cut off from her; her anger sees the Greeks as culpable wrongdoers,[14] and their wrongdoing as bad and serious. This aboutness comes from her active ways of seeing and interpreting: It is not like being given a snapshot of the object but requires looking at the object, so to speak, through her own interpretive window. This perception might contain an accurate vision of the object or it might not. It is what she thinks that matters: If it were not the Greeks but a suddenly invading Scythian army who had killed the boy, she would still be angry at the Greeks until she knew this—for in her view they are the agents of wrong.

This brings out a further point about these emotions: that they embody not just ways of seeing but also beliefs; and, as Aristotle already stressed, they are highly responsive to a change in beliefs.[15] If Hecuba comes to believe that Scythian invaders, not Greeks, killed her grandson, her anger will change its object. If she finds out that Astyanax was not killed but fell from the walls by accident, she will not be angry at anyone, and she will grieve very differently. If she finds out that the body at her feet is not her grandson after all but a dummy dressed in her child's clothes,[16] she will stop grieving altogether.

And this brings me to one last point, in some ways the most important of all. Hecuba's emotions involve various beliefs, including beliefs about what events have and have not taken place and who caused them. But very prominent in the emotions are beliefs of a very particular sort, namely, beliefs about value, worth, and salience. It is because Hecuba has invested her grandson's life with tremendous importance that his death crushes her as it does, and in the way that the death of a stranger would not do. Again, it is because his death is so salient in her life that her anger is so intense; the destruction of a drinking cup would not affect her in the same way. And these beliefs too may alter. The Greek Stoics, teaching the importance of self-sufficiency, claimed that they ought to alter, so that nothing outside one's own virtue would seem to have real importance. A good Stoic father, reports Cicero, responded to the news of his son's death with the words, "I was already aware that I had begotten a mortal."[17]

To show all this about how perceptions and beliefs figure in emotions does not by itself show that there is much social variation in emotional life, or that emotions are in any meaningful sense "socially constructed." It does establish that an emotional repertory is not innate but learned,[18] and that it is in principle possible to alter emotions through altering the beliefs on which they rest.[19] But there might be some beliefs that would almost inevitably be formed by a living creature interacting with an uncertain world, beliefs so central to the creature's whole way of life that the idea of removing them or significantly changing them makes little sense. And this is to a large extent the way things seem to be with the emotions of nonhuman animals.[20] According to the best recent studies, the fear and anger and grief of animals cannot be explained without invoking the animal's own cognitive interpretation of the world, and this interpretation must contain patterns of salience or importance. As psychologists Richard Lazarus and Keith Oatley have put it in the two most acute recent studies of the topic, the emotions are the animal's way of taking in news of how things are going in the world, with respect to its most cherished or most urgent projects and needs. These ways of responding must be learned, because no creature comes into the world knowing what parts of the world are helpful and harmful to it in important ways. On the other hand, the emotional repertory is highly functional and crucial in guiding the animal's actions; it is therefore likely to be pretty uniform, given a type of creature and a general form of life. It would not be plausible, for example, that we should find a "higher animal"[21] who never experienced fear: The belief that one's important projects are threatened is not only true for every mortal living creature at some times but highly useful in prompting evasive behavior.[22]

To some extent, much the same seems to be true of human beings. Fear of death and bodily injury is ubiquitous in some form, because the belief that these are important bad things is ubiquitous[23]; so too with grief at the deaths of loved ones, joy at their presence and safety, anger at the agents of willful damages to them or to oneself. Furthermore, the human body, whose states of pain, hunger, need for warmth and cold, and so on, are so prominent within the emotional life as occasions for fear, anger, joy, relief, and also love and gratitude, is itself ubiquitous. Although infants are from the beginning handled in accordance with cultural rules, there is much about them—their hungry neediness, the way their cognitive capacities develop over time, the shape of their bodies,[24] and the ways in which the body metabolizes nutrients—that is not itself a cultural construct, and that gives emotional experience a common terrain and geography. On the other hand, within this generally shared framework, there is a great deal of room, in the human case, for social shaping and variation. This variation takes four different forms.

(1) *Rules for emotional expression and behavior vary.* Each society teaches rules for the proper expression of emotions such as grief, love, and anger. The public wailing and tearing of clothing and hair that seemed normal to ancient Greeks mourning the death of a loved one would cause a social scandal in contemporary England. The public displays of love and affection that are acceptable among Brown undergraduates would have been regarded as morally hideous in nineteenth-century India. And, of course, most societies also have different rules internally for different types of social actors, dividing them along lines of age, gender, and social class.

(2) *Normative judgments about an emotion vary.* Judgments about the entire emotion type—I have said that most societies contain some species of anger and grief and fear and love because it is hard to find a society whose members do not ascribe to objects outside themselves a salience or importance that leads to these emotions in certain circumstances. But not all societies take the same view about the value of these attachments to objects or the concomitant emotions. Let me focus here on anger. In a remarkable study of an Eskimo tribe, the Utku, anthropologist Jean Briggs[25] carefully showed that these people strongly disapprove of anger, viewing it as all right in children, who feel weak and dependent and therefore ascribe to slights and damages a considerable significance, but as totally defective in an adult, who ought to have a kind of proud self-mastery that would make all such damages seem trivial. (In effect, this society seems to realize quite a lot of what the ancient Greek and Roman Stoics taught

and tried to practice.) The Utku admit that it is hard to get rid of attachments that give rise to anger; they therefore expect anger to occur. But they describe it always in pejorative language, as a socially pernicious force. Contrast the attitude to anger in ancient Rome. It seems that being a truly manly man in the Rome of Seneca's time actually required getting extremely angry at all sorts of slights and damages, to oneself, one's property, one's family, and one's honor and reputation. If one did not get angry, one was being soft. Here I want to say not only that the behavior of angry people in these two cultures will be very different—the Utku trying to cover things up and looking shamefaced, the Roman proudly proclaiming his rage and his vindictive intentions—but also that the experience of anger will differ. For an Utku, being angry will be hooked up to the experience of shame and a sense of diminished adulthood; one will feel infantilized by anger. The Roman, by contrast, will feel his anger accompanied by a feeling of manly self-assertion and full adulthood, and by a quasi-erotic excitement,[26] as he prepares to smash the adversary. In much the same way—to jump ahead to sexuality itself for a minute—one can expect the experience of sexual desire, in a society that has deeply internalized the idea of original sin, to be different from the experience of desire in a society that has no such teaching. The Augustinian Christian will feel desire itself tainted with shame and possibly even revulsion[27]; the ancient Greek has no such general shame to contend with.

Judgments internal to the emotion type—every society teaches norms about the proper objects and occasions for anger, fear, grief, and so forth. Once again, these norms exhibit considerable variation—both across societies and over time in a single society. In the United States, for example, the distinction between first-degree murder and voluntary manslaughter is defined in accordance with normative judgments about the anger of a "reasonable man." The events that are taken to supply this person with "adequate provocation" evolve and change. In the nineteenth century, the paradigm triggering event was a woman's adultery, seen as an invasion of a man's property. Today, the "reasonable man" may be a woman, and her anger may be about domestic violence.[28]

(3) *The taxonomy of emotions recognized varies.* This grows directly out of the observation about variation in norms: We can say that the anger experienced by the Utku is not precisely the same emotion as the anger experienced by the Roman, given its different links to shame and childishness. And, in general, we find that the precise description of the emotion-taxonomy of any society yields subtle variations from that of any other. The fact that Roman taxonomies recognize numerous varieties and subspecies of retributive anger, subtly differentiated according to the type of revenge sought, the length of time one spends planning one's revenge, and the type of slight that occasioned the anger, is not separable from the fact that the Romans are enthusiastic cultivators of this emotional plant and love to observe its every nuance. One assumes that as a result of this cultivation, Romans felt their anger differently, just as a cultivated wine taster tastes wine differently.[29] One can even find categories of emotion that are important for one culture or group but do not occur at all in another, given the differences in forms of life and in metaphysical beliefs. The precise species of

guilt and shame about the body that many Christian cultures experience and cultivate has no one-one equivalent in ancient Greece and Rome. Seneca describes a type of joy that he claims one can only experience when one has become detached from external worldly events and is no longer dependent upon their vicissitudes. (Notice that this Stoic emotion is not likely to be felt by the entirety of a culture and is quite likely to be experienced by individuals in many different cultures who have deeply internalized Stoic teachings. When we speak of "social construction," once again, we must not ignore the fact that cultures are plural, overlapping, and complex.)

Often, a taxonomical difference will be constituted by the different ways in which societies relate elements that are apparently similar, when examined in isolation from one another. Thus, the connections made by Japanese society among apology, exculpation, forgiveness, and guilt seem to be subtly different from similar connections in America. Americans, for example, insist on sincerity and internal emotional consistency in context of apology; Japanese society is more tolerant of the ambivalent and the unexpressed. Americans, again, typically insist on accompanying apology by narratives that at least mitigate blame, if they do not altogether exculpate; in Japanese society such an attempt to mitigate will be a sign that the apology is insincere.[30] These cultural connections express subtle differences in evaluation of what is desirable for persons and society; these differences shape what apology *is* in the two societies, what guilt is, what the desire for restored harmony and acceptance is. These experiences will still be closely related in the two cultures but not precisely the same.

Sometimes, as in the previous cases, such taxonomical variations show differences in evaluation; sometimes they seem attributable, instead, to differences in geography and form of life. I spend part of every summer in Finland and have had described to me an emotion that is connected with the experience of being alone in the forest; it combines awe, the sense of one's own insignificance, a terror of death. It is said to be expressed by certain passages in Sibelius's music. I had never had precisely that emotion, though by now, taking on the form of life (and being anyway a devotee of long solitary walks in the forest) I am beginning to see what it is all about.

(4) *Individual histories vary, and emotions bear traces of their history.* Human emotions are unlike most other animal emotions in that the present object is often not alone: It bears the trace of loved or feared or hated objects from one's past, and the past lends the present some of its wonder or terror. This history is all along culturally mediated; even infants are handled from the beginning in accordance with cultural scenarios. But there is much variation within the general cultural pattern.

Let me now put all this together, focusing on the the case of erotic love. It is not surprising to find that more or less all known societies have some emotion or other that might roughly be called erotic love—a kind of intense attachment to an object connected with sexual feeling. But it is obvious to any devotee of love poetry and love stories that this allegedly single emotion turns up in remarkably different forms in different times and places, forms that do not all share a common core or essence, although they may exhibit many complicated interrelationships. In fact, we find here all four of the types of variation I have identified. First, and most obvious, norms of expression and behavior for lovers vary enormously across cultures and within a culture in connection with differences in age, gender, and social status. A vivid example of this is given in Vikram Seth's novel *A Suitable Boy*, in which the young female university student in Delhi in the 1950s encounters severe conflict with her family when she accepts the role of Olivia in *Twelfth Night* in an English Department production. Her mother is convinced that even to go through the motions of that role is highly improper for a young woman of her class, who should exhibit no erotic behavior until betrothed.

Normative judgments on the emotion also vary: The ancient Greeks seem, on the whole, to have considered *erôs* a fearful and terrible sort of bondage and constraint; medieval courtly lovers think of it as a tender and lofty sentiment issuing from a "gentle heart"; modern Americans tend to think of it as connected with deep projects of self-expression and self-transcendence.[31] Here as with anger, the normative judgment can be expected to enter into the experience itself: The ancient Greek feels bound and made passive by *erôs*; the medieval courtly lover describes his heart as a *cor gentil*, both sensitive and bound by pleasing rules of reverence and courtesy. By contrast, a modern American romantic will be likely to feel love as awesome, something that sweeps one away against one's will.[32] It is also clear that normative judgments internal to the type vary: Ideas about what characteristics make someone an appropriate object of love, and what is an appropriate occasion for love, vary greatly among my three cases. An adult man in ancient Greece will learn from his culture's scenarios and narratives that the paradigm love object is a younger man who exhibits both physical beauty and educability; the same man, born in thirteenth-century Italy, would learn to love a remote ideal lady, seen as chaste and pure; in America, his sources for cultural norms will derive from Hollywood movies, advertisements, and other sources of cultural eroticism. There has been so much recent discussion of these images of ideal desirability that it is unnecessary to comment on them further except to say that they usually do not include the medieval idea of the woman as inaccessible and pure, although they do include a highly ambivalent set of reactions to the absence of those characteristics.

Third, the emotional taxonomy itself exhibits cultural variation. Plato perceptively defined his culture's erotic emotion as a longing for possession of an object one views as good.[33] In that sense it has nothing about mutuality or reciprocity built into its definition; and we can also see that it is closely bound up with jealous wishes to immobilize the object.[34] It is also important that *erôs* is explicitly contrasted in Greek society with *philia*, a type of love defined as involving reciprocity and mutual benefit—and, at least in later texts, with *agapé*, a selfless and usually nonsexual[35] benevolent love. Although a language without a plurality of love words could articulate these distinctions (and authors in the Latin language, using only the term *amor*, try to do so, when they replicate the arguments of Greek philosophers[36]), this highly developed conceptual contrast both represents and shapes, it would seem, real differences in experience:

A Greek will not expect erotic love, as such, to pursue mutuality. Contemporary American conceptions of erotic love, by contrast, place a heavy stress on reciprocity. This means that we really are dealing with subtly different emotions: Plato and John Updike are not describing the same passion. Again, medieval courtly love has some distinctive features that could not be present in contemporary America, such as the idealization of the female object seen as chaste and unapproachable, and the paradigm of selfless devotion to and risk in the service of such a perfect being. Given the changes in cosmology and in women's role in our society, we cannot possibly recover that world (although we should not ignore its continuing influence on our own, shaping men's views, especially, of what women ought to be and are not). What we have to get rid of here is the idea that there is bound to be some one *thing* beneath the surface that is simply being described in different language. For the language itself reproduces (even as it represents) the structure of a form of life; these forms, and the experiences of the agents who inhabit them, have obvious similarities, but also some very important differences.[37]

Finally, of course, all this variation is made vastly more complicated by each person's early history, as intense attachments to parents—themselves impregnated with cultural information—are worked out in individual ways, and color the perception of future objects.

Is this "ontological relativity"[38] in emotion a special case within our metaphysics of experience, or is it simply one example of a phenomenon that is ubiquitous in the human use of categories to interpret the world? The tribe whom W. V. O. Quine famously imagined see a rabbit passing by, and exclaim, "Gavagai!" The external observer, Quine plausibly argues, will be unable to be certain what ontology underlies this utterance. Even after extensive observations, she will not be able to decide whether the utterance is best interpreted as referring to a "rabbit," to a "rabbit stage," a "rabbit part," or even the abstract "Rabbithood." And, like differences in the emotional categories, such ontological differences presumably do color experience at a deep level. What this shows is that ultimately the social-constructionist must engage in exacting metaphysical, and also epistemological, analysis, investigating the twin Quinean claims of the indeterminacy of translation and the underdetermination of theory by empirical evidence.[39] She must take a position in the subtle debates among philosophers such as Quine, Hilary Putnam, Nelson Goodman, and Donald Davidson and come to grips, in particular, with Davidson's argument that the ascription of rationality to a human being from another culture entails a shared conceptual framework. I am clearly not going to solve all these problems in this essay, and I must simply sketch, here, the direction in which I would wish to take the argument. On the one hand, I would agree with Quine, Putnam, and Goodman that our basic theories of the world exhibit variation of the sort social-constructionists find in the areas of emotion and desire. There are multiple theories that are adequate to the data, and these theories employ, in many cases, different basic categories that cut up the world in different ways. On the other hand, I would argue that the area of emotion and desire has particular features that set it apart from our categorizing practices in general. These features point in opposing directions. On the one hand, the evolutionary adaptive significance of emotion and of sexual desire pushes us toward greater commonality of categorization than will be likely to hold in areas that are not so urgently connected with survival. On the other hand, the close connection of these areas to issues of political power leads them to become a scene of cultural manipulation and conflict to a greater degree than may be the case elsewhere—and this will often lead in the direction of greater diversity in categorization. Understanding the emotion and desire categories in any given society will be a matter of understanding the extremely complex interplay between these two dimensions of our categorial activity.

To return, now, to my thesis and to the example of erotic love: What I have said shows that there is considerable relativity in erotic emotion, as in emotion generally. It does not make a case for cultural relativism in the normative sense, that is, for the view that there are no criteria of adjudication by which we can assess these different patterns, asking which are conducive to human flourishing and which are not. Cultural variation, here as elsewhere, means that it will be difficult to ask and answer normative questions, for no language we use will be free of particularity, and there will be many consequent dangers of false translation, of blindness, and of either excessive romanticization of the strange or excessive chauvinism toward the familiar.[40] But there is no reason why these dangers should be taken to defeat the project of normative analysis.[41] We will, of course, have to rule out, as unavailable, any cultural variant that is built on metaphysical beliefs we can no longer accept, or forms of life we can never replicate: In that sense, medieval courtly love is not a live option. But among the many live options, we may still make ethical arguments as we do with anything else in life. We may judge, as the Stoics did, that the value judgments on which the Romans based their conceptions of anger are wrong, that they ascribe too much importance to honor and reputation; we may judge that the negative attitude to sexuality embodied in the Augustinian conception of original sin is without a sound foundation and is an impediment to human flourishing. We must ask these questions holistically, as we attempt to make the best overall coherent sense of our theories and our concrete judgments. (Aristotle and John Rawls have given us good models to follow as we do so.) We may ask ourselves what forms of erotic love are and are not compatible with our other commitments, to justice, to equality, to productive work, to other loves and friendships.

In all these cases, judgment does not lead directly to change. To change beliefs in matters of this depth and importance cannot be a matter of a one-shot argument, but, if at all, of a life's patient effort. As Seneca said of anger, "Slow is the resistance to evils that are continuous and prolific."[42] But this does not mean that change is impossible, that an ironic distance is our only option. First, no cultural scheme is as monolithic and as universally constraining as the social-constructionist story sometimes suggests. In every society there is room to maneuver, room for individuals to wink knowingly at the rules, to play games with the rules, even to improvise mutual love in a situation of distance and hierarchy. (This aspect of the issue has been beautifully treated in some fundamental work on women and men in Greece by the late John J. Winkler.[43]) Second, individuals within societies, and societies themselves, do change, however slowly. One might consider the related case of racist beliefs: One does not change these views overnight in oneself or in another simply as a result of becoming convinced by an ethical argument. On the other hand, once one is convinced, one can go to work on oneself and, I believe, to a significant extent transform oneself—first conduct, then, gradually, the inner world. And at the same time, of course, if one is involved in educating the next generation, one goes to work on them—and, at the same time, on the political and social institutions that shape their experience—with greater optimism. This sort of patient effort is at the core of what morality is.[44] And the payoff of the position that emotions are not given in nature but are socially constructed is that emotions become a part of the domain of moral effort, so construed.[45]

For the social-constructionist, change that does not include structural, institutional, and legal change is likely to be ineffective and short-lived. Social and institutional meanings have no agency and reality on their own, in my view, apart from their role in the judgments and actions of individuals. But there is no doubt that social change may often occur at an institutional level before many of the agents in question have themselves been changed. Thus laws might be made that have implications for the structure of racist emotion even by people who themselves still experience such emotions at one level of their personalities—because they decide, for whatever reason, that it is best for things to be this way, and the institutional meanings themselves will gradually alter the meanings to which individuals attach themselves. Seneca's proposals for judicial institutions have a similar character. People who note in themselves a tendency to vindictive anger and who, as a result of reflection, deplore those tendencies may commit themselves to judicial institutions embodying mercy in their structure and meaning, and this is expected to alter the vindictiveness of individuals, as well as moderating it.

III. The Construction of Desire

This may be all very well for complex emotions such as anger, grief, and even love. But why should we think it true of sexual desire? For surely sexual desire is rooted in our biology, in our animal nature itself. So it must surely be a precultural given in which the cognitive interpretations engendered by social learning play little role.[46]

So one might think. And although the old behaviorist program of reducing every emotion to a single bodily response collapsed long ago in the cases of fear and joy and anger—when it was discovered, to the great surprise of psychologists, that the beliefs people have about the situation they are in affect their identification of their emotional state[47]—it is still alive, in its own peculiar way, in the case of sexual desire. I refer here to the heroic attempts of psychologist James Weinrich to define sexual desire in terms of genital blood volume, as measured by an ingenious machine called a penile plethysmograph.[48] (Weinrich notes that the vaginal plethysmograph is still under development, so there are "few results for women.") If we begin by asking ourselves what is wrong with this elegantly simple device, we can begin to make progress on our problem. The plethysmograph, a metal measuring device, is attached to the man's penis. If the man proves at all able to have an erection with this device around him, it measures changes in penile blood volume. That is precisely all it measures. It is perfectly culture neutral. It brings in nothing about belief or interpretation to mess things up. If we can see why it is not a good measure of sexual desire, we can begin to see where there is room, in sexual desire, for culture to enter in.

Sexual desire does have, it is true, a "drive" component, much like hunger or thirst.[49] It is not terribly clear that the plesthysmograph is a good measure of the bodily need for sexual gratification, or even of immediate sexual arousal; but let me pass over the arguments on that question.[50] What is evident is that the blood volume change measured by the plethysmograph cannot possibly be either necessary or sufficient for (male) sexual desire. Not necessary because it is possible to desire to have intercourse without having an erection: Weinrich cheerfully defines away the whole phenomenon of impotence. (And can't one have desire without even the wish for genital arousal?) Not sufficient because even Weinrich would probably not count as instances of sexual desire erections that occur outside sexual contexts: when one is waking up in the morning, for example, or when a psychologist is being put to death by hanging. What this brings out is that sexual desire is a complicated intentional phenomenon, as well as a drive—a "pull" as well as a "push." Desire, like grief and anger, is *about* an object, and *for* an object. And it does not just take a snapshot of the object; it attends to the object and interprets the object *as desirable*. Desire, in short, is in good part "in the head."

Here, of course, is where culture and cultural variation enter in in a major way. Society shapes a great deal, if not all, of what is found erotically desirable, and social forms are themselves eroticized.[51] We see this quickly in the tremendous variety of what is found erotically appealing in different societies—and, of course, by different individuals in different societies: different attributes of bodily shape,[52] of demeanor and gesture, of clothing, of sexual behavior itself. Social constructions of an attractive sexual object vary enormously, and with these the social meaning of sexual arousal and interaction themselves.[53] To give just one very obvious example, in many societies female submissiveness and male power have become eroticized in such a way that the meaning of male-female sexual interaction itself is, at least in part, an exercise of domination. This is a major theme in the work of Catharine MacKinnon and Andrea Dworkin[54]; and although I would not wish to support a claim that Dworkin has sometimes appeared to endorse, namely that all male-female intercourse must have this feature, I would not deny that intercourse between what many societies construct as male and what many societies construct as female has this feature. Certainly we may agree with MacKinnon and Dworkin that sexual intercourse is, in crucial respects, a meeting of socially constructed fantasies and role enactments more than it is of uninterpreted bodies.[55]

My argument can best be clarified by referring once again to the work of the late John J. Winkler, with whom MacKinnon collaborated at Yale to create grievance procedures for sexual harassment. For Winkler's work on sexuality stresses repeatedly, and I think correctly, that even when hierarchical and oppressive social codes are in place, actors have a certain room to negotiate and to create their own possibilities within these codes, using the resources of their own individual histories, even thumbing their nose at the code in the very process of paying lip service to it. He uses this approach, for example, to argue that men and women in ancient Greece could find ways of expressing a mutual recognition of equality even when the cultural language made it impossible to describe such equality except through the resources of poetic metaphor.[56] He used it in his life to show how a gay man in America might succeed in constructing a life whose terms were not those dictated by those who hate and marginalize gays, the life of a particular person capable of love and joy.

Such claims can only be made good by the detailed analysis of variety and negotiability within a particular culture; I shall not be able to do that here, either for ancient Greece or for contemporary America. But many such studies have shown that even in the most rigid of cultures, one finds internal plurality, dissension, and a certain flexibility for improvisation.[57] (And indeed it is difficult to know how the process of social change in which MacKinnon and Dworkin are leading participants could take place if women and men were all as completely imprisoned by cultural stereotypes as some of their statements sometimes suggest.) One may grant, as I do, that institutional change is a necessary condition for lasting or effective behavioral and attitudinal changes without granting that prior to such large-scale changes there is no room in individual lives for change or variety of perception.

Let me illustrate my general claim about sexuality, however, by taking one complex example, involving both male-female and male-male relations, so as to investigate, in the process, the related claim that homosexuality is itself a cultural construct.[58]

Let us consider, then, the life of a young male in Athens of the fifth century B.C. Let us call this young man Glaukon, after the young Athenian gentleman who is one of the participants in Plato's *Republic*.[59] Glaukon will not be one of Winkler's resourceful real-life actors but, rather, a collection of prevalent social norms, but we can assume that these norms impinge to at least a large degree upon behavior and experience. Glaukon grows up in a culture in which being a real adult man is defined largely in terms of honor and status in the community. Assuming the status of an adult citizen entails a certain attitude toward the needs of the body. Glaukon learns as he grows up that a real man has strong bodily desires, including sexual desire and the desires for food and drink; he exercises them but is not mastered by them. Sexual desire is not specially problematic or an occasion of shame[60]; it is problematic in just the way other strong appetites are. (Already here we see a big difference in experience from the experience of bodily desire in a Christian culture.) What is crucial about sexual desire is, first, that Glaukon should not pursue it in a way that distracts him from his other pursuits or wastes his fortune and, second, that it should be exercised solely in the act of penetration, by entering a suitably receptive body. The crucial opposition Glaukon learns is that of activity and passivity, and he knows that it is a good thing—indeed an exciting and a desirable thing—to be the active penetrator, a shameful and terrible thing to be the passive penetratee.[61] One sphere in which he will exercise his active dominance will be marriage, in order to produce children for the city. But he will not expect much from marriage, either in the way of companionship or in the way of sexual artistry and know-how: An uneducated sixteen-year-old girl who is never permitted to go out of the house[62] may well not completely occupy his imagination. On the other hand, trips to both male and female prostitutes are considered a good thing, as long as he does not spend too much money, and it does not make too much difference which sort he goes to, as long as it is clear that he goes there to penetrate.[63] Finally, given that he is urban and well off, his most intense erotic relationships are likely to be with young males, the *eromenoi*, "beloveds," for whom he is the *erastes*, lover. These young males are future citizens, so he is not to dishonor them by anal penetration; on the other hand, intercrural intercourse (intercourse in which he achieves orgasm by thrusting between the boy's tightly clenched thighs[64]) is all right. And if he is seen to be an intense lover of males, his friends will not judge that he has a "homosexual preference" and dislikes sex with women: On the contrary, they will infer that he is a sexually greedy fellow, and they will run to guard their wives.[65]

Glaukon's world, compared to our own, exhibits with respect to sexual desire all the four types of difference I identified when I talked about emotion. He learns different norms of sexual behavior. He internalizes different normative judgments about sexual activity as such (unaffected by the Christian conception of original sin), and different norms about appropriate sexual acts and desirable sexual objects. He has an individual history of a distinctive sort. And, especially important, the very taxonomy of types of sexual desire exhibits variation from our own: For Glaukon does not conceive of, and therefore in a significant sense does not feel the desire for, males qua males, for females qua females—any more than most modern Americans feel a generalized desire to penetrate, regardless of the gender of the object.

Is Glaukon a homosexual? This is a peculiar question. For unless we suppose that there is buried inside him somewhere a thing called a preference, rather like an extra bodily organ, we have no reason at all, in his behavior or in his statements, for saying that he has a stable disposition toward partners of one gender rather than another. He sees partners as receptive bodies of various sorts: In a sense, women are a species of a class to which anally penetrable male prostitutes also belong, and the citizen boy escapes belonging only by his conventionally ordained anal chastity.[66] On the one hand, he certainly does not have a steady inclination toward males rather than toward females—he likes young men for the conversation they afford, but he likes sex with women also. On the other hand, he is also not simply an "opportunistic homosexual," as Richard Posner has used that term to describe a basically heterosexual man who has intercourse with males in special conditions when females are not available.[67] Glaukon has ready access to women of various educational levels and sexual abilities and does not opt for boys simply out of frustration.[68] The way his desire sees the world, it is a scene for the enactment of various strategies of possession and penetration: That is his role, and it is the possibility of that that excites him.

Ancient Greece, in short, does not divide its sexual actors according to the concept of a stable inner "preference" for objects of a particular gender. In that sense, it lacks the very experience of homosexuality in its modern sense.[69] And this affects the way we cast our normative political arguments. The libertarian ideal articulated in Richard Posner's *Sex and Reason* is that our society contains various sexual kinds, some of them "normal" and some of them not so "normal," but that no moral or legal judgment should be passed on the less normal. We should protect liberty of sexual activity, except where compelling arguments show grave harm to others. But the social-constructionist holds that this way of seeing things does not drive the criticism deep enough: It does not problematize the so-called normal, does not recognize the extent to which the contemporary heterosexual male, like the homosexual male, is the inhabitant of a social role that might have been otherwise.[70] Both are in that sense "unnatural actors."[71] And the heterosexual may well have the more morally problematic role in this social drama, because his role includes the domination of women.[72] Seeing things this way is likely to move one from the combination of complacence about self and slightly condescending tolerance of the other so frequently encountered in liberal rhetoric to a more radical critical scrutiny of society's sexual drama as a whole.

IV. The Social Meaning of the Body

But isn't this all given in the body? And don't bodies come by nature in different kinds? Even if we grant that nobody has shown that "homosexual" bodies are in any biological way different from "straight" bodies, surely we at least have a naturally given division between men and women. Surely this counts for something and provides a "natural" basis for social role divisions.

Yes and no. The body is not simply a cultural sign—as some culture theorists tend to suggest it is.[73] Questions of life and death, of good and bad nutritional status, of fitness and strength, of good and ill health, are not simply matters of cultural advertising, though of course experiences that are culturally shaped may influence them in many ways. And in the domain of sexuality the same is also true: There is much that is independent of cultural representation. The fact that individuals begin to feel sexual desire at a certain age, for example, or that sexual desire fluctuates with fatigue or changing health status—all these things appear to be rooted in the body independently of culture, though at every point they interact with culturally shaped factors in highly complex ways.

On the other hand, culture does enter in, even here. It used to be common to distinguish "sex"—the biological category—from "gender," a socially constructed category, to think of one's sex as "given," one's gender as a socially learned role. But matters are actually not quite so simple. Bodily parts are not self-interpreting. As any woman knows who grew up during the change from the 1950s to the 1960s in the United States, and from Marilyn Monroe and Jayne Mansfield to Twiggy as norms of the woman, the meaning of breasts and legs is not given in nature: What is made of it by social advertising makes all the difference.[74] It is not so different with the so-called sexual organs. They have to some extent a form and a biological function independently of culture's interpretation of them, but much of their role in people's lives depends on what parents and other social actors make of them, what uses they ascribe to them, what metaphors they use about them, what roles and experiences they attach to them. No less a biologist than Charles Darwin, at the conclusion of a lengthy study of sexual dimorphism in plants and animals, expressed the limits of strictly biological knowledge on this topic when he wrote that we "do not even in the least know" what the significance of dimorphic reproduction is, as opposed to a process of parthenogenesis: "The whole subject is as yet hidden in darkness."[75] Nor does today's knowledge seem to have illuminated this mysterious issue in a decisive way.

What we do know a lot about, by contrast, is the insistent way in which parents classify children on the basis of their external genitalia, forcing a binary choice even when the genitalia themselves do not clearly announce their affiliation.[76] What we do know a lot about is the way in which this genital identification leads to pervasive differences in the shaping and interpretation of behavior. Anne Fausto-Sterling has shown, for example, that the same emotional behavior on the part of infants is differently labeled in accordance with the sex announced to the observer: so-called boys are called angry, so-called girls frightened, though the cries they utter are the same.[77] Other "cross-labeling" experiments show that infants are handled and played with differently depending on the perceived sex: Boys are bounced and tossed in the air; girls carefully cradled. These are ways in which societies create men and women.

Genital organs, in short, do not interpret themselves; they do not announce to their bearers what they are and what is salient about them. On the other hand, they are the objects of cultural interpretation and representation from the time an infant is born; they figure in human experience only as mediated through many representations, and these representations interact in many ways with other representations of gender. Historical inquiry has shown that there is, here again, tremendous latitude for differences of reading, even in the apparently neutral domain of science.[78] Historian Thomas Laqueur concludes that the whole question whether there are in a morphologically salient sense two sexes, to be contrasted with one another, or a single sex, whose members vary by degree, is a question to which Western science has given sharply varying answers, even over a rather short period of history.[79] It seems to me that Laqueur pushes the evidence too far: For the Greeks, like all known societies, made a very sharp binary division of humans into two categories in connection with the shape of their genitalia. It would be surprising if any society in which reproduction took its (until now[80]) usual form of insemination and pregnancy did not so divide animals, humans among them. And yet, Laqueur seems right to stress that exactly how we conceptualize these distinctions, and what social significance we attach to them, can vary greatly over time. As sex becomes increasingly divorced from reproduction, this is likely to prove even more evident.

Biological research points both ways on the question of social construction. There have been countless studies of the biology of male-female difference—

but, as Fausto-Sterling has painstakingly argued, these studies are riddled with conceptual and empirical problems. Moreover, given the mounting evidence of differential treatment of infants by gender, it seems clear that separating biology from culture, though in principle possible, is practically next to impossible at this time. Some modern biological research, moreover, lends support to at least some social-constructionist claims by stressing the extent to which human (unlike most animal) sexuality is plastic, not subject to rigid genetic or hormonal patterning but determined by the learning and symbolic areas of the brain.[81]

But this hardly means that there is no biological basis for differences in sexual desire and attraction. The thesis of social construction is good at explaining how societies come to have the sexual categories they do. It is also good at showing how deeply such social patterning enters into the experience of each and every member of society from early infancy on, informing not just reflection but also the very experience of desire and of oneself as desiring. It is far less adequate as an account of how particular social actors come to inhabit the categories they do inhabit. With the male and the female, we can see how parental recognition of differences in external genitalia leads from the start to differences in experience that end up producing a "man" or a "woman." Even in this case, however, it is very likely that biological factors play a significant role in influencing behavioral tendencies, even if we cannot say now what that role is, or how sharply it is divided between the sexes. In the end we are likely to discover a great deal of variation within each sex and consequently much overlap between them.

In the case of sexual orientation, social explanation has even more evident shortcomings. The fact that of two infants whose external genital appearance does not differ in any way, one turns out a "homosexual" and the other a "heterosexual" still seems inadequately explained by social construction all by itself: For the two may be in exactly the same stratum of society and may have had very similar experiences. The feeling of determination and constraint that is such a common feature of self-reports concerning homosexuality in our society suggests that either biological factors or very early individual experiences, or both, need to be invoked to complete the picture.

Biological research in this area is still in its infancy. Le Vay's work on the brain has been much criticized for the small size of his sample, for its complete omission of women, and for the fact that his subjects were all people with AIDS, a disease known to cause massive alterations in the brain.[82] More promising has been Dean Hamer's genetic work.[83] But even here, there is a difficulty, which social constructionist accounts make plain: Exactly what is the explanandum? Is it "homosexuality," that is, the tendency to prefer partners of the same sex? Is it the tendency to prefer the passive role? Will we discover two different genetic markers, one for each of these tendencies (which appear to vary rather independently of one another throughout history)? The genetic marker must be a marker for some culturally invariant tendency: But it is difficult to specify what that invariant something might be, and at the very least we would appear to require a more complex multivariant genetic analysis than we have seen to date.

Biological accounts should still be pursued energetically because there are questions, it seems, that only such an account could answer. But social construction will lead us to ask the right skeptical questions about premature claims in these areas as research evolves and will also show the researcher how complicated the conceptual terrain of her explanandum actually is—that the experiential category one is led to inhabit, by whatever combination of causal factors, is not, in many crucial respects, a transcultural and transhistorical category.

If we accept these arguments, we must also grant that one more category that is sometimes taken to be "natural" is in crucial respects an artifact of human arrangements. Families are homes for love and care; they are also shaped at a very deep level by our conceptions of sex roles, sexual desirability, and the aims of sexual activity. Given the role of culture in constructing what it is to be male; what it is to be female; what it is to love, grieve, and fear; what it is to desire; and even what it is to have a body, it could not fail to follow that what we naively refer to as "*the* family" is a highly various group of social constructs. Showing this is easier, indeed, than showing that desire is socially shaped: For even the most cursory excursion into comparative anthropology and social history makes plain that the "nuclear" family unit headed by a heterosexual couple, dwelling in its own private home and committed to intimate concern for one another and for the well-being of children, is so far from being "natural" that it has hardly ever existed outside Western Europe and North America after the Protestant Reformation.[84] Children are cared for by many different social arrangements: extended kinship structures, same-gender groupings, village cooperation. Indeed, what it is to *be* a parent, and what it is to *be* a child, varies enormously with respect to the type and length of care thought good and its social meaning.

The year 1994 was the United Nations International Year of the Family. No clearer evidence of social variability can be found than the interagency documents that attempt to formulate a definition of "family" to serve as the basis of that year. At first there was an attempt made to treat the family as a "natural unit of socialization" and to offer some definition of its structure. But it quickly became obvious that any simple definition was parochial—leaving out many cultural variants, including single-parent households, lesbian and gay families, and many more traditional forms of polygamous or multiadult bonding that the deliberators wished to include. Even a disjunctive definition proved ridiculous because it would have to be both cumbersomely lengthy and open ended. So the parties settled on no definition at all, using the term "families" without restrictive specification, and stating only that "[a]s basic units of society, families and their well-being are germane to all our organizations."[85]

This does not mean that we cannot ask what role families serve in promoting human flourishing. Once we have given a rough answer to that question, we may be able to see that some of its forms promote those goals better than others. Both John Stuart Mill and Susan Moller Okin, for example, argue, first, that one of the salient roles of the family in society has been to form the moral character of children, preparing them to be just democratic citizens, able to live on terms of reciprocity with their fellow citizens. They then note that families in which females are unequal to males serve those goals badly; for they raise males who are used to a feudal hierarchy within the household and who will therefore have a difficult time tolerating political equality outside the household. A more equal division of power between males and females, by contrast, better serves these larger human interests.[86]

Observing the socially constructed status of the family leads naturally, then, to normative questions about justice (see chapter 2). If we thought the family was simply given in biology, and perhaps unchangeably so, there would be little point to asking about its justice. Once we observe the latitude we have to make and remake the structures that influence our social lives at the most basic level, we have the responsibility of pursuing these questions and doing something about them. I have said that the best way to pursue these larger normative questions is through an Aristotelian inquiry in which we try to make the best sense we can out of all our general beliefs and concrete judgments.

It may be useful, in concluding, to return to ancient Athens, and to a passage from Aristotle's school about the socially constructed meaning of the term "offspring."[87] In the *Problemata*, a work of questions and answers compiled by students in Aristotle's school, a bright pupil asks the following question: Why is it that when a human child is born from one's semen, one calls it one's "offspring" (*ekgonon*), but when one's semen falls on the ground and a worm comes out of it (Aristotelians believed in the spontaneous generation of life from waste products) one does not call it one's "offspring"? The answer comes back: It would be very strange to do so because it seems foreign and unnatural.[88]

Now even if we are not believers in the spontaneous generation of animals from waste products, and even if we have never asked ourselves that particular haunting question, we may see that it does in fact get at an issue of some depth, one that is debated right now in controversies about surrogacy and stepparenthood, family unity and dissolution, the claims of biological versus adoptive parents: the issue, that is, of what really is salient in our practices of naming some creatures "our offspring" and others not, what we think a real parent is and does, what we think a real child is and does.[89] For from Aristotle's biological point of view, the worm is just as physically continuous with the semen as the human child is,[90] and what he, or his student, is really getting at is that being a parent of offspring is a cultural and social matter, a matter of recognition and responsibility not of mere bodily continuity.

The only way to ask this question well is the way Aristotle actually asks it in his ethical writings—holistically, in the context of a larger inquiry into what it is for a human being to flourish. For only when we have a conception, however vague and general, of what the important activities in a human life are, and what support they need to develop, can we even begin to say what role care of various sorts from other human beings does and does not play in getting young human beings to those goals. Only then can we imagine fruitfully the different ways in which the care we want may be instantiated in a society such as ours, with our resources and our history. Only then, as well, can we even begin to ask what material support is required for the kind of care we want and think good, and to take the necessary measures to make such support available to those capable of giving care. Although I shall not present a detailed argument here, my hunch (which I try to defend elsewhere[91]) is that children do need intimate and stable care from a small number of adults who are persistently devoted to the child's well-being, know the child's particularity, and provide the child with a materially secure and emotionally stable environment. One function of the family is to provide such intimate love and care. Another, as Mill and Okin argue, is to prepare young people to become citizens who can take their part in the larger society around them. These conditions can obviously be met, and have throughout history been met, by quite a number of different configurations of caring adults. There is no reason to think our options confined to the nuclear family in its traditional romanticized form. But what is equally clear is that none of them will be adequately met by adults, single or in couples or groups, who are afflicted by severe economic burdens that make it impossible for them to have stable and flourishing and physically healthy lives themselves, much less to create such a context for their children.

The role of society goes very deep, in shaping matters that our tradition has tended to define as outside society, as "private" and "natural." This can feel like a source of constraint, as we come to see to what extent we are artifacts, even in our apparently most internal and intimate lives. On the other hand, and this is what I want to emphasize, it can also feel like a source of freedom, because we can see that many ways of experiencing the body, the emotions, and the care of children that might have seemed given and inevitable are actually made by us and can therefore be otherwise. This freedom, as I have said, is not limitless. For social construction does not deny that biology imposes constraints on the lives both of groups and of individuals, though it encourages a healthy skepticism about research that too quickly discovers a root in "nature" for the social status quo. Even when a social origin for a distinction is agreed, freedom to change does not follow unproblematically: It is difficult to change anything that is as deeply rooted in many people's very ways of seeing the world as is, for example, the perception that sexual relations between men and women are a way of exerting domination over women. With sex as with race, the only changes are likely to be hard-won, slow, and incremental, occurring in individual minds and in the possibilities that these create for the education of the next generation. Such changes are unlikely to take place without broader institutional and legal changes. Nor is it easy even to get agreement on the proper direction for change, for what we are saying is that there is no Archimedean point on which we can unquestioningly rely, that the constraints come not from immutable necessity but from our own ethical convictions and choices, our commitments to justice and equality, our sense of what human flourishing is and should be. Belief in immutable "nature" may be confining, but at least it gets us off the hook without having to make a respectable argument, without having to evaluate the values with which tradition has presented us. The freedom of social construction is a freedom to follow good human arguments, which may lead to the conclusion that tradition is in many ways stupid, oppressive, and bad. And that freedom imposes responsibilities that are all too easy to evade.

In Plato's *Republic*, Socrates, having discussed the radical changes he proposes in the structure of the family and the role of women, remarks to the young

Glaukon that people usually do not pursue such discussions very far because they stop with the agreements people have made over the ages and think that these agreements are sufficient. "They do this," answers Glaukon, "out of laziness." "Laziness, however," replies Socrates, "is a quality that the guardians of a city and of laws can afford to do without." "That's likely to be true," answers Glaukon.[92]

11

"WHETHER FROM REASON OR PREJUDICE"

Taking Money for Bodily Services

Taking leave of Binod, Durga slowly, deliberately walks towards the shack of Sukhlal the contractor, who stared at her even yesterday and flashed ten-rupee notes.

What else can one do, she argues to herself, except fight for survival? The survival of oneself, one's loved ones, and the hopes that really matter.

—Manik Bandyopadhyay,
"A Female Problem at a Low Level" (1963)

If the story is about the peasant wife selling her body, then one must look for the meaning of that in the reality of peasant life. One can't look at it as a crisis of morality, in the sense one would in the case of a middle-class wife.

—Manik Bandyopadhyay,
About This Author's Perspective

I. Body Sellers

All of us, with the exception of the independently wealthy and the unemployed, take money for the use of our body. Professors, factory workers, lawyers, opera singers, prostitutes, doctors, legislators—we all do things with parts of our bodies, for which we receive a wage in return.[1] Some people get good wages and some do not; some have a relatively high degree of control over their working conditions and some have little control; some have many employment options and some have very few. And, some are socially stigmatized and some are not.

The stigmatization of certain occupations may be well founded, based on convincing, well-reasoned arguments. But it may also be based on class prejudice, or stereotypes of race or gender. Stigma may also change rapidly, as these background beliefs and prejudices change. Adam Smith, in *The Wealth of Nations*, tells us that there are "some very agreeable and beautiful talents" that are admirable as long as no pay is taken for them, "but of which the exercise for the sake of gain is considered, whether from reason or prejudice, as a sort of publick prostitution." For this reason, he continues, opera singers, actors, and dancers must be paid an "exorbitant" wage, to compensate them for the stigma involved in using their talents "as the means of subsistence." "Should the publick opinion or prejudice ever alter with regard to such occupations," he concludes, "their pecuniary recompence would quickly diminish."[2] Smith was not altogether right about the opera market,[3] but his discussion is revealing for what it shows us about stigma. Today few professions are more honored than that of opera singer, and yet only two hundred years ago, that public use of one's body for pay was taken to be a kind of prostitution. Looking back at that time, we now think that the judgments and emotions underlying the stigmatization of singers were irrational and objectionable, like prejudices against members of different classes and races. (I shall shortly be saying more about what I think those reasons were.) Nor do we see the slightest reason to suppose that the unpaid artist is a purer and truer artist than the paid artist. We think it entirely right and reasonable that high art should receive a high salary. If a producer of opera should take the position that singers should not be paid, on the grounds that receiving money for the use of their talents involves an illegitimate form of commodification and even market alienation of those talents, we would think that this producer was a slick exploiter, out to make a profit from the ill treatment of vulnerable and impressionable artists.[4] On the whole we think that far from cheapening or ruining talents, the presence of a contract guarantees conditions within which the artist can develop her art with sufficient leisure and confidence to reach the highest level of artistic production.[5]

It is widely believed, however, that taking money or entering into contracts in connection with the use of one's sexual and/or reproductive capacities is genuinely bad. Feminist arguments about prostitution, surrogate motherhood, and even marriage contracts standardly portray financial transactions in the area of female sexuality as demeaning to women and as involving a damaging commodification and market alienation of women's sexual and reproductive capacities.[6] The social meaning of these transactions is said to be both that these capacities are turned into objects for the use and control of men and also that the activities themselves are being turned into commodities, and thereby robbed of the type of value they have at their best.

One question we shall have to face is whether these descriptions of our current judgments and intuitions are correct. But even if they are, what does this tell us? Many things and people have been stigmatized in our nation's history, often for very bad reasons. An account of the actual social meaning of a practice is therefore just a door that opens onto the large arena of moral and legal evaluation. It invites us to raise Adam Smith's question: Are these current beliefs the result of reason or prejudice? Can they be defended by compelling moral arguments? And, even if they can, are these the type of moral argument that can properly be a basis for a legal restriction? Smith, like his Greek and Roman Stoic forebears, understood that the evaluations that ground emotional responses and ascriptions of social meaning in a society are frequently corrupt—deformed by self-interest, resentment, and mere unthinking habit. The task he undertook, in *The Theory of Moral Sentiments*, was to devise procedures and strategies of argument through which one might separate the rationally defensible emotions from the irrational and prejudiced. In so proceeding, Smith and the Stoics were correct. Social meaning does no work on its own: It offers an invitation to normative moral and political philosophy.

My aim in this essay will be to investigate the question of sexual "commodification" by focusing on the example of prostitution.[7] I argue that a fruitful debate about the morality and legality of prostitution should begin from a twofold starting point: from a broader analysis of our beliefs and practices with regard to taking pay for the use of the body, and from a broader awareness of the options and choices available to poor working women. The former inquiry suggests that at least some of our beliefs about prostitution are as irrational as the beliefs Smith reports about singers; it will therefore help us to identify the elements in prostitution that are genuinely problematic. Most, though not all, of the genuinely problematic elements turn out to be common to a wide range of activities engaged in by poor working women, and the second inquiry suggests that many of women's employment choices are so heavily constrained by poor options that they are hardly choices at all. I think that this should bother us—and that the fact that a woman with plenty of choices becomes a prostitute should not bother us provided there are sufficient safeguards against abuse and disease, safeguards of a type that legalization would make possible.

It is therefore my conclusion that the most urgent issue raised by prostitution is that of employment opportunities for working women and their control over the conditions of their employment. The legalization of prostitution, far from promoting the demise of love, is likely to make things a little better for women who have too few options to begin with.[8] The really helpful thing for feminists to ponder, if they deplore the nature of these options, will be how to promote expansion in the option set, through education, skills training, and job creation. These unsexy topics are not common themes in U.S. feminist philosophy, but they are inevitable in any practical project dealing with prostitutes and their female children.[9] This suggests that at least some of our feminist theory may be insufficiently grounded in the reality of working-class lives and too focused on sexuality as an issue in its own right, as if it could be extricated from the fabric of poor people's attempts to survive.

II. Stigma and Wage Labor

Why were opera singers stigmatized? If we begin with this question, we can move on to prostitution with expanded insight. Although we can hardly provide more than a sketch of the background here, we can confidently say that two common cultural beliefs played a role. First, throughout much of the history of modern Europe—as, indeed, in ancient Greece—there was a common aristocratic prejudice against earning wages. The ancient Greek gentleman was characterized by "leisure"—meaning that he did not have to work for a living. Aristotle reproved the Athenian democracy for allowing such base types as farmers and craftsmen to vote, because, in his view, the unleisured character of their daily activities and their inevitable preoccupation with gain would pervert their political judgment, making them grasping and small-minded.[10] The fact that the Sophists typically took money for their rhetorical and philosophical teaching made them deeply suspect in the eyes of such aristocrats.[11] Much the same view played a role in the medieval Church, where it was controversial whether one ought to offer philosophical instruction for pay.[12] Bernard of Clairvaux, for example, held that taking fees for education is a "base occupation" (*turpis quaestus*). (Apparently he did not think this true of all wage labor but only where it involved deep spiritual things.)

Such views about wage labor remained closely linked to class privilege in modern Europe and exercised great power well into the twentieth century. Any reader of English novels will be able to produce many examples of the view that a gentleman does not earn wages, and that someone who does is too preoccupied with the baser things in life, and therefore base himself. Such views were a prominent source of prejudice against Jews, who, not having the same land rights as Christians, had no choice but to earn their living. Even in this century, in the United States, Edith Wharton shows that these attitudes were still firmly entrenched. Lily Bart, impoverished heroine of *The House of Mirth* (1905), is discussing her situation with her friend Gus Trenor. He praises the investment tips he has gotten from Rosedale, a Jewish Wall Street investments expert whose wealth has given him entry into the world of impoverished aristocrats who both use and despise him. Trenor urges Lily to encourage Rosedale's advances: "The man is mad to know the people who don't want to know him, and when a fellow's in that state, there is nothing he won't do for the first woman who takes him up." Lily dismisses the idea, calling Rosedale "impossible" and thinking silently of his "intrusive personality." Trenor replies: "Oh, hang it—because he's fat and shiny and has a shoppy manner! . . . A few years from now he'll be in it whether we want him or not, and then he won't be giving away a half-a-million tip for a dinner!" In the telling phrase "a shoppy manner," we see the age-old aristocratic prejudice against wage work, so deeply implicated in stereotypes of Jews as pushy, intrusive, and lacking in grace.

To this example we may add a moment in the film *Chariots of Fire* when the Jewish sprinter hires a professional coach to help him win. This introduction of money into the gentlemanly domain of sport shocks the head of his college, who suggests to him that as a Jew he does not understand the true spirit of English athletics. Genteel amateurism is the mark of the gentleman, and amateurism demands, above all, not earning or dealing in money. It may also imply not trying too hard, as if it were really one's main concern in life, but this attitude appears to be closely related to the idea that the gentleman does not *need* the activity because he has his living provided already; so the rejection of hard work is a corollary of the rejection of the tradesman. (Even today in Britain, such attitudes have not totally disappeared; people from aristocratic backgrounds frequently frown on working too hard at one's scholarly or athletic pursuits, as if this betrays a kind of base tradesmanly mentality.)

What is worth noting about these prejudices is that they do not attach to activities themselves, as such, but, rather, to the use of these activities to make money. To be a scholar, to be a musician, to be a fine athlete, to be an actor even, is fine—so long as one does it as an amateur. But what does this mean? It means that those with inherited wealth[13] can perform these activities without stigma, and others cannot. In England in the nineteenth century, it meant that the gentry could perform those activities, and Jews could not. This informs us that we need to scrutinize all our social views about money making and alleged commodification with extra care, for they are likely to embed class prejudices that are unjust to working people.

Intersecting with this belief, in the opera singer example, is another: that it is shameful to display one's body to strangers in public, especially in the expression of passionate emotion. The anxiety about actors, dancers, and singers reported by Smith is surely of a piece with the more general anxiety about the body, especially the female body, that has been a large part of the history of quite a few cultures. Thus, in much of India until very recently (and in some parts still), it is considered inappropriate for a woman of good family to dance in public; when Rabindranath Tagore included middle-class women in his theatrical productions early in this century, it was a surprising and somewhat shocking move. Similarly in the West: The female body should be covered and not displayed, although in some respects these conditions could be relaxed among friends and acquaintances. Female singers were considered unacceptable during the early history of opera; indeed, they were just displacing the *castrati* during Smith's lifetime, and they were widely perceived as immoral women.[14] Male actors, singers, and dancers suffered too; and clearly Smith means to include both sexes. Until very recently such performers were considered to be a kind of gypsy, too fleshy and physical, unsuited for polite company. The distaste was compounded by a distaste for, or at least a profound ambivalence about, the emotions that it was, and is, the business of these performers to portray. In short, such attitudes betray an anxiety about the body, and about strong passion, that we are now likely to think irrational, even though we may continue to share them at times; certainly we are not likely to think them a good basis for public policy.

When we consider our views about sexual and reproductive services, then, we must be on our guard against two types of irrationality: aristocratic class prejudice and fear of the body and its passions.

III. Six Types of Bodily Service

Prostitution is not a single thing. It can only be well understood in its social and historical context. Ancient Greek *hetairai*, such as Pericles's mistress Aspasia, have very little in common with a modern call girl.[15] Even more important, within a given culture there are always many different types and levels of prostitution: In ancient Greece, the *hetaira*, the brothel prostitute, the streetwalker; in modern America, the self-employed call girl, the brothel prostitute, the streetwalker (and each of these at various levels of independence and economic success). It is also evident that most cultures contain a continuum of relations between women and men (or between same-sex pairs) that have a commercial aspect—ranging from the admitted case of prostitution to cases of marriage for money, going on an expensive date when it is evident that sexual favors are expected at the other end, and so forth. In most cultures, marriage itself has a prominent commercial aspect: The prominence of dowry murder in contemporary Indian culture, for example, testifies to the degree to which a woman is valued, above all, for the financial benefits one can extract from her family.[16] Let us, however, focus for the time being on contemporary America (with some digressions on India), on female prostitution only, and on explicitly commercial relations of the sort that are illegal under current law.

It will be illuminating to consider the prostitute by situating her in relation to several other women who take money for bodily services:

1. A factory worker in the Perdue chicken factory, who plucks feathers from nearly frozen chickens.
2. A domestic servant in a prosperous upper-middle-class house.
3. A nightclub singer in middle-range clubs, who sings (often) songs requested by the patrons.
4. A professor of philosophy, who gets paid for lecturing and writing.
5. A skilled masseuse, employed by a health club (with no sexual services on the side).
6. A person whom I'll call the "colonoscopy artist": She gets paid for having her colon examined with the latest instruments, in order to test out their range and capability.[17]

By considering similarities and differences between the prostitute and these other bodily actors, we will make progress in identifying the distinctive features of prostitution as a form of bodily service.

Note that nowhere in this comparison am I addressing the issue of child prostitution or nonconsensual prostitution (e.g., young women sold into prostitution by their parents, forcible drugging and abduction, etc). Insofar as these features appear to be involved in the international prostitution market, I do not address them here, although I shall comment on them later. I address only the type of choice to be a prostitute that is made by a woman over the age of consent, frequently in a situation of great economic duress.

The Prostitute and the Factory Worker

Both prostitution and factory work are usually low-paid jobs, but in many instances a woman faced with the choice can (at least over the short haul) make more money in prostitution than in this sort of factory work. (This would probably be even more true if prostitution were legalized and the role of pimps thereby restricted, though the removal of risk and some stigma might at the same time depress wages, to some extent offsetting that advantage for the prostitute.) Both face health risks, but the health risk in prostitution can be very much reduced by legalization and regulation, whereas the particular type of work the factory worker is performing carries a high risk of nerve damage in the hands, a fact about it that appears unlikely to change. The prostitute may well have better working hours and conditions than the factory worker; especially in a legalized regime, she may have much more control over her working conditions. She has a degree of choice about which clients she accepts and what activities she performs, whereas the factory worker has no choices but must perform the same motions again and again for years. The prostitute also performs a service that requires skill and responsiveness to new situations, whereas the factory worker's repetitive motion exercises relatively little human skill[18] and contains no variety.

On the other side, the factory worker is unlikely to be the target of violence, whereas the prostitute needs—and does not always get—protection against violent customers. (Again, this situation can be improved by legalization: Prostitutes in the Netherlands have a call button wired up to the police.) This factory worker's occupation, moreover, has no clear connection with stereotypes of gender—though this might not have been the case. In many parts of the world, manual labor is strictly segmented by sex, and more routinized, low-skill tasks are given to women.[19] The prostitute's activity does rely on stereotypes of women as sluttish and immoral, and it may in turn perpetuate such stereotypes. The factory worker suffers no invasion of her internal private space, whereas the prostitute's activity involves such (consensual) invasion. Finally, the prostitute suffers from social stigma, whereas the factory worker does not—at least among people of her own social class. (I shall return to this issue, asking whether stigma too can be addressed by legalization.) For all these reasons, many women, faced with the choice between factory work and prostitution, choose factory work, despite its other disadvantages.

The Prostitute and the Domestic Servant

In domestic service as in prostitution, one is hired by a client and one must do what that client wants, or fail at the job. In both, one has a limited degree of latitude to exercise skills as one sees fit, and both jobs require the exercise of some developed bodily skills. In both, one is at risk of enduring bad behavior from one's client, although the prostitute is more likely to encounter physical violence. Certainly both are traditionally professions that enjoy low respect, both in society generally and from the client. Domestic service on the whole is likely to have worse hours and lower pay than (at least many types of) prostitution, but it probably contains fewer health risks. It also involves no invasion of intimate bodily space, as prostitution (consensually) does.

Both prostitution and domestic service are associated with a type of social stigma. In the case of domestic service, the stigma is, first, related to class: It is socially coded as an occupation only for the lowest classes.[20] Domestic servants are in a vast majority of cases female, so it becomes coded by sex. In the United States, domestic service is very often racially coded as well. Not only in the South, but also in many parts of the urban North, the labor market has frequently produced a clustering of African-American women in these low-paying occupations. In my home in suburban Philadelphia in the 1950s and 1960s, the only African Americans we saw were domestic servants, and the only domestic servants we saw were African American. The perception of the occupation as associated with racial stigma ran very deep, producing difficult tensions and resentments that made domestic service seem to be incompatible with dignity and self-respect. (It need not be, clearly, and I shall return to this.)

The Prostitute and the Nightclub Singer

Both of these people use their bodies to provide pleasure, and the customer's pleasure is the primary goal of what they do.[21] This does not mean that a good deal of skill and art is not involved, and in both cases it usually is. Both have to respond to requests from the customer, although (in varying degrees depending on the case) both may also be free to improvise or to make suggestions. Both may be paid more or less and have better or worse working conditions, more or less control over what they do.

How do they differ? The prostitute faces health risks and risks of violence not faced by the singer. She also allows her bodily space to be invaded, as the singer does not. It may also be that prostitution is always a cheap form of an activity that has a higher better form, whereas this need not be the case in popular vocal performance (though of course it might be).[22] The nightclub singer, furthermore, does not appear to be participating in, or perpetuating, any type of gender hierarchy—although in former times this would not have been the case, singers being seen as "a type of publick prostitute" and their activity associated, often, with anxiety about the control of female sexuality. Finally, there is no (great) moral stigma attached to being a nightclub singer, although at one time there certainly was.

The Prostitute and the Professor of Philosophy

These two figures have a very interesting similarity: Both provide bodily services in areas that are generally thought to be especially intimate and definitive of selfhood. Just as the prostitute takes money for sex, which is commonly thought to be an area of intimate self-expression, so the professor takes money for thinking and writing about what she thinks—about morality, emotion, the nature of knowledge, whatever—all parts of a human being's intimate search for understanding of the world and oneself. It was precisely for this reason that the medieval thinkers I have mentioned saw such a moral problem about philosophizing for money: It should be a pure spiritual gift, and it is degraded by the receipt of a wage. The fact that we do not think that the professor (even one who regularly holds out for the highest salary offered) thereby alienates her mind, or turns her thoughts into commodities—even when she writes a paper for a specific conference or volume—should put us on our guard about making similar conclusions in the case of the prostitute.

There are other similarities: In both cases, the performance involves interaction with others, and the form of the interaction is not altogether controlled by the person. In both cases there is at least an element of producing pleasure or satisfaction (note the prominent role of teaching evaluations in the employment and promotion of professors), although in philosophy there is also a countervailing tradition of thinking that the goal of the interaction is to produce dissatisfaction and unease. (Socrates would not have received tenure in a modern university.) It may appear at first that the intimate bodily space of the professor is not invaded—but we should ask about this. When someone's unanticipated argument goes into one's mind, isn't this both intimate and bodily (and far less consensual, often, than the penetration of prostitute by customer)? Both performances involve skill. It might plausibly be argued that the professor's involves a more developed skill, or at least a more expensive training—but we should be cautious here. Our culture is all too ready to think that sex involves no skill and is simply "natural," a view that is surely false and is not even seriously entertained by many cultures.[23]

The salary of the professor, and her working conditions, are usually a great deal better than those of (all but the most elite) prostitutes. The professor has a fair amount of control over the structure of her day and her working environment, although she also has fixed mandatory duties, as the prostitute, when self-employed, does not. If the professor is in a nation that protects academic freedom, she has considerable control over what she thinks and writes, although fads, trends, and peer pressure surely constrain her to some extent. The prostitute's need to please her customer is usually more exigent and permits less choice. In this way, she is more like the professor of philosophy in Cuba than like the U.S. counterpart[24]—but the Cuban professor appears to be worse off, because she cannot say what she really thinks even when off the job. Finally, the professor of philosophy, if a female, both enjoys reasonably high respect in the community and also might be thought to bring credit to all women in that she succeeds at an activity commonly thought to be the preserve only of males. She thus subverts traditional gender hierarchy, whereas the prostitute, while suffering stigma herself, may be thought to perpetuate gender hierarchy.

The Prostitute and the Masseuse

These two bodily actors seem very closely related. Both use a skill to produce bodily satisfaction in the client. Unlike the nightclub singer, both do this through a type of bodily contact with the client. Both need to be responsive to what the client wants, and to a large degree take direction from the client as to how to handle his or her body. The bodily contact involved is rather intimate, although the internal space of the masseuse is not invaded. The type of bodily pleasure produced by the masseuse may certainly have an erotic element, although in the type of "respectable" masseuse I am considering, it is not directly sexual.

The difference is primarily one of respectability. Practitioners of massage have fought for, and have to a large extent won, the right to be considered dignified professionals who exercise a skill. Their trade is legal; it is not stigmatized. And people generally do not believe that they degrade their bodies or turn their bodies into commodities by using their bodies to give pleasure to customers. They have positioned themselves alongside physical therapists and medical practitioners, dissociating themselves from the erotic dimension of their activity. As a consequence of this successful self-positioning, they enjoy better working hours, better pay, and more respect than most prostitutes. What is the difference, we might ask? One is having sex, and the other is not. But what sort of difference is this? Is it a difference we want to defend? Are our reasons for thinking it so

crucial really reasons, or vestiges of moral prejudice? A number of distinct beliefs enter in at this point: the belief that women should not have sex with strangers; the belief that commercial sex is inherently degrading and makes a woman
a degraded woman; the belief that women should not have to have sex with
strangers if they do not want to, and in general should have the option to refuse
sex with anyone they do not really choose. Some of these beliefs are worth defending and some are not. (I shall argue that the issue of choice is the really
important one.) We need to sort them out and to make sure that our policies are
not motivated by views we are not really willing to defend.

The Prostitute and the Colonoscopy Artist

I have included this hypothetical occupation for a reason that should by now be
evident: It involves the consensual invasion of one's bodily space. (The example
is not so hypothetical, either: Medical students need models when they are learning to perform internal exams, and young actors do earn a living playing such
roles.[25]) The colonoscopy artist uses her skill at tolerating the fiber-optic probe
without anesthesia to make a living. In the process, she permits an aperture of
her body to be penetrated by another person's activity—and, we might add, far
more deeply penetrated than is generally the case in sex. She runs some bodily
risk, because she is being used to test untested instruments, and she will probably have to fast and empty her colon regularly enough to incur some malnutrition and some damage to her excretory function. Her wages may not be very
good—for this is probably not a profession characterized by what Smith called
"the beauty and rarity of talents," and it may also involve some stigma given
that people are inclined to be disgusted by the thought of intestines.

And yet, on the whole, we do not think that this is a base trade, or one that
makes the woman who does it a fallen woman. We might want to ban or regulate it if we thought it was too dangerous, but we would not be moved to ban it
for moral reasons. Why not? Some people would point to the fact that it does
not either reflect or perpetuate gender hierarchy, and this is certainly true. (Even
if her being a woman is crucial to her selection for the job—they need to study,
for example, both male and female colons—it will not be for reasons that seem
connected with the subordination of women.) But surely a far greater part of
the difference is made by the fact that most people do not think anal penetration
by a doctor in the context of a medical procedure is immoral,[26] whereas lots of
people do think that vaginal or anal penetration in the context of sexual relations is (except under very special circumstances) immoral, and that a woman
who goes in for that is therefore an immoral and base woman.

IV. Sex and Stigma

Prostitution, we now see, has many features that link it with other forms of bodily
service. It differs from these other activities in many subtle ways, but the biggest difference consists in the fact that it is, today, more widely stigmatized.
Professors no longer get told that selling their teaching is a *turpis quaestus*. Opera

singers no longer get told that they are unacceptable in polite society. Even the masseuse has won respect as a skilled professional. What is different about prostitution? Two factors stand out as sources of stigma. One is that prostitution is widely held to be immoral; the other is that prostitution (frequently at least) is bound up with gender hierarchy, with ideas that women and their sexuality are in need of male domination and control, and the related idea that women should be available to men to provide an outlet for their sexual desires. The immorality view would be hard to defend today as a justification for the legal regulation of prostitution, and perhaps even for its moral denunciation. People thought prostitution was immoral because they thought nonreproductive and especially extramarital sex was immoral; the prostitute was seen, typically, as a dangerous figure whose whole career was given over to lust. But female lust was (and still often is) commonly seen as bad and dangerous, so prostitution was seen as bad and dangerous. Some people would still defend these views today, but it seems inconsistent to do so if one is not prepared to repudiate other forms of nonmarital sexual activity on an equal basis. We have to grant, I think, that the most common reason for the stigma attaching to prostitution is a weak reason, at least as a public reason: a moralistic view about female sexuality that is rarely consistently applied (to premarital sex, for example), and that seems unable to justify restriction on the activities of citizens who have different views of what is good and proper. At any rate, it seems hard to use the stigma so incurred to justify perpetuating stigma through criminalization unless one is prepared to accept a wide range of morals laws that interfere with chosen consensual activities, something that most feminist attackers of prostitution rarely wish to do.

More promising as a source of good moral arguments might be the stigma incurred by the connection of prostitution with gender hierarchy. But what is the connection, and how exactly does gender hierarchy explain pervasive stigma? It is only a small minority of people for whom prostitution is viewed in a negative light because of its collaboration with male supremacy; for only a small minority of people at any time have been reflective feminists, concerned with the eradication of inequality. Such people will view the prostitute as they view veiled women, or women in *purdah*: with sympathetic anger, as victims of an unjust system. This reflective feminist critique, then, does not explain why prostitutes are actually stigmatized and held in disdain—both because it is not pervasive enough and because it leads to sympathy rather than to disdain.

The way that gender hierarchy actually explains stigma is a very different way, a way that turns out in the end to be just another form of the immorality charge. People committed to gender hierarchy, and determined to ensure that the dangerous sexuality of women is controlled by men, frequently have viewed the prostitute, a sexually active woman, as a threat to male control of women. They therefore become determined either to repress the occupation itself by criminalization or, if they also think that male sexuality needs such an outlet and that this outlet ultimately defends marriage by giving male desire a safely debased outlet, to keep it within bounds by close regulation. (Criminalization and regulation are not straightforwardly opposed; they can be closely related strategies. Similarly, prostitution is generally conceived as not the enemy but the ally of marriage: The two are complementary ways of controlling women's sexuality.) The result is that social meaning is deployed in order that female sexuality will be kept in bounds carefully set by men. The stigma attached to the prostitute is an integral part of such bounding.

A valuable illustration of this thesis is given by Alain Corbin's valuable and careful study of prostitutes in France in the late nineteenth century.[27] Corbin shows that the interest in legal regulation of prostitution was justified by the alleged public interest in reining in and making submissive a dangerous female sexuality that was always potentially dangerous to marriage and social order. Kept in carefully supervised houses known as *maisons de tolérance*, prostitutes were known by the revealing name of *filles soumises*, a phrase that most obviously designated them as registered, "subjugated" to the law, but that also connoted their controlled and confined status. What this meant was that they were controlled and confined so that they themselves could provide a safe outlet for desires that threatened to disrupt the social order. The underlying aim of the regulationist project, argues Corbin (with ample documentation), was "the total repression of sexuality."[28] Regulationists tirelessly cited St. Augustine's dictum: "Abolish the prostitutes and the passions will overthrow the world; give them the rank of honest women and infamy and dishonor will blacken the universe" (*De ordine* 2.4.12). In other words, stigma has to be attached to prostitutes because of the necessary hierarchy that requires morality to subjugate vice, and the male the female, seen as an occasion and cause of vice. Bounding the prostitute off from the "good woman," the wife whose sexuality is monogamous and aimed at reproduction, creates a system that maintains male control over female desire.[29]

This attitude to prostitution has modern parallels. One instructive example is from Thailand in the 1950s, when Field Marshal Sarit Thanarat began a campaign of social purification, holding that "uncleanliness and social impropriety . . . led to the erosion of social orderliness. . . ."[30] In theory, Thanarat's aim was to criminalize prostitution by the imposition of prison terms and stiff fines; in practice, the result was a system of medical examination and "moral rehabilitation" that shifted the focus of public blame from the procurers and traffickers to prostitutes themselves. Unlike the French system, the Thai system did not encourage registered prostitution, but it was similar in its public message that the problem of prostitution is a problem of "bad" women, and in its reinforcement of the message that female sexuality is a cause of social disruption unless tightly controlled.

In short, sex hierarchy causes stigma, commonly, not through feminist critique but through a far more questionable set of social meanings, meanings that anyone concerned with justice for women should call into question. For it is these same meanings that are also used to justify the seclusion of women, the veiling of women, the genital mutilation of women. The view boils down to the view that women are essentially immoral and dangerous and will be kept in control by men only if men carefully engineer things so that they do not get out of bounds. The prostitute, being seen as the uncontrolled and sexually free woman, is in this picture seen as particularly dangerous, both necessary to society and in need of constant subjugation. As an honest woman, a woman of dignity, she will wreck society. As a *fille soumise*, her reputation in the dirt, she may be tolerated for the service she provides (or, in the Thai case, she may provide an engrossing public spectacle of "moral rehabilitation").

All this diverts attention from some very serious crimes, such as the use of kidnapping, coercion, and fraud to entice women into prostitution. For these reasons, international human rights organizations, such as Human Rights Watch and Amnesty International, have avoided taking a stand against prostitution as such and have focused their energies on the issue of trafficking and financial coercion.[31]

It appears, then, that the stigma associated with prostitution has an origin that feminists have good reason to connect with unjust background conditions and to decry as both unequal and irrational, based on a hysterical fear of women's unfettered sexuality. There may be other good arguments against the legality of prostitution, but the existence of widespread stigma all by itself does not appear to be among them. As long as prostitution is stigmatized, people are injured by that stigmatization, and it is a real injury to a person not to have dignity and self-respect in her own society. But that real injury (as with the comparable real injury to the dignity and self-respect of interracial couples, or of lesbians and gay men) is not best handled by continued legal strictures against the prostitute and can be better dealt with in other ways (e.g., by fighting discrimination against these people and taking measures to promote their dignity). As the Supreme Court said in a mixed-race custody case, "Private biases may be outside the reach of the law, but the law cannot, directly or indirectly, give them effect."[32]

V. Criminalization: Seven Arguments

Pervasive stigma itself, then, does not appear to provide a good reason for the continued criminalization of prostitution, any more than it does for the illegality of interracial marriage. Nor does the stigma in question even appear to ground a sound *moral* argument against prostitution. This is not, however, the end of the issue. There are a number of other significant arguments that have been made to support criminalization. With our six related cases in mind, let us now turn to those arguments.

(1) *Prostitution involves health risks and risks of violence.* To this we can make two replies. First, insofar as this is true, as it clearly is, the problem is made much worse by the illegality of prostitution, which prevents adequate supervision, encourages the control of pimps, and discourages health checking. As Corbin shows, regimes of legal but regulated prostitution have not always done well by women: The health checkups of the *filles soumises* were ludicrously brief and inadequate.[33] But there is no reason why one cannot focus on the goal of adequate health checks, and some European nations have done reasonably well in this area.[34] The legal brothels in Nevada have had no reported cases of AIDS.[35] Certainly risks of violence can be far better controlled when the police are the prostitute's ally rather than her oppressor.

To the extent to which risks remain an inevitable part of the way of life, we must now ask what general view of the legality of risky undertakings we wish to defend. Do we ever want to rule out risky bargains simply because they harm the agent? Or do we require a showing of harm to others (as might be possible in the case of gambling, for example)? Whatever position we take on this complicated question, we will almost certainly be led to conclude that prostitution lies well within the domain of the legally acceptable, for it is certainly far less risky than boxing, another activity in which working-class people try to survive and flourish by subjecting their bodies to some risk of harm. There is a stronger case for paternalistic regulation of boxing than of prostitution, and externalities (the glorification of violence as example to the young) make boxing at least as morally problematic and probably more so. And yet I would not defend the criminalization of boxing, and I doubt that very many Americans would either. Sensible regulation of both prostitution and boxing, by contrast, seems reasonable and compatible with personal liberty.

In the international arena, many problems of this type stem from the use of force and fraud to induce women to enter prostitution, frequently at a very young age and in a strange country where they have no civil rights. An especially common destination, for example, is Thailand, and an especially common source is Burma, where the devastation of the rural economy has left many young women an easy mark for promises of domestic service elsewhere. Driven by customers' fears of HIV, the trade has focused on increasingly young girls from increasingly remote regions. Human rights interviewers have concluded that large numbers of these women were unaware of what they would be doing when they left their country and are kept there through both economic and physical coercion. (In many cases, family members have received payments, which then become a "debt" that the girl has to pay off.)[36] These circumstances, terrible in themselves, set the stage for other forms of risk and/or violence. Fifty to seventy percent of the women and girls interviewed by Human Rights Watch were HIV positive; discriminatory arrests and deportations are frequently accompanied by abuse in police custody. All these problems are magnified by the punitive attitude of the police and government toward these women as prostitutes or illegal aliens or both, although under both national and international law trafficking victims are exempt from legal penalty and are guaranteed safe repatriation to their country of origin. This situation clearly deserves both moral condemnation and international legal pressure, but it is made worse by the illegality of prostitution itself.

(2) *The prostitute has no autonomy; her activities are controlled by others.* This argument[37] does not distinguish prostitution from very many types of bodily service performed by working-class women. The factory worker does far worse on the scale of autonomy, and the domestic servant no better. I think this point expresses a legitimate moral concern: A person's life seems deficient in flourishing if it consists only of a form of work that is totally out of the control and direction of the person herself. Marx rightly associated that kind of labor with a deficient realization of full humanity and (invoking Aristotle) persua-

sively argued that a flourishing human life probably requires some kind of use of one's own reasoning in the planning and execution of one's own work.[38] But that is a pervasive problem of labor in the modern world, not a problem peculiar to prostitution as such. It certainly does not help the problem to criminalize prostitution—any more than it would be to criminalize factory work or domestic service. A woman will not exactly achieve more control and "truly human functioning" by becoming unemployed. What we should instead think about are ways to promote more control over choice of activities, more variety, and more general humanity in the types of work that are actually available to people with little education and few options. That would be a lot more helpful than removing one of the options they actually have.

(3) *Prostitution involves the invasion of one's intimate bodily space.* This argument[39] does not seem to support legal regulation of prostitution, provided that as the invasion in question is consensual; that is, that the prostitute is not kidnapped, or fraudulently enticed, or a child beneath the age of consent, or under duress against leaving if she should choose to leave. In this sense prostitution is quite unlike sexual harassment and rape, and far more like the activity of the colonoscopy artist—not to everyone's taste, and involving a surrender of bodily privacy that some will find repellant—but not for that reason necessarily bad, either for self or others. The argument does not even appear to support a moral criticism of prostitution unless one is prepared to make a moral criticism of all sexual contact that does not involve love or marriage.

(4) *Prostitution makes it harder for people to form relationships of intimacy and commitment.* This argument is prominently made by Elizabeth Anderson, in defense of the criminalization of prostitution.[40] The first question we should ask is, Is this true? People still appear to fall in love in the Netherlands and Germany and Sweden; they also fell in love in ancient Athens, where prostitution was not only legal but also, probably, publicly subsidized.[41] One type of relationship does not, in fact, appear to remove the need for the other—any more than a Jackie Collins novel removes the desire to read Proust. Proust has a specific type of value that is by no means found in Jackie Collins, so people who want that value will continue to seek out Proust, and there is no reason to think that the presence of Jackie Collins on the bookstand will confuse Proust lovers and make them think that Proust is really like Jackie Collins. So, too, one supposes, with love in the Netherlands: People who want relationships of intimacy and commitment continue to seek them out for the special value they provide, and they do not have much trouble telling the difference between one sort of relationship and another, despite the availability of both.

Second, one should ask which women Anderson has in mind. Is she saying that the criminalization of prostitution would facilitate the formation of love relationships on the part of the women who were (or would have been) prostitutes? Or, is she saying that the unavailability of prostitution as an option for working-class women would make it easier for romantic middle-class women to have the relationships they desire? The former claim is implausible, because it is hard to see how reinforcing the stigma against prostitutes, or preventing some poor women from taking one of the few employment options they might have, would be likely to improve their human relations.[42] The latter claim might possibly be true (though it is hardly obvious), but it seems a repugnant idea, which I am sure Anderson would not endorse, that we should make poor women poorer so that middle-class women can find love. Third, one should ask Anderson whether she is prepared to endorse the large number of arguments of this form that might plausibly be made in the realm of popular culture—and, if not, whether she has any way of showing how she could reject those as involving an unacceptable infringement of liberty and yet allowing the argument about prostitution that she endorses. For it seems plausible that making rock music illegal would increase the likelihood that people would listen to Mozart and Beethoven; that making Jackie Collins illegal would make it more likely that people would turn to Joyce Carol Oates; that making commercial advertising illegal would make it more likely that we would appraise products with high-minded ideas of value in our minds; that making television illegal would improve children's reading skills. What is certain, however, is that we would and do utterly reject those ideas (we do not even seriously entertain them) because we do not want to live in Plato's *Republic*, with our cultural options dictated by a group of wise guardians, however genuinely sound their judgments may be.[43]

(5) *The prostitute alienates her sexuality on the market; she turns her sexual organs and acts into commodities.*[44] Is this true? It seems implausible to claim that the prostitute alienates her sexuality just on the grounds that she provides sexual services to a client for a fee. Does the singer alienate her voice, or the professor her mind? The prostitute still has her sexuality; she can use it on her own, apart from the relationship with the client, just as the domestic servant may cook for her family and clean her own house.[45] She can also cease to be a prostitute, and her sexuality will still be with her, and hers, if she does. So she has not even given anyone a monopoly on those services, far less given them over into someone else's hands. The real issue that separates her from the professor and the singer seems to be the degree of choice she exercises over the acts she performs. But is even this a special issue for the prostitute, any more than it is for the factory worker or the domestic servant or the colonoscopy artist—all of whom choose to enter trades in which they will not have a great deal of say over what they do or (within limits) how they do it? Freedom to choose how one works is a luxury, highly desirable indeed, but a feature of few jobs that nonaffluent people perform.

As for the claim that the prostitute turns her sexuality into a commodity, we must ask what that means. If it means only that she accepts a fee for sexual services, then that is obvious, but nothing further has been said that would show us why this is a bad thing. The professor, the singer, the symphony musician—all accept a fee, and it seems plausible that this is a good state of affairs, creating spheres of freedom. Professors are more free to pursue their own thoughts now, as money makers, than they were in the days when they were supported by monastic orders; symphony musicians playing under the contract secured by the musicians' union have more free time than nonunionized musicians, and more opportunities to engage in experimental and solo work that will enhance their art. In neither case should we conclude that the existence of a contract has converted the abilities into things to be exchanged and traded separately from the body of the producer; they remain human creative abilities, securely housed in their possessor. So, if to "commodify" means merely to accept a fee, we have been given no reason to think that this is bad.

If, on the other hand, we try to interpret the claim of "commodification" using the narrow technical definition of "commodity" used by the Uniform Commercial Code,[46] the claim is plainly false. For that definition stresses the "fungible" nature of the goods in question, and "fungible" goods are, in turn, defined as goods "of which any unit is, by nature or usage of trade, the equivalent of any other like unit." Although we may not think that the soul or inner world of a prostitute is of deep concern to the customer, she is usually not regarded as simply a set of units fully interchangeable with other units.[47] Prostitutes are probably somewhat more fungible than bassoon players but not totally so. (Corbin reports that all *maisons de tolérance* standardly had a repertory of different types of women, to suit different tastes, and this should not surprise us.) What seems to be the real issue is that the woman is not attended to as an individual, not considered a special, unique being. But that is true of many ways people treat one another in many areas of life, and it seems implausible that we should use that kind of disregard as a basis for criminalization. It may not even be immoral, for surely we cannot deeply know all the people with whom we have dealings in life, and many of those dealings are just fine without deep knowledge. So our moral question boils down to the question, Is sex without deep personal knowledge always immoral? It seems to me officious and presuming to use one's own experience to give an affirmative answer to this question, given that people have such varied experiences of sexuality.

In general, then, there appears to be nothing baneful or value debasing about taking money for a service, even when that service expresses something intimate about the self. Professors take a salary, artists work on commision under contract—frequently producing works of high intellectual and spiritual value. To take money for a production does not turn either the activity or the product (e.g., the article or the painting) into a commodity in the baneful sense in which that implies fungibility. If this is so, there is no reason to think that a prostitute's acceptance of money for her services necessarily involves a baneful conversion of an intimate act into a commodity in that sense. If the prostitute's acts are, as they are, less intimate than many other sexual acts people perform, that does not seem to have a great deal to do with the fact that she receives money, given that people engage in many intimate activities (painting, singing, writing) for money all the time without loss of expressive value. Her activity is less intimate because that is its whole point; it is problematic, to the extent that it is, neither because of the money involved nor because of the nonintimacy (which, as I have said, it seems officious to declare bad in all cases) but because of features of her working conditions and the way she is treated by others.

Here we are left with an interesting puzzle. My argument about professors and painters certainly seems to imply that there is no reason, in principle, why the most committed and intimate sex cannot involve a contract and a financial exchange. So why doesn't it, in our culture? One reply is that it quite frequently does, when people form committed relationships that include an element of economic dependence, whether one-sided or mutual; marriage has frequently had that feature, not always for the worse. But to the extent that we do not exchange money for sex, why don't we? In a number of other cultures, courtesans, both male and female, have been somewhat more common as primary sexual partners than they are here. Unlike quite a few cultures, we do not tend to view sex in intimate personal relationships the way we view an artist's creation of a painting, namely, as an intimate act that can nonetheless be deliberately undertaken as the result of an antecedent contract-like agreement. Why not? I think there is a mystery here, but we can begin to grapple with it by mentioning two features. First, there is the fact that sex, however prolonged, still takes up much less time than writing an article or producing a painting. Furthermore, it also cannot be done too often; its natural structure is that it will not very often fill up the entire day. One may therefore conduct an intimate sexual relationship in the way one would wish, not feeling that one is slighting it, while pursuing another line of work as one's way of making a living. Artists and scholars sometimes have to pursue another line of work, but they prefer not to. They characteristically feel that to do their work in the way they would wish, they ought to spend the whole day doing it. So they naturally gravitate to the view that their characteristic mode of creative production fits very well with contract and a regular wage.

This, however, still fails to explain cultural differences. To begin to grapple with these we need to mention the influence of our heritage of romanticism, which makes us feel that sex is not authentic if not spontaneous, "natural," and to some degree unplanned. Romanticism has exercised a far greater sway over our ideas of sex than over our ideas of artistic or intellectual production, making us think that any deal or antecedent arrangement somehow diminishes that characteristic form of expression.

Are our romantic ideas about the difference between sex and art good, or are they bad? Some of each, I suspect. They are problematic to the extent that they make people think that sex happens naturally, does not require complicated adjustment and skill, and flares up (and down) uncontrollably.[48] Insofar as they make us think that sex fits badly with reliability, promise keeping, and so forth, these ideas are certainly subversive of Anderson's goals of "intimacy and commitment," which would be better served, probably, by an attitude that moves sex in intimate personal relationships (and especially marriages) closer to the activity of the artist or the professor. On the other hand, romantic views also promote Anderson's goals to some degree, insofar as they lead people to connect sex with self-revelation and self-expression rather than prudent concealment of self. Many current dilemmas concerning marriage in our culture stem from an uneasy struggle to preserve the good in romanticism while avoiding the dangers it poses to commitment. As we know, the struggle is not always successful. There is much more to be said about this fascinating topic. But since (as I've argued) it leads us quite far from the topic of prostitution, we must now return to our primary line of argument.

(6) *The prostitute's activity is shaped by, and in turn perpetuates, male dominance of women.*[49] The institution of prostitution as it has most often ex-

isted is certainly shaped by aspects of male domination of women. As I have argued, it is shaped by the perception that female sexuality is dangerous and needs careful regulation; that male sexuality is rapacious and needs a "safe" outlet; that sex is dirty and degrading, and that only a degraded woman is an appropriate sexual object.[50] Nor have prostitutes standardly been treated with respect, or given the dignity one might think proper to a fellow human being. They share this with working-class people of many types in many ages, but there is no doubt that there are particular features of the disrespect that derive from male supremacy and the desire to lord it over women, as well as a tendency to link sex to (female) defilement that is common in the history of Western European culture. The physical abuse of prostitutes and the control of their earnings by pimps—as well as the pervasive use of force and fraud in international markets—are features of male dominance that are extremely harmful and do not have direct parallels in other types of low-paid work. Some of these forms of conduct may be largely an outgrowth of the illegality of the industry and closely comparable to the threatening behavior of drug wholesalers to their—usually male—retailers. So there remains a question how far male dominance as such explains the violence involved. But in the international arena, where regulations against these forms of misconduct are usually treated as a joke, illegality is not a sufficient explanation for them.

Prostitution is hardly alone in being shaped by, and reinforcing, male dominance. Systems of patrilineal property and exogamous marriage, for example, almost certainly do more to perpetuate not only male dominance but also female mistreatment and even death. There probably is a strong case for making the giving of dowry illegal, as has been done since 1961 in India and since 1980 in Bangladesh[51] (though with little success), for it can be convincingly shown that the institution of dowry is directly linked with extortion and threats of bodily harm, and ultimately with the deaths of large numbers of women.[52] It is also obvious that the dowry system pervasively conditions the perception of the worth of girl children: They are a big expense, and they will not be around to protect one in one's old age. This structure is directly linked with female malnutrition, neglect, noneducation, even infanticide, harms that have caused the deaths of many millions of women in the world.[53] It is perfectly understandable that the governments of India, Bangladesh, and Pakistan are very concerned about the dowry system, because it seems very difficult to improve the very bad economic and physical condition of women without some structural changes. (Pakistan has recently adopted a somewhat quixotic remedy, making it illegal to serve food at weddings—thus driving many caterers into poverty.) Dowry is an institution affecting millions of women, determining the course of almost all girl children's lives pervasively and from the start. Prostitution as such usually does not have either such dire or such widespread implications. (Indeed, it is frequently the product of the dowry system, when parents take payment for prostituting a female child for whom they would otherwise have to pay dowry.) The case for making it illegal on grounds of subordination seems weaker than the case for making dowry, or even wedding feasts, illegal, and yet these laws are themselves of dubious merit and would probably be rightly regarded as involving undue infringement of liberty under our constitutional tradition. (It is significant that Human Rights Watch, which has so aggressively pursued the issue of forced prostitution, takes no stand one way or the other on the legality of prostitution itself.)

More generally, one might argue that the institution of marriage as most frequently practiced both expresses and reinforces male dominance. It would be right to use law to change the most inequitable features of that institution—protecting women from domestic violence and marital rape, giving women equal property and custody rights and improving their exit options by intelligent shaping of the divorce law. But to rule that marriage as such should be illegal on the grounds that it reinforces male dominance would be an excessive intrusion upon liberty, even if one should believe marriage irredeemably unequal. So, too, I think, with prostitution: What seems right is to use law to protect the bodily safety of prostitutes from assault, to protect their rights to their incomes against the extortionate behavior of pimps, to protect poor women in developing countries from forced trafficking and fraudulent offers, and to guarantee their full civil rights in the countries where they end up—to make them, in general, equals under the law, both civil and criminal. But the criminalization of prostitution seems to pose a major obstacle to that equality.

Efforts on behalf of the dignity and self-respect of prostitutes have tended to push in exactly the opposite direction. In the United States, prostitutes have long been organized to demand greater respect, though their efforts are hampered by prostitution's continued illegality. In India, the National Federation of Women has adopted various strategies to give prostitutes more dignity in the public eye. For example, on National Women's Day, they selected a prostitute to put a garland on the head of the prime minister. Similarly, UNICEF in India's Andhra Pradesh has been fighting to get prostitutes officially classified as "working women" so that they can enjoy the child-care benefits local government extends to that class. As with domestic service, so here: Giving workers greater dignity and control can gradually change both the perception and the fact of dominance.

(7) *Prostitution is a trade that people do not enter by choice; therefore the bargains people make within it should not be regarded as real bargains.* Here we must distinguish three cases. First is the case in which the woman's entry into prostitution is caused by some type of conduct that would otherwise be criminal: kidnapping, assault, drugging, rape, statutory rape, blackmail, a fraudulent offer. Here we may certainly judge that the woman's choice is not a real choice, and that the law should take a hand in punishing her coercer. This is a terrible problem currently in developing countries; international human rights organizations are right to make it a major focus.[54]

Closely related is the case of child prostitution. Child prostitution is frequently accompanied by kidnapping and forcible detention; even when children are not stolen from home, their parents have frequently sold them without their own consent. But even where they have not, we should judge that there is an impermissible infringement of autonomy and liberty. A child (and, because of clients' fears of HIV, brothels now often focus on girls as young as ten[55]) cannot give consent to a life in prostitution; not only lack of information and of economic options (if parents collude in the deal) but also absence of adult political rights makes such a "choice" no choice at all.

Different is the case of an adult woman who enters prostitution because of bad economic options: because it seems a better alternative than the chicken factory, because there is no other employment available to her, and so on. This too, we should insist, is a case in which autonomy has been infringed but in a different way. Consider Joseph Raz's vivid example of "the hounded woman," a woman on a desert island who is constantly pursued by a man-eating animal.[56] In one sense, this woman is free to go anywhere on the island and do anything she likes. In another sense, of course, she is quite unfree. If she wants not to be eaten, she has to spend all her time and calculate all her movements in order to avoid the beast. Raz's point is that many poor people's lives are nonautonomous in just this way. They may fulfill internal conditions of autonomy, being capable of making bargains, reflecting about what to do, and so on. But none of this counts for a great deal, if in fact the struggle for survival gives them just one unpleasant option, or a small set of (in various ways) unpleasant options.

This seems to me the truly important issue raised by prostitution. Like work in the chicken factory, it is not an option many women choose with alacrity, when many other options are on their plate.[57] This might not be so in some hypothetical culture, in which prostitutes have legal protection, dignity and respect, and the status of skilled practitioner, rather like the masseuse.[58] But it is true now in most societies, given the reality of the (albeit irrational) stigma attaching to prostitution. But the important thing to realize is that this is not an issue that permits us to focus on prostitution in isolation from the economic situation of women in a society generally. Certainly it will not be ameliorated by the criminalization of prostitution, which reduces poor women's options still further. We may grant that poor women do not have enough options, and that society has been unjust to them in not extending more options while nonetheless respecting and honoring the choices they actually make in reduced circumstances.

How could it possibly be ameliorated? Here are some things that have actually been done in India, where prostitution is a common last-ditch option for women who lack other employment opportunities. First, both government and private groups have focused on the provision of education to women, to equip them with skills that will enhance their options. One group I recently visited in Bombay focuses in particular on skills training for the children of prostitutes, who are at especially high risk of becoming prostitutes themselves unless some action increases their options. Second, nongovernmental organizations have increasingly focused on the provision of credit to women, in order to enhance their employment options and give them a chance to "upgrade" in the domain of their employment. One such project that has justly won international renown is the Self-Employed Women's Association (SEWA), centered in Ahmedabad in Gujerat, which provides loans to women pursuing a variety of informal-sector occupations,[59] from tailoring to hawking and vending to cigarette rolling to agricultural labor.[60] With these loans, they can get wholesale rather than retail supplies, upgrade their animals or equipment, and so forth. They also get skills training and, frequently, the chance to move into leadership roles in the organization itself. Such women are far less likely to need to turn to prostitution to supplement their income. Third, they can form labor organizations to protect women employed in low-income jobs and to bargain for better working conditions—once again making this work a better source of income and diminishing the likelihood that prostitution will need to be selected. (This is the other primary objective of SEWA, which is now organizing hawkers and vendors internationally.) Fourth, they can form groups to diminish the isolation and enhance the self-respect of working women in low-paying jobs; this was a ubiquitous feature of both government and nongovernment programs I visited in India, and a crucial element of helping women deliberate about their options if they wish to avoid prostitution for themselves or their daughters.

These four steps are the real issue, I think, in addressing the problem of prostitution. Feminist philosophers in the United States do not write many articles about credit and employment[61]; they should do so far more. Indeed, it seems a dead end to consider prostitution in isolation from the other realities of working life of which it is a part, and one suspects that this has happened because prostitution is a sexy issue and getting a loan for a sewing machine appears not to be. But feminists had better talk more about getting loans, learning to read, and so forth if they want to be relevant to the choices that are actually faced by working women, and to the programs that are actually doing a lot to improve such women's options.

VI. Truly Human Functioning

The stigma traditionally attached to prostitution is based on a collage of beliefs most of which are not rationally defensible, and which should be especially vehemently rejected by feminists: beliefs about the evil character of female sexuality, the rapacious character of male sexuality, and the essentially marital and reproductive character of "good" women and "good" sex. Worries about subordination more recently raised by feminists are much more serious concerns, but they apply to many types of work poor women do. Concerns about force and fraud should be extremely urgent concerns of the international women's movement. Where these conditions do not obtain, feminists should view prostitutes as (usually) poor working women with few options, not as threats to the intimacy and commitment that many women and men (including, no doubt, many prostitutes) seek. This does not mean that we should not be concerned about ways in which prostitution as currently practiced, even in the absence of force and fraud, undermines the dignity of women, just as domestic service in the past undermined the dignity of members of a given race or class. But the correct response to this problem seems to be to work to enhance the economic autonomy and the personal dignity of members of that class, not to rule off limits an option that may be the only livelihood for many poor women and to further stigmatize women who already make their living this way.

In grappling further with these issues, we should begin from the realization there is nothing per se wrong with taking money for the use of one's body. That's the way most of us live, and formal recognition of that fact through contract is usually a good thing for people, protecting their security and their employment conditions. What seems wrong is that relatively few people in the world have the option to use their body, in their work, in what Marx would call a "truly human" manner of functioning, by which he meant (among other things) having some choices about the work to be performed, some reasonable measure of control over its conditions and outcome, and also the chance to use thought and skill rather than just to function as a cog in a machine. Women in many parts of the world are especially likely to be stuck at a low level of mechanical functioning, whether as agricultural laborers or as factory workers or as prostitutes. The real question to be faced is how to expand the options and opportunities such workers face, how to increase the humanity inherent in their work, and how to guarantee that workers of all sorts are treated with dignity. In the further pursuit of these questions, we need, on balance, more studies of women's credit unions and fewer studies of prostitution.

12

PLATONIC LOVE AND COLORADO LAW

The Relevance of Ancient Greek Norms to Modern Sexual Controversies

I. A Federal Judge Reads Plato

In E. M. Forster's novel *Maurice*, two young men, strongly attracted to one another, begin their university study of Plato:

> They attended the Dean's translation class, and when one of the men was forging quietly ahead Mr Cornwallis observed in a flat toneless voice: "Omit: a reference to the unspeakable vice of the Greeks." Durham observed afterwards that he ought to lose his fellowship for such hypocrisy.
>
> Maurice laughed.
>
> "I regard it as a point of pure scholarship. The Greeks, or most of them, were that way inclined, and to omit it is to omit the mainstay of Athenian society."
>
> "Is that so?"
>
> "You've read the *Symposium*?"
>
> Maurice had not, and did not add that he had explored Martial.
>
> "It's all in there—not meat for babes, of course, but you ought to read it. Read it this vac."
>
> . . . He hadn't known it could be mentioned, and when Durham did so in the middle of the sunlit court a breath of liberty touched him. (51)

In 1990, an American judge, a Reagan appointee to the U.S. Court of Appeals for the Seventh Circuit, fulfills Clive Durham's assignment, reading the *Sym-*

posium for the first time, in order to "plug one of the many embarrassing gaps in my education."[1] In his 1992 book *Sex and Reason*, Richard Posner describes the impact of this experience:

> I knew it was about love, but that was all I knew. I was surprised to discover that it was a defense, and as one can imagine a highly interesting and articulate one, of homosexual love. It had never occurred to me that the greatest figure in the history of philosophy, or for that matter any other respectable figure in the history of thought, had attempted such a thing. It dawned on me that the discussion of the topic in the opinions in *Bowers v. Hardwick* . . . was superficial. . . . [2]

Discussing those opinions later in his book, Posner argues that they betray both a lack of historical knowledge and a lack of "empathy" for the situation of the homosexual, the two being closely connected: "The less that lawyers know about a subject, the less that judges will know, and the less that judges know, the more likely they are to vote their prejudices" (347). Thus he suggests that the "irrational fear and loathing"[3] expressed in the Georgia statute under which Michael Hardwick was prosecuted, and endorsed in the opinions, might have been dispelled by a study of history—beginning, it would appear, with a study of Plato. *Sex and Reason* was his own attempt to advance this educational process, and "to shame my colleagues in the profession" (4) for failing to educate themselves in this area. In at least one subsequent judicial opinion of his own, Posner has shown the effects of his own classical education: In a recent blackmail case, he speaks eloquently and with empathy of the special vulnerability of the closeted homosexual in contemporary American society, describing in some detail the nonnecessary and nonuniversal character of the prejudices that make this class of persons so painfully susceptible to the blackmailer's schemes.[4]

On October 15, 1993, I found myself on the witness stand in a courtroom in Denver, Colorado, telling State District Judge H. Jeffrey Bayless about Plato's *Symposium*. Because I had a very short time to testify as an expert witness, I focused above all on the speech of Aristophanes—which I had elsewhere argued to be one of the speeches in which Plato expresses views that he wishes his reader to take especially seriously.[5] I told the court the story of how human beings were once round and whole—but now, cut in half for their overambitiousness, they feel a sense of lost wholeness and run about searching for their "other half."[6] There are, Aristophanes tells us, three types of search, corresponding to three original species of human beings. There are males whose "other half" is male, females whose "other half" is female, and people whose "other half" is of the opposite sex. The speech describes the feelings of intimacy and joy with which the lost "other halves" greet one another[7] and the activity of sexual intercourse as a joyful attempt to be restored to the lost unity of their original natures. This is so no less for the same-sex than for the opposite-sex couples: In all cases, lovemaking expresses a deep inner need coming from nature, and in all cases the couples, so uniting, have the potential to make a valuable civic contribution.[8] Through this text and many others, I suggested that a study of history reveals a wide variety of judgments about same-sex acts and attachments and a valuable array of reasoned arguments on this topic, which should cause us to ask what our own arguments in this area are and how far they are based on reason.

Taking my Colorado experience as a basis, I shall argue that ancient Greek texts relating to sexuality are radical and valuable for us in just the way Clive Durham and Richard Posner say they are. They have the potential to make a contribution to our contemporary legal and moral thought, and this in four ways. First, they force us to confront the fact that much that we take to be necessary and natural in our own practices is actually local and nonuniversal; this, in turn, forces us to ask whether we have good reasons for what we legislate and judge. Second, they permit us to question certain empirical claims that are commonly made in this domain today, such as the claim that when same-sex acts and relationships are widely tolerated the family and the social fabric will be subverted. Third, the Greek texts provide us with some valuable concrete arguments concerning the important human goods a sexual relationship of this sort may promote. And, fourth, they promote what Posner found so sorely lacking in recent judicial treatments of this topic: empathy for the hopes and fears and human aims of those who are involved in such relationships.

II. Amendment 2 and the Greeks

In 1992, the State of Colorado passed by referendum, with the support of 53% of those who voted, what is now famously known as Amendment 2: an amendment to the state constitution that makes it illegal for any state agency or any local community within the state to "adopt or enforce any statute, regulation, ordinance or policy whereby homosexual, lesbian or bisexual orientation, conduct, practices or relationships shall constitute or otherwise be the basis of, or entitle any person or class of persons to have, any claim of minority status, quota preferences, protected status or claim of discrimination." Since Aspen, Boulder, and Denver had in fact passed civil rights ordinances aimed at protecting lesbians and gays from discrimination, the amendment nullified those ordinances. A group of plaintiffs went to court for a preliminary injunction against the law; such an injunction was granted by Judge Bayless and upheld by the State Supreme Court by a 6–1 vote. The Supreme Court sent the case back for trial, holding that the State must show that Amendment 2's prohibition of special protections on the basis of homosexual or bisexual orientation is "supported by a compelling state interest and narrowly drawn to achieve that interest in the least restrictive manner possible." Both the trial court and, on appeal, the Colorado Supreme Court, found in favor of the plaintiffs, declaring Amendment 2 unconstitutional.

In May 1996, the U.S. Supreme Court declared Amendment 2 unconstitutional, using a different argument that did not depend on showing that such a law must meet strict scrutiny. It was held not to pass rational basis review because it targeted a class of individuals on the basis of a single characteristic and then denied them protection across the board.[9] (See chapter 6 for a discussion of the opinions.)

In the course of attempting to establish its claims of "compelling interest," the State called a wide range of expert witnesses, whose arguments were contested by expert witnesses for the plaintiffs. Among the State's witnesses were several experts on moral philosophy who offered testimony about the views of the ancient Greeks. I was asked to rebut both their historical contentions and their moral arguments.[10] Here I shall focus most closely on the arguments of John Finnis in his two affidavits submitted in the case.

Throughout the trial, the plaintiffs objected to the introduction of this historical/philosophical testimony, arguing that it was irrelevant to the case. I believe that they were correct. Although the trial court admitted the testimony (and the plaintiffs therefore felt the need to introduce rebuttal witnesses), there is reason to think that the Court did not treat it as significant. No opinion in the case mentioned this testimony, although other expert testimony on child abuse and psychology was discussed. In the arguments presented before the Supreme Court it was not discussed, and the whole strategy of argument was different, not focusing any longer on attempts to establish that strict scrutiny was the appropriate level of review. So the testimony was legally irrelevant and performed no function in the case. Nonetheless, it is interesting to examine these arguments for the light they shed on the immutability of our sexual categories in general.

Finnis's moral argument—the argument he traces to "Plato and those many philosophers who followed him" (Affidavit of Oct. 8, para. 47)—begins from the premise that it is morally bad to use the body of another person as an instrument for the purpose of one's own private pleasure or satisfaction (para. 46). Although the legal relevance of this claim remains unclear, it is at least a plausible moral contention.[11] He then continues with the assertion that a sexual relationship is able to avoid this sort of manipulative use of another person only through the openness to procreation characteristic of a marital relationship in which no artificial contraception is used:

> Marriage, with its double blessing—procreation and friendship—is a real common good. Moreover, it is a common good that can be both actualized and experienced in the orgasmic union of the reproductive organs of a man and a woman united in commitment to that good. Conjugal sexual activity, and—as Plato and Aristotle and Plutarch and Kant all argue—*only* conjugal activity is free from the shamefulness of instrumentalization that is found in masturbating and in being masturbated or sodomized. (para. 46)

All beliefs on the part of nonmarried couples that they are in fact actualizing a "common good" such as love or friendship are called "the pursuit of an illusion" (para. 47), on the grounds that there is no "biological reality" to the uniting that takes place, as there is in the "orgasmic union of the reproductive organs of husband and wife" (para. 47). Finnis goes on to argue that such relationships are not merely unproductive but actually destructive of the personalities of the participants[12] and also of the community. Appeal to Greek antiquity is crucial in getting Finnis to this conclusion.

One may wonder what difference it makes whether Finnis did or did not get the Greeks right. For surely his argument must stand or fall on its own merits, not by any such appeal to authority, and so too must the argument that rebuts it. This is all true. And it is possible to rebut the Finnis argument in general philosophical terms as well; my testimony emphasized that point. And yet I shall argue that getting the Greeks right does, in the ways I have suggested, help us in some ways to get our own arguments right—by removing a false sense of inevitability about our own judgments and practices[13] and by showing us moral arguments of great rational power.

III. Ancient Greek Sexuality: Sources and Evidence

It is difficult to study Greek views of sexuality, for the reason so eloquently given by Forster: In this area, scholarly puritanism and evasiveness have exerted a pernicious influence, eclipsing or distorting what Clive Durham quite rightly holds to be a straightforward matter of scholarship. The omissions perpetrated by figures such as Clive and Maurice's imaginary tutor—whether prompted by shame or by the desire to make the revered Greeks look more like proper Victorians[14]—make their way into the editing and translating of ancient texts, into the making of lexica and other technical tools of scholarship, and thence into the interpretation and understanding of the ancient world. Until very recently there were no reliable translations of Greek and Latin texts involving sexuality, and no reliable scholarly discussions of the meanings of crucial words, metaphors, and phrases. As Kenneth Dover writes, in a document addressing the issues of scholarship that arose in the Amendment 2 trial: "On sexual behaviour, and homosexual behaviour in particular, translations and authoritative-sounding statements until quite recent times are not to be relied on, because turbulent irrationality impaired the judgement of translators and scholars."[15] In every instance, then, we need to approach these matters with rigorous scholarship, scrutiny of all the occurrences of a term, and freedom from influence and prejudice.

What, in general, does the Greek evidence show us, so approached?[16] As we approach the evidence, let us bear in mind the claim that Finnis wishes to make about ancient Athenian culture:

> In classical Athens, there was amongst the Athenian upper classes an ideology of same-sex "romantic relationships" which were specifically man-boy relationships (inherently lacking the genuine mutuality of equals) and which in a certain number of cases doubtless resulted in sexual conduct. But even at the height of this ideology, a speaker addressing the Athenian Assembly-Court in 346/5 BC could confidently assume that the bulk of his audience would regard sexual *conduct* between males as involving at least one of the partners in something "most shameful" and "contrary to nature," so that that partner, at least, must "outrage (*hubrizein*) himself." I refer to Aeschines, *Against Timarchus* especially paragraph 185 given in K. J. Dover, *Greek Homosexuality* page 60.[17]

Let us bypass for the present the inherent oddity of citing Dover in connection with an interpretation of Greek norms that Dover painstakingly demolishes, arguing both that this part of Aeschines' speech is in important respects misleading concerning both legal and moral norms and that even Aeschines' antithesis itself "cannot rest on a simple assignation of homosexuality to the category of the unnatural"[18] but rests, instead, on an alleged unnaturalness for males of subordination and passivity. (And, as we shall see, Dover is far from holding that one party in a Greek homosexual relationship must subordinate himself in a shameful way.) But let us instead turn first to more basic matters.

We must begin by enumerating the types of sources on which a scholar can draw in reconstructing the historical picture.[19]

(1) *Visual art.* Of special importance are the numerous vase paintings depicting erotic and sexual activities. Most of these were produced between 570 and 470 B.C., thus prior to most of the literary evidence (the first surviving Greek tragedy being 472). Most derive from Attica. Thus, although caution needs to be exercised in linking the vases with Athenian culture, they can illuminate many aspects of the Athenian cultural scene. Vases have the advantage of explicitness in their depiction of sexual conduct: Literary sources are typically more reticent.[20]

(2) *Oratory.* The central text in Dover's argument is a law-court speech from the year 346 B.C., Aeschines' *Against Timarchus.* Oratory is excellent evidence for popular attitudes, because the speaker had to persuade a jury of citizens chosen by lot, in matters in which much was at stake for his client and for himself.[21] In the absence of rules of relevance, any sort of innuendo or moral rhetoric might be used, and if we often can discern little about what was really true in the case, we can learn a lot about what a jury might have been expected to find persuasive. Dover shows, however, that rhetorical distortions of fact can extend even to the presentation of the legal picture—so, again, caution is needed.

(3) *Comic drama.* The comedies of Aristophanes (and fragments of other comic poets) are filled with frank sexual material.[22] The material is aimed at amusing the average audience, so it relies on some norms of what would be acceptable and what found shocking. But Aristophanes must be used with extreme caution in reconstructing what people seriously thought and did, just as would the humor of a scathing sexual comic of today.

(4) *Other literary evidence.* One may also draw on the poems of Sappho (sixth century B.C.); the erotic poetry ascribed to Theognis, of highly dubious and possibly mixed date (possibly extending from the seventh century B.C. to the Hellenistic period, i.e., after the fourth century B.C.); the erotic poems of the so-called Greek Anthology, composed from the third century B.C. through, probably, early centuries A.D., though the most important texts derive from around 100 B.C.

(5) *Philosophy.* Philosophers are in general not reliable sources for popular thought, but there are exceptions. Plato's dialogues contain, I would argue, no speech that Plato does not wish his reader to ponder seriously. On the other hand, some speakers are identified more clearly than others as spokesmen for popular views of the day. Among these, Dover is right, I think, to single out the speaker Pausanias in the *Symposium;* I would add the speeches of Phaedrus and Aristophanes, though the latter seems to me an especially serious part of Plato's own design—and, as well, though with caution, the speech of Lysias and the first speech of Socrates in the *Phaedrus.*[23] Aristotle's thought can sometimes be used, with caution, to reconstruct the reputable beliefs of his day.

(6) *Artemidoros*. A writer of unusual interest for the student of sexuality is the dream interpreter Artemidoros of Daldis, who wrote during the second century A.D. Dover did not use Artemidoros, because his cutoff date was the end of the Greek Anthology, but the seven or so centuries covered by his reconstruction is a far longer span than the gap of two centuries separating most of the Greek Anthology from Artemidoros. Given the diversity of his clientele, Artemidoros is a fine source for popular thought, and Winkler provides convincing arguments "that Artemidoros' categorization of sexual acts corresponds to widespread and long-enduring social norms—that is, to the public perception of the meaning of sexual behavior."[24] In general, the sexual attitudes and customs of the Greek world do exhibit a remarkable constancy across place and time.[25]

What, then, does this evidence show us? First, it shows us a culture in which the sexual appetite is not found per se problematic or shameful. Here I agree with both Kenneth Dover and Michel Foucault[26]: There is a great distance here from the Christian problematizing of sex, both in the general culture and in the philosophers. No appetite is per se wicked; all appetites need careful management. Sex, like any other pleasure, may be "used" either well or badly.[27]

Second, and again in agreement with the picture presented in Dover, there is neither general condemnation of same-sex acts as such nor a view that the desire to perform such acts is the sign of a wicked or depraved character. Dover's book amply demonstrates that "the Greeks regarded the sexual arousal of an older male by the sight of a beautiful younger male as natural and normal."[28] Homosexual copulation was not viewed as per se immoral or as criticized by the gods. Dover summarizes: "The Greeks in general believed that many kinds of behaviour, notably fraud, perjury, robbery, and the like, were offensive to the gods and incurred divine punishment in this world or the next. They certainly did not include homosexual copulation among these modes of behaviour; indeed, the gods themselves enjoyed it."[29] Dover correctly contrasts Greek attitudes with "the sentiment of a culture which has inherited a religious prohibition of homosexuality and, by reason of that inheritance, has shown (until recently) no salutary curiosity about the variety of sexual stimuli which can arouse the same person. . . ."[30]

We may go further: In Greek culture and practices, the gender of the partner assumes far less importance than it does in our own society and is usually taken as less salient than many other facts about a sexual act. Nor are people very often categorized socially in accordance with their orientation toward partners of a particular gender. It is assumed that abundant appetitive energy may find an outlet in intercourse with either gender, and the two possibilities are frequently treated as more or less interchangeable for moral purposes, youths and women being coupled together as likely pleasures for a man to pursue. To cite just one example analyzed by Dover, in Aristophanes' *Acharnians* the delights of peace are praised in a hymn to Phales, a god in whose honor a phallus is carried in procession. These delights include sex with young men, adultery with married women, and the rape of a pretty Thracian slave girl—all being listed without distinction as more or less interchangeable plea-sures for the male hero.[31]

As for actual practices, in Sparta, we find evidence of a strong encouragement of male-male relations in connection with the military culture and also of female-female relations as evidenced in erotic parts of young girls' choral poetry.[32] For female-female relations elsewhere, the primary evidence is the poetry of Sappho. Like all poetic evidence, this material must be used with caution in reconstruct-ing practices; the difficulty in this case is all the greater on account of the frag-mentary nature of the material. The texts are correctly interpreted by Dover and John J. Winkler as giving clear evidence of sexual acts as well as romantic friend-ship in the world represented; it is difficult to believe that such depictions would be received well by an audience if they in no way corresponded to an accepted reality.[33] Aristophanes' speech in Plato shows that such relationships were fa-miliar to Athenians as well.[34] Although all such arguments must remain rather speculative, the surviving evidence being so slight, Winkler has argued that the lyrics of Sappho give evidence that female-female sexuality was less asymmetri-cal, less governed by the dichotomy of penetrator-penetratee, and more mutu-ally sensuous than other sexual relationships in Greek society.[35] It is interesting to note that Artemidoros, who otherwise does not bother to mention female-female acts in his elaborate list of sex acts (presumably because his clientele was all male), does include in the category of acts "contrary to nature"—a category of weird and counterfactual, rather than vicious acts, and one that includes the perpetual fantasy of making love with a god or goddess—the description "a woman penetrating a woman."[36] He evidently finds this so weird as to be im-possible, though there is no sign that he believes anything one way or the other about other sex acts between women.[37]

For Athens, however, most of our evidence, both literary and artistic, per-tains to male-male relations. Here we find—again I am agreeing with Dover—no general condemnation of male-male relations, a fortiori not a general *moral* condemnation. Indeed Dover, like David Halperin, produces and stresses the evi-dence that visiting both male and female prostitutes was considered perfectly acceptable for a citizen male,[38] and male prostitution is treated as a perfectly routine matter in texts of many kinds. Even in the midst of his moralizing de-nunciation of Timarchus (a citizen) for prostituting himself, Aeschines hastens to reassure his audience that he has no intention of discouraging the general practice of male prostitution; his aim, instead, is to guarantee that people who want casual sex with young men "turn to foreigners and resident aliens so as not to be deprived of what they prefer."[39]

Where relations between two male citizens are concerned, we find, again, no general condemnation, but, instead, a complex system of *caveats* or reservations. We must begin by noting that these relations, even when they involve people close to one another in age, always involve an asymmetry of roles: The *erastês* or "lover" is the older partner, who actively pursues and courts the younger, drawn by the sight of youthful male beauty. He is expected to be keenly inter-ested in sexual contact, and this interest, and the (active, penetrative) conduct that follows from it, is taken to be perfectly normal and natural. The younger partner, the *erômenos* or "beloved," is likely to be pleased at being the object of admiration and interested in benefits such as friendship, education, and political advancement that a relationship with an *erastês* may bestow. The relationship may in this sense involve a real reciprocity of benefits, and mutual affection based on this. But the cultural norm dictates that he is not to have a keen sexual interest in being penetrated or to develop habits of enjoying that sort of penetration; that would be, in effect, to be turned into a woman, and one could expect that this would unfit him from playing, later in life, an active manly role.

This being the case, the relationship between an older and a younger male citizen is hedged round with a complex series of *caveats* and reservations. What are these reservations?

(1) No citizen may receive money for sex. Proof that one does is disqualifying for citizenship because it is connected closely with the idea that one has put one's own body up for sale to and use by the highest bidder, hence with the idea of treason. In a democracy in which most major offices are filled by lot, one does not want to have a citizen who is up for sale.[40] Receipt of many gifts may also give rise to the suspicion that one's favors are being bought.

(2) There are grave strictures against sexual violence and enticement, especially against the young. As Dover shows, *hubris* need not mean actual sexual assault. It usually does mean that, when the subject of the verb *hubrizein* is an adult male and the object a woman or a boy. But the term may be at times extended to include "dishonest enticement, threats, blackmail" and other forms of nonphysical coercion.[41] It seems wrong, however, to assert that a fully consensual relation between *erastês* and *erômenos* could be stigmatized as *hubris*— except by someone alleging that it did after all contain one or more of the forbidden forms of coercion.[42]

(3) Habitual passivity (i.e., being habitually the one who gets penetrated) is much criticized, as I have said, and is taken as evidence that one is not fully manly. (The Aristotelian *Problemata* says it shows that the person is physically malformed, with his fluid-bearing "ducts" going to the anus rather than to the penis.[43]) As a result, there is strong anxiety about passivity in general.

(4) Finally, there is widespread criticism of those who seek casual bodily pleasure in their interactions with younger males without caring for friendship and other values.

Where the relationship between an older and a younger male citizen is concerned, therefore, much care needs to be taken. The penetrative role is per se nonproblematic, and if one goes to penetrate a male prostitute, it is perfectly all right, just as if one goes to penetrate a female prostitute. It was not just common but widely approved for married males to visit prostitutes of either sex. But with a young male who is going to be a citizen, much caution must be exercised not to corrupt him by excessive gifts and not to encourage habits of passivity. For this reason, a cultural ideal, prominently depicted in visual art, prefers intercrural intercourse, that is, intercourse in which the older partner achieves orgasm by friction of the penis between the younger man's tightly clenched thighs.

It is clear, however, that this is not the whole picture. In Greek comedy, anal penetration is taken to be the norm, as Dover stressed in his first edition. In the postscript to his second edition, he now grants that this fact may well indicate that the vase-painters' preference for the intercrural mode may be "highly conventional."[44] In the Greek Anthology and the dream book of Artemidorus, anal intercourse is again taken to be the norm, and intercrural copulation is not mentioned. (Artemidoros classifies both active and passive anal acts as acts that are both "according to nature" and "according to custom.") So it would appear that both in fifth-century Athens and in the later period represented by the Greek Anthology and Artemidoros, anal acts between citizens occurred. How were these acts viewed? The evidence of comedy must be read with much caution, for, as Dover shows, the comic genre depicts human motivation as venal and selfish consistently, not only in the sexual domain. It would be wrong to infer from comedy that in popular thought generally the penetratee was thought to have been bought. On the other hand, it is also clear that the fact of anal passivity would be a source of anxiety and possible shame if it were seen as part of a picture in which the young man is thought to be developing habits of passivity. The best solution to this problem seems to me to be one suggested by David Halperin, invoking conventions of public and literary evidence already demonstrated by Dover.[45] The suggestion is that anal acts were assumed to occur between the *erastês* and his citizen *erômenos*, but they were not in general to be publicly mentioned. To speak publicly of what everyone took for granted would incur shame for the youth, where the fact itself would not. This conclusion is fully consistent with Dover's analysis. The important point to stress, in any case, is that such shame as was potentially at issue was shame not about the fact of same-sex copulation but about the "womanish" position of passivity and its potential connection with being turned into a woman. No such shame, it would seem, attached even potentially to conduct that did not involve this penetration, thus not to conduct involving intercrural intercourse, apparently the most common mode of copulation.

As for oral sex, the Greeks seem to have had some aversion to this form of conduct, and especially to the receptive role, but their condemnation appears to have been aesthetic rather than moral.[46]

We must now insist on the question of age. For Finnis repeatedly called the relationship of *erastês* and *erômenos* a "man-boy" relationship, alleging that nobody has bothered to inquire how young the "boys" actually were.[47] But this is not so: Dover and others have commented on this matter at length, assisted by the clear evidence of visual art. To modern American ears the word "boy" suggests someone between the ages of, say, four and twelve. But the *erômenos* of Greek custom was typically, and ideally, a young man between the time of full attainment of adult height and the full growth of the beard: if we go by modern growth patterns, perhaps sixteen to nineteen, but more likely, since the ancient Greek age of puberty seems to have been slightly later than ours, the age of a modern college undergraduate.

One should also consider what the typical *erômenos* was expected to do and to be, for our own children, although they may reach puberty earlier than ancient Greek youths, are in some respects far less mature and independent in their ways of life once puberty is at hand. Looking at famous couples such as Achilles and Patroclus, the tyrannicides Harmodius and Aristogeiton, and the famous Sacred Band of Thebes, an elite military corps made up of male-male couples, we can conclude that the *erômenos* is generally old enough for mature military and political action.[48] (And because the popular thought of our day tends to focus on the scare image of a "dirty old man" hanging around outside the school waiting to molest young boys, it is important to mention, as well, that the *erastês* might not be very far in age from the *erômenos*. One can begin to play that role, as Halperin correctly insists, even while he is still playing the other role—though he will not play both roles in relation to the same person.) There is, moreover, some evidence of couples in which the *erômenos* was even older than the standard norm, especially in relationships of long duration. Pausanias and Agathon continued for at least twelve years a relationship that began when Agathon was eighteen.[49] The Stoics apparently held that a relationship should continue until the *erômenos* was twenty-eight.[50] We should also consider the relationship between Plato and Dion of Syracuse, which is at any rate widely (and sympathetically) represented in the evidence for Plato's life as a sexual relationship, and which evidently began when the parties were about fifty and thirty-five respectively. We have, as well, the fact that Plato's Pausanias and Aristophanes speaks of their norm as that of a lifelong partnership[51]; Pausanias insists that it should not begin until after the growth of the younger party's beard. Aristotle, finally, following Pausanias, defends a long-term alliance as morally best.

We must now also address the issue of mutuality, because Finnis claimed that the *erastês-erômenos* relationship was inherently exploitative. It is true that the *erômenos* is depicted typically as deriving no *sexual pleasure* from the conduct—although this may well be a cultural norm that conceals a more complicated reality.[52] What is more important is that it is perfectly clear that a successful relationship of this sort produced many advantages for the younger man—education, political advancement, friendship—and that he frequently felt intense affection for the *erastês* as a result. The tales of courageous self-sacrifice with which Plato's Phaedrus regales his audience would not have seemed surprising. Furthermore, the young man can be expected to go promptly on to active sexual pleasures of his own, in a phase of life that will last much longer than his *erômenos* phase lasted.

IV. Same-Sex Desire and Conduct: The Philosophical Evidence

We now turn to the philosophers. Finnis claims that "all three of the greatest Greek philosophers, Socrates, Plato and Aristotle, regarded homosexual *conduct* as intrinsically shameful, immoral and indeed depraved or depraving. That is to say, all three rejected the linchpin of modern 'gay' ideology and lifestyle."[53] He repeatedly suggests that they do so using, or at least suggesting, an argument similar to his own, viz., an argument that relies on the moral centrality of the potentially procreative marital bond. I shall argue that none of the philosophers I discuss takes the position described by Finnis; nor does any endorse his positive view of the marital relationship. Even those texts that do rank nonconsummated same-sex relationships over consummated relationships do so not because they find anything shameful or degrading in homosexual intercourse as distinct from heterosexual intercourse but for other reasons—in the case of some works of Plato, out of a general suspiciousness of the power of sexual passion to interfere with reason and a consequent desire to reduce all orgasmic sexual expression to a minimum. In fact, we shall find that same-sex relationships are usually ranked ahead of heterosexual (and, frequently, marital) relationships on the grounds that they are more likely to be linked with spiritual goals.

Socrates

It is very difficult to reconstruct the views of the historical Socrates on sexual relations. For Socrates' views in general we have four major sources: (1) the dialogues of Plato; (2) several works of the writer Xenophon dealing with Socrates; (3) the Aristophanic comedy *Clouds*, which offers a satire on Socrates; and (4) various scattered statements by Aristotle. From now on we may ignore (3) and (4), which offer no help with the issue of sexuality. Xenophon's testimony is generally recognized as much less reliable than that of Plato, where they conflict; Xenophon, though an able man of affairs, an intrepid military leader, and a literary stylist of some skill, was not a subtle philosopher.[54] Plato, by contrast, was of course a very great philosopher, and he is doubtless the best source we have for Socrates' life and activity. The use of Plato as source, however, poses further problems: for Plato uses Socrates as a character in dialogues of varying dates, in many of which we have independent reason (Aristotle's testimony above all) to think him to be developing ideas of his own that were not Socrates' ideas. Further complexity derives from the fact that in some of the works that are usually judged "Platonic" rather than "Socratic," there may be narrative and biographical material that gives genuine illumination about Socrates.

In brief, I solve this problem as Vlastos solves it—giving the Platonic Socrates pride of place where he and Xenophon do not agree and dividing the works of Plato as Vlastos does, into a group that represents (more or less) the thinking of the historical Socrates, and those that are Platonic. In the former group I would place dialogues such as *Apology, Crito, Laches, Lysis, Charmides, Protagoras,* and *Euthyphro;* in the latter group, *Symposium, Phaedrus, Republic, Philebus, Laws,* and many others that will not concern us here. Unlike Vlastos (and concurring in arguments of T. H. Irwin[55]), I treat *Gorgias* as containing much material that may be called Platonic. Like Vlastos, however—and like Dover—I regard the portrait of Socrates' life and activity painted in the speech of Alcibiades in the *Symposium* as a genuine source for the historical Socrates, if used with proper caution, despite the presence of clearly Platonic doctrines in other portions of that dialogue.

What can we know about Socrates' attitude to same-sex relations? Very little, as it turns out. In Plato's dialogues, Socrates takes his place in the "strongly homosexual ambience" of Athenian society.[56] Socrates' friends are routinely depicted as involved in erotic relationships with younger men, and he responds with sympathy to their situations.[57] Socrates himself is depicted as having strong sexual attractions to younger men; for example, he is "on fire, absolutely beside myself" when he looks inside the cloak of the young Charmides (*Charmides* 155C-E; cf. *Protagoras* 309A).[58] We know that Socrates was married[59] and had children, but he never alludes to his or anyone else's marital sexual life, and in general his sexual interest in women appears to have been slight, so far as Plato's portrait is concerned.[60]

Did Socrates engage in male-male sexual relations? And if he did not, did he have a general reason for this policy, and if so, of what sort? Xenophon provides him with two general reasons against homosexual conduct, which Socrates is prepared to commend to others as well: the pleasures of sex can enslave reason (Xenophon, *Symposium* 3.8–14); and sexual gratification is "not a good thing" because it is something like scratching an itch—that is, a way of relieving a tension but not good in itself (Xenophon, *Memorabilia* i.2.29).[61] We may remark that neither of these arguments singles out homosexual activity for special blame: Xenophon's Socrates would presumably say the same of erotic passion generally, given the reasons he advances. It just happens that his friends are far more passionate about young men than about women and so need more counseling in that regard. Nor do we hear any mention of a view that marital sex is in any way superior to other forms of sex, heterosexual or homosexual (although we may remark that the usual assumption would be that the husband would not be passionately in love with his wife, and marriage would to that extent escape the blame reserved for passion). Finally, the blame involved does not involve the idea that such copulation is wicked or depraved. Like the scratching to which it is compared, it may be inferior, but, as Dover says, apropos of this material, "'Inferior' does not mean 'wicked.'"[62]

As for Plato's Socrates, there is no clear evidence for a general attitude on the matter that Socrates is prepared to recommend to others. In several passages, through a metaphorical use of erotic language, Socrates insists that his own most intense passion is for wisdom, a higher goal that distracts him from the pursuit of bodily intercourse (*Protagoras* 309B–D). As Dover remarks, "It does not follow logically from this that homosexual copulation should be avoided, unless one also believes that any investment of energy and emotion in the pursuit of an inferior end vitiates the soul's capacity to pursue a superior end."[63] Does Socrates think this? Note that even if he does, he would not be singling out homosexual copulation for special condemnation, and the grounds of his condemnation would not be that he finds the activity wicked or shameful. Once again: "inferior" does not mean "wicked." But does he think this? In *GH*, Dover argues in the affirmative—but only by drawing on the *Republic*, an unquestionably Platonic rather than Socratic text, and by putting the evidence of Xenophon together with that of Plato, a method that I would consider defective; Dover now grants my methodological point.[64]

The primary piece of evidence we have is the story told by Alcibiades in Plato's *Symposium*, concerning his own failed attempt to seduce Socrates, in which Socrates sleeps all night beside the beautiful young man without evident arousal (216C–219E). This story must be used with caution as a source for the historical Socrates, given its context in an unquestionably mature Platonic dialogue and its close relation to other arguments of that dialogue, but even scholars such as

Vlastos who insist on the distinction between Plato's Socrates and the historical Socrates as depicted by Plato so use it. What, then, if so used, does the story show? It certainly does not show that Socrates has disgust at Alcibiades' proposal or thinks the orientation of his desire diseased; he clearly treats the proposal as quite natural and normal. Nor does it offer any evidence that he thinks the proposed conduct depraved or wicked, or different in kind from an attempted seduction by an attractive young woman (except that Alcibiades is seen as exceptional in beauty in a way that no woman would probably have been seen by Greek society of the time). Socrates seems to think sexual relations inferior to the course he actually follows—for what reason? Two reasons are suggested in the passage. The first is that (as suggested in the *Protagoras*) he feels the lure of philosophy so strongly that he simply does not get aroused by anything else.[65] The second reason is that he notices Alcibiades' youthful vanity and wants him to find out the hard way that he cannot get what he wants through good looks alone. The seduction of this charismatic teacher would have turned him straight away from philosophy; Socrates' refusal creates a painful stimulus to self-examination.[66] In short, his reasons for refusal are internal to his conception of the value of philosophy and of his role as philosophical teacher.[67] There is no evidence here even for the claim made by Xenophon's Socrates, namely that sexual conduct is always inferior, a distraction from better pursuits. And there is no evidence whatever, even in Xenophon, for Finnis's conclusion that Socrates "regarded homosexual *conduct* as intrinsically shameful, immoral and indeed depraved or depraving."[68]

Plato

Plato is a philosopher of enormous complexity. Because, in his suspiciousness about all appetitive pleasure, he diverges more than any other Greek philosopher from the cultural pattern I have described, his views need to be probed with special care. Sensitivity is also required in posing questions about Plato's own relation to his varied characters; we cannot assume that the character Socrates is the only one whose views we should connect with their author. I shall have my eye on three questions: (1) What, if anything, is said about same-sex desire and conduct? In particular, are they singled out from other forms of sexual desire and conduct as unusually shameful or depraved? (2) What, if anything, is said about the social contribution of same-sex relationships? (3) What, if anything, is said about marriage? Is there any sign of the positive view of the worth of procreative intercourse that Finnis appears to trace to Plato?

Gorgias   Toward the end of this dialogue, Socrates is criticizing Callicles, who has held that the best life is the life with the largest desires, provided one always has the opportunity to satisfy them. Socrates compares this to the wish that one always had the greatest possible itches, provided one always had the power to scratch. In this and the succeeding series of examples, he tries to get Callicles to grant that no pleasure is per se valuable just because, like scratching, it replenishes a lack or removes an antecedent pain. Eventually he will ask Callicles to think this way about the central bodily activities—eating, drinking, and sex. A turning point in this argument is reached when, after Callicles has gamely tried to defend the scratcher's life as a good thing, Socrates provides a further example, the pleasure of the *kinaidos*. Callicles is outraged and tells Socrates he should be ashamed to mention such an example (494E2). Finnis took this case, it would seem, as a reference to same-sex conduct in general.[69] But the *kinaidos* is clearly a person who chronically plays the passive role. Dover translates as "pathic"; in my published treatment of the dialogue, I used the phrase "passive homosexual"[70]—meaning by this to denote someone who habitually plays the passive role. More recently, I have been convinced by arguments of the late John J. Winkler that *kinaidos* usually connotes willingness to accept money for sex, as well as habitual passivity[71]; I therefore would prefer to think of the *kinaidos* as a male prostitute or, at the least, a venal and corrupt male pathic. In any case, there is no doubt that we are dealing here with not an isolated act but a type of person who habitually chooses activity that Callicles finds shameful.[72] That, and no view about same-sex relations per se, is the basis of his criticism. In fact, Callicles is depicted as having a young boyfriend of his own. (It would be assumed that he would practice intercrural intercourse with this boyfriend, thus avoiding putting him in anything like the *kinaidos'* shamed position.) Socrates expresses no view of his own on these matters, although he seems to suggest that all appetitive activities, including eating and drinking, are inferior to activities (whatever they be) that do not simply relieve an antecedent tension or lack. Once again, "inferior" does not mean "'wicked."

The *Gorgias* contains no discussion of the marital bond.

Symposium   The dialogue is set at an all-male drinking party attended by a group that includes pairs of lovers.[73] Its speeches express conventional views about love, most of which Plato depicts in an appealing and serious light. The speech by Phaedrus points to the military advantages that may be derived by including male-male couples in a fighting force: Because of their intense love, each will fight better, wishing to show himself in the best light before his lover (178D–179B). Such an army, he concludes, "though small in size would pretty well conquer all of humanity" (179A).[74] Shame is mentioned as a motive closely connected, in a positive sense, with passionate sexual love: Each will be ashamed of doing anything cowardly before his lover (178E). Phaedrus does mention two cases of marital love and self-sacrifice, giving high praise to the courageous actions of Alcestis, but he expresses some surprise that a male-female love could have the same features he finds in male-male love.[75]

The speech of Pausanias (convincingly argued by Dover to be one of our central pieces of evidence for prevalent Athenian attitudes) criticizes males who seek physical pleasure alone in their relations with younger males, and praises those who seek deeper spiritual and moral goals. Strong interest in sex with women is connected by Pausanias with a preference for the body over the soul (181BC). A sexual act, says Pausanias, like any other act, is not right or wrong in and of itself: Everything depends on the manner in which it is done (180E, 183D). If the *erastês* demonstrates that his primary concern is for the character and education of the *erômenos*, rather than merely for bodily pleasure, then it will be a fine or noble thing (*kalon*)[76] for the younger man to "gratify" the older (*charizesthai*, a word that, as Dover has shown, clearly connotes intercourse). Such a lover should look for a young man whose beard has already started to grow, since that is the age of good judgment (181D): After all, the goal is "to love as people who are going to be together their entire lives and to live together" (181D), and this goal requires careful selection. The young man should not let himself be caught too quickly, because he must test the lover's character and regard for his education (184AB).

Pausanias is aware of a variety of different customs regarding male-male intercourse. He makes fun of regions where it is held *always* to be a good thing to "gratify" a lover, without regard to the moral concerns he has enumerated. This custom, he says, suits unrefined people who lack the capacity to persuade one another of virtue and good intentions (182B). But he also condemns the opposite custom, and more strongly, associating it with Asian despotism. He mentions that tyrants sometimes promulgate the view that same-sex relations are shameful, in order to discourage the sort of devotion to political liberty that such relations, as exemplified by Harmodius and Aristogeiton, can foster (182BC). Marriage plays no part in Pausanias' thinking, except when he mentions laws that forbid sleeping with other people's wives (181E). It would be assumed, however, that the relations he describes could be compatible with marriage on the part of the *erastês*. The lovers Pausanias describes are both happy and socially responsible.

Because Eryximachus' speech is concerned more with cosmology than with human beings, I omit it. Aristophanes' speech I have already described: It situates same-sex longings deep in nature, describes intercourse as a way of being restored to a natural wholeness and unity, and argues for the civic benefits of male-male love in particular. There is absolutely no doubt that lovers of all three types are envisaged as engaging in intercourse—intercourse, indeed, is a central topic of the speech. Although the speech does recognize the distinction between the *erastês* and the *erômenos*, it is remarkable for its suggestion of mutual desire and pleasure: Both partners feel "friendly love and intimacy and passionate love" (192BC), and the younger "halves" of original male-male "wholes" are said to enjoy "lying with and being embraced by men" (192A). (Indeed, the whole conceit of the myth leads the mind in the direction of an uncustomary symmetry and reciprocity.) Relationships between "other halves" are said to endure throughout life (192C). Aristophanes remarks that custom may force such male-male couples to marry, but they "do not turn their thoughts to marriage and begetting of children by nature . . . but it is enough for them to live unmarried with one another" (192AB).

Agathon's speech contains little to interest us. Socrates' speech recounts a process of religious-mystical education in which male-male love[77] plays a central guiding role. Whether or not it is abandoned when one reaches the summit of philosophy's vision, and Anthony Price has now convinced me that it is not,[78] this erotic bond offers a primary insight and inspiration into the nature of the good and beautiful. The speech argues that a preference for women and marriage betrays an inferior type of creativity, focused on bodily rather than spiritual goals: These people want offspring of the body, rather than the mind and character (298E).[79]

Will the lovers in the Socratic ascent have sexual intercourse? Certainly, as they fix their minds increasingly on the whole of beauty, rather than simply on individual exemplars of beauty, the tension and strain involved in erotic passion will cease; Socrates' imaginary instructor Diotima remarks that Socrates will no longer have to pursue the young men that now "strike you out of your mind" (211D). She uses the language of sexual "being with" for the aspiring philosopher's relation to the eternal form of Beauty, having used it earlier of his relation to those same young men (*sunontes*, 211D, *sunontos* 212A)—again, implying that a new form of intercourse displaces the old as the object of the philosopher's most intense interest. One could, of course, imagine intercourse continuing without intense passion—a possibility explored in Plato's *Phaedrus*. But the result is likely to be the stonelike unaroused Socrates of whom Alcibiades so bitterly complains, feeling Socrates' unresponsiveness as a kind of virtual assault.[80] I have argued that the reader of the dialogue is intended to feel more than a little ambivalent about a proposal in which so much of human passion is given up and intended to feel, therefore, some sympathy with Alcibiades' preference for flesh-and-blood intercourse.[81] Through appeals to empathy in both Aristophanes' and Alcibiades' speeches, the text recalls to its reader the world of ordinary Athenian judgments, making clear the costs, as well as the benefits, of Diotima's therapy. But even if we disregard that issue, as we should not, and give Socrates the final word in a simple way, his argument in no way shows the view that homosexual conduct is depraved, wicked, or shameful. It is at least as good as any other sort of sexual conduct, though all such intercourse may be uninteresting once one "has intercourse" with the form.

Republic   In this work (and the roughly contemporaneous *Phaedo*) we first encounter in a clear form that suspiciousness about all appetitive expression that will figure so largely in Plato's thought after this time. The appetitive element in the soul—the one that is responsible for eating, drinking, and sexual activity—is compared to an insatiable "many-headed beast" whose demands grow the more they are gratified (442A) and whose pursuits are a constant threat to good reasoning.[82] People who live by their appetites are said to resemble animals, "[L]ike cattle . . . they pasture, grazing and mounting" (586A). Although the sexual appetite is singled out as the greatest and sharpest and most "madness-producing" of the appetites (402C), the three major appetites are treated in tandem throughout the work (for a typical example, 580E), and Plato's strictures apply to them all. In a passage in which he is making proposals for the control of the dangerous erotic appetite, Socrates suggests that in the Ideal City, the *erastês* should kiss the *erômenos*, if he persuades him, and touch him as a father a son, "for the sake of the *kalon*" (presumably, to encourage his educational development, which would be a morally "fine," *kalon*, result), but go no further (403BC): "[I]f not, he will incur the blame of being uncultivated and lacking comprehension of the beautiful" (*amousias kai apeirokalias*, C1–2). This, of course, is far from the Finnis claim that these sexual relations will be regarded as shameful and depraved. And Plato's argument is altogether different from the Finnis argument, since it applies perfectly generally to all sexual relations, especially those accompanied by real passion.

Notice, as well, that there is no mention of what men will and will not do outside of the *erastês/paidika* relation, which was of special concern to Plato because of the intensities of passion to which it typically gave rise. For example, we are not told that males will not make love with both male and female prostitutes, as in most Greek cities they could routinely be expected to do. This would presumably have been seen as a smaller danger than intercourse with the *erômenos* given that, rather like eating a boring meal, it would be done for release only and not with passion. In the *Phaedo*, Plato does seem to take the position that the wise man will not have sexual intercourse at all, but in the *Republic* he follows a milder program, permitting indulgence in all the appetites "up to the point of health and well-being" (558CD, mentioning sexual intercourse at 559C6, after eating and drinking).[83] Given the tight restrictions on potentially procreative sex that are mandated by Plato's eugenic schemes,[84] it seems logical to suppose that some form of sex for release, presumably with male and/or female prostitutes,[85] would be permitted. As for the positive side of Finnis's sexual program, it is nowhere to be found in a work that sets out in a relentless manner to extirpate the traditional family and the bonds of marriage that sustained it.

Phaedrus   The dialogue contains a praise of the intellectual, political, and spiritual benefits of a life centered around male-male love, with considerable stress on the positive role of bodily desire in awakening the personality to its highest aspirations. It begins with Phaedrus reading to Socrates a speech allegedly written by the well-known orator Lysias.[86] The speech argues that a young man should give his sexual favors not to a person who is passionately in love with him but to one who is not in love with him. The argument plays cleverly on tensions and paradoxes inherent in Athenian conventions of the time. (Notice that "Lysias" begins from the realistic assumption that an attractive young man with many suitors will "gratify" one of them, the only question being which. Rightly or wrongly, he treats the question, "Shall I at all?" as already resolved.) When the speaker holds up the advantages of an alliance that is based on excellence and friendship, on one side, an interest in one's education and advancement on the other, he utters familiar truths. When he argues that these advantages are more likely to be present when the *erastês* is not passionately in love with the younger man but is "in control of myself," he says something not implausible; for his observations concerning the instability and inconstancy of *erôs* would themselves have seemed to the audience familiar truths. The advice to avoid the passionate suitor and to gratify the non-passionate one is, then, on the one hand bound to seem eminently sensible[87]; on the other hand, it leaves out the wonder and divinity of *erôs*, which the Greeks strongly felt, even while they felt its dangers.[88]

After giving his own version of the "Lysias" argument, Socrates tries to leave. He is stopped by his famous *daimôn*, who always stops him when he is going to do something bad. It would be bad, he now acknowledges, to leave the blame of *erôs* unretracted. He now proposes to "purify" himself before *erôs*, whom he asserts to be a god[89], by uttering a speech of recantation. The moving and beautiful speech that follows argues that some forms of "madness" can be the source of the greatest good for human beings, and that among these, the madness of love is the best. The arousal of the soul by a visual response to bodily beauty—a response that is described in unambiguously sexual terms and that is said to involve "the entire soul" (251B–D) (i.e., its appetitive as well as its rational elements) is said to be a crucial step in the soul's progress toward insight and metaphysical understanding.[90] The awakening is imagined throughout as that of an older man by the beauty of a younger; Socrates argues that the highest form of human life is one in which a male pursues "the love of a young man along with philosophy" (249A). He describes the experience of falling in love in moving and erotic language, rich in imagery of receptivity as well as activity (being melted, being watered—even drawing a stream of desire into oneself as through an irrigation trench—251E).

Nor is passionate arousal a mere stage in the soul's progress, for it gives rise to an enduring relationship in which physical infatuation is deepened by conversation and the pursuit of shared spiritual goals, and in which the "mad" lover's state gives rise to generous and stable friendship, rather than to the dangers warned of by "Lysias." Most remarkable of all, it also gives rise to a reciprocation of sexual desire on the part of the younger man,[91] who, taking note of the unparalleled generosity of his lover, finds himself suffused with a stream of desire from "the source of that stream which Zeus, in love with Ganymede, called 'passionate longing'" (255C)[92] and conceives a longing and desire for his *erastês*, "having a 'reciprocal-love' (*anterôs*) that is a replica of the other's love. But he calls it, and thinks that it is, not *erôs* but *philia*. He has desire similar to the other's, albeit weaker, to see, to touch, to kiss, to lie with him" (255D). Greek homosexuality conventionally involves reciprocity of a sort, for the *erômenos* receives kindliness and education in return for his beauty. Plato here constructs—in a way that indicates the culturally unusual nature of the proposal, for the young man does not have a word to use for his own desire—a more thoroughgoing reciprocity, extending to the body's longing for beauty.[93] The relationship is envisaged as a long-lasting one in which the two "associate with touching in the gymnasia and in other places of association" (255C).

Plato expresses views about this touching that will seem to a modern audience rather peculiar. On the one hand, he strongly endorses the lovers' bodily desire as god-sent and good, when it is a response to the way in which a body manifests traces of the soul within. (Thus, like Pausanias, he does not endorse desire that stops short at the body's surface, so to speak.) The dialogue is remarkably erotic, and commentators of many different types have responded to it, rightly, as marking a new stage in Plato's attitude to the passions.[94] The part of the soul that represents the soul's emotions is imagined as good and as motivated by reverence and awe toward the boy's beauty. And the bodily arousal of appetite itself at the sight of bodily beauty is given extraordinary significance in the soul's progress, for it is Plato's contention that this response to bodily beauty is a crucial stage in starting the soul going on its way to truth and understanding (250DE).

But the familiar Platonic suspiciousness of the bodily appetites remains, producing the thesis that it will be best for the contemplative couple, in their search for metaphysical insight, to stop short of orgasmic gratification, although they gratify their bodily desire regularly in caresses that stop short of this. Plato's reasoning seems to be, once again, that orgasmic gratification derails the soul from its pursuit of wisdom and, also, it seems, from reverence toward the image of divinity within the younger partner. In effect he seems to believe, as in the *Republic*, that one must starve one part of the soul in order to feed another. His reasoning applies perfectly generally to all sexual activity, and does not single out homosexual activity in particular, except for special praise and interest; procreative sex was quickly dismissed in a sentence, as the occupation of people deficient in spirituality, rather like animals (250E). Furthermore, Plato shows much sympathy for couples who continue to have full intercourse from time to time and who think of this intercourse as a central element in their relationship.[95] These lovers, too, will recover their wings and reenter the heavens, "so that they carry off no small prize for their erotic madness" (256D). They "will live in the light and be happy traveling around with one another, and will acquire matching plumage, when they acquire it, because of their love" (256DE). Those who have avoided this sort of love will be condemned to "roll around and beneath the earth for nine thousand years" (256E–7A). Plato is very likely wrong to think that sexual activity derails aspiration and even reverent emotion, but the views he does hold here do not come close to the claim that homosexual conduct, as such, is inherently shameful and depraved. Once again, "inferior" clearly does not mean "wicked," as he unambiguously shows in his depiction of the after-life rewards of the sexually indulgent couples.

I must now confront one remaining issue: the occurrence of the difficult phrase "contrary to nature" in an obscure description of sexual activity. The sentence reads as follows:

> The one who has not been recently initiated or whose vision has become corrupted is not sharply carried toward the vision of beauty-in-itself when he sees its earthly counterpart, so that he does not revere it when he looks on it, but, giving himself over to pleasure, attempts to mount in the manner of a four-footed beast and to beget children, and associating with wantonness he neither fears nor is ashamed to pursue pleasure contrary to nature. (250E)

Two things can be insisted on from the start. First, the reference to begetting children is really that, not some more general reference to ejaculation. This has been convincingly argued by Dover, who also points out that the picture of mounting like a four-legged animal would not surprise the Greeks, who by preference depicted (and no doubt practiced) heterosexual copulation in the *a tergo* position.[96] Second, the character who does whatever he does "contrary to nature" is the same person, a fact that most translations obscure. Plato is describing not two distinct types of people but a single type. It is also clear what, in general terms, this type is: The type of person who pursues only bodily pleasure, a type resolutely condemned not only by Plato but by Greek cultural norms.

What, however, is meant by the reference to "contrary to nature"? Commentators have been quick to interpret the passage in the light of modern ideas of the unnaturalness of homosexual copulation in some moral sense. Dover, with greater sensitivity to historical context, reads it in the light of the appeal to the behavior of animals in Plato's *Laws*—which, as we shall see, is itself by no means easy to understand. What we must understand is that the appeal to nature is a very slippery topic in Greek philosophy.[97] To say that something is "in accordance with nature" may indeed mean "in accordance with the behavior of other animals." But such appeals to the animal kingdom are typically associated with hedonism and immoralism—certainly they are so by Plato, who ascribes such appeals to Callicles and Philebus,[98] in defense of their self-serving hedonistic programs. Other prominent examples include the son Pheidippides in Aristophanes' *Clouds*, who learns from his new-fangled philosophical education that appeals to the animal world can help him justify beating his father.[99] To the son's gleeful assertion that the rooster fights its father, the father replies, "Why then, since you imitate the rooster in everything, don't you eat shit and sleep on a perch?" A good question—and Plato would have sympathized with it. In dialogues as diverse in date as *Gorgias, Republic,* and *Philebus,* he shows himself to be resolutely opposed to such appeals to the animal kingdom, which would establish norms for an ethical thinking creature by appeal to the behavior of a nonthinking creature. In the *Philebus,* he concludes that appeal to the animal world does indeed support a hedonist thesis[100] but that we will not give that life the first place

> even if all the cattle and horses and all the other beasts speak in its favor by their pursuit of pleasure—creatures trusting in whom, as diviners trust their birds, the many judge that pleasures are the most important thing in living well, and they think that the passionate loves of beasts (*tous thêriôn erôtas*) are authoritative witnesses, rather than the loves of those arguments that are divined on each occasion by the philosophic muse. (67B)

Nor do nonhuman animals fare well in the *Phaedrus* itself: for Socrates holds that a soul that saw nothing of the eternal Forms would be put into an animal body, because being human requires the intellectual grasp that only a sight of the Forms would deliver (248D, 249B). The people described in 250E, then, are humans who are on the borderline of the human/animal divide, incapable of the loves of those who are further away from the beast. So it would be very odd to find their sexual behavior criticized on the ground that it is *not animal,* and of course the child-begetters have just been criticized, predictably, precisely on the ground that their behavior *is animal.* We may add that the term *phusis* is used elsewhere in Socrates' speech not to designate the animal kingdom but to designate the specific "nature" of the divinity within each human (253A1) and the "nature" of the beauty that each pursues (254B5–6).

The best solution to this problem seems to be the one offered by Christopher Rowe, and now accepted by Kenneth Dover: The pleasure of these people is "against nature" "because it is the pleasure of an animal, not a man."[101] In other words, it is against their specific nature as humans (which Plato, as often, understands in a particularly intellectualistic way). This makes the criticism a unity: Both in child-begetting and in other sexual activity, the person in question behaves like an animal in that he pursues pleasure without an interest in the soul. But what other sexual activities are mentioned in the second part of the sentence? Are they both heterosexual and homosexual, exclusively heterosexual, or exclusively homosexual? There seem to be three possibilities: Either the sentence means "he begets children, and in so doing wantonly pursues pleasure in an animal fashion" or "he begets children, and in general wantonly pursues pleasure in an animal fashion in all of his sexual activities," or it means, "he pursues pleasure animalistically with women, begetting children, and also animalistically with men, having sex for pleasure only, unconstrained by shame and reverence for the soul." The third reading seems to me preferable,[102] and we note that one and the same person, or type of person, may well be envisaged in both roles: It is standard to think of hedonism and wantonness as giving rise to an indiscriminate pursuit of both females and males.[103] What we have, then, is a commonplace of the culture, given a new Platonic sharpness: a stern criticism of the hedonist, who in all his sexual acts behaves like an animal, indifferent to the soul. The departure from standard cultural norms consists in understanding child-begetting itself as a merely animal act; this is to be explained by Plato's tendency to equate human nature with intellectual form-seeing nature. None of this implies that all homosexual copulation is "contrary to nature" in some normative sense, and indeed that suggestion would be hard to square with Plato's treatment of the intercourse of the second-best couples.

In short, the *Phaedrus* offers a stirring defense of male-male desire and love and gives an extraordinary role to erotic love within the life of philosophical aspiration. If full genital intercourse is viewed with standard Platonic suspiciousness, this does not arise from any particular condemnation of homosexual relations; other types of sex fare worse. And bodily acts stopping short of orgasm are endorsed in vivid and moving terms.

Laws   It is sometimes thought that in the *Laws*, Plato offers a general condemnation of homosexual relations in a way that singles them out for special moral blame.[104] Even if this were true, we would at most be able to say that he had for some reason changed his mind, and we would have to look for his reasoning.[105] But I believe that once we establish the Greek text of the two problematic passages in the most accurate way—a difficult paleographical and text-critical challenge—and peel away layers of mistranslation and overtranslation, things look different. Here I can only summarize my conclusions[106]:

1. Plato's overall worry is, once again, about bodily pleasure generally, and its ability to take over the personality, disrupting reason.[107] He appears to have, in addition, a special worry about the loss of male bodily fluids that are important for reproduction, in connection with his persistent worries about population.[108]

2. Homosexual conduct is not singled out for special blame. The final law regulates all forms of extramarital activity. Married sex, furthermore, does

better not because it is thought to *be* better (morally) but simply because it is necessary for the city.[109]

3. Insofar as particular attention is devoted to homosexual relations, it is because they are thought to be especially powerful sources of passionate stimulation, not because they are thought to be especially depraved or shameful.[110] The criticism of those who indulge in the active role is that they are intemperate and overindulgent, not that they are wicked. Nor does Plato suggest that the *desire* for such relations is diseased, depraved, or anything but natural and normal. As for the younger partner, the fear, as elsewhere in Greek culture, is that he will be turned into a woman, and it is this worry about passivity, rather than any worry about same-sex conduct in particular, that inspires that aspect of Plato's critique.

4. Plato's characters suggest that the surrounding society will find regulation of homosexual conduct unacceptable.

5. The passages contain several peculiarities that must make us cautious in our assertions. These include (a) the expression of doubt as to whether the proposed regulations are a joke or in earnest—in close connection to an appeal to animal nature, which might arouse some skepticism in a chronic reader of Plato[111]; (b) the idea—made part of the proposal—that it is "noble" to engage in such conduct provided one does not get caught; and (c) the fact that the eventual legislation is addressed only to males envisaged as having wives and thus has no clear implications for premarital behavior or the behavior of women (whose involvement in same-sex activity has been mentioned before).

6. Plato clearly does not hold Finnis's view either about the high moral worth of marital sex or about openness to procreation. He thinks marital sex necessary, not fine; and elsewhere in the *Laws* he is an enthusiastic supporter of methods traditionally used to keep population size down if it is likely to get too high. Such methods would include contraception and abortion. The "greatest and most honorable" ministry in the city oversees *both* fertility treatment and contraception/abortion (740D).

For all these reasons, it seems wrong to think that we find, even here, any basis either for the positive Finnis view of marital sex or for the view that homosexual conduct is any worse morally than any other sort of sexual conduct.[112] The most important thing to realize about these passages is how difficult they are to interpret, and how mistaken it would be to put forward any simple view without recognizing all the difficulties I have mentioned, and others.

In general, Plato is among the philosophers I consider here by far the most suspicious about the bodily appetites; he thus diverges more from ordinary Greek norms. But the divergence is not total: As I have argued, we may still find ample continuity between his norms and the views of Athenian society, together with a rather extraordinary account of the philosophical dividends of male-male erotic desire. All in all, there is no evidence that Plato regarded same-sex conduct as any worse morally than other forms of sexual conduct.[113]

Aristotle

Aristotle speaks far less about sexual matters than does Plato. It is evident that, like most Greeks, he does not find the sexual appetite per se problematic. Indeed, he argues that the innate desires of a human being incline toward virtue: "All the virtues of character seem to belong to us from birth in a way. For we are just and moderate and courageous and the rest straight from our birth. . . . Even children and animals have these natural dispositions, though they evidently prove harmful without rational guidance" (*Nicomachean Ethics* VI.13, 1144b3–9). The virtue of moderation includes proper balance in choices with respect to sexual conduct: so Aristotle is holding here (among other things) that we are inclined from birth to balanced and appropriate choice in the sexual realm—though of course it requires much education for those inclinations to mature into a fully virtuous disposition.[114] In general, then, Aristotle lacks Plato's intense anxiety about our bodily desires in general, and our sexual desires in particular.

If we turn now to his account of the virtue of moderation, we find that for him it "concerns those pleasures that we have in common with the other animals" (*EN* 1118a23–5): He explicitly mentions eating, drinking, and sexual intercourse and states that the bodily senses involved are, above all, those of touch and taste. Because we share these pleasures with the other animals, it becomes especially important to characterize, and strive for, a specifically human way of performing them (see *EN* 1118a25). This way will be to manage the use of these appetites by one's own practical reason. The vicious person Aristotle imagines is totally indiscriminate in his choice of pleasures (1119a1–3). The virtuous person, by contrast, integrates bodily expression into the framework of an overall plan of life governed by reason. But this does not mean he seeks to reduce bodily expression to a minimum. For there is a deficiency of another sort that a virtuous person must also avoid: having too little pleasure in these forms of bodily expression. Aristotle mentions that this deficiency has no common name in the language, since "that does not happen very often" (*EN* 1119a6, 11). Indeed, he continues, "such a lack of feeling is not human; in fact, even the other animals make selections of food, and take pleasure in some types and not in others. If there is someone to whom none of these things is pleasant, and one thing does not differ from another, he would be far from being a human being" (*EN* 1111a6–10). (Although Aristotle's example here is eating, the passage as a whole leaves no doubt that he is making a general claim about all the bodily appetites, because he generalizes throughout the passage.) The person who strikes the correct balance, he concludes, will "desire as many pleasures as conduce to health or well-beings, in a balanced way and as he should, and other pleasures insofar as they do not impede these or do not contravene the noble or exceed the limits of one's material resources" (*EN* 1119a16–18).[115] In other words, one's sexual choices, like others, should not lead one into excess or ill health or disgrace or extravagance; properly managed, however, sex can actually be a valuable end choiceworthy for its own sake. It is important to note that every virtuous action is, by definition, an end in itself, chosen for its own sake apart from any relation it bears to other ends. This is Aristotle's position about reason-governed sexual activity. It need not be justified by any further end it may promote, such as reproduction; properly chosen, it is good in itself.[116]

Aristotle's views are closely related to the popular Greek norms previously discussed. As in the popular culture, we find (1) a refusal to treat sex as specially problematic in moral terms—it is just one of the appetites to be managed, like the appetite for food; and (2) the absence of any special connection between the management of sexual appetite and the topic of marriage. In fact, marriage is not mentioned in the entirety of the discussion of appetitive moderation. Aristotle nowhere urges husbands to practice sexual monogamy, though they should not go after the wives of other citizens. Nor is any reservation expressed concerning the gender of one's sexual partner.[117]

There is one passage in which Finnis has repeatedly claimed[118] to find an Aristotelian condemnation of same-sex activity. In *Nicomachean Ethics* (VII.5), Aristotle lists some forms of conduct that are not "pleasant by nature" but result from some "deformities or habits or corrupt natures." First he discusses a subclass of these, which he calls "bestial," and the examples are a man who takes pleasure in slitting open pregnant women and eating their children, the cannibalism of the wild people of Pontos, the sale of children for sexual services, and Phalaris, who liked to boil people in cauldrons. That, he says, is the "bestial" category, but then there are other related forms of conduct that come about through disease—for example, someone who ate his mother, and someone else who ate another man's liver, when these people were mad; then, finally, there are some that arise from either sickness or habit, "for example pulling out one's hair and biting one's nails, and eating coal or earth, and, in addition to these, the of [*sic*] sexual intercourse toward men. For some of these things are by nature, some happen from habit, and some to those who are subjected to abuse from childhood" (*EN* 1148b28–31). He continues, "Concerning all those things for which nature is responsible, nobody would hold that these are akratic [cases of blameworthy knowing-the-better and doing-the-worse], just as one would not hold this about women, on the grounds that they do not mount but are mounted" (1148b32–3).

The first thing to notice about this list is the way Aristotle carves it up. In none of the cases does he assign moral blame, because he thinks these people in the grip of a diseased state for which they cannot be held responsible (1148b33–49a2). But the crimes come in various categories, and the male-male case, whatever it is, is grouped not with the hideous and gory crimes but with familiar if somewhat gross habits such as hair-pulling and fingernail biting. There is absolutely no evidence that Aristotle wished to regulate such forms of behavior by law, or that he thought them a danger to society.[119] Second, the treatment of nature in the passage is in fact complex. It appears to me that Aristotle is shifting from a normative and universal sense of nature—these things are not "pleasant by nature" in the sense of "in accordance with our ethical end as human beings"—to a descriptive and particular sense, in which many of these actions are in fact "according to nature" for particular individuals, in the sense of being in accordance with the (odd or diseased) constitution that they happen to have. Once again, we must be on our guard when nature is mentioned, for it is a slippery concept in ancient thought. Aristotle here holds that the fact that something is in accordance with one's "nature" exempts one from moral blame for it—although that will not stop people from rightly regarding the conduct in question as gross or offensive.

What is the conduct in question, in the male-male case? The phrase is simply, "the of sexual intercourse toward men." The "the" is a feminine article, which presumably introduces an unstated noun; this noun, to judge from context, would appear to be *hexis*, "stable state," "disposition." Kenneth Dover, Anthony Price, and Terence Irwin, have all argued independently that what is referred to is a stable or chronic state of preferring passivity toward other men, and that what Aristotle is saying about it is that this state can be produced by repeated sexual abuse in childhood. Dover argues as follows:

> Perhaps distaste for the subject has prevented translators and commentators from discussing the curious words, "the of sexual intercourse for males" and has induced them to translate it as 'pederasty', 'faire l'amour avec les mâles, etc. If that translation were correct, Aristotle would be saying that subjection to a passive role in homosexuality when young disposes one to take an active role when older. This would be a strange thing for a Greek to say; it would also be strange for a Greek to suggest that pleasure in an active homosexual role is 'disease-like' or unlikely to be experienced except in consequence of involuntary habituation; the example of the passive sexual role of women as naturally-determined behaviour which cannot be reproached as a lack of control over bodily pleasure indicates that Aristotle's mind is running on the moral evaluation of sexual passivity.[120]

It should be noted that Dover translates the relevant phrase in the *Ethics* passage as "those who were first outraged in childhood," making it clear that he believes that child abuse or assault is at issue. Dover then goes on to adduce as further evidence a passage in the *Problemata*, a work produced by pupils in Aristotle's school, in which the male taste for *habitual passivity* toward males is explained, in a similar manner, as resulting either from a defective physiology or from habits of passivity.[121] Dover now comments further on Aristotle's cryptic expression of the point at issue. He suggests that the odd dative may mean "the sexual pleasure *of* males," and that it is dative only because *tôn aphrodisiôn* is already in the genitive. He continues:

> It seems to me likely that A. expects us to understand *tôn aphrodisiôn* here as referring to *sexual enjoyment in the passive role*; and it doesn't occur to him that it could be ambiguous, because when he's introduced the subject in the category of things that go wrong he wouldn't expect any reader to regard *penetrating* as going wrong—it's something that all males must naturally like!

In other words, the phrase means a chronic disposition *in a male* to find sexual enjoyment in the passive role.

In a similar manner, Price[122] interprets the passage as referring to a man's "playing the female role" in a way caused by "some pathological state produced by habituation to sexual abuse from boyhood." (By abuse he means not only actual rape but also seduction at an age too young for meaningful consent.) He observes that Dover "rightly stresses that Aristotle is thinking of sexual inversion in particular (which the Greeks disparaged), and not homosexuality in general (which they were far from conceiving as a unitary quasi-medical condition). It is striking that he is not concerned, as we might be, that a sexually abused boy may abuse other boys in his turn; it is habitual passivity, and not imitative activity, that he sees as the danger."

Note that for neither Dover nor Price does the passage condemn the role that an adolescent male might play toward an older male in approved intercrural intercourse (or even, perhaps, the occasional anal act—see section 3, above); the problem is developing *habits* of enjoying passivity.[123]

Aristotle so far, then, does not differ from the standard beliefs of Greek culture regarding homosexuality. But he says so little about the topic that we might remain dissatisfied. Anthony Price has now shown, however, that he in fact says much more than previous commentators realized. By supplementing the meager data of the ethical works with scattered remarks on the topic of erotic love in the logical and rhetorical treatises, Price assembles a composite picture that places Aristotle very close to the speech of Pausanias in Plato's *Symposium*, and close as well (although Price does not say this) to the view of the Greek Stoics who followed Aristotle; all, in turn, are close to the Greek popular norms I discussed. Price's argument has the drawback that it does rely to some extent on examples given in the logical works, where Aristotle is not clearly developing a view of his own but may simply be using hypothetical examples to make a logical point; the use of the *Rhetoric* is open to similar criticism. But insofar as Price has been able to link these remarks to passages in Aristotle's ethical writings—and in most respects he has successfully done this—we may cautiously put the picture forward as what may have formed the contents of Aristotle's lost writings on erotic love.[124]

The picture that emerges, briefly stated, is as follows: Male-male erotic relationships are frequently deficient in mutuality and friendliness because of the inherent inequality of the parties. On the other hand, the real aim of (at least some cases of) *eros* is not intercourse, but friendly love: Intercourse is "an end relative to the receiving of affection" (*Prior Analytics* 68b6). Sexual love, unlike other types of friendly love, must be inspired by a visual response to bodily beauty (*EN* 1171b29–31, 1167a3–4), and the way this beauty awakens imagination (*Rhetoric* 1370b19–25). But lovers naturally seek not just the satisfaction of their desire but also its return (*Eudemian Ethics* 1238b32–9): Thus, erotic love points to a certain degree of mutuality in affection and perhaps also in desire. Thus, over time, "Aristotle envisages the emergence of that reciprocal concern and respect which constitute the best kind of friendship, linking individuals not merely as satisfiers of one another's incidental needs, but as partners in a life of personal self-realization. The moral end of love is to transcend itself in friendship."[125] Or, as Price puts it more recently, "Aristotle allows that a homosexual relationship may fuel a mutual familiarity that leads in time to his ideal of friendship—the cultivation of a shared moral character in and through cooperative activities."[126]

Will sexual intercourse be a part of this picture? Price stresses Aristotle's anxiety (an anxiety that he shares with Greek culture) about the development of habits of passivity in the younger partner. He inclines to the conclusion that—not out of moral or metaphysical concerns but out of medical concerns—Aristotle will want pederasty to focus on "'looking rather than loving,' as Plato had put it" (citing *Laws* 837c4–5). I see no evidence at all in the text for this conclusion, and if Aristotle had intended a conclusion so far from conventional Greek practice one might have expected him to state it. As Price himself states, "Aristotle's moral attitudes, as all agree, were more typical of the Greeks of his time than Plato's."[127] The only evidence for anxiety about the young man's passivity is the passage I have already discussed, in which Price rightly argues that the danger is the production of a certain sort of womanish habit by repeated coercion in childhood. Surely the intercourse envisaged by Pausanias—which begins when the young man has reached the age of judgment, and which presumably carefully avoids engendering "womanish" habits (focusing on intercrural intercourse)—would not court this risk. I see no reason to conclude that Aristotle differed from Pausanias, from the Stoics, and from the prevalent cultural norm, regarding the conditions under which sexual intercourse would be appropriate.[128]

To summarize, it is perfectly clear that the active homosexual role is judged by Aristotle (as interpreted by Dover, by Price, and by me) to be morally unproblematic; for an adult man to visit a male prostitute would incur no blame—except in the sense that it will be better to have, as well, at least some relationships in which one links desire with friendship and kindly intentions.[129] Nor, as Price and I now agree, would sexual conduct between an older male and an adolescent of the appropriate *erômenos* age be problematic, provided it observed the cultural protocols discussed above. We may add that marital fidelity could not supply the Aristotelian husband with a motive for avoiding male-male conduct, as Aristotle never mentions a duty of sexual fidelity in marriage.

The Hellenistic philosophers who followed Aristotle are an extremely important part of the general history of attitudes to sexual conduct in the Greco-Roman world. Because they were not central to Finnis's claims, however, and because I examine their contribution elsewhere, I shall not discuss them here.[130]

To summarize, the major Greek philosophers concur in and develop the Greek popular norm, according to which erotic relationships are better if they focus on the soul rather than simply the body and seek stable friendly love rather than unstable and promiscuous passion. And all believe that same-sex sexual desire, including a characteristic orientation of that desire, can be an extremely valuable element in human life, expressive of goods of love and friendship and powerfully linked to other social and intellectual ends. Relationships that involve sexual desire of this kind can be a major vehicle of human aspiration and are generally deemed more valuable as vehicles than are marital relationships, whose ends are generally assumed to be less profound. Aristotle, like Plato's Pausanias and Aristophanes (and like the later Stoics), has no objection to sexual conduct, either homosexual or heterosexual, provided it is performed with the right motives and ends. Plato's position on orgasmic gratification is complex and varies during his career. He never holds that same-sex touching and caressing are bad things, as far as I can see; nor does he ever hold that orgasmic gratification is wicked and depraved. But he does, in *Phaedrus* and *Laws*, hold it inferior to a nonorgasmic eroticism, in which the appetitive part of the soul offers fewer distractions to reason. He holds this on grounds of his general suspiciousness of appetite, not on grounds of any special worries about same-sex acts. Marital acts fare worse than same-sex acts in *Symposium* and *Phaedrus* (in the latter of which same-sex copulators get rewards from the gods but child-begetters are simply condemned as animal). The position of the *Republic* is unclear, for the reasons I have given. Marital acts fare better than same-sex and extramarital acts in *Laws*—not because they are thought to be finer but because the city has to have them—and the text has the many peculiarities that I noted.

V. Greek Philosophy and Modern Debates

I now return to my four claims about the relevance of the ancient philosophical tradition; in the process I shall be able to answer the moral arguments produced by Finnis.

Looking at ancient Greek culture should have for us today the same result it did for Richard Posner: That is, if we look at the Greeks not as projected images of ourselves but as they really were, in all their difference from us, we will be shaken into seeing that many things we are accustomed to think neutral and natural are actually parochial. As Michel Foucault wrote in the introduction to his study of Greek sexuality, the Greeks "free [our] thought from what it silently thinks, and so enable it to think differently."[131] We see, in particular, that it was possible not to single out the sexual appetite from the other appetites, as a source of special anxiety and shame; that it was possible not to categorize persons in accordance with a binary division between the homosexual and the heterosexual; that it was possible to regard the gender of one's sexual partner as just one factor in a sexual coupling, and not the most morally relevant at that; that it was possible to hold that same-sex relationships are not only not per se shameful but potentially of high spiritual and social value. None of these need make the committed Christian change his judgments; they do, however, make the Christian ask on what evidence and argument the judgments are based. This is especially important for the Catholic natural law tradition, which claims to derive its conclusions from reason not from authority. We need, then, reasoned argument, because we see that our own judgments are not the only ones in the world. We need to be sure that we have distinguished between prejudice and reasoned argument.

Second, when we look at the Greeks—and in general we look at them as a culture that we admire, that we consider successful as a culture, the source of some of our deepest ideas and most cherished cultural artifacts—we notice that the presence of same-sex relationships in both Athens and Sparta did not have the result so frequently mentioned in modern debate, not least in Colorado: the result, that is, of eroding the social fabric, or, as Professor Harvey Mansfield argued, causing the downfall of civilization. In fact we find widespread in Athens—as witness, for example, the speeches in Plato's *Symposium* and *Phaedrus*—the view that encouraging such relationships is a fine way of building up or strengthening the social fabric, because such pairs of lovers, through their special devotion to courage and political liberty, contribute more together than each would separately. Indeed, we notice that Pausanias, in Plato's *Symposium*, spoke of the resistance to such relationships in Asia as a strategy adopted by tyrants, for the purposes of discouraging "high aspirations in the ruled . . . [and] strong friendly loves and associations, which . . . *erôs* is especially likely to create" (182C). (For similar reasons, they discourage gymnastics and philosophy!) Once again, we are put on guard against the possible presence of prejudice and bias in our arguments.

In addition to the use of history to "free thought" and to test social hypotheses, I have said that this particular part of philosophy's history is significant because of the intrinsic interest of the moral arguments it develops on this issue. I believe that, although Finnis's moral argument might be criticized independently, a consideration of ancient Greek arguments gives us great help in developing that critique. For Greek texts show, and show repeatedly, that the passionate love of two people of the same sex may serve many valuable social goals apart from procreation. They may communicate love, friendship, and joy; they may advance shared political, intellectual, and artistic ends. Finnis has no argument to rule this out: He has only the bare assertion that such people are in the grip of an illusion because their reproductive organs are not forming a genuine biological unity. The Greeks show us that this is not the only sort of unity in passion that may promote a human good.[132]

Kenneth Dover, having read Professor Finnis's account of Greek homosexuality, comments on it in the same vein:

> The Greeks were well aware that many homosexual relationships did what the participants hoped and imagined, neither more nor less. If the participants imagined that they were achieving something which for biological reasons they could not achieve, then of course they would have been pursuing an illusion; but why should they have imagined that?[133]

Finally, reading the Greeks has value in our moral and legal deliberations on this issue for the way in which they invite us to share the passionate longing of these same-sex lovers, to be moved by their hopes and anxieties and their eventual joy. Readers of the *Symposium* and the *Phaedrus* are not very likely to go on thinking of people who choose same-sex partners as altogether alien and weird—as do, for example, the majority and concurring opinions in *Bowers v. Hardwick*. Indeed, reading these moving narratives is itself a form of emotional and imaginative receptivity; to allow those stories, those people inside oneself, is not only to gain an education in empathy for those particular people. It is to exemplify some of the very characteristics of receptivity and sympathetic imagination that homophobia seeks to cordon off and to avoid.

I might add that I believe the compassionate imagining of another person's suffering and joy lies at the heart of what is finest in the Christian ethical tradition. In that sense, studying the Greeks might promote Christian virtue.[134]

VI. Objections

There are several objections one might make to this appeal to history. I cannot deal with every possible objection here, but let me address what seem to me to be the most prominent.

The first objection says that the high-minded couplings depicted by Plato have little in common with today's promiscuous gay scene.[135] I think that I do not need to spend much time on this one, since it contains a distorted picture of today's world, and the aspirations of men and women within it. Even in Plato's time, promiscuous relations were well-known, and Pausanias criticizes them; today, on the other hand, deep love and friendship are very well-known, so that, on this side too, the asymmetry has not been demonstrated.

And, in fact, studying the Greek world may tell us something interesting about the issue of promiscuity: It tells us that a society that in general tolerated same-sex relationships could be as critical of promiscuity as any, and as interested in deeper relationships based on friendly love. The Greeks therefore make us ask skeptical questions about any hasty claim that same-sex relations are inherently linked with promiscuity or superficiality, claims that were sometimes made in the context of Amendment 2.

A second objection is far more interesting. It is that the ancient sexual scene is so different in its basic categories from our world that there is no straightforward mapping of today's homosexuals onto ancient Greek actors. What was salient then is different from what is salient now, and to that extent the ancient world lacked the modern conception of "the homosexual," a person with a life-long disposition toward partners of the same gender. This point, which has been developed by some writers I admire, says important things about the two cultures, with many of which I agree. But three observations must now be made. First, this asymmetry does not help the argument of John Finnis, for when he criticizes homosexual conduct in his affidavit, he individuates actions extensionally, not taking into account the thoughts of the parties about the sort of act they are committing. For many people if not most, he holds, are in the grip of illusion; what is really morally relevant is the classification by gender and marital relation that can be performed by a neutral observer. And in this sense there will be no problem in comparing the two cultures, as Finnis enthusiastically does. Second, we must now observe that this asymmetry between cultures is exactly what reading the Greeks is supposed (in my argument) to reveal to us: Namely, it is supposed to reveal to us the fact that a society may tolerate and even encourage sexual acts between members of the same sex *without* regarding this as the most morally salient feature about the act, and without problematizing same-sex desire itself in a special way. The presence of asymmetry does not defeat the comparative project; it is what makes it interesting. Finally, we should note that any characterization of the Greeks that pushes this discontinuity to the limiting point of total noncomparability, denying that the Greeks had any conception of an erotic preference for members of one's own gender, is clearly refuted by the evidence of Plato: For both Pausanias and Aristophanes know and casually refer to people who have such stable preferences, indicating as they do so that they are referring to a widely accepted fact about human life. Such people may, they assert, also marry and have children, while continuing to have same-sex relations: To that extent their form of life is indeed different from that of many modern homosexuals, though certainly not all. But their preference for same-sex acts is held to be both stable and a deep fact about their personalities.

The third and most interesting objection to the cross-cultural comparison is the claim that the Greeks' high evaluation of same-sex activity is inseparable from Greek misogyny and the widespread Greek belief that one's deepest loves and aspirations and political goals could not possibly be shared with a mere woman. To that extent, shouldn't we rule out using the Greeks as a sign of what we might be, even in the very limited sense of that idea suggested by my argument?

I see no reason why one should draw this conclusion. First of all, the historical evidence indicates that encouragement of same-sex relationships varies to a large extent independently of women's role. In Sparta, women had far greater freedom and power than at Athens, but Spartan culture gives especially prominent endorsement to same-sex relationships, both female and male. And we must recall at this point that the existence of same-sex relations among women also complicates the picture.

Second, the philosophers give us strong reasons for doubting that an interest in sex equality need be linked with a tendency to denigrate same-sex relations. Plato probably taught women in his school and certainly argues most seriously for their equal education; he praises relationships that are rich in spiritual and intellectual value, and in his own culture these are most likely to be between males. But there is nothing in his argument itself to prevent an extension of the norm of love in connection with the extension of the educational norm. In Aristotle, too, although the woman remains incompletely equal, there is an ideal of friendly love and reciprocity in both same-sex and opposite-sex relations. As Anthony Price puts it very well in his recent book, *Love and Friendship in Plato and Aristotle*, in both same- and opposite-sex relations "Aristotle envisages the emergence of that reciprocal concern and respect which constitute the best kind of friendship, linking individuals not merely as satisfiers of one another's incidental needs, but as partners in a life of personal self-realization" (249). Such Platonic and Aristotelian norms deeply influenced later Stoic and Epicurean reconceptualizations of marriage as a genuine partnership. And the Stoics evidently wished their ideal city to contain not only male-male but also male-female (and possibly also female-female) sexual partnerships in connection with their norm of gender equality. Indeed, in their view a just city will minimize gender as a salient feature, adopting, for example, a unisex style of dress. All this suggests a close connection between women's equality and an indifference to the gender of one's sexual partner.[136] Equally important, both Platonic and Stoic arguments tell us that the encouragement of same-sex relations of the best sort will promote a general attention to questions of social justice, and that a concerted attention to social justice will lead, down the road, to women's equality. This seems to be a set of connections well worth exploring.

Finally, we can all think for ourselves and see that the Greeks' defense of same-sex relationships as containing important human goods is in fact completely independent of misogyny, both logically and empirically, no matter what the Greeks themselves thought on this point. For we can see, among other things, the great support that feminism has received from same-sex relations, both female and male. And we can notice that desire to enforce traditional gender boundaries has been a major source of resistance to the goals of both feminists and lesbian and gay people in closely connected ways: Thus it seems reasonable to suppose that the historically guided rethinking of the sexual-orientation boundary may also free our minds to think differently about gender more broadly.[137]

In short, the equation of the ancient with the modern should not be done in a facile and historically naive way. Indeed, we will not reap the benefits of the comparison if we do not remain vigilant for difference, for it is difference from which we wish to learn. But with the proper caution the comparison may be extremely fruitful.

VII. Prejudice and Argument

We could draw many morals from this debate. But we should focus above all on one Platonic point, the importance of facing this issue with reason. Plato shows us nothing more clearly, time and time again, than the way in which prejudice can be dispelled by rational argument. His dialogues show us people who intensely disagree. But so long as they are willing to stay in the argument and participate in it sincerely, there is every reason to think that prejudice will eventually fall away and what is of real moral interest will remain. As he has Socrates remark in the *Republic*, apropos of the equal education of women, things that are strange at first inspire mockery or loathing, but over time, this is dispelled by reason's judgment about the best.

Forces impervious to reason can be identified in this situation. The Supreme Court majority opinion in *Romer* was correct when it claimed that Amendment 2 "raises the inevitable inference that it is born of animosity toward the class that it affects."[138] In light of such facts, it is tempting indeed to feel that argument does no work, that politics can only be the struggle of various types of power. But if the game is simply power, the powerless will always lose. If we wish to defend the basic civil rights of the powerless we need, therefore, to hold on to reason, a force whose dignity is not proportional to its sheer strength. Good rational arguments do support basic civil rights on this issue, and these arguments were effective in establishing that a law such as Amendment 2 "cannot be said to be directed to an identifiable legitimate purpose or discrete objective."[139] Moreover, if we fight with any weapon other than rational argument, we will have given our adversaries the greatest victory that they could possibly win, that of debasing our humanity. But if we face the issue with good moral arguments, appropriately illuminated by historical and cross-cultural understanding, there is reason to believe that we can prevail over prejudice, both in the courts and in the larger society of which they are a part.

13

SEX, TRUTH,
AND SOLITUDE

The idea that human sexuality has a history—that it is not altogether biological and immutable, that cultural factors play a central role in determining what is found desirable—is an idea we rightly associate with Michel Foucault's pioneering arguments about ancient Greece. In two volumes published near the end of his life, Foucault argued that a close examination of ancient Greek sexual customs and attitudes shows some contemporary Western norms to be not universal and "natural," as we easily think our deeply rooted habits are, but nonuniversal and of relatively recent origin.[1] Ancient Greek society, for example, he argued, lacked our binary division of human beings into the "heterosexual" and the "homosexual," and its concomitant insistence on the fundamental moral and psychological importance of a stable inner "orientation" of desire toward partners of a particular gender.

Foucault made a powerful argument; the argument has been further developed by some of his followers, including classical scholars David Halperin and the late John J. Winkler.[2] But Foucault was not a professional classical scholar, and he acknowledged openly that for most of his conclusions about the ancient world he was relying (wisely) on the scholarship of a great scholar, Sir Kenneth Dover. Dover's *Greek Homosexuality*[3] is, along with *Greek Popular Morality*[4] one of the most excellent and influential works about the ancient Greek world to be produced in this century. We know a good deal about Foucault's life—

perhaps too much for our own good, in the sense that sensationalizing treatment of its events can impair our intellectual confrontation with the work. Dover's publication of an autobiography (at the age of 74) now gives us an opportunity to reflect about connections between the personal and the professional in a remarkably different life, a life combining stoical restraint and prodigious linguistic talent with a passionate devotion to outspokenness, truthfulness, and scholarly excellence.

Any writer competent to review this sometimes technical scholarly memoir is likely to be acquainted with Sir Kenneth—though, as he tells his readers, few would be likely to be his friends, since throughout most of his life he has concealed his vulnerability beneath a "shell impermeable both to my emotions on the way out and to other people's on the way in." "[T]o this day," he adds, he cannot call someone "emotional" without intending a serious criticism. In consequence both of this fact and of his intense dedication to work, he has "found sociability easy enough, but firm friendship—until fairly recently—difficult, because I have always put work first and friends second. I have never yet experienced what could properly be called grief at anybody's death."[5] Before 1994, I had met Sir Kenneth only once. Intensely though I admired him, I felt his presence forbidding and never pursued the acquaintance further. During 1993–4, however, circumstances led to our corresponding at length about, and then coauthoring, a piece on Greek homosexuality. These common interests led, in turn, to a memorable visit to Kenneth and Audrey Dover's home in St. Andrews, Scotland, in the summer of 1994, during which I read the memoir in page proof on two wet dark July days. Thus, oddly, I learned the most intimate details of Sir Kenneth's life while encountering the person, in effect, for the first time. I cannot separate my description of the memoir from this experience and from the mixture of anxiety, embarrassment, gratitude, and affection it engendered.

Sir Kenneth is a scholar of truly remarkable gifts. Early in his life he would have liked to become a comparative linguist; he devoted himself first to African languages and then to the difficult languages of New Guinea and the Pacific Islands. When his attention turned instead to the Greeks, his fascination with the details of language did not cease, and to the present day the analysis of Greek prose style remains among his most intense fascinations and pleasures. The level of linguistic mastery he has been able to reach eludes all but a few scholars of the present day. The old practice of composing Greek prose and verse, now unhappily in decline, yields an active command of vocabulary, syntax, meter, and style that eludes pupils who practice a dead language only by translating; Dover was from an early age a master in this art, winning a prize in Greek verse in his first year at Oxford by translating into classical Greek a scene from Racine's *Phèdre*. (To give just one example of his versatility, my own copy of *Marginal Comment* bears a Greek verse inscription from its author in which he has managed in one elegiac couplet (1) to use in an apposite and humorous way a Greek word whose meaning we discussed in our coauthored piece, disputing its translation with John Finnis; (2) to express pleasure at the collaboration; and (3) to compare the "daring" outspokenness of our article to that of his own memoir—all with not only impeccable meter and style but also graciousness, wit, and elegance.)

Beyond this considerable talent and a related mastery of historical and textual data, Dover also possesses the ability to think about the Greeks as if they are living people and to ask fresh questions about their civilization without interposing modern prejudices and preoccupations. When Dover approached the topic of Greek homosexuality in order to prepare some university lectures on Plato, he recognized "that practically everything said during the last few centuries about the psychology, ethics, and sociology of Greek homosexuality was confused and misleading" (111): Scholars' modern moral views and personal prejudices had impeded their inquiry into the evidence. This judgment led ultimately to the decision to write a comprehensive book on the subject. When it appeared, it was hailed as the definitive statement on its topic. Scholars of many different types, not all antecedently well disposed to frank treatment of this topic, could not fail to conclude that Dover had written a work of great stature that offered insight both into the ancient Greek world and also into human culture more generally.

In part, Dover's new contribution was methodological, for, in a way that had not been done before, he combined the close study of vase paintings (frequently neglected by scholars whose expertise is literary and philosophical) with examination of evidence from oratory, comedy, and philosophy. In part, it was simply one of excellence: He was just better than anyone before him in this area at figuring out the sense of crucial terms and phrases and at reading crucial texts with the requisite subtlety and nuance. Especially admirable was his close reading of a crucial law-court speech, Aeschines' *Against Timarchus*: Here Dover, unlike some other scholars both before and after him, is alert to the games a speaker is likely to be playing in order to influence the jury in his favor. In a similar way, Dover's use of the evidence of ancient comedy was informed by an acute sense of the genre and its standard ways of depicting human motivation.

Equally important, however, was the scholarly contribution made by Dover's character, free from the "turbulent irrationality" that characterizes, in his view, so many modern pronouncements on the topic of ancient sexuality. Dover does not write with Martian detachment. Frequently he can illuminate an ancient sexual custom by deft modern comparisons, as when he explains contradictory Athenian attitudes to the sexual availability of an adolescent male by comparing them to attitudes about young women in the time of his youth: In both cases we find careful guarding of the potential seducee combined with public approval of the strategies and goals of the seducer. Again, he is able to understand Plato's idea of sexual arousal at the sight of beauty by thinking of an incident from his own experience during the war, when the sight of a beautiful Italian mountain landscape led to arousal and masturbation. "The explanation of such events," he concludes rather anti-Platonically, "is scientific rather than philosophical." (The persistence of the prudery Dover consistently decries can be seen in the fact that, even before publication of the memoir, this episode became the topic of a sensationalizing article in the British press, under the headline "Oxford Don Takes Memoirs in Hand.")

There is one way, however, in which modernity does not obtrude itself: through irrational revulsion and disgust. Dover is not gay, and his life is so conventional that it almost surprises by its sheer lack of surprise. *Marginal Com-*

ment informs us that he has been married with much sexual happiness and exceptionless fidelity to one woman for close to fifty years. The only other interpersonal sexual episodes of which we learn in this remarkably frank life are a single visit to a female prostitute in Cairo, a nonconsummated relationship with a young woman in Italy, and a series of deliberations, at the age of sixty, about whether he ought to permit himself to have an extramarital affair with a younger woman who was pursuing him. (His answer was no.) He is so far from being willing to be thought homosexual that he considered suing a California gay journal for libel when they wrote that he was "president of Christ Church and a practicing homosexual," getting Dover's college wrong as well as his sexual orientation. (His lawyer advised against suing, both on the grounds that he could not prove malicious intent and on the grounds that the journal had no money.)

On the other hand, as he wrote in *Greek Homosexuality*, he is "fortunate in not experiencing moral[6] shock or disgust at any genital act whatsoever, provided that it is welcome and agreeable to all the participants (whether they number one, two, or more than two)" (viii). Aesthetic reactions are another matter, but even they are "not violent" (*Marginal Comment*, 114). As he says in the memoir, "while I have never had any inclination to put my penis into anyone else's anus (or vice versa), I would rather do it (or vice versa) than take melted mutton fat into my mouth" (114). And in a memorable episode Dover reproaches himself for not having allowed a thirteen-year-old friend to sodomize him (when he was the same age) after the friend had shown him how to masturbate. Dover cannot comprehend his own refusal and thinks ill of it. Whereas the sex acts themselves would have had, he concludes, no moral significance, "my failure to do him one morally indifferent favour in return for another *was* a serious delinquency" (19).

It is out of this highly unusual combination of intense seriousness about sex with detachment from conventional disgust and superstition that Dover's magisterial volume was produced. Its central thesis is that for the ancient Greeks, the most salient sexual distinction was the distinction between the active and the passive partner. Being the active partner in a male-male sex act was socially approved and considered no more morally problematic than penetrating a woman. In fact, in some circles male-male relations were more highly regarded than male-female relations (including marriage), because of their apparently greater potential for spiritual exchange and friendship. On the other hand, it was viewed as socially degrading to be the passive partner in an anal sex act, especially if one was thought to enjoy that (inferior, womanish) role. Where the courtship of young citizen males by older males was concerned, therefore, elaborate protocols developed. The older male's desire and pursuit are strongly approved: The gods too enjoy such powerful feelings. And it is all right for the younger man to gratify these desires in carefully circumscribed circumstances, which include a cultural norm of intercrural intercourse. To have established the common occurrence of such intercourse between citizens—largely on the basis of the evidence of visual art—was one of the book's most dramatic and convincing contributions.

The book also establishes that desire for intercourse with a younger male was not thought to be incompatible with desire for women. Not infrequently, a man would be involved in both marriage and a male-male relationship; no concept of an exclusive "orientation" toward partners of a particular gender made this seem odd or unusual. Given the seclusion of women of good class and their relative lack of education, marriage was unlikely to satisfy a man's desire for an intimate relationship containing intellectual friendship and discussion about politics, morals, or art, whereas male-male relationships were frequently associated with education and the communication of civic values.

Other books of Dover's carry his analysis of ancient Greek moral customs further. Even before *Greek Homosexuality* he had published, in 1968, a remarkable commentary on Aristophanes' *Clouds*, the comedy that Socrates, in the *Apology*, mentions as a source of slander against him. This was followed last year by a volume on Aristophanes' *Frogs*, the play in which Aeschylus and Euripides compete before Dionysus to return from the underworld to give advice to Athens. In both cases Dover produces a new edition of the text and a meticulous line-by-line commentary, replete with literary-historical and historical information, as well as original interpretations of the works. *Aristophanic Comedy*, published in 1972, presented Dover's central ideas on this great playwright for a more general audience. I have not yet studied the *Frogs* volume; I must own that early in my career I found the other two works dispiritingly unphilosophical. They gave Aristophanes too little credit, I thought, for having a cohesive social/political view and serious conservative arguments. By now, however, I have come round to agreement with Dover: One can enjoy the humor and the poetry of the plays all the more if one does not try too hard to turn Aristophanes into a philosopher or social theorist.

I am still, however, somewhat at odds with Dover about Plato. His 1980 commentary on the *Symposium* seems to me unduly dismissive of Plato's arguments, unduly disposed to see all the interesting results as dependent on unstated and implausible metaphysical assumptions. Even in *Greek Homosexuality*, the weakest section, it seems to me, remains the one on the philosophers, which in some respects shortchanges Plato, says too little about Aristotle, and completely omits the Hellenistic philosophers, who have rich material to offer us on this topic. In general, I think that Dover has never been inclined toward philosophy. In part, as the memoir tells us, this lack of interest was the result of inadequate teaching at Oxford. It probably also owed something to the absence, at that time, of interesting work in the moral/political areas of the subject, which might have lured Dover in.[7] But there is another cause in Dover's intellectual temperament. I find in the memoir what I frequently also sense in the published works: a sheer distaste for philosophical puzzlement. He announces, for example, that the classic philosophical problem of *akrasia*, or knowing the better but doing the worse, seems to him totally unpuzzling. Of course, he says, people can know what they ought to do and not do it: It happens all the time. Yes, but that is where the philosophical question begins, not where it ends.[8] The question is, what view of desire, choice, and action do we need to have in order to explain *how* this happens? It comes as no surprise that someone who sees no mystery in this issue should be impatient with many Platonic arguments.

On the other hand, precisely this commonsense approach to moral questions becomes an asset when Dover turns to the analysis of popular moral values. In 1974 he published *Greek Popular Morality*, a landmark in the attempt to determine how ordinary Greeks who were not artists or philosophers thought about their values and choices. Other such volumes had focused on literary works such as drama and philosophy, but these cannot be used as reliable evidence for ordinary thought. Dover's approach is to rely, instead, on the evidence of forensic oratory. Law-court speeches concerned matters of urgency: A client's well-being, fortune, even life hung in the balance.[9] And speeches had to persuade a jury of citizens chosen by lot. Because there was no practice of a judge instructing the jury, they played an even larger role than comparable speeches in contemporary court cases. For this very reason, of course, we should often suspect their veracity in matters of fact and even of law. What we can rely on is that the moral values expressed, as the orator tries to make his client look good and his opponent(s) look bad, would be values generally endorsed by the community. This simple but brilliant idea produced the best analyses we have of "the Greek mind" on issues as diverse as revenge, slavery, death, and choice. In the process, Dover is able to make decisive progress beyond the simple Hegelian/progressive views of the development of the Greek character that were misleadingly purveyed in the previous generation by Bruno Snell, and in Dover's own by Arthur Adkins.

Dover's contribution to scholarship includes much more: two volumes on Thucydides, one on the orator Lysias, and numerous articles. (It should be noted that my discussion, focusing as it does on sexuality and popular morality, is unbalanced in ways that reflect its author's expertise. Thucydides, as Dover makes clear, claimed more of his time and energy than did these topics.) He has also been an exceptionally dedicated teacher and administrator. He tells us that he spends on average twenty hours of preparation for each one-hour lecture in a course he is giving for the first time—and he comments: "People who believe . . . that university teachers work only half the year, or that giving a lecture is a matter of improvisation or of simple recall, have much to learn about real life" (71). At St. Andrews, where he spent the largest part of his scholarly career, he served in various administrative roles in addition to holding the Professorship of Greek, and now, in retirement, holds the ceremonial position of Chancellor. The ascending distinction of that institution, now able to retain faculty who have been offered Oxford chairs and to match American salary offers, owes a great deal to his personal prestige and dedication.

Dover was President of the prestigious British Academy during the upheaval occasioned by the revelation of the treason of Anthony Blunt and thus had the responsibility of chairing the meetings that discussed whether Blunt should be expelled from the Academy. Dover's own view was that he would "cheerfully have assisted Blunt to fall from a top-floor window" (213), and certainly favored his expulsion from the Academy, on the grounds that he supported a regime that was hostile to scholarly inquiry and truth. It is characteristic of Dover to focus on that issue, rather than on issues raised by others, such as the fact that Blunt had caused the deaths of British agents and the Academy was a government-funded institution. (Earlier, discussing the Second World War, Dover cites as his central moral objection to the Nazis "not their cruelty and violence per se, but . . . their war against reason" (31).) Equally characteristically, however, when the time for the meeting actually came, Dover judged that he must play a neutral role: Duty obliged him, as Chair, to "ensure that all members of Council had their say and that the outcome truly represented the considered view of the majority."

For ten years, between 1976 and 1986, Dover was President of Corpus Christi College, Oxford. Headships of Oxford colleges are both onerous and personally taxing; it remains mysterious to Americans why so many eminent British scholars should saddle themselves with such jobs at a productive stage of their careers. In Dover's case, the appointment proved trying indeed. In the part of his memoir that has attracted the most public comment, he narrates his long interaction with Trevor Aston, an alcoholic and probably also psychotic historian who served as both fellow and librarian of the college. Aston's deceptiveness and manipulativeness knew no limits. Attempted suicide was only one of many attention-getting devices through which he made colleagues cater to his whims. Dover treated him with almost saintly patience for years, but when he began abusing the college servants Dover found himself wanting to be rid of him. In general, Dover's extremely Stoic memoir relentlessly notes and scrutinizes every wayward impulse and desire. One thinks of Epictetus' Stoic maxim, "Watch over yourself like an enemy lying in wait." At one point in the book he blames himself harshly for allowing himself even to *think* very briefly of moving to America without his family in 1961, during Audrey's long illness from depression.

In this case, he admits to a strong desire for Aston's death, and he consults a lawyer to determine whether a failure to come to his aid in the case of a future suicide attempt would land him in legal difficulty. (Characteristically, he has no moral difficulty contemplating becoming the cause of Aston's death but rules out the prospect of lying about it to a coroner's jury, "whose raison d'être is to discover the truth.") In the end, Dover's aggression was limited to informing Aston of the fact that his fellowship had previously been renewed only with much hesitation; shortly thereafter, he consults Aston's doctor about whether Aston should be committed by force for his own protection, but the doctor rejects the idea. It seems plain that the suicide that ensued shortly thereafter was provoked by Aston's receiving notification of divorce proceedings from his wife, from whom he had very recently been separated.

Here as elsewhere in *Marginal Comment*, Dover writes in a confessional manner that shocks by its very lack of embarrassment or anxiety. This central feature of the book, of which I have already given several examples, had better now be confronted, for it is clearly the book's raison d'être to show the scholarly life as growing out of a particular set of personal experiences. As the title indicates, Dover feels that throughout his life he has stood to one side of immersion in human interaction, protecting himself by an aloofness aided in no small measure by a ferociously competent intellect. He tells us that this aloofness had two causes: bad relations between his parents, and a perception of himself as physically deformed. To the reader who knows Dover as an imposing and physically powerful person, it comes as a considerable surprise to discover that through most of his life he has felt "separated from all my contemporaries by an irreversible deformity" (20). The problem, known as "funnel chest," is described by Dover himself—using a violent language he eschews when speaking of the bodies and acts of others—as "a grotesque and repulsive deformity which caused the centre of my sternum to recede and the bottom ribs to project" (3). He did not know he had it until it was noticed by other boys as he undressed for sports; from this point on, it generated a "deep sense of inferiority . . . which made it hard for me to believe in my own reality" (28).

This cause for self-insulation compounded the already powerful influence of his father's violent temper. Dover's mother emerges in the memoir as a gentle and reasonable person, intensely dedicated to the truth, tightly self-controlled, and protective of her child against her husband's outbursts of rage and contempt. Dover's hatred of his father, on account of the unhappiness his temper caused to both Dover and his mother, is palpable throughout the memoir, not least in this description of his childhood reaction to his father's spitting in the kitchen sink: "The combination of rage, hatred and despair which overwhelmed me on every such occasion is undoubtedly the strongest emotion that I have experienced in my life" (7).

These revelations impress the reader oddly in the context of a life so tightly controlled by reason and, as Dover himself stresses, so insulated from emotion.[10] When a man who until the age of seventy-four has revealed himself very little to others exposes his most private thoughts, wishes, and experiences to the general public, the reader wonders a little about the motive. Is it the love of truth simply, combined with the conventions of the genre?[11] Or is some role played, as well, by a longing for that acceptance by others, that knowledge of one's own reality, which the imagined disgust of his peers had previously denied him? One may wonder whether Dover's lifelong assault on customary prudery and reticence—on all that is subsumed by him under the label of "respectability"—is not itself motivated by a wish to sweep away the forces of convention that stood between Dover the boy and bodily acceptance by others. And frequently, as one reads the memoir, one senses that Dover (with his wife Audrey as, clearly, his approving and loyal partner) is testing his reader's capacity for dispassionate unembarrassed reaction. This reader, who got with equanimity through material on masturbation, sodomy, hatred, and depression (from which both Audrey and he suffer, she most chronically), reached her limit in the chapter dealing with the bodily infirmities of old age, which includes a detailed account of Dover's difficulties with sexual impotence. At this point I thought—and I asked him in a set of comments I sent him later—Would he and Audrey really narrate such facts to me as a guest in their house? And if not, why on earth should he narrate them this way to the whole world? The calm answer was just what I should have expected: If people were not so embarrassed about these things and talked about them more, they would suffer from them a good deal less. True. And yet it made clear to me what is so peculiar about this memoir. Just as most of Dover's life has effaced intimacy by reticence about self, this memoir effaces it just as surely in the opposite way, by refusing to make any distinction at all between what one tells a loved one and what one tells a stranger.[12] The work makes a demand for love and bodily acceptance that it just as insistently repels. One is solicited by its content to have reactions (of acceptance, patience, affection, and even perhaps desire) of the sort one would have to an intimate friend or even a lover—and yet its very form informs one that one is merely in the situation of thousands of others, and that one's emotions are therefore all perfectly unreasonable. For "to this day, despite my unqualified love of my wife and children, if I call someone 'emotional,' I imply: unreasonable, impatient, bad-tempered, unreliable, to be avoided if possible" (28). In the anti-Stoical text is Stoicism's subtle victory.

What, in the end, do we learn about Dover's career from this odd and frequently disturbing document? For, after all, many men have hated their fathers and even their own bodies; what makes this story of interest is the fact that it is the story of someone who has created work of lasting merit and distinction. Dover is a great scholar; his greatness derives in part from his passion for honesty, and the intensity of his passion for honesty, we now see, is probably inseparable from a complicated lifelong project of Stoical self-shaping, which extends into the writing of the memoir itself. Jim Miller's biography of Foucault urged us to look at Foucault's life as an instance of a certain type of Stoic-inspired self-fashioning, a "cultivation of the self."[13] Here Dover's life emerges as a more authentically (and to my mind more admirably) Stoic life, in which the extirpation of emotion goes hand in hand with a ferocious love of truth. The extirpation side is now viewed by even Dover himself as excessive—though with some inconsistency[14]—and to that extent the truth side can be seen as deriving some of its intensity from a pathological detachment and loneliness. But it is a mistake—of which both Foucault and his mentor Nietzsche were probably guilty—to think that the causal analysis of rationality provides us with an "unmasking" of reason's pretentions to objectivity and dignity. To see the will to truth as psychologically caused is not to undermine its dignity; to see these wonderful books as emerging, in some sense, from childhood loathing and self-loathing is not to deny that they express a commitment to reason that is intrinsically noble, worthy of the encomia that Plato devoted to it.

On Dover's final page is an addendum, added in the proof stage, mentioning that he is about to have surgery on his abdominal aorta. The reader who responds to that news with un-Doverian emotion, or even with Doverian curiosity, may wish to know that the operation was remarkably successful and that Dover, after a short convalescence, has resumed his work on Greek prose style with his habitual energy and dedication.

14

SEX, LIBERTY,
AND ECONOMICS

THE STATUE: My experience is that one's pleasures don't bear
thinking about.
DON JUAN: That is why intellect is so unpopular.
                                        —Shaw, *Don Juan in Hell*

I. Sex and Judicial Reasoning

Sex is ubiquitous in American courts, as it is in American life. Judges must deal
with it in civil, criminal, and constitutional cases of many kinds; they are called
on to concern themselves with topics such as prostitution, homosexuality, contraception, nudity, child abuse, and erotic art. And yet, as Richard Posner rightly
observes, judges often know very little about such topics. Proceeding on the assumption that sexual matters are ahistorical and "natural," and therefore sufficiently understood by simply consulting one's own intuitions, they approach these
matters, all too often, with little historical or scientific learning and with a personal experience that is likely, as Posner notes, to be somewhat narrow and uniform, given the effectiveness with which the background checking of judges weeds
out members of sexual minorities. Thus, in deeply important human matters, we
all too often find opinions that combine naiveté with the puritanism and the
moralism that are such a large part of the American cultural heritage.

Consider, for example, the opinions in *Bowers v. Hardwick*,[1] the case in which
the Supreme Court held that a gay man, arrested in his own bedroom while
having oral sex with another man, could not legitimately claim that the Georgia
sodomy law under which he was arrested violated a fundamental personal liberty in connection with the due process clause of the Fourteenth Amendment.[2]

The Court scoffed at the idea that the alleged right to consensual homosexual sodomy was one of "those fundamental liberties that are 'implicit in the concept of ordered liberty' [or] deeply rooted in this Nation's history and tradition."[3] And yet the case bore, on its surface, a close relationship to other privacy cases (dealing with contraception, abortion, and the use of pornographic materials in the home) in which the Supreme Court had upheld the rights of individuals to regulate their sexual conduct by their own choice.[4]

It also invited comparison to earlier cases in which laws forbidding miscegenation had been struck down as violations of both the Due Process Clause and the Equal Protection Clause: Miscegenation in the South a few decades ago, like homosexual conduct in Georgia today, was highly unpopular and not likely to seem to most citizens the sort of thing to which individuals had a fundamental right "implicit in the concept of ordered liberty." And yet the Court had ruled that the Lovings (the remarkably named interracial couple) did in fact have such a right.[5] For, the Court held, miscegenation was a species of a genus—choice of one's own marital partner—that was protected, as a genus, by the Constitution, whether or not one liked all of its species. The same could have been said for homosexual sex acts in *Bowers*. It was not. Pointing to the fact that all the previous privacy cases concerned marriage and/or procreation, the Court concluded that "[n]o connection between family, marriage, or procreation on the one hand and homosexual activity on the other has been demonstrated."[6] But the cases also concerned sex, Posner notes; had the Court taken cognizance of that fact, it "could not have polished them off so easily" (342).

One would have expected the judges deciding such a complex and delicate case to have investigated the phenomenon of homosexuality very thoroughly, finding out what history and science have to say about it, and considering in some depth the lives of homosexuals in American society. None of this happened. The Justices spoke in vague and highly inaccurate terms of a general condemnation of homosexual conduct stretching back to "ancient roots." But in fact their scanty references to the ancient pagan world were largely inaccurate, and even their picture of the history of Christian views on the topic was highly misleading.[7] Nor did they do better when thinking about the way of life of a gay man in America—for they managed to dismiss without argument the notion that what was at stake for Michael Hardwick in choosing a sexual partner bore any relation at all to any of the Court's previous cases. Thus, as Justice Blackmun observed in his dissenting opinion, they all too quickly avoided asking whether there was not indeed a generic right to sexual choice that Hardwick, as much as "straight" Americans, enjoyed; nor did they even reach the point of asking whether the case could be construed as having an equal protection aspect, as Justice Blackmun suggested it did.[8]

The opinions in *Bowers* have drawn a lot of criticism, but the ignorance that they display is not unusual. One could also cite, for example, the opinion of Judge Robert Bork in the case of *Dronenberg v. Zeck*, involving gays in the military.[9] Again, without any argument at all, and without any evidence of interest in learning and research, Bork simply asserted that the presence of gays in the services will lead to problems of sexual harassment in the workplace—never pausing to wonder whether this problem does not obtain similarly between male and female soldiers, whether gays are any more likely to harass their fellow workers than straights, whether all such problems could not best be dealt with by effective regulations governing sexual harassment rather than by the exclusion of an entire class of qualified persons from the services. (Looking at this opinion in the wake of recent revelations about sexual harassment of women by men in both the Navy and the Army, we would surely have to conclude that if any class of persons deserved exclusion on this basis it would be heterosexual males.) And one could also cite the district court ruling by Judge Oliver Gasch in *Steffan v. Cheney,* the case of the talented midshipman at the U.S. Naval Academy who was forced to withdraw shortly before graduation because he admitted to a homosexual orientation (though not to homosexual conduct).[10] Without citing any of the pertinent literature on the topic, Gasch simply asserted that homosexual orientation is a mutable behavioral choice and that homosexuals are not disadvantaged with respect to political power in American society—all this to establish that homosexuals do not constitute a "suspect class" for the purposes of the Equal Protection Clause (see chapter 7).

I have focused on cases involving homosexuality because these are a rich repository of judicial bias and ignorance, but one could find many similarly unargued and insubstantial opinions in cases pertaining to other sexual matters. Prejudice, a lack of curiosity, flawed logic: All these are depressingly common when judges confront the complexities of sex.

Posner wishes to alter this situation. Chief Judge of the U.S. Court of Appeals for the Seventh Circuit, as well as one of the most distinguished and prolific legal thinkers of his generation, he is well-known for opinions that combine broad erudition with clear argument and eloquent, pungent writing. Where sexual matters are concerned, these virtues are combined, in the opinions he has written to date, with a refreshing lack of cant and a passionate concern for artistic liberty of expression. One of his most important opinions—subsequently overturned by the Supreme Court—held unconstitutional, on First Amendment grounds, an Indiana statute that banned nude dancing. Defending the right of the striptease dancers of the Kitty Kat Lounge to keep their nipples uncovered, Posner wrote a learned (and witty) disquisition on the expressive properties of the dance, on the role of the erotic in the history of dance, on expression in the verbal and nonverbal artistic media, on the relationship between "high" and popular culture, and on the limitations of American moralism. He concludes:

> The true reason I think for wanting to exclude striptease dancing from the protection of the First Amendment is not any of the lawyers' classification games that I have been discussing. . . . It is a feeling that the proposition, "the First Amendment forbids the State of Indiana to require striptease dancers to cover their nipples," is ridiculous. It strikes judges as ridiculous in part because most of us are either middle-aged or elderly men, in part because we tend to be snooty, about popular culture . . . in part because we are Americans—which means that we have been raised in a culture in which puritanism, philistinism, and promiscuity are complexly and often incongruously interwoven. . . . But the element of the ridiculous is not all on one side. Cen-

sorship of erotica is pretty ridiculous too. What kind of people make a career of checking to see whether the covering of a woman's nipples is fully opaque, as the statute requires? (These statutes are full of absurd locutions, such as: "'Wholly or substantially exposed to public view,' as it pertains to breasts, shall mean ...."). .... Most of us do not admire the Islamic clergy for their meticulous insistence on modesty in female dress. Many of us do not admire busybodies who want to bring the force of law down on the heads of adults whose harmless private pleasures the busybodies find revolting. The history of censorship is a history of folly and cruelty.[11]

(It is worth reflecting, incidentally, on what might be made of this one paragraph alone in a Supreme Court confirmation hearing. If the confirmation process has evolved in a way that excludes a provocative and brilliant figure such as Posner, but gives us people who either have no opinions or are willing to deny the opinions they have, we are much the worse.)

II. Anti-Puritanism and Naturalism

Out of Posner's dissatisfaction with judicial opinions in cases such as *Bowers* (of which he is highly critical) came this ambitious and complicated book. It has, he announces, three distinct aims. The first, which he describes as his "initial motivation," is to provide the American public, and especially lawyers and judges, with information about sex that is usually lacking in public discussions of the topic by describing the "principal findings" of the "vast multidisciplinary literature" that now exists on human sexuality. In this way he intends "to inform myself in my role as a judge and to dispel some of the clouds of ignorance, prejudice, shame, and hypocrisy that befog the public discussion of sex in America generally and in the American legal system in particular" (442). Posner's second goal, far more ambitious, is to provide a comprehensive explanatory theory of sexual behavior, drawing both on economics and on evolutionary biology. His third goal, finally, is to advance a normative theory of sexual legislation that is "libertarian" in the tradition of John Stuart Mill, defending the rights of individuals to regulate their sexual conduct by their own lights except in those cases in which it can be shown to cause harm to or to infringe on the rights of others.

How are these goals connected? It seems important to ask this question at the outset, because Posner pursues the first and the third with far greater success than the second. Readers of Posner's previous work will have another reason to press the question. For Posner is one of the leading defenders of the thesis that judicial reasoning, properly understood, is really like economic reasoning, that the procedure of judges in torts and contracts, and indeed in constitutional law as well, is actually reasoning that seeks to maximize society's wealth. He advances this thesis as a descriptive thesis (seeing things this way will help us to understand what judges actually do, though they use other language) and as a normative thesis (when judges do not proceed in this way, they are reasoning badly).[12] Posner has used the normative thesis to criticize the privacy jurisprudence of the Supreme Court as "topsy-turvy," suggesting that the only appropriate economic meaning of privacy is "profitable secrecy."[13] A judge who proceeds rationally will build up protections for, say, industrial secrecy, while being far less concerned about the unprofitable privacy of the bedroom. And he has shocked his readers by trying out economic reasoning in the sensitive areas of surrogate motherhood (where he called for a "thriving market in babies")[14] and even rape (where he speculated about whether the special pleasure derived by the rapist from the nonconsensual nature of his act is or is not outweighed by the woman's loss in property rights in her body).[15] Posner defends this apparently crude way of looking at things by asserting, repeatedly, the extremely controversial thesis that whenever individuals (judges or anyone else) are thinking rationally, they are seeking to maximize their satisfactions. Thus, if we are to give individuals (including women) credit for rationality, we had better see how we can cast their reasoning in this "economic" form.[16]

In his economic mode, Posner has struck many of his readers as dogmatic, insensitive to the history and complexity of human phenomena. More recently, in the ambitious *The Problems of Jurisprudence*, Posner seems to waver about whether the economic approach provides a sufficient account of judging, and even of rationality.[17] In his most recent work, *Overcoming Law*, he concludes that it does not: Economic approaches can even be "a potential menace to basic liberties."[18] Moreover, in none of his judicial opinions in the area of sexual conduct does Posner rely on economic notions, or even of cost-benefit analysis. These opinions display a sensitivity and flexibility that were notably lacking in some of his earlier theoretical writing. All of this gives ample reason for Posner's readers to wonder what role economic theorizing will have in his considered account of judicial reasoning about sex.

All three of Posner's projects in this book are connected by an opposition to puritanism and by his closely related view that ethical norms in matters of sex are not "natural" at all but are constructed by societies in different ways, over a basis supplied by a shared biological heritage. This antipuritanism and antinaturalism support Posner's determination to look to other times and places for a more comprehensive understanding of human sexuality than a scrutiny of contemporary American mores might yield. This cross-cultural and scientific study, in turn, lends essential support to his "hands-off" libertarian stance in areas such as homosexuality (where he holds that *Bowers* was wrongly decided and very badly justified), abortion (where he defends the general outcome in *Roe*, if not all the reasoning), and erotic art (where he wishes to give all expressive material full First Amendment protection, whether its content is political or not, propositional or not). The material supports these libertarian judgments by helping us to understand how fundamental sexual choices have been to human beings in many different times and places; by helping us understand what is at stake in a sexual practice or choice that at first seems alien to us; and, above all, by putting judges on notice that they may not invoke current prejudices as if they were timeless, neutral, and natural. If we have a clearer view of the variety of judgments intelligent people have made in this area, Posner believes, we are more likely to be tolerant of the practices of our fellow citizens and reluctant to use the force of law to intrude on them.[19]

The informational and historical part of Posner's book is in many respects its most successful. Although the task of providing, in one hundred pages of text, a short version of what judges ought to know about this topic is a daunting one, Posner, with his broad and accurate erudition, his curiosity and wit, does it remarkably well. He draws on the findings of anthropology, psychology, psychoanalysis, classical scholarship, and cultural history, and although the historical account is thin on material outside the Western tradition, it ranges very widely over times and places within that tradition.

Posner is especially interested in the ancient Greek world, and in analyses of ancient sexuality inspired by Foucault and the "social constructionists." The imaginary judges to whom this segment of the book is addressed would learn from even a cursory study of its contents that sexual categories and normative judgments about those categories are far more various than a modern American perspective might lead one to suppose. He or she would learn, for example, that in ancient Greece the fundamental distinction of sexual roles was between the active partner and the passive partner in the sexual act. For the active partner, the gender of the passive object was a matter of relative indifference. Thus the category of the "homosexual" as we know it—an individual who has an abiding preference for partners of a certain gender, regardless of the distinction between activity and passivity—did not really exist in that society (see chapter 12, in this volume). And in other ways, too, Posner is very good at showing the great diversity of attitudes respectable societies have taken about many highly charged sexual topics, in the process setting contemporary America in perspective, among the cultures of the world, as a society marked by a singular combination of heterogeneity, puritanism, and "machismo."

III. Biology and Social Construction

The dominant position of the book's historical section is "social-constructionist"; that is, it adopts the view that sexual norms do not derive from permanent and immutable laws of nature but are devised by society and tradition. But Posner then goes on to defend as the best explanatory theory of human sexual behavior a theory that combines evolutionary biology with economics. The combined thesis is somewhat elusive, but one might attempt to capture it as follows. Large-scale patterns in sexual behavior—persistent behavioral tendencies and repeated social patterns—are best explained biologically, as ways that the species has found of maximizing its evolutionary fitness. Within the large constraints of biology, on the other hand, individuals, being rational agents (a characteristic that itself is held to derive from evolution), seek to maximize their own satisfactions, computing costs and benefits.

There is no reason in principle why someone who recognizes and stresses the great variety with which societies have constructed sexual categories and norms might not also believe that beneath this variety lie certain "natural" regularities. These regularities might even be invoked to explain why, in each concrete set of circumstances, the specific cultural manifestations take the form they do. Sometimes Posner attempts to integrate his bioeconomic with his historical argument in some such way, as in his attempt to explain ancient Greek homo-sexuals as of two different sorts: some (the "pathics") being males biologically determined to a preference for the passive role (which, quite confusingly, he simply equates with today's people who prefer a same-sex partner, regardless of what sexual role they take), others (the vast majority) being "opportunistic" homosexuals who prefer (young) male partners simply because access to women is difficult.

Still, even such an attempted reconciliation of the two theses runs into diffi-culties. In fact, the evidence shows that women, in the role of prostitutes, were widely available in ancient Athens; nor can Posner's argument explain the thriv-ing business done by male prostitutes in that same city. Posner's account of the ways in which the changing social position of women influences social mores regarding marriage and related sexual matters is stronger and more interesting—though its interest derives far more from its historical than from its bioeconomic component.

In many other cases, Posner does not even try to reconcile his two lines of argument. For example, he asserts that the fact that women frequent prostitutes less often than men shows that women have, by nature, a lower "sex drive" than do men, failing to consider the manifold cultural and emotional factors that play a role in women's distaste for such choices. Again, he asserts that biology deter-mines males to have a preference for women with large breasts and hips, although elsewhere in the book he stresses evidence that the sexual attractiveness of bodily shape is a matter of "social construction," the desirable shape varying a great deal from culture to culture. Some of Posner's bioeconomic assertions seem just as false and unsupported by evidence as those in the judicial opinions he deplores, for example, the assertion that males are more sexually jealous than females—a fact that experience does not appear to bear out—and the assertion that a woman's ideal of an appealing sexual partner is a male who will be likely to protect and care for her offspring. (The plots of many works of fiction, from *Medea* to *Wuthering Heights* to *Casablanca*, might be considered with these two theses in mind.)

And there is a more general problem about the fit between the two projects. The historical project speaks of sexual desire as a phenomenon characterized by a rich and complex intentionality; that is, as fundamentally directed to an object and concerned with the object seen in a certain way.[20] Desire, in that picture, might contain instinctual components, but it is essentially a pull rather than a push, a response to the perception of some value. The biological argument, by contrast, and its economic companion even more clearly, views desire as simply a push, as a force that demands discharge and satisfaction and remains rather constant, whether or not a suitably evocative object is on the scene. It is by making this assumption that Posner can argue, for example, that a male deprived of ac-cess to females will choose an available male partner; that a female who, in the absence of a male partner, does not, like a similarly situated male, frequent a prostitute gives evidence thereby of a lower "sex drive." To have sorted out the "drive" component and the intentional component in sexual desire, and to have described some of the complexities of the interactions between the two, would have been a first step toward an adequate theory of human sexuality. In this sense, Posner's book does not even take the first step.

Consider this typical passage:

> A pretty boy may leave the tepid heterosexual cold but provide an acceptable albeit not ideal outlet for the sex drive of the superheated heterosexual. It is like a passion for apples. The passionate apple eater is more likely to consider a slightly wormy or overripe apple an acceptable substitute for an orange than the person whose enthusiasm for apples is more measured. Replace apples with sex and oranges with television and the point should be clear. The superheated heterosexual may not be able to find enough women to satisfy his sexual desires and, faced with a choice between masturbation and boys may choose boys (124, footnote omitted).

Here as elsewhere, desire is assumed to be fixed in amount, and behavior is explained as a simple function of sex drive with search costs. But there are two sorts of passionate apple-eaters. One is inhabited by a powerful drive toward apples, not much tempered by selective perception; he is willing to wolf down apples until the drive lets up, and if the only apples at hand are wormy or soft, he will put up with that. But another sort loves *apples*. This person is lured by the characteristics of the object; his desire may be dormant until the object itself elicits it. Such a person is unlikely to be attracted by a wormy or soft apple— just as it is the real lover of Mozart piano concertos who would rather wait a year to hear Brendel than go to weekly performances by mediocre musicians, the real lover of novels who will not read Judith Krantz in the airport because Proust is unavailable; the real lover of philosophy who will not choose Alan Watts under any circumstances at all.

Sexual desire is indeed in part a powerful instinctual drive, like the needs for food and drink; insofar as it is such a drive it may demand a lower grade of satisfaction when the preferred form is unavailable. But it also attends to its object and is aroused by the perception of some value or beauty in the object. The more one cares about sex in this intentional way, the more particular one might well be about the objects one chooses for one's satisfaction. Thus from women's failure to frequent prostitutes nothing follows at all about the biological level of their sex drive, so many are the reasons why such an idea might repel someone accustomed to link sex with personal concern and individuality. Posner does not even take the first step toward an account of these complex phenomena.

Nor is it clear that Posner's explanatory theory, such as it is, is really the alternative to moral and religious theories of sexuality that he believes it to be. His strategy is to demonstrate that if one understands that sexual matters have a nonmetaphysical origin, an origin in our animal history, and if one can push this secular explanation far enough, so that it seems to explain what we want to explain at least as well as explanations of sex that invoke divine entities and laws, then we will have put those vestiges of religious moralism at a considerable disadvantage in the American legal process.

But projects of this kind do not establish that biology can displace morality and religion. As Posner himself is well aware, one may hold that biology has constrained human behavior in certain ways without believing that this goes very far in telling us how we ought to behave toward one another in sexual matters. The fact (if it is a fact) that certain forms of behavior promoted the evolutionary fitness of the species at a certain time in its history says nothing at all about whether intelligent reflective creatures should choose to perpetuate these patterns of action. Posner, as I say, knows this, and he insists, for example, on the fact that polygamy, while functional in certain contexts, is unlikely to promote the equality of women, a goal that many modern societies with good reason (in his view) pursue.

But then it is not clear how his theory can be a replacement for moral theorizing—except in the sense that any Darwinian explanation tends to undercut modes of explanation and normative discourse that stress the discontinuity between humans and other animals, and in the sense that some religious views do commit themselves to accounts of the origins of life that are incompatible with Darwinism. But most mainstream religious views in America, and virtually all secular moral views, do not repudiate evolutionary theory: They just hold, reasonably enough, that evolution does not tell us all we need to know about the moral and spiritual aspects of our conduct, or about the norms that should govern it.

To stress the this-worldly and animal nature of sexuality, furthermore, does not go far toward justifying the reductive modes of analysis ("search costs," "transaction costs," etc.) in which Posner takes such pride. As I have said, the acceptance of evolutionary theory does not entail the repudiation of many religious and most ethical views. And even if one should for other reasons repudiate those views, there is no reason to suppose that a secular humanist morality will have to be narrow and reductive in Posner's sense. For there are many ways of being a this-worldly animal, and one of those ways is to be an animal that is ethical. Such an animal will be likely to need a more complex language than Posner offers. Posner does little to show us why naturalistic scientific explanations for the origins of our sexual inclinations should make us prefer to see the world of sexual transactions as a great market and individuals as simply competing to maximize the satisfactions of their subjective preferences.

This is the sort of error that will be made by someone who is in many ways thoroughly fascinated by religion and moral theory and by human dependence on these sources of value—by a type of secular thinker who does not altogether trust human beings to use their own wits to say what has value and how much. Posner, who elsewhere thinks well about the complex inventiveness of human culture, should not make such an error.[21]

He doesn't always. His book, far more quirky and fascinating than this summary of its argument makes it seem, contains constantly surprising reminders of its author's complexity and perceptiveness—as when, in a brief paragraph, he distinguishes between two types of erotic love, giving an account of love that cannot be integrated into the central argument, and is the richer for that (118–9). And at one point he seems to acknowledge that his own theory is simply a crude and shocking theory that will, like an "acid bath," peel away "layers of ignorance, ideology, superstition, and prejudice," and "clear the ground for a normative analysis" of a more complete sort (437).

IV. Biology and Liberty

How important is the bioeconomic theory for the concrete legal reasoning in the book's third section, where Posner unfolds his normative "libertarian" approach? Fortunately, at least as I see it, not very important. Posner frequently refers back to the bioeconomic theory for a general atmosphere of this-worldliness, hardheadedness, and sanity, but he might as well have invoked any secular moral theory. Indeed, there are some theories—say, Dworkin's right-based theory—that would have provided a far more adequate philosophical foundation for Posner's libertarian judgments than his own theory does.

Revealingly, in his first reference to the "libertarian" normative theory, he borrows the language of Mill: Conduct should not be regulated that does not damage another's "*liberty* or property" (3, emphasis added). Later, he says in his own voice that conduct will be regulable only on the basis of "economic or other utilitarian considerations." But protection of fundamental rights and liberties has not generally been a strong point of utilitarianism, which usually holds that such moral considerations are merely instrumental to satisfactions and are to be overridden when the balance of satisfactions goes against them.[22] Posner has more recently granted this point, stating that if people's mental distress at the acts of others is permitted to count in the calculation of social utility, "economics becomes a potential menace to basic liberties" and an excuse for "every manner of discrimination against despised minorities."[23] The "illiberal implications of typical utilitarian and economic thinking" cannot be adequately resisted without supplementing an economic approach with an independent theory of liberty.[24]

Still, one might, with Mill (and contemporary thinker Amartya Sen), defend a general consequentialist conception—a conception in which the right question to ask about an action is whether it promotes the best consequences overall—and yet include the protection of fundamental human rights among the consequences that get promoted.[25] I think that this is what Posner actually does in many cases in *Sex and Reason;* insofar as he follows Mill (and Sen) in this way, he is a lot closer to Dworkin's view of legal reasoning than his own statements suggest. Thus his recent admission that utilitarianism cannot by itself supply an adequate theory of liberty is a welcome clarification of his procedure in *Sex and Reason,* but it need not be seen as a rejection of that book's basic argumentative strategy.

In one respect, however, the bioeconomic theory subverts the libertarian theory. If we have only the account of the value of sexual activity given us in the bioeconomic theory, it seems difficult to say why sex matters to people, or why liberty in this sphere should be taken to be fundamental. If it is just one among many comparable ways of enhancing one's utility, why does it matter that we are free to choose this utility-pursuing strategy rather than some other? And even should the bioeconomic theorist allow sex to be noncommensurable with other sources of satisfaction, Posner's determination to treat it as a drive that needs an outlet, rather than as a form of selective interrelationship with a person, leaves it unclear why shifting the direction and mode of its expression should be an unacceptable interference with a fundamental liberty. If the drive to have sex were just like, say, the desire to urinate—and that is, in effect, the way Posner treats it—any relatively sanitary receptacle would do. We would not feel that a society that forbade people to urinate into receptacles made of fiberglas, holding that only porcelain was in accordance with "nature," had made an error of a sort that would blight people's lives. We can only see what is bad about sodomy laws when we see how sexual object choice goes deeper than that, is hooked up with self-definition and self-expression in more basic ways.

We may, then, approach the libertarian normative theory without seeing it as inseparable from the bioeconomic theory. We should not be misled into supposing that our doubts about the latter undermine the credentials of the former, which can be supported far more strongly from within a more humanistic and intentionalistic view of sexual expression.[26]

Posner's general strategy in this section of the book is to demand that we ask about social costs and benefits calmly and comprehensively, prejudice and disgust aside, using all the information available to us about the practices concerning which we are judging. Proceeding in this way, he arrives at results that will surprise those who are accustomed to making simple distinctions between "left" and "right," and who have long since decided that Posner, in virtue of his pro-market stances, must be a "right wing" thinker. Describing his conclusions will not do justice to his arguments, but the conclusions are remarkable in their own right.

Marriage

On the whole Posner favors the gradual substitution of a secular form of contractual cohabitation (currently available in Scandinavia) for the institution of marriage as it is presently understood. Short of this, he would wish (1) to recognize nonmarital cohabitation by some form of legal contract guaranteeing certain rights and benefits, and (2) to overhaul the system of alimony in order to provide compensatory benefits, in the case of divorce, for women who have sacrificed career opportunities to assist a spouse. He tends to favor allowing homosexuals to marry, although he would really like to solve this problem by "chucking the whole institution of marriage in favor of an explicitly contractual approach that would make the current realities of marriage transparent" (312). Polygamy, he tentatively holds, should continue to be illegal, because it remains connected with hierarchy and the unequal social position of women. But women who have children outside of a recognized marriage should be protected somehow.

Homosexuality

The disgust that many Americans feel toward homosexuals is based on a combination of ignorance and machismo. (The only popular stereotype on this question that Posner finds reliable, on the basis of his cross-cultural study, is that homosexuals have a higher than average probability of having an artistic career, and "it is not the worst fate in the world to be condemned to a career in the arts" [305].) Sodomy laws should be repealed, even if they are not enforced, because they tend to provide a basis for other exclusions—for example, from professions such as that of the judiciary, in which we would be reluctant to see an admitted lawbreaker. He is highly critical of the opinions in *Bowers* for "ignoring the ideological roots" of the Georgia sodomy law: Such statutes "express an irrational fear and loathing of a group that has been subjected to discrimination, much like that directed against the Jews" (346). He also faults the opinions for "lack of knowledge about this history and character of the regulation of sexuality," and, above all, for "a profound lack of empathy for the situation of the male homosexual in America" (346). And he supports the idea of a general constitutional right of sexual autonomy, which would cover this case along with many others. Posner also suggests that homosexuals should count as a suspect class for the purposes of the Equal Protection Clause, and that, even given the *Bowers* result, this avenue of argument might possibly still be used by courts to rule in their favor.

As for the issue of gays in the military, Posner provides a devastating criticism of the arguments most often used to support their exclusion: the security risk argument, the argument that gays are unstable, the sexual harassment argument. The one argument he takes seriously is the view that the presence of gay men (he does not find this problem in the case of women) may well create serious morale problems, given the prevalence and the violence of male homophobia in America (by contrast to other countries, such as the Netherlands, which have unproblematically integrated gays into the services). Posner fears that homophobia is so deep in the self-definition of many American males that the danger of violence against gays is really rather great, and greater than in the parallel case of racial integration. Yet he thinks that the risk should be run, "for it is terrible to tell people they are unfit to serve their country, unless they really are unfit, which is not the case here" (321). He favors a gradual policy of integration, beginning by keeping in the services gays who are already there and "come out," gradually accepting new recruits (314–23).

Finally, on the question of gay marriage, Posner supports the extension to same-sex couples of a Scandinavian-style right of contractual cohabitation but concludes that the present climate of prejudice is too intense to make same-sex marriage "a feasible proposal," even though "[t]he benefits of such marriage may outweigh the costs" (313–4). Posner does not clearly state what features of marriage he has in mind when he says that contractual cohabitation will prove acceptable in a way marriage will not. Nor does he offer criteria that would show us how to decide whether the right to marry is a fundamental right of individuals, and, if it is, when a basic right may be abridged for reasons of social feasibility.

Privacy and the Constitution

Posner holds that the privacy cases involving contraception and abortion were, in general, correctly decided, although he does not approve of all the reasoning in the opinions. He thinks that in the end no compelling basis in the Constitution exists for the recognition of a general right to sexual autonomy, but that the courts should plug this gap and recognize one anyhow:

> A constitution that did not invalidate so offensive, oppressive, probably un-democratic, and sectarian a law [viz., the anticontraception law at issue in *Griswold v. Connecticut*] would stand revealed as containing major gaps. Maybe that is the nature of our, as perhaps of any, written Constitution; but yet, perhaps the courts are authorized to plug at least the more glaring gaps. Does anyone really believe, in his heart of hearts, that the Constitution should be interpreted so literally as to authorize every conceivable law that would not violate a specific constitutional clause? This would mean that a state could require everyone to marry, or to have sexual intercourse at least once a month.
> . . . Yet we do find it reassuring to think that the courts stand between us and legislative tyranny even if a particular form of tyranny was not foreseen and expressly forbidden by the framers of the Constitution. (328–9)

This clarification is particularly welcome in the light of Posner's earlier assault on the Supreme Court's privacy jurisprudence in *The Economics of Justice*. It shows a Posner in whom the libertarian Millean side is increasingly coming to the fore and the tendency to analyze human rights strictly in economic terms is receding. That Posner has by now triumphed, to judge from the clear statement in *Overcoming Law* about the incompleteness of economics as an approach to human liberty.

Pornography

In a discussion closely linked to Posner's opinion in the Kitty Kat Lounge case but ranging more widely, because here he is not constrained by previous Supreme Court pronouncements on obscenity, Posner holds that the only pornography that should be legally restricted is pornography that uses child models or inflicts damage on adult models. (His ruling in the case of *Douglass v. Hustler Magazine, Inc.* 769 F.2d 1128 (7th Cir. 1985), however, also shows that he is willing to support civil damage actions against such publications when photographs are used without consent.[27]) His conclusion here is tentative, and yet, having argued that expressive artistic representations (e.g., Robert Mapplethorpe's photographs) must be protected, he confesses that he can find no evident differences—with respect to the issues of violence and misogyny that are of most concern to feminists—between these "arty" works and the more popular pornographic forms.

Citing the arguments of the feminist historian of religion Margaret Miles concerning the patriarchal and misogynistic dimensions of much of classical art (360), Posner concludes that "if a *Playboy* pinup belongs to the same genre as a Renaissance nude, then since the latter is plainly protected by the First Amendment, so must the former be" (382). In the Kitty Kat opinion, he notes that the category of "established art," sometimes invoked to try to make this distinction, would have excluded from protection Manet's *Déjeuner sur l'herbe*, and much else besides. And that is not his only worry. He plainly wants the dancers of the Kitty Kat Lounge to be free to express themselves in their own low-art way and does not see why the protection of the First Amendment should be extended only to those who meet with the approval of high-brow tastes.

Here Posner is openly at odds with many feminists. It seems to me that he does not fully grapple with their arguments. In particular, he fails to investigate cases of extremely violent and humiliating sexually explicit material, whether on film or on the page. These materials are the real targets of feminist complaint, and it seems evasive not to look closely at some examples of this genre, examining the evidence for the claim that they both cause damage to individual women (through the use of pornography in connection with domestic violence and through the exploitation of actresses and models) and encourage the perpetuation of violent fantasies about women. The striptease dancers of the Kitty Kat Lounge do not adequately represent what feminists are worried about. We might grant him that they are agents and should be allowed to pursue their trade while still being deeply disturbed by the easy availability of materials that represent women as made for abuse and violence. Posner shows a certain amount of puritanism himself, in his unwillingness to quote from or to describe such materials. Because he avoids them, we cannot tell whether he believes that they can do damage and of what type.

Posner would probably conclude that even if pornography does cause general social damage by deforming attitudes toward women, this is insufficient ground for the legal intervention with its production or distribution, given our interest in protecting the freedom of expression. He may be correct, but the book contains no analysis of First Amendment rights that would clearly show exactly how expressive interests figure and how weighty they are when such damages are at issue. Moreover, he gives us no reason at all to reject MacKinnon's actual legal proposal, which is for a civil ordinance under which women who have been personally damaged by pornography can bring a damage action against its makers or distributors. If such harms to nonconsenting individuals can be established, then even a believer in Mill's harm principle could support such a legal proposal. Posner leaves us in considerable doubt about his views and arguments in this important area.

Posner, plainly, is a complex character, difficult to pin down. One might do worse than to think of him as the George Bernard Shaw of American law. Like Shaw, he combines a passion for exposing humbug and pseudo-profundity with an odd but genuine sort of social compassion, a delight in shocking the self-righteous with a love of human diversity and freedom—and all this, one must add, with a good deal of Shaw's inability to get inside the messier human emotions, with his tendency to think of emotion itself as a peculiar sort of religious dogma. Posner's bioeconomic theory is no better than Don Juan's theory of "the Life Force" (which it strongly resembles) as an explanation of the complexities of human sexuality. But as with Shaw, I think, so with Posner: Long after the deeply flawed theories have been forgotten, we will remember, and profit by, the wit and the courage of his attacks on bigotry, folly, and cruelty.

15

THE WINDOW

Knowledge of Other Minds in Virginia Woolf's To the Lighthouse

I. The Dome-Shaped Hive

"How, then, she had asked herself, did one know one thing or another thing about people, sealed as they were?" (80)[1] Sitting close to Mrs. Ramsay, "close as she could get" (78), her arms around Mrs. Ramsay's knees, loving her intensely, Lily Briscoe wonders how to get inside her to see the "sacred inscriptions" in her heart, "which if one could spell them out, would teach one everything, but they would never be offered openly, never made public" (79). She searches for a technique by which these internal tablets might be read: "What art was there, known to love or cunning, by which one pressed through into those secret chambers?" (79). The art eludes her, and yet she continues to long for it:

How, then, she had asked herself, did one know one thing or another thing about people, sealed as they were? Only like a bee, drawn by some sweetness or sharpness in the air intangible to touch or taste, one haunted the dome-shaped hive, ranged the wastes of the air over the countries of the world alone, and then haunted the hives with their murmurs and their stirrings; the hives, which were people. (79–80)

People are sealed hives full of bees that both attract other bees and keep them off. In her complex image Lily Briscoe indicates both that knowledge of the mind of another is a profound human wish—it feels as if to have that knowledge would be to be finally at home, in one's own hive—and, at the same time, that this knowledge is unattainable. The hives are sealed. Their sweetness or sharpness lures us—and then all we can do is to hover round the outside, haunting the hive, listening to the murmurs and stirrings that are the signs of vibrant life within. We can never see whether those murmurs and stirrings really come from other bees like ourselves, rather than, say, some engine constructed to make bee-like noises. And even if we assume there are bees inside, we can never fully decode their messages, can never be certain of what they are thinking and feeling. And yet we pursue the goal obsessively. Knowledge is a project that draws us to one another, and we cannot bear to let that project go.

The first part of Virginia Woolf's *To the Lighthouse* depicts, repeatedly, both our epistemological insufficiency toward one another and our unquenchable epistemological longing. But the first part is also called "The Window." The authorial image of the window stands in tension with Lily's image of the sealed hive, suggesting that Lily is blind to a possibility. And part I ends with a scene in which, or so it would seem, knowledge of another mind is attained. Mrs. Ramsay stands close to her husband, who looks at her as she looks out of the window. "And as she looked at him she began to smile, for though she had not said a word, he knew, of course he knew, that she loved him. He could not deny it. . . . She had not said it: yet he knew" (185–6).

Virginia Woolf tackles a venerable philosophical problem that is also an enduring practical problem. I believe that she makes a contribution both to our understanding of the problem and to its resolution (or perhaps its nonresolution). She may well have discussed this issue with philosophers, and she may well have profited from her philosophical reading. It is not these connections, however, that I wish to investigate. I shall focus here on what is philosophical in the novel itself, both in what it says about the problem of other minds and in the way it says it—for I shall argue that the statement of both problem and "resolution" is made not only by overt statements inside the text but also by the form of the text itself, in its manner of depicting both sealed life and communication.

Woolf's approach to the problem is very different from that of many philosophers who have investigated it: For she suggests that the problem of other minds is not simply an epistemological problem, a problem of evidence and certainty, but, above all, an ethical problem, a problem produced by the motives and desires with which we approach beings who are both separate from us and vital to our projects. Although for many reasons I shall avoid speaking directly of comparisons between Woolf and the thought of Wittgenstein—not least being the knowledge that we would never get started with Woolf if we once tried to get agreement about Wittgenstein on this issue—I shall simply state that her approach can in some respects be fruitfully compared with some interpretations of the later Wittgenstein, particularly that in Stanley Cavell's *The Claim of Reason*, and with Cavell's own approach to the problem of skepticism.[2] In other ways, as I shall indicate, her approach is intimately related to the portrait of skepticism and jealousy in Proust's *Recherche*, which certainly must count as one of the profound philosophical contributions on the topic. Woolf makes a distinctive contribution, however, through her depiction of the sheer many-sidedness of the problem of other minds, by her indication that it is not a single problem at all but many distinct human difficulties that are in complex ways interrelated. She is distinctive, too, in her insistent focus on ethical character and on the virtues of persons that make knowledge possible.

In pursuing these issues, I shall examine, first, the statement of the problem in part I of the novel: Why is it that people are sealed hives to one another? I shall then return to the scene in which Lily Briscoe attempts to know the thoughts and feelings of Mrs. Ramsay, asking how Lily understands the epistemological project and why, so conceived, the project is doomed to failure. I shall then turn to Mr. and Mrs. Ramsay, asking how it comes about that these two people, so deeply dissimilar, so lacking in firsthand understanding of one another's goals and aims, should nonetheless claim, at least, to have solved Lily's problem, communicating and receiving the knowledge of one another's love. On what does Mrs. Ramsay base her claim, and what should we make of it?

II. Complexity and Concealment

If one were to stage the overt actions and interactions of *To the Lighthouse* as a play, one would have hardly enough action and dialogue to fill half an hour. Most of the novel is set inside the minds of its various characters, and its drama is a drama of thought, emotion, perception, and memory. Very little of this thinking and feeling finds expression in language. The reader is thus constantly made aware of the richness of consciousness and of the tremendous gap between what we are in and to ourselves and the part of the self that enters the interpersonal world. Only the prose of the novel bridges the gap—and this, we are made to feel, imperfectly and incompletely. Thinking about Mr. Ramsay and Mr. Bankes, Lily finds a host of thoughts and perceptions crowding in on her, a few of which the authorial voice manages to pin down—but then suggests the limits even of its own accuracy:

> All of this danced up and down, like a company of gnats, each separate, but all marvelously controlled in an invisible elastic net—danced up and down in Lily's mind, in and about the branches of the pear tree . . . until her thought which had spun quicker and quicker exploded of its own intensity. . . . (40–1)

The crowd of gnats in the net become an explosion of uncountable fragments, and we recognize that even the lengthy summary we have been given—none of which any of the other characters will ever know—is no doubt only a crude pinning down, a linguistic simplification, of processes far more elusive and complex.

In this sense, as the novel shows repeatedly, people really are sealed hives—buzzing centers of intense activity, little of which is communicated to any other hive. The novel begins with a single sentence spoken aloud by Mrs. Ramsay. This sentence is followed by a page and a half representing the thoughts of James Ramsay, which is followed in turn by five words spoken aloud by his father, and then one more page from James's thoughts, eleven words aloud from Mrs. Ramsay—and so on. The ratio of internal action to external communication is frequently more lopsided still than this and rarely less so.

What, then, is the problem of access to the other, as the novel presents it? Why are the insides of the hive not made available for the secure grasp of others? First of all, there is the sheer problem of time. The inner world, like the company of gnats, moves extremely rapidly, has many many small pieces, each complexly connected to the others. If one were to set oneself to communicate everything, one would never be done with it, and one would certainly not be able to get on with life. (In this sense the stance of the authorial voice presents itself as radically detached from the ordinary activities of life: By determining to burrow into consciousness and to record its small movements in language, the novel is taking on a task strangely unnatural in the detachment from ordinary activity that it requires and hubristically ambitious in its goal—a task that is hardly fit for a human being, that could be completed, perhaps, only by a god.) Lily thinks of Mr. Bankes and Mr. Ramsay: "Standing now, apparently transfixed, by the pear tree, impressions poured in upon her of those two men, and to follow her thought was like following a voice which speaks too quickly to be taken down by one's pencil . . ." (40).

Human beings cannot even take down the dictation of their own thought, so rapidly and complexly does it move. How much more difficult, then, is it to communicate this thought to another, how impossible, it would seem, by following the signs given by another to attain access to the rapid complex inner world that exists inside another body.

But time, rapidity, and complexity are not the only obstacles to communication of the inner world. The novel shows us, as well, that language, the instrument we must use to make ourselves available to one another, is in some ways a very imperfect instrument of understanding. It is, first, a general medium of exchange, its meanings blunt and serviceable. It appears to be too crude to express what is most personal, what is deepest in the individual consciousness. Mrs. Ramsay thinks of the language of daily social interchange as a crude *lingua franca* that offers uniformity at the cost of suppressing individuality:

> So, when there is a strife of tongues, at some meeting, the chairman, to obtain unity, suggests that every one shall speak in French. Perhaps it is bad French; French may not contain the words that express the speaker's thoughts; nevertheless speaking French imposes some order, some uniformity. (136)

This is not a claim that each person has a language of thought that is in its essence private. The fact that all these thoughts are contained in a novel shows that this is not Woolf's view. The claim is, instead, that the meanings of the common language become inflected with the peculiarities of each person's history and character and taste in such a way that although in principle language might express the peculiar character of an individual's thought (if we waive for a moment our reservations about time and density), in fact the shopworn common language of daily social interchange rarely does so. We also have here a self-referential claim on behalf of the language of the literary artist, which is able to render individuality in a way that most of us, speaking, cannot.[3]

Because the language of daily life is a blunt imperfect medium, and because each of us has a distinctive history and set of experiences, we find ourselves using the same words in different ways, to mean very different things. If we try to gain knowledge of another person's consciousness by listening to his or her words and then asking ourselves what meanings these words conjure up in our own consciousness, we will frequently go wrong. Mr. Ramsay thinks about the universe, with a comfortably self-indulgent fatalism:

> "Poor little place," he murmured with a sigh.
>
> She heard him. He said the most melancholy things, but she noticed that directly he had said them he always seemed more cheerful than usual. All this phrase-making was a game, she thought, for if she had said half what he said, she would have blown her brains out by now.
>
> It annoyed her, this phrase-making, and she said to him, in a matter-of-fact way, that it was a perfectly lovely evening. And what was he groaning about, she asked, half laughing, half complaining, for she guessed what he was thinking—he would have written better books if he had not married. (106)

This highly complex passage reminds us that words, in life, are used to convey meanings that are shaped by an individual history. What Mr. Ramsay means by "poor little place" is not what Mrs. Ramsay would mean if she said something like that about the universe. For her, prone as she is to real depression, such a fatalistic utterance would only be chosen as an expression of despair. To keep herself away from the depression that menaces her, she tries to avoid such phrases. Her husband, by contrast, with his taste for the melodramatic, for "The Charge of the Light Brigade" and other images of courage pitted against disaster, takes a certain delight in characterizing the universe this way. The phrase expresses his image of himself as a courageous solitary voyager pitted against fate. That image pleases him, restores his sense of pride in himself. As she recognizes, the original thought that prompts the phrase is a serious one—he would have written better books if he had not married—but his choice of the quasi-tragic phrase is his way of getting out of the sadness such thoughts might induce, by portraying himself as a victim of fate, to be commended for his courage in sticking it out in a hostile universe. What would for her be a capitulation to depression is his device for keeping depression at bay.

Language, in short, issues from a personal history. It reports the speaker's meanings, which are often highly idiosyncratic, though in principle nonprivate and tellable in the way and to the extent that a novel is told. In some cases we might need a history of novelistic complexity to get at what those meanings are. Moreover, language also does things to and in that history. The words we use to others are not just reports of the inner world; they are also agents. To understand what Mr. Ramsay is saying here we need to know not only how he uses that phrase and phrases like it on many occasions, what actions and other gestures accompany that phrase, we also need to know or guess why he speaks at all, what he is trying to do with and by the phrase—in this case, to distance himself from real personal loss and guilt by the projection of a beloved image of solitary courage. To understand what he means—if, indeed, Mrs. Ramsay does (and we must always remember that her conjectures are shaped by her own needs and desires and are fallible, as any interpretation is fallible)—she does need to know the pattern of his actions and utterances, his history, but she also needs to know his desires and projects, what he wants, what he is seeking to do to himself and his world. To grasp all this, even in an intimate relationship of long duration, is a formidable challenge. Most people lack such information about themselves.

Suppose these problems could be overcome—for example, by taking up the supple fine-tuned language of literary art, together with the literary artist's willingness to tell the story of a unique character so that we can get a grip on that character's idiosyncratic meanings and dynamic goals. We do suppose that we know things about the minds of others when we read novels of consciousness, and we suppose this with good reason, given that novels present us with data requisite for adequate interpretation of a human life, data that social interaction frequently denies us.[4] The novel now shows us, however, that these are not the only obstacles to knowledge of another. For so far we have been supposing that people want to make their meanings known to one another. This, for many different reasons, may not be the case.

This novel contains no Iagos, no evil manipulative characters who systematically deceive, saying one thing and thinking another. In fact, it contains very little dissimulation of a morally blameworthy kind. And yet these characters almost always resist being known; they speak and act in ways that actively impede the encroaching movements of an alien understanding. Social form is one prominent reason for this resistance. The novel is not just incidentally about middle-class English people, who carry with them cultural habits of reticence so long developed that they have become a part of their very character, making it impossible for them to give direct expression to most sentiments, especially deep emotions, especially any socially discordant thought. As Mrs. Ramsay speaks the polite "French" of polite social intercourse, Charles Tansley thinks of the more violent expressive language he would use with his lower-class friends, "there in a society where one could say what one liked" (136) not worrying about decorum. He "suspected the insincerity" (136) of the social language, and thinks of how he will call it "nonsense." But this is not simply a point about English social habits. Any social code, the novel suggests, imposes some discipline on the expression of emotion; in order to achieve order and uniformity, it teaches people to have at least some reticence, some reluctance to be known.

But there are other more personal motives for this reluctance. Above all, the novel shows us the strength of shame as a motive for self-concealment. Behind Charles Tansley's anger and his fantasies of denouncing the Ramsays to the people of his class is a profound feeling of embarrassment and inadequacy that he is not like them, does not belong, has nothing appropriate to say. He desperately conceals this insecurity beneath his angry silence. For Mr. Ramsay, the root of shame is not class-linked but personal—the sense of professional failure that underlies all his bluster and his fatalistic assertiveness. As we learn in a passage that is probably set in Lily Briscoe's consciousness (although it follows seamlessly a passage in which Ramsay himself is contemplating his career), we see him depicted as a man who standardly takes refuge in self-consoling disguises:

But . . . his glory in the phrases he made, in the ardour of youth, in his wife's beauty, in the tributes that reached him from Swansea, Cardiff, Exeter,

Southampton, Kidderminster, Oxford, Cambridge—all had to be deprecated and concealed under the phrase "talking nonsense," because, in effect, he had not done the thing he might have done. It was a disguise; it was the refuge of a man afraid to own his own feelings, who could not say, This is what I like— this is what I am; and rather pitiable and distasteful to William Bankes and Lily Briscoe, who wondered why such concealments should be necessary. . . . (70)

Out of shame at what he feels to be a gap in his attainment, Mr. Ramsay conceals himself systematically from others. Of course they guess at this—and we are led to think their guesses accurate. But the real emotions are not honestly "owned."

The case of Mr. Ramsay shows us something else about concealment: that it is a way of getting power. Mr. Ramsay is not just attempting to cover his shame. That already has a strategic role: Covering one's true weakness and vulnerability is one way people have of trying to exert influence over others. But Mr. Ramsay's strategic use of concealment is more complex: His blusterings and his cheerful fatalisms, which conceal from himself and others what he's really worried about, also have the role of soliciting attention and comfort from others in his circle, especially women. The utterance "poor little place" (106)—which Mrs. Ramsay knows to be a way of distancing himself from the thought of his failure—is also a solicitation, a request that she comfort him. She goes to him, as always, asking "what was he groaning about."[5] After her death, Lily Briscoe feels continually the now unanswered demand for comfort as something "bearing down on her" (221)—"and she pretended to drink out of her empty coffee cup so as to escape him—to escape his demand on her, to put aside a moment longer that imperious need" (219).

Here we arrive at a subtle point. Mr. Ramsay is not only in some respects a concealer; he is also a self-dramatizer. He makes himself more emotionally transparent, in a certain way, than the other characters do, especially in the third part of the novel—but even this transparency is both statement and demand:

Mr. Ramsay sighed to the full. He waited. Was she not going to say anything? Did she not see what he wanted from her? . . . He sighed profoundly. He sighed significantly. All Lily wished was that this enormous flood of grief, this insatiable hunger for sympathy, this demand that she should surrender herself up to him entirely, and even so he had sorrows enough to keep her supplied for ever, should leave her . . . before it swept her down in its flow. (226)

Even the apparently frank statement of grief is not to be taken at face value. Mr. Ramsay does feel grief, but he is also putting on a show to get from Lily the sympathy he wants. It may be impossible for him or for anyone else to say to what extent he exaggerates or changes his grief in the process. Emotions don't stand still to be inspected like so many stones or bricks. The act of bringing them to consciousness frequently changes them; the act of expressing them to another almost always does so.

In fact, one might even ask how clear it is that there is a fact of the matter about Mr. Ramsay's grief that his external statements either do or do not render correctly. The inner world is fluid and dynamic, complexly linked up with the strategies and the aims of the outer. Indeed, it is frequently also undemarcated and in flux, a buzzing of confused conflicting feelings and impulses, which cannot be reported in definite language without being changed. In short, even when we have what seems most like frankness, we may have something far more complicated and strategic. The very concept of frank depiction of the inner may itself involve an oversimplification.

Shame and power are not the only sources of concealment and misrepresentation in the novel. The sheer desire for liberty and privacy is another. Mrs. Ramsay, who lives so much for and toward others, protects her few moments of solitude, cherishing these as what is most real, what is most herself:

> She took a look at life, for she had a clear sense of it there, something real, something private, which she shared neither with her children nor with her husband. . . . [I]t was a relief when they went to bed. For now she need not think about anybody. She could be herself, by herself. And that was what now she often felt the need of—to think; well, not even to think. To be silent; to be alone. All the being and the doing, expansive, glittering, vocal, evaporated; and one shrunk, with a sense of solemnity, to being oneself, a wedge-shaped core of darkness, something invisible to others. . . . This core of darkness could go anywhere, for no one saw it. They could not stop it, she thought, exulting. There was freedom, there was peace, there was, most welcome of all, a summoning together, a resting on a platform of stability. Not as oneself did one find rest ever, in her experience . . . but as a wedge of darkness. Losing personality, one lost the fret, the hurry, the stir; and there rose to her lips always some exclamation of triumph over life when things came together in this peace, this rest, this eternity. . . . (91, 95–6)

Mrs. Ramsay protects her private self. But we notice that it is not the same neatly shaped conscious self that she might communicate to others. Her solitude is not formed for or toward the outer world. We reach here an especially deep difficulty in the way of knowing another mind. This is that what we usually think of as "the mind"—that is, its conscious mental acts, acts that could at least putatively be rendered in language and communicated to another—are only, perhaps, a part of the mind, a part bound up with the outer world of "being and doing," a sort of marshaling of the mind preparatory to communication.

Woolf's depiction thus supports a view of consciousness similar to the one advanced by Nietzsche in *Gay Science*, where he depicts self-consciousness as a relatively late evolutionary arrival, useful only in connection with communication.[6] Most of our mental life, he plausibly stresses, could be carried on without it, at a level of experience and awareness more like that we are accustomed to attribute to other animals. This account has recently received strong support from research in neuroscience and evolutionary biology. Mrs. Ramsay supports this idea: What she feels like in and of herself is something dark, made up of intuition and free-ranging meditation. The more hard, definite verbalizable parts of her are the parts she associates with being at the disposal of others, not with the core of her self. This may not be true of the identities of all individuals. For example, Mr. Ramsay is almost certainly more fully identified with his consciousness than his wife is. He feels most fully himself when he forms himself into words and concepts. But if we admit that Mrs. Ramsay's account of herself is a true account of many people much of the time, we have a very tough obstacle in the way of our knowledge of others: For the very presentation of self as a possible object for knowledge may be a kind of self-change—or even, as Mrs. Ramsay thinks, a making of a nonself, an internalized artifact of the public realm from which she flees.[7]

Woolf supports this outer-inner distinction, but she also calls it into question. For Mrs. Ramsay's identity for the reader is fundamentally constituted by her care for others, her public doings and actings. When she herself uses the language of the "outer" and the "inner," and associates the core of her selfhood with the wedge-shaped core of darkness, the reader both assents and dissents. We understand this distinction not as a universal metaphysical claim but as a very particular psychological fact about Mrs. Ramsay—namely, that she likes to flee at times from the demands of others and to identify herself with her nonverbal meditations. The point about the significance of the nonlinguistic stands, but it is more complex than Mrs. Ramsay's language initially suggests. For the public realm is a crucial constituent of the self; the meditative realm is both the hidden self and, at the same time, the death of the self. Consider the way the passage goes on: "Not as oneself did one find rest ever, in her experience. . . . Losing personality, one lost the fret, the hurry, the stir. . . ." Mrs. Ramsay feels herself at such moments to be very close to, almost identical with, certain inanimate objects, "trees, streams, flowers" (97). But that both is and is not to be Mrs. Ramsay.

III. Knowledge and Possession

In the light of all these obstacles in the way of knowledge, it is no accident that the novel is saturated with images of hiddenness and remoteness: the image of a loved child's mind as a well, whose waters are both receptive and distorting (84); the image of thoughts and feelings hidden as if under veils (160); Lily's images of the loved person as hive, as secret treasure chamber (79). The novel's very structure shows us this hiddenness, by giving us a miraculous access to the thoughts of the characters, an access that they are far from having to one another, though at the same time it is still plainly incomplete—itself too succinct, too strategically plotted, too much a construct of consciousness and language, to constitute in itself a full response to its own challenge.[8]

(As we notice the novel's way of solving a problem human beings seem not to solve so well in life, we should recall that this novel represents Woolf's own personal attempt to know the minds of her own parents—that Mr. Ramsay's anxiety and Mrs. Ramsay's depression are conjectures that fill the hives of Leslie Stephen and Woolf's beautiful remote mother with definite sounds, as the bee haunts their outsides and uses the power of art to represent what may [or may not] have been within.)

Responding to the fact of hiddenness, Woolf's characters try to solve the problem of knowledge by attempts to invade the chambers of the other, to possess, to grab hold, even to become one with the other's thoughts and feelings.

For possession would be, it seems, the most satisfying solution to their episte-mological problem. The most elaborate case of this is Lily Briscoe's attempt to know Mrs. Ramsay, in the passage with which I began. We now need to exam-ine this passage at length:

> Sitting on the floor with her arms round Mrs. Ramsay's knees, close as she could get, smiling to think that Mrs. Ramsay would never know the reason of that pressure, she imagined how in the chambers of the mind and heart of the woman who was, physically, touching her, were stood, like the treasures in the tombs of kings, tablets bearing sacred inscriptions, which if one could spell them out, would teach one everything, but they would never be offered openly, never made public. What art was there, known to love or cunning, by which one pressed through into those secret chambers? What device for be-coming, like waters poured into one jar, inextricably the same, one with the object one adored? Could the body achieve, or the mind, subtly mingling in the intricate passages of the brain? or the heart? Could loving, as people called it, make her and Mrs. Ramsay one? for it was not knowledge but unity that she desired, not inscriptions on tablets, nothing that could be written in any language known to men, but intimacy itself, which is knowledge, she had thought, leaning her head on Mrs. Ramsay's knee.
>
> Nothing happened. Nothing! Nothing! as she leant her head against Mrs. Ramsay's knee. And yet, she knew knowledge and wisdom were stored up in Mrs. Ramsay's heart. How then, she had asked herself, did one know one thing or another thing about people, sealed as they were? Only like a bee, drawn by some sweetness or sharpness in the air intangible to touch or taste, one haunted the dome-shaped hives, ranged the wastes of the air over the countries of the world alone, and then haunted the hives with their murmurs and their stirrings; the hives, which were people. (78–80)

Lily's attempt to know Mrs. Ramsay is, we notice, unilateral: It coexists with her own amused pride in her own self-concealment. This suggests that the project of knowing, as she conceives it, has itself something of the desire for power in it, is just as strategic as the desire to protect herself from knowing. I shall later return to that point.

Lily thinks of the project of knowing as, first, a kind of reading: We go (some-how) inside the room of the other mind and we read the sacred inscriptions that nobody else can see. But reading is not intimate enough, after all. It substitutes an internal object for an external object, but it does not really yield the grasp of what it is like to be that person, to have that person's thoughts and feelings. It is this, not just propositional book knowledge, that Lily desires. She now thinks of the possibility of becoming fused with the person one loves, "like waters poured into one jar, inextricably the same." She conceives of this possibility in a frankly sexual way—as a union to be achieved by either the body or the mind, "subtly mingling"—"loving, as people called it." In this way she alludes to the pervasive idea that sexual intercourse achieves not just intimate responsiveness but an actual oneness. She attempts, through the very intensity of her adoring thought, to achieve some simulacrum of this union. The attempt fails—she has no illusion that she has become closer to Mrs. Ramsay's mind than she was before. She then asks herself the question with which I began: Given that people cannot be entered and possessed, are, in fact, sealed hives, how in fact can we know one thing or another thing about them? Notice that she abandons the goal of complete fusion and also the goal of complete unmediated access to the "sacred tablets," and substitutes a more modest goal—knowing "one thing or another thing."

There is, I think, a progress here, both epistemological and moral. The goal of complete transparent access to the "sacred tablets" is not just unattainable, it is morally problematic because it asks that Mrs. Ramsay surrender her privacy and her boundedness before Lily's curious gaze. We note that Mrs. Ramsay is in fact most unwilling to give up her privacy, which she regards as a central constituent of her selfhood; we also recall that Lily herself wishes to be able to conceal her thoughts from Mrs. Ramsay, even while she dreams of removing from Mrs. Ramsay all possibility of concealment. The move from unmediated reading to fusion deepens the problem: For the wish to be fused with Mrs. Ramsay is not a wish to know her *as other, as Mrs. Ramsay*—as Lily quickly recognizes—it is a wish to incorporate her power, to be that powerful envied presence.[9] But, as Lily soon discovers,[10] having the other person's thoughts and feelings as oneself, in one's own body and mind, is neither necessary nor sufficient for knowledge of the other: Not sufficient, because that would precisely be not to know the *other*, the separateness and externality of that life, those feelings; not necessary because we can conceive of a knowledge that does not entail possession, that *acknowledges*, in fact, the impossibility of possession as a central fact about the lives of persons. That alternative remains to be discussed—and I think that Woolf in many respects anticipates Cavell's argument. But there appears to be wisdom in Lily's shift from the grandiose demand for possession to the modest demand to know "one thing or another thing" about those sealed hives that murmur and buzz as we hover greedily around them. At the very least, Lily's new question involves a more adequate conception of herself—as not a superhuman but a human being, finite in both body and mind, partial and incomplete, separate from other humans of necessity and always.

IV. Knowing and Reading

Woolf's image of the window suggests that people are not completely sealed to one another. There is an opening, one can see through or see in, even if one cannot enter. Part I of the novel ends with a knowledge claim: "She had not said it: yet he knew" (186). In not a trivial but a central matter—a wife's love—Mr. Ramsay is said by his wife to have knowledge. What is the basis for this claim? And to what extent does this case offer a solution to the problems of knowing raised elsewhere in the novel?

Very clearly, Mr. and Mrs. Ramsay do not gain knowledge by any kind of unity or mingling of experience, nor by any violation of one another's solitude and privacy. One of the distinctive features of their relationship is a cautious respect for that which the other wishes to conceal. Mrs. Ramsay senses a good deal about his academic insecurity and his sense of incomplete achievement. But she does not try to get at those insecurities or to show her knowledge of him by dragging them out into the open. Think what it would be for her to demand that he talk about his failures; suppose, in the scene we have examined, she had said to him, "Tell me what's really going on when you say, 'Poor little place'—you aren't worrying about the universe really, are you, you are worrying about your book." We see that such a claim to or demand for "knowledge" would be a way of belittling him and asserting ascendancy over him. She shows him respect and love by allowing him his concealment. She doesn't even try to grasp his failure sharply in her own mind—for it would be incompatible with her love to see him as a failure. We might even say that this respect for hiddenness, and this re-luctance to pry even in imagination, are Mrs. Ramsay's ways of knowing her husband's insecurities in the context of his life—of seeing their importance and their role, of behaving in a way that acknowledges their importance and their role. (Notice that this means that knowing is a very individual thing: In another relationship one might be aware that the person was longing to be "seen through," thrived on that particular kind of intimacy.)

On his side Mr. Ramsay, who is accustomed to burst in on the privacy of others, "bearing down" on Lily and the children, is very careful with his wife's solitude.

> He turned and saw her. Ah! She was lovely, lovelier now than ever he thought. But he could not speak to her. He could not interrupt her. He wanted urgently to speak to her now that James was gone and she was alone at last. But he resolved, no; he would not interrupt her. She was aloof from him now in her beauty, in her sadness. He would let her be, and he passed her without a word, though it hurt him that she should look so distant, and he could not reach her, he could do nothing to help her. (100)[11]

Mr. Ramsay knows his wife, we might say, in a way in which he knows no other character. What do we mean by this? We mean, I think, that he attends to her more fully as a person separate from himself existing in her own right, rather than as an instrument of consolation for himself. His knowledge of her separate being is expressed in, and perhaps also constituted by, such small episodes of noticing and respecting, of refusing to burst in on her. He puts her own mind at the center of the stage and subordinates, for once, the imperious demands of his own. All that may be at least part of what it is to know another mind as other.

Nor do Mr. and Mrs. Ramsay know one another by analogy, or by similar and parallel structures of experience. Of course at a very general level they do analogize—they interpret one another as human beings and as sharing with them certain goals and aims characteristic of human life as they know it. But analogy of that sort doesn't go very far, especially in the context of both idiosyncrasy and socially taught gender differences.[12] We know that they are very dissimi-lar, in thought patterns, in thought content, in patterns of emotional response, in goals and actions, in what they mean by their words. Part of what convinces us that they do have knowledge of one another is the fact that, in case after case, they allow for these differences, they refuse to analogize. He knows that she doesn't want comfort, even though with similar utterances that is exactly what he would be thinking about and wanting. She knows that he is more exhilarated than despairing when he says the words that to her would mean despair. This doesn't even mean that they can vividly imagine what it would be like to be the other person. Sometimes they can, and sometimes they can't. Mr. Ramsay cannot empathetically conceive of her depressed ruminations, though he can learn to respect them; Mrs. Ramsay thinks his mind is strangely different from her own, while recognizing that she cannot really quite imagine what it is like to be him:

> Was it not odd, she reflected? Indeed he seemed to her sometimes made differently from other people, born blind, deaf, and dumb, to the ordinary things, but to the extraordinary things, with an eye like an eagle's. His understanding often astonished her. But did he notice the flowers? No. Did he notice the view? No. Did he even notice his own daughter's beauty, or whether there was pudding on his plate or roast beef? He would sit at table with them like a person in a dream. . . . [T]hen, she thought, stooping down to look, a great mind like his must be different in every way from ours. (107–8)

Here we see that in one sense Mrs. Ramsay has only the most rudimentary knowledge of her husband's mind. She has no idea what he thinks about, nor has she any inclination for the sort of abstract thinking she associates with her vague notion of "the great mind." All she can say about it is what it leaves out, and she herself couldn't think in a way that leaves out those daily things.

How, then, do they know each other, insofar as they do? We might say, they know one another as we know them—by reading. Having lived together for a long time, they have gathered a lot of information about patterns of speech, action, reaction. Among other things, they have learned a lot—partly by making mistakes with one another—about the limits of analogizing, about relevant similarities and differences. They have gathered this information, furthermore, not in the manner of a detached scientist but in the course of interactions to which both ascribe enormous importance. They work hard to "read" the other, to fit the data into a meaningful and predictively accurate pattern, because each loves the other more than anyone else in the world, and it thus matters tremendously that they should get one another right, as far as possible. They spend a good part of their solitude thinking about each other, piecing together what they perceive and think, learning to read not just statements but also gestures, facial expressions, silences. Each learns the idiosyncratic text of the other in the way that one might learn a foreign language—never having a once-for-all guaranteed translation manual but holistically piecing it all together, trying to make the best sense, over time, of all the words and phrases.

The novel suggests that their love for and need of one another play an important role in making them good readers. Because of this love and need, they hover around one another, they allow signals from the other to pull them out of themselves. When Mr. Ramsay, chuckling at the story of Hume stuck in a bog (which comforts him, on account of its metaphorical relation to his intellectual predicament), notices the way she purses her lips while knitting, he quickly reads a good deal in the expression:

> . . . he could not help noting, as he passed, the sternness at the heart of her beauty. It saddened him, and her remoteness pained him, and he felt, as he passed, that he could not protect her, and, when he reached the hedge, he was

sad. He could do nothing to help her. He must stand by and watch her. Indeed, the infernal truth was, he made things worse for her. He was irritable—
he was touchy. He had lost his temper over the Lighthouse. He looked into
the hedge, into its intricacy, its darkness. (98–9)

Here love pulls him toward perceptions and reflections that elude him completely
in the case of other people. A simple facial expression is read in ways that pull
in data from years of knowledge of her sadness—so that he knows, as he passes,
not only what she is likely to be feeling but also what he can and cannot do to
help. And this leads him to a more accurate reading of himself, since to himself
he is a text just as difficult to read correctly as any other mind. Later, at the dinner party, with their focused intensity of mutual concern, the two are able to
carry on complicated conversations about the proceedings simply by small gestures and expressions:

> And why not? Mrs. Ramsay demanded. Surely they could let Augustus have
> his soup if he wanted it. He hated people wallowing in food, Mr. Ramsay
> frowned at her. He hated everything dragging on for hours like this. But he
> had controlled himself, Mr. Ramsay would have her observe, disgusting
> though the sight was. But why show it so plainly, Mrs. Ramsay demanded
> (they looked at each other down the long table sending these questions and
> answers across, each knowing exactly what the other felt). (144)

Once again, both long familiarity and an intensity of focus inspired by love
are at work to make their language vastly more efficient than the clumsy
"French" of social interaction. Because they have been in similar situations together and talked about them afterwards for many years, each caring what the
other feels, the smallest facial sign conveys a history. The theory of truth underlying the knowledge claim is a coherence theory, clearly—they each have no
independent unmediated access to the "sacred tablets," either in self or in the
other. But there is every reason to feel, here, that the demands of coherence have
been well met.

We now need to examine the scene with which "The Window" ends, as it
builds up to its final knowledge claim. Mrs. Ramsay watches her husband as he
reads a novel of Walter Scott. She reads the meaning of his expressions of pleasure and satisfaction—by combining what she knows of his reading habits with
what she knows of his anxieties about his own work, combined with the likely
effect of Charles Tansley's dismissal of Scott at dinner (177). She knows well
the persistence and centrality of his worries about whether his books will be read,
even though at the same time she doesn't quite know what it is like for him to
have those worries. ("It didn't matter, any of it, she thought. A great man, a
great book, fame—who could tell? She knew nothing about it" [177].) She then
thinks in a general way about his truthfulness and outspokenness. "If only he
would speak! She had complete trust in him" (178).

This is an important moment because it reminds us that none of the knowledge either has of the other is immune to skeptical doubt, based as it all is on
reading and interpretation. They get from coherence to knowledge not by any
extra step of grasping or possessing but simply by trusting, by waiving the skep-

tical questions that could arise even about such a complex and carefully sorted fabric of data. Trust, of course, is itself not blind; she trusts his truthfulness because her experience has shown her that he can be trusted. But experience never really shows this; it never really rules out a refined clever deception.[13] So in allowing her experience of him to have this meaning, to lead all the way to trust, Mrs. Ramsay does add to the evidence an extra ingredient—a willingness, we might say, to be at his disposal, to leave her life open to what he says and does.[14] Roused from her reverie by the sound of her husband slapping his thighs with pleasure, she knows that he is delighted by the fact that Scott's novel holds up and gives delight—and so perhaps his writings have some lasting life in them, and perhaps it does not even matter. "Their eyes met for a second; but they did not want to speak to each other. They had nothing to say, but something seemed, nevertheless, to go from him to her" (179).

As she reads a sonnet, she falls into a pleasant trance and feels the peace of a mind swept clean and clear (181). He looks at her, and she feels what he is thinking. The novel itself now shifts rapidly from one center of consciousness to the other, so that we can hardly tell who is having what thought, so rapidly and accurately do they communicate:

> But she was becoming conscious of her husband looking at her. He was smiling at her, quizzically, as if he were ridiculing her gently for being asleep in broad daylight, but at the same time he was thinking, Go on reading. You don't look sad now, he thought. And he wondered what she was reading, and exaggerated her ignorance, her simplicity, for he liked to think that she was not clever, not book-learned at all. He wondered if she understood what she was reading. Probably not, he thought. She was astonishingly beautiful. (182)

If in part the exaggeration of her ignorance is in his mind, it is also, equally, in hers—she knows how he sees her, and perhaps, too, he knows that he exaggerates. (In this odd way, knowledge can be present even when mistakes are clearly being made.) He knows that he finds her beautiful, but she also knows that he finds her beautiful. It is on that account that she puts down her book and responds to his smile. Mrs. Ramsay now mentions the engagement; she wants him to respond, so she tries a joke—"the sort of joke they had together" (183)—another reminder of their long habits of intimate communication.

Mrs. Ramsay now feels the shadow of sadness closing round her. She looks to him, as if to appeal for help, speaking silently. He thinks of Scott and of Balzac, and yet they are responding with ever closer responsiveness and knowledge:

> But through the crepuscular walls of their intimacy, for they were drawing together, involuntarily, coming side by side, quite close, she could feel his mind like a raised hand shadowing her mind. . . . (184)

The image of the shadowy wall shows us that barriers are never removed—but somehow the walls become more like shadow than like substance, and she can feel the action of his mind as if it stands between her and life, casting protection over her mind. He fidgets, thinking how little he likes her "pessimism." He says, in a sharp tone, "You won't finish that stocking tonight." The words are trivial, but they communicate far more. "That was what she wanted—the asperity in his voice reproving her. If he says it's wrong to be pessimistic probably it is wrong, she thought . . ." (184).

Here we are returned to our earlier point about words and actions—but with a difference. For earlier we observed that people use words to conceal vulnerability and to gain power over others. Here, too, the use of words is strategic, but the strategy is one of comfort. His asperity is protection.

Now she senses that his look has changed. "He wanted something—wanted the thing she always found it so difficult to give him; wanted her to tell him that she loved him" (184). She finds it difficult to put her emotions into words. She recognizes their mental difference here—for him verbal articulation of emotion is natural and easy; for her it is not. Instead, she looks for an action through which she can convey the meaning he wants: "Was there no crumb on his coat? Nothing she could do for him?" (185). She stands by the window with the stocking in her hand; he watches her, demanding an expression of love.

> Then, knowing that he was watching her, instead of saying anything she turned, holding her stocking, and looked at him. And as she looked at him she began to smile, for though she had not said a word, he knew, of course he knew, that she loved him. And smiling she looked out of the window and said (thinking to herself, Nothing on earth can equal this happiness)—
>
> "Yes, you were right. It's going to be wet tomorrow. You won't be able to go." And she looked at him smiling. For she had triumphed again. She had not said it: yet he knew. (185–6)

How is knowledge conveyed? The entire pattern of the marriage is the necessary background. A smile, a trivial sentence—all this would mean nothing without the years of intimacy and of daily life that lead up to the moment. In the moment, she conveys her love simply by turning to him and looking at him, only that. It is only after she feels the happiness of knowing that he knows that she says her indulgent words about the weather, healing the slight quarrel that had erupted in the morning. How does he know that she loves him? Only by his experience of her verbal reluctance, her beauty, her willingness to turn to him with her beauty. None of this is beyond skepticism, clearly; and Mr. Ramsay, demanding words, is at times not immune to skeptical doubt and the need for reassurance. But here doubts are put aside and trust, it would seem, enables him to move from interpretation to knowledge. They don't raise doubts not because all grounds for doubt have been extinguished but because that is the way they are, that is the way their marriage is. Skeptical doubt is an attitude, a way of relating, that is just not their way, at least in the context of this history of long intimacy and loyalty.

How far, then, have the problems of knowledge, as the novel presents them, been answered? As fine readers of one another's words, gestures, and actions, the Ramsays have clearly gotten beyond the crudeness of everyday speech as a medium of communication and have also come to a refined understanding of the differences in the personal meanings with which each invests words and gestures. They have not, however, found a magic remedy for the deeper problems with which the novel presents us: problems of shame, of power seeking, of the sheer need for hiddenness. They surmount these problems, to the extent that they do—and we feel that this is considerable, though not total—simply by making a continual patient effort to be a certain sort of person in relation to one another, to be willing to put aside shame or pride, to be willing to use the power of marriage generously rather than manipulatively, to be willing to allow their privacy to be qualified by the needs of another. If Mrs. Ramsay triumphs in conveying the knowledge of love, the triumph is one of yielding generosity—for she has allowed him to summon her out of herself. If Mr. Ramsay triumphs in extracting the much-desired communication, it is again a triumph made possible only by his being the sort of person who is ready to come to her aid. Knowledge, in short, is a function of character.

V. Reading and Loving

As readers of Woolf's novel, we may become aware that our own activity is analogous to that of the Ramsays. We read as the characters read one another, going over the presented features carefully and with emotionally rich attention, trying to develop an interpretation on the basis of both familiarity and concern. The role of novel reading is discussed in this very scene, so that we are invited to explore the parallel. Mr. Ramsay responds to the Scott novel as to a beloved and intimate friend. He allows it to delight him and in a sense he trusts it—he does not read it with detachment in the manner of a skeptical theorist of interpretation. We feel that he "knows" Walter Scott not only in virtue of his familiarity with the novels but also in virtue of the vigor, openness, and unsuspiciousness of his response. But in his love of his wife there are also features that novel reading lacks. There is an intense absorption with a particular being who is seen as necessary for one's own life; there is a willingness to be extremely vulnerable toward her, to put much of his life at risk; there is sexual desire; there is, finally, an intense desire to give protection and love to her.

All these features make personal love in some respects more problematic than novel reading. In the context of these deep needs and vulnerabilities there are ample opportunities for skepticism and jealousy to arise; there are many reasons why one inclined to such love might respond with shame-inspired concealment of self, or with projects of possession and incorporation. We don't really see what those possibilities would be in the case of our relation to the literary text. All this led Proust to hold that it was only in relation to the literary text and its author that we could really have knowledge of another mind. All our relations with real people in real life are marred by a possessiveness and jealous skepticism that are the more or less inevitable outgrowths of our sense of ourselves as needy and incomplete.[15] Proust is convinced that this response to our own weakness obscures any accurate perception of the other person, because we make ourselves the construct we need. It also prevents any sort of trust in the evidence with which the other person presents us. We never rule out the possibility that the whole fabric is an elaborate ruse concealing something altogether different. With the literary text, by contrast, we are intensely concerned but not personally at risk. The author is not going to hurt us, and in a sense we don't really need him. This alone permits us to have what amounts to knowledge of the mind of another living person.

Woolf's response to these points is not exactly epistemological; it is ethical. One can, of course, be the sort of person Proust describes. It is not difficult, in fact, to imagine the Ramsay marriage taking a turn in this direction—if, for example, she had come to feel that his whole relation to her was exploitatively patriarchal, that he underrated her capacity for autonomy, that he was using love and sex to bring about an unequal and unjust division of domestic labor. There is much truth in all these claims, and in some moods I feel she would have been right to focus on them and to be more skeptical of his love. Women frequently buy a kind of domestic harmony at the price of justice. Skepticism in circumstances of inequality is a rational response.

On the other hand, one has to grant that a relationship based on this sort of suspiciousness of the intentions of the other could not be a good marriage *and* would yield little of the interpretive knowledge they attain. And I also want to say that the relationship itself, whatever its deficiencies, has excellences—and the Ramsays, as parties to it, have excellences—that can and should be cultivated, whatever else we seek. If they are cultivated sufficiently, Proust's problem can be overcome. The marriage of the Ramsays has yielded a kind of understanding and trust that is admirable as an ethical norm even if we would prefer to see it realized in the context of greater justice—as indeed it could be, given different upbringing and different expectations on the part of the two partners.[16]

But this means that there simply are possibilities for generosity, for the defeat of shame and anxiety, that Proust has not acknowledged. To develop these possibilities would be the theoretical job of an ethics of character, the practical job of parents and teachers of children, and of friendships of many kinds.

It is no surprise that this account of Woolf's novel should end with broader ethical and social speculations. For it is the distinguished contribution of this novel to show how a problem that philosophy frequently cordons off from the messy stuff of human motivation and social interaction is actually a series of human problems of great complexity, many of them ethical and social, which cannot really be adequately described, much less resolved (where resolution is possible) without reflecting about emotions and desires, without describing a variety of possible human loves and friendships in their historical and social setting, without asking, among other things, how love, politics, power, shame, desire, and generosity are all intertwined in the attempt of a single woman and man to live together with understanding.

Wittgenstein saw, if Cavell is right, that the problem of other minds had to be investigated in some such way, as part of the history of our acknowledgement and avoidance of one another. But there is little concrete pursuit of that investigation in Wittgenstein, nothing to compare with the rich detail we find in Woolf. This, it would seem, is because the concrete pursuit of that particular philosophical investigation requires narrative depiction of individual lives and their interplay, and this was simply not a task in which Wittgenstein was engaged as a writer. (I leave to others the question whether the joy and generosity displayed in Woolf's narrative approach, and so important a part of her "solution," would have been compatible with his personal response to life.) A narrative approach to this set of problems is present in Proust, but in a form that denies the resourcefulness of human generosity and universalizes a primitive longing for comfort as all there really is to love, an obsessive peering at one's own mental constructs as all there is to knowing the loved one. Unlike Wittgenstein, Woolf depicts our searches for knowledge in something like their full human complexity and many-sidedness. Unlike Proust, she does so with an optimism about good character that makes the problem of skepticism a sometimes soluble ethical problem. The mysterious grand problem of other minds thus has, here, a mundane humble tentative answer or rather answers, whose meaning can only be fully grasped in the context of a narrative as complex as this novel: By working patiently to defeat shame, selfish anxiety, and the desire for power, it is sometimes possible for some people to get knowledge of one thing or another thing about some other people, and they can sometimes allow one thing or another thing about themselves to be known.

NOTES

Introduction

1. For Saleha's story, see Martha Chen, "A Matter of Survival: Women's Right to Employment in India and Bangladesh," in *Women, Culture, and Development* (hereafter WCD), ed. M. Nussbaum and J. Glover (Oxford: Clarendon Press, 1995), 37–57; see also Saleha Begum and Martin Greeley, "Rural Women and the Rural Labor Market in Bangladesh: An Empirical Analysis," draft paper prepared in Dhaka for I. D. S. Project (Brighton, UK), 1979.

2. India has no uniform code of civil law, nor are there any secular courts of family law. All family law is therefore handled by the religion of one's birth. See chapter 3 (in this volume).

3. *T. Sareetha v. T. Venkata Subbaiah*, A.I.R. (A.P.) 356 (1983) P.A. Choudary, J). See chapter 3 (in this volume).

4. *Steffan v. Cheney*, 780 F. Supp. 1 (1991); *Steffan v. Aspin*, 8 F.3d 57, 303 U.S. App. D.C. (1993); *Steffan v. Perry*, 41 F.3d 677, 309 U.S. App. D.C. (1994). See chapter 7 (in this volume) for a full discussion of the *Steffan* case.

5. *Romer v. Evans*, 116 S. Ct. 1620 1625, (1996).

6. Women on average live somewhat longer than men, although this is not the case in many parts of the world. See chapter 1 (in this volume). Thus the greatest life expectancy for any discrete group, according to the 1996 *Human Development Report* (United Nations Development Program) is that for women in Japan, 82.5 years. With respect to many other indicators of quality of life women do systematically worse than men. See chapter 1.

7. See John Rawls, *A Theory of Justice* (hereafter TJ) (Cambridge, MA: Harvard University Press, 1971), referring to Hume.

8. The Chinese women were skeptical about using the term "feminist" to describe themselves because they wondered, plausibly enough, whether it was appropriate to speak of feminism where there was no possibility of a free political women's movement.

9. On the complexity of "Asian values," see Amartya Sen, "Human Rights and Asian Values," *The New Republic* July 14/21, 1997, 33–40.

10. See, in a similar vein, Susan Moller Okin, *Justice, Gender, and the Family* (New York: Basic Books, 1989), chap. 8.

11. See chapter 5, with references to work by Amartya Sen, Jon Elster, and others on "adaptive preferences."

12. See chapter 10 for examples and further analysis.

13. Adam Smith, *The Theory of Moral Sentiments* (6th edition, 1790), ed. D. D. Raphael and A. L. Mackie (Indianapolis, IN: Liberty Press, 1979), esp. Part I.

14. TJ; and also J. Rawls, "Fairness to Goodness," *The Philosophical Review* 84 (1975), 536–54.

15. John Stuart Mill, *The Subjection of Women* (1869), ed. Susan M. Okin (Indianapolis, IN: Hackett, 1988).

16. On MacKinnon, see chapters 2, 5, 8, and 9.

17. Catharine MacKinnon, *Feminism Unmodified* (Cambridge, MA: Harvard University Press, 1987), 45.

18. This is not to say that women have always been well served by divorce, which has frequently worsened women's economic position, given the deficient recognition given to women's economic contribution to the family. See chapter 5.

19. On arguments by Sunstein, Law, and Koppelman, and their role in the Hawaii gay-marriage case, see chapter 7.

20. See Philip Blumstein and Pepper Schwartz, *American Couples* (New York: Morrow, 1983).

21. On these traditions, see Roop Rekha Verma, "Femininity, Equality, and Personhood," WCD 433–43.

22. For the full citation, see WCD, 61.

23. A typical, and influential, example is the contrast between "victim feminism" and "power feminism" in Naomi Wolf, *Fire With Fire: The New Female Power and How to Use It* (New York: Fawcett Columbine, 1993), 136–8.

24. Nietzsche, "Skirmishes of an Untimely One," *Twilight of the Idols*, section 38, trans. Kaufmann. He takes a similar view about women's education and about the relief of hunger—see Martha C. Nussbaum, "Is Nietzsche a Political Thinker?" *International Journal of Philosophical Studies* 5 (1997), 1–13.

25. Ibid.

26. See the excellent treatment of this point in Ronald Dworkin, "Liberty and Liberalism," in *Taking Rights Seriously* (Cambridge, MA: Harvard University Press, 1977), 259–65; Dworkin goes on to point out that this understanding of Mill's principle helps us understand why he sharply distinguished between intellectual liberty and economic liberty (Mill was a socialist). See also ibid., 240–58.

27. I discuss stereotypes in chapter 8; because I have made no study of the working conditions of actresses and models, I feel unable to adjudicate the debates about exploitation that arise in this area. For testimonies by women whose abusers acted out scenarios from pornography, see Andrea Dworkin, *Life and Death* (New York: The Free Press, 1997), discussed in chapter 9 (in this volume).

28. See Martha C. Nussbaum, "Kant and Stoic Cosmopolitanism," *The Journal of Political Philosophy* 5 (1997), 1–25, also in *Perpetual Peace*, ed. J. Bohmann and M. Lutz-Bachmann (Cambridge, MA: MIT Press, 1997), 25–58.

29. *Lectures on Ethics*, trans. Louis Infield (Indianapolis, IN: Hackett, 1963), 170; masturbation here is a species of a genus, "crimes of the flesh against nature" of which the other species are homosexual conduct and bestiality. Kant draws no moral distinction among these, and judges them all to be "contrary to natural instinct and to animal nature."

30. See the wonderful discussion in Anthony Price, *Love and Friendship in Plato and Aristotle* (Oxford: Clarendon Press, 1989).

Chapter 1

I have discussed the capabilities approach in several other papers, to which I shall refer: "Nature, Function, and Capability: Aristotle on Political Distribution," *Oxford Studies in Ancient Philosophy* Supplementary Volume 1 (1988), 145–84, hereafter NFC; "Aristotelian Social Democracy," in *Liberalism and the Good*, ed. R. B. Douglass et al. (New York: Routledge, 1990), 203–52, hereafter ASD; "Non-Relative Virtues: An Aristotelian Approach," in *The Quality of Life*, ed. M. Nussbaum and A. Sen (Oxford: Clarendon Press, 1993), hereafter NRV; "Aristotle on Human Nature and the Foundations of Ethics," in *World, Mind and Ethics: Essays on the Ethical Philosophy of Bernard Williams*, ed. J. E. J. Altham and Ross Harrison (Cambridge: Cambridge University Press, 1995), 86–131, hereafter HN; "Human Functioning and Social Justice: In Defense of Aristotelian Essentialism," *Political Theory* 20 (1992), 202–46, hereafter HF; "Human Capabilities, Female Human Beings," in *Women, Culture, and Development*, ed. M. Nussbaum and J. Glover (Oxford: Clarendon Press, 1995), 61–104, hereafter HC; "The Good as Discipline, the Good as Freedom," in *The Ethics of Consumption and Global Stewardship*, ed. D. Crocker and T. Linden (Lanham, MD: Rowman and Littlefield, 1998), 312–41, hereafter GDGF; "Capabilities and Human Rights," *Fordham Law Review* 66 (1997), 273–300, hereafter CHR.

1. For this case and others like it, see Martha Chen, "A Matter of Survival: Women's Right to Employment in India and Bangladesh," in *Women, Culture, and Development* (hereafter WCD), ed. M. Nussbaum and J. Glover (Oxford: Clarendon Press, 1995), 37–57. See also M. Chen, *The Lives of Widows in Rural India* (forthcoming).

2. *Bradwell v. Illinois*, 83 U.S. (16 Wall.) 130 (1873).

3. *Carr v. Allison Gas Turbine Division, General Motors Corp.*, 32 F.3d 1007 (1994). Mary Carr won her case on appeal.

4. Martha Chen, *A Quiet Revolution: Women in Transition in Rural Bangladesh* (Cambridge, MA: Schenkman, 1983), 176.

5. *Human Development Report* (New York: United Nations Development Program, 1996) (hereafter *Report*); see also the 1995 *Report*, which focuses on gender. The countries in which women do best in life quality, according to the Gender Development Index (GDI), a measure using the same variables as the HDI (Human Development Index) but adjusted according to disparities between the sexes (see *Report*, 107, for the technical formulation) are, in order, Sweden, Canada, Norway, the United States, Finland, Iceland, Denmark, France, Australia, New Zealand, the Netherlands, Japan, Austria, the United Kingdom, and Belgium.

6. If we subtract the GDI rank from the HDI rank, we get −10 for Spain, −9 for Japan, 8 for Sweden, 10 for Denmark, and 4 for New Zealand.

7. These variables include percentage shares of administrative and managerial positions, percentage shares of professional and technical jobs, and percentage shares of parliamentary seats.

8. The ranking at the top: Norway, Sweden, Denmark, Finland, New Zealand, Canada, Germany, the Netherlands, the United States, Austria, Barbados, and Switzerland. Spain ranks 25; Japan, 37; France, 40; and Greece, 60.

9. These data are from the 1993 report; later reports disaggregate employment data into jobs of various specific kinds and no longer count unpaid agricultural labor as employment.

10. Again, these are 1993 data; the 1996 report gives the absolute percentages, which are, for these examples, Sierra Leone, 16.7%; Afghanistan, 13.5%; Sudan, 32%; Nepal, 13%. Nations in which the female literacy rate is strikingly out of step with the general level of economic development include Saudi Arabia, 47.6%; Algeria, 45.8%; Egypt, 37.0%; Iraq, 42.3%; Pakistan, 23.0%; and India, 36.0%. Striking progress in female literacy, on the other hand, if one can rely on the figures, has been made in Cuba, 94.6%; Sri Lanka, 86.2%; Philippines, 93.9%; most of the former constituent states of the Soviet Union, in the 90s; Vietnam, 89.5%; and China, 70.9%. On the disparity of achievement between China and India, see Jean Drèze and Amartya Sen, *India: Economic Development and Social Opportunity* (Oxford: Clarendon Press, 1996).

11. Numbers of female students in tertiary education per 100,000 people: Hong Kong, 1,022; Barbados, 1,885; Republic of Korea, 2,866; Philippines, 3,140; Egypt, 499; China, 132; Iran, 764; Laos, 60; Pakistan, 149; Ethiopia, 24; and Rwanda, 19.

12. Countries where women hold a high percentage of parliamentary seats: Norway, 39.4%; Sweden, 40.4%; and Denmark, 33.0%. Bangladesh at 10.6% is ahead of the United States at 10.4%, and India at 8.0% is ahead of Japan at 6.7%.

13. The statistics in this paragraph are taken from Jean Drèze and Amartya Sen, *Hunger and Public Action* (Oxford: Clarendon Press, 1989).

14. This is very likely due to the central role women play in productive economic activity. For a classic study of this issue, see Esther Boserup, *Women's Role in Economic Development* (New York: St. Martin's Press, 1970), 2nd ed. (Aldershot: Gower Publishing, 1986). For a set of valuable responses to Boserup's work, see *Persistent Inequalities*, ed. Irene Tinker (New York: Oxford University Press, 1990).

15. See Drèze and Sen, 52.

16. See Drèze and Sen, *India*.

17. See Sen, "Gender and Cooperative Conflicts," in Tinker, 123–49.

18. See Drèze and Sen, *India*, for graphic evidence of the relative independence of educational and health attainment from economic growth, in comparative regional studies.

19. Gary Becker, *A Treatise on the Family* (Cambridge, MA: Harvard University Press, 1981; 2nd ed. 1991).

20. See Sen, "Gender and Cooperative Conflicts"; Partha Dasgupta, *An Inquiry Into Well-Being and Destitution* (Oxford: Clarendon Press, 1993), chap. 11; on food allocation, see Lincoln C. Chen, E. Huq, and S. D'Souza, "Sex Bias in the Family Allocation of Food and Health Care in Rural Bangladesh," *Population and Development Review* 7 (1981), 55–70. Bargaining models of the family are now proliferating; for two valuable recent examples, see Shelly Lundberg and Robert A. Pollak, "Bargaining and Distribution in Marriage," *Journal of Economic Perspectives* 10 (1996), 139–58, and S. Lundberg, R. Pollak, and T. J. Wales, "Do Husbands and Wives Pool Their Resources? Evidence from the U.K. Child Benefit," *Journal of Human Resources* (forthcoming).

21. See, now, Gary Becker, "The Economic Way of Looking at Behavior," the Nobel Address 1992, in *The Essence of Becker*, ed. Ramón Febrero and Pedro S. Schwartz (Stanford, CA: Hoover Institution Press, 1995), 647, on the role of childhood experiences in shaping preferences.

22. Sen, "Gender and Cooperative Conflicts," argues that Becker's account is much stronger as an account of actual preferences in the household than as an account of the real interests (life and death, good and bad health, good and bad nutrition) that underlie the preferences. (He provides evidence that people's perception of their health and nutritional status may be severely distorted by informational deficiencies.)

23. Becker now admits deficiencies in the model: "Many economists, including me, have excessively relied on altruism to tie together the interests of family members." Motives of "obligation, anger, and other attitudes usually neglected by theories of rational behavior" should be added to the models. Becker, "The Economic Way of Looking at Behavior," 648. Elsewhere, Becker mentions guilt, affection, and fear—his example being a woman's habitual fear of physical abuse from men. Ibid., 647. It is unclear whether he still supports an organic one-actor model, with a more complicated motivational structure, or a "bargaining model," of the sort increasingly used by family economists. See Becker, *A Treatise on the Family*.

24. See Sen, "Gender and Cooperative Conflicts"; Jon Elster, *Sour Grapes* (Cambridge: Cambridge University Press, 1993).

25. See John Rawls, *A Theory of Justice* (hereafter TJ) (Cambridge, MA: Harvard University Press, 1970); *Political Liberalism* (hereafter PL) (New York: Columbia University Press, 1993, paper ed. 1996).

26. The "capabilities approach" was pioneered within economics by Amartya Sen and has been developed by both Sen and me in complementary but not identical ways. For an overview, see David Crocker, "Functioning and Capability: the Foundations of Sen's and Nussbaum's Development Ethic," in WCD, 152–98.

27. See Amartya Sen, "Equality of What?," in *Choice, Welfare, and Measurement* (Oxford: Basil Blackwell, 1982), 353–72; and Nussbaum, ASD.

28. Much of the material described in these examples is now published in *Dominating Knowledge: Development, Culture, and Resistance*, ed. Frédérique Apffel Marglin and Stephen A. Marglin (Oxford: Clarendon Press, 1990). The issue of "embeddedness" and menstruation taboos is discussed in S. A. Marglin, "Losing Touch: The Cultural Conditions of Worker Accommodation and Resistance," 217–82, and related issues are discussed in S. A. Marglin, "Toward the Decolonization of the Mind," 1–28. On Sittala Devi, see F. A. Marglin, "Smallpox in Two Systems of Knowledge," 102–44; and for related arguments see Ashis Nandy and Shiv Visvanathan, "Modern Medicine and Its Non-Modern Critics," 144–84. I have in some cases combined two conversations into one; otherwise things happened as I describe them.

29. For Sen's own account of the plurality and internal diversity of Indian values, one that strongly emphasizes the presence of a rationalist and critical strand in Indian traditions, see M. Nussbaum and A. Sen, "Internal Criticism and Indian Relativist Traditions," in *Relativism: Interpretation and Confrontation*, ed. M. Krausz (Notre Dame: Notre Dame University Press, 1989), 299–325 (an essay originally presented at the same WIDER conference and refused publication by the Marglins in its proceedings); and A. Sen, "India and the West," *The New Republic* June 7, 1993. See also Bimal K. Matilal, *Perception* (Oxford: Clarendon Press, 1995) (a fundamental study of Indian traditions regarding knowledge and logic); and B. K. Matilal,

"Ethical Relativism and the Confrontation of Cultures," in Krausz, ed., *Relativism*, 339–62.

30. S. A. Marglin, "Toward the Decolonization," 22–3, suggests that binary thinking is peculiarly Western. But such oppositions are pervasive in Indian, Chinese, and African traditions (see HC). To deny them to a culture is condescending: for how can one utter a definite idea without bounding off one thing against another?

31. See Eric Hobsbawm and Terence Ranger, eds., *The Invention of Tradition* (Cambridge: Cambridge University Press, 1983). In his *New Republic* piece, Sen makes a similar argument about contemporary India: The Western construction of India as mystical and "other" serves the purposes of the fundamentalist Bharatiya Janata Party (BJP), who are busy refashioning history to serve the ends of their own political power. An eloquent critique of the whole notion of the "other" and of the associated "nativism,"where Africa is concerned, can be found in Kwame Anthony Appiah, *In My Father's House: Africa in the Philosophy of Cultures* (New York: Oxford University Press, 1991).

32. The proceedings of this conference are now published as M. Nussbaum and A. Sen, eds., *The Quality of Life* (Oxford: Clarendon Press, 1993).

33. Marglin has since published this point in "Toward the Decolonization." His reference is to Takeo Doi, *The Anatomy of Dependence* (Tokyo: Kodansha, 1971).

34. See S. A. Marglin, "Toward the Decolonization."

35. See Nussbaum and Sen, "Internal Criticism," and A. Sen, "Human Rights and Asian Values," *The New Republic*, July 10/17, 1997, 33–40.

36. See Roop Rekha Verma, "Femininity, Equality, and Personhood," in WCD.

37. Satyajit Ray, "Introduction," *Our Films, Their Films* (Bombay: Orient Longman, 1976, reprinted New York: Hyperion, 1994), 5.

38. Personal communication, scholars in women's studies at the Chinese Academy of Social Sciences, June 1995.

39. Note that this objection itself seems to rely on some universal values such as fairness and freedom from bias.

40. See HF for a longer version of this discussion.

41. Aristotle, *Nicomachean Ethics* VIII.I. I discuss this passage in HN and NRV.

42. "If my sisters and I were 'children of two worlds,' no one bothered to tell us this; we lived in one world, in two 'extended' families divided by several thousand miles and an allegedly insuperable cultural distance that never, so far as I can recall, puzzled or perplexed us much." Appiah, vii–viii. Appiah's argument does not neglect distinctive features of concrete histories; indeed, one of its purposes is to demonstrate how varied, when concretely seen, histories really are. But his argument, like mine, seeks a subtle balance between perception of the particular and recognition of the common.

43. This point is made by the Marglins, as well as by liberal thinkers, but can they consistently make it while holding that freedom of choice is just a parochial Western value? It would appear not; on the other hand, F. A. Marglin (here differing, I believe, from S. A. Marglin) also held in oral remarks delivered at the 1986 conference that logical consistency is simply a parochial Western value.

44. See Noam Chomsky, in *Cartesian Linguistics* (New York: Harper and Row, 1966). Chomsky argues that Cartesian rationalism, with its insistence on innate essences, was politically more progressive, more hostile to slavery and imperialism, than empiricism, with its insistence that people were just what experience had made of them.

45. The use of this term does not imply that the functions all involve doing something especially "active." See here A. Sen, "Capability and Well-Being," in *The*

Quality of Life, ed. M. Nussbaum and A. Sen (Oxford: Clarendon Press, 1993), 30–53. In Aristotelian terms, and in mine, being healthy, reflecting, and being pleased are all "activities."

46. For further discussion of this point, and for examples, see HN.

47. Could one cease to be one's individual self without ceasing to be human? Perhaps, in cases of profound personality or memory change, but I shall leave such cases to one side here. This is ruled out, I think, in Aristotle's conception but is possible in some other metaphysical conceptions.

48. See HN for a more extended account of this procedure and how it justifies.

49. Nor does it deny that experience of the body is shaped by culture. See NRV.

50. Rawls, TJ, 90–95, 396–7.

51. This was implicit in ASD but has become more prominent in recent essays. See A. Sen, "Freedoms and Needs," *New Republic*, January 10/17, 1994, 31–38; Nussbaum GDGF.

52. In ASD I call it "the thick vague theory of the good."

53. Rawls, PL. Note that the consensus is defined in terms of a normative notion of reasonableness. Thus, the failure of some real individuals to agree will not be fatal to the view.

54. On this relationship, see HN.

55. The current version of this list reflects changes suggested to me by discussions during my visits to women's development projects in India. These include a new emphasis on bodily integrity, on employment, on property rights, and on dignity and nonhumiliation.

56. Although "normal length" is clearly relative to current human possibilities and may need, for practical purposes, to be to some extent relativized to local conditions, it seems important to think of it—at least at a given time in history—in universal and comparative terms, as the *Human Development Report* does, to give rise to complaint in a country that has done well with some indicators of life quality but badly on life expectancy. And although some degree of relativity may be put down to the differential genetic possibilities of different groups (the "missing women" statistics, for example, allow that on the average women live somewhat longer than men), it is also important not to conclude prematurely that inequalities between groups—for example, the growing inequalities in life expectancy between blacks and whites in the United States—are simply genetic variation, not connected with social injustice.

57. The precise specification of these health rights is not easy, but the work currently being done on them in drafting new constitutions in South Africa and Eastern Europe gives reasons for hope that the combination of a general specification of such a right with a tradition of judicial interpretation will yield something practicable. It should be noticed that I speak of health, not just health care; and health itself interacts in complex ways with housing, with education, with dignity. Both health and nutrition are controversial as to whether the relevant level should be specified universally, or relatively to the local community and its traditions. For example, is low height associated with nutritional practices to be thought of as "stunting" or as felicitous adaptation to circumstances of scarcity? For an excellent summary of this debate, see S. R. Osmani, ed., *Nutrition and Poverty* (Oxford: Clarendon Press, WIDER series, 1990), especially the following papers: on the relativist side, T. N. Srinivasan, "Undernutrition: Concepts, Measurements, and Policy Implications," 97–120; on the universalist side, C. Gopalan, "Undernutrition: Measurement and Implications," 17–48; for a compelling adjudication of the debate, coming out

on the universalist side, see Osmani, "On Some Controversies in the Measurement of Undernutrition," 121–61.

58. There is a growing literature on the importance of shelter for health; for example, that the provision of adequate housing is the single largest determinant of health status for HIV-infected persons. Housing rights are increasingly coming to be constitutionalized, at least in a negative form—giving squatters grounds for appeal, for example, against a landlord who would bulldoze their shanties. On this as a constitutional right, see proposed Articles 11, 12, and 17 of the South African Constitution, in a draft put forward by the African National Congress (ANC) committee adviser Albie Sachs, where this is given as an example of a justiciable housing right.

59. Some form of intimate family love is central to child development, but this need not be the traditional Western nuclear family. In the development of citizens it is crucial that the family be an institution characterized by justice as well as love. See Susan Moller Okin, *Justice, Gender, and the Family* (New York: Basic Books, 1989).

60. In terms of cross-cultural discussion, this item has proven the most controversial and elusive on the list. It also properly raises the question whether the list ought to be anthropocentric at all, or whether we should seek to promote appropriate capabilities for all living things. I leave further argument on these questions for another occasion.

61. ASD argues that property rights are distinct from, for example, speech rights, in the sense that property is a tool of human functioning and not an end in itself. See also Nussbaum, CHR.

62. Sen has not endorsed any such specific list of the capabilities.

63. See Sen, "Gender Inequality and Theories of Justice," in WCD, 259–73; Becker, "The Economic Way of Looking at Behavior."

64. With Sen, I hold that the capability set should be treated as an interlocking whole. For my comments on his arguments, see NFC.

65. See ibid., with reference to Aristotle.

66. See HN. This is the core of Marx's reading of Aristotle.

67. See chapter 4.

68. See NFC, referring to Aristotle's similar distinctions.

69. This distinction is related to Rawls's distinction between social and natural primary goods. Whereas he holds that only the social primary goods should be on the list, and not the natural (such as health, imagination), we say that *the social basis of* the natural primary goods should most emphatically be on the list.

70. TJ, 62.

71. Rawls comments that "although their possession is influenced by the basic structure, they are not so directly under its control." TJ, 62. This is of course true if we are thinking of health, but if we think of the social basis of health, it is not true. It seems to me that the case for putting these items on the political list is just as strong as the case for the social basis of self-respect. In "The Priority of Right and Ideas of the Good," *Philosophy and Public Affairs* 17 (1988), 251–76, Rawls suggests putting health on the list.

72. See ASD and GDGF.

73. See HN. For the relation of capabilities to human rights, see CHR.

74. Sen, "Freedoms and Needs," 38.

75. PL 187–8.

76. Though in one form Aristotle had it too. See also GDGF; and CHR.

77. Compare Sen, "Freedoms and Needs," 38: "The importance of political rights for the understanding of economic needs turns ultimately on seeing human beings as people with rights to exercise, not as parts of a 'stock' or a 'population' that passively exists and must be looked after. What matters, finally, is how we see each other."

78. Chapter 3 (in this volume) argues that religious norms should not be imposed without choice on individuals who may not have opted for that religious tradition. In that sense, any religiously based employment restriction is questionable.

79. Chen, *The Lives of Widows in Rural India*. Girls in some regions of India are betrothed at a very young age and at that point become members of their husband's family, although the marriage will not be consummated until puberty. Such a girl is treated as widowed even if the male dies before consummation.

80. Chen, *A Quiet Revolution*.

81. Ibid.

82. Ibid., 202. Married at age seven, abandoned by her husband many years later, Rohima lives with her brother. Four of her children have died; one son and one daughter survive. Her son gives her some financial support.

83. See the account of these in Chen, *The Lives of Widows*.

84. Chen, *A Quiet Revolution*, 216.

85. Sen has stressed this throughout his writing on the topic. For an overview, see "Capability and Well-Being." And for some complications, see GDGF.

86. This is the strategy used by Robert Erikson's Swedish team when studying inequalities in political participation. See Robert Erikson, "Descriptions of Inequality," in Nussbaum and Sen, eds., *The Quality of Life*.

87. Rawls proceeds in a similar way, insisting that satisfactions that are not the outgrowth of one's very own choices have no moral worth. He conceives of the "two moral powers" (analogous to our practical reasoning) and of sociability (corresponding to our affiliation) as built into the definition of the parties in the original position, and thus as necessary constraints on any outcome they will select. See ASD.

88. Chen, *A Quiet Revolution*, 199.

89. The remark was cited by Richard Rorty in "Feminism and Pragmatism," *Michigan Quarterly Review* 30 (1989), 263; it has since been confirmed and repeated by MacKinnon herself.

90. Plato, *Republic*, Book V. Although Plato's proposal is theoretical and utopian, it is closely based on observation of the functioning of women in Sparta. See S. Halliwell, *Plato: Republic V* (Warminster: Aris & Phillips, 1994).

91. See Sen, "Gender and Cooperative Conflicts."

92. On Rousseau, see Susan Moller Okin, *Women in Western Political Thought* (Princeton: Princeton University Press, 1979), and Jane Roland Martin, *Reclaiming a Conversation* (New Haven: Yale University Press, 1985). On some related recent arguments, for example, those of Allan Bloom, see Okin, *Justice*, chap. l.

93. See the convincing summary in Anne Fausto-Sterling, *Myths of Gender*, 2nd ed. (New York: Basic Books, 1992).

94. Ibid.

95. John Stuart Mill, *The Subjection of Women* (1869), ed. Susan Moller Okin (Indianapolis, IN: Hackett, 1988).

96. Here I am in agreement with the general line of argument in Okin, *Women*, and Martin, *Reclaiming*, and with the related arguments in Nancy Chodorow, *The Reproduction of Mothering* (Berkeley: University of California Press, 1978).

97. Jean-Jacques Rousseau, *Emile: or On Education*, trans. Allan Bloom (New York: Basic Books, 1979), Book V.

98. See Okin, *Women*; and Martin, *Reclaiming*.

99. See the discussion in Okin, *Women*.

Chapter 2

1. Roop Rekha Verma, "Femininity, Equality, and Personhood," in *Women, Culture, and Development* (hereafter WCD), ed. M. Nussbaum and J. Glover (Oxford: Clarendon Press, 1995), 433–43.

2. Nahid Toubia, "Female Genital Mutilation," in *Women's Rights, Human Rights* (hereafter WRHR), ed. Julie Peters and Andrea Wolper (New York and London: Routledge, 1995), 224–37, at 235, reprinted from Toubia, *Female Genital Mutilation: A Call for Global Action* (New York: Women, Ink., 1993).

3. *The Hindu*, April 24, 1994.

4. Alison Jaggar, *Feminist Politics and Human Nature* (Totowa, NJ: Rowman and Allanheld, 1983, repr. 1988), 47–8. For related views, see also Carole Pateman, *The Problem of Political Obligation: A Critique of Liberal Theory* (Berkeley: University of California Press, 1979); Nancy C. M. Hartsock, *Money, Sex, and Power* (Boston: Northeastern University Press, 1983). An interesting response to some of the criticisms is found in Marilyn Friedman, "Feminism and Modern Friendship," *Ethics* 99 (1989), 304–19.

5. Among many treatments of these topics, see discussion of the issues in Amartya Sen, "Human Rights and Asian Values," *The New Republic*, July 10/17, 1997, 33–40. See also the exchange between Albie Sachs and Roberto Unger in *Economic and Social Rights and the Right to Health*, Harvard Law School Human Rights Program (Cambridge, MA, 1993), 12–14.

6. Rousseau is, of course, in crucial ways not a liberal, but I shall be referring to those portions of his thought that influenced portions of the liberal tradition.

7. Of course, this power needs development, but the basis for human equality is the possession of the potentiality for that development. Even if individuals possess differing degrees of this basic potentiality, we can say that a sufficient condition for equal moral personality is the possession of a certain basic minimum. See "The Basis of Equality," sec. 77 in John Rawls, *A Theory of Justice* (hereafter TJ) (Cambridge, MA: Harvard University Press, 1970), 504–12; and also the discussion of "basic capabilities," in Martha C. Nussbaum, "Human Capabilities, Female Human Beings," in WCD. This was also the view of the ancient Stoics.

8. See M. Nussbaum, "Kant and Stoic Cosmopolitanism," *The Journal of Political Philosophy* 5 (1997), 1–25. See also Julia Annas, *The Morality of Happiness* (New York: Oxford University Press, 1993).

9. This characterization of the essence of the liberal tradition differs sharply from that given in Ronald Dworkin, "Liberalism," in *A Matter of Principle* (Cambridge, MA: Harvard University Press, 1985), 181–204. Dworkin makes neutrality about conceptions of the good the basic core of liberalism rather than any more positive ideal. I would hold that to the extent that liberals are neutral about the good, this neutrality is explained by the basic intuition about the worth of choice and the respect for the choice-making capacities of the person. Rawls, for example, seems to me to have a far deeper account of the core of liberalism when he begins from an idea of "free and equal moral persons" and derives a measure of neutrality about the good from that idea. See particularly *Kantian Constructivism and Moral Theory: The Dewey Lectures 1980*, Lecture I: "Rational and Full Autonomy," *The Journal*

of Philosophy 77 (1980), 515–72, and "The Priority of Right and Ideas of the Good," *Philosophy and Public Affairs* 17 (1988), 251–76.

10. This idea is central in both the Kantian and the Utilitarian traditions. See the extensive discussion in TJ, 11–16, 118–30, etc. For its relation to U.S. constitutional law, see Cass R. Sunstein, *The Partial Constitution* (Cambridge, MA: Harvard University Press, 1993).

11. Some libertarian offshoots of liberalism might be charged with having lost that central idea insofar as they validate existing distributions that have morally irrelevant origins. Some liberals will claim that personal talents and capacities other than the moral faculties ought to be counted as part of the core of the person and, thus, insofar as they confer advantage, as not morally irrelevant; this is one source of the gulf between Nozick and Rawls. But some libertarian arguments also validate existing hierarchies of wealth and class; unless they do so by deriving those advantages from the moral rights of persons (as Nozick tries to do), they are by my account illiberal. For a judicious analysis of Nozick's relationship to two strands of the liberal tradition, see Barbara Fried, "Wilt Chamberlain Revisited: Nozick's 'Justice in Transfer' and the Problem of Market-Based Distribution," *Philosophy and Public Affairs* 24 (1995), 226–45.

12. Thus there is room for doubt whether classical utilitarianism is not, in the end, illiberal in the sense that it treats the desires of all persons as fusable into a single system and ignores the salience of the separateness of persons. This is the primary criticism of utilitarianism developed in the Kantian tradition. See, for example, TJ, 183–92, 554–9.

13. For some of the opponents, see Stephen Holmes, *The Anatomy of Antiliberalism* (Cambridge, MA: Harvard University Press, 1993).

14. TJ; Nozick, *Anarchy, State, and Utopia* (Oxford: Basil Blackwell, 1974). Both understand themselves to be heirs and rival interpreters of the liberal tradition; in characterizing their difference this way I am not saying anything particularly new or surprising. On this point, see the clear account by Ronald Dworkin in *Men of Ideas*, ed. B. Magee (New York, 1978). Nozick is clear that his own validation of existing differences of wealth and class depends on an argument from basic rights of self-ownership and just transfer, and that inequalities that cannot be so justified are unacceptable. His deepest difference from Kantian liberalism is his unargued assumption that features of persons other than the basis of their moral powers have moral weight and relevance: features such as talent in sports, physical strength, cleverness, etc.

15. On this distinction, see Henry S. Richardson, *Practical Reasoning About Final Ends* (New York: Cambridge University Press, 1994), 69–86, 209–27.

16. Even in this area, liberals will differ. Thus, for example, in the area of legal regulation of speech, Cass Sunstein's view holds that political speech is the central type that government needs to protect in protecting respect for persons; Joshua Cohen argues, in contrast, that artistic speech is also worthy of protection as embodying expressive capacities that are central to personhood. See Cass Sunstein, *Democracy and the Problem of Free Speech* (New York: The Free Press, 1993); Joshua Cohen, "Freedom of Expression," *Philosophy and Public Affairs* 22 (1993), pp. 207–63. Once again, we see here differences not only about strategies to achieve equal respect but, as well, about the more concrete specification of the notions involved, such as personhood and autonomy. On specification, with respect to liberal politics, see Richardson, *Practical Reasoning*, 209–27, esp. 218–27.

A note on U.S. politics: In terms of my discussion here, all major positions represented on the U.S. political scene are to at least some degree liberal positions insofar as they defend the Constitution. The strongest inclinations to antiliberalism can be seen in conservative and communitarian politics, though even these forces are held in check by the Bill of Rights. (Thus, in a recent documentary program on Plato's *Republic* made for the Discovery Channel, William Bennett said that Plato had some very good ideas about the promotion of virtue and the control of art—but then immediately said that of course we think that Plato went too far!) Economic libertarians and their opponents (often called "liberals") are, in terms of my argument, rival heirs of the liberal tradition, who differ about how equal respect and liberty should be embodied in laws and institutions. Things are confused by the fact that the Republican Party houses both libertarians and antiliberals. The Democratic Party used to contain many socialist antiliberals and still contains numerous communitarian critics of liberalism.

17. Jaggar, see above n. 4.

18. This would seem to be the meaning of the claim that "the egoistic model of human nature" is unable to admit "the values of community." Ibid., 45.

19. Jaggar appears to grant this in the case of Rawls (31), but she insists, nonetheless, that the psychological egoism inherent in liberal theory has left its deforming marks on Rawls's normative theory.

20. Amartya Sen, "Rational Fools: A Critique of the Behavioural Foundations of Economic Theory," in *Choice, Welfare, and Measurement* (Oxford: Basil Blackwell, 1982), 84–108, discussed in Jaggar, 45.

21. See Jaggar, 31.

22. Although one probably should not count Hobbes as a part of the liberal tradition.

23. Nor is it correct to think that the liberal conception of "happiness" is simply identical to the satisfaction of self-interested desire; there would appear to be no major liberal theorist, with the possible exception of Bentham, of whom that is unqualifiedly true, and in the Kantian tradition there is no tendency at all in this direction.

24. On these arguments, see Martha C. Nussbaum, *The Therapy of Desire: Theory and Practice in Hellenistic Ethics* (Princeton, NJ: Princeton University Press, 1994), especially chaps. 11–13.

25. Personal communication, Ela Bhatt, March 1997 on a visit to SEWA in Ahmedabad. For a history of the SEWA movement, see Kalima Rose, *Where Women Are Leaders: The SEWA Movement in India* (New Delhi: Vistaar, 1992).

26. See Mill, *On Liberty*, arguing that it is crucial to overcome people's lack of interest in the world and get them engaged in life.

27. We may remark that ancient proponents of self-sufficiency favored masturbation as a way of minimizing dependency on others—see Diogenes Laertius's *Life* of Diogenes the Cynic. No modern liberal thinker follows this view.

28. In these remarks about Buddhism I am much indebted to conversation with Paul Griffiths.

29. Thus I find quite puzzling Jaggar's claim that liberalism rejects human embodiment (31, 40–2). One might, of course, have a metaphysic of separate substances without making embodiment central to it, but then it would be difficult to explain why liberalism would devote so much attention to the feeding of those substances.

30. Putting things in terms of happiness and misery should not be taken to suggest either that liberalism is not critical of existing preferences and desires or that the liberal emphasis on separateness requires Pareto optimality for all policies. It

might well be that we will allow a larger amount of happiness for Q to compensate for a larger amount of misery for X if we judge that X's self-generated taste for luxury and power is at the root of his misery.

31. For statistics, see chapter 1.

32. See chapters 3, 4, and 5.

33. J. S. Mill, *The Subjection of Women*, ed. S. M. Okin (Indianapolis, IN: Hackett, 1988), 33.

34. Mill's reference to *Uncle Tom's Cabin* in this passage makes it clear that he is thinking about America, yet he appears to be ignorant of the sexual situation of American slaves.

35. Mill, *Subjection*, 33–4. Mill here discusses the Infant Custody Act of 1839, which allowed the Court of Chancery to award mothers custody of children under the age of seven and access to those under the age of sixteen; this small beginning shows graphically how bad the legal situation of mothers was previously.

36. Ibid., 86–8. Compare *Considerations on Republican Government*, where Mill observes that a man who takes no pleasure in his wife's pleasure is "stunted." Similar claims are made by Verma. In the context of contemporary India: Verma argues that in this sense, feminism is "the struggle for the liberation of humanity as a whole" (44).

37. See TJ, 128–29. The focus here is on intergenerational justice, and the issue of distribution to the current members of the household is not raised. Rawls states that in a "broader inquiry" the institution of the family "might be questioned, and other arrangements might indeed prove to be preferable" (463).

38. See chapter 1 (in this volume).

39. See Susan Moller Okin, *Women in Western Political Thought* (Princeton, NJ: Princeton University Press, 1979), 282, on the way in which Mill's proposals showed the limitations of previous liberal individualism.

40. See Amartya Sen, "Gender and Cooperative Conflicts," in *Persistent Inequalities*, ed. I. Tinker (New York: Oxford University Press, 1990), 123–49.

41. For one impressive critique of the U.S. tax system's inequities toward women, and a proposal for reform, see Edward McCaffery, *Taxing Women* (Chicago: University of Chicago Press, 1997). McCaffery is a political liberal in the Rawlsian tradition. See, for example, "The Political Liberal Case Against the Estate Tax," *Philosophy and Public Affairs* 23 (1994), 281–312.

42. TJ, 7.

43. Okin, *Justice*, 97. She does not, however, address the issue that is really central to Rawls in the context, namely, the question whether the parties would represent continuing transgenerational lines or simply themselves. See TJ 146, 284–93.

44. Okin, *Justice*, chap. 8. The proposal to make the basic structure of society nongendered does not, of course, imply that gender might not continue to play a role in the private lives of individuals, much in the way that ethnicity or culture could play a role. Among concrete issues, Okin is particularly concerned with the situation of women in the event of divorce; she urges that women who have done housework to facilitate a spouse's career development should be entitled to a substantial share of his income.

45. J. Rawls in "The Idea of Public Reason Revisited," *University of Chicago Law Review* 64 (1997), 765–807. Rawls says that it was always his intention that the parties in the original position do not know the sex of those they represent; he says that distinctions of sex are like distinctions of race and culture: they are based on "fixed natural characteristics" and they often influence people's life chances from

the very start (TJ, 99). It should be clear, he says, that the Veil of Ignorance is designed to ensure the parties' ignorance of all features that have this character. Sex (unlike gender, which is a social and institutional category) is a position in the distribution of natural endowments and abilities. See also "Fairness to Goodness," *Philosophical Review* 84 (1975), 537, where Rawls states that the parties do not know their sex. He also states in TJ and reaffirms in "Public Reason" that the family is certainly a part of the basic structure of society, to be constrained by the principles of justice. These will ensure that women who, for religious or other reasons, wish to choose a traditional role are free to do so; nonetheless, political principles impose constraints on the family as an institution to guarantee the basic rights, liberties, and fair opportunities of all its members. There remains a difference between Rawls and Okin, in that Okin holds, it seems, that the internal workings of the family should be governed by principles of justice, whereas Rawls envisages the principles of justice operating as external constraints on what families may choose but not as governing its internal workings. Where adult women are concerned, the difference may not be great. Rawls agrees with Okin, for example, that equal citizenship for women requires compensation, in the event of divorce, for investments a woman has made in the marriage and also public attention to child care ("Public Reason," 793). Differences are likely to be greater in the requirements concerning children, though, because Rawls has not addressed the specifics of this issue, the extent of the difference remains unknown. I discuss Rawls's view of the family at length in *Feminist Internationalism*, the 1998 Seeley Lectures in Political Theory (Cambridge: Cambridge University Press, forthcoming).

46. See chapter 1 (in this volume).

47. For some representative examples, see Sen, "Gender and Cooperative Conflicts"; Bina Agarwal, *A Field of One's Own: Gender and Land Rights in South Asia* (hereafter *A Field*) (Cambridge: Cambridge University Press, 1994); "'Bargaining' and Gender Relations: Within and Beyond the Household" (hereafter "Bargaining"), *Feminist Economics* 3 (1997), 1–51, and Shelly Lundberg and Robert A. Pollak, "Bargaining and Distribution in Marriage," *Journal of Economic Perspectives* 10 (1996), 139–58.

48. Charlotte Bunch, "Women's Rights as Human Rights: Toward a Re-Vision of Human Rights," *Human Rights Quarterly* 12, 486–98; see also Bunch, "Transforming Human Rights from a Feminist Perspective," in WRHR, 11–17, and Elisabeth Friedman, "Women's Human Rights: The Emergence of a Movement," in WRHR 18–35.

49. See chapter 3 (in this volume), for some examples.

50. See Agarwal, *A Field*; and "Bargaining."

51. Mill notes that when a opinion is grounded in reason, a good counterargument will shake its solidity; when it is grounded in irrational desires and fears, good counterarguments merely intensify the resistance: "The worse it fares in argumentative contest, the more persuaded its adherents are that their feeling must have some deeper ground, which the arguments do not reach; and while the feeling remains, it is always throwing up fresh intrenchments of argument to repair any breach made in the old" (1–2).

52. See Catharine MacKinnon, *Toward a Feminist Theory of the State* (Cambridge, MA: Harvard University Press, 1989), 40–47; "Reflections on Sex Equality Under Law," *Yale Law Journal* 100 (1991), 1281–1328; Jaggar, *Feminist Politics*, 181–85 (noting that liberal feminists have been gradually led to abandon the excessively formal approach).

53. "Toward Neutral Principles of Constitutional Law," *Harvard Law Review* 73 (1959). I discuss Wechsler's argument in detail in *Poetic Justice: The Literary Imagination and Public Life* (hereafter *Poetic Justice*) (Boston: Beacon Press, 1996), chap. 4.

54. See ibid.

55. To some extent, these criticisms are probably inspired by the similar criticism of liberalism made by Marx, for example, in *Critique of the Gotha Program*, where Marx argues that the liberal idea of "equal rights" is "constantly stigmatised by a bourgeois limitation," namely, the neglect of the antecedent role of differences of class and wealth in affecting the productivity of individuals. "It is, therefore, a right of inequality, in its content, like every right. . . . To avoid all these defects, right instead of being equal would have to be unequal." MacKinnon's critique in *Toward a Feminist Theory* is explicitly inspired by the Marxian critique.

56. This would include Gary Becker, who has repeatedly argued for government support for female literacy in connection with global population control.

57. This is not to deny that individual liberal thinkers have made such commitments; and here the libertarian tradition could justly be suspected of having departed from the main line of the liberal tradition, with its strong emphasis on the critique of hierarchies and of the social ascendancy of morally irrelevant distinctions.

58. This is brought out by Amartya Sen, "Freedoms and Needs," *The New Republic*, January 10/17, 1994, and by Martha C. Nussbaum, "The Good as Discipline, the Good as Freedom," in *The Ethics of Consumption and Global Stewardship*, ed. D. Crocker (Lanham, MD: Rowman and Littlefield, 1998), 312–41; also "Capabilities and Human Rights," *Fordham Law Review* 66 (1997), 273–300.

59. See TJ, 83–9, 203–4.

60. *T. Sareetha v. T. Venkata Subbaiah*, AIR 1983 Andhra Pradesh 356.

61. The case was argued primarily as a privacy case, but there was a subsidiary argument that the Hindu Marriage Act violates equal protection.

62. Not all—see the discussion of Sommers in chapter 5 (in this volume).

63. See the discussion of this second criticism in Onora O'Neill, "Justice, Gender, and International Boundaries," in *The Quality of Life*, ed. M. Nussbaum and A. Sen (Oxford: Clarendon Press, 1993), 279–323. The feminists criticized by O'Neill include Carol Gilligan, Eva Kittay, Genevieve Lloyd, Sara Ruddick, and Nel Noddings.

64. This point was well made by Marx in *On the Jewish Question*, where—responding to Bauer's contention that a person could not qua Jew acquire "the rights of man"—he replies that "the incompatibility between religion and the rights of man is so little manifest in the concept of the rights of man that the *right to be religious*, in one's own fashion, and to practise one's own particular religion, is expressly included among the rights of man. The privilege of faith is a *universal right of man*." Unfortunately, Marx (apparently neglecting this insight) goes on to claim that the "rights of man" treat the individual as purely self-centered, "separated from the community, withdrawn into himself, wholly preoccupied with his private interest and acting in accordance with his private caprice." This mistaken claim has probably influenced some feminist critiques.

65. Or, in the case of Rawls, to talents and propensities not integrally bound up with basic rational humanity.

66. These cases are all different. With gender and frequently with race, it is impossible to disregard the identification altogether, because it is imposed by society; some religious identities (e.g., being Jewish) have this aspect as well as a voluntary

aspect. Some (e.g., biological sex and probably sexual orientation) have a biological basis, and some (e.g., race) have none. Nonetheless, in all cases we can say that individuals do have latitude as to how far the identity will be central to their life projects.

67. See, for example, TJ, 207: "To gamble in this way [viz., by allowing the public realm to restrict the liberty of conscience] would show that one did not take one's religious or moral convictions seriously, or highly value the liberty to examine one's beliefs."

68. For a mordant account of those traditions in their relation to feminism, see Verma, in WCD.

69. We should also note that all these traditions view women under some type of universal category and thus cannot attack liberalism simply for its use of an abstract universal. Maistre ridiculed liberalism by saying that "there is no such thing as man in the world. I have seen, during my life, Frenchmen, Italians, Russians, etc. . . . But as far as man is concerned, I declare that I have never in my life met him; if he exists, he is unknown to me" (cited in Holmes, The Anatomy of Antiliberalism, 14). Notice, however, that Maistre is perfectly happy to use high-level abstractions such as "Frenchman," which is, one could argue, far less likely than is "human being" to reveal a set of common features similar across all cases. Compare Catharine MacKinnon, "From Practice to Theory, or What Is a White Woman Anyway?," Yale Journal of Law and Feminism 4 (1991), 13–22, who criticizes antiessentialist feminists for using race and class as legitimate categories while refusing the same legitimacy to gender.

MacKinnon's own degree of "essentialism" about the situation of women has come under sharp attack from communitarian and postmodernist feminists. See the discussion in Elizabeth Rappaport, "Generalizing Gender: Reason and Essence in the Legal Thought of Catharine MacKinnon," in A Mind of One's Own: Feminist Essays on Reason and Objectivity, ed. L. Antony and C. Witt (Boulder, CO: Westview Press, 1993), 127–44, strongly supporting MacKinnon's type of 'essentialism'; and see MacKinnon, "What Is a White Woman Anyway?," criticizing Elizabeth Spelman's Inessential Woman. Charlotte Witt, "Feminist Metaphysics," in A Mind of One's Own, 273–88, argues, plausibly, that MacKinnon needs, and relies on, an idea of the human being, not just an idea of woman. For an excellent discussion of the entire topic, see Charlotte Witt, "Anti-Essentialism in Feminist Theory," Philosophical Topics (1996).

70. See Marilyn Friedman in "Feminism and Modern Friendship," in Friedman, What Are Friends For? (Ithaca: Cornell University Press, 1993), 231–56.

71. Jaggar, Feminist Politics, 28.

72. On Astell, see Margaret Atherton, "Cartesian Reason and Gendered Reason," in A Mind of One's Own, 19–34.

73. See Nussbaum, "Emotions and Women's Capabilities," in WCD; also Anne Fausto-Sterling, Myths of Gender, 2nd ed. (New York: Basic Books, 1992).

74. Some examples include Carol Gilligan, In a Different Voice (Cambridge, MA: Harvard University Press, 1982); Nancy Chodorow, The Reproduction of Mothering (Berkeley: University of California Press, 1978); Virginia Held, Feminist Morality (Chicago: University of Chicago Press, 1993).

75. For criticisms of the reason-emotion contrast, see Martha Minow and Elizabeth Spelman, "Passions Within Reason," Cardozo Law Review 10 (1988), 37–76.

76. See, for example, Catherine Lutz, Unnatural Emotions: Everyday Sentiments on a Micronesian Atoll and their Challenge to Western Theory (Chicago:

University of Chicago Press, 1988); Helen Longino, "To See Feelingly: Reason, Passion, and Dialogue in Feminist Philosophy," in *Feminisms in the Academy*, ed. D. Stanton and A. Stewart (Ann Arbor: University of Michigan Press, 1995), 19–45.

77. This is the theme of my Gifford Lectures at the University of Edinburgh 1993, now entitled *Upheavals of Thought: A Theory of the Emotions* (Cambridge: Cambridge University Press, forthcoming). See also D. Kahan and M. Nussbaum, "Two Conceptions of Emotions in Criminal Law," *Columbia Law Review* 96 (1996), 270–374.

78. See Genevieve Lloyd, *The Man of Reason* (Minneapolis: University of Minnesota Press, 1984); Lutz, *Unnatural Emotions*.

79. Annette Baier, "Hume: The Reflective Woman's Epistemologist," in *A Mind of One's Own*.

80. For a trenchant critique that has not been displaced, see Anthony Kenny, *Action, Emotion, and Will* (London: MacMillan, 1963).

81. For argument that such views derive from a male desire to be free of all strong attachments, see Longino, "To See Feelingly," summarizing the positions of Lloyd and others. A prominent source of this position within feminism is the psychoanalytical work of Chodorow, *The Reproduction of Mothering*.

82. Nel Noddings, *Caring: A Feminine Approach to Ethics and Moral Education* (Berkeley: University of California Press, 1984). I do not discuss the even more influential views of Carol Gilligan because it is very unclear what Gilligan's normative view is and also what analysis she gives to emotions of love and care (to what extent she connects them with thought).

83. Noddings's general position is that the notions of "justification, fairness, justice" are "the language of the father," and that the primary defect in contemporary ethical thought is that it focuses on this voice rather than on the "mother's voice" *passim*.

84. A fruitful comparison would be to the more extensive assault on liberal reciprocity in the work of Emmanuel Levinas. Noddings herself does not discuss Levinas, but she does connect her idea to Martin Buber's account of the I-Thou relation (142).

85. Noddings, 137. This forms part of Noddings's argument against Sartre's claim that emotion always has an intentional object.

86. Perhaps I am handicapped by the fact that I simply do not recognize my own experience of motherhood in Noddings's descriptions of fusing and bonding. My first sharp impression of Rachel Nussbaum was as a pair of feet drumming on my diaphragm with a certain distinct separateness, a pair of arms flexing their muscles against my bladder. Before even her hair got into the world a separate voice could be heard inside, proclaiming its individuality or even individualism, and it has not stopped arguing yet, 23 years later. I am sure RN would be quite outraged by the suggestion that her own well-being was at any time merged with that of her mother, and her mother would never dare to make such an overweening suggestion. This liberal experience of maternity as the give and take of argument has equipped me ill to understand the larger mysteries of Noddings's text.

87. See the acute criticism of Noddings in Diana Fritz Cates, *Compassion for Friends in Fellowship with God* (Notre Dame: Notre Dame University Press, 1997).

88. Nietzsche, *Thus Spoke Zarathustra*, Part I, "On the Teachers of Virtue." (Kaufmann translates *einnicken* as "drop off," but I have substituted a more literal rendering.)

89. This is Bernard Williams's phrase ("Persons, Character, and Morality," in *Moral Luck: Philosophical Papers 1973–80* [Cambridge: Cambridge University Press 1981], 18), used in criticism of impartialist views of responsibility that would urge us to reflect on whether we may or may not give special privileges to our own family. Williams says that if a man on a raft, knowing that he can save either his wife or a stranger but not both, pauses to deliberate at all, he is having "one thought too many." I am not making any claim here about that particular case (Williams may be correct, though it is not obvious that no thought at all should be given to the choice), but it seems likely that a communitarian might say something similar about cases of female self-sacrifice for family, and there I would wish to insist on the relevance of reason, given the social deformation of the norms in question.

90. Chen is an American citizen but grew up in India and has spent half her life there; the other organizers were all Indian.

91. V. Das and R. Nicholas, "'Welfare' and 'Well-Being' in South Asian Societies," ACLS-SSRC Joint Committee on South Asia (New York: Social Science Research Council, 1981); although Das circulated this paper, she has never published it.

92. See also Marcia Homiak, "Feminism and Aristotle's Rational Ideal," in *A Mind of One's Own*, 1–17; Jean Hampton, "Feminist Contractarianism," *ibid.*, 227–55; Susan Moller Okin, "Reason and Feeling in Thinking about Justice," *Ethics* 99 (1989), 229–49.

93. See Catharine MacKinnon, *Feminism Unmodified* (Cambridge, MA: Harvard University Press, 1987); Andrea Dworkin, *Intercourse* (New York: The Free Press, 1988).

94. See chapter 5 (in this volume).

95. J.-J. Rousseau, *Emile*, Book IV.

96. Adam Smith, *The Theory of Moral Sentiments* (rep. Liberty Press, 1976), Parts I and III. The remarks especially critical of greed and competition are primarily from the later editions. On Smith's changing attitudes to acquisitiveness, see Ian Simpson Ross, *The Life of Adam Smith* (Oxford: Clarendon Press, 1995).

97. On Rousseau, see Joshua Cohen, "The Natural Goodness of Humanity," in *Reclaiming the History of Ethics*, ed. Christine Korsgaard, Barbara Herman, and Andrews Reath (Cambridge: Cambridge University Press, 1997). Smith is even more profoundly influenced by Stoicism than is Rousseau, and the primary emphasis in his critique of desire and emotion is placed on distorting social forces.

98. The judgment of naturalness is said by Mill to be made "with that inability to recognise their own work which distinguishes the unanalytic mind" (22–3); see also "Was there ever any domination which did not appear natural to those who possessed it? (12); and "How rarely it is that even men complain of the general order of society; and how much rarer still would such complaint be, if they did not know of any different order existing anywhere else" (84).

99. Both Rousseau and Smith, for example, seem to hold this, although Rousseau's argument about the naturalness of gender distinctions is notoriously difficult to interpret. See Susan Moller Okin, *Women in Western Political Thought* (Princeton, NJ: Princeton University Press, 1979).

100. See chapters 5, 8, and 9.

101. See chapter 8.

102. Kant, *Critique of Practical Reason*, Conclusion. The origin of this passage is probably in Seneca, *Moral Epistle* 40: see Martha C. Nussbaum, "Kant and Stoic Cosmopolitanism," *Journal of Political Philosophy* 5 (1997), 1–25.

Chapter 3

1. See John Rawls, *A Theory of Justice* (hereafter TJ) (Cambridge, MA: Harvard University Press, 1970), 205–21. Rawls holds that restrictions of religious liberty can be justified only when the consequences for the security of public order are "reasonably certain or imminent" (213).

2. See Martha A. Chen, *A Quiet Revolution: Women in Transition in Rural Bangladesh* (Cambridge, MA: Schenkman, 1983), 172–8, 204, 217. This example is on p. 174.

3. In this case, the fact that the women were soon understood to be augmenting the family income won the day for them; husbands and in-laws soon ceased resistance, and the authority of the *mullahs* declined in importance. One woman concludes, "We do not listen to the *mullahs* any more. They . . . did not give us even a quarter kilo of rice. Now we get ten maunds of rice [i.e. through their new employment]. Now, people help us." Ibid., 176. Now, another woman adds, the leaders "know that if they do anything bad with us they will face a problem." Ibid., 177.

4. See the account of the case in Radhika Coomaraswamy, "Women, Ethnicity, and the Discourse of Rights," in *Human Rights of Women: National and International Perspectives* (hereafter HRW), ed. Rebecca J. Cook (Philadelphia: University of Pennsylvania Press, 1994), 39–57.

5. *Mohammed Ahmed Khan v. Shah Bano Begum & Others*, S.C.R. (1985). As the Chief Justice wrote, "Undoubtedly, the Muslim husband enjoys the privilege of being able to discard his wife whenever he chooses to do so, for reason good, bad, or indifferent. Indeed, for no reason at all." Shah Bano's husband had a second wife, both being his first cousins; the three sons from Shah Bano were all employed in managerial and technical jobs, and the son from Halima Begum shared his father's legal practice.

6. Relations enumerated are spouse, minor children, adult handicapped children, and aged parents. On the addition of divorced spouses to the law in 1973, and the controversy at the time that led to an amendment officially exempting Muslim women from the reach of the law, see Kirti Singh, "The Constitution and Muslim Personal Law," in *Forging Identities: Gender, Communities, and the State in India* (hereafter *Forging Identities*) ed. Zoya Hasan (Delhi and Boulder, CO: Westview Press, 1994), 96–107. After 1973 the Supreme Court held that divorced Muslim women were entitled to maintenance in spite of the amendment, since the law had to be interpreted in the light of its social purpose, which was to benefit destitute women. See *Bai Tahira v. Ali Hussain*, S.C.R. (2) 75 (1979).

7. On the controversy, see Kavita R. Khory, "The Shah Bano Case: Some Political Implications," in *Religion and Law in Independent India* (hereafter *Religion and Law*) ed. Robert Baird (Delhi: Manohar, 1993), 121–37, pointing out that in reality the Islamic community was highly divided about the judgment. See also Amartya Sen, "Secularism and Its Discontents," in *Unravelling the Nation*, ed. Kaushik Basu and Sanjay Subrahmanyam (Delhi: Oxford University Press, 1995), 11–43. Kirti Singh, "Obstacles to Women's Rights in India," in HRW, 384–5; Singh, in *Forging Identities*; Zoya Hasan, "Minority Identity, State Policy and the Political Process," in *Forging Identities*, 59–73; relevant documents are collected in Asghar Ali Engineer, ed., *The Shah Bano Controversy* (Delhi: Ajanta Publishers, 1987). See also Veena Das, *Critical Events* (Delhi: Oxford University Press, 1992), chap. 4. On general issues about the Indian legal system and its history, see John H. Mansfield, "The Personal Laws or a Uniform Civil Code?" in *Religion and Law*; Tahir Mahmood,

Muslim Personal Law, Role of the State in the Indian Subcontinent (Delhi: Vikas, 1977); Archana Parashar, *Women and Family Law Reform in India: Uniform Civil Code and Gender Equality* (Delhi: Sage, 1992).

8. The Act, however, contains an option: At the time of marriage, a couple may elect to submit themselves to the maintenance provisions of the Criminal Procedure Code instead of the Islamic law; previously, Islamic law was enforced toward all Muslims, regardless of their choice, and that is still the case, in effect, for most matters. Such options have been a matter of great dispute. Under the Shariat Act, individuals will be governed by the Shariat only if they make an election in its favor, but that choice will be binding on their descendants, who have no choice in the matter. See Mansfield, 169.

9. On the pros and cons of a uniform code, see Sen, "Secularism," 22–24, citing constitutional debates; Mahmood, 115–30, on Muslim opinion. Although Dr. Ambedkar, the leader of the team of constitutional framers, expressed a preference for "uniformity of fundamental laws, civil and criminal," this uniformity was not incorporated in the constitution, and his preference was included only as an unenforceable "Directive Principle of State Policy," stating that "the State shall endeavour to secure for the citizens a uniform civil code throughout the territory of India." It was stated that this principle was "fundamental in the governance of the country," and that "it shall be the duty of the State to apply" it, but that it "shall not be enforceable by any court." *Constitution of India*, Article 44. At the same time, however, Article 13(1) provides that all "laws in force" shall be void insofar as they are in conflict with the constitutionally enumerated Fundamental Rights, among which (Articles 14 and 15) are the right of all persons to the equal protection of the laws and a guarantee of nondiscrimination on the basis of "religion, race, caste, sex, place of birth or any of them." It is thus possible to hold that the personal laws were already rendered void by Article 13(1). See discussion that follows.

10. Cited in Sen, "Secularism," who observes: "This line of reasoning has many problems. . . . Any unfairness that is there is surely one against *Muslim women*, rather than against *Hindu men*" (22).

11. Singh, 380, quoting from *Lok Sabha Debates* Part II, Vol. IV (1955), 6889. Further extracts from parliamentary debates are found in Shaheeda Latif, "Defining Women Through Legislation, in *Forging Identities*, 38–58. For an extensive account of the changes, see Parashar, chap. 3.

12. Akram Mirhosseini, "After the Revolution: Violations of Women's Human Rights in Iran," in *Women's Rights, Human Rights* (hereafter WRHR), ed. Julie Peters and Andrea Wolper (New York: Routledge, 1995), 75.

13. Ibid. (citing Rinaldo Galindo Pohl, Special Representative of the United Nations Commission on Human Rights in the Islamic Republic of Iran, report of January 2, 1992).

14. *Hoffman et al. v. Officer of the Western Wall*, HC 257/89, 2410/90, judgment delivered January 26, 1994, reported in Carmel Shalev, "Women in Israel: Fighting Tradition," in WRHR, 89–95.

15. Data as of January 1994, cited in HRW, 254. See also *Human Development Report* (New York: United Nations Development Program, 1995), 43. Among the countries that will be discussed, Iran, Pakistan, Saudi Arabia, and the Sudan have not ratified the Convention; some of the others, including India, China, and Bangladesh (and many European nations as well) have ratified it only with some "reservation"; in the United States, President Carter signed the treaty in 1980, but the Sen-

ate has still not ratified it. See "Clinton Chides Senate for Not Approving Women's Rights Treaty," *New York Times*, December 11, 1996, A5.

16. Pope John Paul II, Address to the United Nations General Assembly, October 5, 1995.

17. TJ, 206.

18. Pope John Paul II, "Letter to Women," dated June 29, 1995, released July 10, 1995:

> As far as personal rights are concerned, there is an urgent need to achieve real equality in every area: equal pay for equal work, protection for working mothers, fairness in career advancements, equality of spouses with regard to family rights and the recognition of everything that is part of the rights and duties of citizens in a democratic state. . . . The time has come to condemn vigorously the types of sexual violence which frequently have women for their object and to pass laws which effectively defend them from such violence." (2)

Elsewhere, the Pope has spoken explicitly about marital rape, making it clear that he believes it to fall among the violent acts that should be legally prohibited.

19. Constitutional guarantees of rights outside the United States may be merely aspirational for two distinct reasons: (1) because they include a long list of rights, including many economic and social rights, that are extremely difficult to enforce; or (2) because they do not attempt to enforce the very same rights that are enforced in the United States. I am speaking here of the second contrast: Guarantees of equal protection, mobility and assembly rights, speech rights, rights of religious exercise, and others are merely aspirational for many citizens in many nations.

20. See Mary E. Becker, "The Politics of Women's Wrongs and the Bill of 'Rights': A Bicentennial Perspective," *University of Chicago Law Review* 59 (1992), 453–517.

21. An honorable exception to the neglect is certainly Rawls, who, in "The Law of Peoples," in *The Oxford Amnesty Lectures 1993*, ed. S. Shute and S. Hurley (New York: Basic Books), argued that women's equality was one area in which it was legitimate to interfere with the religious or traditional practices of a nation.

22. One may be that even our citizens are not fully convinced of the equal worth of female life. Recent protests from Christian groups against granting most favored nation status to China on grounds of its persecution of Christians have not been accompanied by any similar protest against the far more widespread and horrendous harms to women. See chapter 1.

23. See Jean Drèze and Amartya Sen, *India: Economic Development and Social Opportunity* (Oxford: Clarendon Press, 1996).

24. See Sen, "Secularism"; and Amartya Sen, *On Interpreting India's Past* (Calcutta: Asiatic Society, 1996).

25. Cited by Jawaharlal Nehru, *The Discovery of India* (Calcutta: Signet Press, 1956, centenary ed. Oxford: Clarendon Press, 1989), 75; see discussion in Sen, *Interpreting*, 13–4.

26. For one clear example of this, in her study of reactions to the Shah Bano case, Khory summarizes: "[T]he Shah Bano case is representative of the way in which group divisions within Indian society are increasingly manipulated for political reasons." See also Amartya Sen, "Human Rights and Asian Values," *The New Republic*, July 10/17, 1997, 33–40; and Hasan, in *Forging Identities*.

27. See Sen, "Secularism," 32–39.

28. See Sen, "Secularism," 41 (citing the translation by Rabindranath Tagore in *One Hundred Poems of Kabir* [London: Macmillan, 1915], Verse LXIX); see also Kshiti Mohan Sen, *Hinduism* (Harmondsworth: Penguin Books, 1960), chaps. 18 and 19.

29. For a representative spectrum of positions in the current U.S. debate, see Paul Weithman, ed., *Religion and Contemporary Liberalism* (Notre Dame: University of Notre Dame Press, 1997); and John Rawls, "The Idea of Public Reason Revisited," *University of Chicago Law Review* 64 (1997), 765–807.

30. See Martha C. Nussbaum, "Capabilities and Human Rights," *Fordham Law Review* 66 (1997), 273–300. Other much-discussed questions, concerning the precise relationship between rights and interests, rights and theories of the good, and rights and duties do not affect the analysis to be presented here and can therefore be deferred.

31. Women's Convention, Article 2.

32. See chapter 1, on "missing women."

33. On Islam, see Chen, *A Quiet Revolution*; Valentine Moghadam, *Gender, Development, and Policy: Toward Equity and Empowerment*, UNU/WIDER Research for Action series, November 1990; on the Confucian tradition, see Xiarong Li, "Gender Inequality in China," in *Women, Culture, and Development* (hereafter WCD), ed. M. Nussbaum and J. Glover (Oxford: Clarendon Press, 1995), 407–25; on Hindu traditions, see Roop Rekha Verma, "Femininity, Equality, and Personhood," in WCD, 433–43, with ample references to traditional texts.

34. See Martha Chen, "A Matter of Survival: Women's Right to Employment in India and Bangladesh," in WCD, 37–57.

35. See Chen, "A Matter of Survival," 37.

36. See A. Sen, "Gender and Cooperative Conflicts," in *Persistent Inequalities: Women and World Development*, ed. I. Tinker (New York: Oxford University Press, 1990).

37. For an account of the case, see Coomaraswamy, in HRW, 48–50.

38. Pressure can be either spiritual or financial; in the past, many such cases clearly involved financial motives by family members eager to avoid dowry payment and also by in-laws eager to avoid having another mouth to feed.

39. See Das, "Communities as Political Actors," in *Critical Events*, 84–117.

40. Coomaraswamy, p. 49.

41. See the discussion of the legal developments in Indira Jaising, "Violence Against Women: The Indian Perspective," in WRHR, 51–6; the 1983 Cruelty to Women act (similar to the 1983 Bangladesh law, see discussion later) has somewhat improved women's bargaining situation. A UNICEF report estimates that 5,000 women a year die from such abuses in India. *Progress of the Nations* (UNICEF, July 1997). For a nuanced contemporary analysis, see Uma Narayan, "Cross-Cultural Connections, Border-Crossings, and 'Death by Culture': Thinking About Dowry-Murders in India and Domestic-Violence Murders in the United States," in U. Narayan, *Dislocating Cultures: Identities, Traditions, and Third World Feminism* (New York and London: Routledge, 1997), 81–118.

42. *Khatoon v. State* 38 D.L.R. 348 (1986).

43. Drèze and Sen, *India*, 173.

44. See Drèze and Sen, *India*, 172–5; M. Chen, *The Lives of Widows in Rural India* (forthcoming).

45. See Chen, "A Matter of Survival," 37.

46. See Das, "National Honour and Practical Kinship," in *Critical Events*, 55–83. The document states: "No civilized people can recognize such conversions and there is nothing more heinous than abduction of women." Ultimately, however, the women's interests and rights took a back seat to questions of national and religious-group honor: Laws governing the return of abducted women gave the women no choice at all in the matter, despite the protests of some politicians who pointed out that forcible return seemed to conflict both with international law and with Indian law.

47. Das, citing information given to the House in the context of legislative debates. These figures may well be inflated, given the political context, but the numbers certainly were very large.

48. *Double Jeopardy: Police Abuse of Women in Pakistan* (New York: Women's Rights Project, and Asia Watch, Human Rights Watch, 1992).

49. Indira Jaising, The Lawyers' Collective, New Delhi, personal communication, March 1997.

50. Witnesses need not always be eyewitnesses, so the requirement is not as absurd as it seems, but a woman whose guardian or other male relatives do not approve of her general demeanor is highly vulnerable.

51. It is explicitly forbidden to beat on the face or in a way that permanently marks the body; this leaves a lot of ground open.

52. Chief Justice Chandrachud in the Shah Bano case cites the *Laws of Manu* statement that "[t]he woman is utterly unfit for independence."

53. See Indira Jaising, "Violence Against Women: The Indian Perspective," in WRHR, 51–6.

54. A.I.R. (A.P.) 356 (1983).

55. Article 21 states, "No person shall be deprived of his life or personal liberty except according to procedure established by law." The history of the interpretation of this article, described in detail by Judge Choudary in his opinion, parallels that of the interpretation of the Due Process Clause of the Fourteenth Amendment of the U.S. Constitution and indeed is heavily influenced by that history; major U.S. cases establishing a "right to privacy" are cited by the judge as having shaped the interpretation of the terms "life" and "liberty" to recognize a right to choice in intimate matters of sex and reproduction.

56. Choudary cites a 1927 case from Bombay, A.I.R. (Bom.) 264 (1927), which makes the same point.

57. A.I.R. (S.C.) 152 (1984); see Singh, 388.

58. *Nelly Zaman v. Ghiyasuddin*, 34 D.L.R. 221 (1982).

59. For a review of these documents, see Abdullahi A. An-Na'im, "Toward a Cross-Cultural Approach to Defining International Standards of Human Rights: The Meaning of Cruel, Inhuman, or Degrading Treatment or Punishment," in *Human Rights in Cross-Cultural Perspectives*, ed. A. An-Na'im (Philadelphia: University of Pennsylvania Press, 1992), 19–43.

60. See ibid., 36.

61. See ibid., 35.

62. Ibid., 36, citing parallels from the orthodox Jewish tradition.

63. Women's Convention, art. 11.

64. Mirhosseini, 73.

65. Ayatollah Mutahari, *The Question of the Veil*, quoted in Mirhosseini, 73.

66. See "Guerillas Take Afghan Capital as Troops Flee," *New York Times*, September 28, 1996, A1; John F. Burns, "Walled in, Shrouded and Angry in Afghani-

stan," *New York Times*, October 4, 1996; Burns, "Afghanistan's Professional Class Flees Rule by Ultra-Strict Clerics," *New York Times*, October 7, 1996; Barbara Crossette, "Afghans Draw U.N. Warning Over Sex Bias," *New York Times*, October 8, 1996; Burns, "Afghan Says Restriction Will Not Be Eased," *New York Times*, October 9, 1996, A8; Susan Moller Okin, "U.S. Should Protest Afghan Women's Plight" (Letter to the Editor), *New York Times*, October 7, 1996.

67. *Bradwell v. Illinois*, 83 U.S. (16 Wallace) 130 (1872).

68. Cornelia Sorabji, *India Calling* (London: Nisbet and Co., 1934), 68. Though rich and pampered, this woman (one of three or four wives of the local Thakur) was also illiterate, "the theory being that if women learnt to write they would get themselves into trouble" (67).

69. See Neil MacFarquhar, "Backlash of Intolerance Stirring Fear in Iran," *New York Times*, September 20, 1996, A1.

70. Ann Elizabeth Mayer, "Cultural Particularism as a Bar to Women's Rights," in WRHR, 176–88.

71. Marsha A. Freeman, "The Human Rights of Women in the Family," in WRHR, 149–64.

72. See Asma Mohamed Abdel Halim, "Challenges to Women's International Human Rights in the Sudan," in HRW, 397–421.

73. See Mayer, 180, with documentation.

74. Mayer, 180–81.

75. On the United States, in comparison to other developed countries, see chapter 5.

76. "Subject to public order, morality and health and to the other provisions of this Part, all persons are equally entitled to freedom of conscience and the right freely to profess, practice and propagate religion" (Art. 25). Article 17, however, abolishes "untouchability," arguably a core feature of the Hindu tradition. Article 26 gives the religions management of their own affairs and property; article 28 guarantees freedom to attend religious instruction; articles 27 and 28 forbid the use of tax money for religious purposes and religious instruction in state-funded schools.

77. See also Hasan, in *Forging Identities*, on violations of the constitutional provision against discrimination on the basis of religion, when women lose a benefit on account of being classified as Muslim.

78. See Bina Agarwal, *A Field of One's Own: Gender and Land Rights in South Asia* (Cambridge: Cambridge University Press, 1994), chap. 5, which describes the situation for all the major religions; see also Chen, *Widows*, chap. 9.

79. *Mrs Mary Roy v. the State of Kerala and Others*, A.I.R. (SCC) 1011 (1986b); see Agarwal, 224, Parashar, 190–1.

80. P. J. Kurien, cited in Agarwal, 225.

81. See Agarwal, 225, with references.

82. *Dow v. Attorney General*, Ct. App. Civ. App. No. 4/91 (1992): Unity Dow challenged the Botswana nationality law, under which by marrying an American she lost her ability to transfer Botswana nationality to the children of the marriage and thereby the free university education to which the children would otherwise be entitled. The Court ruled in her favor by a 3–2 vote. In the majority opinion, Judge President Amissah cites Article 2 of the Universal Declaration of Human Rights of 1948, which states that everyone is entitled to all the rights contained in the Declaration "without distinction of any kind, such as race, colour, sex, language, religion, political or other opinion, national or social origin, property, birth, or other status." In a concurring opinion, Judge Agudah cites the Women's Convention as binding,

saying that it "has created an international regime" that must be considered in considering whether national laws were constitutional.

83. And also, in India today, to non-Muslim men—a fact that has given rise to some interesting free exercise jurisprudence in Indian courts. Polygamy is of course not required in Islam, but criticisms of the practice are met with intense opposition.

84. "Egyptian Court Forces Professor to Divorce for Writings on Islam," *New York Times*, August 6, 1996.

85. *Abu Baker Siddique v. S. M. A. Bakar*, 38 D.L.R. (AD) (1986).

86. Hindu Guardianship and Minority Act, reported in Singh, 382.

87. See Mahmood, 110–14.

88. Mahmood, 113 (citing his letter of 15 September 1974, addressed to Mrs. Tara Ali Beg, President, Indian Council for Child Welfare).

89. Metha Bai almost lost her small farm because a mortage notice arrived and she put it aside, knowing that she was unable to read it.

90. See Drèze and Sen, *India*, on the India/China contrast and its importance for overall welfare. They emphasize that the Chinese achievement has its basis in the policies of the older regime, highly egalitarian toward women, and long pre-exist the current era of market expansionism; in Iran, the discrepancy between female and male education becomes much sharper as we move higher up: Iranian women have only 47 percent the tertiary education (i.e. college) of males.

91. Data from *Human Development Report* (New York: United Nations Development Program, 1995); the data are from 1992.

92. See Drèze and Sen, *India*.

93. Mirhosseini, 74.

94. *Wisconsin v. Yoder*, 406 U.S. 205 (1972). The sex-equality aspect of the issue was not discussed in any of the opinions.

95. See Sen, "Population: Delusion and Reality," *New York Review of Books*, September 22 (1994); and "Fertility and Coercion," *University of Chicago Law Review* 63 (1996), 1035–61.

96. Compare Article 16 of the Women's Convention, which guarantees women "the same rights to decide freely and responsibly on the number and spacing of their children and to have access to the information, education and means to enable them to exercise these rights."

97. For the equality-based defense of abortion rights, see Cass R. Sunstein, *The Partial Constitution* (Cambridge, MA: Harvard University Press, 1993).

98. See Vina Mazumdar, in *Reproductive Technology and Women's Equality*, ed. J. Glover and M. Nussbaum (forthcoming).

99. Compare a moment in Lincoln's Second Inaugural, where, commenting on the use of religious discourse by southern slaveholders, he observes that it "may seem strange that any men should dare to ask a just God's assistance in wringing their bread from the sweat of other men's faces."

100. Nor is the British legal system fully symmetrical: Blasphemy laws protect Christianity and no other religion, just as in Pakistan blasphemy laws protect only Islam.

101. The most detailed and comprehensive recent treatment of conflicts between women's rights and systems of personal law is in Indira Jaising, ed., *Justice for Women* (Mapusa, Goa: The Other India Press, 1996), with meticulous accounts of all the major provisions of all the personal codes, and leading court cases, in the areas of marriage, divorce, maintenance, custody and guardianship, matrimonial property, and hereditary family property. Particularly helpful general summaries are in three

articles by Jaising: "Introduction" i–v; "The Politics of Personal Laws," 1–8; and "Towards an Egalitarian Civil Code," 24–7.

102. Article 15, which prohibits employment discrimination on grounds of religion, race, caste, sex, or place of birth, explicitly states that this shall not prevent the State from making special provision for "the advancement of any socially and educationally backward classes of citizens or for the Scheduled castes and the Scheduled Tribes."

103. See Mahmood, 80–82 (citing Mohammad Ismail). Some Muslim leaders took the rather different position that the uniform code was a good thing but "in advance of its time." Still others were openly in favor of uniformity: see Hasan, in *Forging Identities*; and Heera Nawaz, "Toward Uniformity," in Jaising, ed., 14–18; Danial Latifi, "After Shah Bano," in Jaising, ed., 213–15. Ironically, some speakers invoked the Raj, holding that one of the "secrets of success" of the British rulers was their willingness to retain the personal laws: Pocker Saheb, cited in Mahmood, 82.

104. See Sen, "Secularism."

105. Chowdry Hyder Hussain, "A Unified Code for India," A.I.R. (j) 68, 71–2 (1949), cited in Mahmood, 115.

106. M. C. Chagla, *Proceedings of the 26th Congress of Orientalists*, 79–80 (1964); and "Plea for a Uniform Civil Code," *Weekly Round Table*, March 25, 1969, 7, both cited in Mahmood, 116. As the *Sareetha* case shows, it is not just the idea of separate codes that is British, it is also some of the most controversial provisions of the codes themselves.

107. Engineer, 158. See *Forging Identities*.

108. Excerpt from *The Times of India*, March 12–13, 1986, reprinted in Engineer, 107.

109. Latifi, "After Shah Bano," in Jaising, ed., 213–15; see also Latifi, "Women, Family Law, and Social Changes," in Jaising, ed., 216–22, criticizing Tahir Mahmood's writings in the Shah Bano case, where he took a conservative position and criticized the Supreme Court ruling in writings that Latifi describes as "rabble-rousing," and guilty of "*suppressio veri* and *suggestio falsi*." "Actually," Latifi writes, "it is un-Islamic not to respect the court verdict."

110. Indira Jaising, personal communication, March 1997; see Jaising, ed., 7.

111. Will Kymlicka, *Multicultural Citizenship: A Liberal Theory of Minority Rights* (Oxford: Clarendon Press, 1995).

112. See ibid., 165, arguing that intervention with the policies of Saudi Arabia denying political rights to women and non-Muslims would be unjustified.

113. In 1996, 110 million.

114. Chagla, "Plea for a Uniform Civil Code," in Mahmood, 116.

115. Interestingly, the coalition has become a major defender of women's equality, at least in the political arena: Mr. Deve Gowda, the Prime Minister, proposed a bill in the Lok Sabha (the lower house of parliament) to reserve a full third of seats in parliament and state assemblies for women; this bill is parallel to a 1947 bill that reserved a third of seats for Dalits and tribal people. The bill would boost the number of female representatives from 38 to about 180. Mr. Gowda scrapped plans to refer the bill to a committee for further study, after female MP's complained that this would kill the Bill. All major parties publicly support sex equality, though many individuals hoped to delay action on the measure. See "Women Score Historic Victory in Indian Parliament," *Times of London* (on-line), September 13, 1996. For bringing this report to my attention, I am grateful to John Lott.

116. Joyce, *Ulysses*, in the "Cyclops" episode in which Bloom confronts an antisemitic Irish nationalist in Barney Kiernan's bar.

117. Kymlicka's principle suggests that the United States should permit segregated schools in the South because of the sad history of quasi-national division.

118. Only one woman dared to come forward to claim that Yantra had fathered her child, but many complained of sexual harassment.

119. "Yantra May Be Drummed out of Monkhood," *The Bangkok Post*, February 4, 1995; "Phra Yantra's Back to the Wall," *The Bangkok Post*, February 5, 1995. The latter article summarizes: "The nagging Yantra fiasco has in fact shown that there is no official agency with real authority and willingness to deal decisively and rightly with such a high-profile scandal. . .The buck has been passed to and from with no one fully authorised or equipped to deal with the case." For these articles, and discussion of the case, I am grateful to Suwanna Satha-Anand, Philosophy Department, Chulalongkorn University.

120. See *United States v. Seeger*, 380 U.S. 163 (1965): The intent of the law is understood to be "to embrace all religions and to exclude essentially political, sociological, or philosophical views. " The Court held that where a set of beliefs "occupies a place in the life of its possessor parallel to that filled by the orthodox belief in God," the person may be considered for the exemption, and much of the argumentation about Seeger's non-orthodox system of belief proceeded by comparing it to beliefs that would be orthodox for a practicing Buddhist.

121. A classic case is *Sherbert v. Verner*, 374 U.S. 398 (1963), in which it was held that a state's refusal to grant unemployment benefits to a woman who had been dismissed because she refused, for religious reasons, to work on Saturday violated the free exercise clause. As Justice Stewart pointed out in his concurring opinion, the state would be within its rights to refuse unemployment benefits to a woman whose dismissal from employment resulted from inability to find a Saturday babysitter: "[T]he Court . . . holds that the State must prefer a religious over a secular ground for being unavailable for work." Stewart argues that this creates grave difficulties for the Establishment clause. *Sherbert* was overruled in *Employment Division v. Smith*, 110 S. Ct. 1595 (1990), which very much narrowed the scope of free exercise exemptions to "generally applicable law[s]." *Smith*, in turn, was overruled by the Religious Freedom Restoration Act of 1993 (RFRA), Pub. L. No. 103–41, H.R. 1308, S. 578, 103d Cong. (1993), which restores the "compelling interest" test set out in *Sherbert*, again with an exclusive focus on religious interests. In June 1997, RFRA was declared unconstitutional by the Supreme Court.

122. In *Evans v. Romer*, the case dealing with the constitutionality of Colorado's Amendment 2, which denied local communities and state agencies the right to pass nondiscrimination laws for sexual orientation, Judge Bayless, ruling that the law did not survive strict scrutiny, recognized the interest in religious liberty as a compelling interest, but pointed out that the way to protect that interest in a "narrowly tailored" way was to do as Denver had done, and exempt religious organizations from the law. (These issues were not addressed in the Supreme Court's discussion of the case in *Romer v. Evans* [see chapter 7, in this volume] because strict scrutiny was not at issue and the entire mode of argumentation was different.)

123. 413 U.S. 455 (1973).

124. 461 U.S. 574, 103 S. Ct. 2017 (1983).

125. Although not affiliated with any specific denomination, its stated purpose is "to conduct an institution of learning . . . , giving special emphasis to the Christian religion and the ethics revealed in the Holy Scriptures." Ibid., 2922.

126. The primary focus of the institution was on preventing interracial dating. Until 1973, the institution completely refused to admit black students; from 1971 to 1975 it admitted only black students "married within their race," giving a few exceptions to longterm members of the university staff. Since 1975, unmarried black students have been permitted to enroll, but a disciplinary rule forbade interracial dating and marriage, stating that violators would be expelled.

127. There is an interesting question, however, whether the *fatwah* would not be protected under the current U.S. law of free speech. In *Brandenburg v. Ohio*, 395 U.S. 444 (1969), the Court required three things in order for speech to forfeit protection: (1) express advocacy of law violation; (2) the advocacy must call for *immediate* law violation; and (3) the immediate law violation must be likely to occur. The *fatwah* may not satisfy (2), and yet a number of individuals connected with the publication and translation of Rushdie's book have, over the years, been murdered. See the discussion in G. R. Stone, L. M. Seidman, C. R. Sunstein, and M. V. Tushnet, *Constitutional Law*, 3rd ed. (Boston: Little, Brown, 1996), 1127 (citing Schwartz, "Holmes versus Hand: Clear and Present Danger or Advocacy of Unlawful Action?" *Supreme Court Review* 209, 240–41 [1994], who argues that the *Brandenburg* test would protect the Ayatollah's speech). If one holds, as I do, that the Ayatollah's speech should be punishable, one may feel that the *Brandenburg* test is too protective.

128. There was a recent case of this type in an Arab family in northern Israel, in which a woman who came home to visit her family was murdered for allegedly bringing shame on the family by her short skirts, and so on.

129. See C. Sunstein, *Democracy and the Problem of Free Speech* (New York: The Free Press, 1993), 202–204, arguing that the Stanford speech code would be constitutional even in a public university. Under the Stanford code, speech qualifies as regulable "harassment" if it "(1) is intended to insult or stigmatize an individual or a small number of individuals on the basis of their sex, race, color, handicap, religion, sexual orientation, or national and ethnic origin, (2) is addressed directly to the individual or individuals whom it insults or stigmatizes, and (3) makes use of insulting or 'fighting' words or nonverbal symbols." To qualify under (3), the speech must by its "very utterance inflict injury or tend to incite to an immediate breach of the peace," and must be "commonly understood to convey direct and visceral hatred and contempt for human beings on the basis of" one of the grounds enumerated in (2). I cannot comment extensively on the complexities involved in applying this useful paradigm to the cases I have been talking about, but one surely is the contestability of "hatred and contempt": For speech that might legitimately be seen by women as expressing hatred and contempt of them may be seen by the speaker as expressing a protective kind of love, the kind of love one has for a child who is prone to error.

130. Article 19 of the Indian Constitution protects the right "to freedom of speech and expression" but allows "reasonable restrictions" for the sake of "the sovereignty and integrity of India, the security of the State, friendly relations with foreign States, public order, decency or morality, or in relation to contempt of court, defamation or incitement to an offence."

131. John Rawls (New York: Columbia University Press, 1996), l–lii; see now the fuller development of the new view in Rawls, "Public Reason." Because Rawls's view is highly protective of the liberty of conscience, all his argument pertains to moral, not legal, restrictions on religious speech.

132. Whether this is, in the Rawlsian sense, a speech about constitutional fundamentals or issues of basic justice remains unclear.

133. Sen, "Secularism," notes, however, that the attitude to Rama taken in Hindu activist politics (that he is the central god of the tradition) is far from universal: In Bengal, Rama is traditionally thought of as simply a good king, not divinity incarnate. (Thus, even the idea that the *Ramayana* is in any sense a religious text is contestable.) Furthermore, in the classic Bengali dramatic poetry of Madhusudhan Dutt, Rama's adversary Meghad is the hero, while Rama and his brothers are not even especially admirable.

134. Thus, Chief Justice Chandrachud, in the Shah Bano case, arguing (in his opening paragraph) that women are a class "traditionally subjected to unjust treatment":

> *Na stree swatantramarhati* said Manu, the Law-giver: The woman does not deserve independence. And, it is alleged that the "fatal point in Islam is the degradation of woman." [footnote to Edward William Lane, *Selections from the Kuran*]. To the Prophet is ascribed the statement, hopefully wrongly, that "Woman was made from a crooked rib, and if you try to bend it straight, it will break; therefore treat your wives kindly."

This appearance of balance in criticism, however, did not prevent a storm of protest over the Chief Justice's treatment of Islam, and citing a British critic of Islam was certainly not the most prudent or courteous thing to do.

135. For one good recent example, see *Religion and Human Rights*, ed. John Kelsay and Sumner B. Twiss (New York: The Project on Religion and Human Rights, 1994).

Chapter 4

1. See Celia W. Dugger, "U.S. Gives Asylum to Woman Who Fled Genital Mutilation," *New York Times*, June 20, 1996; and "A Refugee's Body Is Intact but Her Family Is Torn," *New York Times*, September 11, 1996. For related stories, see Neil MacFarquhar, "Mutilation of Egyptian Girls: Despite Ban, It Goes On," *New York Times* August 8, 1996, A3; Celia W. Dugger, "African Ritual Pain: Genital Cutting," *New York Times*, October 5, 1996; Celia W. Dugger, "New Law Bans Genital Cutting in United States," *New York Times*, October 12, 1996, A1.

2. Moreover, the male operation, in both Judaism and Islam, is linked with membership in the dominant male community rather than with subordination.

3. Nahid Toubia, *Female Genital Mutilation: A Call for Global Action* (hereafter *FGM*) (New York: UNICEF, 1995), 5. Toubia was the first woman surgeon in the Sudan. She is an advisor to the World Health Organization, vice chair of the Women's Rights Project of Human Rights Watch, and director of the Global Action against FGM Project at the Columbia University School of Public Health. Other medical discussions include Toubia, "Female Circumcision as a Public Health Issue," *New England Journal of Medicine* 331 (1994), 712 ff. Amy O. Tsui, Judith N. Wasserheit, and John G. Haaga, eds., *Reproductive Health in Developing Countries: Expanding Dimensions, Building Solutions* (Washington, DC: National Academy Press, 1997), 32–3 with bibliography; N. El-Saadawi, "Circumcision of Girls," and R. H. Dualeh and M. Fara-Warsame, "Female Circumcision in Somalia," in *Traditional Practices Affecting the Health of Women and Children*, ed. T. Baasher, R. H. Bannerman, H. Rushwan, and I. Sharif (Alexandria, Egypt: the World Health Organization, 1982); C. P. Howson et al., eds., *In Her Lifetime: Female Morbidity and Mortality in Sub-Saharan Africa* (Washington, DC: National Academy Press, 1996);

World Health Organization, "WHO Leads Action Against Female Genital Mutilation," *World Health Forum* 15 (1994), 416 ff; L. Heise, "Gender-based Violence and Women's Reproductive Health," *International Journal of Gynecology and Obstetrics* 46 (1994), 221–9.

4. See *FGM*, 10, stating that ritualistic circumcisions never involve only the removal of the skin around the glans, without damage to the sensitive part of the organ—although such "male style female circumcisions" have been documented in modern surgical settings. In this sense, one lengthy recent contribution to the debate appears to bypass the main issue. Leslye Obiora, "Bridges and Barricades: Rethinking Polemics and Intransigence in the Campaign Against Female Circumcision," *Case Western Reserve Law Review* 47 (1997), 275–378, begins by attacking the campaign against the operation as an example of Western paternalism and condescension, but in the end it emerges that what she herself would accept may be limited to a merely symbolic pricking. She recommends "clinicalizing" the practice, that is, permitting it but requiring it to be done in a hospital or clinic setting; she strongly implies that in such a setting no tissue would be removed, and a symbolic pricking would be the only thing that would occur. However, her own normative position remains extremely unclear because she does not ask what is in fact occurring in clinical settings in Djibouti, which has adopted the medicalization solution, and where there is no reason at all to suppose that a mere pricking is being preferred to traditional forms of the practice. See Isabelle Gunning, "Commentary," *Case Western Law Review* 47 (1992), 445–460, which emphasizes that the Djibouti campaign has focused on a shift from infibulation to any lesser surgery; given this emphasis, a considerable amount of tissue is still removed under the medicalized form of the procedure; nor does Obiora state that her own approval of medicalization would be contingent upon the operation's being merely symbolic.

5. See *FGM*, 10–11, with anatomical drawings.

6. Twenty-four countries have legislation or ministerial regulations against FGM per se; several others cover FGM under laws relating to child abuse; it is also illegal under the Convention on the Rights of the Child (CRC) and the Convention to Eliminate All Forms of Discrimination Against Women (CEDAW), which most of the countries in question have ratified. See *FGM*, 44.

7. See *FGM*, 25, reporting WHO data. Another valuable source of data is the *Country Reports on Human Rights Practices for 1996*, report submitted to the Committee on Foreign Relations, U.S. Senate and Committee on International Relations, U.S. House of Representatives by the Department of State (Washington, DC: U.S. Government Printing Office, 1997). The data, arranged by individual countries, are similar to the WHO data. See also *Human Rights are Women's Right* (London: Amnesty International, 1995), 131–4.

8. See *FGM*; and also N. Toubia, "Female Genital Mutilation," in *Women's Rights, Human Rights* (hereafter WRHR), ed. J. Peters and A. Wolper (New York: Routledge, 1994), 224–37, bibliography.

9. See Amnesty International, 132–4.

10. An African defense that has influenced many Western commentators is that of Jomo Kenyatta, *Facing Mount Kenya* (London: Secker and Warburg, 1938), 130–62. For a related anthropological account, see J. S. La Fontaine, *Initiation* (Manchester: Manchester University Press, 1985), 109–12, 166–80. Obiora gives an overview of other anthropological perspectives; unfortunately, however, she fails to acknowledge the extent of African women's resistance to FGM. See Gunning's commentary, with references, and also comments by African activist Seble Dawit, cited in

"Preface," *Case Western Law Review* 47 (1997), 28. A recent U.N. report shows that the request to use the term "female genital mutilation" rather than "female circumcision" to describe the practice came from African women, not from outsiders. See *Report of the United Nations Seminar on Traditional Practices Affecting the Health of Women and Children*, Subcommission on Prevention of Discrimination and Protection of Minorities, Commission on Human Rights, 43d Sess. 32, U.N. Doc. E/CN.4/ Sub.2/1991/48 (1991). At times, Obiora appears to recognize that "culture" includes contestation and resistance; at other times she seems to treat all resistance and protest as evidence of an alien "Western" ideology. Other African critiques of FGM can be found in Asma A'Haleem, "Claiming Our Bodies and Our Rights: Exploring Female Circumcision as an Act of Violence," *Freedom from Violence*, ed. Margaret Schuler (OEF International: 1992), available from United Nations/UNIFEM; Raqiya H. D. Abdalla, *Sisters in Affliction: Circumcision and Infibulation of Women in Africa* (London: Zed Books, 1982); Olayinko Koso-Thomas, *The Circumcision of Women: A Strategy for Eradication* (London: Zed Books, 1992); Efua Dorkenoo, *Cutting the Rose: Female Genital Mutilation—The Practice and Its Prevention* (Minority Rights Publication, 1994); Marie B. Assad, "Female Circumcision in Egypt: Social Implications, Current Reserach, and Prospects for Change," *Studies in Family Planning* 11 (1980). For a general treatment of human rights issues in Islamic perspective, see Abdullahi An-Na'im, *Toward an Islamic Reformation: Civil Liberties, Human Rights, and International Law* (Syracuse, NY: Syracuse University Press, 1990).

11. For further discussion of student writing in a course on practices of control and shaping of the female body at St. Lawrence University, see *Cultivating Humanity: A Classical Defense of Reform in Higher Education* (Cambridge, MA: Harvard University Press, 1997), chap. 6. One example of an academic article that could easily be read as advancing such claims is Tamir, "Hands off Clitoridectomy," *The Boston Review* 21(3/4) (1996), 21–2. See also Tamir's response to critics in the following issue, where she clarifies her position, suggesting that she did not intend to endorse any of the four claims in the form in which I have stated them here.

12. Quotations from student writing are from the St. Lawrence course.

13. For analysis of a (typical) student essay that advanced this thesis, see *Cultivating Humanity*, chap. 4.

14. Tamir, 21. Compare Obiora, 318–20.

15. Tamir, 21.

16. FGM, 21.

17. Ibid., 7.

18. See Toubia, in WRHR, 233.

19. "African Ritual Pain."

20. Toubia has encountered rare cases in which women who have undergone clitoridectomy and even intermediate infibulation convince her that they have experienced orgasm. She attributes this to unusual psychological resourcefulness, together with the capacities of secondary sources of sexual stimulation.

21. For valuable reflections on this point I am indebted to Grant Cornwell's "Suffering and Sexuality," a description of his experience in Kenya, as a part of a faculty group from St. Lawrence University.

22. Toubia suggests the more pertinent analogy to artificial breast implants, which do involve serious health risks but do not impair functioning in a similar way.

23. For accounts of such views in a Kenyan village, I am indebted to manuscripts by Eve Stoddard, Grant Cornwell, and the members of the St. Lawrence University Culture Encounters Group.

24. For an especially vivid description of this practice, see Jung Chang, *Wild Swans: Three Daughters of China* (London and New York: HarperCollins, 1992). See also Andrea Dworkin, *Woman Hating* (New York: Dutton, 1974), 95–116, with citations to scholarly studies and memoirs.

25. On the two styles of agricultural organization, the classic work is Esther Boserup, *Women's Role in Economic Development* 2nd ed. (Aldershot, England: Gower Publishing, 1986). (Original work published 1971)

26. See Toubia, in WRHR, 236; cf. *FGM*, 31. Mohammed told his listeners to "circumcise" but not to "mutilate," for not destroying the clitoris would be better for the man and would make the woman's face glow—a directive that many interpret as calling for "a male-type circumcision where the prepuce is removed, making the clitoris even more sensitive to touch." Toubia, in WRHR, 236. See also Marie Aimée Hélie-Lucas, "Women Living Under Muslim Laws," in *Ours By Right: Women's Rights as Human Rights*, ed. Joanna Kerr (London: Zed Books, 1993), 53. Obiora attacks this argument against the religion-based defense, saying, "The originating claim for the position holds only for persons favorably disposed to denigrating indigenous African religion as a farce" (350). But the bare fact that the practice predates the arrival of Islam and Christianity into Africa does not show that it is religious rather than cultural, and Obiora offers no argument that would help us to distinguish these two spheres. Furthermore, the legal question must be whether today the practice is defended as part of a religious system of belief, not whether at one time it had such a connection. In any case, as Obiora notes, even in the United States, with its very liberal understanding of religious freedom, the protection of the well-being and health of children has typically been understood to override the parent's interest in initiating the child into a religious practice. See *Prince v. Massachusetts*, 321 U.S. 158 (1944).

27. Kenyatta, *Facing Mount Kenya*.

28. *FGM*, 29.

29. Tamir, 21.

30. Of course, in the past many women were forced to become nuns by their families; in this situation (which may still exist today in some countries), Christian celibacy is more directly comparable to FGM.

31. Thus it is not surprising that Christians have been among the leading opponents of the practice. See *FGM*, 32, stressing the role of Christian leaders in raising the issue in the British parliament. Toubia notes, however, that the Coptic church has been silent about FGM, and the Ethiopian Orthodox Church actively supports it.

32. See, however, Catullus poem 65, where a devotee of an Asian cult castrates himself in the service of the goddess—and is promptly referred to by the female pronoun!

Chapter 5

1. Christina Hoff Sommers, *Who Stole Feminism?: How Women Have Betrayed Women* (New York: Simon and Schuster, 1994). For related arguments against feminism, see Rene Denfield, *The New Victorians: A Young Woman's Challenge to the Old Feminist Order* (New York: Warner Books, 1996); Katie Roiphe, *The Morning After: Sex, Fear, and Feminism on Campus* (1993); Elizabeth Fox Genovese, *"Feminism Is Not the Story of My Life"* (New York: Doubleday, 1996).

2. *Reed v. Reed*, 404 U.S. 71 (1971); *Frontiero v. Richardson*, 411 U.S. 677 (1973).

3. *Frontiero*, the Court repudiated the "attitude of 'romantic paternalism' which, in practical effect, put women, not on a pedestal, but in a cage"—and then went on

to assert that, though things have recently improved, pervasive discrimination still exists, "in part because of the high visibility of the sex characteristic. . . ."

4. Asymmetry of power plays a crucial role in the law of sexual harassment. For one clear case, see Judge Richard Posner's opinion in *Carr v. Allison Gas Turbine Division, General Motors*, 32 F.3d 1007 (1994).

5. These were the issues at stake in *Reed* and *Frontiero*.

6. See *Carr v. Allison Gas Turbine Division, General Motors*. Rejecting the lower court judge's finding that Carr's use of occasional obscenities constituted provocation for the harassment she received, Posner wrote, "The asymmetry of positions must be considered. . . ."

7. New York: United Nations Development Program, 1995 and 1996. I use 1996 except where a particular set of data are available only in the 1995 report.

8. Nineteen nations do better than the United States in male life expectancy, which is 72.6 to women's 79.4.

9. I omit Cuba and China, where parliamentary representation is not the result of free elections; I make no comment on the quality of elections in the cases I do cite.

10. Here I am indebted to Susan Moller Okin, "Inequalities between the Sexes in Different Cultural Contexts," in *Women, Culture, and Development*, ed. M. Nussbaum and J. Glover (Oxford: Clarendon Press, 1995), 274–97.

11. On Mexico, where rape is rarely reported, see analysis in "Mexican Woman Who Killed Would-Be Rapist to Turn to Activism," Associated Press (on-line), February 12, 1997. The story concerns a 30-year-old housewife who shot her would-be rapist and faced murder charges. Public debate about the case led to widespread concern about the treatment of female complainants by police and the legal system. For bringing this story to my attention, I am grateful to John Lott.

12. For a review of the literature on underreporting, see Richard A. Posner, *Sex and Reason* (Cambridge, MA: Harvard University Press, 1994), 384–5, with notes.

13. I am grateful to Edward Laumann for comments on Sommers's chapter about earlier surveys. He concludes that she has accurately identified some serious flaws in those studies.

14. Edward O. Laumann et al., *The Social Organization of Sexuality* (Chicago: University of Chicago Press, 1994; and Robert T. Michael, et al., *Sex in America* (Boston: Little, Brown, 1994). The study came out after Sommers's book, and she did not have access to the data.

15. They deliberately did not use the word "rape" in questioning people because they believed that there are differences between the legal and the popular meaning of the term, because people would not want to own up to committing a crime, and because many women who believe that they have had forced sex may be reluctant to apply a term with such strong emotional connotations. See *Sex in America*, 221.

16. Ibid., 221.

17. Some 20 percent of the women who had been forced said that they were sometimes or usually unhappy, as opposed to only 12 percent of the women who had not been forced.

18. *Life and Death* (New York: The Free Press, 1997).

19. In one particularly strident part of her analysis, Sommers reports with sympathy Katie Roiphe's debunking of Mary Koss's statistic that 25 percent of women have experienced rape or attempted rape at some time in their lives: "If 25 percent of my women friends were really being raped, wouldn't I know it?" But this is silly: Roiphe is in her early twenties, and Koss's claim is that this will happen to one in

four women *at some time in their lives*. The number of post-twenty-two-year-olds who are raped is surely substantial. This is the sort of error in analysis that Sommers should have pilloried, and does pillory when it is made by the other side.

20. See also Steven Schulhofer, "Taking Sexual Autonomy Seriously: Rape Law and Beyond," *Law and Philosophy* 11 (1992), 35–94; and Schulhofer, "The Feminist Challenge in Criminal Law," *University of Pennsylvania Law Review* 143 (1995), 2151–2207. For another valuable summary, see Kathryn Abrams, "Sex Wars Redux: Agency and Coercion in Feminist Legal Theory," *Columbia Law Review* 95 (1995), 304–76.

21. William Blackstone, *Commentaries*, no. 210.

22. For an excellent introduction to the law in this area, see Sanford H. Kadish and Steven J. Schulhofer, *Criminal Law and Its Processes*, 6th ed. (Boston: Little, Brown, 1995), chap. 4.

23. *House of Lords* [1976] A.C. 182.

24. See Robin D. Weiner, "Shifting the Communication Burden: A Meaningful Consent Standard in Rape," *Harvard Women's Law Journal* 6 (1983), 143, 147–9; Stephen J. Schulhofer, "The Gender Question in Criminal Law," *Social Philosophy and Policy* 7 (1990), 105, 132–3, claiming that debate about the *mens rea* standard sweeps the most important question under the rug; Catharine MacKinnon, *Toward a Feminist Theory of the State* (Cambridge, MA: Harvard University Press, 1989), chap. 171.

25. *People v. Hughes*, 343 NYS 2d 240 (App. Div. 1973). For discussion, see S. Schulhofer, *Unwanted Sex: The Culture of Intimidation and the Failure of Law* (Cambridge, MA: Harvard University Press, 1998), chap. 2.

26. A pamphlet published by the U.S. Department of Justice, and cited in *State v. Rusk*, 289 Md. 230, 424 A.2d 270 (1980): "If you are confronted by a rapist, stay calm and maximize your chances for escape.... You should not immediately try to fight back. Chances are, your attacker has the advantage." The judge also cited studies showing that victims who resist are far more likely to be injured than those who do not.

27. Ibid.

28. *State v. Lima*, 64 Hawaii 470, 643 P.2d 536, 540 (1982).

29. *People v. Warren*, 113 Ill. App. 3d 1, 446 N.E.2d 491 (1983).

30. *State in the Interest of M.T.S.*, 129 J.J. 422, 609 A.2d 1266 (1992).

31. *Tyson v. State*, 619 N.E.2d 276 (Ind. Ct. App. 1993).

32. *Commonwealth v. Lefkowitz*, 20 Mass. App. 513, 481 N.E.2d 277, 232 (1985).

33. A vivid description of the gang rape of a young woman of lower class and bad reputation, spurred on by the mythology in question, is in Joyce Carol Oates, *We Were the Mulvaneys* (New York: Dutton, 1996).

34. Schulhofer, "Taking Sexual Autonomy Seriously."

35. See ibid.

36. See Richard Posner, *Sex and Reason* (Cambridge, MA: Harvard University Press, 1992), 390–1.

37. Ibid., 390 (citing Diana E. H. Russell, *Rape in Marriage* [expanded and rev. ed. with new introduction, 1990], 59). See also Kadish and Schulhofer, 363–8.

38. See Posner, 391 (citing Irene Hanson Frieze and Angela Browne, "Violence in Marriage," in *Crime and Justice: A Research Review*, ed. Lloyd Ohlin and Michael Tonry [1989], 163, 188–90).

39. These states are Alabama, Colorado, Delaware, Florida, Georgia, Hawaii, Indiana, Kansas, Maine, Massachusetts, Minnesota, Mississippi, Missouri, Montana,

Nebraska, New Hampshire, New Jersey, New Mexico, North Dakota, Oregon, Utah, Vermont, Wisconsin. In addition, Alaska, Arkansas, Michigan, and Rhode Island exempt the married only from those laws governing intercourse with a mentally disabled partner. See Richard A. Posner and Katharine B. Silbaugh, *A Guide to America's Sex Laws* (Chicago: University of Chicago Press, 1996).

40. See Rebecca M. Ryan, "The Sex Right: A Legal History of the Marital Rape Exemption," *Law and Social Inquiry* 20 (1995), 941–1004. As an example of prevalent attitudes, Ryan discusses the case of Soames Forsyte in John Galsworthy's *The Forsyte Saga*: Having been disturbed about his behavior in raping his spouse, Soames calms his "odd, intolerable feelings of remorse and shame" by thinking about his legal rights and privileges, until the night of shame becomes, in his mind, "a certain night on which Soames at last asserted his rights and acted like a man."

41. See Ryan, 996.

42. Catharine MacKinnon (New Haven: Yale University Press, 1979).

43. See Jerome Stokes and D. Frank Vinik, "Consensual Sexual Relations between Faculty and Students in Higher Education," *Education Law Reporter* 96 (1995), 899–905.

44. "Student-Professor Sexual Relations: A Forum Discussion," *Harper's Magazine*, September 1993, 87–98.

45. Title VII, Civil Rights Act of 1964, 42 U.S.C. §§ 2000e et seq. (1988 & Supp 1993).

46. See *Harris v. Forklift Systems, Inc.*, 510 U.S. 17, 114 S. Ct. 367, 126 L. Ed. 2d. 295 (1993).

47. See *Carr v. Allison Gas Turbine Division, General Motors Corp*, 32 F.3d 1007 (7th Cir 1994).

48. See Amartya Sen, "Internal Consistency of Choice," Presidential Address of the Econometric Society 1984, *Econometrica* 1993.

49. Catharine MacKinnon, "From Practice to Theory, or What Is a White Woman Anyway?," *Yale Journal of Law and Feminism* 4 (1991), 13–22, discussed in chapter 2 (in this volume); C. MacKinnon, "Feminism and Human Rights: An Answer to Postmodernism," speech given in Valencia Spain, July 4, 1996, and forthcoming in conference proceedings.

50. John C. Harsanyi, "Morality and the Theory of Rational Behaviour," in *Utilitarianism and Beyond*, ed. A. Sen and B. Williams (Cambridge: Cambridge University Press, 1982), 39–62.

51. Jon Elster, *Sour Grapes* (Cambridge: Cambridge University Press, 1983); see also Elster, "Sour Grapes: Utilitarianism and the Genesis of Wants," in Sen and Williams, 219–38.

52. See especially Sen, "Gender Inequality and Theories of Justice," in *Women, Culture, and Development: A Study of Human Capabilities*, ed. M. Nussbaum and J. Glover (Oxford: Clarendon Press, 1995).

53. See Sen, "Freedoms and Needs," *The New Republic* January 10/17, 1994.

54. "Why the Third World Should Stress the Three R's," and "Let's Defuse the Population Bomb—with Free Markets," rep. in Gary S. Becker and Guity Nashat Becker, *The Economics of Life* (New York: McGraw Hill, 1996), 67–8, 287–9; the former defends increased public spending on education and health for the poor in Brazil and other developing countries; the latter echoes the now familiar point that education is a key to holding down population growth.

55. See, for example, Cass R. Sunstein, *The Partial Constitution* (Harvard: Harvard University Press, 1993), 133–45; David Estlund, "Who's Afraid of De-

liberative Democracy?," *Texas Law Review* 71 (1993), 1437–77; Amy Gutmann and Dennis Thompson, *Democracy and Disagreement* (Cambridge, MA: Harvard University Press, 1996).

56. See the discussion of this issue in John Rawls, "Fairness to Goodness," *The Philosophical Review* 74 (1975), 536–54.

57. Gary Becker, "The Economic Way of Looking at Behavior," in *The Essence of Becker*, ed. Ramón Febrero and Pedro S. Schwartz (Stanford, CA: Hoover Institution Press, 1995), 633–58.

58. It is not made clear here whether the preferences are deformed or whether the women are led to make choices that are contrary to what they really prefer (since Becker, unlike Paul Samuelson and other advocates of the "revealed-preference" view of choice, makes a conceptual distinction between preference and choice). Probably one should distinguish two levels of generality: At a general level, the woman's preference for a flourishing life is not distorted but frustrated by the counterproductive choice she makes; at a more concrete level, however, her preference for not getting very much education—which may seem to her the best route available to a flourishing life—can be held to be distorted by the false beliefs she holds.

59. For the Kantian antecedents of the ideas of Catharine MacKinnon and Andrea Dworkin, see Barbara Herman, "Could it be Worth Thinking About Kant on Sex and Marriage?" in *A Mind of One's Own: Feminist Essays on Reason and Objectivity*, ed. Louise Antony and Charlotte Witt (Boulder: Westview Press, 1993), 49–67; cf. chapter 8 (in this volume).

60. See especially "Should the Academy Support Academic Feminism?", *Public Affairs Quarterly* 2 (1988), 97–118.

61. See the libertarian critique of Aristotle in Jonathan Barnes, "Aristotle and Political Liberty," in *Aristoteles' "Politik"*, ed. G. Patzig (Göttingen: Vandenhoeck & Ruprecht, 1990), 250–64.

62. For a summary of this history, see Catharine A. MacKinnon, "Reflections on Sex Equality under Law," *Yale Law Journal* 100 (1991), 1281–1328.

Chapter 6

1. Andrea Dworkin, *Mercy* (New York: Four Walls, Eight Windows, 1991); see further treatment of Dworkin's ideas in chapters 8 and 9. *Life and Death* by Andrea Dworkin," *The New Republic*, 1997. *Life and Death* contains a valuable autobiographical essay going over the same events depicted in the novel, to my mind more powerfully.

2. We do not find this refusal in some of Dworkin's best essays on sexuality, in particular the essays on Tennessee Williams and James Baldwin in *Intercourse* (New York: The Free Press, 1987), showing that she thinks differently about relationships that unfold in a context of rough social equality. See also the autobiographical essay in *Life and Death*.

3. For an excellent discussion of the term and its philosophical/legal history in Greece and Rome, see Francesco D'Agostino, *Epieikeia: Il Tema Dell'Equità nell'Antichità Greca* (Milan: A. Giuffre, 1973). An excellent study that focuses on fourth-century B.C. oratory and its relationship to Aristotle is John Lawless, *Law, Argument, and Equity in the Speeches of Isaeus*, Ph.D. Dissertation, Brown University, 1991. Both D'Agostino and Lawless have extensive bibliographies. *Epieikeia* is usually translated into Latin by *clementia*—see op. cit. Modern scholars gener-

ally render it into German with *Billigkeit,* Italian by *equità,* French by *équité* or (translating the Latin) *clémence.*

4. Both equity and mercy can be spoken of as attributes of persons, as features of judgments rendered by a person, or as moral abstractions in their own right. Thus a person may be praised as *epieikês;* his or her judgments or decisions display *to epieikes,* or show a respect for *to epieikes.*

5. Herodotus III.53; for discussion, see D'Agostino, *Epieikeia,* 7.

6. Gorgias, *Epitaphios,* fragment Diels-Kranz 82B6. The passage has occasioned much comment and controversy. See D'Agostino, *Epieikeia,* 28–31, for some examples. It seems crucial to understand the passage as pertaining to the civic virtue of the fallen, not their military attributes.

7. See P. Chantraine, *Dictionnaire etymologique de la langue grecque: Histoire des mots,* tome II (Paris 1970), 355. For other references, see D'Agostino, *Epieikeia,* 1–2. *Eikos* is the participle of *eoika,* "seems." (The English word "seemly" is an instructive parallel.) In early poetry, the opposite of the *epieikes* is the *aeikes,* "outrageous," "totally inappropriate," "horrible."

8. In addition to the passages to be discussed later, see Pseudo-Plato, *Definitiones* 412A, the first known definition of *epieikeia,* which defines it as "good order of the reasoning soul with respect to the honorable and shameful," as "the ability to hit on what is appropriate in contracts," and also as "mitigation of that which is just and advantageous."

9. Plato, *Laws* 867d, on regulations about bringing an exiled homicide back from exile.

10. Justice Scalia, in *Walton v. Arizona,* 110 S.Ct. 3047 (1990): "Our cases proudly announce that the Constitution effectively prohibits the States from excluding from the sentencing decision *any* aspect of a defendent's character or record or *any* circumstance surrounding the crime: [for example] that the defendant had a poor and deprived childhood, or that he had a rich and spoiled childhood" (at 3062).

11. Anaximander DK fragment B1, the first surviving verbatim fragment of ancient Greek philosophy. (We know it to be verbatim because Simplicius, who reports it, also comments with some embarrassment about its language, saying "as he said using rather poetic terms.") For an excellent account of Anaximander's idea, and its connection with ideas of justice and equality in law and morals, see Gregory Vlastos, "Equality and Justice in Early Greek Cosmologies," in *Studies in Presocratic Philosophy,* vol. I, ed. David Furley and Reginald Allen (London: Routledge, 1970).

12. See G. Vlastos, "Plato's Theory of Social Justice," in *Interpretations of Plato: A Swarthmore Symposim,* ed. H. North (Leiden: Brill, 1977).

13. *Ton drasanta pathein,* Aeschylus, *Choephoroi,* I. 313. A similar idea is expressed in many places. See, for example, Aeschylus, *Agamemnon* 249, 1564.

14. That is the way Oedipus interprets the requirement. There was no religious or secular law that prescribed such a punishment for incest.

15. Sophocles fr. 770 (Pearson). See D'Agostino, *Epieikeia,* 8–10 for other related passages.

16. See *Statesman* 294A-95A; *Laws* 757E, 867D, 876A-E, 925D-926D. Like Aristotle, Plato recognizes the importance of *epieikeia* both in the judgment of whether or not a certain offense was committed and in the assessment of penalties. He suggests that laws are written deliberately in such a way as to leave gaps to be filled in by the judgment of juries. He compares the prescriptions of law to the general instructions that an athletic trainer has to give when he cannot deal with each pupil one by one—and also to a trainer or a medical doctor who has to go out of

town and therefore leaves instructions that cannot anticipate all the circumstances that may arise. This being so, it is in the spirit of law that when one *does* look into the particular case, one will modify the prescription to suit the differing conditions.

17. See Lawless, *Speeches of Isaeus*, bibliography; for some particulars, see op. cit.

18. Strictly speaking, there is another possibility: that they are both valuable norms that pervasively conflict in their requirements. Aristotle does recognize contingent conflicts of obligation, but not this sort of more deep-seated value conflict.

19. *Epanorthôma* suggests both things: The image is of straightening up something that has fallen over or gone crooked a bit. So the suggestion is that equity is putting law into the condition to which it aspires in the first place.

20. On the role of this passage in Aristotle's ethical theory generally, see Martha C. Nussbaum, "The Discernment of Perception: An Aristotelian Model for Public and Private Rationality," in *Love's Knowledge: Essays on Philosophy and Literature* (New York: Oxford University Press, 1990). There I discuss in greater detail Aristotle's reasons for thinking that general rules cannot be sufficient for the complexities of particular cases.

21. See *Nicomachean Ethics* VII.I on ethical excellence in general; *Politics* I.I on the social excellences, and *EN* X.8, 1178a9–b18, on virtue and justice as purely human and not divine.

22. See Kenneth J. Dover, "Father, Sons and Forgiveness," *Illinois Classical Studies* 16 (1991), 173–82. Dover shows that *suggnômê* is a category of judgment or opinion about what has been done, and is persistently opposed to a revenge-taking attitude, often in the context of a view about the origins of error as in obstacles common in human life, rather than in essential evil. A characteristic passage, discussed by Dover, is Xenophon *Cyrus* 3.1.38–40, where a wrongly sentenced man, about to be executed, asks the son of his enemy to forgive his father, since "[h]e does this not from ill-will (*kakonoia*) but from ignorance (*agnoia*), and all the wrong that people do from ignorance I regard as action under constraint." Cyrus, hearing this story, agrees that the father's fault is only human, and urges forgiveness on the son.

23. Cf. also *EN* 1143a19–20, connecting *suggnômê* and equity, and both with perception of the particular; cf. also *EN* 1110a24–5, 1111a1–2, on *suggnômê* in tragic situations.

24. For the link between *suggnômê* and *eleos*, see, for example, *EN* 1109b32, 1111a1. On *eleos* and obstacles, see *Rhetoric* II.8. Dover similarly, in describing tragic occasions for *suggnômê*, writes that it is frequently accompanied by the thought that the person did wrong through some error such as "[i]gnorance; duress; poverty, alcohol, lust, provocation . . . the mortal propensity to err."

25. As Aristotle evidently is, in his account of "corrective justice," in *EN* V.

26. See Stephen Halliwell, *Aristotle's Poetics* (London: Duckworth, 1986); and "Pleasure, Understanding, and Emotion in Aristotle's *Poetics*," in *Essays on Aristotle's Poetics*, ed. A. Rorty (Princeton: Princeton University Press, 1992), 241–60.

27. See *Poetics*, chap. 9, and the excellent discussion in Halliwell, "Pleasure." Aristotle remarks that neither pity nor fear will be experienced by a person who believes that he or she is above the uncertainties of life and can suffer no serious reversal. See *Rhetoric* 1382b30–32, 1385b21–2, 31: He calls this state of mind a *hubristikê diathesis*, an "overweening disposition."

28. Among the legal/rhetorical figures to be mentioned, Lysias predates Aristotle, and is active in the late fifth century; both Isaeus and Isocrates are contemporaries of Aristotle, and their period of activity overlaps with the likely period of composi-

tion of Aristotle's *Rhetoric*, which is prior to Aristotle's first departure from Athens in 347. Isaeus' earliest and latest works, for example, can be dated approximately to 389 and 344/3 B.C.

29. On all this, see Lawless, with copious references to sources ancient and modern.

30. See Michael Hillgruber, *Die zehnte Rede des Lysias: Einleitung, Text und Kommentar mit einem Anhang über die Gesetzesinterpretation bei den attischen Rednern* (Berlin and New York: Walter de Gruyter, 1988), 116–7. Hillgruber cites passages in the orators where an appeal to *ta dikaia* is used to persuade the dikasts that obedience to the letter of the law is not required by their oath. These passages are: Andocides I.31, Lysias 15.8, Demosthenes 21.4, 21.212, 23.194, 24.175, [Dem.] 58.61. Lawless, 78, discusses this material and adds Isaeus I.40 to the list.

31. See K. Seeliger, "Zur Charackteristik des Isaios," *Jahrb. für Philologie* 113 (1876), 673–9, translated in Lawless: "The principle of equity is almost always maintained, while the letter of the law is not infrequently circumvented, however much the orator is accustomed to holding his opponents to it."

32. For examples of such contrasts, see Richard Posner, *Law and Literature* (Cambridge: Harvard University Press, 1988), 108 ff., to be discussed in a later section.

33. I am translating *orgizesthai* this way because Aristotle defines *orgê* as a desire for retribution, on account of the pain of a believed slight.

34. I have discussed Seneca's views on mercy in "Seneca on Anger in Public Life," *The Therapy of Desire: Theory and Practice in Hellenistic Ethics* (Princeton: Princeton University Press, 1994), chap. 11.

35. One possible difference: Aristotle's ethical schema makes a big distinction between *adikêmata*, for which it is necessary to have a bad *character*, and lesser wrongdoings that will be classified as among the blameworthy *hamartêmata*; the latter class will include bad acts done from weakness of will with respect to some passion. Stoic moral theory is harsher toward the passions, treating them as types of false judgment that it is always in an agent's power to refuse. Thus the distinction between *akrasia* and wrongdoing from bad character is significantly weakened, if not altogether eroded.

36. Diogenes Laertius VII.117 = *Stoicorum Veterum Fragmenta* (*SVF*) III.637.

37. Clement, *Strom.* VII.7 = *SVF* III.639.

38. *SVF* III.640.

39. Plutarch, *On How the Young Person Should Listen to Poetry*, 15CD. I argue that this work represents some of the contents of Chrysippus' lost work of the same title, in M. C. Nussbaum, "Poetry and the Passions: Two Stoic Views," in *Passions & Perceptions*, ed. J. Brunschwig and M. Nussbaum (Cambridge: Cambridge University Press, 1993), 97–149.

40. Epictetus, *Diss.* 2.26.31; though a Roman Stoic, Epictetus is loyal to the Greek Stoics.

41. Epictetus, 1.24.16–18, 2.17.19–22.

42. The proper view is that virtue by itself is sufficient for *eudaimonia*.

43. Most of my argument in this passage is based on the *De Ira* (*On Anger*), though there are many similar passages in other works.

44. Insofar as she punishes people who are totally innocent of crime, she is not even a good Greek Stoic judge, for whom the particulars of the crime and offender must be correct. But the Greek Stoic would say that once some basic criteria of responsibility are met, a tough punishment is in order without a search for mitigating factors; and here her judicial procedure is like theirs.

45. Cf. K. Dover, *Greek Popular Morality in the Time of Plato and Aristotle* (Oxford: Clarendon Press, 1974), 270–2.

46. Unlike Aristotle, Seneca does not endorse *pity* or compassion as a correct response to the misfortunes of human life: for in his view, to do so would be to give too little credit to the person's own will and dignity, and, frequently, too much importance to external events.

47. One should not ignore the fact that some ameliorative punishments, according to Seneca, can be extremely harsh. Indeed, in a peculiar move, he defends capital punishment itself as in the interest of the punished, given that a longer bad life is better than a shorter one: he compares it to merciful euthanasia.

48. See J. Fillion-Lahille, *Le De Ira de Sénèque* (Paris, 1984), and the summary of the evidence in Nussbaum, *Therapy*, chap. 11.

49. These issues are discussed in more detail in "Steerforth's Arm," in *Love's Knowledge*.

50. All citations from the novel are taken from the Penguin edition, ed. Trevor Blount (Harmondsworth: Penguin, 1966).

51. These are not precisely the same, because the mature novelist has achieved an integration of the erotic and the moral that eludes the character earlier on.

52. Compare the ideas on moral responsibility developed in Susan Wolf, *Freedom Within Reason* (New York: Oxford University Press, 1990). Wolf holds—like the ancient tradition described here—that there is an asymmetry between praise and blame, that it is legitimate to commend people for achievements that are in large part the outgrowth of early education and social factors but not legitimate to blame them when such forces have made them into bad characters who are unable to respond to reason. In Wolf's view, as in mine, this asymmetry will sometimes mean not holding individuals responsible for their bad acts. Unlike her, however, I make a distinction between culpability and punishment, holding that a defendant's life story may give reasons for mitigating punishment even when requirements for culpability are met.

53. See especially, shortly preceding the discovery of Steerforth's death: "As plainly as I behold what happened, I will try to write it down. I do not recall it, but see it done; for it happens again before me" (855).

54. Of course, the novelist's stance is traditionally linked with compassion, as well as with mercy. Sometimes, that is, the response will be to sympathize with the plight of a character without blaming, whereas in other cases there may be both blame and a merciful punishment. The line is, and should be, difficult to draw, for the factors that make mercy appropriate also begin to cast doubt on full moral responsibility. (In other cases, of course, there is not even a prima facie offense, and therefore we will have pity without mercy.)

55. The development of this idea begins in "The Discernment of Perception," in *Love's Knowledge*; it continues in *Poetic Justice* (Boston: Beacon Press, 1996).

56. Or the spectator at a play. I discuss some reasons for focusing above all on the novel in *Poetic Justice*, chap. 1.

57. Discussed in "Steerforth's Arm," in *Love's Knowledge*.

58. The citation is from the opening pages of *The Princess Casamassima*.

59. John Roemer suggests the following important point: Insofar as my literary judge treats many of a person's abilities, talents, and achievements as products of circumstances beyond his or her control, this reinforces and deepens the novel's commitment to egalitarianism. (In "The Literary Imagination" I had argued that the novel is already egalitarian in asking us to identify successively with members

of different social classes, and to see their needs, without being aware of where, in the social scheme we are to choose, we ourselves will be.) For we will then see the talents and dispositions in virtue of which people earn their greater or lesser social rewards as not really theirs by desert, or not fully so, given the large role played by social advantages and other external circumstances in getting to these dispositions; and we will be more inclined to treat them as social resources that are subject to allocation as are other resources. (Not, obviously, in the sense that we will take A's talents from A and give them to B; but we will regard A's talents as like a certain level of wealth, on account of which we may require A to give back more to society in other ways.) On all this, see Roemer, "Equality of Talent," *Economics and Philosophy* I (1985), 151–86; "Equality of Resources Implies Equality of Welfare," *The Quarterly Journal of Economics* (November 1986), 751–83; "A Pragmatic Theory of Responsibility for the Egalitarian Planner," *Philosophy and Public Affairs* 22 (1993), 146–66.

60. The most important sources for Holmes's view are "The Path of the Law" and "The Common Law," now printed (the latter in extracts) in *The Essential Holmes*, ed. Richard A. Posner (hereafter Posner ed.) (Chicago: University of Chicago Press, 1992), 160–77, 237–64. For Posner's views, see *The Problems of Jurisprudence* (Cambridge, MA: Harvard University Press, 1990), chap. 5.

61. Posner commenting on Holmes's view, with approval: "We would deal with criminals as we deal with unreasonably dangerous machines.... [I]nstead of treating dangerous objects as people, he was proposing to treat dangerous people as objects" (168).

62. See especially "The Common Law," Posner ed. 247–53. Holmes does not mention the ancient Greek debate; he focuses on Hegel's account of retributivism.

63. See, for example, Posner ed., 247: "The desire for vengeance imports an opinion that its object is actually and personally to blame. It takes an internal standard, not an objective or external one, and condemns its victim by that."

64. Holmes notes that the retributive view of the criminal law has been held by such eminent figures as Bishop Butler and Jeremy Bentham. He then quotes, without comment, Sir James Stephen's view that "[t]he criminal law stands to the passion of revenge in much the same relation as marriage to the sexual appetite" (248). Presumably this means that it allows for the satisfaction of this passion in an institutionalized and civilized form, not that it causes the passion's decline.

65. See especially Posner, *Law and Literature: A Misunderstood Relation* (Cambridge, MA: Harvard University Press, 1988), 25–70.

66. Posner, *Problems of Jurisprudence*, 393–419. See also Posner, *Law and Literature*, 105–15.

67. Posner, *Law and Literature* 108–15.

68. There is another reason for Posner's skepticism about mercy: He feels that it implies a kind of interfering scrutiny of the "insides" that sits uneasily with the libertarian hands-off attitude to government intervention he has long defended. I think this is wrong: Wanting to know the relevant facts in no way entails additional curtailment of individual liberty of choice.

69. Here he advances his famous "bad man" theory of the law: In order to figure out the deterrent aspect of punishment correctly, the judge should think, in each case, of what a bad person, completely insensitive to legal or moral requirement except in calculating personal costs and benefits, would do in response to a particular set of legal practices. Thus he endorses the basic strictness in assessing penalties that gave rise to our asymmetry in the ancient tradition.

70. Posner ed., 59–60.

71. Senecan influence on Christianity begins with the work of writers such as Clement of Alexandria and Augustine. I mean to point to a resemblance—which is later developed in explicitly Stoic terms.

72. For the distinction between forgiveness and mercy, see my previous discussion of Seneca; a good modern discussion is in Jean Hampton and Jeffrie Murphy, *Forgiveness and Mercy* (Cambridge: Cambridge University Press, 1988). The attitude of Jesus toward sinners appears to be more one of mercy than of forgiveness: For sinners will certainly be condemned and punished, not let off the hook.

73. And in many cases it is harsher than the retributivist view, because a deterrence-based view often punishes attempts at crime that do not succeed; and a relatively minor crime may be punished harshly if there is reason to think the offender a dangerous repeat offender.

74. *Small v. Commonwealth*, 91 Pa. 304, 306, 308 (1879). See generally Dan M. Kahan and Martha C. Nussbaum, "Two Conceptions of Emotion in Criminal Law," *Columbia Law Review* 96 (1996), 269–374.

75. See Kahan and Nussbaum on the relationship of changing social norms to these ideals of appropriateness. Of particular interest is the contested area of homophobic killings, where some courts have refused as a matter of law to admit evidence of strong hatred and disgust as potentially mitigating, and others have in fact judged them to be mitigating factors.

76. *Woodson v. North Carolina*, 428 U.S. 280, 304 (1976) (opinion of Stewart, Powell, and Stevens, J.J.).

77. 110 S. Ct. 3047 (1990).

78. 479 U.S. 538 (1987). For discussion of both of these cases I am indebted to Ronald J. Allen, "Evidence, Inference, Rules, and Judgment in Constitutional Adjudication: The Intriguing Case of *Walton v. Arizona*," *Journal of Criminal Law and Criminology* 81 (1991), 727–59. For later thoughts about the role of logic in judicial inference, see Allen, "The Double Jeopardy Clause, Constitutional Interpretation and the Limits of Formal Logic," *Valparaiso University Law Review* 26 (1991), 281–310.

79. The murder was committed in an "especially heinous, cruel or depraved manner," and it was committed for pecuniary gain. Note that even here, in the nondiscretionary and codified portion of the judgment, intentional notions are prominently used.

80. *Mills v. Maryland*, 486 U. S. 367 (1988); and *McKoy v. North Carolina*, 110 S. Ct. 1229 (1990).

81. I have not committed myself here on the ideal scope for discretion in other areas of the law. This is an issue I feel I need to study further before making concrete claims. I focus on the capital cases because they have been the focus of an especially interesting debate about mercy, in which the penalty-setting phase has a special weight. But I think that a similar approach could be tried in another group of cases to which a finding of aggravation is pertinent, namely hate crimes. Here I think one would want to describe the grounds for aggravation very explicitly and systematically, either by setting up a special class of crimes or in the guidelines for sentencing. Once one had determined that the particular offense was of this particularly severe kind, one could then consider whether the defendant's youth, family background, and so forth gave any grounds for mitigation.

82. See Allen, "*Walton*," 741. I agree with this point against Stevens but disagree with an earlier one. Allen argues that "the primary thrust of [Stevens's] argument . . . is for categorical rather than discretionary sentencing" (736). This

seems to me inaccurate: It is, instead, a statement about the conditions under which discretionary sentencing can be well done.

83. See also Allen, "A Reconceptualization of Civil Trials," in *Probability and Inference in the Law of Evidence*, ed. P. Tillers and E. D. Green (Dordrecht: Kluwer, 1988), 21–60.

84. See Allen, "*Walton*," 734–5. This is the assumption that the current test in effect makes. If they are not independent, this probabilistic analysis does not follow, but there is also, then, no justification at all for treating them in isolation from one another, the conclusion for which I am arguing.

85. One might also point out that different jurors might be convinced by different factors, as long as they are treated as isolated units; thus one could have a situation in which all jurors agree that there is at least one mitigating factor present, but, if they disagree enough about which one that is, the defendant's attempt fails. I owe this point to Cy Wasserstrom.

86. Here the similarity to the ancient tradition is striking—especially to Seneca's insistence on separating the determination of guilt, and its level, from the assignment of (merciful) punishment.

87. 110 S. Ct. at 3062.

88. See Allen, "*Walton*," 739, also 742: "Any particular fact is of very little consequence standing alone. The web of facts is what matters." In *David Copperfield* we see a very clear example of a rich and spoiled childhood as a mitigating factor: Steerforth has no opportunity to learn moral self-restraint and is encouraged to use his talent and charm in a reckless manner.

89. I am not claiming that knowledge of the whole story should never give rise to aggravation of punishment, and by focusing on capital cases I have left undiscussed a number of lesser cases in which such thinking might figure. Consider, for example, *United States v. Lallemand*, discussed loc. cit.

90. Another point against Scalia is the structure of the pardon power: A governor can pardon a criminal but not increase a criminal's sentence or condemn someone who was acquitted. Indeed, asymmetry is built into the entirety of the criminal justice system, in the requirement to prove guilt beyond a reasonable doubt, in the safeguards surrounding the admissibility of confessions, and so forth.

91. Note that for a juror, the case at issue is likely to be a rare event, and thus there is reason to think that jury deliberations will be free from at least some of the problems of callousness and shortness of time that may limit the advisability of discretion in cases involving judges. On the other hand, the limits of juror sympathy with people who are unlike themselves remains a clear difficulty, and this is why I sympathize, to the extent that I do, with parts of the warning in the California juror instruction.

92. Compare the advice given to the prospective juror in the state of Massachusetts, in the "Juror's Creed" printed in the *Trial Juror's Handbook*: "I am a JUROR. I am a seeker of truth . . . I must lay aside all bias and prejudice. I must be led by my intelligence and not by my emotions. . . ."

93. *California v. Brown*, 479 U.S. at 542–3.

94. Thus I agree in part with Allen, "*Walton*," 747—although I do think it reasonable to stipulate this restriction on sentiment, and believe that it is possible to think of cases where sentiments would be of the inappropriate sort.

95. 479 U.S. at 545.

96. Ibid. at 548–50.

97. Ibid. at 561–3. Thus I do not agree with Allen that Blackmun "gets it right" (750). Allen, like Blackmun, is willing to give the normative term "rational" to the

opposition, granting that merciful sentiment is not rational. Why not? It is based on judgments that are (if the deliberative process is well executed) both true and justified by the evidence.

98. *Saffle v. Parks*, 110 S. Ct. 1257 (1990), at 1261.

99. See Paul Gewirtz, "Victims and Voyeurs," in *Law's Stories: Narrative and Rhetoric in the Law*, ed. Peter Brooks and Paul Gewirtz (New Haven: Yale University Press, 1996), 135–61.

100. See *United States v. Lallemand*, 989 F.2d 936 (7th Cir. 1993), where Judge Posner argues that a married homosexual is an "unusually vulnerable victim," given the current level of prejudice against gays in American society.

101. See Susan Bandes, "Empathy, Narrative, and Victim Impact Statements," *University of Chicago Law Review* 63 (1996), 361–412.

102. Ibid., 400 (citing psychological literature).

103. James Lindgren, "Defining Pornography," *University of Pennsylvania Law Review* 141 (1993), 1153–1275, has shown that none of the standard definitions of pornography work very well in separating feminist fiction from pornography if (as MacKinnon has urged—see chap. 8, this volume) the test is applied to passages taken out of context of the whole work. MacKinnon's and Dworkin's definition worked better than others in one test to separate Dworkin's own fiction from pornography, but only because Lindgren selected a rare Dworkin passage in which the woman is in control of what happens and is not subordinated. When he chose a nonconsensual episode from *Mercy*, it was judged more pornographic (by the Dworkin/MacKinnon definition) than other materials in the test (1201–2, 1242–3).

104. *Mercy*, 328.

105. Miriam Hallbauer, a University of Chicago law student who worked with battered women who had committed crimes of violence against their abusers, wrote an impressive paper demonstrating these connections, from which I have learned much.

106. See, in this connection, Elaine Scarry, *The Body in Pain: The Making and Unmaking of the World* (New York: Oxford University Press, 1985).

107. One might argue that Dworkin's style of retributivism, even if not morally precise, has strategic value, in publicizing the pervasiveness of harms done to women. There is some truth in this. See chap. 9, this volume. But there are dangers: In equating justice with a permanent state of hostility, Dworkin obscures possibilities for progress and education.

108. Contrast Dworkin, *Mercy*, 334, where, in an epilogue entitled "Not Andrea," a liberal feminist attacks Andrea Dworkin as "a prime example, of course, of the simpleminded demagogue who promotes the proposition that *bad things are bad*."

109. For Seneca's use of this animal imagery elsewhere, see Nussbaum, "Serpents in the Soul: A Reading of Seneca's *Medea*," in Nussbaum, *Therapy*, chap. 12. On related imagery in Lucretius, see Nussbaum, *Therapy*, chap. 7.

110. Cf. also *De Clementia* I.17.1: "No animal has a more troublesome temperament, none needs to be handled with greater skill, than the human being; and to none should mercy more be shown.

Chapter 7

1. E. M. Forster, *Maurice: A Novel* (New York: W. W. Norton & Company, 1971), 250.

2. *Romer v. Evans*, 116 S. Ct. 1620 (1996).

3. *The Subjection of Women* (1869), ed. Susan Moller Okin (Indianapolis, IN: Hackett, 1988), 1–2.

4. See Anne B. Goldstein, "Reasoning about Homosexuality," *Virginia Law Review* 79 (1993), 1781–1804. It was only after the Oscar Wilde trials that U.S. courts interpreted their "sodomy" and "crime against nature" statutes to prohibit fellatio.

5. 487 U.S. 186 (1986).

6. See Robert T. Michael, et al., *Sex in America* (Boston: Little, Brown, 1994); and E. O. Laumann, et al., *The Social Organization of Sexuality* (Chicago: University of Chicago Press, 1994).

7. *Watkins v. U.S. Army*, 837 F.2d 1428 (9th Cir. 1988), *amended*, 847 F.2d 1329, *different results reached on reh'g*, 875 F.2d 699 (9th Cir. 1989) (en banc), *cert. denied*, 111 S. Ct. 384 (1990). This and other related cases are collected in W. B. Rubenstein, ed., *Lesbians, Gay Men, and the Law* (New York: The New Press, 1993), which also includes an interview with Watkins about his history. Mary Ann Humphrey, "Interview with Perry Watkins," in Rubenstein, 368–75.

8. See Goldstein, 1802.

9. "Interview," 370.

10. *High Tech Gays v. Defense Indus. Sec. Clearance Office*, 895 F.2d 563 (9th Cir. 1990), reprinted in Rubenstein.

11. All citations are from *Watkins v. U.S. Army* (emphasis in the original).

12. "Interview," 371.

13. *Steffan v. Aspin*, 8 F.3d 57, 383 U.S. App. D.C. 411 (1993).

14. See Kenneth J. Dover, *Greek Homosexuality* (Cambridge, MA: Harvard University Press, 1986); and chapters 10, 12, 13, and 14 (in this volume).

15. *Loving v. Virginia*, 388 U.S. 1 (1967).

16. See William N. Eskridge, Jr., "A Social Constructionist Critique of Posner's *Sex and Reason*: Steps toward a Gaylegal Agenda," *Yale Law Journal* 102 (1990), 333–86.

17. See chapter 10 on Le Vay's work.

18. Richard Posner, *Sex and Reason* (Cambridge, MA: Harvard University Press, 1992), 418; for further discussion of Posner, see chapter 14 (in this volume).

19. Gary David Comstock, *Violence Against Lesbians and Gay Men* (New York: Columbia University Press, 1991), 31–55.

20. *Commonwealth v. Carr*, 580 A.2d 1362 (Pa. Super. 1990). See Claudia Brenner, *Eight Bullets: One Woman's Story of Surviving Anti-Gay Violence* (1995), written by the surviving woman. These and related cases are discussed in Dan M. Kahan and Martha C. Nussbaum, "Two Conceptions of Emotion in Criminal Law," *Columbia Law Review* 96 (1996), 269–374.

21. See generally R. B. Mison, "Homophobia in Manslaughter: The Homosexual Advance as Insufficient Provocation," *California Law Review* 80 (1992), 133–78.

22. "Victim's Family, Gays Say Killer Got Off Too Easy," *Salt Lake Tribune*, August 1994, C1; "Judge Draws Protest after Cutting Sentence of Gay Man's Killer," *New York Times*, August 17, 1994, A15.

23. "Panel to Examine Remarks by Judge on Homosexuals," *New York Times*, December 21, 1988, A16; see Mison, 163–4.

24. Robert Lindsey, "After Trial, Homosexuals Say Justice Is Not Blind," *New York Times* March 21, 1988, A17; see Mison, 164.

25. Suzanne Bryant, National Lesbian and Gay Law Association, remarks before the A.B.A. Judicial Conduct Subcommittee, September 22, 1989, quoted in Mison, 163.

26. Paul Gibson, "Gay and Lesbian Youth Suicide," in *U.S. Department of Health and Human Services Youth Suicide Report* (1989), 110 ff., rep. in Rubenstein, 163–6.

27. Gibson, 164.

28. Donna Dennis and Ruth Harlow, "Gay Youth and the Right to Education," in Rubenstein, 156–9.

29. Roger Scruton, "Gay Reservations," in *The Liberation Debate: Rights at Issue*, ed. Michael Leahy and Dan Cohn-Sherbok (London: Routledge, 1995), 121.

30. "No person shall be excluded from or discriminated against in admission to a public school of any town, or in obtaining the advantages, privileges and course of study of such public school on account of race, color, sex, religion, national origin or sexual orientation." Massachusetts General Laws Annotated, chapter 76, section 5 (West, 1996). Similar "sexual orientation" provisions appear in statutes governing charter schools and admission of nonresident students. All the sexual orientation provisions were enacted in 1993, under the leadership of Governor William Weld.

31. On the shaping of norms by law, see Cass R. Sunstein, "Social Norms and Social Roles," *Columbia Law Review* 96 (1996), 904–68; for the idea that emotions respond to changes in social norms, see Kahan and Nussbaum, "Two Conceptions."

32. See Richard A. Posner and Katharine B. Silbaugh, *A Guide to America's Sex Laws* (Chicago: University of Chicago Press, 1996), 65–71. The states are Arkansas, Kansas, Kentucky, Missouri, Tennessee, and Texas. Usually definitions refer to oral-genital and anal-genital contact, or, more vaguely, to "a lewd and lascivious act" or "the crime against nature"; Arkansas defines the crime in terms of penetration: Thus, in the female-female case, it is "the penetration, however slight, of the anus or vagina of a female by any body member of another female." (Thus, technically speaking, a gynecological examination by a female doctor is a crime.)

33. Alabama, Arizona, DC, Georgia, Idaho, Louisiana, Maryland, Massachusetts, Michigan, Minnesota, Mississippi, Montana, New York, Oklahoma, Pennsylvania, Rhode Island, Utah, and Virginia.

34. *Shahar v. Bowers*, 836 F. Supp. 859 (D. Ga. 993).

35. "Interview with Michael Hardwick," in Rubenstein, 125–31.

36. Posner, *Sex and Reason*, 311.

37. The data gathered in Laumann et al. show that frequency of both oral and anal intercourse among heterosexuals increases with level of education.

38. Posner, *Sex and Reason*, 346.

39. *Romer v. Evans*, 1625. Note that one may accept this line of reasoning even if one objects on principle to all antidiscrimination laws. Thus Richard Epstein, who opposed all such laws as unacceptable interference with freedom of association (*Forbidden Grounds: The Case Against Employment Discrimination Laws* [Cambridge, MA: Harvard University Press, 1992]), argues that in a world in which such laws are accepted for race and sex, it is reasonable to suggest that Amendment 2 "could be viewed as an effort to impose second-class citizenship on some persons for the benefit of others." Epstein, "Caste and the Civil Rights Laws: From Jim Crow to Same-Sex Marriages," *Michigan Law Review* 92 (1994), 2456–78.

40. In this way, the Court implicitly distinguished the case at hand from a hypothetical case in which a state might forbid smokers the narrow and specific right to overturn local antismoking laws. Here, by contrast, the minority is denied rights to nondiscrimination in multiple areas of life.

41. For an excellent treatment of the case, see C. Sunstein, "Foreword: Leaving Things Undecided," *Harvard Law Review* 110 (1996), 6–101.

42. *Romer v. Evans*, 1629.

43. Sunstein, "Foreword," 62–3.

44. See evidence presented in *Romer* at the trial court stage by a representative of the state's department of child welfare.

45. On colleges and universities in the United States, see Martha C. Nussbaum, *Cultivating Humanity: A Classical Defense of Radical Reform in Higher Education* (Cambridge, MA: Harvard University Press, 1997), chap. 7.

46. Local Government Act 1986, cited in Goldstein, "Reasoning about Homosexuality."

47. Posner, *Sex and Reason*, 302.

48. A similar religious exemption is in Title VII of the Civil Rights Act of 1964.

49. Randy Shilts, *Conduct Unbecoming: Lesbians and Gays in the US Military* (Harmondsworth: Penguin, 1992); see also Posner, *Sex and Reason*, 317.

50. *Steffan v. Cheney* , 780 F. Supp. 1, 13 (1991).

51. See Shilts, *Conduct Unbecoming*.

52. Posner, *Sex and Reason*, 321.

53. See Janet Halley, "The Status/Conduct Distinction in the 1993 Revisions to Military Anti-Gay Policy: A Legal Archaeology," *Gay/Lesbian Quarterly* 3 (1996), 159–252, including an analysis of the multiple meanings given, in discharge hearings, to the slippery word "propensity" and of inconsistencies in types of evidence admitted.

54. Scruton, "Gay Reservations," 116.

55. In numerous cases, college students on ROTC scholarships who realized and announced their sexual orientation as undergraduates were required to refund the entirety of the scholarship—even though it was not alleged that they had accepted them in bad faith.

56. *Steffan v. Aspin*, 8 F.3d 57, 303 U.S. App. D. C. 406 (1993).

57. *Steffan v. Cheney*, 780 F. Supp. 1, 3 (1991).

58. Ibid., 16.

59. Discussing the scope of discovery, Gasch said, "'The most I would allow is what relates to this plaintiff, not every "homo" that may be walking the face of the earth at this time.'" "Judge Denies Recusal Motion Over 'Homo' Remark," *Lesbian and Gay L. Notes* (1991), 34, quoted in Mison, 164, n. 213.

60. *Steffan v. Aspin*, 417.

61. *Steffan v. Perry*, 41 F.3d 677, 309 U.S. App. D.C. 281 (1994).

62. Rejecting the idea that an affirmative answer to the question, "Are you a homosexual?" could mean only "that he harbored homosexual desires and that by desires he referred to something so removed from an intention as to constitute a pure thought." Ibid., 302.

63. Ibid., 324.

64. See *Baehr v. Lewin*, 852 P.2d 44 (Hawaii 1993); Richard Mohr, *A More Perfect Union: Why Straight America Must Stand Up for Gay Rights* (Boston: Beacon Press, 1994), 72–3; Michael Nava and Robert Dawidoff, *Created Equal: Why Gay Rights Matter to Americans* (New York: St. Martins Press, 1994), 155; Williams Eskridge, Jr., *The Case for Same-Sex Marriage* (New York: The Free Press, 1996), 66–7.

65. Eskridge, *The Case for Same-Sex Marriage*, 12.

66. For Epstein's own libertarian argument in favor of gay marriage, see "Caste and the Civil Rights Laws: From Jim Crow to Same-Sex Marriages": "The arguments in favor of their legalization are strong as a matter of political theory. . . .

[T]he key point is that outsiders cannot point to their own distaste for the practices, or to their strong religious convictions and objections, as public reasons to render these unions unlawful. . . . It follows that these married couples should be allowed to participate on equal footing with other couples in the benefits the state confers on marriages. . . ." Epstein compares the argument in favor of gay marriage to the arguments against antimiscegenation laws: "It should hardly matter that there are lots of people who are deeply offended by either kind of union or who regard them as violating every sacred religious belief."

67. Thus registered partners in Norway and Sweden do not have the same adoption rights that married couples have.

68. Norwegian Act on Registered Partnerships for Homosexual Couples, 1993, Ministry of Children and Family Affairs.

69. See *Baehr v. Miike*, 1996 Haw. App. (Dec. 3, 1996): One of the State's central experts testified that "the absence of the intent or the ability to have children does not weaken the institutution of marriage"; the plaintiff's experts offered extensive testimony on these goals, which the Judge found "especially credible." Pepper Schwartz, for example, described marriage as involving "an aspiration for intimacy and security . . . a high state of hope and effort for people."

70. See Martha Minow, "All in the Family and In All Families: Membership, Loving, and Owing," in *Sex, Preference, and Family: Essays on Law and Nature*, ed. David Estlund and Martha Nussbaum (New York: Oxford University Press, 1997), 249–76; also William N. Eskridge, Jr., "Beyond Lesbian and Gay 'Families We Choose,'" in *Sex, Preference, and Family*, 277–89.

71. Scruton, "Gay Reservations."

72. P. Blumstein and P. Schwartz, *American Couples: Money, Work, Sex* (New York: William Morrow, 1983).

73. See Eskridge, *The Case for Same-Sex Marriage*, 9–12.

74. See ibid., 9–10, 70–85.

75. 388 U.S. 1 (1967).

76. Andrew Koppelman, "Why Discrimination against Lesbians and Gay Men is Sex Discrimination," *New York University Law Review* 69 (1994), 197–287; Sylvia Law, "Homosexuality and the Meaning of Gender," *Wisconsin Law Review* 1988; Cass R. Sunstein, in Estlund and Nussbaum.

77. See Eskridge, *The Case for Same-Sex Marriage*, 168–72.

78. See chapter 3 on the role of this right in the United Nations Convention on the Elimination of All Forms of Discrimination against Women. President Clinton recently reproved the Senate for not ratifying this treaty. See *New York Times*, December 11, 1996.

79. Scruton, "Gay Reservations," 117–8.

80. Paul Weithman, "Natural Law, Morality, and Sexual Complementarity," in Estlund and Nussbaum.

81. See the essays collected in S. Olyan and M. Nussbaum, *Sexual Orientation and Human Rights in American Religious Traditions* (New York: Oxford University Press, 1998).

82. Posner, *Sex and Reason*, 417–8. California study cited p. 417.

83. 457 S.E.2d 102 (Va. 1995).

84. Ibid., 109, citing the trial court; the issue was obscured by the fact that the majority opinion of the Supreme Court mentioned a precedent establishing that a lesbian mother is not per se an unfit parent and failed to emphasize the fact that the trial court's finding of unfitness was based on a disregard of this precedent.

85. The "social condemnation" attached to such a relationship will "inevitably afflict the child's relationships" with both peers and community." See ibid., 108.

86. 466 U.S. 429 (1984).

87. S. N. E. v. R. L. B., 669 P.2d (1985), 875, 878.

88. See Mison, 175 (citing *Seebol v. Farie*, No. 90–923–CA-13 (Fla. Cir. Ct. Monroe County, March 15, 1991).

89. *Seebol v. Farie*, 12 (testimony of Kenneth Pruett). Similar statements were made by the other witnesses for the state.

90. See Posner, 420.

91. 50 Ohio St. 3d 88, 552 N.E.2d 884 (1990).

92. Scruton, "Gay Reservations," 122.

93. See *Sex in America*; and *Social Organization of Sexuality*.

94. See *Sex in America*, 103–5: Blacks were more likely than whites to have had multiple partners during the past year, but the number of blacks or whites with multiple partners was small; 3 percent of whites said they had more than five partners during the past year, as opposed to 6 percent of blacks. When the team examined the number of sexual partners over a lifetime, there were no significant racial differences. The authors conclude: "The popular myth is that poor people have many partners, blacks have many partners, and conservative Christians have few. But when we looked at our respondents' education, race, and religion, these patterns did not emerge."

95. Twenty-four percent of college graduates report having more than ten partners in a lifetime, as opposed to 15 percent of those with less than a high school education. The team explained this difference as resulting from the later age of marriage in the college-educated group. There is no correlation between higher educational level and a higher number of partners during the previous year.

96. See Eskridge, *The Case for Same-Sex Marriage*.

97. Roger Scruton, *Sexual Desire* (New York: The Free Press, 1986), 305–10.

Chapter 8

1. Catharine MacKinnon, *Feminism Unmodified* (Cambridge, MA: Harvard University Press, 1987), 174.

2. See ibid., 262 n. 1. The Indianapolis ordinance struck down in *American Booksellers, Inc. v. Hudnut* (598 F. Supp. 1316 [S.D. Ind. 1984]) uses the related category: "[W]omen are presented as sexual objects for domination, conquest, violation, exploitation, possession, or use. . . ."

3. MacKinnon, *Toward a Feminist Theory of the State* (Cambridge, MA: Harvard University Press, 1989), 124.

4. Cass R. Sunstein, *The Partial Constitution* (Cambridge, MA: Harvard University Press, 1993), 257–90; also "Neutrality in Constitutional Law (With Special Reference to Pornography, Abortion, and Surrogacy)," *Columbia Law Review* 92 (1992), 1–52.

5. *Defending Pornography: Free Speech, Sex, and the Fight for Women's Rights* (New York: Scribner, 1995).

6. Review of Strossen, *The New Republic*, January 9, 1995, 42–46.

7. Passages are taken from D. H. Lawrence, *The Rainbow* (London: Penguin, 1989, first publication 1915), 132–3; James Joyce, *Ulysses* (New York, Modern Library, 1961, first copyright 1914), 742; James Hankinson, writing under the pseudonym Laurence St. Clair, *Isabelle and Véronique: Four Months, Four Cities* (New

York: Blue Moon Books, 1989), 2–4 (of 181 pages); Alan Hollinghurst, *The Swimming-Pool Library* (New York: Vintage, 1989, first published 1988), 20; Henry James, *The Golden Bowl* (New York: Penguin Books, 1985, first published 1904), 574.

8. On the artist's creative activity as an example of morally assessible conduct, see the discussion of Henry James in Martha C. Nussbaum, "'Finely Aware and Richly Responsible: Literature and the Moral Imagination," in *Love's Knowledge* (New York: Oxford University Press, 1990).

9. See Wayne Booth, *The Company We Keep: An Ethics of Fiction* (Berkeley: University of California Press, 1988).

10. See ibid., chap. 3. Booth uses Aristotle's account of friendship to ask about the ethical value of spending time in the company of texts of different sorts.

11. I want to emphasize that I speak only of the text and make no claim about the motives and views of Hankinson himself, who may for all we know have had any number of different motives for writing in this genre. We should scrupulously observe Booth's distinction between the "implied author" and the "real-life author."

12. Each of these seven would ultimately need more refinement, in connection with debates about the proper analysis of the core notions. There are, for example, many theories of what autonomy and subjectivity are.

13. I put this in quotes because I am conscious that the word is not ideal; it is too anthropomorphic for things such as ballpoint pens.

14. The same is true of "violability"—see ibid.—although if I had chosen a term such as "breakability" it would not be.

15. It is interesting to consider in this regard the legal doctrine of "moral rights" of the creators of artworks, which, in much of Europe and increasingly in the United States, protects creators against objectionable alterations in an artwork even after they have relinquished ownership. Technically speaking, these are rights of the artist, not of the artwork, and may be waived by the artist, though not, in a jointly produced work, by one artist without the consent of the others, but the resulting situation is one in which the work itself has, in effect, rights against being defaced or destroyed or in nonpermitted ways altered. For a good summary of the doctrine, see Martin A. Roeder, "The Doctrine of Moral Right: A Study in the Law of Artists, Authors and Creators," *Harvard Law Review* 53 (1940), 554–78; see also Peter H. Karlen, "Joint Ownership of Moral Rights," *Journal, Copyright Society of the U.S.A.* 1991, 242–75; for criticism of some recent U.S. state laws, see Thomas J. Davis, Jr., "Fine Art and Moral Rights: The Immoral Triumph of Emotionalism," *Hofstra Law Review* 17 (1989), 317–21. I am grateful to William Landes for these references.

16. *Gay Ideas: Outing and Other Controversies* (Boston: Beacon Press, 1992), especially the essay "'Knights, Young Men, Boys': Masculine Worlds and Democratic Values," 129–218.

17. See Gayle Rubin, "Thinking Sex," in *The Lesbian and Gay Studies Reader*, ed. H. Abelove et al. (New York: Routledge, 1993); Mohr, "Knights." See Roger Scruton, *Sexual Desire: A Moral Philosophy of the Erotic* (New York: The Free Press, 1986).

18. In an interesting sense, the norm of unconditional love of children may lead love to disregard the particularizing qualities of the individual; this may be seen as a good feature of parental love. See Gregory Vlastos, "The Individual as Object of Love in Plato," in *Platonic Studies*, 2nd ed. (Princeton: Princeton University Press, 1973, 1981).

19. For MacKinnon's account of the relation between this account and her feminist account of objectification, see *Feminist Theory*, 124, cf. also ibid., 138–9. It is

fairly clear from this discussion that the term "objectification" is intended by MacKinnon to correspond to Marx's language of *Versachlichung* or *Verdinglichung* in *Das Kapital*, and is closely connected with the notion of *Entaüsserung*, closely linked by Marx to *Entfremdung*, usually translated "alienation." MacKinnon explains Marx's argument that the "realization" of the self in private property is really a form of alienation of the self, and then says that in the case of property "alienation is the socially contingent distortion" of a process of realization, whereas in sexuality as currently realized, women's objectification just *is* alienation: "[F]rom the point of view of the object, women have not authored objectifications, they have been them."

20. One might certainly wonder whether Marx has underestimated the distinction between the worker's situation, based on a contract in which there is at least some kind of consent, and the situation of the slave, which lacks any sort of consent. This tendency to equate relations that may be subtly distinct is closely related to MacKinnon and Dworkin's tendency to efface distinctions among different types of sexual relations.

21. *Feminism Unmodified*, 48. See also *Feminist Theory*, 124, 138–9. MacKinnon understands Marx to mean that the worker puts his selfhood into the "products and relationships" he creates; he "becomes embodied in" these products. So read, Marx's idea is a version of Diotima's idea, in Plato's *Symposium*, that human beings seek to create items in which their identity may be extended and prolonged.

22. This is also the way in which I would regard the incentive of manumission as a reward for hard work: It is an incentive that is not exactly part of the institution, offered to the slave as human. Other incentives for hard work do not involve a recognition of autonomous agency and purpose.

23. Though, once again, we shall see that a certain sort of keen attention to subjective experience may be entailed by certain sorts of instrumental use of persons.

24. One way of cashing this out further would be to ask to what extent my use of him as a pillow prevented him from either attaining or acting on important capacities with which he identifies his well-being. Am I preventing him from getting up to eat? From sleeping? From walking around? From reading a book? And so forth.

25. "Could It Be Worth Thinking about Kant on Sex and Marriage?" in *A Mind of One's Own: Feminist Essays on Reason and Objectivity*, ed. Louise Antony and Charlotte Witt (Boulder, CO: Westview, 1993), 49–67.

26. See *Lectures on Ethics*, esp. the following passage "Taken by itself [sexual love] is a degradation of human nature; for as soon as a person becomes an Object of appetite for another, all motives of moral relationship cease to function, because as an Object of appetite for another a person becomes a thing and can be treated and used as such by every one." Quoted by Herman, "Kant on Sex and Marriage," 55.

27. See Andrea Dworkin, *Intercourse* (New York: The Free Press, 1987), 122–3:

There is a deep recognition in culture and in experience that intercourse is both the normal use of a woman, her human potentiality affirmed by it, and a violative abuse, her privacy irredeemably compromised, her selfhood changed in a way that is irrevocable, unrecoverable. . . . By definition, she [has] a lesser privacy, a lesser integrity of the body, a lesser sense of self, since her body can be physically occupied and in the occupation taken over.

28. Thus sex for Kant is not like a contractual relation in which one can use the other person as a means in an overall context of mutual respect: For sexual desire,

according to his analysis, drives out every possibility of respect. This is so even in marriage (see later), although there the legal context ensures that at least in other parts of the relationship respect will be present.

29. See, for a very Kantian example, Dworkin, *Intercourse*:

It is especially in the acceptance of the object status that her humanity is hurt: it is . . . an implicit acceptance of less freedom, less privacy, less integrity. In becoming an object so that he can objectify her so that he can fuck her, she begins a political collaboration with his dominance; and then when he enters her, he confirms for himself and for her what she is: that she is something, not someone; certainly not someone equal. (140–1)

30. See, for example, MacKinnon, *Feminist Theory*: "Women have been the nature, the matter, the acted upon to be subdued by the acting subject seeking to embody himself in the social world" (124); and "The acting that women are allowed is asking to be acted upon" (198).

31. Both fungibility and ownership, for example, are implicit in MacKinnon's description of males as "consumers" and "women as things for sexual use." *Feminist Theory*, 138–9.

32. See the convincing discussion of MacKinnon's ideas in Sally Haslanger, "On Being Objective and Being Objectified," in *A Mind of One's Own*, 85–125, esp. 111, where she argues that instrumentality is at the heart of MacKinnon's concept of objectification.

33. See Herman's excellent discussion: "The rules are not so much to restrain or oblige action as to construct moral regard. That is, they make the sexual interest in another person possible only where there is secure moral regard for that person's life, and they do this by making the acceptance of obligations with respect to that person's welfare a condition of sexual activity" "Kant on Sex and Marriage," 62–3.

34. Compare MacKinnon, *Feminist Theory*: "[O]bjectification itself, with self-determination ecstatically relinquished, is the apparent content of women's sexual desire and desirability" (138–9).

35. Andrea Dworkin, *Woman Hating* (New York: E. P. Dutton, 1974), 58, 62. Dworkin does not take account of the increasing prevalence of dual-ring ceremonies, which would appear to be changing the meaning of the ring from one of ownership to one of nonavailability.

36. Dworkin points to the prevalence of anal penetration in the novel as evidence that O is a surrogate for René.

37. See, for example, MacKinnon, *Feminist Theory*, objecting that the "as a whole" test legitimates publications such as *Playboy*: "[L]egitimate settings diminish the injury perceived to be done to the women whose trivialization and objectification it contextualizes. Besides, if a woman is subjected, why should it matter that the work has other value? Perhaps what redeems a work's value among men enhances its injury to women" (202).

38. In this particular case, it does not seem to be connected with a willingness to be broken or smashed, but one should see, I think, a close link between this sort of boundary surrender and the boundary surrender involved in at least some sadomasochistic relationships.

39. I mean here to say that a working-class man in England of that time is roughly comparable in social power to an upper-class woman. As for Brangwen and his wife, her higher-class origins and her property give her a rough parity with him.

40. This point is only slightly weakened by the fact that "John Thomas" is a traditional name for the penis and is not original with Mellors. The entire exchange has a very personal character, and it is at any rate clear that this is the first time that Constance has heard the name, and that for her it is a fully proper name. The fact that the genital organ is given a personal proper name, and yet a name distinct from the name of the rest of Mellors, is itself complexly related to my earlier point about loss of individuality: It alludes to the fact that in allowing this part to take over one does cease to be oneself.

What should one make of the fact that Constance's cunt is not given a proper name but is simply called "the cunt of Lady Jane," with a joking allusion to the tension between sex and class? One could, of course, argue that Mellors is treating her genitals less personally than he treats his own, but then I think it would be a jarring note in the scene if he did simply invent a name for her cunt—presumably that is a game in which she ought to play a role, and she is too frightened at this point to play that game.

41. I think that this position is subtly different from the position developed in Scruton's *Sexual Desire*. Scruton holds that in a good sexual encounter the individual people encounter one another in one another's bodies, because they allow their respective bodies to be illuminated by their own personalities—"the body of the other becomes the other self, and is illuminated in the moment of arousal by the 'I'" (Scruton, letter of April 1, 1995). I feel that in Scruton's attitude to the body there is always a sense that just as it is it is not a part of our personhood—it needs to be transfigured, and in a sense redeemed from mere animality, by a momentary and mysterious "illumination." The view I share with Lawrence holds, instead, that it was always, just as it is, a part of personhood, and does not need to be transfigured, or rather, that the only transfiguration it needs is shame-free attention and love. The difference comes out clearly in our respective attitudes to the bodies of animals, as shown in Scruton's expression "mere animality"; whereas in my view animality is one part of what a human being is, and often a delightful part. See Martha C. Nussbaum, Review of *Sexual Desire*, *The New York Review of Books*, January 1987.

42. "The Uses of the Erotic," in *Sister Outsider* (Freedom, CA: Crossing Press, 1984), 53–9.

43. See also ibid.: "The erotic . . . has been made into the confused, the trivial . . . the plasticized sensation" (54).

44. "For once we begin to feel deeply all the aspects of our lives, we begin to demand from ourselves and from our life-pursuits that they feel in accordance with that joy which we know ourselves to be capable of." Ibid., 57.

45. In that sense, the proposal is in the spirit of the attitude to sexuality expressed in the writings of the late John J. Winkler, especially *The Constraints of Desire: The Anthropology of Sex and Gender in Greece* (New York: Routledge, 1990).

46. See Martha C. Nussbaum, "The Transfiguration of Everyday Life," *Metaphilosophy* 25 (1994), 238–61.

47. In *Macho Sluts: Lesbian Erotic Fiction*. See also *Sexual Desire*, references.

48. Things are made more complex by the fact that the two Hankinson *characters* are in a sense quite Lawrentian—it is the implied author, not Macrae, who seems to be proceeding in bad faith, ascribing to the woman a subjectivity desirous of pain and humiliation. Why, then, do I move so quickly in the Hankinson case to a critique of the construction of the fiction as a whole, given that both cases are apparently equally fictional? The answer lies in the formulaic character of the Hankinson

text, which invites us to see the characters as mere pretexts for the implied author's expression of a view about women's sexuality. It seems pointless to discuss their conduct independently of a discussion of the genre, and the author's participation in it.

49. *The Subjection of Women*, ed. Susan M. Okin (Indianapolis, IN: Hackett, 1988), 86–7; see chapter 2 (in this volume).

50. For MacKinnon's accounts of this, see references in *Feminism Unmodified* and *Only Words*. See also Cohen, "Freedom, Equality, Pornography," in *Justice and Injustice in Law and Legal Theory*, ed. Auston Sarat and Thomas R. Kearns (Ann Arbor: University of Michigan Press, 1996), 99–137. Compare Mill's account of the way in which domination is "inoculated by one schoolboy upon another" (*Subjection*), though with no explicit reference to specifically erotic education.

51. One might complain about the possible bad influence of the unrepresentative portrayal of women even in a narrative that contextualized the portrayal in a way inviting criticism or distancing; thus it is not obviously mistaken of MacKinnon and Dworkin to reject appeal to context in defense of objectionable passages. But their ideas about the construction of desire take on more power when the work as a whole encourages the belief that this is the way all male-female relations are or can be. This point about the unrepresentative portrayal of women is logically independent of and has implications beyond the objectification issue: One could, similarly, object to a work that, without objectifying women in any of the senses discussed here, portrayed all its female characters as stupid, or greedy, or unreliable.

52. See discussion in "Introduction."

53. It is an interesting question to what extent a critical context of reading can impede the formation of the patterns of desire constructed by the work as it addresses its implied reader. The ancient Greek Stoics, unlike Plato, wanted to keep tragic poetry around as a source of moral warning about the pain that would ensue from the overestimation of the "goods of fortune"—as Epictetus defined tragedy, "What happens when chance events befall fools." Rejecting Plato's banishment of the poets, they thought they could domesticate them by moral critique. Were they right? See Martha C. Nussbaum, "Poetry and the Passions: Two Stoic Views," in *Passions & Perceptions*, ed. J. Brunschwig and M. Nussbaum (Cambridge: Cambridge University Press, 1993), 97–149.

54. See the very good discussion in Alison Assiter, "Autonomy and Pornography," in *Feminist Perspectives in Philosophy*, ed. Morwenna Griffiths and Margaret Whitford (London: MacMillan, 1988), 58–71, who argues that the person who frequently experiences satisfaction in connection with such limited relationships is less likely to seek out less distorting, more complicated relationships. Assiter's article contains a valuable parallel to Hegel's master-slave dialectic.

55. "The Uses of the Erotic," 54: "But pornography is a direct denial of the power of the erotic, for it represents the suppression of true feeling. Pornography emphasizes sensation without feeling."

56. See Assiter, 66–9. One may accept this criticism of *Playboy* even if one is not convinced that its portrayal of women is sufficiently depersonalizing to count as objectification. And of course, none of these arguments entails moral criticism of masturbation.

57. See Homer, *Iliad* IX.121–30: This is the offer Agamemnon makes to assuage the anger of Achilles.

58. At Brown in 1995, the essence of the controversy was over the ethical question whether women should allow themselves to be hired as models, given that they

would be cast in the role of representing Brown women generally, and given that Brown women generally did not want to be represented in that way. Issues were also raised about whether the student newspaper should have run an ad for the recruitment, given that campus sentiment was against it; and students sponsored a forum to discuss the more general ethical and legal issues involved. Because the actual recruitment took place off campus, there was nothing else to say, and in fact Brown produced the largest number of applicant models of any Ivy League campus.

59. I am thinking of bad influence in Wayne Booth's way (see *The Company We Keep*) as a bad way of spending one's time thinking and desiring during the time one is reading. I make no claims in this chapter about causal connections between those times and other times, though I do find convincing Assiter's claim that the habit of having pleasure in connection with fantasies of this type is likely to lead one to seek out such undemanding relationships in life, rather than those involving a fuller recognition of women's subjectivity and autonomy.

60. *Gay Ideas*, 196.

61. I think that this is the point made by Roger Scruton in *Sexual Desire*, when he holds that a context of intimacy and mutual regard promote the sexual attention to individuality.

62. See I.i (Maggie to the Prince): "You're a rarity, an object of beauty, an object of You're not perhaps absolutely unique, but you're so curious and eminent that there are very few others like you. . . . You're what they call a *morceau de musée*."

63. See the impressive Marxist reading of the novel in Ed Ahearn, *Marx and Modern Fiction* (New Haven: Yale University Press, 1989), 76–99.

64. "[T]he celebration of the aesthetic and the misuse of persons, two forms of acquisition, are rooted in that original accumulation, the money of the amiable Adam Verver." Ibid., 99.

65. This double etiology is suggested in some parts of Dworkin's *Intercourse*, especially "Dust/Dirt"; and in the episode in *Mercy* in which the Greek lover of Andrea abuses her after discovering that she has been having sex with other men.

Chapter 9

1. See Plato, *Sophist* 229B-D , where the Eleatic Stranger, who stands in for Socrates in that dialogue, so characterizes one species of the *kathartikê technê* (the art that cleans things up) among the subclass whose function it is to clean up the soul. The description of the operations of the questioner are a clear reference to the Socratic elenchus (the term is used at 230D1), and one that seems intended to characterize the way its practitioners see themselves. Of course, any idea attributed to Socrates in a dialogue as late as this can be ascribed to the historical Socrates only with greatest tentativeness, even more tentativeness than one must have about all Platonic evidence concerning Socrates; but it is an excellent characterization of Socrates' method and its effects, no matter whether or not Socrates invented it. (The idea of philosophy as purgative was used in a different and more radical way by the later Greek Skeptics, who intended the image to convey that philosophy carries away *all* beliefs, because they considered that it was the disease of belief *as such* that produced the ills of human life.)

2. John Rawls, *A Theory of Justice* (Cambridge, MA: Harvard University Press, 1971), 587 (the final sentence of the book): "Purity of heart, if one could attain it, would be to see clearly and to act with grace and self-command from this point of view."

3. Ibid., 7.

4. This chapter was originally a review of Andrea Dworkin, *Life and Death: Unapologetic Writings on the Continuing War Against Women* (New York: The Free Press, 1997).

Chapter 10

1. Philo, *De Animalibus*, ed. and trans. A. Terian (*Studies in Hellenistic Judaism* 1 Chico, CA: 1981), discussed in John J. Winkler, *The Constraints of Desire: The Anthropology of Sex and Gender in Ancient Greece* (New York: Routledge, 1990), 23. Philo is a Jewish Platonist living in Alexandria whose views are in some key ways different from those held by both philosophers and nonphilosophers in classical Athenian culture; he does, however, reflect views rather broadly shared in his own later time.

2. See Winkler, 23.

3. See the discussion of this passage in Kenneth J. Dover, *Greek Homosexuality* 2nd ed. (Cambridge, MA: Harvard University Press, 1989), 61. The younger man's love is *philia*, not *erôs*.

4. See John Stuart Mill, *The Subjection of Women* (1869), ed. Susan M. Okin (Indianapolis, IN: Hackett, 1988). Similar points are made in Mill's essay "On Nature."

5. Strictly speaking, he says only that this is what he wants, but the context suggests that he means that this is what he has decided to pursue, and that (by both character and author) an ethical point is being made.

6. These problems include having a body of a certain type that demands a certain sort and quantity of nutrition; in that way biological commonality does shape the experience of emotion and desire. See the discussion to follow.

7. The material in this section is presented much more fully, and with more complete references to relevant philosophical and anthropological studies, in Martha C. Nussbaum, *Upheavals of Thought: A Theory of the Emotions* (The Gifford Lectures, University of Edinburgh, 1993) (Cambridge: Cambridge University Press, forthcoming).

8. The argument in what follows is closely related to the argument of Gifford Lecture 1, a version of which is published as "Emotions as Judgments of Value and Importance," in *Relativism, Suffering and Beyond: Essays in Memory of Bimal K. Matilal*, ed. P. Bilimoria and J. N. Mohanty (Delhi: Oxford University Press, 1997), 231–51. See also the related account of ancient Greek Stoic views in *The Therapy of Desire: Theory and Practice in Hellenistic Ethics* (Princeton: Princeton University Press, 1994) chap. 10.

9. There is much confusion here between two importantly distinct claims: (1) the claim that emotions are "irrational" in the sense of "noncognitive," and (2) the claim that they are "irrational" in a normative sense, meaning "ill-suited to guide us when we wish to think well." One might, of course, hold (2) without (1); and indeed most of the major philosophical holders of (2)—such as Plato, the ancient Greek and Roman Stoics, Spinoza, and Kant—were all defenders of some type of cognitive view of emotion. They just thought that the cognitions in question were inaccurate because they ascribed too much importance to aspects of the world outside ourselves that we do not control.

10. In the Gifford Lectures, I discuss related views from Chinese and Indian traditions.

11. Richard Lazarus, *Emotion and Adaptation* (New York: Oxford University Press, 1991).

12. There might be a very different type of social-construction project that would accept the adversary's view and still think of emotions as material to be formed by a noncognitive process of behavioral conditioning. See D. Kahan and M. Nussbaum, "Two Conceptions of Emotion in Criminal Law," *Columbia Law Review* 96 (1996), 270–374.

13. Euripides, *Trojan Women*, 1158–207.

14. Hecuba's criticism focuses on the gratuitous exercise of overwhelming power to crush a helpless small child who could have been rendered politically ineffectual by less brutal means—in particular, by sending him off into exile with his mother. Hecuba sees in the Greek action a sign of cowardice and weakness, not of political good sense.

15. This does not mean that a person who has a certain emotion—and therefore the beliefs that go with that—could not also have contradictory beliefs about the same matter. For example, if I am trying to become a good Stoic, I may find myself grieving at the death of a loved one (and having the beliefs about the badness of that event and the importance of the person that this grief entails) while also believing that the Stoics are correct—that these things have no real importance. What my view says about these cases is that they are instances of internal conflict in which the conflict has the form of a debate about what is really true, not the form of a noncognitive struggle between forces.

16. An intermediate case would be one in which she discovered that it was a real child but not her grandchild. Here she would presumably have some emotion, but not of this intensity. I discuss this problematic unevenness in the emotions in several of the Gifford Lectures.

17. Cicero, *Tusculan Disputations* III.30.

18. I am assuming here that the relevant beliefs and other cognitive activities are not innate, but learned. This has in fact been experimentally confirmed in some very interesting work by Martin Seligman on animal learning. See Martin Seligman, *Helplessness* (New York: W. H. Freeman, 1975).

19. Here I have only argued that beliefs are necessary for emotions—and necessary as constituent parts of what a given emotion is. (One cannot say what grief *is* without mentioning the typical beliefs that differentiate grief from anger and fear and pity.) I do not argue here for the thesis that cognitions of a certain type are sufficient conditions for the emotion. But in fact I am prepared to argue for that thesis, and I do argue for it in Gifford Lecture 1. Indeed, I argue (though with some qualification) that the emotion is identical with a cognition of this sort.

20. I discuss this in Gifford Lecture 2. The works on which I most prominently rely in constructing my account are Seligman, *Helplessness*; Lazarus, *Emotion and Adaptation*; Keith Oatley, *Best-Laid Schemes* (Cambridge: Cambridge University Press, 1992). See also Nico Frijda, *The Emotions* (Cambridge: Cambridge University Press, 1986). Of particular importance for my purposes here is the work of James Averill, which combines cognitive-psychological analysis with an analysis of socially constructed role playing. See "Grief: Its Nature and Significance," *Psychological Bulletin* 70 (1968), 721–48; and *Anger and Aggression: An Essay on Emotion* (New York: Springer, 1982). Within philosophy, an excellent and rigorous account of the cognitive dimensions of emotion, with an analysis of their adaptive significance in the lives of animals generally, is in Ronald de Sousa, *The Rationality of Emotion* (Cambridge, MA: MIT Press, 1987).

It should be noted that a good deal of the psychological literature implicitly commits itself to mental "representationalism"—that is, to the view that the way in which

the world impinges upon animals is through mental representations that they produce and that then have causal properties. Because the psychologists who use this
language do not offer arguments in favor of representationalism or against other
ways of understanding the animal/world relation, and because I myself have grave
doubts about the adequacy of representationalism as a view of mind, I shall simply
speak here of the animal's "interpretation" of the world, remaining neutral concerning the mental mode of the interpreting. The psychologists' basic argument is
untouched by this change, and one may note that more philosophically trained psychologists such as Lazarus and Oatley do not use representationalist language.

21. How far "down" do emotions go? Experimental evidence suggests that it is
not possible to give adequate explanations of the behavior even of rats without pos-
iting cognitive representations of the sort involved in fear. See Seligman, *Helplessness*. And Darwin long ago discovered remarkable cognitive complexity in the
activities of worms. See James Rachels, *Created From Animals* (New York: Oxford
University Press, 1990). But Darwin also argued convincingly that evasive behavior in some insects could be explained without invoking cognitive interpretations,
and the issue clearly needs to be resolved by prolonged inspection of the behavior
of each species.

22. My cognitive position is perfectly compatible with the thesis that emotions
have evolved as they have *because* of their adaptive value. (I stress this thesis in
Gifford Lecture 2.) Evolutionary biologists who offer functional accounts of emotion do not presently hold that such accounts require us to believe that emotions
are "hard-wired" rather than learned in interaction with other animals. The best
philosophical investigation of this issue is in de Sousa, *The Rationality of Emotion*.
And see also Oatley, Lazarus, and Seligman, op. cit. Because emotions can be shown
to require cognitive interpretations that must be learned, and that can—as Seligman
shows with painstaking experimental work—be disrupted by a disruption of ordinary learning processes, they occupy a different status from that of reflex activities
such as sneezes.

23. This does not mean that individuals could not be taught to lose that fear—
either through religious belief or through becoming so hardened to risk that it no
longer seems terrible, or through losing the love of life. But no known society is, as
a whole, totally without that fear.

24. Although, as we shall shortly see, cultural manipulation of bodily shape begins very early in life.

25. Jean Briggs, *Never in Anger* (Cambridge, MA: Harvard University Press,
1970); for a related anthropological study, see Catherine Lutz, *Unnatural Emotions*
(Chicago: University of Chicago Press, 1988).

26. On the close connection between erotic excitement and anger in Roman life,
see *The Therapy of Desire*, chaps. 11 and 13. A full study of this phenomenon would
include a study of Roman erotic language—very different from Greek erotic language in the role played by invective, enemy smashing, and humiliation, and a study
of the sexual activities reported in Roman biography—in which assertions of power
over one's male enemies are very frequently linked with sexual arousal. Here one
may note that the *Penthouse* magazine film of Suetonius' life of Caligula, which
looked obscene to many American eyes, looked evasive and prettified to a student
of ancient Rome, because consensual sexual activity between adults was again and
again substituted for the exercise of vindictive sexual humiliation and mutilation
against powerless inferiors (usually male). At the trial of the film, historian Glen
Bowersock, pressed by the district attorney to describe the divergences between film

and "book" (in the expectation that we would find that the film had introduced gratuitous obscenity), repeatedly demonstrated how the sensibility of *Penthouse* lacked the connection between arousal and revenge that is intrinsic to Suetonius' narrative. There is not a really good account of Roman sexuality corresponding to Dover's work on Greece, but for a start, see J. Adams, *The Latin Sexual Vocabulary* (Baltimore: Johns Hopkins University Press, 1982). For related observations about the role of cruelty in the "social construction" of Roman parenthood, see Richard Saller's excellent studies of child-beating and related phenomena, including "Pietas, Obligation and Authority in the Roman Ramily," *Festschrift Karl Christ* (Darmstadt: Wissenscheftliche Buchgesellschaft, 1988), 393–410.

27. For a wonderful literary embodiment of this idea, see Samuel Beckett's *Molloy* trilogy; I discuss its emotion taxonomy in Martha C. Nussbaum, "Narrative Emotions," in *Love's Knowledge* (New York: Oxford University Press, 1990). Consider, for example, the following passage:

> The idea of punishment came to his mind, addicted it is true to that chimera and probably impressed by the posture of the body and the fingers clenched as though in torment. And without knowing exactly what his sin was he felt full well that living was not a sufficient atonement for it or that this atonement was in itself a sin, calling for more atonement, and so on, as if there could be anything but life, for the living. And no doubt he would have wondered it if was really necessary to be guilty in order to be punished but for the memory, more and more galling, of his having consented to live in his mother, then to leave her. And this again he could not see as his true sin, but as yet another atonement which had miscarried and, far from cleansing him of his sin, plunged him in it deeper than before. And truth to tell the ideas of guilt and punishment were confused together in his mind, as those of cause and effect so often are in the minds of those who continue to think. And it was often in fear and trembling that he suffered, saying, This will cost me dear. . . . (Beckett, *Molloy* [New York: Grove Press, 1955], 239–40)

Here we see a specifically Irish-Christian taxonomy of emotions in which desire, guilt, fear, disgust, self-hatred, and the desire for atonement are all interwoven in a characteristic way.

28. See Kahan and Nussbaum, "Two Conceptions."

29. It is not simply that they give names to emotions that we experience but do not bother to name. A longer study of the example would show, I think, that the zealous interest in and pride concerning anger that emerges in this taxonomic activity also enters into the experience of the emotion, tinging it with a manly pride and a self-conscious classificatory zeal that would be no part of the Utku experience.

30. See Hiroshi Wagatsuma and Arthur Rossett, "The Implications of Apology: Law and Culture in Japan and the United States," *Law and Society Review* 20 (1986), 461–98. Unfortunately, the authors do not distinguish between mitigation and exculpation, and present American explanations as "exculpatory." This is unlikely to be the case, given the long tradition of linking explanation with mercy as opposed to acquittal. See chapter 12 (in this volume).

31. See Winkler, "The Constraints of Desire: Erotic Magic Spells," *The Constraints of Desire* (New York: Routledge, 1990), 71–98.

32. I am not claiming that this is universally true. Our culture, where *erôs* is

concerned, stands at the confluence of quite a few different traditions, prominently including the Christian and the Romantic, both of which have darker understandings of *erôs*.

33. Plato, *Symposium*, 199E. On the close relationship of this definition to popular understandings, see Winkler, *The Constraints of Desire*; and David M. Halperin, *One Hundred Years of Homosexuality and Other Essays on Greek Love* (New York: Routledge, 1990). Plato's primary departure from tradition is in holding that *erôs* is all along really directed toward an object—the form of the *kalon*—that is immortal and unchanging; popular accounts take it for granted that the object is a human being, and that the goal of *erôs* is intercourse with that human being.

34. Lucretius describes a closely related cultural pattern in which fusion with a divine or quasi-divine object is the goal. See Nussbaum, *Therapy of Desire*, chaps. 5 and 7.

35. But we should not forget the topless *hetaira* called Agape on an early red-figure vase, R20 in Dover's list (in *Greek Homosexuality*).

36. Cicero complains that he has only one term to use to capture these varied experiences; and yet he still thinks his audience knows well what the experiences are: see *Tusculan Disputations* IV. Japanese, more like Greek than like Latin and English, contains a plurality of words for love: *ai*, used to translate *agapê* in the Bible, is strictly nonsexual and is appropriate for parental love; *koi* is strictly sexual; *suki* is connected with liking. (I owe these observations to Mark Ramseyer.)

37. All this could be pursued further by discussing Wittgenstein's ideas of "family resemblance" and his views about the connections between meanings and forms of life.

38. I take this term from W. V. O. Quine, "Ontological Relativity," in *Ontological Relativity and Other Essays* (New York: Columbia University Press, 1969).

39. On the importance of metaphysics and epistemology for feminist inquiries in these areas, see Charlotte Witt, "Feminist Metaphysics," and Louise Antony, "Quine as Feminist," in *A Mind of One's Own: Feminist Essays on Reason and Objectivity*, ed. Louise Antony and Charlotte Witt (Boulder, CO: Westview Press, 1993).

40. See the excellent discussion of these pitfalls in Lee Yearley, *Mencius and Aquinas: Comparing Virtues and Theories of Courage* (Albany: SUNY Press, 1990).

41. See Nussbaum, "Non-Relative Virtues," in *The Quality of Life*, ed. M. C. Nussbaum and Amartya Sen (Oxford: Clarendon Press, 1993), 242–69.

42. Seneca, *On Anger*, II.10.

43. See Winkler, *The Constraints of Desire*, esp. "Penelope's Cunning and Homer's," and "The Laughter of the Oppressed."

44. See Iris Murdoch, *The Sovereignty of Good* (London: Routledge, 1970).

45. See Seneca, *On Anger*, esp. I.5. It is important to qualify this optimistic claim, in three ways, for constraints of two different sorts may make the success (or the complete success) of such a project impossible: (1) It may turn out that the experience in question does indeed have a biological component that cannot itself be changed by change of thought; I shall discuss this further below. (2) It may turn out that the structure of human life makes it impossible not to have experiences that engender the emotion—unless one withdraws one's cares from the world in such a radical way as to lose all motives for action. This is, I think, Seneca's final

position about anger. (3) The roots of the emotion may lie so deep in infancy, and may so permeate the personality, that change will not know where to locate its target, or, if it does, may find the costs of alteration too high.

46. Note that the "argument" here assumes an erroneous view of animal psychology, in which cognitive interpretation plays no important role. On this, see Seligman, Lazarus, and Oatley, op. cit.

47. I am thinking here of the famous Schachter-Singer experiments, described in S. Schachter and J. E. Singer, "Cognitive, Social, and Physiological Determinants of Emotional State," *Psychological Review* 69 (1982), 379–99. Subjects were injected with adrenalin while at the same time being given different views about their situation—as to whether they were being threatened, or insulted, or amused. Their identification of fear, and anger, and joy followed the beliefs.

48. See James Weinrich, "Toward a Sociobiological Theory of the Emotions," in *Emotion: Theory, Research, and Experience*, ed. R. Plutchik and H. Kellerman (New York: Academic Press), 13–35.

49. I do not mean to grant here that hunger and thirst are *only* "drives," lacking in all intentional or interpretive content. I mean only that they do arise "from behind," so to speak, from the state the body is in, whether or not there is any suitable object on the scene, even in fantasy, though of course the presence of an object may alter both intensity and experience, and cultural beliefs about suitable objects may play a large role here as well.

50. Briefly put, they include the observation that one may have frequent erections without any sexual feeling or pleasure, and, indeed, with a diminished capacity for sexual feeling: This is a common side effect, for example, of some medications. On the other hand, one may have intense sexual feeling and orgasm without erection, or at least without a full erection, so that even the claim of necessity seems unsuccessful. Weinrich's way of phrasing his claims has other difficulties. For example, it appears that he is committed to the view that a man with a larger penile blood volume is more aroused (and more desirous) than a man with a smaller blood volume, and thus that penis size is a measure of the capacity for arousal and desire.

51. See the good statement of this point in Sherry B. Ortner and Harriet Whitehead, *Sexual Meanings: The Cultural Construction of Gender and Sexuality* (Cambridge: Cambridge University Press, 1981).

52. See Anne Hollander, *Seeing Through Clothes* (New York: Viking, 1978). The slender female figure that is considered desirable in contemporary America would be regarded as altogether without sexual interest in many parts of the world, past and present. And, in general, stories abound about siblings of different figure types whose erotic fortunes are reversed by a change of geographical location. A valuable recent study of the American body norm, in all of its cultural contradictions, is Susan Bordo, *Unbearable Weight* (Berkeley: University of California Press, 1993). Through analysis of advertisements and other cultural signs, Bordo argues that the American female learns to eroticize incompatibles: on the one hand, susceptibility to the seductive lure of consumer commodities of many sorts, but foods above all; on the other hand, iron control over the body, manifested in an ideal form with no "wiggles."

53. Some wonderful material on this is in Ortner and Whitehead, *Sexual Meanings*; see also Jane Collier and Sylvia Yanagisako, *Gender and Kinship: Essays Toward a Unified Analysis* (Stanford: Stanford University Press, 1987). For ancient

Greece, see the essays in *Before Sexuality*, ed. D. Halperin, J. Winkler, and F. Zeitlin (Princeton: Princeton University Press, 1990).

54. Catharine MacKinnon, especially *Feminism Unmodified: Discourses on Life and Law* (Cambridge, MA: Harvard University Press, 1987); Andrea Dworkin, esp. *Intercourse* (New York: The Free Press, 1987).

55. See chapter 5 (in this volume).

56. Winkler, "Penelope's Cunning and Homer's," *The Constraints of Desire*, 129–61; see also "The Laughter of the Oppressed," 188–209.

57. See, for example, Briggs's subtle account of variations in children's responses to the Utku cultural norms; and similar material in Lutz, *Unnatural Emotions*. On the general issue of internal plurality and contestation, see, among others, Seyla Benhabib, in *Women, Culture, and Development*, ed. M. Nussbaum and J. Glover (Oxford: Clarendon Press, 1995). Amartya Sen and I have argued the point for India in "Internal Criticism and Indian Rationalist Traditions," in *Relativism*, ed. M. Krausz (Notre Dame: Notre Dame University Press, 1988). And see now Sen's "India and the West," *The New Republic*, June 7, 1993, 27–33, and "Human Rights and Asian Values," *The New Republic*, July 10/17, 1997, 33–40.

58. This claim is associated above all with the work of Michel Foucault: especially *The Use of Pleasure* Vol. 2: *The History of Sexuality*, trans. Robert Hurley (New York: Pantheon, 1984); for ancient Greece, it has also been well discussed by Halperin, *One Hundred Years*. The best historical account of Greek sexual customs is Dover, *Greek Homosexuality*.

59. Glaukon is also Plato's own half-brother.

60. Although the other bodily appetites are contrasted with the desire *to be penetrated* in respect of shamefulness. See Ps.-Aristotle, *Problemata* IV.27.

61. See Winkler, "Laying Down the Law: The Oversight of Men's Sexual Behavior in Classical Athens," in *The Constraints of Desire*, 45–70: "The concept of a *kinaidos* was of a man socially deviant in his entire being, principally observable in behavior that flagrantly violated or contravened the dominant social definition of masculinity" (45–6). For a fascinating attempt to explain how such a creature could ever be produced, see Ps.-Aristotle, *Problemata* IV.27, brilliantly analyzed by Winkler, 67–9. After a lengthy appeal to innate biological difference supported by a theory that the ducts that in most men run to the penis run, in some, to the anus by mistake, the author throws up his hands and says, "Besides, in some people habit is a second nature."

62. There are occasional exceptions for religious festivals, and possibly the theater, a religious institution. But on the whole even the complex operations of a woman who manages her husband's estate—like the young wife described in Xenophon's *Oeconomicus*—are carried on indoors. Xenophon's advice to her is to get some exercise dusting the pots and pans so that her complexion will glow without makeup.

63. See Halperin, "The Democratic Body," in *One Hundred Years*. The evidence makes it clear that prostitutes were available at a price within any man's means. A comic fragment (Philemon fr. 3 K.-A.) opines that the existence of low-price public brothels was the idea of Solon the lawgiver himself, in order to reinforce the idea of democratic equality by guaranteeing to all citizens regardless of means a way of exercising manly domination in matters of pleasure.

64. For the visual evidence on this point, with many reproductions, see Dover, *Greek Homosexuality* and chapter 12 (in this volume). It is worthy of note that the apparently obvious alternative of oral sex is disdained in Greek culture in both male-female and male-male relationships. The activity is considered "unclean," and the

performer of either fellatio or cunnilingus is thought to be humiliated by the act. Artemidoros, the second-century A.D. dream interpreter, explains at length that dreams of oral sex are always ill-omened—unless the dreamer is a person who "makes his living by his mouth," such as "trumpet players, rhetoricians, sophists, and the like." In that case, the dream is a happy sign of the profitable exercise of one's chosen profession. Ancient India also had a strong taboo against oral sex: The permissive *Kama Sutra* is sternly negative.

65. On this, see the evidence in the title essay of Halperin, *One Hundred Years*.

66. On the boy's lack of sexual arousal, see Dover on the artistic evidence, which displays cultural norms if not invariable cultural practices.

67. Richard Posner, *Sex and Reason* (Cambridge, MA: Harvard University Press, 1992); see chapter 14 (in this volume).

68. The most recent version of Posner's thesis about Greek homosexuality is "The Economics of Homosexuality," in *Sex, Preference, and Family: Essays on Law and Nature*, ed. David Estlund and Martha Nussbaum (New York: Oxford University Press, 1997); and also (under the title "Economics and the Social Construction of Homosexuality") in Posner, *Overcoming Law* (Cambridge, MA: Harvard University Press, 1996), 552–80. Here Posner makes a more complicated and, I think, much more plausible argument. Given, Posner says, that relationships with women could rarely involve companionship and friendship, the male formed relations of that sort with other males and then felt in some cases the desire to "cement" that companionship with sex. I think that this represents a marked departure from the book's analysis of opportunistic homosexuality, because it represents the desire for sex with the young male as arising not from frustrated desire for (unavailable) women but from the boy's own attractiveness in other respects, and thus it recognizes the intentional and interpretive character of sexual desire to a far greater degree than Posner's book usually does. On the other hand, it seems to me still to recognize the role of culture too little. The Greek male did not just find himself desiring to make love with a male friend: In fact, the entire culture saturated his experience with images proclaiming the beauty of young males, as well as their suitability for friendship. And the relationship thus constructed was different in all sorts of ways from Posner's image of "companionate marriage" (in its asymmetry and nonmutuality, for example, and its intense focus on a particular sort of bodily beauty), whereas Posner's analysis tends to assimilate the two.

69. Compare to both the Greek and the modern cases the case of the Navajo "berdache," discussed in Harriet Whitehead, "The Bow and the Burden Strap: A New Look at Institutionalized Homosexuality in Native North America," in Ortner and Whitehead, 80–115; and also in Walter Williams, *The Spirit and the Flesh: Sexual Diversity in American Indian Culture* (Boston: Beacon Press, 1988). This male who shows a preference for female work (especially basket weaving) gets classified as socially female *on that account*, and for this reason is steered into wearing female dress. "She" will become the wife of some male, usually one too poor to pay the usual bride-price. Whereas Christian missionaries who encountered this custom recoiled in horror, seeing "sodomy" and "unnatural activity" before their eyes, the Navajo clearly regard the intercourse of such a couple as male-female intercourse, albeit of a peculiar sort, since the berdache has been previously classified as female. And occupational classification is the central *definiens*, on which sexual role follows; there is no reason to see the berdache as having an antecedent preference for sex with males. To read the evidence this way is to impose our sexual categories a priori.

70. This does not mean that there is no biological element involved in explaining how, given the society one is in, one gets assigned to this sexual category rather than that. See section IV to follow.

71. See the excellent article by William Eskridge, "A Social Constructionist Critique of Posner's *Sex and Reason*: Steps Toward a Gaylegal Agenda," *Yale Law Journal* 102 (1992), 333–86. It should be noted that although Posner's libertarianism traces its origins to Mill, Posner on the whole does not follow Mill in his radical criticism of the current erotic preferences of men and women, which Mill holds to be distorted and highly irrational. See chapter 5 (in this volume).

72. See Cass R. Sunstein, in Estlund and Nussbaum, chap. 10.

73. This is the main defect of Bordo's imaginative analysis. For example, she criticizes those who call extremely obese people self-destructive, saying that such people are in the grip of cultural images of thinness, although of course extreme obesity is linked to various causes of death, in a causal chain that does not run through cultural perceptions—although, of course, the cultural discrimination experienced by obese people may make their health worse in a variety of ways. Again, she treats exercise as simply a matter of sculpting one's bodily "signifier," without recognizing that a person who is fitter and stronger can actually do certain things that she could not do before, say, lift a heavy object without damaging herself. The fact that lifting weight has a certain effect on the muscles and on their ability to perform certain tasks appears to be independent of the muscles' cultural symbolism.

74. For much more along these lines, see Hollander, *Seeing Through Clothes*. It is instructive to note that the first Miss America (in the 1920s) had a bust measurement of 28 inches. To take another case in point, the most cursory reading of classical Indian poetry reveals an eroticization of fleshy thighs (so fleshy that they make it hard to walk) that strikes contemporary American readers as peculiar and even a bit disgusting, rather like a praise of decaying food. Again, see Bordo, *Unbearable Weight*, for the current American norm.

75. Charles Darwin, "On the Two Forms, or Dimorphic Condition, in the Species of *Primula*, and on Their Remarkable Sexual Relations," in *The Collected Papers of Charles Darwin: Volume Two* (Chicago: University of Chicago Press, 1977), 61.

76. See Judith Butler, *Gender Trouble: Feminism and the Subversion of Identity* (New York: Routledge, 1990); M. Foucault, *Herculine Barbin, Being the Recently Discovered Memoirs of a Nineteenth Century Hermaphrodite*, trans. Richard McDongall (New York: Pantheon, 1980).

77. Anne Fausto-Sterling, *Myths of Gender* (New York: Basic Books, 1985; 2nd ed., 1992).

78. Here my argument connects with a broader set of issues in contemporary metaphysics, concerning the "interest relativity" of all categorization, in science and elsewhere. I cannot defend a general position in this complex debate here, but the position I would wish to defend is close to that of Hilary Putnam, who argues that all distinctions are in a significant sense made by human beings and relative to human interests—but that there are many constraints on the ways in which this can be done, and some categorizations are therefore superior to others. In the area of emotion and sexuality, however, I think we see considerably more variation of schematization than we do in many of the areas investigated by Putnam, given the intensity of the political interests in the outcome. This does not mean that we cannot still argue cogently that some categorizations are better than others; it does mean that it will be a long and difficult process.

79. Thomas Laqueur, *Making Sex: Body and Gender from the Greeks to Freud* (Cambridge, MA: Harvard University Press, 1990). Laqueur's treatment of the ancient Greek evidence does not seem to me very satisfactory, but the later chapters, which deal with his real period of expertise, appear convincing.

80. On February 24, 1995, the successful cloning of an adult sheep was first announced to the world.

81. This research also stresses that insofar as hormones govern sexual arousal, the operative hormone, androgen, is the same for "men" and for "women." For a good summary of recent research, see Salvatore Cucchiari, "The Origins of Gender Hierarchy," in Ortner and Whitehead, 31–79. Among the studies whose results are discussed are: John Money, "Psychosexual Differentiation," in *Sex Research: New Developments*, ed. John Money (New York: Holt, Rinehart, and Winston, 1965) 3–23; Money and Patricia Tucker, *Sexual Signatures: On Being a Man or a Woman* (Boston: Little, Brown, 1975); Frank A. Beach, "Evolutionary Changes in the Physiological Control of Mating Behavior in Mammals," *The Psychological Review* 54 (1947), 346–55; Saul Rosenzweig, "Human Sexual Autonomy as an Evolutionary Attainment, Anticipating Proceptive Sex Choice and Idiodynamic Bisexuality," in *Contemporary Sexual Behavior: Critical Issues for the 70's*, ed. J. Zubin and J. Money (Baltimore: Johns Hopkins University Press, 1973), 189–229. And for a brilliant and persistent account of the misreading of biological evidence on the question of sex difference, see Fausto-Sterling, *Myths of Gender*.

82. Simon Le Vay, "Difference in Hypothalamic Structure between Heterosexual and Homosexual Men," *Brain Research* 253 (1991), 1034–7, *The Sexual Brain* (Cambridge, MA and London: MIT Press, 1994). One good criticism is in Fausto-Sterling, *Myths of Gender*, 223–59.

83. Dean H. Hamer *et al.*, "A Linkage between DNA Markers on the X Chromosome and Male Sexual Orientation," *Science* 261 (1993), 321 ff.

84. See Charles Taylor, *Sources of the Self: The Making of the Modern Identity* (Cambridge, MA: Harvard University Press, 1989), with historical references. For comparative data, see Ortner and Whitehead, Collier and Yanagasako, and many others. For America, see Martha Minow, "All in the Family," in Estlund and Nussbaum. Of course many societies do have separate dwelling places for groupings that are in some sense "nuclear." But the peculiar Western emphasis on the moral worth of the intimate bonds of the family and on the privacy of the dwelling place as scene for this intimate moral bonding is virtually unique.

85. "Interagency Statement on the International Year of the Family, 1994," jointly issued by the concerned organizations and specialized agencies of the United Nations system.

86. Mill, *The Subjection of Women* (1869); Okin, *Justice, Gender, and the Family* (New York: Basic Books, 1989).

87. I thank my own offspring, Rachel Nussbaum, for bringing the passage to my attention.

88. "Aristotle," *Problemata*, Greek text (with English translation by W. Hett), Loeb Classical Library (Cambridge, MA: Harvard University Press, 1970), IV.13, 878A.

89. For another fascinating Greek example on this issue, see the dialogue between father and son about father beating in Aristophanes' *Clouds*; I discuss this in "Sophistry about Conventions" in *Love's Knowledge* (New York: Oxford University Press, 1990).

90. This is so because he denies that the maternal matter makes any contribution to reproduction beyond that of keeping the growing creature warm.

91. In Gifford Lecture 3.
92. *Republic*, 504 A–D.

Chapter 11

Both epigraphs to this chapter are translated from the Bangali by Kalpana Bardhan, in *Women, Outcastes, Peasants, and Rebels: A Selection of Bengali Short Stories* (Berkeley: University of California Press, 1990). Bandyopadhyay (1908–56) was a leading Bengali writer who focused on peasant life and issues of class conflict.

1. Even if one is a Cartesian dualist, as I am not, one must grant that the human exercise of mental abilities standardly requires the deployment of bodily skills. Most traditional Christian positions on the soul go still further: Aquinas, for example, holds that souls separated from the body have only a confused cognition and cannot recognize particulars. So my statements about professors can be accepted even by believers in the separable soul.

2. Smith, *The Nature and Causes of the Wealth of Nations*, I.x.b.25. Elsewhere, Smith points out that in ancient Greece acting was "as creditable . . . as it is discreditable now" (LRBL ii.230).

3. He expresses the view that the relevant talents are not so rare, and that when stigma is removed, many more people will compete for the jobs, driving down wages; this is certainly true today of acting, but far less so of opera, where "the rarity and beauty of the talents" remains at least one dominant factor.

4. Such arguments have often been used in the theater; they were used, for example, in one acting company of which I was a member, in order to persuade actors to kick back their (union-mandatory) salaries to the owners. This is fairly common in theater, where the union is weak and actors are so eager for employment that they are vulnerable to such arguments.

5. The typical contract between major U.S. symphony orchestras and the musicians' union, for example, guarantees year-round employment to symphony musicians, even though they do not play all year; this enables them to use summer months to play in low-paying or experimental settings in which they can perform contemporary music and chamber music, do solo and concerto work, and so forth. It also restricts hours of both rehearsal and performance during the performing season, leaving musicians free to teach students, attend classes, work on chamber music with friends, and in other ways to enrich their work. It also mandates blind auditions (i.e., players play behind a curtain)—with the result that the employment of female musicians has risen dramatically over the past twenty or so years since the practice was instituted.

6. See Elizabeth Anderson, *Value in Ethics and Economics* (Cambridge, MA: Harvard University Press, 1993); and Anderson, "Is Women's Labor a Commodity?" *Philosophy and Public Affairs* 19 (1990), 71–92; Margaret Jane Radin, *Contested Commodities: The Trouble with the Trade in Sex, Children, Bodily Parts, and Other Things* (Cambridge, MA: Harvard University Press, 1996); and Radin, "Market-Inalienability," *Harvard Law Review* 100 (1987), 1849–1937; Cass R. Sunstein, "Neutrality in Constitutional Law (With Special Reference to Pornography, Abortion, and Surrogacy)," *Columbia Law Review* 92 (1992), 1–52; and Sunstein, *The Partial Constitution* (Cambridge, MA: Harvard University Press, 1993), 257–90. For contrasting feminist perspectives on the general issue of contract, see Jean Hampton, "Feminist Contractarianism," in *A Mind of One's Own: Feminist Essays on*

Reason and Objectivity (Boulder, CO: Westview, 1993), 227–55; Susan Moller Okin, *Justice, Gender, and the Family* (New York: Basic Books, 1989).

7. I use this term throughout because of its familiarity, although a number of international women's organizations now avoid it for reasons connected to those in this essay, preferring the term "commercial sex worker" instead. For one recent example, see Report of the Panel on Reproductive Health, National Research Council, *Reproductive Health in Developing Countries: Expanding Dimensions, Building Solutions*, ed. Amy O. Tsui, Judith N. Wasserheit, and John G. Haaga (Washington, DC: National Academy Press, 1997), 30, stressing the wide variety of practices denoted by the term "commercial sex" and arguing that some studies show economic hardship as a major factor but some do not.

8. Among feminist discussions of prostitution, my approach is close to that of Sibyl Schwarzenbach, "Contractarians and Feminists Debate Prostitution," *New York University Review of Law and Social Change* 18 (1990–1), 103–29, and to Laurie Shrage, "Prostitution and the Case for Decriminalization," *Dissent* (Spring 1996), 41–5 (in which Shrage criticizes her earlier view expressed in "Should Feminists Oppose Prostitution?," *Ethics* 99 [1989]: 347–61).

9. To give just one example, the Annapurna Mahila Mandel project in Bombay offers job training and education to the daughters of prostitutes, in a residential school setting; they report that in five years they have managed to arrange reputable marriages for 1,000 such girls.

10. Aristotle, *Politics*, III.5 and VII.9–10.

11. See Plato, *Apology* 19D–20C, *Protagoras* passim, *Gorgias* passim.

12. I have profited here from reading an unpublished paper by Dan Klerman, "Slavery, Simony and Sex: An Intellectual History of the Limits of Monetary Relations."

13. Or those supported by religious orders.

14. Mrs. Elizabeth Billington, who sang in Arne's *Artaxerxes* in London in 1762, was forced to leave England because of criticisms of her morals; she ended her career in Italy. Another early *diva* was Maria Catalani, who sang for Handel (d. 1759), for example, in *Samson*. By the time of the publication of *The Wealth of Nations*, female singers had made great headway in displacing the *castrati*, who ceased to be produced shortly thereafter. For Smith's own attitudes to the female body, see *The Theory of Moral Sentiments* I.ii.1.3, where he states that as soon as sexual passion is gratified it gives rise to "disgust," and leads us to wish to get rid of the person who is their object, unless some higher moral sentiment preserves our regard for (certain aspects of) this person. "When we have dined, we order the covers to be removed; and we should treat in the same manner the objects of the most ardent and passionate desires, if they were the objects of no other passions but those which take their origin from the body." Smith was a bachelor who lived much of his life with his mother and did not have any lasting relationships with women.

15. Aspasia was a learned and accomplished woman who apparently had philosophical and political views; she is said to have taught rhetoric and to have conversed with Socrates. On the other hand, she could not perform any of the functions of a citizen, both because of her sex and because of her foreign birth. On the other hand, her son Pericles was subsequently legitimated and became a general. More recently, it has been doubted whether Aspasia was in fact a *hetaira*, and some scholars now think her a well-born foreign woman. But other *hetairai* in Greece

had good education and substantial financial assets; the two women recorded as students in Plato's Academy were both *hetairai*, as were most of the women attested as students of Epicurus, including one who was apparently a wealthy donor.

16. See chapter 3.

17. As far as I know, this profession is entirely hypothetical, though not by any means far-fetched. It is clear, at any rate, that individuals' abilities to endure colonoscopy without anesthesia and without moving vary considerably, so one might well develop (or discover) expertise in this area.

18. It is probably, however, a developed skill to come to work regularly and to work regular hours each day.

19. Consider, for example, the case of Jayamma, a brick worker in Trivandrum, Kerala, India, discussed by Leela Gulati, *Profiles of Female Poverty* (Delhi: Hindustan Publishing Corp., 1981) and whom I met on March 21, 1997, when she was approximately sixty-five years old. For approximately forty years, Jayamma worked as a brick carrier in the brick-making establishment, carrying heavy loads of bricks on her head all day from one place to another. Despite her strength, fitness, and reliability, she could never advance beyond that job because of her sex, whereas men were quickly promoted to the less physically demanding and higher-paying tasks of brick molding and truck loading.

20. Indeed, this appears to be a ubiquitous feature: In India, the mark of "untouchability" is the performance of certain types of cleaning, especially those dealing with bathroom areas. Mahatma Gandhi's defiance of caste manifested itself in the performance of these menial services.

21. This does not imply that there is some one thing, pleasure, varying only by quantity, that they produce. With Mill (and Plato and Aristotle), I think that pleasures differ in quality, not only in quantity.

22. This point was suggested to me by Elizabeth Schreiber. I am not sure whether I endorse it: It all depends on whether we really want to say that sex has one highest goal. Just as it would have been right, in an earlier era, to be skeptical about the suggestion that the sex involved in prostitution is "low" because it is nonreproductive, so too it might be good to be skeptical about the idea that prostitution sex is "low" because it is nonintimate. Certainly nonintimacy is involved in many noncommercial sexual relationships and is sometimes desired as such.

23. Thus the *Kama Sutra*, with its detailed instructions for elaborately skilled performances, strikes most Western readers as slightly comic, because the prevailing romantic ideal of "natural" sex makes such contrivance seem quite unsexy.

24. We might also consider the example of a skilled writer who writes advertising copy.

25. See Terri Kapsalis, *Public Privates: Performing Gynecology from Both Ends of the Speculum* (Durham: Duke University Press, 1997); and Kapsalis, "In Print: Backstage at the Pelvic Theater," *Chicago Reader*, April 18, 1997, 46. While a graduate student in performance studies at Northwestern, Kapsalis made a living as a "gynecology teaching associate," serving as the model patient for medical students learning to perform pelvic and breast examinations.

26. The same goes for vaginal penetration, according to Kapsalis: She says that the clinical nature of the procedure more than compensates for "society's queasiness with female sexuality."

27. *Women for Hire: Prostitution and Sexuality in France After 1850*, trans. Alan Sheridan (Cambridge, MA: Harvard University Press, 1990).

28. Ibid., 29. Representative views of the authors of regulationism include the view that "[d]ebauchery is a fever of the senses carried to the point of delirium; it leads to prostitution (or to early death) . . ." and that "[t]here are two natural sisters in the world: prostitution and riot." Ibid., 373.

29. For a more general discussion of the relationship between prostitution and various forms of marriage, see Richard Posner, *Sex and Reason* (Cambridge, MA: Harvard University Press, 1992), 130–3.

30. Sukanya Hantrakul, "Thai Women: Male Chauvinism à la Thai," *The Nation* November 16, 1992, cited with further discussion in Asia Watch Women's Rights Project, *A Modern Form of Slavery: Trafficking of Burmese Women and Girls into Brothels in Thailand* (New York: Human Rights Watch, 1993).

31. See *A Modern Form of Slavery; the Human Rights Watch Global Report on Women's Human Rights* (New York: Human Rights Watch, 1995), 196–273, esp. 270–3. The pertinent international human rights instruments take the same approach, including the International Covenant on Civil and Political rights, the Convention on the Elimination of All forms of Discrimination against Women, and the Convention for the Suppression of Traffic in Persons and the Exploitation of the Prostitution of Others.

32. *Palmore v. Sidoti*, 466 U.S. 429 (1984).

33. See Corbin, 90: In Paris, Dr. Clerc boasted that he could examine a woman every thirty seconds, and estimated that a single practitioner saw 400 women in a single twenty-four-hour period. Another practitioner estimatated that the average number of patients per hour was fifty-two.

34. For a more pessimistic view of health checks, see Posner, *Sex and Reason*, 209, pointing out that they frequently have had the effect of driving prostitutes into the illegal market.

35. See Richard Posner, *Private Choices and Public Health: The AIDS Epidemic in an Economic Perspective* (Cambridge, MA: Harvard University Press, 1993), 149, with references.

36. See *Human Rights Watch Global Report*, 1–7.

37. See Anderson, *Value in Ethics and Economics*, 156: "Her actions under contract express not her own valuations but the will of her customer."

38. This is crucial in the thinking behind the "capabilities approach" to which I have contributed in *Women, Culture, and Development* and other publications. For the connection between this approach and Marx's use of Aristotle, see Martha C. Nussbaum, "Aristotle on Human Nature and the Foundations of Ethics," in *World, Mind, and Ethics: Essays on the Philosophy of Bernard Williams*, ed. J. E. J. Altham and R. Harrison (Cambridge: Cambridge University Press, 1993).

39. Made frequently by my students, not necessarily to support criminalization.

40. *Value in Ethics and Economics*, 150–8; Anderson pulls back from an outright call for criminalization, concluding that her arguments "establish the legitimacy of a state interest in prohibiting prostitution, but not a conclusive case for prohibition," given the paucity of opportunities for working women.

41. See K. J. Dover, *Greek Homosexuality*, 2nd ed. (Cambridge, MA: Harvard University Press, 1978); and David Halperin, "The Democratic Body," in *One Hundred Years of Homosexuality and Other Essays on Greek Love* (New York: Routledge, 1990). Customers were all males, but prostitutes were both male and female. The evidence that prostitution was publicly funded is uncertain because it derives from comic drama, but it is clear that both male and female prostitution enjoyed broad public support and approval.

42. For a similar point, see M. J. Radin, "Market-Inalienability," 1921–25; and *Contested Commodities*, 132–6; Anderson refers to this claim of Radin's, apparently as the source of her reluctance to call outright for criminalization.

43. I would not go quite as far as John Rawls, however, in the direction of letting the market determine our cultural options. He opposes any state subsidy to opera companies, symphony orchestras, museums, and so on, on the grounds that this would back a particular conception of the good against others. I think, however, that we could defend such subsidies, within limits, as valuable because they preserve a cultural option that is among the valuable ones, and that might otherwise cease to exist. Obviously much more argument is needed on this entire question.

44. See Radin, "Market-Inalienability"; and Anderson, 156: "The prostitute, in selling her sexuality to a man, alienates a good necessarily embodied in her person to him and thereby subjects herself to his commands."

45. On this point, see also Schwarzenbach, with discussion of Marx's account of alienation.

46. See Richard Epstein, "Surrogacy: The Case for Full Contractual Enforcement," *Virginia Law Review* 81 (1995), 2327.

47. Moreover, the UCC does not cover the sale of services, and prostitution should be classified as a service rather than a good.

48. It is well-known that these ideas are heavily implicated in the difficulty of getting young people, especially young women, to use contraception.

49. See Shrage's earlier article; Andrea Dworkin, "Prostitution and Male Supremacy," *Life and Death* (New York: The Free Press, 1997).

50. An eloquent examination of the last view, with reference to Freud's account (which endorses it) is in William Miller, *The Anatomy of Disgust* (Cambridge, MA: Harvard University Press, 1997), chap. 6.

51. The Dowry Prohibition Act of 1961 makes both taking and giving of dowry illegal; in Bangladesh, demanding, taking, and giving dowry are all criminal offenses. See chapter 3 (in this volume).

52. It is extremely difficult to estimate how many women are damaged and killed as a result of this practice; it is certainly clear that criminal offenses are vastly underreported, as is domestic violence in India generally, but that very problem makes it difficult to form any reliable idea of the numbers involved. See Indira Jaising, *Justice for Women* (Bombay: The Lawyers' Collective, 1996); and chapter 3 (in this volume).

53. See Amartya Sen and Jean Drèze, *Hunger and Public Action* (Oxford: Clarendon Press, 1989), 52; and chapter 1 (in this volume). Kerala, the only Indian state to have a matrilineal property tradition, also has an equal number of men and women (contrasted with a 94/100 sex ratio elsewhere), and 97% both male and female literacy, as contrasted with 32% female literacy elsewhere.

54. See, for example, *A Modern Form of Slavery: Trafficking of Burmese Women; Human Rights Watch Global Report*, 1296–373; Amnesty International, *Human Rights Are Women's Right* (London: Amnesty International, 1995), 53–6.

55. See *Human Rights Watch Global Report*, 197, on Thailand.

56. Joseph Raz, *The Morality of Freedom* (Oxford: Clarendon Press, 1986), 374.

57. See Posner, *Sex and Reason*, 132 n. 43 on the low incidence of prostitution in Sweden, even though it is not illegal; his explanation is that "women's opportunities in the job market are probably better there than in any other country."

58. See Schwarzenbach.

59. An extremely high proportion of the labor force in India is in the informal sector.

60. SEWA was first directed by Ela Bhatt, who is now involved in international work to improve the employment options of informal-sector workers. For a valuable description of the movement, see Kalima Rose, *Where Women Are Leaders: The SEWA Movement in India* (Delhi: Sage Publications, 1995).

61. But see, here, Schwarzenbach and Shrage (op. cit.). I have also been very much influenced by the work of Martha Chen, *A Quiet Revolution: Women in Transition in Rural Bangladesh* (Cambridge, MA: Schenkman, 1983); Chen, "A Matter of Survival: Women's Right to Work in India and Bangladesh," in *Women, Culture, and Development*, ed. M. Nussbaum and J. Glover (Oxford: Clarendon Press, 1995); and Bina Agarwal, *A Field of One's Own: Gender and Land Rights in South Asia* (Cambridge: Cambridge University Press, 1994); and also "'Bargaining' and Gender Relations: Within and Beyond the Household," FCND Discussion Paper No. 27, Food Consumption and Nutrition Division, International Food Policy Research Institute, Washington, DC.

Chapter 12

This version is basically the same as that published in R. Louden, ed., *The Greeks and Us* (Chicago: University of Chicago Press, 1996). The full version of the piece, published in the *Virginia Law Review* (1994), (hereafter VALR), is considerably longer and includes both more examples and numerous further discussions of issues surrounding the use of classical evidence in courts of law. Appendices omitted here include a more detailed discussion of the passages in the *Laws* and the full evidence concerning Plato's use, throughout his writings, of disputed lexical items. At Dover's suggestion, I have incorporated material from our coauthored appendix in the VALR, which makes a joint statement of our position on central issues, into the text itself.

1. Richard A. Posner, *Sex and Reason* (Cambridge, MA: Harvard University Press, 1992), 2.

2. Ibid., 2. Posner here says that the superficiality of the opinions does not imply that the decision is wrong, but later in the book he does argue for the latter position, as we shall see.

3. Ibid., 346:

[S]tatutes which criminalize homosexual behavior express an irrational fear and loathing of a group that has been subjected to discrimination, much like that directed against the Jews, with whom indeed homosexuals . . . were frequently bracketed in medieval persecutions. . . . There is a gratuitousness, an egregiousness, a cruelty, and a meanness about the Georgia statute that could be thought to place it in the same class with Connecticut's anticontraceptive law. . . .

4. *United States v. Lallemand*, 989 F.2d 936 (7th Cir. 1993). The question before Posner was whether Lallemand, who had deliberately set out to blackmail a married homosexual, deserved an upward departure in sentencing under the federal guidelines for what is called an "unusually vulnerable victim": Given that all blackmail victims are persons with guilty secrets, what was special about this one, a married government employee with two grown children (who had attempted suicide when approached by Lallemand with the blackmail demand)? The answer lies, Posner argues, in current American mores, which do treat this sexual secret as different from many others.

5. See Martha C. Nussbaum, *The Fragility of Goodness: Luck and Ethics in Greek Tragedy and Philosophy* (hereafter *FG*) (Cambridge: Cambridge University Press, 1986), chap. 6.

6. Plato, *Symposium* 189C–193D.

7. "[T]hey are struck in a wonderful way with friendly love and intimacy and passionate desire, and are hardly willing to be apart from one another for even a short time" (192BC).

8. Aristophanes clearly prefers the male-male pairs, whom he characterizes as motivated to intercourse "not by shamelessness but by bravery and courage and manliness, welcoming one who is similar to themselves" (192A). He claims that only this sort become *politikoi*—and says that they will marry only if coerced by the law. But his description of the joyful love of the reunited "other halves" is explicitly said to apply to all three types: "both the lover of youths and any other one" (192B7). Kenneth J. Dover (*Plato: Symposium* [Cambridge: Cambridge University Press, 1980], note on this passage) argues that Aristophanes' remark about the *erômenoi* in male-male couples becoming *politikoi* is a joke, along the lines of other jokes in comedy that make fun of an alleged similarity between politicians and those who give sex for money. But in that case we would not expect Aristophanes to say, as he does, that the *erômenoi*, when older, become active *erastai*; we would expect him to focus on chronic passivity, as he does not. See, e.g., Aristophanes, *Clouds* 1088–1104, where the joke is that the politicians (and most of the audience) are all *eauprôktoi*, "wide-anused." Nor would we expect him to insist as he does, apparently seriously, that these are the bravest and most manly of lovers (192A). Since Aristophanes' statements about the manliness of male-male couples are so much in line with what Phaedrus and Pausanias seriously say, it would be difficult for a reader to take them as joking without a much clearer signal. I would therefore argue that we have Plato making fun of his foe Aristophanes by putting his own serious ideas (ideas Aristophanes would have treated cynically) into Aristophanes' own mouth. Dover now agrees with this argument.

9. *Romer v. Evans*, 116 S. Ct. 1620 (1996).

10. Much of my testimony, and by far the most relevant part, concerned an entirely different issue, the status of same-sex domestic partner law in Scandinavia, where I spent some years as a consultant with a United Nations institute concerned with quality-of-life issues.

11. Finnis, para. 46. Far less plausible, however, is the premise that Finnis also endorses, that it is always morally bad to use one's own body as an instrument of one's pleasure. As Kenneth Dover and I argue in our coauthored appendix, VALR, Finnis has no consistent way of assailing masturbation while approving of such innocuous activities as feeling the wind in one's face, going for a swim, or smelling a rose.

12. Cf., for example, para. 34: "[I]t harms the personalities of its participants by its dis-integrative manipulation of different parts of their one personal reality. . . ."

13. Here see Kenneth J. Dover, "Greek Sexual Choices" (a review of David Halperin's *One Hundred Years of Homosexuality*), *The Classical Review* (1991): "[C]hoice of sexual object has a history which becomes intelligible in proportion to our readiness to shed our belief in the inescapable naturalness of our own assumptions. . . ."

14. Cf. Kenneth J. Dover, *Greek Homosexuality* (hereafter *GH*) 2nd ed. (Cambridge, MA: Harvard University Press, 1989), vii:

A combination of love of Athens with hatred of homosexuality underlies the judgments that homosexual relations were "a Dorian sin, cultivated by a tiny minority at Athens" (J. A. K. Thomson, ignoring the evidence of the visual arts) or that they were "regarded as disgraceful both by law and . . . by general opinion" (A. E. Taylor, ignoring the implications of the text to which he refers in his footnote).

In a personal communication of February 11, 1994, Dover calls Taylor's statement a "grossly false statement." On the history of British classical scholarship on this topic, see Linda Dowling, *Hellenism and Homosexuality in Victorian Oxford* (Ithaca, NY: Cornell University Press 1994).

15. Dover, letter, February 11, 1994 (on file with VALR). In the longer version of this essay (VALR), I give numerous examples of these phenomena, many of them taken from my experience as assessor of the philosophical translations of the Loeb Classical Library—which, as it happens, was the series of translations relied on throughout by Finnis.

16. On all major points I am in agreement with the conclusions of Dover, *GH*; see also Dover, *Plato: Symposium*, a work less fully available to the lawyer because it is a commentary on the Greek text, but the main points can be easily grasped.

17. Finnis, Affidavit, para. 32.

18. Dover, *GH*, 67–8.

19. See Dover, *GH*, 1–17; and also Dover, *Greek Popular Morality in the Time of Plato and Aristotle* (hereafter *GPM*) (Oxford: Basil Blackwell, 1974).

20. The degree of reticence varies, of course, with the genre, and even in lyric and tragedy, one discovers passages of an explicitly sexual character (see my later remarks on Sappho and Aeschylus' *Myrmidons*). Interestingly, these two examples of explicitness are both homosexual; I cannot recall a case of similar heterosexual explicitness in early lyric or in tragedy.

21. See Dover, *GPM*.

22. Aristophanes' surviving plays were produced at Athens between 425 and 388 B.C.; few surviving comic fragments in general can be positively dated earlier.

23. See Martha C. Nussbaum, "Eros and the Wise: The Stoic Response to a Cultural Dilemma," *Oxford Studies in Ancient Philosophy* (1995).

24. The best treatment of Artemidoros on sex is in John J. Winkler, "Unnatural Acts," *The Constraints of Desire* (New York: Routledge, 1990), 17–44. Winkler also translates the relevant passages in an appendix (210–16). The only complete English translation (Robert White, Park Ridge, NJ: Noyes Press, 1975) is seriously defective and should not be trusted. The passage cited here is from *Constraints* p. 24.

25. See Dover, *GH*, 8; David Halperin, "Homosexuality," in *The Oxford Classical Dictionary*, 3rd ed., ed. S. Hornblower and A. Spawforth (Oxford: Oxford University Press, 1996).

26. In *The Use of Pleasure*, vol. II of *The History of Sexuality*, trans. R. Hurley (New York: Pantheon, 1985), 38–52.

27. For some examples from the philosophers, see my later discussion, and Aristotle, *EN* III.5–6; Plato, *Republic* 436B–439E; *Phaedrus* 238AB; *Laws* book I, which moves rapidly from a discussion of sexual *sôphrosunê* to a discussion of drunkenness. Other examples are cited in Foucault, op. cit., passim.

28. Dover, letter, February 11, 1994 (on file with VALR), summarizing the argument of *GH*, 60–8, where much evidence of the perceived naturalness of this desire is assembled. For just one example, Xenophon *Hieron* 1.33, where Hiero tells the poet Simonides that his passion for a youth "is for what human nature perhaps compels us to want from the beautiful."

29. Dover, letter, February 11, 1994 (on file with VALR); cf. *GH*, 196–203. Dover notes that "Pindar's gods are too refined to digest anything but ambrosia, but never so insensitive that their genitals cannot be aroused."

30. Dover, *GH*, 203.

31. Aristophanes *Acharnians* 263–79; see Dover, *GH*, 136. For many more examples, see Dover, *GH*, passim; and see David Halperin, "One Hundred Years of Homosexuality," in *One Hundred Years of Homosexuality and Other Essays on Greek Love* (New York: Routledge, 1990), 15–40.

32. See Dover, *GH*, 179–82, 183–8.

33. Dover, *GH*, 171–80; Winkler, *Constraints*, 162–87; Dover, *GH*, 175–6, argues that one fragment refers to an orgasm.

34. Plato, *Symposium* 191E. This would appear to be the only passage in Athenian literature to describe female-female relationships.

35. Winkler, *Constraints*, 162–87.

36. Artemidoros, in Winkler, *Constraints*, 221. The acts are "contrary to nature," it would seem, because to perform them would involve violating the usual rules of what is possible. The other main examples in this section are self-*fellatio*, presumed to be physically impossible; sex with the moon; sex with a dead person—again, presumed impossible (Artemidoros is presumably thinking not of necrophilia but of the fantasy that one actually succeeds in having regular intercourse with someone who is lost); and sex with various animals, especially wild animals. This last case may be possible in a way the others are not—though it all depends how wild the animals are! It is not too clear what leads Artemidoros to classify it with the impossibles, except that he may be concentrating on the vast majority of cases, where the animals are too wild or are otherwise unavailable.

37. As to the sex acts that occurred or were believed to occur, Dover, *GH*, on the basis of the evidence about the sexual practices of the women of Lesbos (involving both men and other women), concludes as follows: "[T]hey are likely to have been credited with all such genital acts as the inventive pursuit of a piquant variety of pleasure can devise, including homosexual practices together with fellation, cunnilinctus, threesomes, copulation in unusual positions and the use of olisboi" (184). On *olisboi* (dildoes) and female masturbation, see *GH*, 176 n. 9.

38. The most extensive treatment of the evidence on this point is in "The Democratic Body," in Halperin, *One Hundred Years*, 88–112, and endnotes to these pages, esp. 180 n.3.

39. Aeschines, *Against Timarchus* 1.195; see Halperin, *One Hundred Years*, 180 n.3.

40. For the best treatment of this set of connections, see Dover, *GH*, 20–109. See also John J. Winkler, "Laying Down the Law: The Oversight of Men's Sexual Behavior in Classical Athens," *Constraints*, 45–70.

41. Dover, *GH*, 36.

42. David Cohen, *Law, Sexuality, and Society: The Enforcement of Morals in Classical Athens* (Cambridge: Cambridge University Press, 1991), argues that a father could bring a prosecution of *hubris* against the consensual lover of his son. Dover points out in his recent review of Cohen (*Gnomon* 1993, 657–60) that we know of not a single case in which this actually occurred. He also criticizes Cohen for generalizing hastily from passages in Aeschines that are likely to contain self-serving distortions of popular norms. Cohen's book was repeatedly cited as a central authority by Finnis, although it appears to offer no support to Finnis's positive thesis regarding the marital bond, and although it insists, consistently with Dover's analysis, that

the penetrative homosexual role is not per se problematic (see Cohen, 182). Like Dover, Cohen insists that it is passivity that involves stigma—although he differs from Dover in his account of the circumstances under which such stigma was incurred. Dover's two counterarguments show, I believe, that Cohen has not given us any good reason to diverge from Dover's own analysis. On the other hand Dover gives Cohen's book high praise, as I would also, for its treatment of the seclusion of women.

A larger issue should now be mentioned, as David Cohen has emphasized to me (letter, April 27, 1994 [on file with VALR]). The thesis of Cohen's book, and especially of its final chapter, is that the notion of a private sphere, immune from interference by the state, was absolutely essential to the Athenian notion of radical democracy. *Law, Sexuality, and Society*, 218–40. The Introduction to the book opens with a strong attack on contemporary American and English statutes that penalize consensual sexual behavior, and, specifically, homosexual conduct. Cohen holds that the proper way to use his book in the context of these public issues is to argue that the state has no business trying to use the law to enforce morality. To this end he deliberately drew attention to the contrast between ancient Greek views on privacy and modern sexual legislation.

43. *Problemata* iv.26, see op. cit.

44. Dover, *GH*, 133–51, 204.

45. Halperin, *Oxford Classical Dictionary*.

46. See discussion in the longer version of this essay (VALR).

47. For example:

Nussbaum is further inviting the Court to admire a culture in which the primary, and perhaps the only, socially approved sorts of same-sex sex acts were between adult men on the one side and boys on the other. Nussbaum herself, and the several pro-"gay" writers on classical Greek sex whom she praises in her publications, display no noticeable interest whatever in the question whether there was an age of consent for the young boys between whose thighs grown men (with or more likely without social approval) performed what she calls "inter-crural intercourse" (graphically described by Dover at page 98). Neither she nor the others inquire how young such boys might therefore be in practice. (Rebuttal Affidavit, para. 23)

Note that Finnis, as usual, completely bypasses the possibility of penetrating a prostitute or a noncitizen, which would be widespread and socially approved forms of same-sex conduct; and he also, as usual, omits same-sex relations among women.

48. On Achilles and Patroclus, see Plato, *Symposium* 180AB: Phaedrus says that Aeschylus is wrong to make Achilles the older, on the grounds that Achilles was clearly beardless and was also the most beautiful of all the heroes. (The *erômenos* is assumed to be more beautiful than the older *erastês*.) The fragments of Aeschylus' lost *Myrmidons* give clear evidence that he saw the relationship as one involving sexual conduct, presumably intercrural intercourse: Achilles, mourning for the dead Patroclus, speaks of the "many kisses" they have shared, and of "god-fearing converse with your thighs." See translation of the fragments in Dover, *GH*, 197–8. Aeschines interprets Homer's silence on the sexual side of the relationship as a kind of cultivated knowing reticence about what would have been obvious to "educated" hearers. See Dover, *GH*, 41, 53. In Xenophon *Symposium* Socrates denies that Homer intended any erotic element in the portrayal of the friendship; as Dover and I agree, he is correct about the heroic age, but, as Dover remarks, Socrates "lived in an age

when legend owed its continued hold on the imagination at least in part to the steady importation of homosexual themes" (*GH*, 199). On Harmodius and Aristogeiton, see Dover, *GH*, 41; and especially Plato *Symposium* 182C. On the Sacred Band, see the discussion of Plato's *Symposium* in this chapter.

49. For the evidence, see this chapter's discussion on Plato's *Symposium*; and Dover, *GH*, 84.

50. See this chapter's discussion of the Stoics.

51. It would not be obvious that the partners would be expected to continue sexual relations throughout that time—although Aristophanes' picture, which makes intercourse central to the benefits of the relationship, strongly suggests this. But it is also not obvious that in long-term marriages the parties continue having sex throughout.

52. Dover aptly compares the situation of the *erômenos* to that of a young woman in Britain in the time of his adolescence (the 1930s) (*GH*, 88). He might have extended the comparison to take in this point: Just as a proper British woman, from the Victorian era until rather recently, was publicly expected not to enjoy sex but frequently did in private, so, too, it is possible that the *erômenos* derived more pleasure than is publicly depicted. In his Postscript to the second edition, Dover grants that there is some literary evidence that the *erastês* stimulated the penis of the *erômenos*, and that one vase shows an *eromenos* with an erection (205).

53. Affidavit, para. 35.

54. The best treatment of the entire issue of sources is Gregory Vlastos, *Socrates: Ironist and Moral Philosopher* (Cambridge: Cambridge University Press, 1991); Xenophon's testimony is discussed at 99–106. See also T. H. Irwin, "Xenophon's Socrates" (review of Leo Strauss), *Philosophical Review* 83 (1974), 409–13.

55. *Plato's Moral Theory* (Oxford: Clarendon Press, 1977).

56. Dover, *GH*, 154.

57. See the discussion in Dover, *GH*, 154 ff., and especially *Lysis* 205D-206A.

58. As Dover notes in *Symposium*, 5, there is a tradition—reported by Aristoxenus in the fourth century—that Socrates' heterosexual appetite was abnormally strong; it is conspicuous that Plato does not represent this version of the tradition—which, of course, would not have been incompatible with showing Socrates to have, as well, unusually strong homosexual responses.

59. To at least one woman: For the story that he had a second wife on account of laws intended to remedy underpopulation, see Diogenes Laertius, "Life of Socrates," in Diogenes Laertius, *Lives of the Philosophers*, Greek text (with English translation by R. D. Hicks), Loeb Classical Library, vol. I (Cambridge, MA: Harvard University Press, 1925).

60. At *Apology* 41C, however, he does announce his attention to engage women as well as men in philosophical questioning—when he reaches the underworld, where, presumably, women would be less secluded! And he does, of course, converse with the learned Aspasia in *Menexenus*.

61. See Dover, *GH*, 159–60. Note the close resemblance of this argument to Socrates' argument against Callicles in the *Gorgias*—see op. cit.

62. Dover, in Dover/Nussbaum appendix, VALR, discussing both the Xenophonic and the Platonic Socrates; we add that "[s]omeone who says, 'Polonius condemns borrowing,' does not imply that Polonius regards borrowing as wicked or depraved."

63. *GH*, 159.

64. Ibid., 159–60; compare Dover, letter, March 15, 1994 (on file with VALR): "I accept the criticism that in *GH* 153–164 I ought to have drawn a distinction be-

tween Plato's Socrates and Xenophon's Socrates. I think there were two reasons why I failed to do so. One was my long habituation to thinking of Socrates in terms of the contrast between the Socrates of comedy and the Socrates of serious literature (Plato, Xenophon, Lysias, etc.); the other was that in *GH* I was not primarily interested in the real Socrates, but simply in the views of homosexuality to be found in philosophical contexts, no matter to whom they were attributed. However, this is a suitable opportunity to sort things out."

65. See Vlastos, *Socrates*, 40: "A maxipassion keeps all the minipassions effortlessly under control."

66. See ibid., 42: "The irony in his love for Alcibiades, riddling from the start, persisted until the boy found the answer the hard way, in a long night of anguished humiliation, naked next to Socrates, and Socrates a block of ice."

67. In *Symposium*, Dover argues in a similar way, writing of the incident (165): "Plato undoubtedly wishes to suggest that physical relations are inimical to the pursuit of metaphysical truth with the same partner on other occasions. This may not be true, and even if it is true not everyone will regard it as a good advertisement for metaphysics, but it is dictated by Plato's psychology. . . ." Dover now clarifies:

> In that passage of my *Symposium* commentary I did not intend any inference, positive or negative, to be drawn about the views of Plato's Socrates on homosexual copulation in circumstances where no philosophical teaching or co-operation is contemplated. Since he consistently assumes that homosexual temptation is universal, natural and normal (and in *Charmides* 155C-E he amusingly describes its impact on himself), we can hardly imagine that he regarded its consummation as "monstrous," "evil," "depraved," or any adjective stronger than would be applied nowadays to a heterosexual "lapse."

68. Finnis, Affidavit, para. 35; see discussion earlier in this chapter. As for Xenophon's own attitudes to homosexual conduct, see the excellent discussion in Dover, *GH*, 61–64, where he argues that "evidently Xenophon did not think the impulse to those relations a blemish in a character for which he had an unreserved admiration" (64); the worries about conduct expressed by Xenophon's characters focus on the issue of passion as threat to reason, not on any notion of intrinsic shamefulness, wickedness, or depravity.

69. At the conclusion of his general line of argument that homosexual conduct can never actualize a genuine good because it lacks "biological unity," Finnis writes: "Hence Plato's judgment, at the decisive moment of the *Gorgias*, that there is no important distinction in essential moral worthlessness between solitary masturbation, being sodomized as a prostitute, and being sodomized for the pleasure of it." It seems very dubious that any reference to masturbation is intended in the passage. Dover (letter, March 15, 1994 [on file with VALR]) writes that he knows of "no explicit reference to masturbation in Plato or Aristotle." He points out that if Plato had intended such a reference to be understood from 494C–E, Callicles' protest would have come at D1 rather than at E7, after the reference to the *kinaidos*. (I note here that masturbation would have elicited protest for a different reason: It was thought to be a habit of slaves who did not have the means to find a sexual outlet. See Dover, *GH*, 97.)

70. Dover, letter, March 15, 1994 (on file with VALR). Nussbaum, *FG*, chap. 5, 142–3.

71. Winkler, "Laying Down the Law," in *Constraints*, 45–70; on the idea that addiction to this sort of pleasure will lead one to sell oneself, see esp. 57. Winkler

stresses that the *kinaidos* is a scare image defined contextually, usually as the polar opposite of the stouthearted patriotic manly soldier (45–54).

72. Finnis accuses me of "inherent unreliability" (Rebuttal Affidavit, 17) on the grounds that I say one thing in my book and another in the trial; he interprets the book's term "passive homosexual" to mean a person who is anally receptive in a single act. All I can say is that if my statement in the book was indeed ambiguous enough to permit this interpretation, it should not have been ambiguous; no scholar will doubt that a *kinaidos* is a type of person who habitually behaves as a pathic. And it seems reasonable enough that I should be allowed to learn from the work of others and modify my claims accordingly.

73. Pausanias is the *erastês* of Agathon. See 177D, 193B7–C2, and also *Protagoras* 315DE; the relationship is historical and was well-known for its long duration: It is attested both when Agathon is eighteen and twelve years later, when Pausanias followed him to Macedon. See Dover, *GH*, 84; *Symposium*, 3. Intimacy between Phaedrus and Erixymachus is less clearly suggested (177A). Finnis asserts without evidence that all the relationships depicted in the dialogue are "intended by the author to be understood as consistent with Socrates' and his own firm repudiation of all forms of homosexual genital activity" (Rebuttal Affidavit, para. 19). Surely if Plato wished to make such a point he would hardly have introduced Pausanias as a character, because he not only is well-known for a sexual relationship but gives the rationale for it eloquently in his speech. Dover remarks, justly, that the language of serious Greek literature is "always circumspect" in matters of sex but that this should not mislead the reader: "The ultimate 'service' or 'favour' desired by the older male is bodily contact leading to orgasm, though no doubt a smile or a friendly word would be treasured by the besotted lover as an interim favour." *Symposium*, 3.

74. This is likely to be a reference to the well-known Sacred Band of Thebes, formed around 378 B.C. Dover (*Symposium*, 10 and *Phronesis* 10 [1965], 1–20) argues that the dialogue must have been composed after that date, since Phaedrus describes the idea in "entirely hypothetical terms." But Plato more than once plays on the gap between dramatic date and date of composition, making his characters hint at things that, by the date of composition, would have been known to be reality. Thus the *Republic*'s allusions to the abuse of justice by those seeking power, on the part of characters who somewhat after the dramatic date would have been embroiled on opposite sides of a bitter political struggle with those very features, would have been heard by its audience to contain ironic reference to those events, which had in the meantime occurred. Similarly, the fact, in the *Charmides*, that characters known to the audience for their lack of moderation are shown (at a dramatic date well before the relevant events) calmly discoursing on moderation would likely be read as containing ironic reference to those well-known (to the reader) events. I believe that the reference here is like that: Phaedrus, at the dramatic date 416, refers in entirely hypothetical terms to what an audience of the 370s would know to be a current reality. Dover (letter, May 11, 1994 [on file with VALR]) now accepts this point.

75. "And indeed lovers are the only ones who are willing to give their lives— not only the males, but even women" (179A). It is culturally interesting that Alcestis is depicted as the *erastês* of her husband, though no doubt she was imagined as younger and as behaving sexually in the usual female way. The reason seems to lie in the intensity of her love, as contrasted with her husband's self-absorption—so Phaedrus maps them onto the *erastês-erômenos* dichotomy in a way that makes this distinction paramount and sexual role subordinate.

76. Dover points out (letter, May 11, 1994 [on file with VALR]) that *kalos* sometimes means just "okay," "in order," "(perfectly) all right," etc. I am happy enough with this; but in a dialogue whose central topic is the *kalon*, and in which the high moral connotations of the word that are common in Platonic philosophy predominate, I would be still be inclined to render the terms as I have. This is certainly the only way to translate the term consistently throughout the dialogue, something that translators have on the whole rightly sought, despite the dialogue's plurality of speakers.

77. As often in Plato, we simply do not know whether some of the insights developed using this example might be intended to be generalizable to male-female and female-female loves as well.

78. *Love and Friendship in Plato and Aristotle* (Oxford: Clarendon Press, 1989), 15–54, esp. 47–9, where Price argues that a type of close personal intimacy characterized by "educative pederasty" is present throughout the ascent. (By "pederasty" Price means something quite different from pedophilia, sex with young children; he means sex with adolescents of [roughly] college age). In American usage, these terms are not kept distinct, and "pederasty" is thus a misleading term for what Price is talking about.

79. See the comments of Dover, *GH*, 163; and Vlastos, "The Individual as Object of Love in Plato," in *Platonic Studies*, 2nd ed. (Princeton: Princeton University Press, 1981).

80. *Hubrisen* 219C5; on these metaphors, see the excellent treatment in M. Gagarin, "Socrates' *Hubris* and Alcibiades' Failure," *Phoenix* 31 (1977), 22–37. His charge against Socrates seems unfounded. *Being used* seems an essential feature of rape, and Socrates has humiliated him in a way that expresses not only no intent to use but probably also a sincere concern for his well-being.

81. *FG*, chap. 6.

82. My own account of these familiar issues is in *FG*, chaps. 5 and 7; see especially 436–439E, 583C–84A, 533CD, 586AB.

83. This passage is in the middle of the discussion of the oligarchic city and man, but it is introduced as a digression, necessary to clarify a concept that will be used in that discussion. There is no reason to think that Socrates' articulation of the concept of "necessary desire" itself holds good only for the oligarchic city. He says simply that such desires "might justly be called necessary" (558E).

84. The best treatment of these, with all their contradictions, is in Halliwell.

85. But the latter only if Plato thought he could rely on the contraceptive devices in use at the time; see VALR, appendix 3, for his concern about this. Masturbation would be another possibility, but I am not certain that the term *aphrodisia* could, without strain, designate masturbation.

86. Scholars are not agreed on whether the speech is a real speech by the historical Lysias or a Platonic invention that captures Lysias's style well. I am inclined to the latter view.

87. One might here register another complaint against A. E. Taylor (see Dover's critique cited in n.15 above), who writes, "The thesis of Lysias, we must remember, would be an offensive paradox even to the section of Athenian society which practiced 'unnatural' aberrations" (*Plato*, 302).

88. One excellent place to study this is Euripides' *Hippolytus*, in which *erôs* is depicted as bringing an extraordinary mixture of beauty and danger to human life, and in which the hero's decision to avoid its claims is shown to be both impious and impoverishing.

89. In contrast to the *Symposium,* which had denied the divinity of *erôs.* On all these issues I have presented a fuller argument in *FG,* chap. 7.

90. See Dover, *GH,* 163–5, who comments on the extraordinary emphasis given to the erotic response to bodily beauty in Plato's metaphysical system. In his autobiography, Dover comments further on this theme (see chapter 13, in this volume).

91. See David Halperin, "Plato and Erotic Reciprocity," *Classical Antiquity* 5 (1986), 60–80; and Halperin, "Plato and the Metaphysics of Desire," and Nussbaum, "Commentary on Halperin," in *Proceedings of the Boston Area Colloquium for Ancient Philosophy* 5 (1989), 27–72.

92. What is at issue is a complicated etymological play in which the word *himeros,* "passionate longing," has been etymologized (251C) as deriving from "particles" (*merê*) that flow (*rhein*) from the beloved to the lover. The dialogue is suffused with this sort of word play, much of it erotic. See also *Cratylus* 419E.

93. We need not suppose that such reciprocity was unknown before this; Socrates describes the experience as one that is likely to follow upon the young man's perception of his lover's generosity. But what is clear is that the cultural vocabulary lacks a description for it.

94. For an excellent treatment of the shift from *Republic* and *Symposium* to *Phaedrus* in this respect, see Vlastos, *Socrates,* chap. 1; and "The Individual as Object of Love in Plato," in Vlastos, *Platonic Studies,* 2nd ed. (Princeton: Princeton University Press, 1981), especially appendix, "Sex in Platonic Love." See also Price, *Love and Friendship,* 54–102; *FG,* chap. 7; and the briefer comments by Dover, *GH,* 164–5, who describes well the persistent sexual imagery of the dialogue.

95. Interpreting 256D, "thinking that they have given and received the greatest pledges," with Price (following a suggestion by Edward Hussey), to refer to their sex acts, which they believe (wrongly) to be the greatest thing they have exchanged with one another. See Price, 92–3, criticizing Dover, *GH,* 163 n. 16, who takes the "pledges" to be the rest of their relationship and their "thinking," therefore, to be correct. Dover now accepts correction on this point. Letter, May 11, 1994 (on file with VALR).

96. Dover, *GH,* 163 n. 15, critciizing Vlastos, "Individual," 23 n. 76. Concurring see Christopher Rowe, ed. and trans., *Plato, Phaedrus* (Warminster: Aris and Phillips, 1986), 184. I would add that in *Republic* IX (see op. cit.) "mounting" has been used as a general description of animalistic sexual activity, just as "grazing" is used of animalistic eating.

97. For one sensitive exploration of a passage using "nature," see Dover, *GH,* 60–68. I am in effect arguing that Dover has not read the present Plato passage with the same sensitivity to context and argument that he there argues to be an essential requisite of interpreting the appeal to nature.

98. Callicles, in *Gorgias* 483C8–484C3; Philebus, in *Philebus,* passim.

99. *Clouds* lines 1421–32. There are many similar examples. For a good overview of the "nature/convention" debate, see W. K. C. Guthrie, *A History of Greek Philosophy* vol. III (Cambridge: Cambridge University Press, 1969).

100. What is probably in question here is the hedonism of Eudoxus, who is reported by Aristotle (*Nicomachean Ethics* 1172b9–11) to have argued that pleasure is the supreme good by appealing to the behavior of "all creatures, both those endowed with reason and those without it."

101. Rowe, commentary, 184; see Dover, letter, May 11, 1994 (on file VALR), praising Rowe's suggestion as "certainly excellent."

102. The first is now defended by Price. May 7.

103. See, for example, Pausanias' speech at 181B.

104. Here it is especially important to note that problems of establishing the Greek text correctly and problems in translating it beset all available versions. Thomas Pangle's is by far the most adequate, going well beyond Bury and especially Saunders in accuracy, but in the crucial passage he reverts to inadequate manuscript readings at a pivotal juncture.

105. In any case, it is certainly wrong to assert that "to know or tell Plato's views on the morality, the immorality, of all such non-marital conduct as homosexual sex acts, one need go no further than these unmistakably clear passages in the *Laws*, texts with which every other text of Plato can readily be seen to be consistent" (John Finnis, "Law, Morality and 'Sexual Orientation,'" *Notre Dame Law Review* 69 [1994], at 1061).

106. See VALR, appendix 3, for a full philological and philosophical discussion, including the new translation of the Book I passage by Christopher Bobonich and numerous references to new work of Dover and other scholars.

107. See Dover, *GH*, 167: "Plato's main concern is to reduce to an unavoidable minimum all activity of which the end is physical enjoyment, in order that the irrational and appetitive element of the soul may not be encouraged and strengthened by indulgence. . . ." He spends at least as much time on drunkenness as on sex.

108. Dover (May 11) suggests that loss of semen plays such a large role in folklore and psychopathology that one may wonder whether Plato thought that semen is a nonrenewable resource. The Dover/Nussbaum appendix, VALR, states that "we can agree that the Book I passage criticizes same-sex conduct as a violation of norms of moderation, and blames this conduct for ruining people's pleasure in marital sex. We can also agree that the disputed term *tolmêma* in that passage should be translated 'venture,' 'daring,' or 'having-the-nerve' rather than 'crime.'

109. Plato does not always distinguish these two categories, certainly, but he is capable of doing so, as in the notorious discussion of the rule of the ideal city by the philosophers, a task they view "not as something *kalon* (fine, noble) but as a necessity." *Republic* 540B.

110. See here Dover, *GH*, 164.

111. The Dover/Nussbaum appendix, VALR, states that these two features "complicat[e] any attempt to take the passage as a major Platonic statement."

112. Compare Price, 230–35; Price, who had simply used Dover's translation in the first edition of his book, has now altered his translation of the relevant passage for the forthcoming new edition, agreeing with my view and Dover's current view: *Tolmêma* should be translated as "venture" or "daring," not as "crime."

113. This last sentence is from the Dover/Nussbaum appendix, VALR.

114. This does not imply a belief in infantile sexuality, which does not seem to be present in any ancient thinker. What Aristotle means is that things are in good order at our birth, in such a way that with the proper support and development virtue will in due time result.

115. The word I have, for want of a perfect equivalent, translated "material resources" is *ousia*, which means one's estate, fortune, property, possessions. In other words, "material" is not meant to refer to one's own body.

116. "Given that Aristotle thinks male-male arousal natural and also thinks the indulgence of sexual desire acceptable, we regard it as inconceivable that he would think it incorrect to act on one's same-sex arousal." Dover/Nussbaum appendix, VALR.

117. Marriage is mentioned only twice in the entirety of the *Nicomachean Ethics*: as the occasion for an especially big party (1123a1) and as an occasion, like a

funeral, to which one will want to invite one's relatives (1165a18). There are, of course, numerous references to the (friendly) relation of husband and wife, but not in contexts where the end of sexual activity is discussed. In two passages Aristotle cites sleeping with someone else's wife as an instance of unjust or wrongful action (1134a20–1, 1137a19–20), but this should be understood not as a reference to any intrinsic immorality in nonmarital relations, but rather as a violation of the rights of the woman's husband. Aristotle does hold that *moicheia* is bad in itself (see *Eudemian Ethics* 1221b; *EN* 1134a19, 118a25; *Rhetoric* 1375a), but *moicheia* includes only sleeping with someone else's wife or concubine, or with an unmarried woman of good family who is a citizen's daughter or ward. See M. J. Dover, *GPM*, 209; the narrower definition argued for by Cohen, 98–132, is refuted in Dover's review. *Moicheia* is seen as an injury against "the husband's claim to exclusive sexual access to his wife" (Cohen, 109); thus it does not bear on the propriety of a married man's visiting a prostitute or *hetaira*, neither of which would be disapproved at the time. The only passage I know of where Aristotle calls a form of sexual conduct "contrary to piety" is in a reference to incest at *Politics* 1262a27, criticizing Plato's ideal city.

118. Affidavit of Oct. 8, para. 38; Rebuttal Affidavit, para. 18. He follows Thomas Aquinas' interpretation of the passage.

119. Finnis fails to note these distinctions in his affidavit, simply saying that the male-male case is "the last item on the list of unnatural pleasures"; nail biting and hair pulling receive no mention in his account. In fact, in Affidavit, para. 38, he cites the present passage as evidence that "Aristotle . . . represents such conduct [by which Finnis means all homosexual conduct] as intrinsically perverse, shameful and harmful both to the individuals involved and to society itself." Will we have a new referendum on the civil rights of nail biters?

120. Dover, *GH*, 169.

121. Ibid., 169–70, discussing *Problemata* IV.26. This being Dover's interpretation, Finnis's summary in his Affidavit of Oct. 8, para. 38, is very odd:

> Dover's discussion of the views of Aristotle (born 384, died 322 BC) is incomplete and may be judged evasive, discussing only one of several relevant passages in Aristotle's works. But even Dover does not contradict the scholarly consensus that Aristotle rejected homosexual conduct. In fact, Aristotle on a number of occasions (in some cases directly and in other cases by a lecturer's hint) represents such conduct as intrinsically perverse, shameful and harmful both to the individuals involved and to society itself. I refer to his *Nicomachean Ethics* VII,5: 1148b29, his *Politics* II,1: 1262a33–39, together with the hints in II,6: 1269b28 and II,7: 1272a25.

But, of course, it was precisely Dover's purpose to argue that the *EN* passage *does not* contain a general condemnation of homosexual conduct but rather a condemnation of child abuse leading to chronic passivity; nor does Dover mention any of the other three passages cited by Finnis. These passages would not have changed his case if he had. *Politics* 1262a33–39 is a discussion of the danger of incest in Plato's ideal city. Aristotle notes that, making all children in the city the children of all the adults, Plato seeks to prevent incest by prohibiting intercourse between the generations, but he does not prohibit "passionate love and the other practices that would be most unfitting between a father and a son, or between a brother and a brother." This hardly amounts to a general condemnation of homosexual conduct, and it does not have to do with conduct at all, in Finnis's narrowly defined sense; 1269b28 is a discussion of the warlike customs of Sparta and Crete, which Aristotle links with sexual excess. He mentions that most warlike peoples are excessively bossed around by their women at home (1269b24–5), "with the exception of the Celts and others who clearly give honor to male-male intercourse." Honoring male-male intercourse, it would seem, is here seen as a way some warlike nations have of not being excessively woman-dominated. Next, in the line actually cited by Finnis, he says that it is reasonable that mythographers linked Ares to Aphrodite: "[F]or all people of that kind [viz., warlike people] are dependent on intercourse either with males or with women." I fail to see what Finnis thinks he finds here to support his claims, since male-male and male-female intercourse are treated exactly alike. The last passage mentioned by Finnis is 1272a 25. Here Aristotle has been discussing the Cretan custom of public meals; he mentions that the Cretan lawgiver holds *oligositia*, deliberate undereating, to be healthful and "philosophizes" about it at length; he also philosophizes about holding down the population size by having men reside separately from their wives, "making them associate with the males" (*tên pros tous arrenas poiêsas homilian*). Aristotle concludes, "concerning which [i.e. this associating], as to whether it is an inferior custom or not inferior, there will be another occasion to conduct a thorough inquiry." Now presumably Finnis understands *homilia* to refer to sexual intercourse with males and takes Aristotle to be hinting that he is going to condemn it somewhere else. Of course the bare statement that one is going to look into something, as to whether it is good or not, hardly tells us how the inquiry will come out. But a more important difficulty is that the passage is plainly discussing the custom that men do not *reside* with wives, but *reside*, military fashion, in all-male barracks. This custom is neither necessary nor sufficient for sexual intercourse with males. We know that an army may have single-sex barracks without encouraging same-sex sexual conduct; on the other hand, sexual intercourse between males, at Athens and elsewhere, standardly occurred while the older party was residing with a wife. And, of course, it is the custom of separate residence that Aristotle actually does discuss elsewhere, producing arguments that it is good for the upbringing of children for families to dwell together. Finally, *homilia* is not, as *sunousia* is, a standard euphemism for sexual intercourse, and the statement that the legislator "makes" or "causes" this "associating" would surely be odd if it meant sexual intercourse—we know of no laws for mandatory male-male intercourse, whereas it would not be odd if it meant what I think it clearly means, requiring men to reside with their fellow males.

122. *Love and Friendship*, 248–9.

123. Translator Terence Irwin concurs in this reading of the passage. See the longer version of this article (VALR).

124. Diogenes Laertius, reproducing a list of Aristotle's writings that probably reflects an early collection in the Peripatetic school, lists an "*Eroticus*, 1 book," and a "*Theses on love*, 4 books" (DL V.22–7).

125. Price, 249.

126. Letter, December 16, 1993 (on file with VALR).

127. Ibid. Later in the same document (an Open Letter), Price describes those Greek attitudes as follows: "As Nussbaum correctly asserts, what generally troubled the Greeks (like all macho Mediterranean males) was that a man should play the woman's role, especially habitually. It is that, and not the non-procreativity, which the orator Aeschines, for instance, once calls 'unnatural' (i.185)."

128. In correspondence, Price now accepts this point, saying that his remarks about chaste pederasty were meant to apply only to relations with boys too young for meaningful consent.

129. And, as Dover points out (letter, May 11, 1994 [on file with VALR]) except in the sense in which men who pay because they are no good at seducing "incur a certain degree of ridicule and contempt in all cultures."

130. See VALR version of this article; but also Martha C. Nussbaum, *The Therapy of Desire: Theory and Practice in Hellenistic Ethics* (Princeton: Princeton University Press, 1994), chaps. 5 and 12; and Nussbaum, "*Eros* and the Wise," 231–67.

131. *The Use of Pleasure*, 9.

132. For a related critique of Finnis's position on sexual complementarity, see Paul Weithman, "Natural Law, Morality, and Sexual Complementarity," in *Shaping Sex, Preference, and Family: Essays on Laws and Nature*, ed. D. Estlund and M. Nussbaum (New York: Oxford University Press, 1996), 227–46.

133. Kenneth Dover, personal communication, March 15, 1994.

134. Dover and Nussbaum make several more general observations about the issues (related to points I pursue in chapter 7, in this volume): First, we argue that there is nothing wrong with using one's body for the purpose of getting pleasure. Going for a swim, hiking, and masturbating are all ways of using the human body for pleasure, and we see nothing intrinsically objectionable about any of them. Even if one grants that interpersonal sex is superior to masturbation, it is not immoral to choose an inferior form of pleasure when the superior one is unavailable, or as a preparation for engaging in the superior form. If Finnis responds that the sexual use of one's body differs from other uses of one's body in games or skilled performances, we reply that this distinction is unconvincing. Sexual activity can certainly be a skilled performance. To assert that because it involves sexual organs and sexual pleasure, it must be different from other activities, is to introduce metaphysical premises for which no argument has been given. Interpersonal sex, moreover, may pursue many different ends in addition to procreation and physical pleasure: joy, the expression of love and friendship. There is no reason to suppose that openness to procreation is a sine qua non of these other goods.

135. For a related point, see Finnis, Rebuttal Affidavit, para. 29.

136. For the evidence on gender equality, see Malcolm Schofield, *The Stoic Idea of the City* (Cambridge: Cambridge University Press, 1991).

137. See Introduction and chapter 7.

138. *Romer*, 1622; cf. also 1628, where this claim is elaborated.

139. *Romer* 1622; cf. also 1628.

Chapter 13

A review of Kenneth Dover, *Marginal Comment: A Memoir* (London: Duckworth, 1994). Page numbers in parentheses refer to this work, unless otherwise noted.

1. M. Foucault, *The Use of Pleasure*. Vol. 2: *The History of Sexuality*, trans. Robert Hurley (New York: Pantheon, 1985); and *The Care of the Self*. Vol. 3: *The History of Sexuality*, trans. R. Hurley (New York: Pantheon, 1986).

2. See David Halperin, *One Hundred Years of Homosexuality and Other Essays on Greek Love* (New York: Routledge, 1990); and John J. Winkler, *The Constraints of Desire: the Anthropology of Sex and Gender in Ancient Greece* (New York: Routledge, 1990).

3. K. J. Dover, *Greek Homosexuality*. (Cambridge, MA: Harvard University Press, 1978; 2nd ed., 1989).

4. K. J. Dover, *Greek Popular Morality in the Time of Plato and Aristotle* (Oxford: Basil Blackwell, 1974).

5. In correspondence, Dover has told me that he now believes that he did not draw enough chronological distinctions in this paragraph. In fact, he says, the remark about grief has not been true of him since 1984. (The significance of that year is not explained by any event I can locate in the book.) Moreover, he points out that in the very same paragraph in which he denies having felt grief, he remarks that his regret for not having made his mother (who died in 1973) more aware of his affection is "anguished."

6. Dover now notes (January 16, 1997) that he wishes he had italicized the word "moral" in this sentence.

7. Dover now adds that some of the problems that were discussed seemed to him to be discussed incompetently in the sense that nonexistent problems were created by neglect, for example, of the context or point of an utterance.

8. Dover now observes that it ends pretty quickly if either "fatigue or shyness" is the cause of not doing the good thing. My view is that we still need an account of the relationship between desiring and acting that makes it clear how such impediments occur, but Dover seems right to suggest that these impediments should occupy philosophers more than they do, because they may operate differently from the standard case of desire for pleasure.

9. Speeches were put into circulation, and are in that sense also literary works, but it is on account of their practical role that Dover judges them superior to drama as evidence.

10. Dover writes (January 1997): "I see (not for the first time!) that what I said about friendship etc. may have given the impression that I am a 'reserved' and 'private' person, whereas I am actually inclined to treat everyone as a friend and speak about myself with a degree of candour which can alarm people who don't consider that they know me well."

11. Dover notes that he considers himself to have broken with the "conventions of the genre" and has been complimented for doing so. Perhaps he is thinking of conventions of English autobiography until the rather recent present. I was thinking of Augustine and Rousseau.

12. Dover now points out (letter, March 11, 1995 [on file with author]) that telling the whole world such facts is in one sense easier than telling a guest because then "no individual guest is involved in an embarrassing interplay of facial expression."

13. James Miller, *The Passion of Michel Foucault* (New York: Simon and Schuster, 1993).

14. See the discussion of Dover's emotions in n. 5. The remarks about emotion are brought right up into the present, as my citation shows, although at the same time Dover states that his aloofness from friendship persisted only "until very recently."

Chapter 14

A review of Richard Posner, *Sex and Reason* (Cambridge, MA: Harvard University Press, 1992).

1. 487 U.S. 186 (1986).

2. See Posner, 341–50. Posner notes that in common law, sodomy did not include fellatio but was limited to anal intercourse; the extension took place in the nineteenth century. For background to the case, see chapter 7 (in this volume).

3. *Bowers*, 190–1.

4. See Posner, 342; *Griswold v. Connecticut*, 381 U.S. 479 (1965) (contraception for married couples); *Eisenstadt v. Baird*, 405 U.S. 483 (1972) (contraception

for unmarried adults); *Stanley v. Georgia*, 394 U.S. 557 (1969) (use of pornography in the home); *Roe v. Wade* 410 U.S. 113 (1973) (abortion). See also Thomas Grey, "Eros, Civilization and the Burger Court," *Law and Contemporary Problems* 43 (1980), 83–100.

5. *Loving v. Virginia*, 388 U.S. 1 (1967).

6. *Bowers*, 190.

7. Ibid., 186, 192–4, 196–7.

8. See Cass R. Sunstein, "Sexual Orientation and the Constitution: A Note on the Relationship between Due Process and Equal Protection," *University of Chicago Law Review* 55 (1988), 1161–79.

9. 741 F.2d 1388 (D.C. 1984).

10. 780 F. Supp. 1 (1991).

11. *Miller v. Civil City of South Bend*, 904 F.2d 1080, 1100 (7th Cir 1990), *rev'd sub nom., Barnes v. Glen Theatre, Inc.*, 111 S. Ct. 2456 (1991).

12. For discussion of the relationship of these two aims, see Martha C. Nussbaum, *Poetic Justice: The Literary Imagination and Public Life* (Boston: Beacon Press, 1996), 46–9.

13. Posner, *The Economics of Justice* (Cambridge, MA: Harvard University Press, 1981).

14. See Elisabeth M. Landes and Richard A. Posner, "The Economics of the Baby Shortage," *Journal of Legal Studies* 7 (1978), 323–48. Posner corrects misreadings of that article in "The Regulation of the Market in Adoptions," *Boston University Law Review* 67 (1987), 59–72.

15. Posner, "An Economic Theory of the Criminal Law," *Columbia Law Review* 85 (1985), 1193, 1198–9; see *Sex and Reason*, 386, for a more nuanced treatment of the issue.

16. See *Economics of Justice*, 3.

17. *The Problems of Jurisprudence* (Cambridge, MA: Harvard University Press, 1990), 353–92.

18. *Overcoming Law* (Cambridge, MA: Harvard University Press, 1996), 222–4.

19. See Posner interview in *The Advocate*.

20. For a good discussion of this aspect of sexual desire, see Roger Scruton, *Sexual Desire* (New York: The Free Press, 1986).

21. For example, in *Law and Literature: A Misunderstood Relation* (Cambridge, MA: Harvard University Press, 1988), and in *Law and Literature: The Relationship Rethought* (Cambridge, MA: Harvard University Press, 1997), Posner offers a fascinating account of the role of revenge in culture and the overcoming of revenge by law.

22. This is John Rawls's central objection to Utilitarianism in *A Theory of Justice* (Cambridge, MA: Harvard University Press, 1971).

23. *Overcoming Law*, 23.

24. Ibid., 23. Posner's point is similar to that of Amartya Sen, "The Impossibility of a Paretian Liberal," *Journal of Political Economy* 78 (1970), 152–7, reprinted in Sen, *Choice, Welfare, and Measurement* (Oxford: Basil Blackwell, 1982), 285–90.

25. Sen, "Rights and Agency," *Philosophy and Public Affairs* 11 (1982), 3–39.

26. This point is missed by Roger Scruton, in "Gay Reservations," in *The Liberation Debate: Rights at Issue*, ed. M. Leahy and D. Cohn-Sherbok (London and New York: Routledge, 1996), 108–29, at 110–3: Scruton takes Posner's Millean libertarianism to entail the bioeconomic theory and thus takes refutation of the latter to be sufficient to refute the former.

27. *Douglass v. Hustler Magazine, Inc.*, 769 F.2d 1128 (7th Cir. 1985).

Chapter 15

1. *To the Lighthouse* (New York: Harcourt Brace, 1955). All references are to page numbers of the Harvest paperback edition.

2. Stanley Cavell, *The Claim of Reason: Wittgenstein, Skepticism, Morality, and Tragedy* (New York: Oxford University Press, 1979), esp. part IV.

3. Compare Proust, *Recherche*: "Style for the writer, no less than colour for the painter, . . . is the revelation . . . of the qualitative difference, the uniqueness of the fashion in which the world appears to each one of us" (Marcel Proust, *Remembrance of Things Past*, vol. III, trans. Andreas Mayor and Terence Kilmartin [New York: Vintage, 1981], 931–2). Proust, however, focuses here on the unconscious expression of individuality by the artist in the creation of the work as a whole, whereas Woolf draws attention to the power of the artist consciously to represent individuality in the creation of characters, each with a different texture of consciousness.

4. Note, however, that novels frequently do this by making meanings more definite and coherent than they are in real life. To put a meaning into words is already to impose an interpretation on what may have been an undemarcated buzzing.

5. See also 59: "But he must have more than that. It was sympathy he wanted, to be assured of his genius, first of all, and then to be taken within the circle of life, warmed and soothed, to have his senses restored to him, his barrenness made fertile. . . ."

6. Nietzsche, *The Gay Science*, trans. W. Kaufman (New York: Vintage, 1974), 354.

7. We should compare the posing of this problem in Beckett's *The Unnamable*, where the attempt to "say myself" is shown to contain a self-contradiction: Putting himself into language, the narrator feels himself becoming a public nonself, a generalized "pupil Mahood"; and yet (as with Mrs. Ramsay here) to cease to use the categories of consciousness is in a significant way to cease to be.

8. Part II takes on the task of depicting reality from the point of view of nonconscious nature—a paradoxical task, given that the novelist's tools must still be words and concepts, but a task that shows us Woolf's sense of the importance of a reality that is alive but nonconscious.

9. See related argument about sexual fusion in Martha C. Nussbaum, *The Therapy of Desire* (Princeton: Princeton University Press, 1994), chap. 5. On Proust's related arguments, and their defects, see Martha C. Nussbaum, "Love's Knowledge," in *Love's Knowledge* (New York: Oxford University Press, 1990).

10. See the similar argument in Stanley Cavell, "Knowing and Acknowledging," in *Must We Mean What We Say?* (New York: Charles Scribner's Sons, 1969, repr. Cambridge: Cambridge University Press, 1976), 238–66. See also Cavell, *The Claim of Reason*, part IV. On the way in which a desire for knowledge can generate a desire for incorporation, but then, in turn, the realization that incorporation would precisely *not* be knowledge, one might fruitfully compare aspects of Hegel's master-slave dialectic.

11. Cf. 103.

12. What this brings out, among other things, is that the common "analogy" solution to the problem of other minds is too crude to be really informative: For what makes all the difference is to say what analogies are helpful and what analogies are not. The novel suggests that there is no single answer to this question—one just has to learn by experience.

13. On all this, see Cavell, *The Claim of Reason*, especially the reading of *Othello* at the end of part IV.

14. Could hate generate knowledge of another? In some respects, it might; for it could motivate a close intense focusing on the pattern of the other person's sayings and actions that would make the hater a good reader. On the other hand, if the hatred is mutual and known to be such, skepticism about the evidence would always be a reasonable response, and would defeat the epistemological aim. In an asymmetrical hatred—for example, in the relationship of Iago with Othello, perhaps one-way knowledge might be attained—but note that its condition is Othello's openhearted trust in his "friend," and Iago's consequent trust in the evidence with which Othello presents him.

15. See Nussbaum, "Love's Knowledge."

16. Here I have in mind the discussion of love and justice in Susan Moller Okin's *Justice, Gender, and the Family* (New York: Basic Books, 1989).

NAME INDEX

SUBJECT INDEX

467